Functional Bakery Products: Technological, Chemical and Nutritional Modification

Functional Bakery Products: Technological, Chemical and Nutritional Modification

Guest Editors

Anna Wirkijowska
Piotr Zarzycki
Agata Blicharz-Kania
Urszula Pankiewicz

Basel • Beijing • Wuhan • Barcelona • Belgrade • Novi Sad • Cluj • Manchester

Guest Editors

Anna Wirkijowska
Department of Engineering
and Cereals Technology
University of Life Sciences
in Lublin
Lublin
Poland

Piotr Zarzycki
Department of Engineering
and Cereals Technology
University of Life Sciences
in Lublin
Lublin
Poland

Agata Blicharz-Kania
Department of Biological
Bases of Food and Feed
Technologies
University of Life Sciences
in Lublin
Lublin
Poland

Urszula Pankiewicz
Department of Analysis and
Food Quality Assessment
University of Life Sciences
in Lublin
Lublin
Poland

Editorial Office
MDPI AG
Grosspeteranlage 5
4052 Basel, Switzerland

This is a reprint of the Special Issue, published open access by the journal *Applied Sciences* (ISSN 2076-3417), freely accessible at: http://www.mdpi.com.

For citation purposes, cite each article independently as indicated on the article page online and as indicated below:

Lastname, A.A.; Lastname, B.B. Article Title. *Journal Name* **Year**, *Volume Number*, Page Range.

ISBN 978-3-7258-3191-3 (Hbk)
ISBN 978-3-7258-3192-0 (PDF)
https://doi.org/10.3390/books978-3-7258-3192-0

© 2025 by the authors. Articles in this book are Open Access and distributed under the Creative Commons Attribution (CC BY) license. The book as a whole is distributed by MDPI under the terms and conditions of the Creative Commons Attribution-NonCommercial-NoDerivs (CC BY-NC-ND) license (https://creativecommons.org/licenses/by-nc-nd/4.0/).

Contents

Preface vii

Piotr Zarzycki, Anna Wirkijowska and Urszula Pankiewicz
Functional Bakery Products: Technological, Chemical and Nutritional Modification
Reprinted from: *Appl. Sci.* **2024**, *14*, 12023, https://doi.org/10.3390/app142412023 1

Anna Diowksz, Przemysław Kopeć and Anna Koziróg
The Inactivation of Microscopic Fungi in Bakery Products Using Hurdle Technology—A Case Study
Reprinted from: *Appl. Sci.* **2024**, *14*, 10648, https://doi.org/10.3390/app142210648 5

Piotr Lewko, Agnieszka Wójtowicz and Marek Gancarz
Application of Conventional and Hybrid Thermal-Enzymatic Modified Wheat Flours as Clean Label Bread Improvers
Reprinted from: *Appl. Sci.* **2024**, *14*, 7659, https://doi.org/10.3390/app14177659 21

Krzysztof Juś, Mateusz Ścigaj, Daniela Gwiazdowska, Katarzyna Marchwińska and Wiktoria Studenna
Innovative Fermented Beverages Based on Bread Waste—Fermentation Parameters and Antibacterial Properties
Reprinted from: *Appl. Sci.* **2024**, *14*, 5036, https://doi.org/10.3390/app14125036 45

Iuliana Banu and Iuliana Aprodu
Assessment of the Performance of Oat Flakes and Pumpkin Seed Powders in Gluten-Free Dough and Bread Based on Rice Flour
Reprinted from: *Appl. Sci.* **2024**, *14*, 3479, https://doi.org/10.3390/app14083479 63

Iva Burešová, Romana Šebestíková, Jaromír Šebela, Anna Adámková, Magdalena Zvonková, Nela Skowronková and Jiří Mlček
The Effect of Inulin Addition on Rice Dough and Bread Characteristics
Reprinted from: *Appl. Sci.* **2024**, *14*, 2882, https://doi.org/10.3390/app14072882 76

Angelika Bieniek and Krzysztof Buksa
The Influence of Arabinoxylan on the Properties of Sourdough Wheat Bread
Reprinted from: *Appl. Sci.* **2024**, *14*, 2649, https://doi.org/10.3390/app14062649 88

Aneta Sławińska, Ewa Jabłońska-Ryś and Waldemar Gustaw
Physico-Chemical, Sensory, and Nutritional Properties of Shortbread Cookies Enriched with *Agaricus bisporus* and *Pleurotus ostreatus* Powders
Reprinted from: *Appl. Sci.* **2024**, *14*, 1938, https://doi.org/10.3390/app14051938 101

Agata Blicharz-Kania, Kostiantyn Vasiukov, Agnieszka Sagan, Dariusz Andrejko, Weronika Fifowska and Marek Domin
Nutritional Value, Physical Properties, and Sensory Quality of Sugar-Free Cereal Bars Fortified with Grape and Apple Pomace
Reprinted from: *Appl. Sci.* **2023**, *13*, 10531, https://doi.org/10.3390/app131810531 126

Salih Salihu, Njomza Gashi and Endrit Hasani
Effect of Plant Extracts Addition on the Physico-Chemical and Sensory Properties of Biscuits
Reprinted from: *Appl. Sci.* **2023**, *13*, 9674, https://doi.org/10.3390/app13179674 136

Anna Wirkijowska, Piotr Zarzycki, Dorota Teterycz, Agnieszka Nawrocka, Agata Blicharz-Kania and Paulina Łysakowska
The Influence of Tomato and Pepper Processing Waste on Bread Quality
Reprinted from: *Appl. Sci.* **2023**, *13*, 9312, https://doi.org/10.3390/app13169312 . . . . **147**

Grażyna Cacak-Pietrzak, Katarzyna Sujka, Jerzy Księżak, Jolanta Bojarszczuk and Dariusz Dziki
Sourdough Wheat Bread Enriched with Grass Pea and Lupine Seed Flour: Physicochemical and Sensory Properties
Reprinted from: *Appl. Sci.* **2023**, *13*, 8664, https://doi.org/10.3390/app13158664 . . . . **162**

Agata Marzec, Patrycja Kramarczuk, Hanna Kowalska and Jolanta Kowalska
Effect of Type of Flour and Microalgae (*Chlorella vulgaris*) on the Rheological, Microstructural, Textural, and Sensory Properties of Vegan Muffins
Reprinted from: *Appl. Sci.* **2023**, *13*, 7632, https://doi.org/10.3390/app13137632 . . . . **178**

Piotr Zarzycki, Anna Wirkijowska, Dorota Teterycz and Paulina Łysakowska
Innovations in Wheat Bread: Using Food Industry By-Products for Better Quality and Nutrition
Reprinted from: *Appl. Sci.* **2024**, *14*, 3976, https://doi.org/10.3390/app14103976 . . . . **193**

Joanna Stasiak, Dariusz M. Stasiak and Justyna Libera
The Potential of Aquafaba as a Structure-Shaping Additive in Plant-Derived Food Technology
Reprinted from: *Appl. Sci.* **2023**, *13*, 4122, https://doi.org/10.3390/app13074122 . . . . **229**

Preface

Bakery products are a vital part of modern diets, offering nutrients like complex carbohydrates, proteins, vitamins, and minerals. This reprint delves into the latest research on modifying these products using advanced technologies to enhance their health benefits; it is an essential resource for anyone interested in food innovation and healthy living.

Anna Wirkijowska, Piotr Zarzycki, Agata Blicharz-Kania, and Urszula Pankiewicz
Guest Editors

Editorial

Functional Bakery Products: Technological, Chemical and Nutritional Modification

Piotr Zarzycki [1], Anna Wirkijowska [1,*] and Urszula Pankiewicz [2]

[1] Department of Engineering and Cereals Technology, Faculty of Food Science and Biotechnology, University of Life Sciences in Lublin, Skromna 8, 20-704 Lublin, Poland; piotr.zarzycki@up.lublin.pl
[2] Department of Analysis and Food Quality Assessment, Faculty of Food Science and Biotechnology, University of Life Sciences in Lublin, Skromna 8, 20-704 Lublin, Poland; urszula.pankiewicz@up.lublin.pl
* Correspondence: anna.wirkijowska@up.lublin.pl

Citation: Zarzycki, P.; Wirkijowska, A.; Pankiewicz, U. Functional Bakery Products: Technological, Chemical and Nutritional Modification. *Appl. Sci.* **2024**, *14*, 12023. https://doi.org/10.3390/app142412023

Received: 19 November 2024
Accepted: 20 December 2024
Published: 23 December 2024

Copyright: © 2024 by the authors. Licensee MDPI, Basel, Switzerland. This article is an open access article distributed under the terms and conditions of the Creative Commons Attribution (CC BY) license (https://creativecommons.org/licenses/by/4.0/).

Increasing consumer interest in the health benefits of various foods has driven the development of new food products and prompted modifications to the recipes and technologies used for the production of traditional items. Nutritional claims such as "source of...", "rich in...", and "light" have become increasingly common, reflecting a stronger focus on health benefits [1,2]. Current research trends emphasize the nutritional and technological advancements reflected in cereal-based products, including the incorporation of novel additives and production processes aimed at achieving clean-label recognition [3,4]. Functional foods provide a valuable platform for introducing new ingredients, offering benefits from economic, nutritional, technological, and environmental perspectives. This approach not only enhances nutritional value but also addresses dietary deficiencies in the population. Moreover, in response to the global challenge of food waste, extensive research has been conducted to explore the potential for utilizing by-products from the food industry—such as those from fruit, vegetable, or oil processing—as well as underutilized mill streams rich in fiber fractions. Developing technological solutions to integrate these by-products into higher-quality products will lead to an enhancement in their economic value, improve resource efficiency, and support zero-waste principles, advancing a circular economy [5–7].

These trends also extend to bakery products, which are typically made from flour or meal derived from a variety of both cereal and non-cereal grains. Depending on the ingredients present, bakery products can serve as excellent sources of complex carbohydrates (including starch and dietary fiber), proteins, vitamins, minerals, and phytochemicals with specific health benefits. Bakery items such as bread, cookies, cereal bars, biscuits, and muffins play a central role in the modern diet, representing numerous opportunities to enhance their nutritional value, functionality, and alignment with current health and sustainability values [8–11].

One common strategy with which to enhance the nutritional value of bakery products is the partial or complete substitution of wheat flour. This approach is particularly effective for products in which wheat flour is a primary ingredient, such as refined (low-extraction) wheat bread. Refined flour, depending on its extraction rate, is characterized by low levels of dietary fiber, protein, minerals, and bioactive compounds. Additionally, the proteins in wheat flour are incomplete, lacking certain essential amino acids, particularly lysine, limiting their digestibility [12–15]. Bread, one of the most widely consumed bakery products, has an average per capita consumption of around 250 g per day [16] and plays a vital role in human nutrition due to its accessibility and nutritional value. Wheat bread, the most common type of bread, has been a dietary staple for centuries. It provides a substantial energy source through its high carbohydrate content (70–80% dry matter) and also supplies protein (10–14% dry matter) and minerals (0.5–0.8% dry matter). However, the dietary fiber content in white wheat bread is relatively low, typically at around 2–3% [17]. To address these nutritional limitations, there is a rising trend of incorporating non-traditional raw materials, including high-protein by-products from the plant food industry, into bread and other bakery products traditionally made using white wheat flour [18].

While partially substituting wheat flour with another ingredient can improve the chemical composition of baked goods, this method also poses significant challenges, particularly in maintaining the quality characteristics of the final product, which are critical for consumer acceptance. Wheat flour is unique because of its gluten content, a structural protein essential for the appearance, crumb structure, and overall texture of many baked goods. The gluten matrix plays a crucial role in determining the rheological properties of dough, making it challenging to replace wheat flour without compromising product quality. Enriching raw materials often need to be used in limited amounts, as excessive additions can negatively impact the dough quality, microstructure, and texture of the final product [19]. Developing dough with desirable properties becomes even more challenging when formulating gluten-free bakery products. This issue is particularly significant considering the rising global incidence of celiac disease, which has reached annual rates of 21.3 cases per 100,000 individuals among children and 12.9 per 100,000 individuals among adults in recent years [20]. Patients with celiac disease often face limited access to suitable products, which are frequently characterized by lower nutritional and sensory quality compared with their gluten-containing counterparts. This presents specific challenges, not only in achieving the desired dough quality but also in ensuring that the final product meets appropriate nutritional standards [21].

Recent studies in the field of functional bakery products have increasingly focused on incorporating unconventional ingredients and innovative technologies to enhance the nutritional, sensory, and technological properties of baked goods. Examples include the use of industrial by-products, such as fruit pomace, vegetable processing waste, and underutilized mill streams rich in fiber fractions, as well as ingredient modifications like inulin, microalgae, or mushroom powders. Additionally, enriching products with gluten-free or clean-label alternatives as a strategy has gained attention. Such strategies aim not only to improve the health benefits of bakery products but also to align with sustainability trends by minimizing waste and promoting eco-friendly practices in the food industry.

One promising area of research explores the application of enzymatic, thermal, hydrothermal, and enzyme-assisted hybrid modifications in underutilized mill streams [22]. These modifications aim to incorporate wheat flour fractions, which account for about 10% of milling production, into bread-making while maintaining desirable properties. Thermal treatments, especially when combined with enzymes, were found to enhance bread yield and water absorption without compromising texture or color. The treatments reduced amylase activity and starch retrogradation, improved bread volume (up to 16%), and lowered baking and weight losses by 8% compared to standard wheat bread. However, hydrothermal treatments negatively impacted dough structure and crust formation despite increasing bread volume and yield. Flour blends containing up to 20% of modified fractions proved effective as clean-label bread improvers, though higher levels reduced product quality. These findings have practical applications for milling companies, enabling them to reduce waste and create ready-to-use bakery blends with clean-label benefits. Future research should aim to optimize production processes and explore additional enzymes and flour types to further enhance bread quality.

Another innovative study examined the fortification of cereal bars with grape and apple pomace, by-products of the fruit industry, to enhance their nutritional value, physical properties, and sensory characteristics [23]. Replacing 10 or 20 g of sultanas with these pomaces increased the bars' moisture and soluble dietary fiber content while reducing their antioxidant levels. Fortification improved their mechanical strength and visual appeal, though noticeable color changes and less acceptable aroma and texture were also observed in some cases. Cereal bars fortified with grape pomace and up to 10 g of apple pomace demonstrated high dietary fiber content, desirable sensory properties, and suitability for industrial production. However, bars containing 20 g of apple pomace exhibited excessive moisture and lower mechanical integrity, raising concerns about storage stability and transportation. Future studies should evaluate the shelf life and stability of fortified bars and explore methods to minimize color changes during storage.

The impact of inulin (5–40%) on the rheological, textural, and sensory properties of rice bread was also explored to assess its potential for enhancing gluten-free bakery products [24]. Inulin addition softened the dough, raised the gelatinization temperature, and improved bread characteristics, including the specific loaf volume (1.16–1.48 mL/g), crumb porosity (36–58%), and sensory appeal. The optimal inulin level was found to be 30%; this produced bread with superior texture, porosity, and sensory properties, while aligning with dietary recommendations by providing approximately 23 g of inulin per serving. However, higher inulin levels (40%) led to a deterioration in bread texture and cohesiveness, along with increased baking losses. These findings highlight the potential to use inulin in gluten-free bread production and suggest that further research on its application in other bakery products, such as pastries, be conducted.

Functional bakery products provide an excellent platform for enhancing human health and promoting sustainability through ingredient modifications and innovative processing techniques. The reviewed studies highlight the potential of utilizing industrial by-products and functional ingredients, such as inulin, to improve the nutritional, sensory, and technological properties of bakery products while simultaneously addressing waste reduction and sustainability objectives. Future research should focus on developing scalable production methods for the incorporation of modified flours and by-products into bakery formulations without compromising product quality, assessing the long-term stability and shelf life of fortified products, investigating consumer preferences, especially for products with noticeable changes in sensory characteristics such as color, texture, or aroma, and evaluating the bioavailability of nutrients in functional products and their potential health benefits. With continued advancements in ingredient utilization and processing technologies, functional bakery products have the potential to make a significant contribution to health, sustainability, and waste reduction in the food industry.

Author Contributions: P.Z.: writing—original draft preparation; A.W.: writing—original draft preparation and editing; U.P.: writing—review. All authors have read and agreed to the published version of the manuscript.

Conflicts of Interest: The authors declare no conflicts of interest.

References

1. Verhagen, H.; Vos, E.; Francl, S.; Heinonen, M.; Van Loveren, H. Status of Nutrition and Health Claims in Europe. *Arch. Biochem. Biophys.* **2010**, *501*, 6–15. [CrossRef] [PubMed]
2. Duarte, P.; Teixeira, M.; Costa, E.; Silva, S. Healthy Eating as a Trend: Consumers' Perceptions towards Products with Nutrition and Health Claims. *Rev. Bras. Gest. Neg.* **2021**, *23*, 405–421. [CrossRef]
3. Cappelli, A.; Bettaccini, L.; Cini, E. The kneading process: A systematic review of the effects on dough rheology and resulting bread characteristics, including improvement strategies. *Trends Food Sci. Technol.* **2020**, *104*, 91–101. [CrossRef]
4. Vargas, M.C.A.; Simsek, S. Clean label in bread. *Foods* **2021**, *10*, 2054. [CrossRef]
5. Jung, J.-M.; Kim, J.Y.; Kim, J.-H.; Kim, S.M.; Jung, S.; Song, H.; Kwon, E.E.; Choi, Y.-E. Zero-waste strategy by means of valorization of bread waste. *J. Clean. Prod.* **2022**, *365*, 132795. [CrossRef]
6. Jimenez-Moreno, N.; Esparza, I.; Bimbela, F.; Gandia, L.M.; Ancin-Azpilicueta, C. Valorization of selected fruit and vegetable wastes as bioactive compounds: Opportunities and challenges. *Crit. Rev. Environ. Sci. Technol.* **2020**, *50*, 2061–2108. [CrossRef]
7. Dymchenko, A.; Geršl, M.; Gregor, T. Trends in bread waste utilisation. *Trends Food Sci. Technol.* **2023**, *132*, 93–102. [CrossRef]
8. Goubgou, M.; Songré-Ouattara, L.T.; Bationo, F.; Lingani-Sawadogo, H.; Traoré, Y.; Savadogo, A. Biscuits: A systematic review and metaanalysis of improving the nutritional quality and health benefits. *Food Prod. Process. Nutr.* **2022**, *3*, 26. [CrossRef]
9. Cacak-Pietrzak, G.; Dziki, D.; Gawlik-Dziki, U.; Sułek, A.; Kalisz, S.; Sujka, K. Effect of the Addition of Dried Dandelion Roots (*Taraxacum officinale* F. H. Wigg.) on Wheat Dough and Bread Properties. *Molecules* **2021**, *26*, 7564. [CrossRef] [PubMed]
10. Bianchi, F.; Cervini, M.; Giuberti, G.; Rocchetti, G.; Lucini, L.; Simonato, B. Distilled grape pomace as a functional ingredient in vegan muffins: Effect on physicochemical, nutritional, rheological and sensory aspects. *Int. J. Food Sci. Technol.* **2022**, *57*, 4847–4858. [CrossRef]
11. Borges, M.S.; Biz, A.P.; Bertolo, A.P.; Bagatini, L.; Riego, E.; Cavalheiro, D. Enriched cereal bars with wine fermentation biomass. *J. Sci. Food Agric.* **2020**, *101*, 542–547. [CrossRef] [PubMed]

12. Villarino, C.B.J.; Jayasena, V.; Coorey, R.; Chakrabarti-Bell, S.; Johnson, S. Nutritional, Health, and Technological Functionality of Lupin Flour Additionto Bread and Other Baked Products: Benefits and Challenges. *Crit. Rev. Food Sci. Nutr.* **2016**, *56*, 835–857. [CrossRef] [PubMed]
13. Shewry, P.R.; Hey, S.J. The contribution of wheat to human diet and health. *Food Energy Secur.* **2015**, *4*, 178–202. [CrossRef] [PubMed]
14. Rawat, M.; Varshney, A.; Rai, M.; Chikara, A.; Pohty, A.L.; Joshi, A.; Binjola, A.; Singh, C.P.; Rawat, K.; Rather, M.A.; et al. A comprehensive review on nutraceutical potential of underutilized cereals and cereal-based products. *J. Agric. Food Res.* **2023**, *12*, 100619. [CrossRef]
15. Sułek, A.; Cacak-Pietrzak, G.; Różewicz, M.; Nieróbca, A.; Grabiński, J.; Studnicki, M.; Sujka, K.; Dziki, D. Effect of Production Technology Intensity on the Grain Yield, Protein Content and Amino Acid Profile in Common and Durum Wheat Grain. *Plants* **2023**, *12*, 364. [CrossRef] [PubMed]
16. Mollakhalili-Meybodi, N.; Ehrampoush, M.H.; Hajimohammadi, B.; Mosaddeg, M.H. Formulation optimization of functional wheat bread with low glycemic index from technological and nutritional perspective. *Food Sci. Nutr.* **2023**, *11*, 284–294. [CrossRef] [PubMed]
17. Almeida, E.L.; Chang, Y.K.; Steel, C.J. Dietary fibre sources in bread: Influence on technological quality. *LWT* **2013**, *50*, 545–553. [CrossRef]
18. Zarzycki, P.; Wirkijowska, A.; Nawrocka, A.; Kozłowicz, K.; Krajewska, M.; Kłosok, K.; Krawęcka, A. Effect of Moldavian dragonhead seed residue on the baking properties of wheat flour and bread quality. *LWT* **2022**, *155*, 112967. [CrossRef]
19. Azadfar, E.; Rad, A.H.; Sharifi, A.; Armin, M. Effect of olive pomace fiber on the baking properties of wheat flour and flat bread (Barbari Bread) quality. *J. Food Process. Preserv.* **2023**, *2023*, 1405758. [CrossRef]
20. Celiac Disease Foundation. Incidence of Celiac Disease Steadily Increasing. 2020. Available online: https://celiac.org/about-the-foundation/featured-news/2020/02/incidence-of-celiac-disease-steadily-increasing/ (accessed on 15 November 2024).
21. See, J.A.; Kaukinen, K.; Makharia, G.K.; Gibson, P.R.; Murray, J.A. Practical insights into gluten-free diets. *Nat. Rev. Gastroenterol. Hepatol.* **2015**, *12*, 580–591. [CrossRef]
22. Lewko, P.; Wójtowicz, A.; Gancarz, M. Application of Conventional and Hybrid Thermal-Enzymatic Modified Wheat Flours as Clean Label Bread Improvers. *Appl. Sci.* **2024**, *14*, 7659. [CrossRef]
23. Blicharz-Kania, A.; Vasiukov, K.; Sagan, A.; Andrejko, D.; Fifowska, W.; Domin, M. Nutritional Value, Physical Properties, and Sensory Quality of Sugar-Free Cereal Bars Fortified with Grape and Apple Pomace. *Appl. Sci.* **2023**, *13*, 10531. [CrossRef]
24. Burešová, I.; Šebestíková, R.; Šebela, J.; Adámková, A.; Zvonková, M.; Skowronková, N.; Mlček, J. The Effect of Inulin Addition on Rice Dough and Bread Characteristics. *Appl. Sci.* **2024**, *14*, 2882. [CrossRef]

Disclaimer/Publisher's Note: The statements, opinions and data contained in all publications are solely those of the individual author(s) and contributor(s) and not of MDPI and/or the editor(s). MDPI and/or the editor(s) disclaim responsibility for any injury to people or property resulting from any ideas, methods, instructions or products referred to in the content.

Article

The Inactivation of Microscopic Fungi in Bakery Products Using Hurdle Technology—A Case Study

Anna Diowksz [1], Przemysław Kopeć [2] and Anna Koziróg [1,*]

[1] Institute of Fermentation Technology and Microbiology, Faculty of Biotechnology and Food Sciences, Lodz University of Technology, 90-530 Lodz, Poland; anna.diowksz@p.lodz.pl

[2] Dakri Ltd., 90-349 Lodz, Poland; przemkop1@tlen.pl

* Correspondence: anna.kozirog@p.lodz.pl

Abstract: The issue of the microbiological spoilage of bakery products with an extended shelf life declared by the producer was the reason for searching for an effective solution. The aim of the investigation was to find the sources of infection, identify microorganisms causing product spoilage, and propose ways to eliminate the problem without the use of chemical preservatives in the product. It was found that the dominant contaminating microorganisms are yeasts of the genus *Hyphopichia* sp., *Saccharomyces* sp., and *Candida* spp., as well as molds—*Aspergillus* spp. and *Penicillium* spp. The microbiological quality of the production environment was assessed, and as a remedial action, a disinfection process was carried out. The influence of gas composition in MAP (modified atmosphere packaging) and the use of ethanol during packaging on the incidence of yeast or mold occurrence was checked. The effectiveness of using sourdough was also tested. The best results were achieved by using sourdough obtained with selected starter cultures and using a gas mixture for packaging in the proportion of 70% carbon dioxide and 30% nitrogen, without the addition of ethanol. These conditions ensured the expected shelf life of bakery products while maintaining their quality.

Keywords: bakery products; microscopic fungi; modified atmosphere packaging (MAP); starter cultures

1. Introduction

In recent decades, there has been a dramatic increase in the scale of bread production and the extension of the supply chain. The resulting need to extend the shelf life of baked goods is a major challenge for the bakery industry.

For the consumer, constant access to fresh bread is important. However, transporting finished bread to stores does not ensure the expected quality and freshness of the products. Processes occurring from the moment of baking, i.e., loss of aroma, moisture, and, above all, staling causing hardening of the crumb, resulting mainly from starch retrogradation, limit the freshness period of bread to 24 h. The next day unsold breads are returned to the bakery or discarded. Due to the short shelf life of bread, the availability of fresh products is limited to regional areas. Production increased to an industrial scale and the resulting extension of the distribution chain requires the use of methods that extend the shelf life of products. The use of preservatives, although preventing microbiological spoilage, not only does not inhibit the staling process but is also poorly accepted by consumers. A convenient solution seems to be the production of bread using the so-called half-baking (HB) method. This method involves pre-baking the products to such a stage as to fix their quality and then transporting the half-baked products to the stores, where they will be heated and browned, which further promotes the maintenance of freshness. The use of this technology in combination with the modified atmosphere packaging (MAP) technique makes it possible to effectively extend the shelf life of semi-finished products, which improves the economics of production [1,2].

A limiting factor in the shelf life of such intermediates is their susceptibility to microbial infections. Manufacturers are trying to develop newer and newer methods of eradicating

microorganisms. These include innovative ways of packaging products or preservatives that prevent the growth of bacteria, mold, and yeast. In the case of packaging, it is possible to use the already mentioned modified atmosphere, where inert gases like CO_2 or N_2 are used [3,4]. However, the use of synthetic chemicals is currently poorly perceived by consumers due to the "clean label" market trend. The lack of consumer acceptance of synthetic additives is forcing manufacturers to use alternatives that will meet the relevant technological functions as well as market requirements. One possible solution is the use of natural additives in the form of essential oils, plant extracts, and starter cultures containing lactic acid bacteria [5–10].

In the process of food preservation, a single agent is often used, the dosage of which most often exceeds the required level. Increasingly, hurdle technology is being used, where several preserving agents are applied. By doing so, it is possible to achieve a higher level of food safety and at the same time better quality despite the use of lower quantities of preservative agents [11].

The microbiological quality of food is also greatly influenced by the production environment, such as surfaces, air, substrates used, and personnel. Although bread is free from microorganisms after baking, contamination is possible during the process of packaging, storage, or transportation [12,13]. One possible solution is to use cooling spirals with air handling units equipped with HEPA filters and a cleaning-in-place (CIP) system. To further protect the product, carbon dioxide can be injected into the coils. In further processing, packaging rooms can be designed to meet "clean room" requirements and be equipped with airlocks for workers. Such a room layout works best for long-run production. At the company under review, 30 different products are packed in the MAP packing room. Mainly, there is a hot dog, which is subjected to freezing during one of the stages of the production process. Such a production scheme precludes the use of technology in which the product is transported directly to the packing room after baking.

The aim of the research was to determine the sources of microbial contamination occurring in baked goods produced using HB technology and MAP packaging, identify spoilage microorganisms and search for solutions aimed at microbiological protection of the products meeting the expectations of customers reluctant to use chemical preservatives.

2. Materials and Methods

The research was performed in an SME bakery specializing in the production of frozen and MAP-packed semi-products.

2.1. Microbiological Testing of the Environment in a Bakery

2.1.1. Air Mycological Analysis

Air microbiological analysis was performed using the impact method using an MAS-100 (Merck; Darmstadt, Germany) air sampler. Its suction speed equals 100 L/min. In the tests, 50-L air samples were collected in the locations shown in Table 1. In both halls, the measurement was performed in three repetitions in different locations in the rooms at a height of approximately 1.5 m from the floor.

Air contamination with fungi was checked by collecting samples on Petri dishes with dichloran–glycerol agar (DG-18, Merck, Darmstadt, Germany) medium with chloramphenicol (Angene, London, UK). All samples were then left at 25 °C. After 2–3 days, the colonies that had grown were counted, taking into account the correction included in the positive sample correction table attached to the air sampler and the volume of the air sample taken. The results were given as cfu/m^3.

Table 1. Designation and description of the locations where air samples were taken.

Room Type	Sample Number	Impact Air Sampling Location
Drilling room	1	On the right side of the hall, at the entrance from the packing room
	2	At drilling machine A
	3	At drilling machine B
MAP packing room	4	At the pole located next to the packing machine T10
	5	Between the machines, in the middle of the hall
	6	In the corner of the hall, under the conveyor belt suspended from the ceiling
Atmospheric air		Right in front of the entrance to the plant through the gate

2.1.2. Mycological Analysis of Surfaces

Samples were taken by swabbing the surface of 25 cm^2, a description of which is included in Table 2.

Table 2. Markings and description of locations where samples were taken from production areas.

Room Type	Sample Number	Impact Air Sampling Location
Drilling room Driller	1	Drilling machine—the troughs on which hot dogs lie during drilling
	2	Drilling machine—the top at the front on which the hot dogs lie before drilling
	3	Drilling machine—the surface that presses the hot dog during drilling
MAP packing room	4	Swab from the surface of the top of the T 10 machine
	5	Swab from the surface of the T 17 machine
	6	Swab from the bread conveyor belt suspended from the ceiling

The swabs were taken with sterile swabs previously moistened in saline solution. After sampling, the swab was placed in 20 mL of 0.85% saline solution (Eurochem, Tarnów, Poland). In a further step, serial 10-fold dilutions were prepared. A 1 mL suspension was taken from each and introduced into a Petri dish by pouring with dichloran–glycerol agar (DG-18, Merck, Germany) medium with chloramphenicol (Angene, London, UK) to determine the number of fungi. The plates were incubated at 25 °C for 3 days, and then the grown colonies were counted. Each test was performed in triplicate. The result is given in cfu/25 cm^2 area.

2.2. Mycological Testing of Bakery Products

The amount of microscopic fungi was also determined in the bakery products. A 10 g sample was taken from each of the four types of bread (Section 2.4) and transferred to 90 mL of 0.1% peptone water (BTL, Lodz, Poland) and placed in stomacher bags with a side filter (MERCK, Germany). The whole sample was homogenized for 5 min in a stomacher BagMixer 400 (Interscience, Saint Nom la Bretêche, France) at a speed of 8 beats per second. The resulting solution was diluted by making successive 10-fold dilutions (10^{-1}–10^{-5}). From each dilution, 1 mL was taken, added to Petri dishes, and dichloran–glycerol agar (DG-18, Merck, Darmstadt, Germany) medium with chloramphenicol was poured into the dishes (Angene, London, UK). The plates were incubated at 25 °C for 3 days and then the grown colonies were counted. Tests were performed on the samples after half baking and 24 h after packaging the products in MAP (70% CO_2/30% N_2). The number of microscopic fungi was determined both in the crumb and in the outer crust of the bread. Each test was performed in triplicate, with the detection level equal to 1.0×10^1 cfu/g. The result is given in cfu/g of product.

2.3. Characterization of Microscopic Fungi in the Production Environment and in the Product

Microorganisms were isolated from bakery products packaged in a modified atmosphere. In the first stage, pure cultures of single strains were isolated. Subsequently, for microscopic observations, life-size slides were prepared and observed under a light microscope, Olympus CX41 (Olympus, Poland), at $100\times$ and $400\times$ total magnification. Characteristic structures and systems were observed and compared with diagnostic keys [14]. In the case of yeast, identification was also made based on API 20C AUX tests (Biomerieux, France). The strains were inoculated on dichloran–glycerol agar (DG-18, Merck, Darmstadt, Germany). The suspension of yeast cells in 0.85% saline solution with a turbidity equal to 2 McFarland scale was prepared. From this suspension, 0.1 mL was transferred into API C medium (Biomerieux, France) and used to inoculate the API 20 C AUX kits (Biomerieux, France). The tests were performed according to the instructions of the manufacturer. After incubation, the reactions were read by comparing them to the growth controls.

2.4. Bread Samples

The following bakery goods produced using half-baked technology were used in the research:
- Ciabatta (300 g), individually packaged (product A);
- Wheat hot dogs (60 g), packed four to a package (product B);
- Graham hot dogs (60 g), packed four to a package (product C);
- Wheat kaiser rolls (50 g), packaged six to a package (product D).

2.5. Bakery Recipes and Process Parameters

Basic test samples were prepared according to the standard recipes used at the company. The composition of the dough and process parameters remain the plant's secrets. These samples were used to conduct MAP storage trials with or without ethanol in the package. Laminated foil with an ethylene vinyl alcohol copolymer (EVOH) layer was used in the packaging process. EVOH has excellent barrier properties for oxygen, water vapor, and a variety of other gases and volatiles.

2.6. Influence of the Composition of the Gas Mixture Used in MAP Technology and the Use of Ethanol on the Development of Microscopic Fungi in Bakery Products

Test samples of four products, ciabatta (product A), a wheat hot dog (product B), a graham hot dog (product C), and a wheat roll (product D), were packed in three different modified atmosphere conditions (70% CO_2/30% N_2; 100% CO_2; and 100% N_2). Ethanol was also added to some variants at concentrations of 1.5, 4.5, and 9%. The dose of ethanol added to the packaging was calculated in relation to the weight of the products in the packaging. Ethanol was injected into the package manually just before sealing the package.

MAP-packed products were stored at room temperature for seven (product A) or five weeks (products B, C, and D).

Three packages of each variant were observed macroscopically every 2–4 days for potential yeast or mold growth. If so, contamination was confirmed by microscopic observations.

In each variant, three packages with no alcohol added were also checked for the residual oxygen content at weekly intervals using an O_2/CO_2 OxyBaby gas analyzer (WITT—Gasetechnik GmbH & Co, Witten, Germany) (Table A1). The maximum allowable percentage of residual oxygen inside the packages was set at 0.5%.

2.7. Effectiveness of Bakery Sourdoughs in Preventing the Occurrence of Microbial Infections

The modifications in the recipes and the process parameters (Table 3) were developed for the purpose of the presented study. Commercial preparations of lyophilized starter cultures containing selected strains of lactic acid bacteria (LAB) were used to study the effect of sourdough on product shelf life. Two starter cultures used in the study contained strains of lactic bacteria isolated from bakery sourdoughs: (1) a starter culture consisting of three different strains of *Lactiplantibacillus plantarum* bacteria and (2) a starter culture containing *Lactiplantibacillus plantarum* and *Fructilactobacillus sanfranciscensis* bacteria (Table 3). In accordance with the plant's policy and confidentiality agreements, the authors are not authorized to disclose the names of the products used in the research.

Table 3. Production specifications for sourdough-containing baked goods.

Raw Material Composition	Amount [kg]	Parameters
Wheat flour	19.60	Flour type 550. Parameters: gluten 30–32, falling number: 280–320 p/L, and alveograph: 0.77–0.90
Water	5.50	It is permitted to reduce or add water up to 1 L, depending on the water absorption capacity of the flour
Yeast	0.25	
Salt	0.50	
Sourdough	10	Wheat flour (5 kg), water (5 kg), and starter culture 1 or 2 (8 g) fermentation at 28 °C, 16 h
Gluten	0.56	

Yeast or mold growth and residual oxygen content were checked in the same way as in the previous paragraph.

2.8. Statistical Analysis

The experiments were performed in triplicate, and the microbiological results are presented as the arithmetic mean ± standard deviation. The significance of differences between means was determined in Excel using analysis of variance (one-way ANOVA) and Tukey's test, with $p \leq 0.05$.

3. Results

The problem of microbiological infections appearing on bakery products with a declared extended shelf life was the reason for taking corrective actions to eliminate product spoilage. In the first stage, measures were taken to define the potential source of these microorganisms. Subsequently, solutions were sought, aimed at the microbiological protection of baked goods made with half-baking technology and packaged with MAP technology, without the use of chemical preservatives.

Raw materials for bakery products did not cause microbiological problems until sale selling. After eliminating them as a possible source of microscopic fungi in the plant, attention was turned to the production environment.

3.1. Microbiological Testing of the Environment in a Bakery

At this stage of the work, analyses were carried out to assess the occurrence of microscopic fungi in the production space in two zones—the drilling room and the MAP packaging hall—in the bread production plant. The study included quantitative analysis of microscopic fungi in the air and on production surfaces.

In the drilling room, the number of fungi in the air was at level 10^2–10^3 cfu/m^3 (Table 4). The average fungi content in this room compared to outside air is not statistically significant. On the other hand, in the hall where MAP packaging takes place, compared to the drilling room, the number of tested microorganisms decreased to an average level of 7.6×10^1 cfu/m^3. In this case, there are statistically significant differences in the number of microscopic fungi between the halls.

Table 4. The number of microscopic fungi on production surfaces and in the air.

Sampling Location	Number of Sample	Air [cfu/m^3]	Production Area [cfu/25 cm^2]
Drilling room	1	$1.9 \times 10^2 \pm 1.1 \times 10^1$	$3.2 \times 10^4 \pm 6.1 \times 10^1$
	2	$2.0 \times 10^2 \pm 1.9 \times 10^1$	$7.4 \times 10^3 \pm 2.5 \times 10^1$
	3	$1.6 \times 10^3 \pm 2.5 \times 10^1$	$6.8 \times 10^4 \pm 5.5 \times 10^1$
	mean	$6.6 \times 10^{2\ a;\ A,B}$	$3.6 \times 10^{4\ c}$
MAP packaging plant	4	$1.4 \times 10^2 \pm 1.3 \times 10^1$	$3.1 \times 10^2 \pm 2.6 \times 10^1$
	5	$6.0 \times 10^1 \pm 0.0$	$5.6 \times 10^3 \pm 4.5 \times 10^1$
	6	$2.7 \times 10^1 \pm 1.1 \times 10^1$	$2.4 \times 10^3 \pm 2.0 \times 10^1$
	mean	$7.6 \times 10^{1\ b;\ B}$	$2.8 \times 10^{3\ d}$
Atmospheric air	7	$1.6 \times 10^3 \pm 5.2 \times 10^{1\ A}$	not applicable

Means within individual categories (air or production area in the drilling room and the MAP packaging plant) followed by different lowercase letters are significantly different. Means in the air category (air in the drilling room, the MAP packaging plant, and atmospheric air) followed by different capital letters are significantly different (Tukey's test, $p < 0.05$).

On the surface of the hot dog drilling machines (samples 1–3), the number of microscopic fungi was between 7.4×10^3 and 6.8×10^4 cfu/25 cm^2. In contrast, in the MAP packaging plant, on the surface of the machines and on the conveyor belt, the number is more than 1 log lower. The differences between the average number of fungi on surfaces in the two halls studied are statistically significant. It can therefore be concluded that both the air and surfaces in the packaging hall are significantly ($p < 0.05$) less contaminated.

In most manufacturing plants, internal limits are being developed to allow a certain number of microorganisms both in the air and on surfaces, taking into account the specifics of production. Nevertheless, the level of surface contamination, especially in the driller, with microscopic fungi of the order of 10^3–10^4 cfu/25 cm^2 is high.

3.2. Mycological Testing of Bakery Products

Microbiological analysis was also performed on the bread samples. The amount of microscopic fungi was checked both in the half-baked products and in their packaging process.

Regardless of the type of bread, after the half-baking process, the amount of microscopic fungi was below the detection threshold (Table 5). However, after the packaging process, the content of the tested microorganisms in the crumb was at the level of 4.8–9.8×10^1 cfu/g. Higher content was found on the crust, which may indicate that the microscopic fungi come from the external environment.

Table 5. Number of microscopic fungi in the products.

Type of Bread	After Half Backing	Microscopic Fungi [cfu/g] After Packaging	
		Crust on Bread	Bread Crumb
Ciabatta	<10^1	$1.4 \times 10^2 \pm 1.1 \times 10^1$	$5.0 \times 10^1 \pm 1.0 \times 10^1$
Wheat hot dog		$7.5 \times 10^2 \pm 3.3 \times 10^1$	$7.8 \times 10^1 \pm 1.6 \times 10^1$
Graham hot dog		$1.3 \times 10^3 \pm 4.3 \times 10^1$	$9.8 \times 10^1 \pm 1.3 \times 10^1$
Wheat kaiser roll		$1.8 \times 10^2 \pm 2.3 \times 10^1$	$4.8 \times 10^1 \pm 8.4 \times 10^0$

3.3. Characterization of Microscopic Fungi in the Production Environment and in the Product

The predominant strains of mold and yeast were isolated from the production environment as well as from the surface of the contaminated product and identified. Macroscopic and microscopic observations of characteristic structures and arrangements (for mold and yeast) and API 20C AUX tests (for yeast) made it possible to identify the tested isolates. Among the molds, two genera, *Aspergillus* spp. and *Penicillium* spp., predominated, which grew as colored colonies: black *Aspergillus niger*, green *Penicillium* spp., or yellowish-brown *Aspergillus ochraceus*. The microscopic images of the molds show conidiophores arrangements characteristic of these genera (Figure 1).

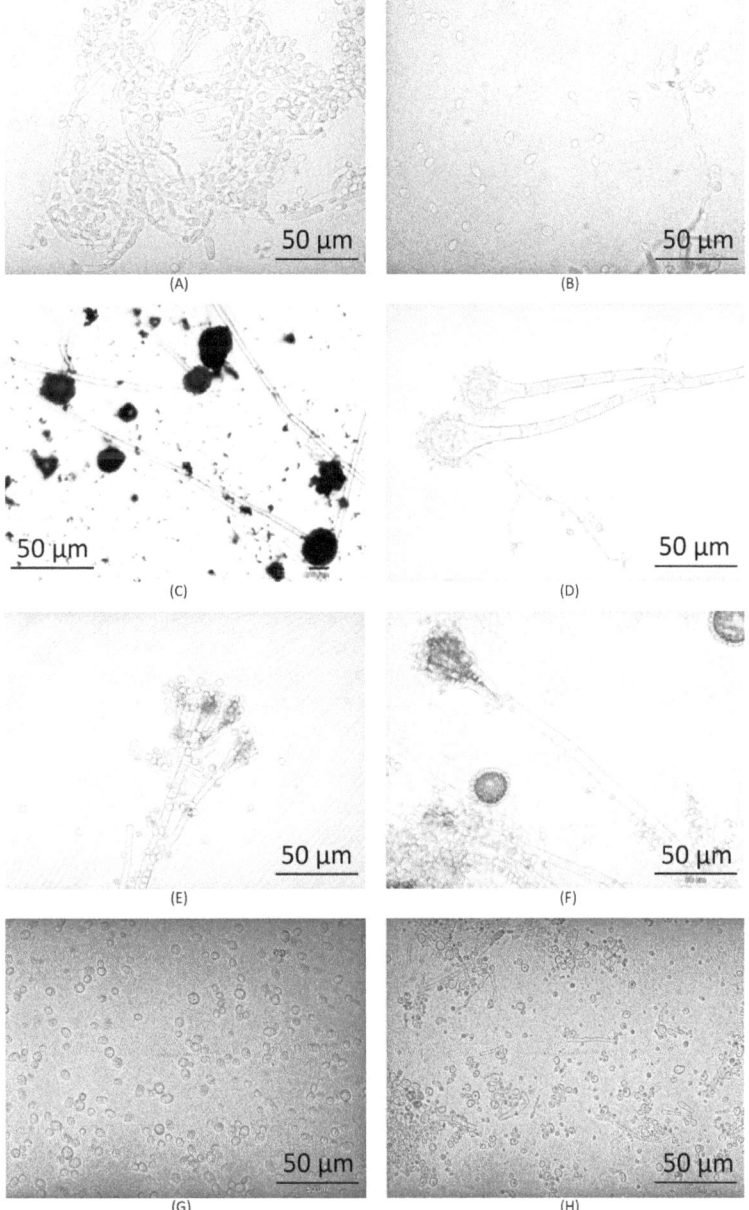

Figure 1. Microscopic observation of microscopic fungi isolated from the environment in a bakery (**C,F,G**) and the surface of baked goods (**A,B,D,E,H**) (**A**)—*Candida guilliermondii*; (**B**)—*Candida pelliculosa*; (**C**)—*Aspergillus niger*; (**D**)—*Aspergillus ochraceus*; (**E**)—*Penicillium* sp., (**F**)—*Penicillium* sp.; (**G**)—*Saccharomyces cerevisiae*; (**H**)—*Hyphopichia burtonii*.

Yeast isolates, on the other hand, were mainly the genera *Hyphopichia* sp.; *Saccharomyces* sp.; and *Candida* spp. During their microscopic observation, pseudomycelium as well as elongated or oval cells capable of vegetative reproduction by budding were observed. The yeast *Hyphopichia burtonii* on the surface of the product also formed a characteristic powdery, white, spreading coating (Figure 2).

Figure 2. Macroscopic observation of yeast growth on the ciabatta surface.

In order to eliminate microscopic fungi from the surface of various types of baked goods packaged in MAP, several modifications were made to both the packaging and product preparation processes.

3.4. Influence of the Composition of the Gas Mixture Used in MAP Technology and the Use of Ethanol on the Development of Microscopic Fungi in Bakery Products

Microscopic fungal growth was observed in almost every type of baked good packaged in a modified atmosphere but without the addition of ethanol. The data collected in Table 6 indicate the day of contamination occurrence (first number in the column) and the number of contaminated samples (the digit after the slash). In most samples, there was visible growth of single, spotty, creamy-white yeast colonies, and in the case of hot dogs, there were also more extensive, often colorful colonies of molds. In ciabatta, these appeared after 7–9 days regardless of the type of gases contained in the packages. However, in the remaining types of products (both hot dogs and wheat kaiser rolls) packaged with 100% CO_2, the development of microscopic fungi was completely inhibited. In contrast, in packages with 70% CO_2/30% N_2 and 100% N_2, the time at which the first infections appeared was 12–33 days.

Table 6. The occurrence of microscopic fungi on baked goods packed in different atmospheric conditions and ethanol concentrations during storage (day of the contamination occurrence/number of infected samples).

Type of Bread	Gases in Packaging	Ethanol Concentration [%]			
		0	1.5	4.5	9.0
Ciabatta	70% CO_2/30% N_2	9/3	11/1 (16/3)	49/0	49/0
	100% CO_2	7/2 (9/3)	49/0	49/0	49/0
	100% N_2	7/3	17/1	49/0	49/0
Wheat hot dog	70% CO_2/30% N_2	25/1 (32/3)	35/0	35/0	35/0
	100% CO_2	35/0	35/0	35/0	35/0
	100% N_2	12/1 (17/3)	35/0	35/0	35/0
Graham hot dog	70% CO_2/30% N_2	26/1 (35/2)	35/0	35/0	35/0
	100% CO_2	35/0	35/0	35/0	35/0
	100% N_2	12/1(14/3)	35/0	35/0	35/0
Wheat kaiser roll	70% CO_2/30% N_2	20/1	23/2	35/0	35/0
	100% CO_2	35/0	30/1	35/0	35/0
	100% N_2	33/1	35/0	35/0	35/0

Only the absence of infection in any sample was considered a positive result, as it reflects the level of acceptance adopted in industrial reality.

The use of 100% CO_2 was effective in protecting the products, but severe packaging deformation was observed. Package collapse results from the decrease in gas volume due to CO_2 absorption. In addition, the oxygen concentration was checked in samples packaged without added ethanol. It was found that there were no exceedances of residual oxygen standards in the packaging. Its value was below 0.5%.

The addition of ethanol at a concentration of 1.5% completely protected the hot dogs (wheat and graham) from microscopic fungal growth, in all three gas modifications. However, in the case of ciabatta as well as the wheat kaiser roll, there were single infected samples. Increasing the ethanol concentration to $\geq 4.5\%$ contributed to the complete inhibition of microscopic fungal growth in all samples tested. However, the addition of ethanol has the disadvantage of an intense alcohol smell when opening the package.

3.5. Effectiveness of Sourdoughs in Preventing the Occurrence of Microbial Infections

At this stage of the work, starter cultures containing selected strains of lactic acid bacteria (LAB) were used for the production of the examined goods. Their effect on the shelf life of half-baked goods during 30 days of storage was determined by checking the inhibition of the growth of microscopic fungi causing spoilage. The starter cultures used in the study contained strains of lactic acid bacteria isolated from baker's sourdoughs: starter cultures consisting of three different strains of *Lactiplantibacillus plantarum* (1) or *Lactiplantibacillus plantarum* and *Fructilactobacillus sanfranciscensis* (2) (Table 7). After packaging in MAP (gas mixture of 30% N_2/70% CO_2), the products were stored for 30 days.

Table 7. The number of sourdough-containing samples infected by microscopic fungi during storage.

Time [Day]	Control Without Sourdough	Starter Cultures	
		3 Different Strains of *L. plantarum* (1)	*L. plantarum* and *F. sanfranciscensis* (2)
1	0		
8	3		
15	3	0	0
26	3		
27	3		
30	3		

In the control samples without the addition of sourdough, the growth of microscopic fungi was observed in all three samples after 8 days. In turn, the activity of lactic acid bacteria effectively protected the products, and no mold or yeast growth was observed in any of the samples.

Analyzing the appearance of baked goods produced with *L. plantarum* starter and those produced with the *L. plantarum* + *F. sanfranciscensis* starter, clear differences in the appearance of the products were observed (Figure 3). The surface of the product obtained with the starter containing only one species of bacteria was smooth and uniform (Figure 3(1A)), while the usage of the starter containing two LAB species caused cracks to appear on the surface of the rolls during baking (Figure 3(2A)). However, it was considered that such a product might be perceived as a more attractive, rustic type.

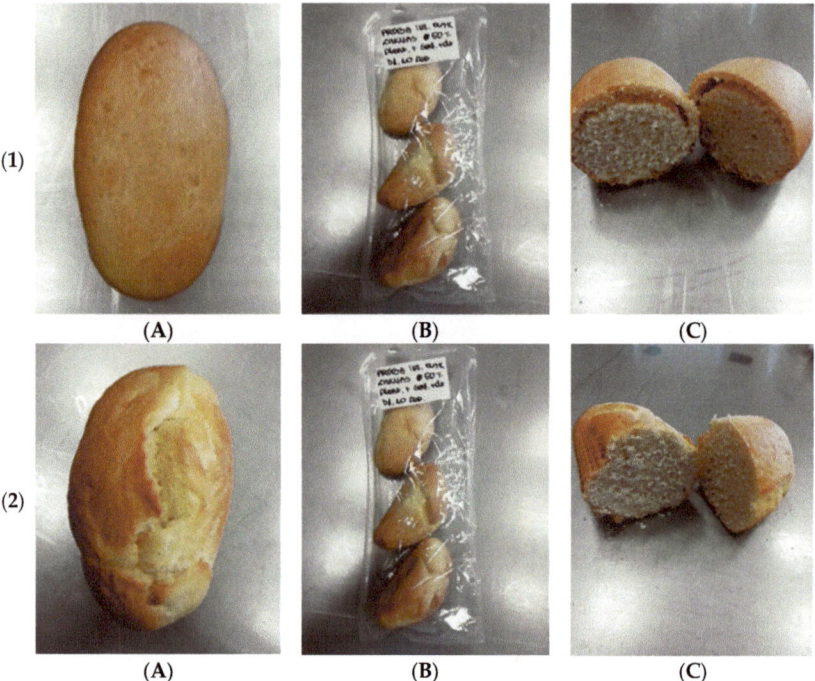

Figure 3. Appearance of products obtained with a starter containing (**1**) *L. plantarum* and (**2**) *L. plantarum* and *F. sanfranciscensis* bacteria (**A**)—before packaging in MAP; (**B**)—in MAP packaging after storage; (**C**)—after storage and removal from packaging.

The samples prepared with the *L. plantarum* + *F. sanfranciscensis* starter also had a better crumb structure after storage than the samples with the mono-culture starter. In the case of all samples, porosity was poorer than in the control sample, but in the case of sample 2 (Figure 3(2C)), no projection of the crust over the crumb was observed, as in the case of sample 1 (Figure 3(1C)).

4. Discussion

Microscopic fungal growth can occur in the bakery environment, mainly in the air and on work surfaces, equipment, personnel, and ingredients, which can contaminate products after baking and ultimately contribute to food spoilage [12,13].

Bernardi et al. (2019); Dantigny et al. (2005); Garcia et al. (2019 b), and Ollinger et al. (2020) [13,15–17] found mold in bakery air samples, where *Cladosporium*, *Aspergillus*, and *Penicillium* genera predominated. However, few studies have focused on contamination control in bakery processing plants. Verifying mold contamination in the food industry involves a complex process. It is very important to study key environmental issues, such as hygiene related to microbiological air quality in factories [13] and contamination of food-contact surfaces [18]. Therefore, in the first stage of the study, microbiological analysis of the air and surfaces in the MAP drilling and packaging room of the manufacturing plant was carried out. The microbiological tests helped determine the level of contamination in the respective production areas. Based on the results obtained, the number of microscopic fungi in the air was found to range from 3.0×10^1 to 1.6×10^3 cfu/m^3. On the surfaces, on the other hand, the values were in the 3.1×10^2–6.8×10^4 cfu/25 cm^2 range. The number of microorganisms tested in both rooms was therefore high, especially on the production surfaces.

Baked goods have a sterile surface after the baking process, and mold spores are inactivated during baking [19,20]. Also, in the presented study, in all samples, regardless of the type of bread, after the half-baking process, the level of contamination with microscopic fungi was below 10^1 cfu/g. Further cooling, packaging, and slicing procedures, however, can quickly lead to the microbial contamination of products. Air, as well as contact with surfaces and equipment, is also often a source of contamination. This is confirmed by the results obtained, indicating a significant deterioration in the quality of bread after contact with the environment in the plant. The level of contamination, especially of hot dogs, increased to $7.5 \times 10^2 \div 1.3 \times 10^3$ cfu/g. This is not a high level compared to the data presented by Garcia et al. (2019 b), where the amount of mold in bread ranges from 2.6×10^7 to 9×10^8 cfu/g. However, it should be remembered that the tested products were intended for long-term storage, and what is more, molds are potential toxin-producing microorganisms. Also noteworthy is the fact that a ready-to-eat hot dog is not just the bread itself, but also cut, fresh vegetable. These ingredients are also very often highly contaminated [21]. Repeating the process of cutting such vegetables increases the number of bacteria, because the knife, contaminated during cutting, comes into contact with the vegetable several times. In the final product, the amount of microorganisms is therefore the sum of all contaminants and makes the product unfit for consumption.

The reason for the increasing contamination of products after half baking is the poor quality of the production environment. Microscopic fungi present in the air and on production surfaces enter products both during the drilling and packaging processes. It is therefore important to prevent contamination after the baking process. Sanitary practices during the subsequent stages of production are of great importance here in particular.

Mold causes not only changes in the color or taste of baked goods but also a loss of food quality due to the possible production of mycotoxins. Among the genera that contaminate bread, the following are listed: *Alternaria* and *Cladosporium*—often found in the air, *Aspergillus* and *Penicillium*—so-called storage molds, and *Rhizopus, Mucor*, or *Geotrichum*. One of the most common species is *Rhizopus stolonifer*, called "bread mold" [6,13,19,22–24]. In the work presented herein, among the isolated strains of mold, two genera predominated—*Aspergillus* and *Penicillium*—which are also mentioned by other authors [25–27] as the main cause of bread spoilage.

Various types of yeast were also identified in the analyzed samples. In the not-fully-thawed MAP-packaged products, high condensation of moisture in the packaging was observed. This contributed to a very intensive development of yeast forming white, rather extensive colonies macroscopically similar to mold, which were identified as *Hyphopichia burtoni*. According to Legan and Vosey [28], this yeast is capable of developing at low a_w = 0.85, where it forms white or pink spots on the surface of products. It is a species that is very often isolated from baked goods and can rapidly multiply to form a pseudomycelium. Together with *Pichia anomala* and *Saccharomycopsis fibuligera*, they cause spoilage of pre-baked, MAP-packed baked goods, which is known as "chalk mold" [29,30]. As Cauvain (2015) [31] points out, modified atmosphere packaging can extend the shelf life of bakery products but is ineffective against spoilage by chalk mold.

In the presented work, two species of *C. guilliermondii* and *C. parapsilosis*, which are known as potential human pathogens, were also isolated from the surface of the examined samples. So-called non-albicans *Candida* have recently found increasing interest as a growing cause of infection [32]. Although not considered a source of foodborne infection, both isolated species were found in more than 20% of bread samples collected in Europe [28]. Unlike mold, where the risks associated with mycotoxin production are known, the health significance of yeast-contaminated foods is not well recognized. However, there are some reports indicating that the above-mentioned yeast species can also cause disease in humans [33].

The use of half-baking technology in combination with MAP packaging technology makes it possible to effectively extend the shelf life of baked goods, which improves the economics of production. However, a limiting factor in the shelf life of such semi-baked products is their susceptibility to the occurrence of microbial infections, mainly related to the growth of microscopic fungi.

Three different modifications of the gas composition were used in the study. The best results were achieved for packages containing only CO_2, where fungal growth was observed only on ciabatta. However, this resulted in the collapse of the packaging and ultimately the shrinking of the foil around the products. Therefore, it is necessary to add nitrogen, which has a filling function in the packaging.

The effectiveness of carbon dioxide in MAP-packaged bakery products was confirmed by Guynot et al. (2003) [34], who observed no mold growth after 28 days of storing samples at 25 °C. The gas acts as a fungistatic agent by inhibiting metabolism and disrupting enzymatic activity and can also react with proteins [1]. In the other two variants, where a mixture of 70% CO_2/30% N_2 or 100% N_2 was used, infected samples were present in all types of products.

Soares et al. (2002) [35] conclude that the use of MAP technology to extend the shelf life of baked goods has some drawbacks. According to them, the highly porous structure does not allow for the complete elimination of oxygen and its migration from the product to the package; therefore, the oxygen concentration may increase in the package. Meanwhile, the results obtained in the course of repeated tests several times contradict the described results. They did not confirm the migration of oxygen from the product into the package. The vacuum created during packaging is unable to completely remove the gases from the product. However, the lack of increase in oxygen concentration in the package during storage may be due to the fact that during fermentation, carbon dioxide, which is one of the products of fermentation, dominates in the pores of the bread.

In order to protect the bakery samples from the growth of microscopic fungi, ethanol was administered to the packages during MAP packaging.

The addition of ethanol is one of the methods of preserving bread. Dao and Dantigny (2011) [36] indicate that the presence of this compound in the concentration range of 0.2–20% extends the shelf life of baked goods. However, ethanol is very often ineffective against yeast [20,28]. This is confirmed by the results obtained in this study, where microbial infections occurred in some samples with 1.5% ethanol, but in all cases, it was yeast.

Legan and Voysey (1991) [28] found that ethanol can significantly extend the shelf life of bakery products without mold contamination when ethanol is added to their surfaces or packaging in an amount of up to 2% by weight of the product. The compound also has a moderate effect in preventing the darkening of baked goods. However, the use of ethanol in food packaging has some limitations. The disadvantage is the strong, undesirable odor of alcohol [20], which was also found in the presented work. For bread and other bakery products, active ethanol-emitting systems can be used to extend shelf life, and vanilla and other compounds can be used to mask the ethanol odor.

The last of the modifications tested for the potential to reduce the development of microscopic fungi in baked goods were starter cultures. The use of lactic acid bacteria in the form of sourdough effectively protected MAP-packed products from microscopic fungal growth. Bread produced with starters also had other advantages: better taste and aroma and delayed darkening process.

The antifungal properties of LAB strains of the former genus *Lactobacillus* (*L. plantarum*, *L. brevis*, or *L. reuteri*) in bakery products have been reported, among others, by Valerio et al. (2009) [37], Gerez et al. (2009) [25], and Cizeikiene et al. (2013) [38]. They tested more than a dozen strains of lactic acid bacteria, which showed a strong inhibitory effect on the growth of molds such as *Aspergillus niger*, *Penicillium roqueforti*, and *Endomyces fibuliger*, comparable to the effect of the commonly used preservative calcium propionate. Some lactic acid bacteria also have the ability to react with secondary metabolites of fungi that contaminate food, causing decontamination of mycotoxins [39,40].

Ceresino et al. (2024) [41] also emphasize that microorganisms contained in sourdough can be used as part of a natural food preservation strategy through the development of antimicrobial metabolites such as short-chain carboxylic acids, ethanol, and bacteriocins.

The antifungal activity of *Lactiplantibacillus plantarum* described by Liu et al. (2022) [42] is caused, among others, by (a) cationic peptides—their antifungal activity results from interactions with negatively charged molecules of the fungal cell membrane, which leads to cell death [43] or (b) unsaturated fatty acids with hydroxyl groups (HUFA)—the antifungal activity is related to their structure [44]. Lactic acid bacteria and their metabolites are a valuable source of antifungal compounds, making them increasingly used in bakery products as natural preservatives

5. Conclusions

Yeasts of the genus *Hyphopichia* sp., *Saccharomyces* sp., and *Candida* spp. as well as molds—*Aspergillus* spp. and *Penicillium* spp.—were found to be predominant as the spoilage microorganisms of half-baked products. Due to a large number of microscopic fungi found both in the air and on production surfaces, the plant disinfection and implementation of hygienization process procedures were required. In order to effectively prevent the growth of yeast and mold on the surface of the packaged products, the hurdle method of protection (Figure 4) was necessary.

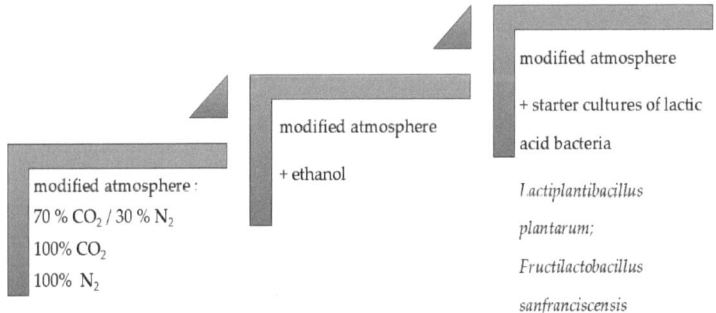

Figure 4. Application of hurdle technology in the prevention of bakery goods spoilage.

Modified atmosphere packaging alone turned out to be ineffective. The additional application of ethanol, although protecting the products quite well, contributed to the unpleasant smell of the product. The best solution to protect baked goods against microbiological contamination was to combine packaging in a modified atmosphere with the use of LAB starter cultures.

Author Contributions: Conceptualization, A.K. and A.D.; methodology, A.K., P.K. and A.D.; formal analysis, A.K. and P.K.; investigation, P.K. and A.K.; data curation, A.K.; statistical analysis, A.K.; writing—original draft preparation, A.K., A.D. and P.K; writing—review and editing, A.K. and A.D.; visualization, A.K.; supervision, A.K. and A.D. All authors have read and agreed to the published version of the manuscript.

Funding: This research was funded by the "Industrial Doctorate" project implemented at the Faculty of Biotechnology and Food Sciences of the Lodz University of Technology (TUL), contract No. 40/DW/2017/01/1, financed by Ministry of Science and Education in Poland.

Data Availability Statement: The original contributions presented in the study are included in the article, further inquiries can be directed to the corresponding author.

Conflicts of Interest: Author Przemysław Kopeć was employed by the company Dakri Ltd. The remaining authors declare that the research was conducted in the absence of any commercial or financial relationships that could be construed as a potential conflict of interest.

Appendix A

Table A1. Summary of the number of samples packaged in different atmospheric modifications and with different amounts of alcohol.

Type of Bread	Gases in Packaging	Ethanol Concentration [%]			
		0	1.5	4.5	9.0
Ciabatta	70% CO_2/30% N_2	24	3	3	3
	100% CO_2	24	3	3	3
	100% N_2	24	3	3	3
Wheat hot dog	70% CO_2/30% N_2	18	3	3	3
	100% CO_2	18	3	3	3
	100% N_2	18	3	3	3
Graham hot dog	70% CO_2/30% N_2	18	3	3	3
	100% CO_2	18	3	3	3
	100% N_2	18	3	3	3
Wheat roll	70% CO_2/30% N_2	18	3	3	3
	100% CO_2	18	3	3	3
	100% N_2	18	3	3	3

References

1. Ooraikul, B. Modified Atmosphere Packaging of Bakery Products. In *Modified Atmosphere Packaging of Food*; Ooraikul, B., Stiles, E., Eds.; Ellis Horwood: New York, NY, USA, 1991; pp. 49–117.
2. Kotsianis, I.S.; Giannou, V.; Tzia, C. Production and packing of bakery products using MAP technology. *Trends Food Sci. Technol.* **2002**, *13*, 319–324. [CrossRef]
3. Czerwiński, K.; Rydzkowski, T.; Wróblewska-Krepsztul, J.; Thakur, V.K. Towards Impact of Modified Atmosphere Packaging (MAP) on Shelf-Life of Polymer-Film-Packed Food Products: Challenges and Sustainable Developments. *Coatings* **2021**, *11*, 1504. [CrossRef]
4. Degirmencioglu, N.; Göcmen, D.; Inkaya, A.N.; Aydin, E.; Guldas, M.; Gonenc, S. Influence of modified atmosphere packaging and potassium sorbate on microbiological characteristics of sliced bread. *J. Food Sci. Technol.* **2011**, *48*, 236–241. [CrossRef] [PubMed]
5. Vermelho, A.B.; Moreira, J.V.; Junior, A.N.; da Silva, C.R.; Cardoso, V.D.S.; Akamine, I.T. Microbial Preservation and Contamination Control in the Baking Industry. *Fermentation* **2024**, *10*, 231. [CrossRef]
6. Garcia, M.V.; Copetti, M.V. Alternative Methods for Mould Spoilage Control in Bread and Bakery Products. *Int. Food Res. J.* **2019**, *26*, 737–749.
7. Islam, F.; Saeed, F.; Imran, A.; Shehzadi, U.; Ali, R.; Nosheen, F.; Chauhan, A.; Asghar, A.; Ojukwu, M. Bio-Preservatives and Essential Oils as an Alternative to Chemical Preservatives in the Baking Industry: A Concurrent Review. *J. Food Sci. Technol.* **2023**, *61*, 609–620. [CrossRef]
8. Illueca, F.; Moreno, A.; Calpe, J.; Nazareth, T.D.M.; Dopazo, V.; Meca, G.; Quiles, J.M.; Luz, C. Bread Biopreservation through the Addition of Lactic Acid Bacteria in Sourdough. *Foods* **2023**, *12*, 864. [CrossRef]
9. Gonçalves, N.D.; de Lima Pena, F.; Sartoratto, A.; Derlamelina, C.; Duarte, M.C.T.; Antunes, A.E.C.; Prata, A.S. Encapsulated thyme (*Thymus vulgaris*) essential oil used as a naturalpreservative in bakery product. *Food Res. Int.* **2017**, *96*, 154–160. [CrossRef]
10. Sadeghi, A.; Ebrahimi, M.; Mortazavi, S.A.; Abedfar, A. Application of the selected antifungal LAB isolate as a protective starter culture in pan whole-wheat sourdough bread. *Food Control* **2019**, *95*, 298–307. [CrossRef]
11. Kour, M.; Gupta, N.; Sood, M.; Bandral, J.D.; Hameed, F.; Kour, P. Hurdle Technology: A Review. *Int. J. Chem. Stud.* **2019**, *7*, 2579–2585.
12. Dijksterhuis, J. Fungal spores: Highly Variable and Stress-Resistant Vehicles for Distribution and Spoilage. *Food Microbiol.* **2019**, *81*, 2–11. [CrossRef] [PubMed]
13. Garcia, M.V.; Bernardi, A.O.; Parussolo, G.; Stefanello, A.; Lemos, J.G.; Copetti, M.V. Spoilage Fungi in a Bread Factory in Brazil: Diversity and Incidence Through The Bread-Making Process. *Food Res. Int.* **2019**, *126*, 108593. [CrossRef] [PubMed]
14. Samson, R.A.; Hoekstra, E.S.; Frisvad, J.C. *Introduction to Food and Airborne Fungi*, 7th ed.; Centraalbureau voor Schimmelcultures: Utrecht, The Netherlands, 2004.
15. Bernardi, A.O.; Garcia, M.V.; Copetti, M. Food Industry Spoilage Fungi Control Through Facility Sanitization. *Curr. Opin. Food Sci.* **2019**, *29*, 28–34. [CrossRef]
16. Dantigny, P.; Guilmart, A.; Bensoussan, M. Basis of Predictive Mycology. *Int. J. Food Microbiol.* **2005**, *100*, 187–196. [CrossRef]

17. Ollinger, N.; Lasinger, V.; Probst, C.; Pitsch, J.; Sulyok, M.; Krska, R.; Weghuber, J. DNA Barcoding for The Identification of Mold Species in Bakery Plants and Products. *Food Chem.* **2020**, *318*, 126501. [CrossRef]
18. Britton, B.C.; Sarr, I.; Oliver, H.F. Enterobacteriaceae, Coliform, Yeast, and Mold Contamination Patterns in Peanuts Compared to Production, Storage, Use Practices, and Knowledge of Food Safety Among Growers in Senegal. *Int. J. Food Microbiol.* **2021**, *360*, 109437. [CrossRef]
19. Saranraj, P.; Geetha, M. Microbial Spoilage of Bakery Products and Its Control by Preservatives. *Int. J. Pharm. Biol. Arch.* **2012**, *3*, 38–48.
20. Melini, V.; Melini, F. Strategies to Extend Bread and GF Bread Shelf-Life: From Sourdough to Antimicrobial Active Packaging and Nanotechnology. *Fermentation* **2018**, *4*, 9. [CrossRef]
21. Sun, Y.; Zhao, X.; Ma, Y.; Ma, Z.; He, Z.; Zhao, W.; Wang, P.; Zhao, S.; Wang, D. Investigation on the Microbial Diversity of Fresh-Cut Lettuce during Processing and Storage Using High Throughput Sequencing and Their Relationship with Quality. *Foods* **2022**, *11*, 1683. [CrossRef]
22. Vagelas, I.; Gougoulias, N.; Nedesca, E.D.; Liviu, G. Bread Contamination with Fungus. *Carpathian J. Food Sci. Technol.* **2011**, *3*, 1–6.
23. Viljpen, C.R.; von Holy, A. Microbial Populations Associated with Commercial Bread Production. *J. Basic Microbiol.* **1997**, *37*, 439–444. [CrossRef] [PubMed]
24. Chou, K.; Liu, J.; Lu, X.; Hsiao, H.I. Quantitative Microbial Spoilage Risk Assessment of Aspergillus Niger in White Bread Reveal That Retail Storage Temperature and Mold Contamination During Factory Cooling are The Main Factors to Influence Spoilage. *Food Microbiol.* **2024**, *119*, 104443. [CrossRef] [PubMed]
25. Gerez, C.L.; Torino, M.I.; Rollán, G.; Font de Valdez, G. Prevention of Bread Mold Spoilage by Using Lactic Acid Bacteria with Antifungal Properties. *Food Control* **2009**, *20*, 144–148. [CrossRef]
26. Demirel, R.; Sariozlu, N.Y. Mycotoxigenic Moulds and Mycotoxins in Flours Consumed in Turkey. *J. Sci. Food Agri.* **2013**, *94*, 1577–1584. [CrossRef]
27. Weidenbörner, M.; Wieczorek, C.; Appel, S.; Kunz, B. Whole Wheat and White Wheat Flour-The Mycobiota and Potential Myco-Toxins. *Food Microbiol.* **2000**, *17*, 103–107. [CrossRef]
28. Legan, J.D.; Voysey, P.A. Yeast Spoilage of Bakery Products and Ingredients. *J. Appl. Bacteriol.* **1990**, *70*, 361–371. [CrossRef]
29. Deschuyffeleer, N.; Audenaert, K.; Samapundo, S.; Ameye, S.; Eeckhout, M.; Devlieghere, F. Identification and Characterization of Yeasts Causing Chalk Mould Defects on Par-Baked Bread. *Food Microbiol.* **2011**, *28*, 1019–1027. [CrossRef]
30. Burgain, A.; Bensoussan, M.; Dantigny, P. Validation of a Predictive Model for The Growth of Chalk Yeasts on Bread. *Int. J. Food Microbiol.* **2015**, *204*, 47–54. [CrossRef]
31. Cauvain, S. Bread spoilage and staling. In *Technology of Breadmaking*; Springer: Cham, Switzerland, 2015; pp. 279–302.
32. Riesute, R.; Salomskiene, J.; Moreno, D.S.; Gustiene, S. Effect of Yeasts on Food Quality and Safety and Possibilities of Their Inhibition. *Trends Food Sci. Technol.* **2021**, *108*, 1–10. [CrossRef]
33. Chamroensakchai, T.; Kanjanabuch, T.; Saikong, W.; Panya, W.; Thaweekote, S.; Eiam-Ong, S.; Hurdeal, V.G.; Hyde, K.D. The First Human Report of *Hyphopichia Burtonii*, Initially Misdiagnosed as Sterile Peritonitis in a Patient on Peritoneal Dialysis. *Med. Mycol. Case Rep.* **2021**, *33*, 26–29. [CrossRef]
34. Guynot, M.E.; Marin, S.; Sanchis, V.; Ramos, A.J. Modified Atmosphere Packaging for Prevention of Mold Spoilage of Bakery Products with Different pH and Water Activity Levels. *J. Food Prod.* **2003**, *10*, 1864–1872. [CrossRef] [PubMed]
35. Soares, N.F.F.; Rutishauser, D.M.; Melo, N.; Cruz, R.S.; Andrade, N.J. Inhibition of Microbial Growth in Bread Through Active Packaging. *Packag. Technol. Sci.* **2002**, *15*, 129–132. [CrossRef]
36. Dao, T.; Dantigny, P. Control of Food Spoilage Fungi By Ethanol. *Food Control* **2011**, *22*, 360–368. [CrossRef]
37. Valerio, F.; Favilla, M.; De Bellis, P.; Sisto, A.; de Candia, S.; Lavermicocc, P. Antifungal Activity of Strains of Lactic Acid Bacteria Isolated from a Semolina Ecosystem Against *Penicillium roqueforti*, *Aspergillus niger* and *Endomyces fibuliger* Contaminating Bakery Products. *Syst. Appl. Microbiol.* **2009**, *32*, 438–448. [CrossRef]
38. Cizeikiene, D.; Juodeikiene, G.; Paskevicius, A.; Bartkiene, E. Antimicrobial Activity of Lactic Acid Bacteria against Pathogenic and Spoilage Microorganism Isolated from Food and Their Control in Wheat Bread. *Food Control* **2013**, *31*, 539–545. [CrossRef]
39. Piotrowska, M. Microbiological Decontamination of Mycotoxins: Opportunities and Limitations. *Mycotoxins* **2021**, *13*, 819. [CrossRef]
40. Dalié, D.K.D.; Deschamps, A.M.; Richard–Forget, F. Lactic Acid Bacteria–Potential for Control of Mould Growth and Mycotoxins: A Review. *Food Control* **2010**, *21*, 370–380. [CrossRef]
41. Ceresino, E.B.; Juodeikiene, G.; Schwenninger, S.M.; Ferreira da Rocha, J.M. *Sourdough Microbiota and Starter Cultures for Industry*; Springer: Cham, Switzerland, 2024. [CrossRef]
42. Liu, A.; Xu, R.; Zhang, S.; Wang, Y.; Hu, B.; Ao, X.; Li, O.; Li, J.; Hu, K.; Yang, Y.; et al. Antifungal Mechanisms and Application of Lactic Acid Bacteria in Bakery Products: A Review. *Front. Microbiol.* **2022**, *13*, 924398. [CrossRef]

43. Muhialdin, B.J.; Algboory, H.L.; Kadum, H.; Mohammed, N.K.; Saari, N.; Hassan, Z.; Hussin, A.S.M. Antifungal Activity Determination for The Peptides Generated By *Lactobacillus plantarum* TE10 Against *Aspergillus flavus* in Maize Seeds. *Food Control* **2020**, *109*, 106898. [CrossRef]
44. Liang, N.; Cai, P.; Wu, D.; Pan, Y.; Curtis, J.M.; Gänzle, M.G. High-Speed Counter-Current Chromatography (HSCCC) Purification of Antifungal Hydroxy Unsaturated Fatty Acids from Plant-Seed Oil and Lactobacillus Cultures. *J. Agric. Food Chem.* **2017**, *65*, 11229–11236. [CrossRef]

Disclaimer/Publisher's Note: The statements, opinions and data contained in all publications are solely those of the individual author(s) and contributor(s) and not of MDPI and/or the editor(s). MDPI and/or the editor(s) disclaim responsibility for any injury to people or property resulting from any ideas, methods, instructions or products referred to in the content.

Article

Application of Conventional and Hybrid Thermal-Enzymatic Modified Wheat Flours as Clean Label Bread Improvers

Piotr Lewko [1,2], Agnieszka Wójtowicz [1,*] and Marek Gancarz [3,4,5]

1 Department of Thermal Technology and Food Process Engineering, University of Life Sciences in Lublin, Głęboka 31, 20-612 Lublin, Poland; piotr.lewko@up.lublin.pl
2 PZZ Lubella GMW Sp. z o.o., Wrotkowska 1, 20-469 Lublin, Poland
3 Faculty of Production and Power Engineering, University of Agriculture in Krakow, Balicka 116B, 30-149 Krakow, Poland; marek.gancarz@urk.edu.pl
4 Institute of Agrophysics, Polish Academy of Sciences, Doświadczalna 4, 20-290 Lublin, Poland
5 Center of Innovation and Research on Healthy and Safe Food, University of Agriculture in Krakow, Balicka 104, 30-149 Krakow, Poland
* Correspondence: agnieszka.wojtowicz@up.lublin.pl

Abstract: A new flour blend (F) composed of selected milling and leaving passages with a high content of non-starch polysaccharides underwent thermal (T), hydrothermal (H) or hybrid processing and was used along with cellulase (C) and cellulase-xylanase complex (CX) to produce bread. This modified flour can be considered a clean label product. In this study, blends of common and treated flours were tested for dough properties and rheology. The modified flours were added at 10 and 20% to the base wheat flour. A pan bread was then prepared to test their suitability for bread baking. Dough and bread properties were subsequently assessed. Accordingly, dough with added thermally, hydrothermally, and hybrid modified flours revealed differences in rheology. Addition of hybrid enzymatic-hydrothermal treated flour increased dough tenacity by 23% and baking strength by 26%, but decreased dough extensibility by 19%, whereas hybrid enzymatic-thermal modification increased water absorption by 6% and bread yield from 146.77% to 150.02% when modified flour was added at 20%. Breads with added modified flours demonstrated a 16% increase in bread volume, 8% lower baking loss, and 14% greater density, with no negative effect on color and texture. Thus, hybrid thermal-enzymatic treatment of the developed flours can be recommended as a suitable method for enhancing the utilization of waste flour fractions and increasing their value by enabling them to be considered as clean label bread improvers.

Keywords: thermal treatment; enzymatic treatment; hydrothermal; wheat flour; dough rheology; bread quality

1. Introduction

Bread, as one of the most common food products in the world, is considered crucial in human nutrition due to its accessibility and nutritional value. It is a very good source of carbohydrates, protein, dietary fiber, vitamins, and minerals [1]. Progress in the milling and bakery industries has resulted in the development of technology for the production of bakery products. These products are constantly improved, which allows industry to introduce wheat-based products with special health-promoting and functional values to the food market. Current research trends are focused on nutritional and technological improvements in cereal-based products using various additives and production processes that, ideally, allow these products to be recognized as clean label products [2,3]. The outcome of such work is that the addition of alternative components to standard wheat flour (insects, legumes, fruits, vegetables, herbs, microalgae, or by-products from the agri-food industry) [4–9], as well as the use of modern grain processing technologies [10,11] has enabled improvement of bakery products, especially of whole grain flours and breads [12].

To improve the functional properties of wheat flour through physical modification, various flour treatment technologies can be used. The most popular are dry heating or hydrothermal treatment with steam [13–17]. Additional modifications may be supported by utilizing selected enzymes such as cellulase or xylanase [18,19]. Modern technologies that can be applied to change or improve cereals' properties include steam explosion (SE), high-hydrostatic-pressure (HHP), high-pressure homogenization (HPH), pulsed electric field (PEF), and plasma processing. The use of these technologies has significant effects on the resulting flour's chemical, rheological, and hydration properties, as reported by Li and Niu [20]. Introducing specific physical modifications to grains or flours could reduce the negative effects of supplementation with wholegrain flour or unmodified bran-rich fractions on bread quality, especially with regard to dough rheology and bread quality [21–23]. Processes for extracting selected ingredients and components with desired properties from grains, mostly based on soluble and insoluble dietary fiber or beta-glucans, vitamins, and antioxidants, are under intense development [6,24,25].

Heating, as a physical treatment, via various methods (dry heating, hydrothermal, extrusion) may effectively modify the techno-functional properties of wheat grain and flour without the introduction of undesirable chemical additives. Hence, the developed products can be considered clean label additives [7]. Even if enzymes are used in such modification processes, after drying, the enzymes are inactivated, so enzymatically assisted modification can also be considered a clean label approach in bread production [12,13]. Each of the aforementioned modifications are intended to improve the various attributes of bakery products, especially their nutritional attributes, but, unfortunately, they often also have a negative impact on the technological and production properties of dough and, consequently, bakery products, e.g., bread [2].

Mill streams richest in fiber fractions come from the outer parts of the grain. As we described in our previous studies [26], differences in the composition of individual main milling streams of wheat result directly from the origin of specific fractions from the anatomical parts of the grain and the influence of grinding processes such as the mechanical damage of starch. Fractions containing bran parts, also of various sizes, are considered undesirable as a component of standard bread flours due to lower overall quality of dough and a decrease in dough elasticity and bread volume [26–29]; as such, they are sold as bran-rich products and supplements or animal feed [30]. Such items bring in less profit to the mill owners. These underutilized fractions amount to about 10% of the total production in a milling company, so it is economically important to find technological solutions for reducing the quantity of these underutilized fractions by increasing their use in higher quality products.

Economics and growing consumer concerns about food ingredients and clean labelling have had an impact on industrial bread production, resulting in enhanced efficiency and new recipes [3]. Consumers are looking for clean label products, without E-marked additives, but also with proper quality [20]. Unfortunately, some bread improvers are perceived as being unknown and harmful chemicals that may be unhealthy to consume [3]. In contrast, thermal processing methods may have a positive impact on the final quality of bakery products while enabling these to be considered "clean label". In this present study, we investigate the possibility of using a developed wheat flour with an increased content of non-starch polysaccharides [26], fortified with baking enzymes, and additionally treated via various physical methods for bread production. Such modifications may offset the negative effects of treatments on the final quality of flour and help in the utilization of unused flour fractions as clean label additives to commercial bread flour blends.

The aim of the study was to investigate the impact of the addition of flours subjected to enzymatic, thermal, hydrothermal, and enzyme-assisted hybrid modifications on the quality of bread dough during mixing and fermentation, and on the characteristics of bread, as compared to the use of conventional flour.

2. Materials and Methods

2.1. Materials

Common wheat flour type 750 produced in PZZ Lubella was used as the base raw material suitable for the production of wheat bread. This was characterized by a moisture content of 14.3%, a gluten content of 28.2%, an ash content of 0.77%, and a falling number of 280 s. The developed flour before modifications was characterized as having a moisture content of 13.7%, a gluten content of 31.0%, an ash content of 0.78%, and a falling number of 340 s. The functional flours were prepared by undergoing thermal and hydrothermal treatments as described in Section 2.2 and were added in amounts of 10 and 20% of the total common flour base. The quantities of the incorporated modified flours were selected based on a preliminary study and on economic profitability. In the preliminary study, at over 20% of modified flours, the tested bread showed a tendency to collapse during fermentation and baking, thus 20% was considered the upper limit in the full study (any greater amount would lower the final product quality, hence lowering the profitability of production).

Selected batches of the functional flours underwent hybrid enzyme-assisted treatments. Commercial baking enzymes were employed to fortify the flour (the amount of the enzyme was determined based on preliminary tests and on the suggestions of the enzyme manufacturer). The following baking enzymes were used in the experiment: Bakezyme® WholeGrain-cellulase from *Trichoderma reesei* (DSM Food Specialities B.V., Delft, The Netherlands) with declared enzyme activity 1475 EGU/g (+/−5%); VERON 292-xylanase from *Aspergillus niger*, (AB Enzymes GmbH, Darmstadt, Germany) with declared enzyme activity min 1701 XylH/g. The cellulase enzyme was added in the amount of 120 ppm (samples marked as C), and the complex of cellulase and xylanase enzyme was incorporated in amounts of 60 ppm and 50 ppm, respectively (samples marked CX). Salt (Ciech S.A., Warszawa, Poland) and commercial bakery yeast (Lallemand, Lublin, Poland) were also used in the recipe.

2.2. Flour Modification Procedure

Enzymatic modification of the developed wheat flour (F) [31] was performed through the addition of 120 ppm of powdered cellulase (FC) and a combined 50 + 60 ppm of cellulase-xylanase complex (FCX). Components were mixed for 5 min at room temperature using a laboratory ribbon mixer (Konstal-Zakład Mechaniczny CNC Zbigniew Własiuk, Lublin, Poland) and left for 2 h to start enzymatic action.

A prototype installation (owned by PZZ Lubella) with an efficiency of 650 kg/h was used to obtain the modified flours. This consisted of cylindrical barrels with heating jackets that incorporated screw transporting-mixing elements.

Dry thermal treatment (T) was carried out for the tested wheat flour (TF) and for the flours incorporating the enzymes (TFC and TFCX) after mixing in a continuous ribbon mixer for 2 min at 25 °C. The processed flours underwent 5 min of dry heating at 15% moisture content inside the barrel, wherein the heating jacket temperature was set to 100 °C; the product temperature was measured during the tests so as not to exceed 50 °C.

Hydrothermal modification (H) of base wheat flour (HF) and the flours incorporating the enzymes (HFC and HFCX) was performed after mixing in a continuous ribbon mixer for 2 min at 25 °C using a prototype installation equipped with an additional steam-assisted preconditioner. Herein, flour samples without/with enzymes were mixed at 30 °C for 2 min and transferred to a single-screw preconditioner with 20 L/h of water, with a set jacket temperature of 100 °C, and were subjected to steam injection for 5 min. The product temperature measured during the tests did not exceed 65 °C.

The heated or hybrid enzymatic-assisted treated samples were subsequently dried in an air dryer at 100 °C for at least 15 min to end enzyme activity. A final moisture content of below 9% was achieved.

All samples were ground and sieved using a square sifter (Toruńskie Zakłady Urządzeń Młyńskich Spomasz S.A., Toruń, Poland) to homogenize the material and remove aggregates to obtain particle sizes below 300 µm. The samples were then stored at room temperature in closed plastic bags before tests.

2.3. Rheological Properties of Flours and Dough with Added Modified Flours

Rheological tests were performed with the following devices: Mixolab (Chopin Tech-nologies, Villeneuve-la-Garenne, France) according to ICC method 173, Brabender Farinograph-E apparatus (Duisburg, Germany) according to ICC method 115/1, and Alveograph (Chopin Technologies, Villeneuve-la-Garenne, France) according to ICC method 121 [32].

Rheological properties of blends prepared with additions of the modified flours were studied using a Chopin Mixolab based on the Chopin+ flour protocol with some modifications. The device was equipped with an additional attachment (the set includes a dough feeder and a special nozzle for this application) to control the quality of the prepared dough. For this purpose, 75 g of dough prepared during the bread preparation procedure described in Section 2.4 was transferred directly to the mixer and the test was begun according to the standard protocol at the following settings: dough weight—75 g, total analysis time—45 min, mixing speed—80 rpm, hydration water temperature 30 °C [33]. The Mixolab test was performed using a standard protocol: 8 min at 30 °C, heating for 15 min at a rate of 4 °C/min, holding at 90 °C for 7 min, cooling for 10 min to 50 °C at a rate of 4 °C/min, and holding at 50 °C for 5 min [14]. The following rheological features were evaluated via the Mixolab procedure: protein weakening (C2), starch gelatinization (C3), amylase activity (C4), starch retrogradation (C5) [34].

The rheological properties of the dough prepared without and with modified flours were determined using the Farinograph procedure [16] with some modification according to preparation of bread by way of the pan method. Water absorption (WA) was tested at the consistency of 400 BU, as recommended for this type of bread as prepared with pans (% of water needed to obtain a dough consistency of 400 BU or corrected at 14%).

Standard testing procedure was applied using Alveograph (Chopin Technologies, Villeneuve-la-Garenne, France) to investigate the blends with the addition of modified flours. The following features were assessed: the baking strength (W) as the surface area under the curve obtained, dough strength (P) as the maximum pressure needed to blow the dough bubble expressing dough resistance, dough extensibility (L) as the length of the curve expressing dough extensibility, elasticity index (Ie) [35], strain hardening index (SH), and P/L as configuration ratio [36]. All rheological tests were performed in triplicate.

2.4. Bread Preparation

The control bread sample (K) was prepared without the addition of modified flours. The control bread preparation was as follows: common wheat bread flour 750 type was mixed with 2% of salt and 3% of yeast, and water was added to obtain a dough consistency of 400 BU. The bread dough was prepared by way of the direct one-step method [7] with slight modifications. To prepare the tested breads, common bread wheat flour was replaced with developed flour (F), enzymatically modified flours (FC, FCX), as well as with thermal, hydrothermal, and hybrid enzymatic-assisted modified flours (TF, TFC, TFCX and HF, HFC, HFCX, respectively) in amounts of 10 and 20% (w/w). All ingredients were mixed in a laboratory mixer for 6 min (JMP12, Fimar Food Processing Equipment, Vericchio, Italy). The prepared dough was then divided into 300 g pieces and placed in loaf pans (approx. 10 × 10 × 10 cm) and fermented at 30 °C and 75% relative humidity (RH) for 50 min in a climatic chamber (MIWE US 2.0, Arnstein, Germany) controlled by an incorporated automatic temperature and humidity control system with an accuracy of 1 °C and 1% RH, respectively. After fermentation, the bread was then baked at 210/200/190/210 °C for 30 s/2 min/20 min/3.5 min—for a total of 26 min in a MIWE AERO backcombi oven (Arnstein, Germany). After loaf placement, steam was introduced for 30 s in an amount of 0.08 L. The temperature inside the baking oven was controlled by an incorporated automatic temperature control system with an accuracy of 1 °C. Post-baking, the loaves were removed from the tins and weighed. The breads were then cooled down for 1 h and weighed again, packed in polyethylene bags, and stored at 21 °C before the tests. All procedures were repeated in triplicate for each flour sample.

2.5. Proximate Composition Analysis of Bread

The chemical composition of ground dried bread samples was determined according to standard methods: AACC 46-10 method for protein (Nx6.25), AACC 30-10 method for fat, and AACC 08-01 method for ash [37]. The 991.43 method was applied to evaluate soluble (SDF) and insoluble (IDF) fractions and the content of total dietary fiber (TDF) [38]. Total carbohydrates and caloric values with Atwater energy equivalents were calculated for the tested breads [39]. All tests were performed in triplicate.

2.6. Bread Quality Tests

Specific bread volume (mL) was tested by way of the rapeseed displacement method according to AACC 10-05 standard [37] by using a known volume/mass of rapeseeds replaced by bread loaf and calculated as bread volume to bread weight [40]. Bread density (g/cm^3) was calculated as the weight to volume ratio of single loaf. Baking loss (%) was evaluated as the difference of dough and loaf mass directly after baking to proper dough mass [6]. Weight loss (%) was checked as the difference between mass of the hot bread just after baking and after 24 h of storage. Bread yield (%) was calculated as the ratio of dough mass multiplied by dough yield to the mass of cold bread after baking [41]. Data were given as the averages of three independent experiments.

2.7. Water Absorption Index and Water Solubility Index Assessment

Water absorption index (WAI) and water solubility index (WSI) in breads were determined according to Soja et al. [42]. WAI was expressed as g of water absorbed by g of bread. WSI was expressed as % of components soluble in water after WAI testing. Measurements were conducted in triplicate.

2.8. Color Profile of Bread

To evaluate the color characteristics of bread crumb and crust 24 h after baking, the NH310 colorimeter was used (3NH TECHNOLOGY Co., Ltd., Guangzhou, China). Color assessment followed the CIE-Lab system, where L^* describes the lightness and ranged from 0 (black) to 100 (white), the a^* chromatic coordinate is determined as the balance between red (positive values) and green (negative values), and the b^* chromatic coordinate is ascertained as the balance between yellow (if positive) and blue (if negative) [7]. The final values of the L^*, a^*, and b^* coordinates of bread crumb and crust were expressed as the means of at least five measurements of each color determinant from three individual bread loaves. ΔE was calculated as the total color difference [7]. Before each measurement, the colorimeter was calibrated using a supplied white calibration plate.

2.9. Bread Crumb Texture Analysis

The textural properties of control bread and samples prepared with modified flours were determined in triplicate using a ZwickRoell BDO-FB0.5TH (Zwick GmbH and Co., Ulm, Germany) instrument, according to the TPA protocol, and testXpert®13.3 software. Bread samples were cut from the middle part of the crumb ($3 \times 3 \times 1$ cm). An Ottawa cell was employed for the testing, and had a working head speed of 100 mm/min in the double compression test to 50% of sample height and 10 s distance between cycles. TPA curves were analyzed, and textural properties were evaluated as mean values of five replications. The following features were determined: firmness as the highest peak during the first compression run, adhesion as the work needed to separate crumb and piston, springiness as the distance of the detected height during the second compression cycle divided by the original compression distance, gumminess and chewiness calculated on the base of firmness, cohesiveness, and springiness, and cohesiveness as the area of work during the second compression cycle divided by the area of work during the first compression [43].

2.10. Statistical Analysis

The obtained data were subjected to one-way analysis of variance (ANOVA) via the Statistica 13.3 software (StatSoft, Inc., Tulsa, OK, USA) application, followed by Tukey post hoc test to compare means at the 0.05 significance level. Pearson's correlation coefficients were found to evaluate the correlations between the tested properties using Statistica 13.3 software (StatSoft, Inc., Tulsa, OK, USA) within the 95% confidence interval.

Statistica software (version 12.0, StatSoft Inc., Tulsa, OK, USA) was used for statistical analyses. Principal component analysis (PCA), analysis of variance, and determination of correlations were performed at the significance level of $\alpha = 0.05$. Principal component analysis was applied to determine the relationship between conventional and hybrid thermal-enzymatic modified wheat flours and the studied parameters. The PCA data matrix for statistical analysis of the research results consisted of 40 columns (parameters) and 20 rows (Type of material). The input matrix was automatically rescaled. The optimal number of principal components obtained in the analysis for each matrix was determined based on the Cattel criterion.

3. Results

3.1. Flour and Dough Features Analysis

The developed flour was characterized as having an increased content of proteins, polysaccharides, and arabinoxylans due to it containing mostly the outer fractions of the wheat grain [14]. The composition of the NSP-rich developed wheat flour before modifications was as follows (%): protein—14.62 ± 0.06, fat—1.31 ± 0.01, ash—0.78 ± 0.02, insoluble dietary fiber—3.94 ± 0.04, soluble dietary fiber—2.86 ± 0.02, and total dietary fiber—6.80 ± 0.03. The composition of polysaccharides in the developed flour before modifications was as follows (%): total arabinoxylans—1.91 ± 0.06, which consisted of 1.31 ± 0.04 of insoluble fraction and 0.60 ± 0.02 of soluble fraction, and total non-starch polysaccharides—3.40 ± 0.00, which consisted of 2.06 ± 0.01 of insoluble fraction and 1.34 ± 0.00 of soluble fraction [31].

The following rheological features were evaluated through the Mixolab procedure: protein weakening (C2), starch gelatinization (C3), amylase activity (C4), and starch retrogradation (C5) [34]. In order to qualitatively assess individual samples, using the Mixolab device, an analysis of the dough taken from the mixer was carried out just before forming the dough in pans. This allowed us to check whether the dough had proper consistency and the flour was properly hydrated. This is made evident by reading the dough resistance at point C1 of the graph [5]. The properties of the finished dough, prepared for shaping, were tested at specific analysis points in accordance with the adopted methodology for the Chopin + protocol, i.e., C2, C3, C4, C5. Additional analysis allowed for effective control of the dough consistency, as the calculated average consistency for all dough samples at point C1 was 0.763 Nm ± 0.01 Nm. Figure 1 presents the rheological properties of the tested doughs with added modified flours in amounts of 10 and 20%.

The results of the analyses confirmed that the addition of flours modified by the addition of FC and FCX enzymes did not significantly affect the tested features, such as the level of C2 protein weakening, C3 starch gelatinization, C4 amylase activity, or the level of C5 starch retrogradation (Figure 1).

In tests with the addition of flour modified by thermal treatment, a slight increase in the C2 point value was observed for flours without the use of enzymes TF10 and TF20, indicating greater stiffness of the dough (Figure 1a). Incorporating hybrid enzymatic-thermal modified flours TFC10-TFCX20 resulted in a reduction of the C2 parameter values to the level of the control flour K. Mixtures with the addition of TF, TFC, and TFCX flours after thermal treatment were characterized by a reduction in C4 amylase activity without a significant effect of enzyme activity (Figure 1c), and the level of retrogradation of C5 starch was similar to the value for the control flour (Figure 1d).

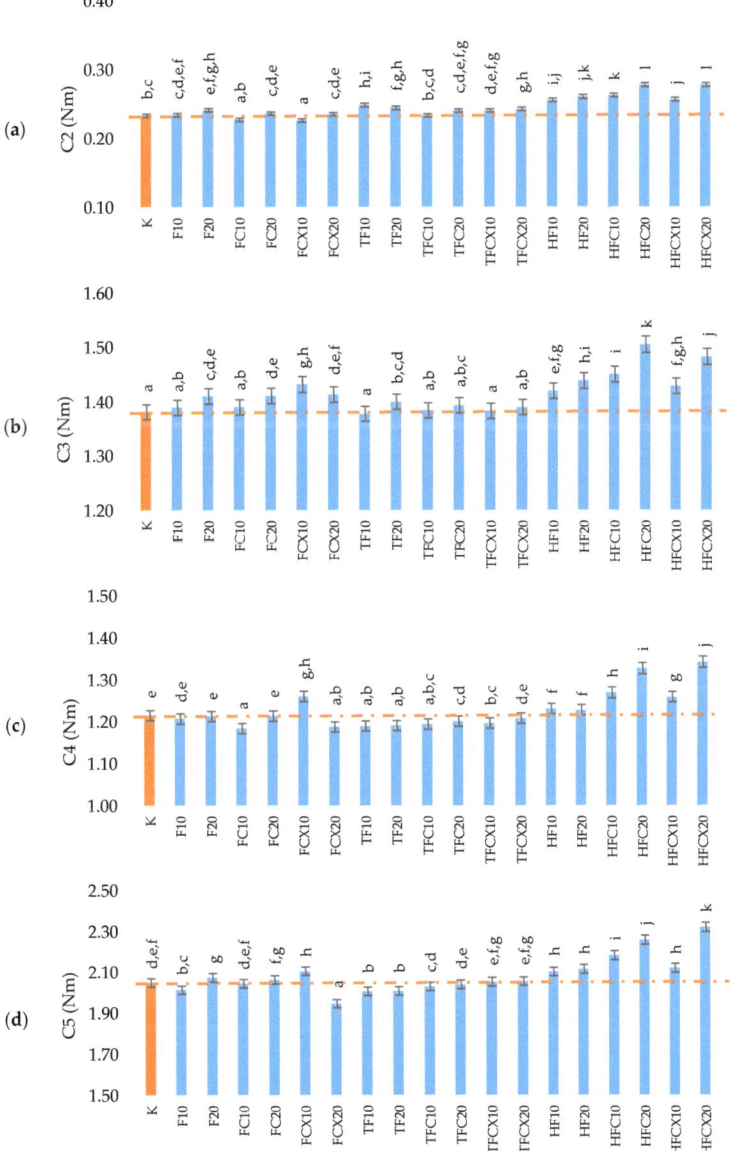

Figure 1. Rheological features of raw materials composition with added modified flours as compared to control common bread flour: (**a**) protein weakening (C2); (**b**) starch gelatinization (C3); (**c**) amylase activity (C4); (**d**) starch retrogradation (C5); K—control; F—flour; T—dry thermal treatment; H—hydrothermal treatment; C—cellulase enzyme; CX—cellulase-xylanase enzyme complex; 10 and 20—% of modified flour in bread recipe; dash line—level for control sample; [a–l]—means indicated with similar letters in columns do not differ significantly at α = 0.05.

The greatest differences in the values indicated via the Mixolab procedure were observed for mixtures with the addition of the hydrothermally processed flours–HF, HFC, and HFCX–where the values of all tested parameters–C2, C3, C4, C5–increased, as compared to the control flour, which indicates the large impact of flours modified with this method on the dough's protein and starch complexes. These flours were characterized by a higher level of protein weakening, starch gelatinization, reduced activity of amylolytic enzymes, and a higher level of starch retrogradation than the control flour K. High-temperature treatment with steam and water had a negative effect on the protein-starch complex of the tested HF, HFC, and HFCX flours. Partial denaturation of gluten proteins occurred, thus bringing about difficulties in creating a gluten network matrix (unpublished data) and affecting an increase in the C2 parameter of protein weakening. The hydrothermal process induced initial starch gelatinization, hence, generating, through inactivation of amylolytic enzymes, a significant increase in starch gelatinization (C3), amylase activity (C4), and starch retrogradation (C5). These observations are supported by the PCA analysis presented in Section 3.5, which showed a commonality of effect in all the hydrothermally treated flours.

The addition of developed flour treated with enzymes in the hybrid processing increased this effect. Of note, the parameters from this analysis were well correlated with the parameters obtained in the alveographic analysis of bread composition mixtures consistency features. We found significant correlations between C2, C3, C4, C5 and dough tenacity (P) values with coefficients of 0.842, 0.825, 0.773, and 0.785, respectively, as well as dough configuration index (P/L) with r values of 0.845, 0.850, 0.812, and 0.794, respectively. Slightly lower but still significant negative correlations were noted between C2–C5 and dough extensibility L (range of r coefficients form -0.601 to -0.687). Starch gelatinization (C3), amylase activity (C4), and starch retrogradation (C5) were also significantly negatively correlated with water absorption (WA), with values of r ranging from -0.706 to -0.723.

Jurkaninová et al. [7] tested unfermented bread dough using the Mixolab procedure and they reported a negligible effect of herb extract addition on dough rheological characteristics, whereas their C2–C5 results were higher than that of our tested bread dough. Mahmoud et al. [8] assessed bread products with the addition of microalgae, and the results of their Mixolab rheological tests were similar, the C2 range being 0.23–0.44 Nm and the C3 being 2.12–2.74 Nm, while the C4 varied from 2.00 to 2.41 Nm, and, finally, C5 ranged between 3.06–4.27 Nm.

Upon analyzing the tested flour mixtures via farinographic analysis (Table 1), we observed that the improved tendency to absorb water seen in the modified developed flours had the greatest impact on the increase in water absorption (WA) within the bread mixtures. This was especially noticeable in the doughs created from flours incorporating thermally treated flours at both 10 and 20% values. Thus, for TFCX10 flour, WA increased by 3.5%, for TFCX20 by 5.4% and for TFC20 by 5.7%, as compared to the control K recipe. An increase in water absorption of the analyzed flour blends was also found for samples incorporating hydrothermally processed flours, but without significant differences when baking enzymes were used during this treatment. The results allowed the selection of the appropriate amount of water to prepare pan method bread dough with a constant consistency of 400 BU, enabling comparison of the impact of the addition of modified flours on the quality and bread yield.

Cacak-Pietrzak et al. [44] tested the addition of dried crushed roots of *Taraxacum officinale* to wheat flour and observed decreased WA from 57.5% (control sample) to 55.5% (sample with 6% TO), but significant differences were found even if 1% TO rich in inulin content was applied. Inulin, as a dietary fiber fraction rich in soluble components (such as inulin-type fructans), has a limited ability to absorb water [45]. In our samples, the increased level of non-starch polysaccharides in the developed flour rich in arabinoxylans (especially the insoluble fractions that came mostly from the final fractions of the reduction and sorting passages, as well as from filtration stream flours) was positively correlated with the water absorption [26]. Hence, the increased water absorption ability in blends with 10 and 20% of developed modified flour content may be connected with the presence of non-starch polysaccharides that were slightly modified by thermal or hydrothermal and hybrid treatments.

Table 1. Consistency characteristics of tested bread dough compositions with 10 and 20% w/w added modified flours treated through various methods.

Bread Sample	WA (%)	P (mm)	L (mm)	W (J10^{-4})	P/L (-)	Ie (%)	SH (-)
K	62.5 ± 0.2 [a]	92 ± 2 [d,e]	73 ± 3 [d,e,f,g]	212 ± 3 [c,d]	1.26 ± 0.06 [f,g]	47.67 ± 0.55 [e,f]	1.60 ± 0.04 [e]
F10	62.8 ± 0.1 [a,b]	93 ± 1 [e,f]	89 ± 3 [j,k]	235 ± 3 [g]	1.05 ± 0.04 [a,b,c]	46.97 ± 0.35 [d,e]	1.52 ± 0.01 [b,c]
F20	64.1 ± 0.1 [e,f]	97 ± 2 [g]	87 ± 1 [j,k]	239 ± 4 [g,h]	1.10 ± 0.01 [b,c,d,e]	45.77 ± 0.12 [b,c]	1.52 ± 0.02 [b,c]
FC10	63.5 ± 0.2 [c,d]	88 ± 0 [b,c]	78 ± 1 [g,h,i]	212 ± 2 [c,d]	1.13 ± 0.02 [c,d,e,f]	48.13 ± 0.15 [f,g]	1.61 ± 0.01 [e,f]
FC20	63.0 ± 0.1 [b]	95 ± 1 [f,g]	72 ± 2 [d,e,f,g]	223 ± 2 [e,f]	1.32 ± 0.05 [g]	48.83 ± 0.06 [g]	1.64 ± 0.02 [f]
FCX10	63.2 ± 0.2 [b,c]	92 ± 1 [d,e]	73 ± 2 [e,f,g]	212 ± 6 [c,d]	1.26 ± 0.03 [f,g]	47.23 ± 0.42 [d,e,f]	1.59 ± 0.01 [d,e]
FCX20	64.0 ± 0.1 [e,f]	92 ± 1 [d,e]	70 ± 1 [d,e,f]	205 ± 6 [b,c]	1.32 ± 0.01 [g]	47.00 ± 0.46 [d,e]	1.60 ± 0.01 [e]
TF10	64.1 ± 0.2 [e,f]	91 ± 1 [d,e]	74 ± 2 [f,g]	201 ± 2 [b]	1.23 ± 0.03 [e,f,g]	43.93 ± 0.15 [a]	1.47 ± 0.00 [a]
TF20	65.3 ± 0.2 [i]	86 ± 1 [b]	68 ± 4 [c,d,e]	184 ± 3 [a]	1.26 ± 0.09 [f,g]	45.50 ± 0.10 [b]	1.55 ± 0.03 [c,d]
TFC10	64.3 ± 0.2 [f,g]	80 ± 0 [a]	81 ± 2 [h,i]	186 ± 2 [a]	0.99 ± 0.03 [a,b]	44.33 ± 0.15 [a]	1.49 ± 0.01 [a,b]
TFC20	66.0 ± 0.1 [j]	86 ± 0 [b]	91 ± 1 [k]	221 ± 2 [d,e,f]	0.94 ± 0.01 [a]	47.33 ± 0.21 [d,e,f]	1.53 ± 0.01 [b,c]
TFCX10	64.7 ± 0.1 [g,h]	90 ± 0 [c,d]	83 ± 1 [i,j]	225 ± 2 [f]	1.08 ± 0.02 [a,b,c,d]	47.43 ± 0.06 [d,e,f]	1.58 ± 0.01 [d,e]
TFCX20	65.9 ± 0.2 [j]	92 ± 1 [d,e]	77 ± 3 [g,h]	213 ± 3 [c,d,e]	1.19 ± 0.05 [d,e,f,g]	46.63 ± 0.23 [c,d]	1.55 ± 0.01 [c,d]
HF10	64.1 ± 0.1 [e,f]	107 ± 1 [h]	67 ± 1 [b,c,d]	244 ± 1 [g,h]	1.59 ± 0.03 [h]	50.37 ± 0.15 [h]	1.70 ± 0.01 [g]
HF20	65.1 ± 0.2 [h,i]	113 + 1 [j]	68 + 1 [c,d,e]	268 ± 3 [j]	1.66 ± 0.01 [h,i]	51.97 ± 0.12 [i]	1.74 ± 0.00 [g,h]
HFC10	63.9 ± 0.1 [d,e]	110 ± 1 [i]	62 ± 1 [a,b]	246 ± 3 [h]	1.78 ± 0.01 [i,j]	52.03 ± 0.12 [i]	1.77 ± 0.01 [h,i]
HFC20	64.3 ± 0.2 [f,g]	114 ± 2 [j]	62 ± 2 [a,b]	257 ± 5 [i]	1.83 ± 0.08 [j]	53.10 ± 0.61 [j]	1.79 ± 0.01 [i]
HFCX10	64.0 ± 0.1 [e,f]	106 ± 1 [h]	63 ± 3 [a,b,c]	237 ± 6 [g,h]	1.68 ± 0.07 [h,i]	50.63 ± 0.68 [h]	1.74 ± 0.01 [g,h]
HFCX20	64.3 ± 0.2 [f,g]	111 ± 2 [i,j]	59 ± 2 [a]	242 ± 1 [g,h]	1.88 ± 0.08 [j]	52.13 ± 0.40 [i,j]	1.79 ± 0.00 [i]

K—control; F—flour; T—dry thermal treatment; H—hydrothermal treatment; C—cellulase enzyme; CX—cellulase-xylanase enzyme complex; 10 and 20—% of modified flour in bread recipe; WA—water absorption; P—dough tenacity; L—extensibility; W—baking strength; P/L—dough configuration index; Ie —elasticity index; SH—strain hardening index; [a–k]—means indicated with similar letters in columns do not differ significantly at α = 0.05.

Tayefe et al. [11] reported increased WA in dough with the addition of hydrothermally treated bran. Their explanation for this outcome is that hydrothermal treatment causes interaction between water molecules and structural fibers through hydrogen bonding and thus increases the WA. Moreover, this hydrothermal processing may convert the starch present in developed flour to pregelatinized starch, which is characterized by improved retention of water molecules. They also reported an increase in dough development time and a decrease in dough stability when 6 and 9% of HT treated bran were added to the component bread flour. Similarly, when extruded at 50, 60, and 70 °C, wheat starch added to bread flour caused increased water absorption, as tested with Farinograph by Tao et al. [46].

The results of dough property testing utilizing an Alveograph are presented in Table 1 for control common bread flour and for blends with enzymatic, thermally, hydrothermally, and hybrid enzyme-assisted modified methods. The tested base common bread flour (K) was characterized by appropriate parameters for baking bread, wherein the baking force W was 212 J 10^{-4}, with the dough elasticity and extensibility coefficient P/L being 1.26. After the addition of flour with increased content of non-starch polysaccharides (F), in amounts of both 10 and 20%, a slight increase in dough extensibility (L) was observed, and thus an improvement in baking value (W). However, with the addition of enzymatically modified flours, the flours had these values at a level similar to the control flour. When modified heat-treated raw materials (TF) were employed as additions to the control flour, a deterioration in the baking value (W) was found, mainly due to a decrease in dough elasticity (P). Here, the dough elasticity parameters (Ie) and (SH) also deteriorated. Of note, when thermally modified flours with enzymatic fortification were used as an additive, the elasticity parameters (P) increased to those observed for the control flour.

Improvement in dough elasticity (L), baking value (W), and elasticity index (Ie) was also observed; the improvement in these properties was more visible in the tests with the addition of the enzyme complex (TFCX). Buscella et al. [15] analyzed wheat cakes and bread flours that differed in quality and baking value and were subjected to heat treatment without water and to hydrothermal treatment. They conducted analyses of both the suspension and the dough matrix and observed that heat treatment improved the stability of the dough, albeit more intensively for the flour with weaker baking value, and that the viscosity properties of bread flour also changed [15]. The sedimentation value indicating the quality of gluten protein of bread flour subjected to dry heat treatment also showed a significant decrease compared to untreated bread flour [15]. This outcome was attributed to changes in the gluten structure due to the rearrangement of disulfide bonds [15]. We also observed that the addition of bread flour subjected only to dry heating worsened the quality parameters determined by alveographic analysis. The use of the hybrid modification method through the participation of bakery enzymes in the mixture, especially TFCX with the cellulase-xylanase complex, allowed us to obtain a level of quality that improved the overall quality of gluten proteins, evident in the improvement of dough elasticity, as well as in the notable improvement of the hydration properties of the flour (increased water absorption) (Table 1). In the case of the addition of flours modified by hydrothermal treatment, a decrease in dough extensibility and a significant increase in its elasticity were found in all tested blends. This resulted in a significant change in the configuration of the P/L chart, the value of which increased by 26% compared to the control flour and for dough with the addition of 10% of hydrothermally processed (HF10) flour, and to 49% if 20% of hybrid enzymatic-hydrothermal flour (HFCX20) was added to the blend.

Hydrothermal treatment carried out in the developed flour also brought about significant changes in the conformation of gluten proteins by reducing their elasticity. We did not observe significant differences between the addition of hydrothermally treated flours or those treated with enzyme assisted modification. Although both the baking value W and the SH coefficient increased to a higher level than in the control flour (K), this was due to increased dough stiffness and not due to improvement in flour blend quality, as we did not observe an increase in flour water absorption. Similar results were obtained in the work of Martinez et al. [22], who used extruded flours as additives to bread. Here, the addition of extruded flours significantly increased the elasticity of the dough and reduced its extensibility [22].

3.2. Bread Proximate Composition

Table 2 summarizes the main chemical components present in bread made with a common bread flour and when 10 and 20% w/w was replaced by modified flours without or with enzymatic assistance. The level of protein in common bread flour was 13.22% and all breads with added modified flours were higher in protein content than the control bread. This is the effect of the composition of the developed flour (F), which was characterized by higher protein content (14.62%) due to selection of appropriate milling passages, as well as to the contribution of selected fractions [31]. The bread formed from the developed flour, whether modified enzymatically, thermally, or hydrothermally without or with enzyme assistance, when replacing common flour at 10 and 20%, had increased total protein content, with higher values when 20% was added to the basic bread recipe.

Moreover, fat content in the developed flour was $1.31 \pm 0.01\%$, and, after thermal modification or enzymatic modifications, was similarly ranged—at 1.30–1.38. Bucsella et al. [47], when testing aleurone-rich flour, found a different composition (20% protein, 15% dietary fiber) to that of commercial fiber-rich wheat fractions (9–13% protein, 9% dietary fiber). They noted that the presence of a higher content of inner layers of the seed coat than seen in white or wholegrain flour also resulted in a high fat content (4%). In our work, we saw that the fortified bread was lower in fat if modified flours were added, especially following HFC and HFCX application at 20%. Accordingly, significantly lowered fat content was found to be extractable during bread analysis. This limitation may be the effect of the formation complexes with amylose that usually come about during hydrothermal or extrusion treatment at increased temperatures [48]. The final temperature of these flours was around 65 °C, hence the temperature effect was more intense than that which occurs under dry thermal treatment (TF). Additionally, during baking temperatures, formation of fat-induced complexes may take place.

Table 2. Proximate composition of bread obtained with addition of modified flours.

Bread Sample	Protein [%]	Fat [%]	Ash [%]	IDF [%]	SDF [%]	TDF [%]	Carbohydrates [%]	Caloric Value [kcal/100 g]
K	13.22 ± 0.06 [a]	0.30 ± 0.01 [g,h]	1.02 ± 0.02 [a,b,c]	5.43 ± 0.02 [c]	2.79 ± 0.01 [f,g]	8.21 ± 0.02 [c]	77.25 ± 0.05 [m]	397.40 ± 0.13 [g,h]
F10	13.46 ± 0.06 [b,c]	0.27 ± 0.01 [f,g]	1.04 ± 0.02 [a,b,c,d]	7.10 ± 0.02 [l]	3.08 ± 0.01 [h,i]	10.17 ± 0.02 [l]	75.06 ± 0.03 [d]	397.19 ± 0.13 [f,g,h]
F20	13.54 ± 0.02 [c,d]	0.22 ± 0.01 [e]	0.98 ± 0.02 [a]	7.19 ± 0.02 [m]	3.38 ± 0.02 [j]	10.57 ± 0.02 [o]	74.69 ± 0.02 [c]	397.20 ± 0.09 [f,g,h]
FC10	13.28 ± 0.02 [a]	0.13 ± 0.02 [b,c]	1.05 ± 0.02 [a,b,c,d]	5.28 ± 0.01 [b]	2.64 ± 0.02 [d,e,f]	7.93 ± 0.02 [b]	75.76 ± 0.02 [g]	396.47 ± 0.16 [b,c,d]
FC20	13.86 ± 0.04 [g,h]	0.23 ± 0.01 [e,f]	1.02 ± 0.02 [a,b,c]	6.76 ± 0.01 [j]	3.01 ± 0.02 [h]	9.78 ± 0.02 [j]	76.96 ± 0.07 [k]	397.09 ± 0.11 [e,f,g]
FCX10	13.25 ± 0.05 [a]	0.22 ± 0.02 [e]	1.15 ± 0.01 [e]	6.51 ± 0.02 [i]	2.40 ± 0.02 [b,c]	8.91 ± 0.01 [e]	76.40 ± 0.05 [j]	396.28 ± 0.21 [a,b]
FCX20	13.72 ± 0.04 [e,f]	0.20 ± 0.01 [d,e]	1.08 ± 0.02 [c,d]	5.50 ± 0.02 [d]	3.43 ± 0.01 [j]	8.94 ± 0.01 [e]	76.05 ± 0.05 [h,i]	396.68 ± 0.13 [b,c,d,e]
TF10	13.42 ± 0.04 [b]	0.27 ± 0.02 [f,g]	1.03 ± 0.01 [a,b,c]	5.28 ± 0.01 [a]	2.60 ± 0.02 [d,e]	7.88 ± 0.02 [a]	77.47 ± 0.00 [n]	397.25 ± 0.04 [g,h]
TF20	13.43 ± 0.03 [b]	0.29 ± 0.01 [g,h]	1.03 ± 0.02 [a,b,c]	6.73 ± 0.02 [j]	2.53 ± 0.02 [c,d]	9.27 ± 0.01 [h]	76.14 ± 0.01 [i]	397.55 ± 0.04 [h]
TFC10	13.43 ± 0.01 [b]	0.20 ± 0.02 [d,e]	1.01 ± 0.02 [a,b,c]	5.91 ± 0.03 [f]	2.44 ± 0.01 [b,c]	8.35 ± 0.02 [d]	76.93 ± 0.02 [k]	397.36 ± 0.18 [g,h]
TFC20	13.56 ± 0.03 [d]	0.28 ± 0.03 [g]	1.07 ± 0.02 [b,c,d]	7.72 ± 0.02 [o]	3.21 ± 0.02 [i]	10.92 ± 0.02 [p]	74.24 ± 0.03 [a]	396.74 ± 0.16 [c,d,e]
TFCX10	13.81 ± 0.04 [f,g]	0.09 ± 0.02 [a,b]	1.11 ± 0.03 [d]	6.18 ± 0.01 [g]	2.81 ± 0.01 [g]	9.02 ± 0.02 [f]	75.97 ± 0.05 [h]	396.01 ± 0.22 [a]
TFCX20	13.92 ± 0.02 [h]	0.12 ± 0.01 [a,b]	1.06 ± 0.02 [b,c,d]	7.34 ± 0.02 [n]	3.07 ± 0.01 [h,i]	10.40 ± 0.02 [n]	74.50 ± 0.02 [b]	396.34 ± 0.09 [a,b,c,d]
HF10	13.44 ± 0.02 [b,c]	0.20 ± 0.02 [d,e]	1.05 ± 0.03 [a,b,c,d]	6.94 ± 0.01 [k]	2.33 ± 0.03 [b]	9.27 ± 0.01 [h]	76.04 ± 0.04 [h,i]	396.77 ± 0.08 [d,e,f]
HF20	13.64 ± 0.04 [d,e]	0.28 ± 0.01 [g]	1.01 ± 0.06 [a,b,c]	6.46 ± 0.02 [h]	2.72 ± 0.20 [e,f,g]	9.07 ± 0.01 [g]	76.00 ± 0.06 [h]	397.38 ± 0.20 [g,h]
HFC10	13.43 ± 0.03 [b]	0.08 ± 0.02 [a]	1.00 ± 0.02 [a,b]	7.09 ± 0.02 [l]	3.19 ± 0.01 [i]	10.26 ± 0.02 [m]	75.23 ± 0.04 [e]	396.38 ± 0.16 [a,b,c,d]
HFC20	13.70 ± 0.02 [e]	0.13 ± 0.02 [b,c]	1.01 ± 0.02 [a,b,c]	5.81 ± 0.01 [e]	2.09 ± 0.02 [a]	7.89 ± 0.02 [b]	77.07 ± 0.04 [l]	397.63 ± 0.18 [h]
HFCX10	13.70 ± 0.01 [e]	0.07 ± 0.02 [a]	1.02 ± 0.02 [a,b,c]	7.16 ± 0.02 [m]	2.80 ± 0.01 [g]	9.95 ± 0.01 [k]	75.26 ± 0.02 [e]	396.29 ± 0.16 [a,b,c]
HFCX20	13.82 ± 0.02 [f,g,h]	0.18 ± 0.02 [c,d]	1.05 ± 0.03 [a,b,c,d]	6.55 ± 0.01 [i]	2.96 ± 0.01 [h]	9.52 ± 0.02 [i]	75.43 ± 0.02 [f]	396.67 ± 0.17 [b,c,d,e]

K—control; F—flour; T—dry thermal treatment; H—hydrothermal treatment; C—cellulase enzyme; CX—cellulase-xylanase enzyme complex; 10 and 20—% of modified flour in bread recipe; TDF—total dietary fiber; IDF—insoluble dietary fiber; SDF—soluble dietary fiber; [a–p]—means indicated with similar letters in columns do not differ significantly at α = 0.05.

Our work saw that ash content in common bread was 1.02%, but that in the developed flour, ash content was lower (0.78%) [31]. Thus, the substitution of common flour with 10 and 20% of the developed F flour decreased ash content in the prepared bread. The ash content in treated flours varied from 1.00 to 1.15%, with a slight decreasing effect of C and CX enzymes addition on ash content in the produced bread (Table 2). In our work, dietary fiber and its fractions were tested in bread composed according to control (K) and modified recipes. The content of fibrous fractions in the developed flour showed IDF 3.94%, SDF 2.86%, and TDF 6.80% [31]. In contrast, the TDF in control bread was 8.21% and demonstrated a predominance of insoluble fraction IDF. In breads fortified with untreated developer flour (F10, F20), the content of TDF was significantly higher due to the incorporation of passages rich in non-starch polysaccharides derived from the outer layer of the original wheat grains [26].

As mentioned previously, increased content of fibrous fractions, especially insoluble, may have an effect on dough properties through an increase in water binding ability [49]. We also found high correlation between insoluble fractions and the TDF content (r = 0.933 at $p < 0.05$). In all breads with added hydrothermally treated flour at 20% content, both without and with enzymes, a lower level of TDF was noted than that for 10% of the additive, in addition to significantly lower amounts of insoluble fiber fractions. This may be the effect of enhanced enzymes activity being improved upon by temperature and steam action, because cellulases and xylanases act mostly on fibrous fractions of polysaccharides, causing partial hydrolysis of pentosanes [19,48,49]. In contrast, replacement of 20% of bread composition by modified flours resulted in higher content of TDF in bread than if 10% was applied—no matter the treatment or supplementation. In all cases, the effect of the addition of enzymes was ambiguous or similar in all dietary fiber fractions analysis. Analysis of carbohydrates content showed a slight decrease if modified flours were added to the bread mixture, and thus some slight changes in caloric values were noted (Table 2).

3.3. Bread Quality and Appearance

Bread quality and appearance are important factors for both producers and consumers [1,3–9]. Breads made from whole grain flour or supplemented with unmodified bran addition, due to the reduced ability of the dough to retain gases, are characterized by having smaller loaf volume and, hence, deteriorated baking quality [27,28]. Producers prefer a high yield of bread with high loaf volume and increased water absorption ability during bread dough making, but consumers prefer a regular crust structure and homogenous pores distribution in the bread crumb. Adding more water to dough recipes is a common approach to increasing bread production. However, increasing the amount of water in the dough can result in a deterioration of the dough's kneading ability, as it becomes too wet and sticky, and this affects the final volume and texture of the bread [21]. Additionally, a higher water content in the dough can reduce the shelf life of the bread due to microbiological hazards. The addition of physically modified flours rich in fibrous fractions have been demonstrated to bring about changes in the bread quality [20]. The results of selected quality characteristics of baked bread prepared with the addition of modified flours are presented in Table 3.

Table 3. Selected quality characteristics of baked bread prepared with the addition of modified flours.

Bread Sample	Bread Volume (mL)	Specific Volume (cm^3/g)	Bread Density (g/cm^3)	Baking Loss (%)	Weight Loss (%)	Bread Yield (%)
K	755 ± 10 [a,b]	2.84 ± 0.02 [a,b]	0.35 ± 0.00 [g,h]	9.79 ± 0.49 [a]	2.80 ± 0.21 [a,b]	146.77 ± 0.64 [b,c,d,e]
F10	778 ± 8 [b,c]	2.95 ± 0.03 [b,c]	0.34 ± 0.00 [f,g]	9.33 ± 0.33 [a]	3.06 ± 0.20 [a,b,c]	147.21 ± 0.32 [b,c,d,e,f]
F20	832 ± 13 [d,e,f,g]	3.12 ± 0.05 [d,e]	0.32 ± 0.01 [c,d,e]	9.34 ± 0.47 [a]	3.13 ± 0.19 [b,c,d,e]	147.72 ± 0.70 [b,c,d,e,f,g]
FC10	860 ± 9 [g,h,i]	3.28 ± 0.04 [g,h,i]	0.31 ± 0.00 [a,b]	9.48 ± 0.09 [a]	3.63 ± 0.10 [e]	146.30 ± 0.02 [b]
FC20	880 ± 10 [i]	3.34 ± 0.05 [i]	0.30 ± 0.00 [a]	9.48 ± 0.19 [a]	2.98 ± 0.12 [a,b,c]	146.93 ± 0.31 [b,c,d,e,f]
FCX10	750 ± 17 [a]	2.77 ± 0.08 [a]	0.35 ± 0.01 [g,h]	9.31 ± 0.34 [a]	3.46 ± 0.30 [c,d,e]	147.28 ± 0.41 [b,c,d,e,f,g]
FCX20	847 ± 12 [f,g,h]	3.21 ± 0.03 [e,f,g,h]	0.31 ± 0.00 [a,b,c,d]	9.64 ± 0.43 [a]	3.22 ± 0.10 [b,c,d,e]	146.48 ± 0.55 [b,c]
TF10	810 ± 10 [d,e]	3.13 ± 0.05 [d,e,f]	0.32 ± 0.01 [c,d,e]	9.39 ± 0.26 [a]	3.64 ± 0.27 [f]	146.77 ± 0.04 [a]
TF20	817 ± 3 [d,e,f]	3.11 ± 0.01 [d,e]	0.32 ± 0.00 [d,e]	9.61 ± 0.56 [a]	3.58 ± 0.25 [d,e]	147.46 ± 0.76 [b,c,d,e,f,g]
TFC10	873 ± 6 [h,i]	3.32 ± 0.03 [h,i]	0.30 ± 0.00 [a]	9.42 ± 0.06 [a]	3.61 ± 0.08 [e]	146.59 ± 0.17 [b,c,d]
TFC20	813 ± 6 [d,e]	3.07 ± 0.01 [c,d]	0.33 ± 0.00 [e,f]	9.40 ± 0.39 [a]	2.80 ± 0.24 [a,b]	150.02 ± 0.28 [i]
TFCX10	828 ± 3 [d,e,f]	3.12 ± 0.01 [d,e]	0.32 ± 0.00 [c,d,e]	9.44 ± 0.62 [a]	2.79 ± 0.11 [a,b]	148.13 ± 0.96 [e,f,g,h]
TFCX20	837 ± 6 [e,f,g]	3.16 ± 0.03 [d,e,f,g]	0.32 ± 0.00 [b,c,d,e]	9.30 ± 0.38 [a]	2.92 ± 0.15 [a,b]	149.60 ± 0.45 [h,i]
HF10	833 ± 15 [d,e,f,g]	3.14 ± 0.07 [d,e,f]	0.32 ± 0.01 [b,c,d,e]	9.08 ± 0.26 [a]	3.18 ± 0.18 [b,c,d,e]	147.90 ± 0.34 [c,d,e,f,g]
HF20	860 ± 17 [g,h,i]	3.25 ± 0.06 [f,g,h,i]	0.31 ± 0.01 [a,b,c]	9.11 ± 0.22 [a]	3.47 ± 0.04 [c,d,e]	147.58 ± 0.30 [b,c,d,e,f,g]
HFC10	803 ± 6 [c,d]	3.03 ± 0.03 [c,d]	0.33 ± 0.00 [e,f]	9.58 ± 0.18 [a]	2.60 ± 0.17 [a]	148.05 ± 0.12 [d,e,f,g]
HFC20	810 ± 1 [d,e]	3.05 ± 0.02 [c,d]	0.33 ± 0.00 [e,f]	9.53 ± 0.17 [a]	2.89 ± 0.05 [a,b]	148.40 ± 0.23 [f,g,h]
HFCX10	833 ± 15 [d,e,f,g]	3.13 ± 0.05 [d,e,f]	0.32 ± 0.00 [c,d,e]	9.27 ± 0.47 [a]	3.10 ± 0.10 [a,b,c,d]	148.76 ± 0.77 [g,h,i]
HFCX20	823 ± 6 [d,e,f]	3.11 ± 0.00 [d,e]	0.32 ± 0.00 [c,d,e]	9.17 ± 0.23 [a]	3.08 ± 0.11 [a,b,c]	148.43 ± 0.41 [f,g,h]

K—control; F—flour; T—dry thermal treatment; H—hydrothermal treatment; C—cellulase enzyme; CX—cellulase-xylanase enzyme complex; 10 and 20—% of modified flour in bread recipe; [a–i]—means indicated with similar letters in columns do not differ significantly at $\alpha = 0.05$.

In analyzing the quality and performance characteristics of the baked bread obtained from recipes with the addition of modified flours, it can be noticed that the addition of enzymatically and process-modified flours had a significant impact on the volume of the tested bread. This effect was also evident in the specific loaf volume values. Bread volume increased significantly when treated flours were added to the bread composition, in most cases, when 20% of modified flours were added.

Very good results in increasing the loaf volume were obtained when only flours subjected to enzymatic fortification (FC10, FC20, and FCX20) were used as additives. Hilhorst et al. [50] reported that the addition of xylanases may enhance the handling properties of wheat dough, the ovenspring, and the bread volume. The addition of process-modified flours or flours treated using hybrid enzyme-assisted methods to the bread mixtures also improved the bread volume, but without significant differences among the applied processing methods. Significant increase in bread volume was also demonstrated if thermally and hydrothermally treated TFC10 and HF20 flours were added to the bread recipe.

It should be noted that the higher loaf volume of breads prepared with the addition of hydrothermally treated flour with enzymes was also the result of uneven distribution of gas bubbles, which were located in large numbers under the bread crust, causing it to stand aside and bringing about the collapse of the loaf in the final stage of baking, as visible in the obtained bread pictures presented in Figure 2. This suggests that the consistency of the dough may have been too loose, and that the amount of water added to the recipes should be reduced when adding hydrothermally modified flours [47].

When flours modified hydrothermally were used as an additive for baking, a negative impact on the final quality of the produced bread was evident. The problems with gas retention in bread were probably due to flours modified in this way losing their gluten network formation properties. According to Hong et al. [51], modification of wheat flour via superheated steam treatment causes protein denaturation and brings about the initial gelatinization of its contained starch granules, thus reducing the access of water to the protein phase due to its greater absorption. The resulting problem with the formation of a continuous network by starch is that it results in a weakening of the gluten quality and a reduction in its elasticity. This effect was noted in the alveographic analyses. The presence of HF, HFC, and HFCX flour components in the bread dough induced a lowering of dough strength and a problem with gas bubble containment in the dough matrix. Despite the use of bakery enzymes for processing, which increased the soluble fiber fraction, this did not eliminate the negative impact of the process on gluten protein quality.

In our work, specific bread volume increased significantly with the addition of thermal, hydrothermal, and hybrid treated developed flour, or if FC10 and FC20 was incorporated within the bread recipe (Table 3). A significant decrease in bread density (0.30–0.33 g/cm^3) was also observed in these samples, as compared to control (0.35 g/cm^3), due to the larger number of pores in the crumb than in the control bread.

We also found that bread volume and specific volume were highly negatively correlated with bread density (r = −0.997 and 0.987, respectively, at $p < 0.05$). Accordingly, Tao et al. [46] reported increased specific bread volume (from 1.63 to 2.15 cm^3/g) when low temperature extrusion was applied to process wheat starch added to a bread recipe. Moreover, in our work, the addition of modified flours did not cause an increase in baking loss compared to the control bread, while an increase in weight loss after 24 h was observed. The increase in baking loss after 24 h was, however, slightly greater, albeit statistically insignificant, when modified and control flour recipes were compared. The greatest baking loss was observed in the control breads. The loss during baking of bread incorporating modified flours was lower, which indicates a heightened ability to retain water during baking; however, after 24 h, the weight loss was slightly higher, which may be the effect of retrogradation of starch treated via T and H methods after baking and cooling. The WAI values were also lower in the control bread and higher in that made with the modified additives. The addition of dry thermal heating reduced the retrogradation of the dough, as illustrated by the results of the C5 measurement, while the addition of hydrothermally treated flour increased the retrogradation, which is confirmed by the C5 results. Here, after cooling, the internal consistency was less springy, as confirmed by texture measurements.

Figure 2. Bread samples with the addition of modified flours: K—control; F—flour; T—dry thermal treatment; H—hydrothermal treatment; C—cellulase enzyme; CX—cellulase-xylanase enzyme complex; 10 and 20—% of modified flour in bread recipe.

In related work, Kurek et al. [52] found that values of a specific volume of wheat bread depend on the flour type used, with the lowest specific volume observed in wholegrain bread (0.82 cm^3/g) and the highest in control white bread samples (1.60 cm^3/g). Ma et al. [13] investigated the effect of superheated steam treatment on enhancing the physicochemical properties of flour for baked products. They noted that steam treatment could improve certain dough quality characteristics, such as volume and crumb quality. In their research, they found that the superheated steam treatment increased the starch gelatinization level and weakened the gluten strength due to denaturation, and that changes in these physicochemical properties of flour showed an effect on dough quality [13,16]. In our research, treatment with enzymes eliminated the negative aspects of the physical processes. In contrast, Hydrothermal treatment, despite the use of an enzyme complex, negatively affected the quality of the modified flour, the addition of which caused problems with bread dough gas bubble retention during rising and baking.

From an economic and quality point of view, the most desired outcome of flour/recipe modification is generating the highest specific volume. Alamri et al. [53] reported a specific volume between 2.55 and 3.14 cm^3/g for bread with addition of 1 and 2% of plant gums, with the lowest value obtained for common wheat flour control bread. Wholegrain or fiber enriched dough generally has more phytic acid, which reduces alpha-amylase activity, which, in turn, causes a decrease in bread specific volume. A much higher specific bread volume was obtained by Zhan et al. [5] for whole wheat bread (3.82 cm^3/g), and replacement of wheat flour by pulses decreased the specific volume of supplemented bread because of the lower water absorption of pulse flour.

In our study, change in the yield of the obtained bread was calculated for individual baked loaves. A significant increase was observed in breads made with recipes containing the addition of HFC20, HFCX20, HFCX10, TFCX 20, and TFC20 flours; however, as mentioned earlier, breads baked with the addition of HF flours were characterized by a lower ability to retain gases during fermentation, especially when 10% HFC and HFCX flours were added, and the bubbles moved under the crust, causing it to stand apart after baking (Figure 2). Such changes were not observed when dry heat-treated flour was used as an additive.

As shown in Figure 2, breads with TF, TFC, and TFCX additions were characterized by an increased or similar number of pores as in the control bread K; these were located evenly in the crumb, increasing the overall volume of the loaves. Ambrosewicz-Walacik et al. [41], in a related work, tested bread yield of yeast or sourdough fermented bread based on various compositions of doughs. They reported that bread yield varied from 131.1% if yeast were used in white wheat bread to 134.8% in wholemeal wheat bread, whereas bread yield ranged from 152.8% to 162.4%, respectively, when natural sourdough was applied. A much higher bread yield was obtained if rye flour was used, especially wholegrain (188.3%), with natural sourdough being used for bread preparation.

3.4. Bread Physical Properties

The color profile of bread crumb and crust are quality parameters mostly associated with the attractiveness of bakery products to the consumer. Development of non-enzymatic browning, as the effect of sugars caramelization or the Maillard reaction, on the surface of baked goods is important because of the formation of a marketable beige-brown color and specific flavor [7]. Table 4 presents the results of color profile evaluation of bread crumb and crust depending on the addition of the developed flour (F) as modified via the researched methods.

In our work, the control bread crumb and crust had L^* values 65.26 and 45.60, respectively. Breads with the addition of TH20 and HF20 were lighter than other samples with added modified flours, and the color profile was similar to the control. The use of modified flours with enzymes significantly decreased bread crumb lightness, and breads with the addition of FC10, FCX10, and FCX20 and HFC10 and HFC20 showed L^* values ranging between 61.92 and 62.77. Other results were comparable with negligible effects of processing methods and enzymes used.

Table 4. Color profile evaluation of bread crumb and crust.

Bread Sample	Bread Crumb				Bread crust			
	L^*	a^*	b^*	ΔE	L^*	a^*	b^*	ΔE
K	65.29 ± 0.74 [a,b]	1.97 ± 0.13 [a]	10.48 ± 0.34 [a,b,c]	ref	45.60 ± 1.66 [c,d]	13.45 ± 0.20 [a,b,c]	22.69 ± 0.90 [c,d,e]	ref
F10	65.02 ± 2.59 [a,b]	1.95 ± 0.17 [a]	10.61 ± 0.38 [a,b,c]	0.30	45.33 ± 1.55 [c,d]	13.54 ± 0.27 [b,c,d]	23.36 ± 1.17 [c,d,e]	0.73
F20	63.75 ± 1.37 [a,b]	2.13 ± 0.20 [a]	10.48 ± 0.79 [a,b,c]	1.55	45.75 ± 2.51 [c,d]	13.07 ± 0.85 [a,b,c]	22.50 ± 2.47 [c,d,e]	0.46
FC10	62.51 ± 1.99 [a]	1.85 ± 0.23 [a]	9.80 ± 0.72 [a,b]	2.86	43.20 ± 1.16 [a,b,c]	13.07 ± 0.42 [a,b,c]	20.84 ± 1.47 [a,b,c,d]	3.05
FC20	64.06 ± 2.95 [a,b]	2.01 ± 0.22 [a]	10.44 ± 0.19 [a,b,c]	1.23	48.46 ± 1.92 [d]	12.87 ± 0.30 [a,b]	23.84 ± 0.85 [d,e]	3.14
FCX10	62.36 ± 1.86 [a]	1.83 ± 0.20 [a]	10.16 ± 0.40 [a,b,c]	2.95	41.13 ± 2.02 [a,b]	13.10 ± 0.33 [a,b,c]	19.48 ± 1.56 [a,b]	5.52
FCX20	61.95 ± 1.11 [a]	2.17 ± 0.26 [a]	10.26 ± 0.71 [a,b,c]	3.35	44.05 ± 1.48 [a,b,c]	13.72 ± 0.25 [b,c,d]	22.42 ± 0.31 [b,c,d,e]	1.59
TF10	62.52 ± 1.92 [a]	2.08 ± 0.20 [a]	10.47 ± 0.43 [a,b,c]	2.77	46.61 ± 1.90 [c,d]	13.90 ± 0.49 [c,d]	24.14 ± 0.80 [e]	1.82
TF20	64.97 ± 0.66 [a,b]	2.04 ± 0.07 [a]	10.70 ± 0.42 [b,c]	0.39	44.62 ± 1.68 [b,c]	12.98 ± 0.45 [a,b,c]	21.90 ± 1.88 [a,b,c,d,e]	1.34
TFC10	64.46 ± 0.90 [a,b]	1.98 ± 0.15 [a]	10.48 ± 0.54 [a,b,c]	0.83	43.39 ± 1.68 [a,b,c]	13.07 ± 0.62 [a,b,c]	20.68 ± 2.01 [a,b,c]	3.01
TFC20	62.42 ± 1.08 [a]	1.91 ± 0.24 [a]	10.04 ± 0.64 [a,b,c]	2.90	44.95 ± 1.82 [c,d]	13.69 ± 0.51 [b,c,d]	22.51 ± 1.42 [c,d,e]	0.71
TFCX10	65.53 ± 1.91 [b]	2.08 ± 0.16 [a]	10.82 ± 0.35 [c]	1.33	43.76 ± 1.90 [a,b,c]	13.38 ± 0.43 [a,b,c]	21.50 ± 1.50 [a,b,c,d,e]	2.19
TFCX20	63.50 ± 1.77 [a,b]	2.03 ± 0.24 [a]	10.88 ± 0.55 [c]	1.83	41.90 ± 1.15 [a,b]	12.82 ± 0.30 [a,b]	19.93 ± 0.52 [a,b]	6.09
HF10	63.14 ± 2.37 [a,b]	1.91 ± 0.22 [a]	10.75 ± 0.32 [b,c]	2.17	44.86 ± 1.85 [c,d]	12.93 ± 0.54 [a,b]	21.78 ± 1.59 [a,b,c,d,e]	1.29
HF20	64.28 ± 2.42 [a,b]	1.81 ± 0.27 [a]	10.06 ± 0.60 [a,b,c]	1.10	45.63 ± 1.92 [c,d]	12.81 ± 0.31 [a,b]	21.49 ± 1.04 [a,b,c,d,e]	1.37
HFC10	62.77 ± 1.66 [a]	2.00 ± 0.13 [a]	9.95 ± 0.40 [a,b,c]	2.57	45.81 ± 1.43 [c,d]	13.53 ± 0.36 [b,c]	22.87 ± 1.65 [c,d,e]	0.28
HFC20	62.31 ± 1.90 [a]	1.88 ± 0.14 [a]	9.64 ± 0.36 [a]	3.10	44.19 ± 1.25 [a,b,c]	12.76 ± 0.44 [a,b]	20.86 ± 1.15 [a,b,c,d]	2.41
HFCX10	63.58 ± 0.42 [a,b]	1.86 ± 0.14 [a]	10.45 ± 0.41 [a,b,c]	1.71	45.38 ± 1.31 [c,d]	13.50 ± 0.36 [b,c]	22.99 ± 1.76 [c,d,e]	0.37
HFCX20	63.64 ± 0.42 [a,b]	1.96 ± 0.08 [a]	10.10 ± 0.23 [a,b,c]	1.69	45.13 ± 2.68 [c,d]	14.49 ± 0.74 [d]	23.45 ± 1.48 [c,d,e]	1.37

K—control; F—flour; T—dry thermal treatment; H—hydrothermal treatment; C—cellulase enzyme; CX—cellulase-xylanase enzyme complex; 10 and 20—% of modified flour in bread recipe; L^*—lightness (0–100); a^*—greenest (−)—redness (+) balance; b^*—blueness (−)—yellowness (+) balance; ΔE—total color change; [a–e]—means indicated with similar letters in columns do not differ significantly at $\alpha = 0.05$.

Bread crust color profiles were similar in lightness and a^* values; however, a wider range of results were noted if the crust yellowness b^* was evaluated (19.93–24.14). The more intensive redness or yellowness and darker crust color seen in some resulting breads may be the effect of nonenzymatic browning reactions or surface caramelization occurring under high temperature baking, especially when an increased content of reducing sugars is present in the bread composition [21]. In our work, ΔE was calculated separately for bread crumb and crust, and the results were, in almost all tested breads, below a value of 5, which is an easily recognized color difference.

Some differences were found between the tested breads and control sample if CX enzyme complex was added to the developed flour modifications. Especially in FCX10 and TFCX20, bread crust total color change values notably differed from the control. This could have come about due to the action of the enzyme complex upon the contained polysaccharides (which were hydrolyzed into simple sugars). This effect was not observed in the hydrothermally treated samples, probably due to the intensiveness of the treatment, which resulted in the complete deactivation of the enzymes. In the tested breads, however, no clear trend was observed, and the obtained breads were visually very similar. This confirms the appropriate quality of the resulting breads and that the additives did not have a deteriorating effect.

In a related work, Zhang et al. [5] tested the color of bread crumb prepared with whole what and supplemented with various pulse flours up to 25%. Here, the addition of pulse flour limited L^* and b^* coordinates, but, similarly, no significant trend was observed. Jurkaninová et al. [7] observed L^* values from 59.0 to 69.8 for bread crust of breads fortified with herb extracts, which is within the standard range of lightness. They determined that a^* ranged from 8.79 to 15.70 and b^* from 32.98 to 38.33, which, while indicating a red–yellow area of crust color that is favorable for baked goods, demonstrated that the color profile of the crumb was much less intensive in redness and more yellow. Mahmoud et al. [8], in turn, tested the addition of microalgae to bread and they reported twice as much a decrease of crust and crumb lightness and a more intensive green and more yellow tint of crumb when various algaes were added. In our bread with the developed treated flour, the lightness and yellowness of crust and crumb were lower, but redness was more intensive than in the control.

Testing of WAI and WSI is helpful in identifying the integration of components in products that undergo variable heat-related treatments, for example, thermal treatment, baking, or extrusion [17,42]. In all the tested breads fortified with the modified developed flours, an increased WAI was obtained as compared to control bread K (Table 5). This confirms the ability of the dough to absorb more water when the developed modified flour was added to breads. When starch granules are partly gelatinized, they have tendency to absorb and hold water, but after exceeding the gelatinization point temperature, the starch granules become broken, and they do not have the ability to absorb water [54]. Of additional interest, thermal and hydrothermal treatment may be responsible for increasing swelling capacity; in our work, the addition of treated flours showed the tendency to increase WAI. During the steam process, wheat flour components are restructured and may present different affinities with water, because strong water binding capacity can be related to interactions between water and the carbohydrates and proteins present inside the flour. Delatte et al. [17] noted some differences in the WAI and WSI of untreated and modified flours when steam treated. They reported WAI of 0.929 to 2.089 g/g in the former, and up to 4.169 to 7.450 g/g in the latter, depending on the amount of steam added during treatment. In our study, increased WAI was noted if thermally, hydrothermally, and enzyme-assisted modified flours were incorporated into the basic bread recipe, as compared to control common wheat bread (Table 5), but differences were not strictly dependent on treatment method. WAI varied from 2.668 g/g in control bread K to 3.754 g/g in the TFC10 fortified bread.

Table 5. WAI and WSI of breads.

Bread Sample	WAI (g/g)	WSI (%)
K	2.668 ± 0.044 [a]	6.847 ± 0.276 [d,e]
F10	2.930 ± 0.019 [b]	7.199 ± 0.087 [e,f]
F20	2.692 ± 0.046 [a]	7.840 ± 0.148 [g]
FC10	3.093 ± 0.078 [c,d]	6.700 ± 0.290 [c,d,e]
FC20	3.362 ± 0.010 [g]	6.710 ± 0.148 [c,d,e]
FCX10	2.691 ± 0.046 [a]	7.133 ± 0.143 [d,e,f]
FCX20	3.266 ± 0.065 [e,f,g]	6.985 ± 0.148 [d,e,f]
TF10	3.290 ± 0.035 [f,g]	7.173 ± 0.355 [e,f]
TF20	2.694 ± 0.071 [a]	7.270 ± 0.137 [e,f,g]
TFC10	3.754 ± 0.031 [i]	6.548 ± 0.289 [b,c,d]
TFC20	3.086 ± 0.062 [c,d]	7.555 ± 0.005 [f,g]
TFCX10	3.209 ± 0.024 [d,e,f]	6.143 ± 0.286 [a,b,c]
TFCX20	3.144 ± 0.048 [d,e,f]	7.046 ± 0.209 [d,e,f]
HF10	3.125 ± 0.039 [c,d,e]	6.981 ± 0.162 [d,e,f]
HF20	2.673 ± 0.061 [a]	6.904 ± 0.228 [d,e]
HFC10	3.521 ± 0.081 [h]	5.832 ± 0.276 [a]
HFC20	3.118 ± 0.016 [c,d]	6.847 ± 0.143 [d,e]
HFCX10	2.978 ± 0.018 [b,c]	7.539 ± 0.011 [f,g]
HFCX20	3.147 ± 0.016 [d,e,f]	5.974 ± 0.008 [a,b]

K—control; F—flour; T—dry thermal treatment; H—hydrothermal treatment; C—cellulase enzyme; CX—cellulase-xylanase enzyme complex; 10 and 20—% of modified flour in bread recipe; WAI—water absorption index; WSI—water solubility index; [a–i]—means indicated with similar letters in columns do not differ significantly at $\alpha = 0.05$.

WSI, as an indicator of degradation of molecular components, is usually employed to measure the degree of starch conversion during baking and may be an indicator of the amount of soluble polysaccharide released from the starch component after processing [55].

The decrease in WSI may be because of the reduction of carbohydrates, especially starch, in the recipe as replaced by the developed modified flour (Table 2), and thus limited gelatinization is one of the important effects of utilized baking procedure. Since WSI indicates the water solubility of non-bounded food components into water after WAI measurements, a tendency towards WSI increase with lowering of WAI was observed for most of the obtained results. Soluble components evaluated after bread testing indicated enhanced solubility if F developed flour was added to bread at 10 and 20%; here, the increase was associated with higher TDF in bread (Table 2) produced from fibrous fractions of selected passages in this new flour [26]. The highest WSI results were noted in bread with the addition of FC20 (Table 5). This outcome confirms the cellulase enzyme action on polysaccharides fractions in enzyme modified flour. Quite low WSI values were noted in breads with added enzyme-hydrothermal hybrid treated flour, both with cellulase and cellulase-xylanase complex application. All WSI values were below 8%. This confirms that the breads have both an appropriate internal structure and combination of most components within the protein-starch matrix of the bread dough after baking.

Texture measurements of the bread crumb showed some differences in the main textural properties of the tested breads, with the results from double-compression tests being presented in Table 6. Accordingly, control bread firmness was 15.47 N, springiness was 0.81, chewiness was 5.00 N, and cohesiveness was 0.40. Substitution of bread wheat flour with thermal, hydrothermal, or enzyme-assisted hybrid treated developed flour induced slight changes in the textural properties of the bread crumb. Most of the tested breads showed higher firmness values when thermal and hydrothermal modification of the added flour was applied. Moreover, the addition of untreated F flours increased bread hardness. Furthermore, lower compression forces were noted if enzymes were added to the developed flour. This outcome may be the effect of enzyme action on the fibrous flour fractions and subsequently on loosening the internal structure of bread crumb fortified with FC and FCX flours. Adhesion, as the work needed to separate the measuring element from the crumb surface, was very low in all the tested breads and differences were insignificant. Similarly, low values and insignificant differences were found for bread springiness.

Table 6. Texture of bread with the addition of modified flours.

Bread Sample	Firmness (N)	Adhesion (mJ)	Springiness (−)	Gumminess (N)	Chewiness (N)	Cohesiveness (−)
K	15.47 ± 1.22 [a,b,c,d]	0.09 ± 0.06 [a,b]	0.81 ± 0.07 [a]	6.19 ± 0.28 [a,b,c,d]	5.00 ± 0.61 [a]	0.40 ± 0.02 [a,b]
F10	20.20 ± 1.59 [f,g]	0.04 ± 0.06 [a]	0.86 ± 0.01 [a]	7.70 ± 0.51 [c,d,e]	6.65 ± 0.51 [a,b]	0.38 ± 0.01 [a,b]
F20	17.47 ± 3.21 [c,d,e,f,g]	0.07 ± 0.06 [a,b]	0.72 ± 0.14 [a]	7.25 ± 1.51 [b,c,d,e]	5.18 ± 1.25 [a,b]	0.41 ± 0.03 [a,b]
FC10	13.67 ± 0.80 [a,b,c]	0.08 ± 0.02 [a,b]	0.82 ± 0.01 [a]	5.44 ± 0.18 [a,b]	4.44 ± 0.17 [a]	0.40 ± 0.02 [a,b]
FC20	13.77 ± 1.67 [a,b,c]	0.07 ± 0.01 [a,b]	0.86 ± 0.02 [a]	5.89 ± 0.30 [a,b,c]	5.04 ± 0.35 [a]	0.43 ± 0.03 [b]
FCX10	14.67 ± 0.15 [a,b,c,d,e]	0.13 ± 0.00 [a,b]	0.78 ± 0.07 [a]	6.15 ± 0.15 [a,b,c,d]	4.77 ± 0.49 [a]	0.39 ± 0.02 [a,b]
FCX20	12.93 ± 1.02 [a]	0.08 ± 0.03 [a,b]	0.85 ± 0.03 [a]	5.25 ± 0.17 [a]	4.46 ± 0.14 [a]	0.41 ± 0.03 [a,b]
TF10	20.97 ± 1.29 [g,h]	0.06 ± 0.06 [a,b]	0.67 ± 0.10 [a]	7.94 ± 0.36 [d,e]	5.36 ± 0.97 [a,b]	0.38 ± 0.01 [a,b]
TF20	17.43 ± 0.86 [b,c,d,e,f,g]	0.08 ± 0.05 [a,b]	0.69 ± 0.21 [a]	6.63 ± 0.48 [a,b,c,d]	4.67 ± 1.66 [a]	0.38 ± 0.04 [a,b]
TFC10	15.53 ± 0.38 [a,b]	0.09 ± 0.02 [a,b]	0.86 ± 0.01 [a]	5.45 ± 0.14 [a,b]	4.69 ± 0.11 [a]	0.40 ± 0.00 [a,b]
TFC20	24.83 ± 0.99 [h]	0.09 ± 0.01 [a,b]	0.87 ± 0.01 [a]	9.02 ± 1.47 [e]	7.79 ± 1.26 [b]	0.36 ± 0.06 [a,b]
TFCX10	19.53 ± 0.46 [e,f,g]	0.03 ± 0.02 [a]	0.72 ± 0.13 [a]	7.04 ± 0.70 [a,b,c,d]	5.04 ± 0.76 [a]	0.36 ± 0.03 [a,b]
TFCX20	15.63 ± 1.70 [a,b,c,d,e]	0.20 ± 0.05 [b]	0.74 ± 0.06 [a]	5.55 ± 0.30 [a,b]	4.06 ± 0.31 [a]	0.36 ± 0.03 [a,b]
HF10	18.07 ± 0.31 [d,e,f,g]	0.11 ± 0.03 [a,b]	0.70 ± 0.12 [a]	6.95 ± 0.48 [a,b,c,d]	4.89 ± 1.13 [a]	0.39 ± 0.04 [a,b]
HF20	16.13 ± 0.12 [a,b,c,d,e]	0.09 ± 0.04 [a,b]	0.72 ± 0.10 [a]	6.44 ± 0.27 [a,b,c,d]	4.66 ± 0.82 [a]	0.40 ± 0.01 [a,b]
HFC10	17.20 ± 0.20 [b,c,d,e,f,g]	0.06 ± 0.06 [a,b]	0.74 ± 0.17 [a]	6.63 ± 0.33 [a,b,c,d]	4.94 ± 1.31 [a]	0.39 ± 0.03 [a,b]
HFC20	18.17 ± 1.40 [d,e,f,g]	0.16 ± 0.14 [a,b]	0.76 ± 0.07 [a]	6.27 ± 0.26 [a,b,c,d]	4.78 ± 0.63 [a]	0.34 ± 0.02 [a]
HFCX10	16.07 ± 0.72 [a,b,c,d,e]	0.08 ± 0.05 [a,b]	0.75 ± 0.08 [a]	6.13 ± 0.32 [a,b,c,d]	4.60 ± 0.73 [a]	0.38 ± 0.01 [a,b]
HFCX20	16.30 ± 1.35 [a,b,c,d,e,f]	0.06 ± 0.02 [a,b]	0.67 ± 0.08 [a]	6.41 ± 0.47 [a,b,c,d]	4.29 ± 0.77 [a]	0.39 ± 0.02 [a,b]

K—control; F—flour; T—dry thermal treatment; H—hydrothermal treatment; C—cellulase enzyme; CX—cellulase-xylanase enzyme complex; 10 and 20—% of modified flour in bread recipe; [a–h]—means indicated with similar letters in columns do not differ significantly at α = 0.05.

Chewiness of breads supplemented with F10 and F20, and those which contained unchanged fibrous fractions in the developed flour, was slightly higher than that of the control bread K. For other bread samples, the results did not differ significantly, except for the addition of TFC20. This increased bread chewiness. All baked breads were similar in cohesiveness, which confirms the visual observations of bread crumb presence of a compact internal structure (Figure 2). In general, the addition of modified flours did not significantly deteriorate the texture of the bread, while bread yield, bread volume, and specific volume of prepared breads with the modified developed flour were improved significantly. Zhang et al. [5] found that increasing the substitution level of pulse flours significantly enhanced the starch retrogradation value and resulted in a harder bread texture, as both polysaccharides and protein in the pulse flours have an effect on bread hardness. Tao et al. [46], in turn, found that the hardness of the bread crumb is limited if extruded flour was added; this is because bread containing extruded starch had a softer texture and a more porous crumb structure. The addition of plant gums to bread recipes also significantly reduces the firmness of bread via a clear effect of crumb-softening, as reported by Alamri et al. [53].

3.5. PCA Analysis

From the PCA analysis performed to determine the parameters that have the greatest influence on the variability of the system, eighteen new variables were obtained, of which the first three principal components explain more than 50% of the variability of the system. Indeed, the first two principal components explain 40.16% of the variability of the system (PC1 in 24.95% and PC2 in 15.21%), and the parameters that are contained between the two circles have the greatest influence on the variability of the system. As a result of this procedure, fourteen parameters were determined from the forty parameters examined: C2, C3, C4, C5, L, IDF, TDF, bread yield, W, Ie, SH, P, P/L, and carbohydrates (Figure 3a). The remaining parameters have a weak influence on the variability of the system. Moreover, C2, C3, C4, C5, W, Ie, SH, P, and P/L are strongly and positively correlated. The same relationship was observed for IDF, TDF, and bread yield. A strong but negative correlation occurs between parameters C2, C3, C4, C5, W, Ie, SH, P, P/L, and L, while a strong and negative correlation was also determined for IDF, TDF, bread yield, and carbohydrates. There is no correlation between C2, C3, C4, C5, W, Ie, SH, P, P/L, and IDF, TDF, bread yield, and carbohydrates. There is also no correlation between L and IDF, TDF and bread yield, and between L and carbohydrates.

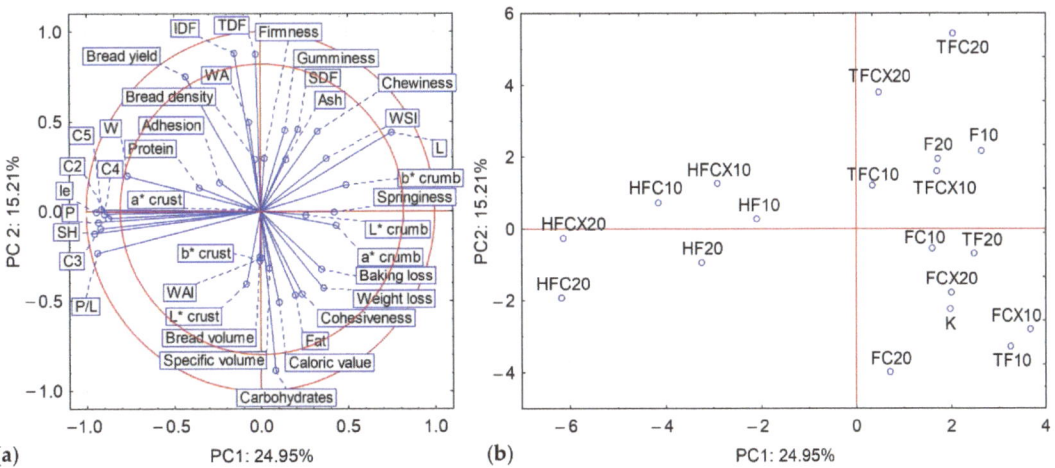

Figure 3. PCA analysis: (**a**) projection of variables all parameters on the PC1 and PC2 loadings plot; (**b**) projection of modified wheat flours on the PC1 and PC2 scores plot.

The PCA analysis also shows (Figure 3a,b) that HF, HFC, and HFCX are strongly and positively correlated with C2, C3, C4, C5, W, Ie, SH, P, and P/L, and strongly and negatively with L. In turn, F10, F20, TFC, and TFCX are strongly and positively correlated with L. In turn, K, FC, TF, and FCX are strongly and positively correlated with carbohydrates. The PCA analysis shows that the first principal component PC1 distinguishes hybrid thermal-enzymatic flour from control flour and thermal-enzymatic flour by 24.95% (Figure 3b). Positive values of the principal component PC1 describe the results of F and T and the control, and negative values of the principal component PC1 describe the results for H. The second principal component PC2 characterizes F, TF, and TFCX (positive values of PC2) and K, FC, and FCX (negative values of PC2) to 15.21%.

The first and third principal components explain 36.99% of the variability of the system (PC1 to 24.95% and PC2 to 15.21%). The parameters that are contained between the two circles have the greatest influence on the variability of the system. As a result of the analysis, twelve parameters were determined from the forty parameters studied: C2, C3, C4, C5, bread yield, W, Ie, SH, P, P/L, specific volume, and bread volume (Figure 4a). The remaining parameters have a weak influence on the variability of the system. C2, C3, C4, C5, W, Ie, SH, P, and P/L are strongly and positively correlated. The same relationship was observed for specific volume and bread volume. A strong but negative correlation occurs between the parameters: specific volume, bread volume, and bread yield. There is no correlation between C2, C3, C4, C5, W, Ie, SH, P, P/L, and bread yield, specific volume, and bread volume.

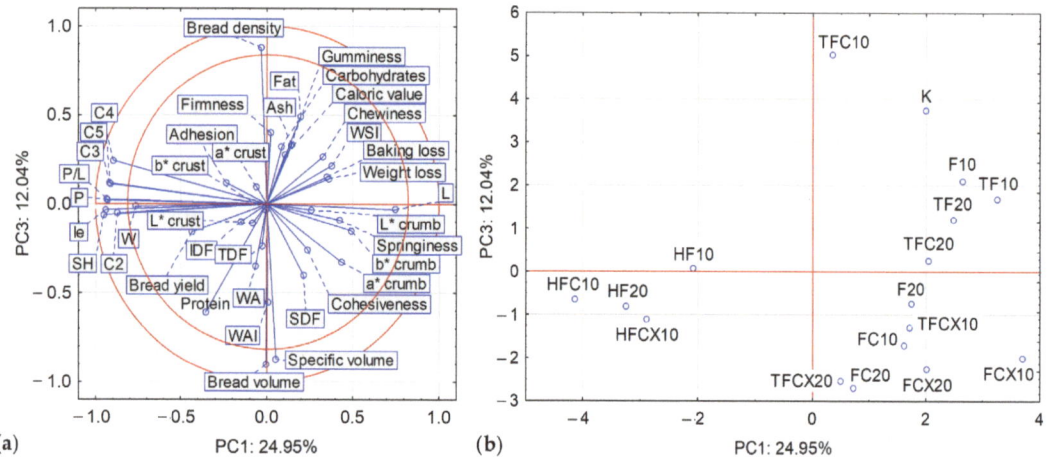

Figure 4. PCA analysis: (**a**) projection of variables parameters on the PC1 and PC3 loadings plot; (**b**) projection of modified wheat flours on the PC1 and PC3 scores plot.

The PCA analysis also shows (Figure 4a,b) that HF, HFC, and HFCX are strongly and positively correlated with C2, C3, C4, C5, W, Ie, SH, P, and P/L. In turn, F10, F20, TFC, and TFCX are strongly and positively correlated with specific volume and bread volume. In turn, K, FC, TF, and FCX are strongly and positively correlated with bread yield.

The PCA analysis shows that the first principal component PC1 distinguishes hybrid thermal-enzymatic flour from flour and thermal-enzymatic flour to 24.95% (Figure 4b). Positive values of the PC1 principal component describe the results of F and T and the control, and negative values of the PC1 principal component describe the results for H. The third principal component PC3 characterizes F20, FC, FCX, and TFCX (negative PC2 values) and K F, TF, and TFC (positive PC2 values) to 12.04%.

4. Conclusions

The presented research has both scientific and practical impact due to it providing the possibility to find technological solutions for reducing the amount of underutilized wheat flour fractions (10% of production in a milling company) by incorporating it into blends that may be applicable for bread making with appropriate properties. Moreover, new knowledge acquired about the characteristics of developed flour modified with thermal, hydrothermal, and enzyme-assisted hybrid treatment and its application in bread is valuable for the baking industry and in providing food for a fast-growing population.

The presented research results confirmed the possibility of substituting standard wheat flours with flours treated via thermal, hydrothermal, or enzyme-assisted hybrid methods in bread recipes for the purpose of improving bread yield in a clean label manner. The investigated modification processes brought about some significant changes in dough rheology when 10 or 20% of modified flours replaced common wheat flour in bread composition. According to our research results, bread dough properties varied depending on modification process and level of added modified flour. Treatment with enzymes allowed us to eliminate the negative aspects of the physical processes. The hydrothermal treatment, despite the use of an enzyme complex, negatively affected the quality of modified flour, the addition of which caused problems with gas bubble retention in the bread dough during rising and baking. When modified flours were introduced, the protein weakening values increased by 19%. This indicates that the resulting bread product showed enhanced bread dough stiffness. However, dry thermal heated flours without or with enzymes showed significantly decreased amylase activity and starch retrogradation results by 2–11% and 2–13%, respectively, as compared to the control sample or to the hydrothermally modified flours. This indicates that thermal treatment deteriorated the flour parameters, but the addition of enzymes resulted in a dough quality similar to control, with increased bread efficiency related to the higher water absorption of the flour.

Bread properties, in terms of chemical composition, quality features, texture, and color, were slightly different if modified flours were added. Application of thermal treated modified flours to a common wheat bread recipe gave the highest bread yield of 150.02% and increased water absorption of the dough by 6%, especially when the enzyme-assisted method was applied to the developed flour; this was achieved without a negative impact on the texture or color of the obtained breads. It should be noted that the developed flours modified via hydrothermal method or hybrid enzyme-assisted method, when added to bread composition, did not produce a desired dough structure, and the addition resulted in a deteriorated bread crust formation, despite the increasing of bread volume and yield, as compared to control common wheat flour bread. However, all types of additives lowered baking loss and weight loss of the produced bread by 8% as compared to control sample. The resulting doughs with added thermally modified flour may be suitable for processing, mixing, and fermentation without deterioration of the quality of the bread and with improved bread volume (16%).

The presented results can be readily implemented in practice by milling companies as a solution for reducing the amount of underutilized fractions. Moreover, the composition of the new flour blends with the added developed modified flour (with its specific properties) may be offered as a ready-to-use bakery blend with a clean label as a bread improver. As a limitation in the use of the obtained modified flours, it should be noted that the addition of more than 20% of the total blend would not be profitable for bread producers as such amounts lower the final product quality. Future research, however, will be focused on production optimization, as well as exploring the possibilities of incorporating other flours into bread-making and evaluating the effects of the aforementioned additions on dough and bread quality. Moreover, additional tests will be carried out using other baking enzymes (e.g., bacterial xylanase) that could modify the processed flours more effectively.

Author Contributions: Conceptualization, P.L. and A.W.; methodology, P.L., A.W. and M.G.; software, P.L., A.W. and M.G.; validation, P.L. and A.W.; formal analysis, P.L. and M.G.; investigation, P.L.; resources, P.L.; data curation, P.L. and A.W.; writing—original draft preparation, P.L. and A.W.; writing—review and editing, P.L., A.W. and M.G.; visualization, P.L. and M.G.; supervision, A.W.; project administration, A.W.; funding acquisition, P.L. All authors have read and agreed to the published version of the manuscript.

Funding: This research was financially supported from the founds of the Polish Ministry of Education and Science as a part of Implementation doctorate project (agreement number DWD/4/84/2020).

Institutional Review Board Statement: Not applicable.

Informed Consent Statement: Not applicable.

Data Availability Statement: Data presented in this study are available on request from the corresponding author.

Acknowledgments: Particular acknowledgements to Marek Goldsztejn from PZZ Lubella GMW Sp. z o.o., for his kind support during the research.

Conflicts of Interest: The authors declare no conflicts of interest. The funders had no role in the design of the study; in the collection, analyses, or interpretation of data; in the writing of the manuscript; or in the decision to publish the results.

References

1. Cauvain, S.P. (Ed.) *Breadmaking: Improving Quality*; Series: Food Science, Technology and Nutrition; Woodhead Publishing: Cambridge, UK, 2012. Available online: https://www.sciencedirect.com/book/9780857090607/breadmaking (accessed on 3 June 2024).
2. Cappelli, A.; Bettaccini, L.; Cini, E. The kneading process: A systematic review of the effects on dough rheology and resulting bread characteristics, including improvement strategies. *Trends Food Sci. Technol.* **2020**, *104*, 91–101. [CrossRef]
3. Vargas, M.C.A.; Simsek, S. Clean label in bread. *Foods* **2021**, *10*, 2054. [CrossRef]
4. Campbell, L.; Euston, S.R.; Ahmed, M.A. Effect of addition of thermally modified cowpea protein on sensory acceptability and textural properties of wheat bread and sponge cake. *Food Chem.* **2016**, *194*, 1230–1237. [CrossRef] [PubMed]
5. Zhang, Y.; Hu, R.; Tilley, M.; Siliveru, K.; Li, Y. Effect of pulse type and substitution level on dough rheology and bread quality of whole wheat-based composite flours. *Processes* **2021**, *9*, 1687. [CrossRef]
6. Wójcik, M.; Bieńczak, A.; Woźniak, P.; Różyło, R. Impact of watermelon seed flour on the physical, chemical, and sensory properties of low-carbohydrate, high-protein bread. *Processes* **2023**, *11*, 3282. [CrossRef]
7. Jurkaninová, L.; Švec, I.; Kučerová, I.; Havrlentová, M.; Božik, M.; Klouček, P.; Leuner, O. The use of thyme and lemongrass essential oils in cereal technology — Effect on wheat dough behavior and bread properties. *Appl. Sci.* **2024**, *14*, 4831. [CrossRef]
8. Mahmoud, N.; Ferreira, J.; Raymundo, A.; Nunes, M.C. Enhancing the protein, mineral content, and bioactivity of wheat bread through the utilisation of microalgal biomass: A comparative study of *Chlorella vulgaris*, *Phaeodactylum tricornutum*, and *Tetraselmis chuii*. *Appl. Sci.* **2024**, *14*, 2483. [CrossRef]
9. Zarzycki, P.; Wirkijowska, A.; Teterycz, D.; Łysakowska, P. Innovations in wheat bread: Using food industry by-products for better quality and nutrition. *Appl. Sci.* **2024**, *14*, 3976. [CrossRef]
10. Lee, Y.Y.; Ma, F.; Byars, J.A.; Felker, F.C.; Liu, S.; Mosier, N.S.; Lee, J.H.; Kenar, J.A.; Baik, B.K. Influences of hydrothermal and pressure treatments on compositional and hydration properties of wheat bran and dough mixing properties of whole wheat meal. *Cereal Chem.* **2021**, *98*, 673–682. [CrossRef]
11. Tayefe, M.; Shahidi, S.A.; Milani, J.M.; Sadeghi, S.M. Development, optimization, and critical quality characteristics of new wheat four dough formulations fortified with hydrothermally treated rice bran. *J. Food Meas. Charact.* **2020**, *14*, 2878–2888. [CrossRef]
12. Tebben, L.; Shen, Y.; Li, Y. Improvers and functional ingredients in whole wheat bread: A review of their effects on dough properties and bread quality. *Trends Food Sci. Tech.* **2018**, *81*, 10–24. [CrossRef]
13. Ma, F.; Lee, Y.Y.; Park, E.; Luo, Y.; Delwiche, S.; Baik, B.-K. Influences of hydrothermal and pressure treatments of wheat bran on the quality and sensory attributes of whole wheat Chinese steamed bread and pancakes. *J. Cereal Sci.* **2021**, *102*, 103356. [CrossRef]
14. Keppler, S.; Bakalis, S.; Leadley, C.E.; Sahi, S.S.; Fryer, P.J. Evaluation of dry heat treatment of soft wheat flour for the production of high ratio cakes. *Food Res. Int.* **2018**, *107*, 360–370. [CrossRef] [PubMed]
15. Bucsella, B.; Takács, Á.; Vizer, V.; Schwendener, U.; Tömösközi, S. Comparison of the effects of different heat treatment processes on rheological properties of cake and bread wheat flours. *Food Chem.* **2016**, *190*, 990–996. [CrossRef]
16. Hu, J.; Wang, L.; Zhu, H.; Li, Z. Superheated steam treatment improved flour qualities of wheat in suitable conditions. *J. Food. Process. Pres.* **2017**, *41*, 13238. [CrossRef]
17. Delatte, S.; Doran, L.; Blecker, C.; Mol, G.; Roiseux, O.; Gofflot, S.; Malumba, P. Effect of pilot-scale steam treatment and endogenous alpha-amylase activity on wheat flour functional properties. *J. Cereal Sci.* **2019**, *88*, 38–46. [CrossRef]

18. de Souza, T.; Kawaguti, H.Y. Cellulases, hemicellulases, and pectinases: Applications in the food and beverage industry. *Food Bioprocess Technol.* **2021**, *14*, 1446–1477. [CrossRef]
19. Melim Miguel, A.S.; Souza, T.; da Costa Figueiredo, E.V.; Paulo Lobo, B.W.; Maria, G. Enzymes in Bakery: Current and Future Trends. In *Food Industry*; Muzzalupo, I., Ed.; IntechOpen: London, UK, 2013. [CrossRef]
20. Li, M.; Niu, M. New technologies in cereal processing and their impact on the physical properties of cereal foods. *Foods* **2023**, *12*, 4008. [CrossRef]
21. Gómez, M.; Jiménez, S.; Ruiz, E.; Oliete, B. Effect of extruded wheat bran on dough rheology and bread quality. *LWT-Food Sci. Technol.* **2011**, *44*, 2231–2237. [CrossRef]
22. Martinez, M.; Oliete, B.; Gómez, M. Effect of the addition of extruded wheat flours on dough rheology and bread quality. *J. Cereal Sci.* **2013**, *57*, 424–429. [CrossRef]
23. Jiang, X.; Wang, X.; Zhou, S. Effect of flaxseed marc flour on high-yield wheat bread production: Comparison in baking, staling, antioxidant and digestion properties. *LWT-Food Sci. Technol.* **2022**, *169*, 113979. [CrossRef]
24. Cingöz, A.; Akpinar, O.; Sayaslan, A. Rheological properties of dough by addition of wheat bran hydrolysates obtained at different temperatures. *J. Cereal Sci.* **2023**, *109*, 103612. [CrossRef]
25. Li, X.; Wang, L.; Jiang, P.; Zhu, Y.; Zhang, W.; Li, R.; Tan, B. The effect of wheat bran dietary fibre and raw wheat bran on the flour and dough properties: A comparative study. *LWT-Food Sci. Technol.* **2023**, *173*, 114304. [CrossRef]
26. Lewko, P.; Wójtowicz, A.; Gancarz, M. Distribution of arabinoxylans and their relationship with physiochemical and rheological properties in wheat flour mill streams as an effective way to predict flour functionality. *Appl. Sci.* **2023**, *13*, 5458. [CrossRef]
27. Schmiele, M.; Jaekel, L.; Patricio, S.; Chang, Y.; Steel, C. Rheological properties of wheat flour and quality characteristics of pan bread as modified by partial additions of wheat bran or whole grain wheat flour. *Int. J. Food Sci. Tech.* **2012**, *47*, 2141–2150. [CrossRef]
28. Bucsella, B.; Molnár, D.; Harasztos, A.; Tömösközi, S. Comparison of the rheological and end-product properties of an industrial aleurone-rich wheat flour, whole grain wheat and rye flour. *J. Cereal Sci.* **2016**, *69*, 40–48. [CrossRef]
29. Noort, M.; Haaster, D.; Hemery, Y.; Schols, H.A.; Hamer, R. The effect of particle size of wheat bran fractions on bread quality –Evidence for fibre–protein interactions. *J. Cereal Sci.* **2010**, *52*, 59–64. [CrossRef]
30. Kaur, A.; Yadav, M.; Singh, B.; Bhinder, S.; Simon, S.; Singh, N. Isolation and characterization of arabinoxylans from wheat bran and study of their contribution to wheat flour dough rheology. *Carbohyd. Polym.* **2019**, *221*, 166–173. [CrossRef]
31. Lewko, P.; Wójtowicz, A.; Różańska-Boczula, M. Effect of extruder configuration and extrusion cooking processing parameters on selected characteristics of non-starch polysaccharide-rich wheat flour as hybrid treatment with xylanase addition. *Processes* **2024**, *12*, 1159. [CrossRef]
32. *ICC Standard Methods*, online version; International Association for Cereal Science and Technology: Vienna, Austria, 2018.
33. Dubat, A.; Boinot, N. *MIXOLAB Applications Handbook*; Chopin Technologies: Villeneuve-la-Garenne, France, 2012; p. 148. [CrossRef]
34. Dubat, A. A New AACC International Approved Method to measure rheological properties of a dough sample. *Cereal Foods World* **2010**, *55*, 150–153. [CrossRef]
35. Codină, G.G.; Mironeasa, S.; Bordei, D.; Leahu, A. Mixolab versus Alveograph and falling number. *Czech J. Food Sci.* **2010**, *28*, 185–191. [CrossRef]
36. Jødal, A.S.; Larsen, K.L. Investigation of the relationships between the alveograph parameters. *Sci. Rep.* **2021**, *11*, 5349. [CrossRef]
37. *Approved Method of the AACC*, 9th ed.; American Association of Cereal Chemists: St. Paul, MN, USA, 2009. Available online: https://www.scirp.org/(S(czeh2tfqyw2orz553k1w0r45))/reference/ReferencesPapers.aspx?ReferenceID=1316335 (accessed on 2 August 2023).
38. McCleary, B.; DeVries, J.; Rader, J.; Cohen, G.; Prosky, L.; Mugford, D.C.; Champ, M.; Okuma, K. Determination of insoluble, soluble, and total dietary fiber (CODEX Definition) by enzymatic-gravimetric method and liquid chromatography: Collaborative study. *J. AOAC Int.* **2012**, *95*, 824–844. [CrossRef] [PubMed]
39. Charrondiere, U.R.; Chevassus-Agnes, S.; Marroni, S.; Burlingame, B. Impact of different macronutrient definitions and energy conversion factors on energy supply estimations. *J. Food Compos. Anal.* **2004**, *17*, 339–360. [CrossRef]
40. Cingöz, A.; Akpinar, Ö.; Sayaslan, A. Effect of addition of wheat bran hydrolysate on bread properties. *J. Food Sci.* **2024**, *89*, 2567–2580. [CrossRef]
41. Ambrosewicz-Walacik, M.; Tańska, M.; Rotkiewicz, D.; Piętak, A. Effect of various sodium chloride mass fractions on wheat and rye bread using different dough preparation techniques. *Food Technol. Biotechnol.* **2016**, *54*, 172–179. [CrossRef] [PubMed]
42. Soja, J.; Combrzyński, M.; Oniszczuk, T.; Biernacka, B.; Wójtowicz, A.; Kupryaniuk, K.; Wojtunik-Kulesza, K.; Bąkowski, M.; Gancarz, M.; Mołdoch, J.; et al. The effect of fresh kale (*Brassica oleracea* var. *sabellica*) addition and processing conditions on selected biological, physical and chemical properties of extruded snack pellets. *Molecules* **2023**, *28*, 1835. [CrossRef]
43. Nishinari, K.; Fang, Y. Perception and measurement of food texture: Solid foods. *J. Texture Stud.* **2018**, *49*, 160–201. [CrossRef]
44. Cacak-Pietrzak, G.; Dziki, D.; Gawlik-Dziki, U.; Sułek, A.; Kalisz, S.; Sujka, K. Effect of the addition of dried dandelion roots (*Taraxacum officinale* F. H. Wigg.) on wheat dough and bread properties. *Molecules* **2021**, *26*, 7564. [CrossRef]
45. Peressini, D.; Sensidoni, A. Effect of soluble dietary fibre addition on rheological and breadmaking properties of wheat doughs. *J. Cereal Sci.* **2009**, *49*, 190–201. [CrossRef]

46. Tao, H.; Zhu, X.-F.; Nan, B.-X.; Jiang, R.-Z.; Wang, H.-L. Effect of extruded starch on the structure, farinograph characteristics and baking behavior of wheat dough. *Food Chem.* **2021**, *348*, 129017. [CrossRef]
47. Bucsella, B.; Takács, Á.; von Reding, W.; Schwendener, U.; Kálmán, F.; Tömösközi, S. Rheological and stability aspects of dry and hydrothermally heat treated aleurone-rich wheat milling fraction. *Food Chem.* **2017**, *220*, 9–17. [CrossRef] [PubMed]
48. Alam, M.S.; Kaur, J.; Khaira, H.; Gupta, K. Extrusion and extruded products: Changes in quality attributes as affected by extrusion process parameters: A review. *Crit. Rev. Food. Sci. Nutr.* **2016**, *56*, 445–475. [CrossRef] [PubMed]
49. Leys, S.; De Bondt, Y.; Bosmans, G.; Courtin, C.M. Assessing the impact of xylanase activity on the water distribution in wheat dough: A ^{1}H NMR study. *Food Chem.* **2020**, *325*, 126828. [CrossRef]
50. Hilhorst, R.; Dunnewind, B.; Orsel, R.; Stegeman, P.; van Vliet, T.; Gruppen, H.; Schols, H.A. Baking performance, rheology, and chemical composition of wheat dough and gluten affected by xylanase and oxidative enzymes. *J. Food Sci.* **1999**, *64*, 808–813. [CrossRef]
51. Hong, T.; Ma, Y.; Wu, F.; Jin, Y.; Xu, D.; Xu, X. Understanding the effects of dry heat treatment on wheat flour pasting: Insights from protein and starch structural changes. *J. Cereal Sci.* **2023**, *113*, 103740. [CrossRef]
52. Kurek, M.A.; Wyrwisz, J.; Karp, S.; Brzeska, M.; Wierzbicka, A. Comparative analysis of dough rheology and quality of bread baked from fortified and high-in-fiber flours. *J. Cereal Sci.* **2017**, *74*, 210–217. [CrossRef]
53. Alamri, M.S.; Mohamed, A.A.; Hussain, S.; Ibraheem, M.A.; Qasem, A.A.A.; Shamlan, G.; Hakeem, M.J.; Ababtain, I.A. Functionality of cordia and ziziphus gums with respect to the dough properties and baking performance of stored pan bread and sponge cakes. *Foods* **2022**, *11*, 460. [CrossRef]
54. Thomas, D.; Atwel, W. *Starches. America Association of Cereal Chemists*; Eagan Press: St. Paul, MN, USA, 1999.
55. Kumar, K.; Kumar, N. Development of vitamin and dietary fibre enriched carrot pomace and wheat flour based buns. *J. Pure Appl. Sci. Technol.* **2012**, *2*, 107–115.

Disclaimer/Publisher's Note: The statements, opinions and data contained in all publications are solely those of the individual author(s) and contributor(s) and not of MDPI and/or the editor(s). MDPI and/or the editor(s) disclaim responsibility for any injury to people or property resulting from any ideas, methods, instructions or products referred to in the content.

Article

Innovative Fermented Beverages Based on Bread Waste—Fermentation Parameters and Antibacterial Properties

Krzysztof Juś [1], Mateusz Ścigaj [2], Daniela Gwiazdowska [1,*], Katarzyna Marchwińska [1] and Wiktoria Studenna [2]

[1] Department of Natural Science and Quality Assurance, Institute of Quality Science, Poznań University of Economics and Business, Al. Niepodległości 10, 61-875 Poznań, Poland; krzysztof.jus@ue.poznan.pl (K.J.); katarzyna.marchwinska@ue.poznan.pl (K.M.)

[2] Scientific Student Association "Inventum", Department of Natural Science and Quality Assurance, Institute of Quality Science, Poznań University of Economics and Business, Al. Niepodległości 10, 61-875 Poznań, Poland; 82625@student.ue.poznan.pl (M.Ś.)

* Correspondence: daniela.gwiazdowska@ue.poznan.pl

Featured Application: In response to the contemporary and future challenges for the food production sector in achieving sustainable development goals, this work presents an innovative solution for the management of problematic food waste, such as bakery waste. Prepared beverages based on unused wheat–rye bread fermented using lactic acid bacteria, may be a good starting point for the further development of an innovative, functional food product. Moreover, fermented drinks based on waste from the bakery industry are consistent with the assumptions of sustainable production, and the results obtained in this work may provide interesting information for the circular economy and waste management development.

Abstract: Faced with challenges related to environmental degradation and the growing need for sustainable development, the food sector must look for innovative and ecological production solutions. One of the increasingly popular directions is the zero-waste approach, which limits waste generation and enables its reuse. This research aimed to evaluate selected quality indicators of the lactic acid fermentation process of beverages based on waste from the bakery industry (wheat–rye bread) to determine the optimal fermentation conditions using two strains of lactic acid bacteria: *Lacticasibacillus paracasei* and *Lactiplantibacillus plantarum*. Preliminary process optimization was carried out, taking into account the beverage composition, fermentation time, and starter culture. The process evaluation and the selection of the optimal variant were based on the microbiological quality, pH value, and antimicrobial activity of fermented beverages. The results showed that the bread waste may constitute a base for obtaining fermented beverages as evidenced by the high number of lactic acid bacteria, above 10^8 CFU/mL, and low pH values (≤ 3.5) after the appropriate incubation time. Fermented beverages exhibited antibacterial properties against tested indicator microorganisms, which confirmed their functional properties. The analysis of the obtained results and the adopted assumptions enabled the selection of the most optimal variant—the beverage with ground flaxseed, fermented by *L. paracasei* for 24 h. The conducted research indicates great potential for lactic acid fermentation in the management of bakery waste to create innovative, sustainable food products with probiotic potential.

Keywords: circular economy; waste management; zero waste; fermented beverages; lactic acid bacteria; bread waste; innovative beverages; functional properties; sustainable food production

1. Introduction

Food waste is a global problem, causing significant economic losses around the world and negatively affecting the environment [1]. The problem is deepened by the fact that the world population may reach approximately 10 billion in 2050, resulting in a growing demand for various types of products, especially food [2]. It is estimated that food production, including agricultural production, will increase from approximately 47% to 102% during this time to meet the growing demand for food [3]. However, it should be taken into account that the intensification of food production largely contributes to the degradation of the natural environment. The negative effects of food production include, among others, excessive greenhouse gas emission, associated with increasingly frequent weather anomalies, loss of biodiversity, bioaccumulation of toxic substances, reduction in forest area, and depletion of natural resources [4,5]. Consumerism also contributes to the intensification of production, which, regardless of social, climatic, or ecological costs, leads to overproduction and generates excessive waste amounts. It is estimated that approximately one-third of food produced is wasted annually on a global scale, which results in social costs (including waste of resources) and negatively affects the financial results of producers [6]. Food waste losses may occur at various stages of the food supply chain, from primary production, including agriculture and animal production, through processing, packaging, and distribution processes, to losses caused by the consumer [7]. Food loss and waste generation depend on the type of food, with greater loss and waste occurring in perishable foods such as fruit and vegetables. However, bakery waste is also a serious global problem.

Bread is one of the most important products consumed around the world, and its global production reaches >100 million tons per year. Therefore, it is a commonly wasted food in most developed countries, which is a particularly serious problem in Europe [8]. It is difficult to determine the exact amount of wasted bread, as the use of water and energy in the production and transport process should also be taken into account; however, it is estimated that 10% of all bread produced is wasted worldwide [9]. For example, in the United Kingdom (UK), bread is the second most frequently wasted food. It is estimated that every day in UK homes, the equivalent of 25 million slices of bread or 1,300,000 loaves is thrown away [10]. In Poland, research carried out by the Federation of Polish Food Banks in 2012–2018 indicates that bread is the most frequently thrown-away product, and the percentage of respondents declaring waste of bread ranged from 49 to 62% in this period [11].

Therefore, various ways of using bakery waste are being undertaken towards valorization into value-added products considering that bread contains a wide range of nutrients. In 100 g of bread, there are approximately 50–70 g of carbohydrates, 8–10 g of protein, 1–5 g of fat, and trace amounts of phosphorus [12]. Bread waste can be used as biomass for the production of biohydrogen, regarded as clean and renewable energy [13], as well as for the production of ethanol, considered one of the most promising fuel sources [14,15]. Dubrovskis and Plume [16] described biogas production from damaged bread. Moreover, bread waste can be used as feed for livestock [17,18] as well as a substrate for hydroxymethylfurfural synthesis and for the production of pigments, proteins, or aroma compounds [19–21]. Many researchers emphasize that bakery waste usage should largely focus on processing it into new food products. This is possible to achieve by using the fermentation processes with various microorganisms. Lactic acid fermentation is considered a safe and practical way to acidify food products and extend their shelf life because the metabolites produced and the low pH inhibit the growth of undesirable microorganisms. The nutritional, health-promoting, and sensory values of fermented products are also important. The increase in nutritional value is related, among others, mainly to the production of amino acids and different bioactive compounds [22,23]. The health benefits associated with consuming fermented foods and beverages include increased digestibility, antimicrobial [24], antihypertensive, antioxidant [25], and even immunostimulating [26] properties. Some lactic acid bacteria (LAB) strains also produce exopolysaccharides (EPS), which increase the viscosity of the fermented product [27,28]. An example of using lactic acid fermentation to reuse bread waste is research conducted by Immonen et al. [29]. The authors assessed the potential of two LAB strains (*Weissella confusa* A16 and *Pediococcus claussenii* E-032355T) to transform bakery waste into an EPS-enriched bread slurry dedicated as an ingredient in the production of baked goods.

It is worth emphasizing that fermented products are considered functional foods, which constitutes a valuable part of the food market, especially in highly developed countries. A constant development and increase in the value of this branch of the food industry is expected around the world [30]. There are many definitions of functional food in the literature, but generally this product category includes unmodified (natural) food as well as food in which ingredients have been modified (including those increasing their bioavailability), added or removed using cultivation conditions or technological/biotechnological processes, which make it possible to obtain specific health-promoting effects or improve general well-being after consumption [31]. Beverages are one of the most popular products in the functional food category mainly due to the convenience of consumption as well as easier distribution and storage [32]. A wide range of traditional, non-dairy fermented drinks are produced around the world [33]. Examples of such products are *Boza* made from wheat, rye, millet, maize, and other cereals, known in Bulgaria, Albania, Turkey, and Romania [34], *Bushera* from sorghum consumed in Uganda [35], or *Togwa* prepared by fermentation of maize flour in Africa [36]. In the case of fermented beverages with potential probiotic properties, it is important to maintain the cell count at an appropriate level throughout the shelf life of the product [37] as well as during the passage through the digestive system [38]. One of the basic procedures aimed at increasing the survival of LAB in a product is the addition of various types of products/substances with prebiotic effects [39]. An interesting example is ground flaxseed, which, in addition to its high content of dietary fiber (prebiotic effect), is also a valuable source of substances such as α-linolenic acid, omega-3 acid, proteins, and lignan, making it an ingredient with functional potential [40]. The literature contains research results showing the positive effect of ground flaxseed on the stability of LAB in various types of products. For example, Vesterlund et al. [41] (2012) found a positive effect of adding ground flaxseed to the matrix on the increased viability of *Lacticaseibacillus rhamnosus* GG during storage for a period of 14 months. A positive effect of flaxseed on LAB survival was also reported by HadiNezhad et al. [42] (2013), who found a significantly higher number of LAB in kefir with the addition of flaxseed mucilagate after 28 days of storage at 4 °C compared to unfortified kefir. In turn, Bialasová et al. [43] (2018) reported a higher number of *Lactobacillus acidophilus* CCDM 151 in milk with the addition of ground flaxseed (by 0.8 log CFU/mL) after 16 h of fermentation compared to milk without the addition of flaxseed.

Despite studies confirming the positive impact of LAB fermentation on food waste reuse, it should be emphasized that products obtained through spontaneous fermentation are not repeatable and may differ in composition and sensory characteristics. Standardization of the process requires specific starter cultures. However, this involves selecting the appropriate strain with specific properties. Therefore the present study aimed to design innovative beverages produced by lactic acid fermentation of waste from the bakery industry and to evaluate selected quality characteristics of the beverages for the initial selection of optimal fermentation conditions. Appropriately selected LAB strains and the addition of ground flaxseed to increase the nutritional value of bakery waste for bacteria were used in the fermentation process.

2. Materials and Methods
2.1. Chemicals, Materials, and Microorganisms
2.1.1. Chemicals

Microbiological media used for the studies were obtained from BioMaxima (Poland) and included as follows: de Man, Rogosa, and Sharpe (MRS) broth and MRS LAB-AGAR™, nutrient broth, Sabouraud dextrose with chloramphenicol LAB-AGAR™, Mueller-Hinton broth, trypticasein soy broth (TSB), and TBX LAB-AGAR™. Chemical reagents such as glucose (Stanlab, Lublin, Poland), sodium chloride (POCh, Gliwice, Poland), and pH buffers (Sigma-Aldrich, Steinheim, Germany), used for the tests were of analytical grade.

2.1.2. Research Material

Wheat–rye crushed stale bread was the base for the preparation of fermented beverages. Research material was stored in sealed bags in a dry location at room temperature (±20 °C). Ground flaxseed (LenVitol®, Oleofarm, Wrocław, Poland) was purchased from a local pharmacy in Poland.

2.1.3. Microorganisms

Bread-waste beverages (BWBs) were fermented using two strains of lactic acid bacteria as starter cultures: *Lactiplantibacillus plantarum* DKK 003 and *Lacticaseibacillus paracasei* DKK 002. Both strains were from the collection of the Department of Natural Science and Quality Assurance, Poznań University of Economics and Business. The starter microorganisms were cultured before each use on MRS liquid medium at 30 °C for 24 h, and long-term storage was maintained in cryoprobes on MRS broth with 80% glycerol (in a 1:1 ratio) at −22 °C.

The antimicrobial properties of the fermented BWBs were tested against four indicator bacteria, namely *Staphylococcus saprophyticus* ATCC 49453, *Micrococcus luteus* ATCC 4698, *Escherichia coli* ATCC 25922, and *Pseudomonas fluorescens* ATCC 13525 from the American Type Culture Collection (ATCC). Tested bacteria were freshly cultured before the experiments on nutrient broth or trypticasein soy broth (for *M. luteus*) for 24 h at a temperature of 30 or 37 °C (depending on the strain), according to ATCC data. Indicator strains were stored long-term at −22 °C using Microbank® cryogenic beads (BioMaxima, Lublin, Poland).

2.2. Methods

2.2.1. Bread-Waste Beverage Fermentation

BWBs were prepared using 10 g of wheat–rye crushed stale bread with or without 5 g of ground flaxseed, depending on the variant. Next, 200 mL of boiling water was added and samples were left for 24 h to soften the ingredients. An amount of 5 g of glucose was added to all samples, which were then inoculated with 1 mL of LAB cultures per 100 mL. Two strains were used to inoculate the beverages: *L. plantarum* and *L. paracasei*, as well as a mixture of both strains (1:1, *v:v*); the density of the inoculum was 10^{10} CFU/mL. Finally, the inoculated beverages were incubated at 30 °C for 6, 8, 12, 24, and 48 h. After fermentation, the liquid phase was poured off from the solid phase (pulp), and the obtained beverage was used for testing. The selection of the optimal BWB variant involved the selection of strains and fermentation time, as well as chosen quality characteristics: microbiological quality, pH value, and antimicrobial activity (Figure 1).

2.2.2. Determination of Microbiological Quality of Fermented BWBs

The microbiological quality of the prepared fermented BWB samples was determined by the standard plate method. The tested samples were placed in sterile blender bags (BagFilter S, Interscience, Saint Nom, France) and mixed with sterile saline solution (in ratio 10:90, *v:v*) and homogenized in a stomacher (BagMixer 400 W, Interscience, Saint Nom, France) for 5 min. The tests were performed included determining the total number of LAB on MRS agar (30 °C for 48 h), the total number of fungi (yeast and molds) on Sabouraud agar with chloramphenicol (25 °C for 5 days), and the presence of *E. coli* bacteria on TBX agar (37 °C for 24 h). The results are presented as average values from three parallel repetitions.

2.2.3. Measurement of the pH of Fermented BWBs

The pH value of the fermented BWBs was measured using an Orion Star A111 pH meter from Thermo Scientific, Waltham, MA, USA. The glass electrode was placed in the well-stirred test sample and the result was read after the readings stabilized. The measurement was carried out in three repetitions at room temperature (22.0 ± 2.0 °C).

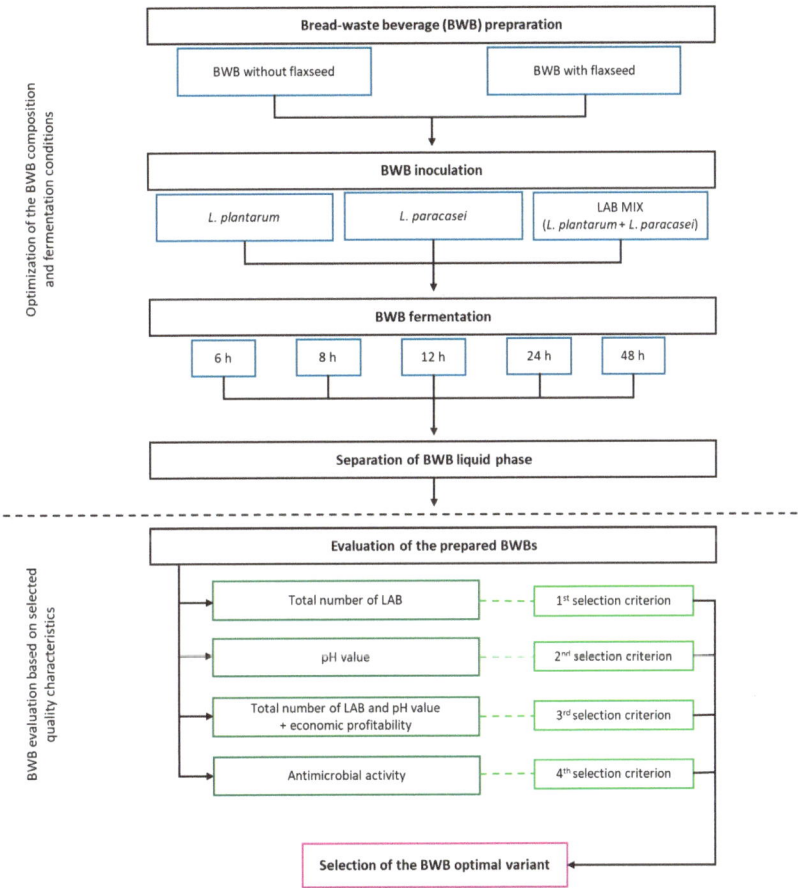

Figure 1. Scheme of the bread-waste beverage (BWB) selection procedure.

2.2.4. Antimicrobial Properties of Fermented BWBs

The antimicrobial activity of the prepared fermented BWBs was determined using the microdilution method on 96-well microtiter plates according to the methodology described by Kaczmarek et al. [44] with some modifications. Samples of fermented BWBs were centrifuged twice at 10,000 rpm/min for 10 min using a Centrifuge 5804R. Next, a series of two-fold dilutions was prepared on 96-well microplates in MH broth medium (for *S. saprophyticus*, *E. coli*, and *P. fluorescens*) and TSB (for *M. luteus*) at a ratio of 80:80 μL. Fresh, 24 h cultures of indicator microorganisms were then used to prepare suspensions in broth mediums with a final density of 0.5 McFarland which corresponds 10^5 CFU/mL. The prepared plates were incubated for 24 h at 30 or 37 °C, depending on the indicator microorganism. After incubation, the optical density of the prepared cultures was measured at 600 nm using a BioTek EPOCH2 Microplate Reader (Agilent, Santa Clara, CA, USA). The antimicrobial activity of the BWBs was tested in the concentration range of 6.25–50%. The results are expressed as the average (from three parallel repetitions) percentage of inhibited growth of indicator microorganisms calculated based on the formula described by Marchwińska et al. [45]:

$$A\% = \left(1 - \left(\frac{(\underline{X}_{OD_B} - \underline{X}_{OD_C})}{(\underline{X}_{OD_I} - \underline{X}_{OD_M})}\right)\right) \times 100\% \quad (1)$$

where $A\%$ is the antibacterial properties of the tested BWBs, $\underline{X}_{OD_B}$ is the mean optical density of bacterial culture with the addition of fermented BWBs, $\underline{X}_{OD_C}$ is the mean optical density of the culture medium with the addition of fermented bread beverage, $\underline{X}_{OD_I}$ is the mean optical density of bacterial inoculate (without fermented BWB), and $\underline{X}_{OD_M}$ is the average optical density of the pure medium.

The minimal inhibitory concentration (MIC) was determined next based on the previously calculated antibacterial activity of the fermented BWBs, assuming that the inhibition of the indicator microorganisms' growth had to be no less than 90%.

2.2.5. Statistical Analysis

The results of the studies are presented as the arithmetic mean (±standard deviation) from three parallel replicates. The results obtained from the microbiological quality and pH value determination were subjected to one-way analysis of variance (ANOVA) using Tukey's test with a significance level of $p < 0.05$. Microsoft Excel® (Microsoft 365 MSO) and IBM SPSS Statistics 28 (PS IMAGO PRO 8.0) programs were used for statistical analyses.

3. Results

3.1. Microbiological Quality and pH of BWBs

In the first part of the experiment, the suitability of the *L. plantarum* and *L. paracasei* strains as starter cultures for the fermentation of bread waste was assessed. Microbiological quality including the number of LAB, the number of fungi, and the presence of *E. coli* as well as the pH value were monitored at specific intervals during 48 h fermentation as the basic quality parameters chosen to evaluate the process (Table 1). It was crucial to determine the minimal fermentation time in which the LAB population would reach at least 10^8 CFU/mL so that the beverage could provide health-promoting properties and inhibit the development of undesirable microorganisms.

Table 1. Total number of lactic acid bacteria (LAB) and pH values of fermented BWBs.

Incubation Time	*L. plantarum*		*L. paracasei*		MIX of LAB	
	[CFU/mL]	pH	[CFU/mL]	pH	[CFU/mL]	pH
	BWBs without flaxseed					
0 h	7.41 ^{CDE} ± 0.13	5.21 ^{n} ± 0.02	7.39 ^{CDE} ± 0.09	5.09 ^{m} ± 0.01	6.79 ^{A} ± 0.01	5.02 ^{m} ± 0.04
6 h	8.23 ^{HIJ} ± 0.46	4.30 ^{hi} ± 0.05	8.06 ^{GH} ± 0.03	4.28 ^{hi} ± 0.03	7.20 ^{CD} ± 0.14	4.23 ^{gh} ± 0.01
8 h	8.38 ^{IJK} ± 0.25	3.87 ^{f} ± 0.02	8.47 ^{JKL} ± 0.01	3.63 ^{e} ± 0.03	8.11 ^{GHI} ± 0.05	4.13 ^{g} ± 0.02
12 h	8.51 $^{J-M}$ ± 0.13	3.66 ^{e} ± 0.13	8.63 $^{K-O}$ ± 0.04	3.59 ^{e} ± 0.01	8.12 ^{GHI} ± 0.01	3.89 ^{f} ± 0.01
24 h	8.60 $^{K-O}$ ± 0.01	3.37 ^{d} ± 0.02	9.53 ^{TU} ± 0.03	3.05 ^{b} ± 0.01	8.95 ^{RS} ± 0.07	3.01 ^{b} ± 0.02
48 h	8.80 $^{M-R}$ ± 0.01	3.22 ^{c} ± 0.02	8.75 $^{L-R}$ ± 0.03	2.77 ^{a} ± 0.03	8.60 $^{K-N}$ ± 0.12	2.81 ^{a} ± 0.05
	BWBs with flaxseed					
0 h	7.39 ^{CDE} ± 0.18	5.29 ^{no} ± 0.03	7.12 ^{BC} ± 0.02	5.30 ^{no} ± 0.02	6.82 ^{AB} ± 0.02	5.34 ^{o} ± 0.04
6 h	7.84 ^{FG} ± 0.01	4.43 ^{j} ± 0.06	8.41 ^{IJK} ± 0.07	4.80 ^{l} ± 0.02	7.63 ^{EF} ± 0.09	4.99 ^{m} ± 0.05
8 h	8.26 ^{HIJ} ± 0.04	4.24 ^{gh} ± 0.03	8.24 ^{HIJ} ± 0.18	4.21 ^{gh} ± 0.05	7.50 ^{DE} ± 0.03	4.63 ^{k} ± 0.01
12 h	8.88 $^{N-R}$ ± 0.03	3.86 ^{f} ± 0.03	8.87 $^{N-R}$ ± 0.02	4.15 ^{g} ± 0.02	8.64 $^{K-P}$ ± 0.03	4.36 ^{ij} ± 0.01
24 h	8.94 ^{PR} ± 0.03	3.64 ^{e} ± 0.02	9.24 ST ± 0.02	3.21 ^{c} ± 0.01	8.9 ^{OPR} ± 0.03	3.23 ^{c} ± 0.01
48 h	9.63 ^{U} ± 0.39	3.37 ^{d} ± 0.00	8.83 $^{N-R}$ ± 0.07	2.94 ^{b} ± 0.01	8.93 ^{PR} ± 0.08	2.99 ^{b} ± 0.01

Averages with different lowercase letters ($^{a-o}$) are significantly different at $p < 0.05$ (comparison of pH value of BWBs). Averages with different capital letters ($^{A-U}$) are significantly different at $p < 0.05$ (comparison of the LAB amount in BWBs).

The obtained results showed that the expected level of bacterial counts—10^8 log CFU/mL—was achieved in most of the prepared fermented beverages after 8 h of fermentation, except for the beverage with the addition of ground flaxseed inoculated with a mixture of LAB cultures, where the LAB concentration was 7.50 log CFU/mL. It is worth emphasizing that in some variants, including BWBs with *L. plantarum* and *L. paracasei* as well as BWBs with flaxseed inoculated with *L. paracasei*, the level of 10^8 log CFU/mL was reached after 6 h. The highest number of LAB (at the level of 10^9 CFU/mL) was obtained after 24 h of fermentation in beverages fermented with *L. paracasei* with and without the addition of ground flaxseed as well as after 48 h in beverages with the addition of flaxseed inoculated with *L. plantarum*, for which the results were 9.24, 9.53, and 9.63 log CFU/mL, respectively. It should be underlined that only the result for the BWB with flaxseed fermented by *L. plantarum* after 48 h was significantly different from all obtained results. It is also worth noting that the BWBs inoculated with the LAB mixture achieved lower numbers, with the highest result of 8.95 in the BWB after 24 h and 8.93 in the BWB with flaxseed after 48 h of fermentation. No presence of *E. coli* or fungi (both yeast and filamentous fungi) was detected in all prepared BWBs variants.

During fermentation, as the number of bacteria increased, a significant decrease in the pH value of all beverages was observed. No significant differences in pH values were observed only in the case of BWBs fermented with LAB mixture (between 6 and 8 h of fermentation) as well as BWBs with and without flaxseed inoculated with *L. plantarum* (between 8 and 12 h of fermentation). The lowest pH values were recorded in BWBs fermented by *L. paracasei* and LAB mixture after 48 h of fermentation, with pH of 2.77 and 2.81, respectively. The beverages with the addition of ground flaxseed inoculated with *L. paracasei* and LAB mixture after 48 h of fermentation were also characterized by pH values < 3.0; however, these values were significantly higher compared to BWBs without the addition of flaxseed. It is worth noting that the addition of ground flaxseed increased the pH value of the beverages regardless of the inoculant (pH values were significantly higher at each hour of fermentation compared to samples without ground flaxseed). Lower pH values were observed in beverages fermented by *L. paracasei* (with and without the addition of ground flaxseed) and the mixture compared to the *L. plantarum* strain.

3.2. Antimicrobial Properties of BWBs

3.2.1. Minimal Inhibitory Concentration Determination

One of the parameters characterizing fermented beverages is antimicrobial activity, with the determining minimum inhibitory concentration (MIC) of the indicator microorganisms' growth (Table 2). The results indicate that the main factor determining the MIC values was fermentation time. It was found that the determination of the MIC value of BWBs in the tested concentration range (from 6.25 to 50%) was possible as the fermentation process was extended. For most BWB variants, the MIC against *E. coli*, *S. saprophyticus*, and *P. fluorescens* was >50% (from 6 to 12 h of fermentation) and 25 or 50% (BWBs after 24 and/or 48 h fermentation). The exception was the BWB variant with the addition of ground flaxseed fermented with *L. paracasei*, where MIC against *P. fluorescens* was determined at 12.5% concentration after 48 h fermentation. The lowest MIC value was determined for *M. luteus*, indicating the highest sensitivity of this microorganism. The MIC value in the tested range of BWB concentrations was determined for BWBs after 6 h of fermentation (25 to 50%), while after 24 and 48 h the MIC value for all prepared variants of fermented drinks was 6.25%.

Table 2. Minimal inhibitory concentration (%) of fermented BWBs towards indicator microorganisms.

Variant	Incubation Time	BWBs Inoculated with *L. plantarum*			
		E. coli	*P. fluorescens*	*S. saprophyticus*	*M. luteus*
BWBs without flaxseed	6 h	>50	>50	>50	25
	8 h	>50	>50	>50	25
	12 h	>50	>50	>50	12.5
	24 h	>50	50	50	6.25
	48 h	50	50	50	6.25
BWBs with flaxseed	6 h	>50	>50	>50	25
	8 h	>50	>50	>50	12.5
	12 h	50	50	50	6.25
	24 h	50	50	50	6.25
	48 h	25	25	25	6.25
		BWBs inoculated with *L. paracasei*			
BWBs without flaxseed	6 h	>50	>50	>50	50
	8 h	>50	>50	>50	50
	12 h	>50	>50	>50	50
	24 h	>50	50	50	6.25
	48 h	50	50	50	6.25
BWBs with flaxseed	6 h	>50	>50	>50	50
	8 h	>50	>50	>50	50
	12 h	>50	50	>50	50
	24 h	50	25	50	6.25
	48 h	25	12,5	25	6.25
		BWBs inoculated with MIX of LAB strain			
BWBs without flaxseed	6 h	>50	>50	>50	50
	8 h	>50	>50	>50	50
	12 h	>50	>50	>50	25
	24 h	>50	50	>50	6.25
	48 h	50	50	50	6.25
BWBs with flaxseed	6 h	>50	>50	>50	50
	8 h	>50	>50	>50	50
	12 h	>50	>50	>50	50
	24 h	50	50	>50	6.25
	48 h	25	25	50	6.25

3.2.2. Effect of Fermented BWBs on Bacterial Growth Inhibition

The antimicrobial activity of BWBs was considered an added value of prepared products and was examined against both gram-positive and gram-negative bacteria (Figures 2–4). Since the exact MIC value was not determined for many samples, indicating that it was higher than the highest concentration of the beverage used, antibacterial activity is presented as the degree of inhibition of the growth of indicator microorganisms by the tested concentrations. This also enables the observation of activity changes during the fermentation process.

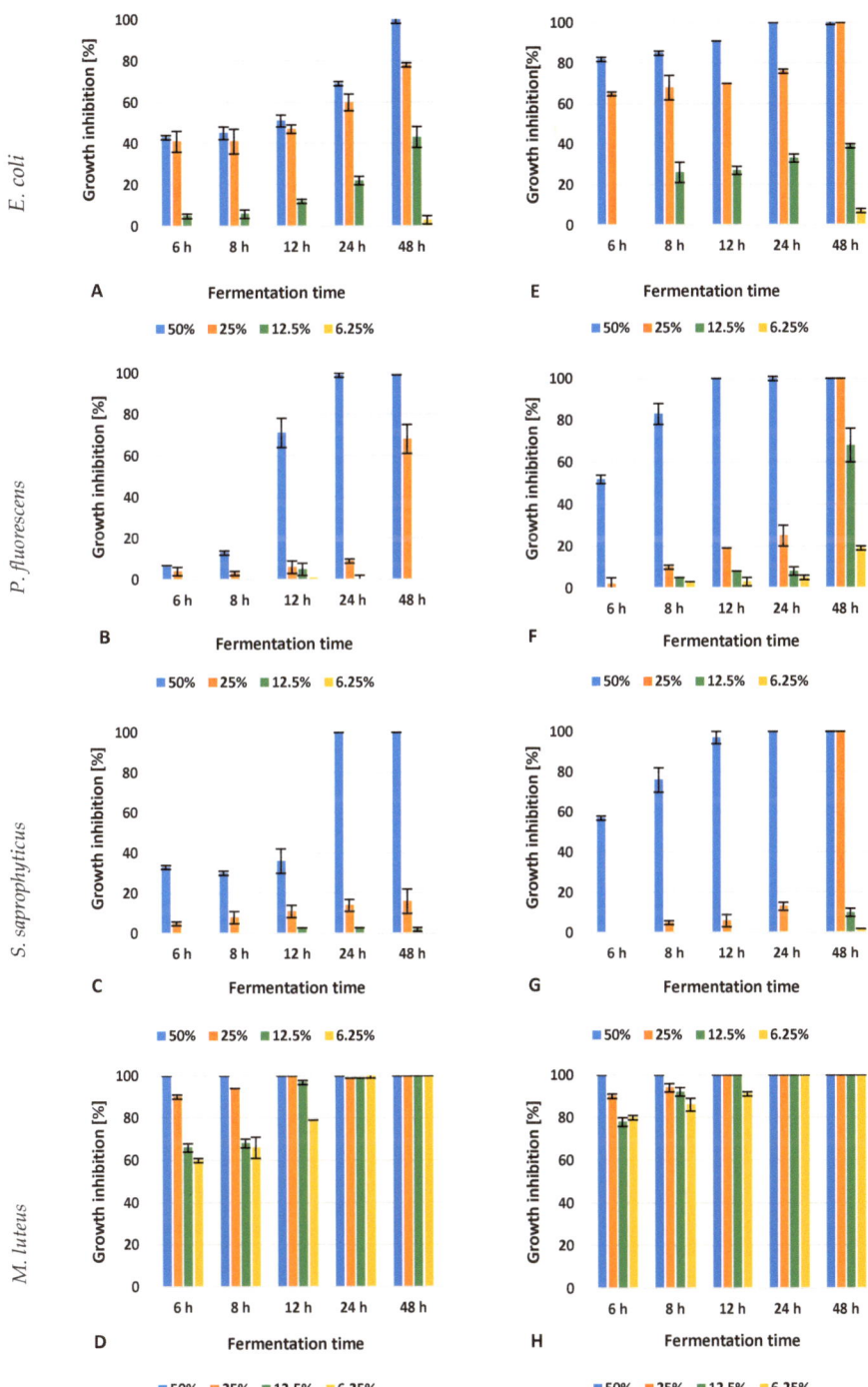

Figure 2. Antimicrobial activity of BWBs inoculated with *L. plantarum* against indicator microorganisms. (**A**–**D**)—BWBs without flaxseed; (**E**–**H**)—BWBs with flaxseed.

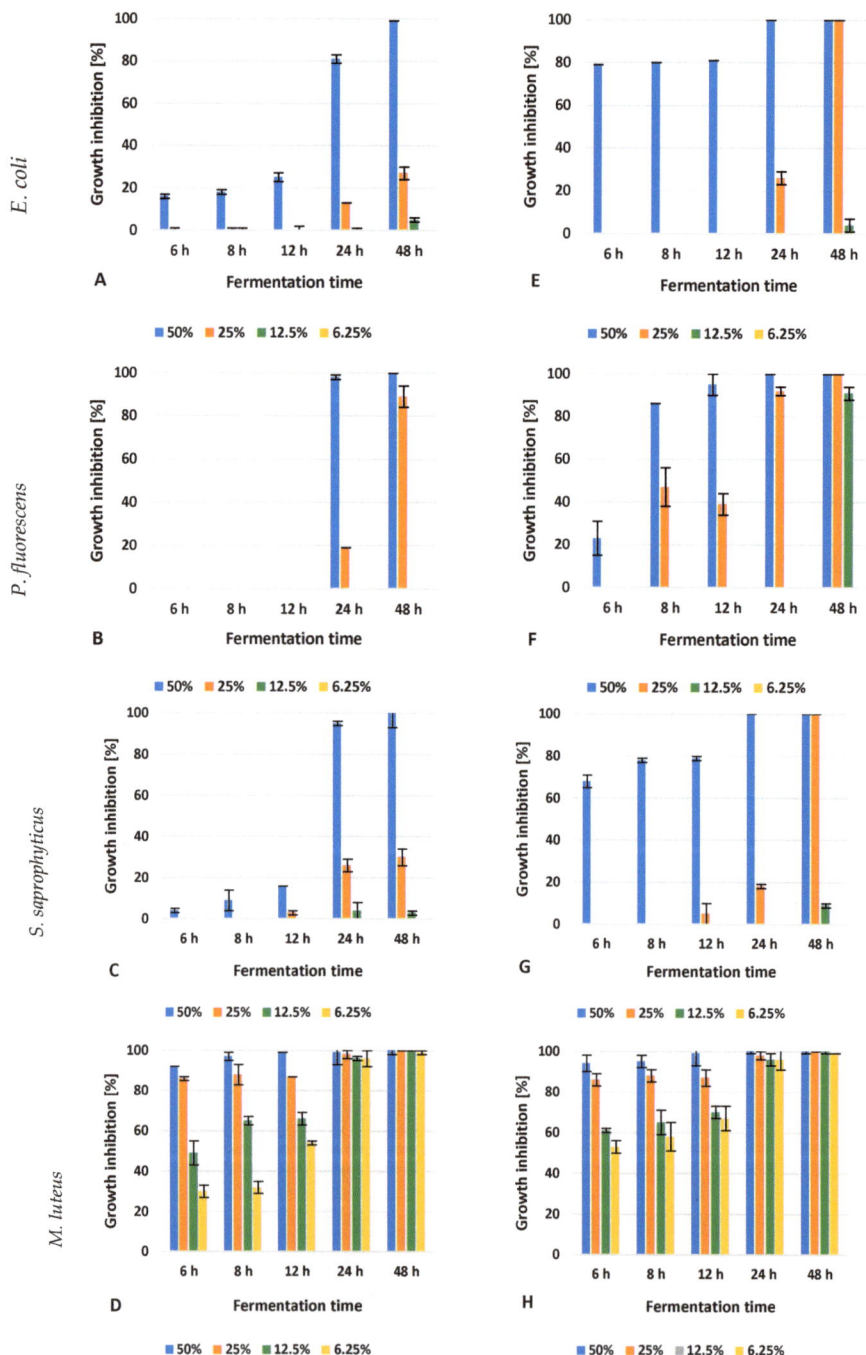

Figure 3. Antimicrobial activity of BWBs inoculated with *L. paracasei* against indicator microorganisms. (**A–D**)—BWBs without flaxseed; (**E–H**)—BWBs with flaxseed.

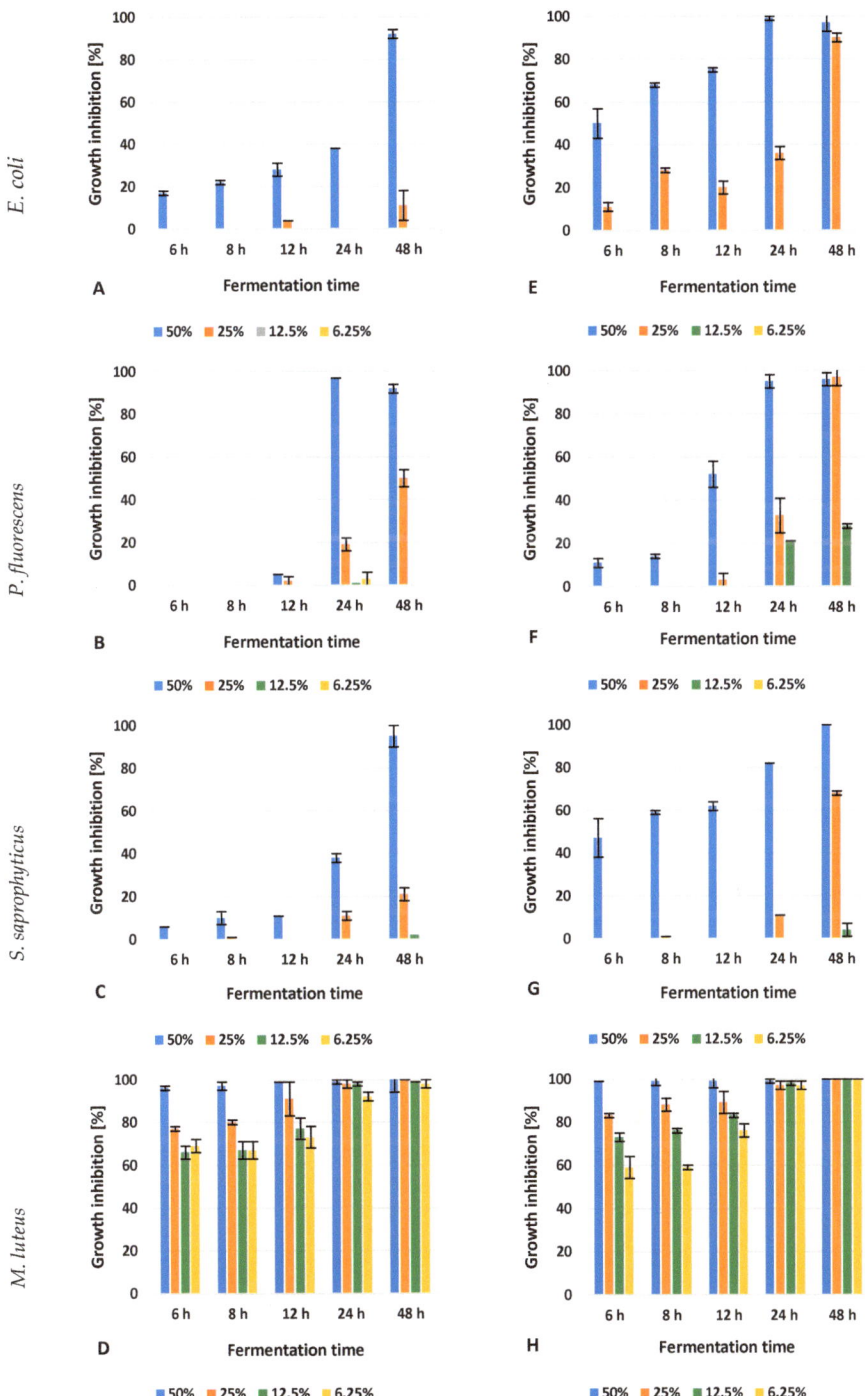

Figure 4. Antimicrobial activity of BWBs inoculated with a mixture of LAB strains against indicator microorganisms. (**A**–**D**)—BWBs without flaxseed; (**E**–**H**)—BWBs with flaxseed.

The strongest antibacterial effect of fermented BWBs inoculated with *L. plantarum* (Figure 2) was recorded for beverages with the addition of ground flaxseed at 50% concentration, which inhibited bacterial growth of all tested microorganisms at a level exceeding 70% starting from 6 h of fermentation. The exception was *S. saprophyticus,* whose growth was inhibited at this level by BWBs from 8 h of fermentation. The greatest sensitivity to BWBs inoculated with *L. plantarum,* both without and with the addition of flaxseed, was demonstrated by *M. luteus,* the growth of which was inhibited by 90 to 100% at BWB concentrations of 25 and 50% from 6 h of fermentation. A strong antagonistic effect was also observed against *E. coli,* inhibited by BWBs after 6 h fermentation at levels of 43 and 41% (BWBs without flaxseed) and 82 and 65% (BWBs with flaxseed) at 25 and 50% concentrations, respectively. *P. fluorescens* showed similar sensitivity; however, strong inhibition of bacterial growth was observed with BWBs at a 50% concentration. A longer fermentation time increased the antibacterial activity of BWBs against both gram-negative bacteria, with higher activity demonstrated by beverages with ground flaxseed. The least sensitivity to BWBs with *L. plantarum* was demonstrated by *S. saprophyticus,* the growth of which was inhibited to a significant extent (>90%) only after BWBs fermented for 24 h (BWB without flaxseed) and after 12 h of fermentation (BWB with flaxseed) mainly at 50% concentration.

In Figure 3, antimicrobial activity of BWBs inoculated with *L. paracasei* is presented. Similarly to beverages with *L. plantarum,* the highest antibacterial activity towards all tested indicator bacteria was demonstrated by BWBs fermented for 24 and 48 h. BWBs without ground flaxseed inhibited the growth of *E. coli, P. fluorescens,* and *S. saprophyticus* at a significant level (>80%) at 50% concentrations after 24 and 48 h fermentation. In comparison, at 25% concentration, high growth inhibition (89%) was observed only against *P. fluorescens* by BWBs fermented for 48 h. In turn, BWBs with the addition of ground flaxseed demonstrated higher antimicrobial activity than those without. The significant inhibition of the growth of microorganisms was observed at a 50% concentration (above 60% of growth inhibition) after 6 h fermentation (towards *E. coli* and *S. saprophyticus*) and after 8 h fermentation (towards *P. fluorescens*). Concerning *P. fluorescens*, the effect of the drink increased significantly after 8 h fermentation, while after 48 h, a high (>90%) inhibition of bacterial growth was found by the lower concentration of the beverages—12.5%. The most sensitive microorganism to the effects of drinks fermented with *L. paracasei* (both without and with the addition of flaxseed) was *M. luteus,* for which growth inhibition in a wide range of beverage concentrations (6.25–50%) was observed after 6 h of fermentation.

The BWBs fermented with the LAB mixture had similar antimicrobial activity to beverages fermented with single LAB cultures; however, the spectrum of activity at individual concentrations and incubation times was noticeably lower (Figure 4). Only in relation to *M. luteus,* BWBs fermented with the LAB mixture exhibited a strong inhibitory effect (in the range of 60–100%) after just 6 h fermentation in the entire range of tested concentrations (6.25–50%). The addition of ground flaxseed increased antimicrobial activity, but this relationship was observed mainly at 50% BWB concentration (against *P. fluorescens* and *S. saprophyticus*) and 50 and 25% concentrations (against *E. coli*). BWBs without the addition of ground flaxseed showed a strong antibacterial effect (above 90% growth inhibition) against *E. coli* and *S. saprophyticus* after 48 h of fermentation (at 50% concentration), while against *P. fluorescens*, such a high level of growth inhibition was obtained both after 24 and 48 h fermentation at 50% beverage concentration.

3.3. Selection of the Optimal BWB Variant

The assessment of the BWB fermentation process based on chosen quality features enabled the selection of a beverage variant that would constitute the basis for further development of the innovative product. The selection process included several steps, which are presented in Figure 5.

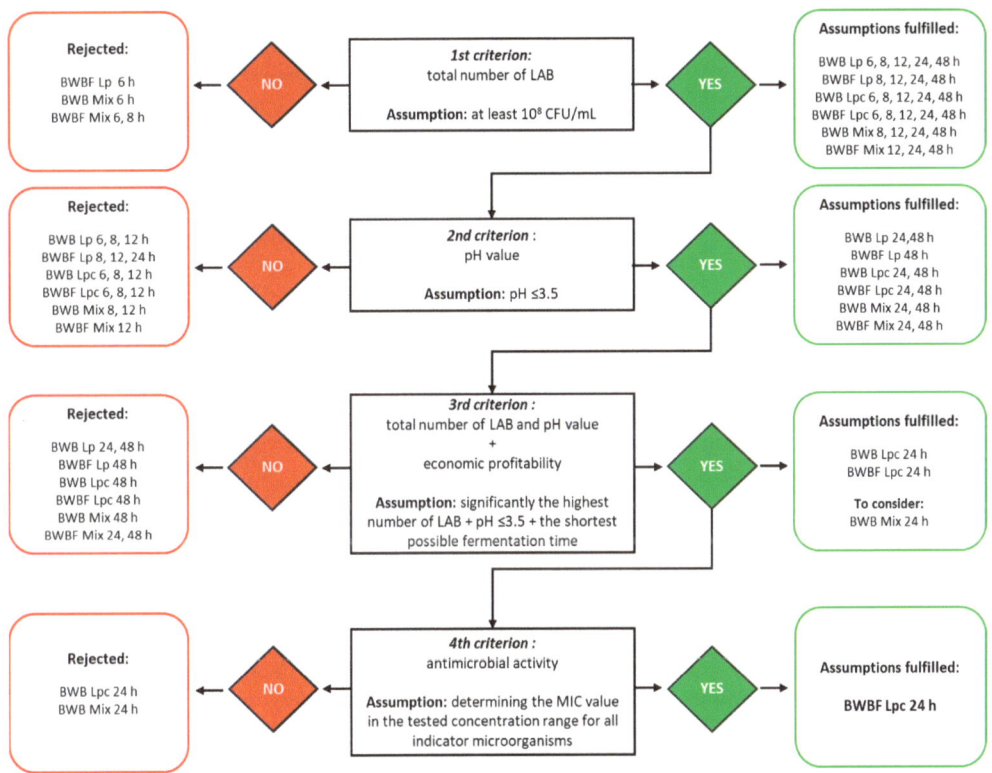

Figure 5. Selection of the optimal BWB variant based on the adopted assumptions. BWB: bread waste beverages without flaxseed; BWBF: bread waste beverages with flaxseed; Lp: fermented by *L. plantarum*; Lpc: fermented by *L. paracasei*; Mix: fermented by a mixture of LAB; 0–48 h: fermentation time.

First, the success of the fermentation process and microbiological quality were assessed based on LAB amount and pH value. In most BWB variants, the LAB amount reached the satisfactory level of 10^8 CFU/mL after 8 h of fermentation. The LAB number will determine, among others, the shelf life and health benefits of the product, so this value should be as high as possible. Therefore, the best variants are BWB with flaxseed fermented with *L. plantarum* for 48 h and BWBs without and with flaxseed fermented by *L. paracasei* for 24 h, in which the LAB count reached 10^9 cfu/mL. Statistical analysis confirmed the significantly higher LAB amount in these variants, although the LAB number in BWB with flaxseed fermented by *L. paracasei* for 24 h and BWB without flaxseed fermented with the LAB mixture for 24 h did not differ significantly.

The second quality criterion chosen to evaluate the prepared BWBs was the pH value. The appreciable acidity of the beverages indicates that the fermentation process is proceeding correctly and positively affects the microbiological safety and stability of the final product. Therefore, the study assumed that the optimally prepared fermented BWBs should have a pH of ≤3.5. Obtaining the desired degree of acidity depended on the fermentation time. In most variants, a pH level below 3.5 was achieved after 24 h, except for BWB with flaxseed fermented by *L. plantarum*, where a pH of 3.37 was achieved after 48 h fermentation. The lowest pH values (<3.0) were obtained for BWBs without and with the addition of flaxseed, fermented by *L. paracasei* and the LAB mixture after 48 h of fermentation. Interestingly, the highest LAB population was not recorded in the BWB variants with the lowest pH. For example, in the BWB with flaxseed fermented by *L. plantarum* for 48 h (the highest LAB number), the pH value (3.37) did not differ significantly from BWBs with flaxseed fermented by *L. paracasei* (3.21) and BWBs fermented with LAB mixture (3.01 and 3.23 with and without flaxseed, respectively) for 24 h, for which LAB amount was significantly lower.

The LAB number and pH were used together as the third criterion, emphasizing the economic aspect of the process. As BWBs fermented for both 24 and 48 h had good and comparable quality parameters, it can be assumed that it will be more profitable from a production point of view to carry out fermentation in a shorter time, reducing the production costs. Taking into account these parameters, the optimal variants were BWBs without and with the addition of ground flaxseed, fermented with *L. paracasei* and a LAB mixture for 24 h.

The last parameter for selecting the optimal BWB variant was its antimicrobial activity. The results confirmed that to obtain the best functional properties (in the context of antibacterial properties), it is necessary to carry out fermentation for at least 24 h. After this fermentation time, it was possible to determine the MIC values for most variants, and a broader spectrum of the activity of the beverages against indicator microorganisms was observed. Additionally, the conducted research indicated that the ground flaxseed addition resulted in increased antagonistic activity of the fermented BWBs. These observations indicated that adding a nutrient-rich ingredient could increase the product's functional properties.

Taking into account the antibacterial properties of the fermented BWBs, as well as the previous premises, the optimal variant was the BWB with the addition of flaxseed fermented with *L. paracasei* for 24 h. For this variant, it was possible to determine the MIC against all indicator microorganisms, and for *P. fluorescens* this value was the lowest (MIC = 25%) compared to the other variants. Since these types of products are most often consumed without dilution (100% concentration), the criterion for selecting other variants for further development may be the LAB number and pH value. The stronger antibacterial effect of fermented BWBs with flaxseed indicates that these variants meet the product functional criterion to a greater extent. BWBs with flaxseed fermented by LAB mixture are also worth considering, as multi-strain fermented products may be more acceptable by consumers.

4. Discussion

In response to contemporary and future challenges for the food production sector in achieving sustainable development goals, the work presents an innovative solution for managing problematic food waste, such as bakery waste. It is also in line with current trends concerning the development of non-dairy fermented products including fermented beverages, which is associated with the increase in various health problems such as lactose intolerance.

Applying lactic acid fermentation to cereal raw materials may be problematic due to the fact that LAB does not have good properties in converting starch into lactic acid, although some strains, including *L. plantarum*, show such activity [46]. However, the beneficial properties of LAB make them an attractive subject of research for new fermented products. It is worth emphasizing that bakery waste is rarely used as a matrix for composing a fermented beverage, so literature data in this area are strongly limited.

Zamfir et al. [47] used wheat bran, a major by-product of wheat processing, containing different nutritional constituents, such as proteins, carbohydrates, vitamins, and minerals, together with red beetroot/carrots to prepare fermented beverages. As the starter culture, two strains of *L. plantarum* (BR9 and P3) and *L. acidophilus* IBB801 were used. Similar to the results obtained in our work, in the final product the pH was, in most cases, below 3.5 and spoilage microbiota such as enterobacteria were not detected. Sigüenza-Andrés et al. [48] described beverages based on flour from bread waste fermented using commercial starters Nu-trish® LGG® and Nu-trish® BY-01 DA. Regarding the number of LAB and *Bifidobacterium* in beverages after 24 h of fermentation, the authors recorded values similar to the present study. Beverages fermented with Nu-trish® LGG® starter reached bacterial levels above 10^8 CFU/g, while beverages fermented with the Nu-trish® BY-01 DA saturator acquired lower values of 10^3–10^7 CFU/g, depending on the prepared variant. Moreover, Sigüenza-Andrés et al. [48] found that the content of organic acids in the tested beverages ensures the pH value of the beverages, allowing the microbiological stability of the product to be maintained. Lactic acid fermentation of bread slurries using the *L. rhamnosus* GG ATCC 53103 strain was also carried out by Nguyen et al. [49]. In the prepared fermented bread slurries (2.5% w/w, dry weight) after 16 h of fermentation, the authors recorded *L. rhamnosus* at a concentration of 7.7 log CFU/g and a pH close to 3.5. The authors obtained a higher number of *L. rhamnosus*, above 10^8 CFU/g, with an increased share of bread slurry (to 5% w/w, dry weight) after 16 and 24 h of fermentation. While the pH value of the fermented bread slurries prepared by Nguyen et al. [49] was close to the pH of the BWBs tested in this study (after 24 h fermentation), the LAB number obtained by Nguyen et al. [49] was lower.

Determining the antimicrobial activity of the fermented beverages was crucial due to their potential health-promoting properties; however, the presented data also indicate that the activity of fermented BWBs depended mostly on the genus of indicator bacteria, as well as on the concentration of the beverages. The higher degree of growth inhibition of indicator microorganisms was also observed with the extension of the fermentation time. In most cases, the addition of ground flaxseed to beverages had a positive effect on increasing the antimicrobial activity of BWBs.

The antibacterial properties of fermented drinks are rarely an evaluation criterion. Very few data apply to products made from waste. Typically, antimicrobial properties are determined for strains subsequently used to produce the beverages. Nevertheless, some authors have also evaluated these properties. Similar to our results, Zamfir et al. [47] observed inhibition of *Listeria monocytogenes*, *Salmonella enterica*, *Staphylococcus aureus*, and *E. coli* by fermented beverages made from wheat bran and root vegetables. Singh et al. [50] reported the antimicrobial activities of whey-based fermented soy beverages with the addition of curcumin. The product obtained by fermentation with *L. acidophilus* NCDC 195 (LA195) and *Streptococcus thermophilus* NCDC323 (ST323) demonstrated activity towards *E. coli*, *B. cereus*, *S. aureus*, *L. monocytogenes*, *Shigella dysenteriae*, and *Salmonella typhi*. The authors observed that with the increasing storage time, the antibacterial activity decreased. Undhad et al. [51] studied the antimicrobial activity of fermented soy-based beverages towards some pathogenic strains and found higher antimicrobial activity against gram-positive bacteria (*S. aureus*, *B. cereus*, and *L. monocytogenes*) than against gram-negative pathogens (*E. coli*, *S. typhi*, and *S. dysenteriae*). The antimicrobial properties of fermented beverages can be explained by the presence of metabolites produced by LAB, such as organic acids or bacteriocines, although some components of the raw materials as well as additives may also affect the activity. Antimicrobial properties were also described for non-dairy beverages fermented by microorganisms other than LAB such as kombucha. Al-Mohammadi et al. [52] observed inhibition of the growth of *S. aureus* and *E. coli*, while other authors also reported activity against different species of *Candida* (*C. krusei*, *C. glabrata*, *C. albicans*, *C. tropicalis*), *Haemophilus influenzae* [53], *Staphylococcus epidermidis*, *S. aureus*, *M. luteus*, *Salmonella typhimurium*, *L. monocytogenes*, or *Pseudomonas aeruginosa* [54].

The antimicrobial properties of such products are related to the presence of metabolites such as organic acids, mainly acetic acid and catechins [55]. It should be emphasized that antimicrobial activity constitutes a significant added value not only due to their connection with the potentially probiotic properties of bacteria, but also because they protect against the development of undesirable microorganisms.

5. Conclusions

Current and future challenges facing the food production sector in terms of environmental and social aspects (ensuring food security) encourage producers to look for more sustainable solutions both in the area of production processes and the design of new products. This work attempts to preliminarily optimize the process of lactic acid fermentation of beverages based on waste from the bakery industry. Our research is consistent with current trends related to waste management and sustainable food production. The obtained results indicate that bakery waste (wheat–rye bread) may constitute the basis for obtaining beverages through lactic acid fermentation. Very interesting and important results were obtained in studies on the antimicrobial properties of prepared fermented BWBs, which were significantly influenced by fermentation time, composition, and LAB culture. Extending fermentation time and adding ground flaxseed had a key impact on increasing the antibacterial activity of fermented BWBs. The research has shown that when developing new fermented products, it is important to select the appropriate composition and production conditions to obtain products with the best possible quality parameters. The omission of any of the assessed parameters may lead to the selection of inappropriate process conditions or beverage composition, thus contributing to the deterioration of the quality or functionality of the final product.

Our research is also a good starting point for further work on product development. Prior to the product-testing stage, it is necessary to develop flavor proposals for BWBs as well as determine their microbiological stability during storage to ensure an appropriate level of product safety. The finally developed beverages should also be fully analyzed to determine the content of macro- and microelements, and LAB survival tests should be performed (e.g., metagenomic analysis) to ensure appropriate quality characteristics of BWBs. Additionally, further LAB strains can still be tested in terms of the effectiveness of fermentation of bread waste in order to possibly create a multi-strain beverage that could be an interesting proposition for consumers. Marketing research such as consumer acceptance and preferences and unit packaging design should be considered as interesting and valuable complementary research. Conducting the above-mentioned complementary research would provide the basis for attempting to commercialize the designed innovative beverages based on bread waste.

Author Contributions: Conceptualization, K.J. and M.Ś.; methodology, K.J., M.Ś. and D.G.; validation, K.J., D.G. and K.M.; formal analysis, K.J., M.Ś., D.G., K.M. and W.S.; investigation, K.J., M.Ś., D.G. and W.S.; resources, K.J., D.G. and K.M.; data curation, K.J., M.Ś. and D.G.; writing—original draft preparation, K.J., M.Ś., D.G., K.M. and W.S.; writing—review and editing, K.J., D.G. and K.M.; visualization, K.J., M.Ś. and D.G.; supervision, K.J. and M.Ś.; project administration, K.J. and D.G. All authors have read and agreed to the published version of the manuscript.

Funding: This research was funded by the Polish Ministry of Science and Higher Education (MNiSW) as part of the "Student Scientific Association Create Innovations" program, project number SKN/SP/569408/2023.

Institutional Review Board Statement: Not applicable.

Informed Consent Statement: Not applicable.

Data Availability Statement: The data presented in this study are available in the article.

Conflicts of Interest: The authors declare no conflict of interest.

References

1. Narisetty, V.; Cox, R.; Willoughby, N.; Aktas, E.; Tiwari, B.; Matharu, A.S.; Salonitis, K.; Kumar, V. Recycling bread waste into chemical building blocks using a circular biorefining approach. *Sustain. Energy Fuels* **2021**, *5*, 4842–4849. [CrossRef] [PubMed]
2. Pawlak, K.; Kołodziejczak, M. The Role of Agriculture in Ensuring Food Security in Developing Countries: Considerations in the Context of the Problem of Sustainable Food Production. *Sustainability* **2020**, *12*, 5488. [CrossRef]
3. Fukase, E.; Martin, W. Economic growth, convergence, and world food demand and supply. *World Dev.* **2020**, *132*, 104954. [CrossRef]
4. Krajnc, D.; Glavic, P. Indicators of sustainable production. *Clean Technol. Environ. Policy* **2003**, *5*, 279–288. [CrossRef]
5. Wünsche, J.F.; Fernqvist, F. The Potential of Blockchain Technology in the Transition towards Sustainable Food Systems. *Sustainability* **2022**, *14*, 7739. [CrossRef]
6. FAO. *Food Wastage Footprint: Impacts on Natural Resources*; Summary Report; FAO: Rome, Italy, 2013; ISBN 9251077525.

7. Chauhan, C.; Dhir, A.; Akram, M.U.; Salo, J. Food loss and waste in food supply chains. A systematic literature review and framework development approach. *J. Clean. Prod.* **2021**, *295*, 126438. [CrossRef]
8. Dymchenko, A.; Geršl, M.; Gregor, T. Trends in bread waste utilisation. *Trends Food Sci. Technol.* **2023**, *132*, 93–102. [CrossRef]
9. Demirci, A.S.; Palabiyik, I.; Gumus, T. Bread wastage and recycling of waste bread by producing biotechnological products. *J. Biotechnol.* **2016**, *231*, S13. [CrossRef]
10. WRAP. UK Food Waste & Food Surplus—Key Facts. 2023. Available online: https://wrap.org.uk/sites/default/files/2024-01/WRAP-Food-Surplus-and-Waste-in-the-UK-Key-Facts%20November-2023.pdf (accessed on 11 March 2024).
11. Mitka, M. Marnowanie żywności w gospodarstwach domowych w Polsce. *Probl. Econ. Law* **2020**, *4*, 1–14. [CrossRef]
12. Mihajlovski, K.; Rajilić-Stojanović, M.; Dimitrijević-Branković, S. Enzymatic hydrolysis of waste bread by newly isolated Hymenobacter sp. CKS3: Statistical optimization and bioethanol production. *Renew. Energy* **2020**, *152*, 627–633. [CrossRef]
13. Han, W.; Huang, J.; Zhao, H.; Li, Y. Continuous biohydrogen production from waste bread by anaerobic sludge. *Bioresour. Technol.* **2016**, *212*, 1–5. [CrossRef] [PubMed]
14. Pietrzak, W.; Kawa-Rygielska, J. Ethanol fermentation of waste bread using granular starch hydrolyzing enzyme: Effect of raw material pretreatment. *Fuel* **2014**, *134*, 250–256. [CrossRef]
15. Datta, P.; Tiwari, S.; Pandey, L.M. Bioethanol production from waste breads using *Saccharomyces cerevisiae*. In *Utilization and Management of Bioresources: Proceedings of 6th IconSWM 2016*; Springer: Singapore, 2018; pp. 125–134. [CrossRef]
16. Dubrovskis, V.; Plume, I. Biogas potential from demaged bread. In Proceedings of the International Conference Engineering for Rural Development, Jelgava, Latvia, 24–26 May 2017; pp. 437–442. [CrossRef]
17. Al-Ruqaie, I.; Swillam, S.; Al-Batshan, H.; Shafey, T. Performance, Nutrient Utilization and Carcass Characteristics and Economic Impact of Broiler Chickens Fed Extruded Bakery Waste. *J. Anim. Veter- Adv.* **2011**, *10*, 2061–2066. [CrossRef]
18. Pedro, F.M.S.; Vara, I.A.D.; Bórquez, J.L.; Gonzalez-Ronquillo, M. The effect of feeding fresh swine manure, poultry waste, urea, molasses and bakery by-products ensiled for lambs. *Int. J. Recycl. Org. Waste Agric.* **2015**, *4*, 273–278. [CrossRef]
19. Daigle, P.; Gélinas, P.; Leblanc, D.; Morin, A. Production of aroma compounds by Geotrichum candidum on waste bread crumb. *Food Microbiol.* **1999**, *16*, 517–522. [CrossRef]
20. Aggelopoulos, T.; Katsieris, K.; Bekatorou, A.; Pandey, A.; Banat, I.M.; Koutinas, A.A. Solid state fermentation of food waste mixtures for single cell protein, aroma volatiles and fat production. *Food Chem.* **2014**, *145*, 710–716. [CrossRef]
21. Madrera, R.R.; Bedriñana, R.P.; Valles, B.S. Production and characterization of aroma compounds from apple pomace by solid-state fermentation with selected yeasts. *LWT* **2015**, *64*, 1342–1353. [CrossRef]
22. Łopusiewicz, Ł.; Drozłowska, E.; Siedlecka, P.; Mężyńska, M.; Bartkowiak, A.; Sienkiewicz, M.; Zielińska-Bliźniewska, H.; Kwiatkowski, P. Development, Characterization, and Bioactivity of Non-Dairy Kefir-Like Fermented Beverage Based on Flaxseed Oil Cake. *Foods* **2019**, *8*, 544. [CrossRef] [PubMed]
23. Verni, M.; Demarinis, C.; Rizzello, C.G.; Baruzzi, F. Design and Characterization of a Novel Fermented Beverage from Lentil Grains. *Foods* **2020**, *9*, 893. [CrossRef]
24. Cordeiro, M.; Souza, E.; Arantes, R.; Balthazar, C.; Guimarães, J.; Scudino, H.; Silva, H.; Rocha, R.; Freitas, M.; Esmerino, E.; et al. Fermented whey dairy beverage offers protection against Salmonella enterica ssp. enterica serovar Typhimurium infection in mice. *J. Dairy Sci.* **2019**, *102*, 6756–6765. [CrossRef]
25. Luz, C.; Izzo, L.; Graziani, G.; Gaspari, A.; Ritieni, A.; Manes, J.; Meca, G. Evaluation of biological and antimicrobial properties of freeze-dried whey fermented by different strains of *Lactobacillus plantarum*. *Food Funct.* **2018**, *9*, 3688–3697. [CrossRef] [PubMed]
26. Garcia, G.; Agosto, M.E.; Cavaglieri, L.; Dogi, C. Effect of fermented whey with a probiotic bacterium on gut immune system. *J. Dairy Res.* **2020**, *87*, 134–137. [CrossRef] [PubMed]
27. Ruas-Madiedo, P.; Hugenholtz, J.; Zoon, P. An overview of the functionality of exopolysaccharides produced by lactic acid bacteria. *Int. Dairy J.* **2002**, *12*, 163–171. [CrossRef]
28. Tieking, M.; Korakli, M.; Ehrmann, M.A.; Gänzle, M.G.; Vogel, R.F. In Situ Production of Exopolysaccharides during Sourdough Fermentation by Cereal and Intestinal Isolates of Lactic Acid Bacteria. *Appl. Environ. Microbiol.* **2003**, *69*, 945–952. [CrossRef] [PubMed]
29. Immonen, M.; Maina, N.H.; Wang, Y.; Coda, R.; Katina, K. Waste bread recycling as a baking ingredient by tailored lactic acid fermentation. *Int. J. Food Microbiol.* **2020**, *327*, 108652. [CrossRef] [PubMed]
30. Granato, D.; Barba, F.J.; Kovačević, D.B.; Lorenzo, J.M.; Cruz, A.G.; Putnik, P. Functional Foods: Product Development, Technological Trends, Efficacy Testing, and Safety. *Annu. Rev. Food Sci. Technol.* **2020**, *11*, 93–118. [CrossRef] [PubMed]
31. Pravst, I. Functional foods in Europe: A focus on health claims. In *Scientific, Health and Social Aspects of the Food Industry*; Valdez, B., Ed.; InTech: Rijeka, Croatia, 2012; pp. 165–208.
32. Corbo, M.R.; Bevilacqua, A.; Petruzzi, L.; Casanova, F.P.; Sinigaglia, M. Functional Beverages: The Emerging Side of Functional Foods: Commercial trends, research, and health implications. *Compr. Rev. Food Sci. Food Saf.* **2014**, *13*, 1192–1206. [CrossRef]
33. Prado, F.C.; Parada, J.L.; Pandey, A.; Soccol, C.R. Trends in non-dairy probiotic beverages. *Food Res. Int.* **2008**, *41*, 111–123. [CrossRef]
34. Blandino, A.; Al-Aseeri, M.E.; Pandiella, S.S.; Cantero, D.; Webb, C. Cereal-based fermented foods and beverages. *Food Res. Int.* **2003**, *36*, 527–543. [CrossRef]
35. Muyanja, C.M.B.K.; Narvhus, J.A.; Treimo, J.; Langsrud, T. Isolation, characterisation and identification of lactic acid bacteria from bushera: A Ugandan traditional fermented beverage. *Int. J. Food Microbiol.* **2003**, *80*, 201–210. [CrossRef]

36. Oi, Y.; Kitabatake, N. Chemical Composition of an East African Traditional Beverage, *Togwa*. *J. Agric. Food Chem.* **2003**, *51*, 7024–7028. [CrossRef] [PubMed]
37. Walsh, H.; Cheng, J.; Guo, M. Effects of Carbonation on Probiotic Survivability, Physicochemical, and Sensory Properties of Milk-Based Symbiotic Beverages. *J. Food Sci.* **2014**, *79*, M604–M613. [CrossRef]
38. Champagne, C.P.; Gomes da Cruz, A.; Daga, M. Strategies to improve the functionality of probiotics in supplements and foods. *Curr. Opin. Food Sci.* **2018**, *22*, 160–166. [CrossRef]
39. Saarela, M.; Virkajärvi, I.; Nohynek, L.; Vaari, A.; Mättö, J. Fibres as carriers for Lactobacillus rhamnosus during freeze-drying and storage in apple juice and chocolate-coated breakfast cereals. *Int. J. Food Microbiol.* **2006**, *112*, 171–178. [CrossRef]
40. Ganorkar, P.M.; Jain, R.K. Flaxseed—A nutritional punch. *Int. Food Res. J.* **2013**, *20*, 512–525.
41. Vesterlund, S.; Salminen, K.; Salminen, S. Water activity in dry foods containing live probiotic bacteria should be carefully considered: A case study with Lactobacillus rhamnosus GG in flaxseed. *Int. J. Food Microbiol.* **2012**, *157*, 319–321. [CrossRef]
42. HadiNezhad, M.; Duc, C.; Han, N.F.; Hosseinian, F. Flaxseed Soluble Dietary Fibre Enhances Lactic Acid Bacterial Survival and Growth in Kefir and Possesses High Antioxidant Capacity. *J. Food Res.* **2013**, *2*, 152–163. [CrossRef]
43. Bialasová, K.; Němečková, I.; Kyselka, J.; Štětina, J.; Solichová, K.; Horáčková, Š. Influence of flaxseed components on fermented dairy product properties. *Czech J. Food Sci.* **2018**, *36*, 51–56. [CrossRef]
44. Kaczmarek, D.K.; Gwiazdowska, D.; Juś, K.; Klejdysz, T.; Wojcieszak, M.; Materna, K.; Pernak, J. Glycine betaine-based ionic liquids and their influence on bacteria, fungi, insects and plants. *New J. Chem.* **2021**, *45*, 6344–6355. [CrossRef]
45. Marchwińska, K.; Gwiazdowska, D.; Juś, K.; Gluzińska, P.; Gwiazdowska, J.; Pawlak-Lemańska, K. Innovative Functional Lactic Acid Bacteria Fermented Oat Beverages with the Addition of Fruit Extracts and Lyophilisates. *Appl. Sci.* **2023**, *13*, 12707. [CrossRef]
46. Giraud, E.; Gosselin, L.; Marin, B.; Parada, J.; Raimbault, M. Purification and characterization of an extracellular amylase from *Lactobacillus plantarum* strain A6. *J. Appl. Bacteriol.* **1993**, *75*, 276–282. [CrossRef]
47. Zamfir, M.; Angelescu, I.-R.; Voaides, C.; Cornea, C.-P.; Boiu-Sicuia, O.; Grosu-Tudor, S.-S. Non-Dairy Fermented Beverages Produced with Functional Lactic Acid Bacteria. *Microorganisms* **2022**, *10*, 2314. [CrossRef] [PubMed]
48. Sigüenza-Andrés, T.; Mateo, J.; Rodríguez-Nogales, J.M.; Gómez, M.; Caro, I. Characterization of a Fermented Beverage from Discarded Bread Flour Using Two Commercial Probiotics Starters. *Foods* **2024**, *13*, 951. [CrossRef] [PubMed]
49. Nguyen, T.-L.; Toh, M.; Lu, Y.; Ku, S.; Liu, S.-Q. Biovalorization of Market Surplus Bread for Development of Probiotic-Fermented Potential Functional Beverages. *Foods* **2022**, *11*, 250. [CrossRef] [PubMed]
50. Singh, D.; Vij, S.; Singh, B.P. Antioxidative and antimicrobial activity of whey based fermented soy beverage with curcumin supplementation. *Indian J. Dairy Sci.* **2016**, *69*, 171–177.
51. Undhad, T.; Hati, S.; Makwana, S. Significance of storage study on ACE inhibitory, antioxidative, antimicrobial activities, and biotransformation of isoflavones of functional fermented soy-based beverage. *J. Food Process. Preserv.* **2020**, *45*, e15062. [CrossRef]
52. Al-Mohammadi, A.-R.; Ibrahim, R.A.; Moustafa, A.H.; Ismaiel, A.A.; Zeid, A.A.; Enan, G. Chemical Constitution and Antimicrobial Activity of Kefir Fermented Beverage. *Molecules* **2021**, *26*, 2635. [CrossRef]
53. Ivanišová, E.; Meňhartová, K.; Terentjeva, M.; Harangozo, Ľ.; Kántor, A.; Kačániová, M. The evaluation of chemical, antioxidant, antimicrobial and sensory properties of kombucha tea beverage. *J. Food Sci. Technol.* **2020**, *57*, 1840–1846. [CrossRef] [PubMed]
54. Battikh, H.; Bakhrouf, A.; Ammar, E. Antimicrobial effect of Kombucha analogues. *LWT* **2012**, *47*, 71–77. [CrossRef]
55. Watawana, M.I.; Jayawardena, N.; Gunawardhana, C.B.; Waisundara, V.Y. Health, Wellness, and Safety Aspects of the Consumption of Kombucha. *J. Chem.* **2015**, *2015*, 591869. [CrossRef]

Disclaimer/Publisher's Note: The statements, opinions and data contained in all publications are solely those of the individual author(s) and contributor(s) and not of MDPI and/or the editor(s). MDPI and/or the editor(s) disclaim responsibility for any injury to people or property resulting from any ideas, methods, instructions or products referred to in the content.

Article

Assessment of the Performance of Oat Flakes and Pumpkin Seed Powders in Gluten-Free Dough and Bread Based on Rice Flour

Iuliana Banu and Iuliana Aprodu *

Faculty of Food Science and Engineering, Dunarea de Jos University of Galati, 111 Domneasca Street, 800201 Galati, Romania; iuliana.banu@ugal.ro
* Correspondence: iuliana.aprodu@ugal.ro

Abstract: The performance of oat flake flour and pumpkin seed protein powder in gluten-free dough and bread based on rice flours was assessed in this study. After studying the thermo-mechanical properties of the rice and oat flake flours at different water absorption capacities, two composite flours obtained by mixing the rice and oat flake flours with and without pumpkin seed protein powder were investigated. Regardless of the sample subjected to thermo-mechanical behavior analysis, the increase in the water adsorption level when preparing the dough caused a decrease in protein weakening, as well as starch retrogradation. The dough with added oat flake flour had a higher resistance to kneading compared to the control prepared with rice flour. Additionally, the substitution of rice flour with oat flake flour produced important changes in the gelatinization temperature, which decreases from 84–86 °C to 76 °C. The addition of pumpkin seed protein powder increased the maximum torque during kneading at 30 °C and decreased breakdown and starch retrogradation compared to the composite flour based on rice flour and oat flake flour. The higher amount of water used for preparing the dough improved the specific volume and crumb firmness of the bread prepared with the pumpkin seed protein-enriched composite flours.

Keywords: rice; oat flakes; pumpkin seed protein; Mixolab; bread

Citation: Banu, I.; Aprodu, I. Assessment of the Performance of Oat Flakes and Pumpkin Seed Powders in Gluten-Free Dough and Bread Based on Rice Flour. *Appl. Sci.* **2024**, *14*, 3479. https://doi.org/10.3390/app14083479

Academic Editors: Anna Wirkijowska, Piotr Zarzycki, Agata Blicharz-Kania and Urszula Pankiewicz

Received: 22 March 2024
Revised: 17 April 2024
Accepted: 19 April 2024
Published: 20 April 2024

Copyright: © 2024 by the authors. Licensee MDPI, Basel, Switzerland. This article is an open access article distributed under the terms and conditions of the Creative Commons Attribution (CC BY) license (https://creativecommons.org/licenses/by/4.0/).

1. Introduction

Celiac disease has a rising incidence worldwide, with reported annual values in recent years of 21.3 people with celiac disease per 100,000 persons among children and 12.9 per 100,000 persons among adults [1]. Because of this high incidence, the need to ensure an appropriate diet for people with celiac disease has increased, a goal for which researchers and the food industry must closely collaborate. The most important problems faced by patients with celiac disease in ensuring a gluten-free diet are related to the scarce availability, rather low nutritional and sensorial quality, high cost, and safety of gluten-free foods, associated with possible cross-contamination [2].

Ensuring the nutritional and sensorial quality of these foods needs to start with an adequate selection of the ingredients based on valuable nutritional qualities and technological functionalities, while considering their compatibility within gluten-free blends. Most often, gluten-free bakery products are obtained from composite flours based on cereal or/and pseudocereal flours and other ingredients such as starch, protein, and dietary fibers from different sources [3].

Rice flour is known to be a basic ingredient for baking gluten-free products. Because of the hypoallergenic properties of its proteins and its overall good digestibility [4,5], rice flour is considered the most suitable ingredient to be used as a base for gluten-free baking products, in spite of the poor technological and functional properties which are important for the overall quality of the final products. In addition, rice flour has nutritional limitations, residing in its low content of vitamins, minerals, and fiber [6].

Most of the people with celiac disease tolerate oats well [7]. Therefore, oats can be used as an ingredient in gluten-free products, but their label must include the mention of "OATS". Because of its high content of nutrients, the oat grain is considered a functional ingredient. According to the USDA [8], the average values of the main chemical components per 100 g of oats are the following: carbohydrates 69.9 g, proteins 13.2 g, total dietary fibers 12.9 g, and lipids 6.31 g, varying with the genetic features and growing conditions of the oats. The major fraction of oat proteins consists of globulins (70–80%), and, compared to other cereals, this fraction, together with albumin, has a higher lysine concentration [9]. Oats have a low glycemic index because they include high amounts of resistant starch (25%), followed by slowly digestible starch (22%) and only a small amount of rapidly digestible starch (7%) [9]. The particularities of the pasting properties of oat starch are related to the shorter time needed to achieve peak viscosity and lower pasting temperatures [10]. Regarding dietary fibers, oats are a good source of soluble β-glucans (82% of the total β-glucans content of 3–8 g/100 g dry weight). The importance of oat β-glucan is reinforced by the EFSA health claims regarding balancing blood glucose, increasing fecal bulk, and reducing blood cholesterol [11]. Additional heart and vascular system health claims have been assigned to high amounts of unsaturated fatty acids, residing mainly in oat grain endosperm [9,11]. A wholegrain diet based on oats is also recommended because of its important contents of polyphenols and avenanthramides, with antioxidant and anti-inflammatory properties [11]. A limitation in the utilization of oat flour is related to its stability. Oat flour processing through fermentation, germination, defatting, and hydrothermal treatment proved to be efficient for improving its stability, whereas extrusion and treatments based on pulsed electric field or enzymes can additionally increase the antioxidant properties and soluble dietary fiber content of oat flours [9].

Pumpkins are rich in nutrients and compounds with human health-promoting benefits, such as proteins, peptides, amino acids, essential oils, fibers, pectins, vitamins, minerals, phenolic compounds with antioxidant activity, carotenoids, tocopherols, and phytosterols [12]. Of particular importance for producing functional food ingredients are pumpkin seeds because of their high content of oil, proteins, fibers, minerals, and phenolic compounds [12]. The main products obtained by processing pumpkin seeds are oil and proteins. According to Vinayashreea and Vasu [13], pumpkin seed protein isolates are rich in essential amino acids and have good functional properties, comparable to those of soybean protein isolates. Regarding their amino acid profile, pumpkin seed protein isolates have high amounts of Arg, Glu, and Gln, and their essential amino acids comply with the requirements of the FAO/WHO for pre-school children and adults. The major fraction of pumpkin proteins is globulins, about 68%, while the prolamin fraction is about 4% [14]. Pumpkin seed protein isolates offer the advantage of a low presence of antinutritional factors. Vinayashreea and Vasu [13] reported the absence of trypsin inhibitors in pumpkin seed protein isolates, while their amount of phytic acids and tannins was rather low.

The objective of this study was to evaluate the possibility of using oat flake flour and pumpkin seed proteins for improving the rheological properties of rice flour-based dough and gluten-free bread-making potential. The thermo-mechanical properties of the individual and composite flours at various water absorption levels was tested, as well as the physical-chemical properties of the gluten-free breads enriched with valuable compounds from oat flakes and pumpkin seed proteins.

2. Materials and Methods

2.1. Materials

Whole rice flour (distributed by Adam Vision SRL, Targu Mures, Romania), and oat flakes (Solaris Plant SRL, Bucharest, Romania) were purchased from the Galati market (Galati, Romania). The pumpkin seed protein powder was provided by Kuk SRL (Bucharest, Romania). Oat flake flour was obtained using a blade mill grinder (Bosch MKM6003, Gailingen, Germany).

2.2. Proximate Compositions

The proximate composition of whole rice flour (RF), oat flake flour (OFF), and pumpkin seed protein powder (PP) was assessed as follows: moisture content through the SR ISO 712:2005 method [15], ash content through the SR ISO 2171/2002 method [15], protein content by means of semimicro-Kjeldahl (Raypa Trade, R Espinar, SL, Barcelona, Spain), fat content using Soxhlet (SER-148; VELP Scientifica, UsmateVelate (MB), Italy) extraction, and the crude fiber content using the Fibretherm Analyser (C. Gerhardt GmbH & Co. KG, Königswinter, Germany). The starch content was finally calculated by subtracting, from 100 g of RF or OFF, the amount of compounds determined as indicated before.

2.3. Thermo-Mechanical Properties

The thermo-mechanical behavior of the dough prepared with RF, OFF, and flour blends consisting of RF and OFF with and without PP addition was determined using the Mixolab device (Chopin Technology, Villeneuve La Garenne, France). The RF + OFF blend was obtained by mixing RF with OFF in the ratio of 80:20. In the RF + OFF + PP blend, the RF:OFF:PP ratio was 65:20:15, such as to obtain a total protein content of the flour blend within the 15–20% range.

The Chopin+ protocol was used to investigate the thermo-mechanical behavior of the dough samples at different water absorption (WA) levels. All the investigated dough samples were prepared in the mixing bowl of the Mixolab device. The weight of the dough prepared in the Mixolab bowl was always 90 g per batch. The RF doughs were prepared using three WA levels of 65, 70, and 75%, while for the OFF-based dough samples WA levels of 70, 80, and 90% were considered. Larger WA levels of the OFF, compared to the RF, were considered due the higher amounts of total and soluble fibers in OFF [9,16,17]. The thermo-mechanical behavior of the dough samples obtained using the two composite flours, RF + OFF and RF + OFF + PP, were investigated at WA levels of 70 and 75%.

The torque values registered while running the Chopin+ protocol were used to assess the behavior of the proteins and starch within the investigated dough samples: maximum C1 torque during initial mixing at 30 °C; CS consistency of the dough measured after 8 min of mixing at 30 °C; minimum C2 torque associated with the thermal weakening of the proteins in the matrix; C3 and C4 torques related to starch gelatinization and the stability of the gel at high temperatures, respectively; and C5 registered when starch retrogradation occurred during the cooling phase [18,19]. Furthermore, starch gelatinization (pasting), breakdown, and starch retrogradation were estimated based on (C3-C2), (C3-C4), and (C5-C4) values, respectively. The mechanical weakening of the proteins (MWPs) and the thermo-mechanical weakening of the proteins (TMWPs) were calculated using the following equations:

$$\text{MWP} = \frac{C1 - CS}{C1} \quad (1)$$

$$\text{TMWP} = \frac{CS - C2}{C1} \quad (2)$$

2.4. Bread-Making Procedure and Bread Characterization

The baking test was carried out, as indicated by Patraşcu et al. [20], using the one-stage method to prepare the dough. The ingredients used for preparing the breads were 100 g flour (100 g RF; 80 g RF and 20 g OFF; 65 g RF, 20 g OFF, and 15 g PP), 1.5 g salt, 1.5 g sugar, 3 g fresh baker's yeast (Rompak SRL, Pascani, Romania), and water according to the WA levels mentioned above for each type of flour.

A gas oven (Electrolux, Poland) was used to bake the breads for 35 min at 200 °C. Bread sample characterization was further carried out after equilibration to room temperature.

The specific volume of the breads was determined using the rapeseed displacement method SR 91:2007 [15]. Two slices selected from the center of each bread loaf were used to measure the crumb firmness, with the MLFTA apparatus (Guss, Strand, South Africa) fitted with a probe with ø 7.9 mm. The maximum force needed for a 25 mm wide penetration of the bread slices at a penetration speed of 5 mm/s and a trigger threshold force of 20 g was registered to estimate the crumb firmness.

The brightness (L*), redness (a*), and yellowness (b*) of the crumb were measured using the Chroma Meter CR-410 (Konica Minolta Inc, Tokyo, Japan) colorimeter. The total color difference (ΔE) obtained upon partial replacement of the RF by OFF and PP in the bread formulation was calculated as follows:

$$\Delta E = \sqrt{\left(L^*_{sample} - L^*_{control}\right)^2 + \left(a^*_{sample} - a^*_{control}\right)^2 + \left(b^*_{sample} - b^*_{control}\right)^2} \quad (3)$$

The color intensity was estimated by calculating chroma (C*) using Equation (4):

$$C^* = \sqrt{a^{*2} + b^{*2}} \quad (4)$$

2.5. Statistical Analysis

The results of triplicate measurements were reported as the mean ± standard deviation. One-way ANOVA was applied using the Minitab 19 (Minitab Inc., State College, PA, USA) software to identify the significant differences among the samples. A post hoc analysis using Tukey's method at a confidence of 95% was applied ($p < 0.05$).

3. Results and Discussion

3.1. Proximate Composition

The proximate composition of RF and OFF is presented in Table 1. The RF had a low protein content of 7.40% and a medium fiber content of 4.20%. RF was chosen as the basis for the gluten-free composite flour and bread due to its high content of starch and particular pasting properties. Significantly higher contents of protein (13.10%), fiber (9.80%), and fat (6.33%) were found in the OFF (Table 1). Because of the high protein concentration of 9–20% with respect to other gluten-free flours, Mao et al. [9] indicated that oat is a good source of low-cost protein. Additional reasons for choosing OFF in this study were related to its high fiber content and high antioxidant potential [21]. Finally, PP was selected as a vector for increasing the protein content of the composite flour consisting of RF and OFF.

Table 1. Proximate composition of rice flour (RF), oat flake flour (OFF), and pumpkin seed protein powder (PP).

Sample	Moisture, %	Proteins, %	Fat, %	Fiber, %	Ash, %	Carbohydrates, %
RF	11.45 ± 0.01 [a]	7.40 ± 0.10 [c]	2.50 ± 0.08 [c]	4.20 ± 0.10 [c]	1.52 ± 0.02 [a]	72.93 [a]
OFF	11.35 ± 0.01 [b]	13.10 ± 0.10 [b]	6.33 ± 0.05 [b]	9.80 ± 0.15 [b]	1.49 ± 0.02 [a]	57.86 [b]
PP	9.55 ± 0.01 [c]	62.15 ± 0.17 [a]	12.67 ± 0.06 [a]	12.90 ± 0.10 [a]	0.62 ± 0.02 [b]	2.11 [c]

n.d.—not determined. Different superscript letters accompanying mean values in the same column indicate statistically significant differences at $p < 0.05$, based on Tukey's post hoc test.

3.2. The Thermo-Mechanical Properties of RF and OFF

The primary and secondary Mixolab parameters, registered while running the Chopin+ protocol, are presented in Table 2.

The investigation of the thermo-mechanical properties for RF and OFF was performed at different WA levels, decided based on the assumption that high dough consistencies are not necessary for gluten-free breads, as in the case of dough systems based of wheat [22]. Considering the higher fiber and protein contents but also the fact that the OFF had been obtained from extruded oats, the WA levels selected for the OFF were higher compared to those for the RF.

Table 2. Primary and secondary Mixolab parameters of the dough prepared with rice flour (RF) and oat flake flour (OFF) at different water absorption (WA) levels.

Parameter/ Sample and WA	Rice Flour			Oat Flake Flour		
	65	70	75	70	80	90
Primary Mixolab parameters						
C1, Nm	0.70 ± 0.01 [a]	0.38 ± 0.01 [b]	0.29 ± 0.01 [c]	2.20 ± 0.01 [a]	1.49 ± 0.01 [b]	0.85 ± 0.01 [c]
CS, Nm	0.68 ± 0.01 [a]	0.34 ± 0.01 [b]	0.18 ± 0.01 [c]	1.93 ± 0.02 [a]	1.34 ± 0.01 [b]	0.84 ± 0.02 [c]
C2, Nm	0.33 ± 0.01 [a]	0.19 ± 0.01 [b]	0.11 ± 0.01 [c]	1.20 ± 0.01 [a]	0.86 ± 0.02 [b]	0.59 ± 0.01 [c]
C3, Nm	2.20 ± 0.01 [a]	1.97 ± 0.01 [b]	1.76 ± 0.02 [c]	2.16 ± 0.01 [a]	1.86 ± 0.02 [b]	1.69 ± 0.01 [c]
C4, Nm	2.16 ± 0.02 [a]	1.92 ± 0.01 [b]	1.69 ± 0.01 [c]	1.33 ± 0.02 [a]	1.13 ± 0.01 [b]	0.97 ± 0.01 [c]
C5, Nm	3.57 ± 0.02 [a]	3.08 ± 0.02 [b]	2.77 ± 0.02 [c]	1.95 ± 0.01 [a]	1.73 ± 0.02 [b]	1.46 ± 0.02 [c]
Secondary Mixolab parameters						
C3-C2, Nm	1.87 ± 0.02 [a]	1.78 ± 0.02 [b]	1.65 ± 0.03 [c]	0.95 ± 0.03 [b]	1.00 ± 0.03 [b]	1.10 ± 0.02 [a]
C3-C4, Nm	0.04 ± 0.03 [a]	0.05 ± 0.02 [a]	0.07 ± 0.01 [a]	0.82 ± 0.01 [a]	0.73 ± 0.01 [b]	0.72 ± 0.02 [b]
C5-C4, Nm	1.41 ± 0.02 [a]	1.16 ± 0.01 [b]	1.08 ± 0.03 [c]	0.62 ± 0.01 [a]	0.60 ± 0.02 [a]	0.49 ± 0.01 [b]
MWP, %	3.32 ± 1.74 [b]	10.46 ± 4.26 [b]	38.57 ± 4.15 [a]	12.42 ± 1.09 [a]	10.09 ± 0.53 [a]	1.57 ± 1.47 [b]
TMWP, %	50.01 ± 0.58 [a]	39.49 ± 3.79 [b]	23.97 ± 3.53 [c]	32.88 ± 1.25 [a]	32.07 ± 0.46 [a]	29.01 ± 2.31 [a]

For a flour sample, different superscript letters accompanying means values on the same line indicate statistically significant differences at $p < 0.05$, based on Tukey's post hoc test.

Analyzing the Mixolab parameters registered during mixing at 30 °C, it can be seen that WA increase caused a decrease in the C1 and CS values (Table 2). In the case of RF, the maximum value of C1 was 0.70 Nm at 65% WA and decreased to 0.29 Nm at 75% WA, while, in the case of OFF, the maximum value of C1 was 2.20 Nm, which decreased to 0.85 Nm at 90% WA. For the same WA level of 70%, the C1 registered for OFF was about 5.8 times higher compared to RF. In case of RF dough, the CS was significantly lower ($p < 0.05$) compared to the C1 for 75% WA; smaller differences between C1 and CS were found for WA levels of 65 and 70%. As a consequence, the MWP values increased with the WA (Table 2), suggesting that, at lower values of WA, the RF dough was more stable, having a higher resistance to kneading at a constant temperature of 30 °C. On the other hand, although WA increases caused the decrease in the C1 and CS values of the OFF dough, the dough was more stable at a WA level of 90%, because of the closer C1 and CS values, which resulted in a lower MWP (Table 2). These important differences between the behaviors of the OFF and RF doughs at increasing WA levels were most likely due to the different protein and fiber profiles and contents. OFF has higher protein and fiber contents than RF (Table 1). High-molecular-weight glutelins are the major protein fraction in milled rice, representing 79–93% of the total protein, followed by globulins (6–13%), albumins (4–6%), and prolamins (2–7%) [23]. The main proteins in oats are globulins (50–80%), followed by prolamins, albumins, and glutelins, representing 4–15%, 1–12%, and 10%, respectively, or the total proteins content [24,25]. Nonetheless, it is important to mention that their physicochemical properties are modified in oat flakes because of hydrothermal treatment and shearing. As mentioned by Gates [26], flaking changes the structure of oat groats, affecting the cell walls' integrity. Moreover, because of the high shear and work inputs, damages in the starch granules and protein bodies have been noticed. In addition, Gu et al. [27] reported that the use of gelatinized oat flour with increased water absorption and swelling allowed them to obtain oat dough with an improved elastic behavior. The changes observed in the rheological behavior of the dough are related to the changes observed in the ratio between the main forces involved in stabilizing the matrix: a higher contribution of the hydrogen and covalent bonds and a lower participation of the hydrophobic and ionic interactions were reported in the dough samples based on gelatinized oat flour compared to the control dough.

Regarding the fiber content, it should be noted that oats have the highest content of β-glucans among all cereals, largely distributed in the endosperm cell wall (75%) [9]. The ratio between soluble and insoluble β-glucans as well as the properties of the soluble fraction of β-glucans suffer changes in oat flake flour compared to native oat flour. Torbica et al. [17] noted that oat flour prepared by hydrothermal pre-treatment needed a high water level for dough preparation, compared to native flour, such as to avoid obtaining a hard and sticky dough. A high level of WA improves the protein and carbohydrate network. An improvement in the functionality of the soluble fiber content was noted by Zhang et al. [28]. They studied the effect of oat bran extrusion on soluble fibers' properties and reported an improvement in water-related properties like solubility, solvent retention capacity, swelling ability, and apparent viscosity. In addition, the presence of resistant starch most likely influences the level of water addition needed during kneading. Oats have a high resistant starch content [9], which increases during extrusion as a result of shearing and the thermal treatment meant to improve the gelatinization, retrogradation, and recrystallization properties of the starch [29].

In the second phase of the Mixolab curves, characterized by temperature increases while keeping the dough's mixing constraint, a torque decrease in all the tested dough samples was noticed (Figure 1). Regardless of the tested flour type, the values of the minimum C2 torques varied significantly ($p < 0.05$) with the WA level (Table 2). The C2 of the RF-based dough decreased from 0.33 to 0.11 Nm, and from 1.20 to 0.59 Nm in case of the OFF-based dough, with the increase in the WA level. An important decrease in the TMWP from 50.01 to 23.97% with a WA level increase from 65% to 75% was registered in case of the RF dough samples, whereas no significant differences were noticed in the case of the OFF dough (Table 2). These differences between RF and OFF dough behavior might be partially assigned to the differences regarding the quality of the proteins from the two sources. In addition, considering the important changes regarding the properties of the main oat constituents occurring during flaking, as discussed before, the influence of the way in which water is bound within the dough matrix during kneading at 30 °C [17] should not be neglected.

The results from Tables 2 and 3, as well as from Figure 1, indicate very different behaviors of the starch in the two flours during heating and cooling. This behavior was determined, on the one hand, by the structural particularities of the starch of the two investigated cereals—rice and oats—and, on the other hand, by the modifications that the starch underwent during the oats' flaking process. The size of starch granules is similar in the two cereals [10], and amylose has a similar molecular weight [30], but the amylopectin chains are longer in oats compared to rice [31]. For this reason, oat starch has unique pasting properties that require a shorter time to reach maximum gelatinization and a lower temperature at which this maximum is reached [10]. From Figure 1, it can be seen that C3 was achieved much faster (after 20 min) and at a lower temperature (67–71 °C) in the case of OFF, compared to RF (after 28 min, at 84–86 °C). The increasing WA level led to significantly lower C3 and C4 values ($p < 0.05$) in the case of both investigated flours (Table 2). However, the larger amount of water available in the dough system led to changes in starch gelatinization behavior, depending on the flour type: the WA increase caused a significant reduction in the (C3-C2) values in the RF-based dough ($p < 0.05$), whereas a significant increase in the (C3-C2) from 1 to 1.1 Nm ($p < 0.05$) was noticed when raising the WA level of the OFF dough from 80 to 90% (Table 2). The heat treatment applied during oat flakes' processing influenced the pasting properties and the moisture of the OFF, limiting starch gelatinization. It was also found that the heat treatment during drying and steaming led to the decrease in the temperature and enthalpy of gelatinization, determined by differential scanning calorimetry, but also to the increase in the viscosity after pasting, and this could be explained by enzyme inactivation [26].

As can be observed in Figure 1 and Table 2, the breakdown (C3-C4) was significantly higher in OFF compared to RF, suggesting that gelatinized OFF starch had a lower stability to heating and kneading compared to RF. However, the (C3-C4) values registered for OFF (0.72–0.73 Nm at WA levels of 80 and 90%) were lower compared to those of native oat flour (1.01 Nm at 85% WA) [32].

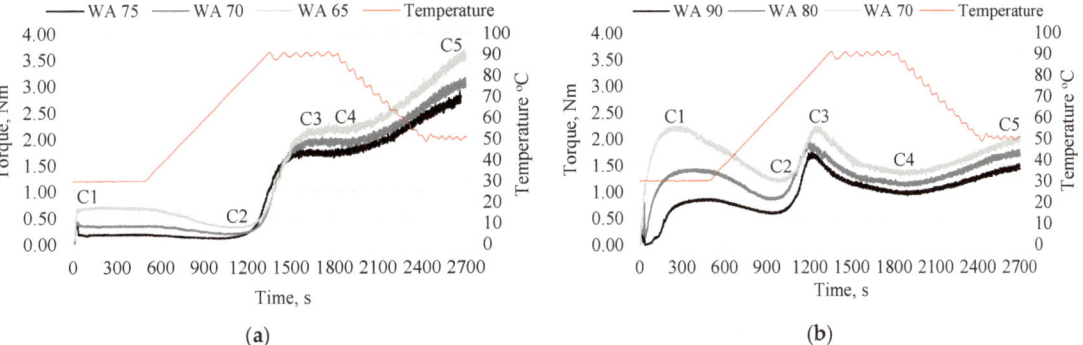

Figure 1. Mixolab curve of the dough samples prepared with rice flour (**a**) and oat flake flour (**b**) at various water absorption (WA) levels.

Table 3. Primary and secondary Mixolab parameters of the dough prepared with composite flours at different water absorption (WA) levels. RF + OFF consisted of 80% rice flour and 20% oat flake flour, while RF + OFF + PP consisted of 65% rice flour, 20% oat flake flour, and 15% pumpkin seed protein powder.

Parameter/ Sample and WA	RF + OFF	RF + OFF + PP	RF + OFF	RF + OFF + PP
	70		75	
Primary Mixolab parameters				
C1, Nm	0.81 ± 0.02 [b]	0.94 ± 0.01 [a]	0.46 ± 0.01 [d]	0.58 ± 0.02 [c]
CS, Nm	0.80 ± 0.02 [b]	0.93 ± 0.03 [a]	0.43 ± 0.01 [d]	0.56 ± 0.01 [c]
C2, Nm	0.46 ± 0.02 [a]	0.48 ± 0.01 [a]	0.27 ± 0.01 [b]	0.31 ± 0.02 [b]
C3, Nm	1.95 ± 0.02 [a]	1.85 ± 0.02 [b]	1.81 ± 0.02 [c]	1.66 ± 0.01 [d]
C4, Nm	1.66 ± 0.02 [a]	1.63 ± 0.02 [a]	1.51 ± 0.01 [b]	1.45 ± 0.02 [c]
C5, Nm	2.88 ± 0.01 [a]	2.52 ± 0.01 [b]	2.38 ± 0.02 [c]	2.18 ± 0.01 [d]
Secondary Mixolab parameters				
C3-C2, Nm	1.50 ± 0.03 [a]	1.37 ± 0.03 [b]	1.54 ± 0.03 [a]	1.35 ± 0.03 [b]
C3-C4, Nm	0.30 ± 0.02 [a]	0.22 ± 0.03 [b]	0.30 ± 0.02 [a]	0.21 ± 0.01 [b]
C5-C4, Nm	1.21 ± 0.01 [a]	0.88 ± 0.01 [b]	0.87 ± 0.01 [b]	0.73 ± 0.02 [c]
MWP, %	1.19 ± 3.27 [a]	1.42 ± 2.22 [a]	7.25 ± 1.27 [a]	3.33 ± 5.06 [a]
TMWP, %	42.15 ± 4.17 [a,b]	47.52 ± 2.15 [a]	34.01 ± 3.79 [b]	43.77 ± 5.48 [a,b]

For a flour sample, different superscript letters accompanying mean values on the same line indicate statistically significant differences at $p < 0.05$, based on Tukey's post hoc test.

3.3. The Thermo-Mechanical Properties of the Composite Flours

Table 3, as well as Figure 2, presents the results registered from the Mixolab curves corresponding to the dough samples prepared using the composite flours. The use of WA levels of 70 and 75% for preparing the doughs based on composite (RF + OFF) flour was decided upon analyzing the results of the investigations carried out on the individual flours.

The RF + OFF composite flour showed major differences in terms of C1, CS, and C2 compared to RF and OFF, as, in this area of the Mixolab curve, the largest differences between the three types of flours were observed. Briefly, by substituting 20% of the RF with OFF, s significant increase ($p < 0.05$) in C1, CS, and C2 (Table 3) was observed with respect to the RF (Table 2). This thermo-mechanical behavior of the dough based on composite flour was due to presence of higher amounts of protein and fiber in the OFF compared to the RF. The dough based on composite flour exhibited a higher resistance to kneading compared to the RF, as evidenced by lower MPW values (Table 3). The C2 value increase in the case of the RF + OFF samples could be attributed to the β-glucan intake from the OFF, with Duta et al. [33] reporting a positive correlation between protein weakening and β-glucan content. The TMWT increased relative to both the RF and the OFF, indicating that the dough presented a lower resistance to kneading and heating.

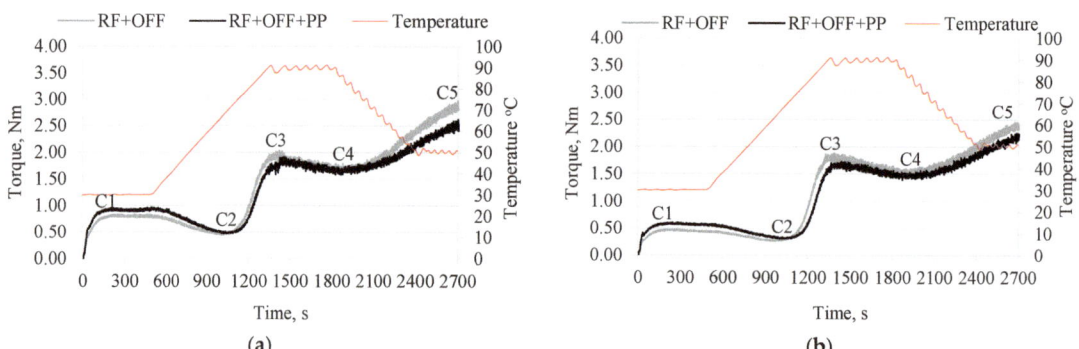

Figure 2. Mixolab curve of the dough samples prepared with composite flour consisting of 80% rice flour + 20% oat flake flour (RF + OFF) and 65% rice flour + 20% oat flake flour + 15% pumpkin seed protein powder (RF + OFF + PP). Measurements were carried out at water absorption (WA) levels of 70 (**a**) and 75% (**b**).

Regardless of the water absorption level, the addition of PP caused an increase in the C1 and CS values with respect to the RF + OFF composite flour, most probably as the result of high protein and fiber intakes from the PP which had been used to substitute 15% of the RF. Alshehry [34] noted that the ratio of insoluble-to-soluble fiber in pumpkin seed powder is 2:1, and this may explain the high C1 and CS values compared to the RF dough. Vinayashreea and Vasu [13] reported water holding capacity values of 1.29–1.35 mL/g for PP. They highlighted that the water-related properties of the proteins are influenced by intrinsic and extrinsic properties like structural properties of the proteins, namely, amino acid composition, conformation particularities, and surface hydrophobicity, protein concentration, temperature, pH, and ionic strength [13]. Regarding the particular influence of the secondary structure elements, Litvynchuk et al. [14] indicated that the α-helical content is mainly responsible for the viscosity of the dough. Analyzing the secondary structure of proteins from pumpkin seed protein isolates, Du et al. [35] observed the presence of 38.2% α-helix conformation, while Vinayashreea and Vasu [13] reported, for the water-soluble fraction in the protein isolate, the presence of 38.8% α-helical content, whereas the rest of the amino acids were organized as β-strands (17.7%), turns (8.4%), or random coils (35.0%). One could assume that kneading and the heat treatment resulted in structural changes in the proteins, causing the TMWT to increase from 42.15 to 47.52% in the case of the dough with a WA level of 70% and from 34.01 to 43.77% for the samples with a WA level of 75% (Table 3). Mechanical action, combined with the temperature increase, most likely caused disulfide bonds' breaking, therefore exposing more sulfhydryl groups on the surface of the protein molecules. It should be noted that the C2 value was obtained at a temperature of about 53 °C, which was higher compared to that required for the RF + OFF composite flour, for which C2 was obtained at 49–50 °C.

Compared to the RF samples, the addition of OFF produced small effects on C3 but significantly decreased the (C3-C2) and increased the (C3-C4) ($p < 0.05$). These changes were due to the properties of starch and non-starch polysaccharides from the OFF. The dough with a WA level of 70% had higher C5 and (C5-C4) values compared to the sample with a WA of 75%. One could estimate that, in the dough prepared with 70% WA, the amount of water was insufficient to well hydrate the flour matrix rich in non-starch polysaccharides originating from the OFF. The addition of OFF also produced important changes in the gelatinization temperature, which decreased from 84–86 °C to 76 °C upon substituting 20% of the RF with the OFF. The addition of PP decreased the C3, (C3-C2), and (C3-C4) values compared to the RF + OFF (Tables 2 and 3). The C3 decrease could also be attributed to the high lipid content of the PP (Table 1) but also to starch dilution by substituting 15% RF with the PP [4]. Marco and Rosell [4] reported a 23% decrease in C3, from 0.82 to 0.63 Nm, by substituting 13% RF with soy protein isolate at 95% WA. In the case of our experiment, the RF substitution with 15% PP resulted in a smaller C3 decrease, from 1.95 to 1.85 Nm, in the case of the dough prepared with a WA level of 70%, and from 1.81 to 1.66 Nm in the case of the samples with a WA level of 75%. These observations are in good agreement with Zheng et al. [36], who reported on the higher strength of the gel based on native pumpkin seed protein isolate compared to soybean or pea protein isolates.

PP addition to the RF + OFF composite flour caused a significant decrease in C5 and (C5-C4) (Tables 4 and 5), which may be a good premise for using this high protein content composite flour for obtaining bakery products. When comparing the PP-containing dough samples with WA levels of 70 and 75%, one could observe that (C3-C2), (C3-C4), and C4 had very close values, while (C5-C4) was lower in the case of the dough with a higher amount of water. Therefore, one can expect a better crumb firmness quality from bread at a WA level of 75% compared to bread at a WA level of 70%.

Table 4. Specific volume and firmness of the gluten-free bread samples prepared at different water absorption (WA) levels. RF + OFF consisted of 80% rice flour and 20% oat flake flour, while RF + OFF + PP consisted of 65% rice flour, 20% oat flake flour, and 15% pumpkin seed protein powder.

Bread Sample	WA, %	Specific Volume, cm³/g	Firmness, g Force
RF	70	2.43 ± 0.03 [a]	1366.03 ± 21.23 [a]
RF + OFF	70	2.40 ± 0.02 [a,b]	1414.64 ± 47.98 [a]
RF + OFF + PP	70	2.34 ± 0.04 [b]	1462.22 ± 43.35 [a]
RF	75	2.84 ± 0.04 [a]	716.09 ± 16.47 [c]
RF + OFF	75	2.61 ± 0.04 [b]	1007.44 ± 49.96 [b]
RF + OFF + PP	75	2.47 ± 0.03 [c]	1263.38 ± 37.21 [a]

Different superscript letters accompanying mean values in the same column indicate statistically significant differences at $p < 0.05$, based on Tukey's post hoc test.

Table 5. Color characteristics of gluten-free bread samples prepared at different water absorption (WA) levels. RF + OFF consisted of 80% rice flour and 20% oat flake flour, while RF + OFF + PP consisted of 65% rice flour, 20% oat flake flour, and 15% pumpkin seed protein powder.

Bread	WA, %	L*	a*	b*	ΔE	C*
RF	70	55.42 ± 0.02 [a]	2.89 ± 0.01 [c]	14.45 ± 0.04 [c]	-	14.74 ± 0.03 [c]
RF + OFF	70	49.98 ± 0.79 [b]	3.06 ± 0.01 [b]	15.38 ± 0.18 [b]	5.53 ± 0.73 [b]	15.68 ± 0.18 [b]
RF + OFF + PP	70	37.87 ± 0.12 [c]	4.66 ± 0.03 [a]	15.91 ± 0.03 [a]	17.70 ± 0.13 [a]	16.58 ± 0.04 [a]
RF	75	54.69 ± 0.09 [a]	3.00 ± 0.01 [c]	15.20 ± 0.01 [c]	-	15.49 ± 0.01 [c]
RF + OFF	75	49.01 ± 0.10 [b]	3.18 ± 0.01 [b]	15.90 ± 0.02 [b]	5.72 ± 0.19 [b]	16.21 ± 0.02 [b]
RF + OFF + PP	75	37.49 ± 0.26 [c]	4.43 ± 0.03 [a]	16.21 ± 0.19 [a]	17.29 ± 0.25 [a]	16.81 ± 0.18 [a]

Different superscript letters accompanying mean values in the same column indicate statistically significant differences at $p < 0.05$, based on Tukey's post hoc test.

3.4. Breads' Characterization

The physical properties of the gluten-free bread samples prepared with composite flour with and without pumpkin seed protein powder are shown in Tables 4 and 5.

The breads prepared with higher amounts of water presented higher specific volumes, regardless of the flour used. The specific volume was positively correlated with C2 (R^2 of 0.787 and $p < 0.05$). The breads prepared with the composite flours (RF + OFF and RF + OFF + PP) presented lower values of specific volumes compared to the control breads prepared with the RF. Martinez et al. [37] also reported specific volume decrease when using extruded flour to replace 10% of rice flour in gluten-free breads' formulation. Nonetheless, the specific volume of the breads prepared using the composite flours at a WA level of 75% was higher compared to the control bread with a lower amount of water (WA of 70%). Dabash et al. [38] reported the reduction in the specific volume of bread when partially substituting rice flour with pumpkin flour. They explained these results through the high fiber content derived from pumpkin flour, which weakened the dough structure, interfering with its ability to retain CO_2 while baking. This observation is also supported by the study of El-Soukkari [39], who compared the effect of pumpkin seed meal and pumpkin protein isolate addition on the bread-making properties of wheat flour and reported a lower reduction in the specific volume of bread in the latter case.

No significant differences in terms of firmness were registered between the bread samples with a WA level of 70%, whereas at a higher WA level of 75%, RF substitution with OFF or OFF and PP had a stronger effect on crumb firmness, which increased significantly from 716.09 to 1263.38 g force (Table 4). Nonetheless, it should be noted that the firmness of the bread sample prepared with the RF + OFF + PP composite flour was better at WA 75% compared to WA 70%. The firmness of the bread prepared at 70% WA was correlated with C5 (R^2 of 0.986 and $p < 0.05$), while the firmness of the bread with 75% WA was correlated with (C5-C4) (R^2 of 0.997 and $p < 0.05$). Gallagher et al. [40] tested the effect of different levels of gluten-free flour substitution with various dairy protein products on the quality of the bread and indicated a significant crumb softness reduction compared to the control. Moreover, Patrașcu et al. [20] reported the important increase in crumb hardness when supplementing wholegrain rice flour with 15% soy protein concentrate or powdered egg. Gormley and Morrissey [41] reported that the addition of oat flakes to wheat flour supplemented with gluten resulted in an improvement in the specific volume and crumb firmness. Nonetheless, they reported a crumb firmness increase and a specific volume decrease for the sample with no gluten addition. The authors explained away these results by the large particle size of the oat flakes compared to that of wheat flour, with the presence of higher amounts of gluten being able to blur their effect. Additionally, Huttner et al. [42] investigated the bread-making potential of different oat varieties and found that the most important differences in bread quality were related to the crumb properties.

Regardless of the WA level used for dough preparation, the substitution of RF with OFF and PP significantly decreased the brightness (L*) ($p < 0.05$) and increased the redness (a*) and yellowness (b*) ($p < 0.05$) of the gluten-free breads (Table 5, Figure 3). Our results are in good agreement with those of Belc et al. [43], who tested the quality of high-protein breads and reported significant darkness, redness, and yellowness increases when incorporating soy and pea protein concentrates at various levels, ranging from 5 to 15%, into the wheat flour. The color difference (ΔE) between the control breads, prepared with RF, and the breads with RF + OFF was 5.53–5.72, which is visible to the human eye [38]. The ΔE significantly increased to 17.70–17.29 ($p < 0.05$) when PP was used in the composite flour's formulation. These differences were mainly due to the L* values, even though OFF addition induced a more pronounced red tone (higher a* values), and PP contributed to the yellow tone's intensification (higher b* value) compared to the RF. The color intensity (C*) increased when increasing the percentage of RF substituted by OFF and OFF + PP, with higher values being obtained in the case of the bread samples prepared with higher amounts of water (WA of 75%).

(a) RF (b) RF + OFF (c) RF + OFF + PP (d) RF (e) RF + OFF (f) RF + OFF + PP

Figure 3. Appearance of the crumbs of breads prepared at 70% WA with RF (**a**), RF + OFF (**b**), and RF + OFF + PP (**c**) and at 75% WA with RF (**d**), RF + OFF (**e**), and RF + OFF + PP (**f**).

4. Conclusions

The influence of oat flake flour and pumpkin seed protein powder addition on the thermo-mechanical and bread-making performance of rice flour was investigated. The oat flake flour presented a higher maximum consistency during kneading at 30 °C and after 8 min of kneading at the same temperature and a lower mechanical weakening protein value compared to the rice flour. Moreover, the oat flake flour presented a higher breakdown and lower starch retrogradation compared to the rice flour. The substitution of rice flour with oat flake flour caused starch retrogradation decreases, with the breakdown being lower compared to that recorded for the oat flake flour. Pumpkin seed protein powder addition enhanced the thermo-mechanical protein weakening observed. In addition, decreases in starch gelatinization, breakdown, and starch retrogradation were observed when substituting rice flour with pumpkin seed protein powder. The breads prepared with higher amounts of water presented better specific volumes and crumb firmness.

Author Contributions: Conceptualization, I.A. and I.B.; methodology, I.B.; validation, I.A.; formal analysis, I.B.; investigation, I.B. and I.A.; writing—original draft preparation, I.B.; writing—review and editing, I.A.; supervision, I.A. All authors have read and agreed to the published version of the manuscript.

Funding: This research received no external funding.

Data Availability Statement: Data are contained within the article.

Acknowledgments: The Integrated Center for Research, Expertise, and Technological Transfer in the Food Industry is acknowledged for providing technical support.

Conflicts of Interest: The authors declare no conflicts of interest.

References

1. Celiac Disease Foundation. Incidence of Celiac Disease Steadily Increasing. 2020. Available online: https://celiac.org/about-the-foundation/featured-news/2020/02/incidence-of-celiac-disease-steadily-increasing/ (accessed on 23 February 2023).
2. See, J.A.; Kaukinen, K.; Makharia, G.K.; Gibson, P.R.; Murray, J.A. Practical insights into gluten-free diets. *Nat. Rev. Gastroenterol. Hepatol.* **2015**, *12*, 580–591. [CrossRef] [PubMed]
3. Badiu, E.; Aprodu, I.; Banu, I. Trends in the development of gluten-free bakery products. *Ann. Univ. Dunarea Galati Fascic. VI-Food Technol.* **2014**, *38*, 21–36.
4. Marco, C.; Rosell, C.M. Breadmaking performance of protein enriched, gluten-free breads. *Eur. Food Res. Technol.* **2008**, *227*, 1205–1213. [CrossRef]
5. Ghanghas, N.; Mukilan, M.T.; Sharma, S.; Prabhakar, P. Classification, composition, extraction, functional modification and application of rice (*Oryza sativa*) seed protein: A comprehensive review. *Food Rev. Int.* **2022**, *38*, 354–383. [CrossRef]
6. Kadan, R.S.; Bryant, R.J.; Miller, J.A. Effects of milling on functional properties of rice flour. *J. Food Sci.* **2008**, *73*, 151–154. [CrossRef] [PubMed]
7. AOECS. *AOECS Standard for Gluten-Free Foods*; Association of European Coeliac Societies: Brussels, Belgium, 2016.
8. USDA. 2022. Available online: https://fdc.nal.usda.gov/fdc-app.html#/food-details/2261421/nutrients (accessed on 23 February 2023).
9. Mao, H.; Xu, M.; Ji, J.; Zhou, M.; Li, H.; Wen, Y.; Wang, J.; Sun, B. The utilization of oat for the production of wholegrain foods: Processing technology and products. *Food Front.* **2022**, *4*, 28–45. [CrossRef]

10. Punia, S.; Sandhu, K.S.; Dhull, S.B.; Siroha, A.K.; Purewal, S.S.; Kaur, M.; Kidwai, M.K. Oat starch: Physico-chemical, morphological, rheological characteristics and its applications—A review. *Int. J. Biol. Macromol.* **2020**, *154*, 493–498. [CrossRef] [PubMed]
11. Smulders, M.J.M.; van de Wiel, C.C.M.; van den Broeck, H.C.; van der Meer, I.M.; Israel-Hoevelaken, T.P.M.; Timmer, R.D.; van Dinter, B.-J.; Braun, S.; Gilissen, L.J.W.J. Oats in healthy gluten-free and regular diets: A perspective. *Food Res. Int.* **2018**, *110*, 3–10. [CrossRef] [PubMed]
12. Hussain, A.; Kausar, T.; Sehar, S.; Sarwar, A.; Ashraf, A.H.; Jamil, M.A.; Noreen, S.; Rafique, A.; Iftikhar, K.; Aslam, J.; et al. Utilization of pumpkin, pumpkin powders, extracts, isolates, purified bioactives and pumpkin based functional food products: A key strategy to improve health in current post COVID 19 period: An updated review. *Appl. Food Res.* **2022**, *2*, 100241. [CrossRef]
13. Vinayashreea, S.; Vasu, P. Biochemical, nutritional and functional properties of protein isolate and fractions from pumpkin (*Cucurbita moschata* var. Kashi Harit) seeds. *Food Chem.* **2021**, *340*, 128177. [CrossRef]
14. Litvynchuk, S.; Galenko, O.; Cavicchi, A.; Ceccanti, C.; Mignani, C.; Guidi, L.; Shevchenko, A. Conformational Changes in the Structure of Dough and Bread Enriched with Pumpkin Seed Flour. *Plants* **2022**, *11*, 2762. [CrossRef] [PubMed]
15. *SR ISO 712:2005, SR ISO 2171:2002 and SR 91:2007*; Romanian Standards Catalog for Cereal and Milling Products Analysis. ASRO: Bucharest, Romania, 2008.
16. Flander, L.; Salmenkallio-Marttila, M.; Suortti, T.; Autio, K. Optimization of ingredients and baking process for improved wholemeal oat bread quality. *LWT-Food Sci. Technol.* **2007**, *40*, 860–870. [CrossRef]
17. Torbica, A.; Belovic, M.; Tomic, J. Novel breads of non-wheat flours. *Food Chem.* **2019**, *282*, 134–140. [CrossRef] [PubMed]
18. Dubat, A.; Boinot, N. *Mixolab Applications Handbook. Rheological and Enzymes Analyses*; Chopin Technology: Villenueve, France, 2012; p. 14.
19. Svec, I.; Hruskova, M. The Mixolab parameters of composite wheat/hemp flour and their relation to quality features. *LWT-Food Sci. Technol.* **2015**, *60*, 623–629. [CrossRef]
20. Pătrașcu, L.; Banu, I.; Vasilean, I.; Aprodu, I. Effect of gluten, egg and soy proteins on the rheological and thermo-mechanical properties of wholegrain rice flour. *Food Sci. Technol. Int.* **2017**, *23*, 142–155. [CrossRef] [PubMed]
21. Hüttner, E.K.; Dal Bello, F.; Arendt, E.K. Rheological properties and bread making performance of commercial wholegrain oat flours. *J. Cereal Sci.* **2010**, *52*, 65–71. [CrossRef]
22. Cappa, C.; Lucisano, M.; Mariotti, M. Influence of Psyllium, sugar beet fibre and water on gluten-free dough properties and bread quality. *Carbohydr. Polym.* **2013**, *98*, 1657–1666. [CrossRef] [PubMed]
23. Amagliani, L.; O'Regan, J.; Kelly, A.L.; O'Mahony, J.A. The composition, extraction, functionality and applications of rice proteins: A review. *Trends Food Sci. Technol.* **2017**, *64*, 1–12. [CrossRef]
24. Boukid, F. Oat proteins as emerging ingredients for food formulation: Where we stand? *Eur. Food Res. Technol.* **2021**, *247*, 535–544. [CrossRef]
25. Yue, J.; Gu, X.; Zhu, Z.; Yi, J.; Ohm, J.B.; Chen, B.; Rao, J. Impact of defatting treatment and oat varieties on structural, functional properties, and aromatic profile of oat protein. *Food Hydrocoll.* **2021**, *112*, 106368. [CrossRef]
26. Gates, F. *Role of Heat Treatment in the Processing and Quality of Oat Flakes*; University of Helsinki: Helsinki, Finland, 2007.
27. Gu, Y.; Qian, X.; Sun, B.; Wang, X.; Ma, S. Effects of gelatinization degree and boiling water kneading on the rheology characteristics of gluten-free oat dough. *Food Chem.* **2023**, *404*, 13471. [CrossRef] [PubMed]
28. Zhang, M.; Bai, X.; Zhang, Z. Extrusion process improves the functionality of soluble dietary fiber in oat bran. *J. Cereal Sci.* **2011**, *54*, 98–103. [CrossRef]
29. Huth, M.; Dongowski, G.; Gebhardt, E.; Flamme, W. Functional properties of dietary fibre enriched extrudates from barley. *J. Cereal Sci.* **2000**, *32*, 115–128. [CrossRef]
30. Li, H.Y.; Wen, Y.Y.; Wang, J.; Sun, B.G. Relations between chain length distribution, molecular size, and amylose content of rice starches. *Int. J. Biol. Macromol.* **2018**, *120*, 2017–2025. [CrossRef] [PubMed]
31. Li, H.Y.; Lei, N.Y.; Yan, S.; Gao, M.Y.; Yang, J.Y.; Wang, J.; Sun, B.G. Molecular causes for the effect of cooking methods on rice stickiness: A mechanism explanation from the view of starch leaching. *Int. J. Biol. Macromol.* **2019**, *128*, 49–53. [CrossRef] [PubMed]
32. Banu, I.; Aprodu, I. Investigations on functional and thermo-mechanical properties of gluten free cereal and pseudocereal flours. *Foods* **2022**, *11*, 1857. [CrossRef] [PubMed]
33. Duta, D.E.; Culetu, A. Evaluation of rheological, physicochemical, thermal, mechanical and sensory properties of oat-based gluten free cookies. *J. Food Eng.* **2015**, *162*, 1–8. [CrossRef]
34. Alshehry, G.A. Preparation and nutritional properties of cookies from the partial replacement of wheat flour using pumpkin seeds powder. *World J. Environ. Biosci.* **2020**, *9*, 48–56.
35. Du, H.; Zhang, J.; Wang, S.; Manyande, A.; Wang, J. Effect of high-intensity ultrasonic treatment on the physicochemical, structural, rheological, behavioral, and foaming properties of pumpkin (*Cucurbita moschata* Duch.)-seed protein isolates. *LWT-Food Sci. Technol.* **2022**, *155*, 112952. [CrossRef]
36. Zheng, L.; Wang, Z.; He, Z.; Zeng, M.; Qui, F.; Chen, J. Physicochemical and gel properties of pumpkin seed protein: A comparative study. *Int. J. Food Sci. Technol.* **2023**, *58*, 1639–1651. [CrossRef]
37. Martinez, M.M.; Oliete, B.; Roman, L.; Gomez, M. Influence of the addition of extruded flours on rice bread quality. *J. Food Qual.* **2014**, *37*, 83–94. [CrossRef]

38. Dabash, V.; Buresova, I.; Tokar, M.; Zacharova, M.; Gal, R. The effect of added pumpkin flour on sensory and textural quality of rice bread. *J. Microbiol. Biotechnol. Food Sci.* **2017**, *6*, 1269–1271. [CrossRef]
39. El-Soukkary, F.A.H. Evaluation of pumpkin seed products for bread fortification. *Plant Foods Hum. Nutr.* **2001**, *56*, 365–384. [CrossRef]
40. Gallagher, E.; Gormley, T.R.; Arendt, E.K. Crust and crumb characteristics of gluten free breads. *J. Food Eng.* **2003**, *56*, 153–161. [CrossRef]
41. Gormley, T.R.; Morrissey, A. A note on the evaluation of wheaten breads containing oat flour or oat flakes. *Ir. J. Agric. Food Res.* **1993**, *32*, 205–209.
42. Huttner, E.K.; Dal Bello, F.; Zannini, E.; Titze, J.; Beuch, S.; Arendt, E.K. Physicochemical properties of oat varieties and their potential for breadmaking. *Cereal Chem.* **2011**, *88*, 602–608. [CrossRef]
43. Belc, N.; Duta, D.E.; Culetu, A.; Stamatie, G.D. Type and amount of legume protein concentrate influencing the technological, nutritional, and sensorial properties of wheat bread. *Appl. Sci.* **2021**, *11*, 436. [CrossRef]

Disclaimer/Publisher's Note: The statements, opinions and data contained in all publications are solely those of the individual author(s) and contributor(s) and not of MDPI and/or the editor(s). MDPI and/or the editor(s) disclaim responsibility for any injury to people or property resulting from any ideas, methods, instructions or products referred to in the content.

Article

The Effect of Inulin Addition on Rice Dough and Bread Characteristics

Iva Burešová [1], Romana Šebestíková [1], Jaromír Šebela [1], Anna Adámková [2], Magdalena Zvonková [2], Nela Skowronková [2] and Jiří Mlček [2,*]

[1] Department of Food Technology, Faculty of Technology, Tomas Bata University in Zlín, nám. T. G. Masaryka 5555, 760 01 Zlín, Czech Republic; buresova@utb.cz (I.B.); r_sebestikova@utb.cz (R.Š.); j_sebela@utb.cz (J.Š.)
[2] Department of Food Analysis and Chemistry, Faculty of Technology, Tomas Bata University in Zlín, nám. T. G. Masaryka 5555, 760 01 Zlín, Czech Republic; aadamkova@utb.cz (A.A.); m1_zvonkova@utb.cz (M.Z.); n_skowronkova@utb.cz (N.S.)
* Correspondence: mlcek@utb.cz; Tel.: +420-576-033-030

Featured Application: The obtained results may be applied in gluten-free bread production.

Abstract: Inulin may be widely used in in the food industry due to its many health benefits. It has the potential to increase the insufficient nutritional quality of gluten-free bread. Therefore, the aim of this study was to test the applicability of inulin in rice baking. The impact of added inulin (5%, 10%, 20%, 30%, and 40%) on the dough's rheological, bread's textural and sensory characteristics was evaluated. The extensibility of rice dough during uniaxial deformation tests (8.5 mm) was improved by the added inulin (10.2–12.3 mm). The presence of inulin softened the dough and shifted the gelatinization temperature toward higher values. The added inulin also increased the loaf's specific volume (1.16–1.48 mL/g), tenderized the breadcrumbs, increased the crumb porosity (36–58%), and generally improved the crumb structure. The panelists favored the sensory characteristics of breads with inulin. However, baking losses were increased in these breads as well (15.1–18.5%). The effect of the added inulin on the dough and bread characteristics generally rose with an increasing addition of inulin, reaching the maximum in samples with 30% inulin. The presence of 40% inulin deteriorated some characteristics of the bread. Therefore, the addition of up to 30% of inulin seemed to be optimal for rice bread.

Keywords: dough extensibility; bread texture; bread volume; baking losses; sensory characteristics; oligofructose

Citation: Burešová, I.; Šebestíková, R.; Šebela, J.; Adámková, A.; Zvonková, M.; Skowronková, N.; Mlček, J. The Effect of Inulin Addition on Rice Dough and Bread Characteristics. *Appl. Sci.* **2024**, *14*, 2882. https://doi.org/10.3390/app14072882

Academic Editors: Anna Wirkijowska, Piotr Zarzycki, Agata Blicharz-Kania and Urszula Pankiewicz

Received: 27 February 2024
Revised: 25 March 2024
Accepted: 26 March 2024
Published: 29 March 2024

Copyright: © 2024 by the authors. Licensee MDPI, Basel, Switzerland. This article is an open access article distributed under the terms and conditions of the Creative Commons Attribution (CC BY) license (https://creativecommons.org/licenses/by/4.0/).

1. Introduction

Inulin is widely found in more than 36,000 plant species as a reserve polysaccharide. It is commonly extracted from inulin-containing plant sources, such as chicory roots (*Cichorium intybus* L.) and Jerusalem artichoke tubers (*Helianthus tuberosus* L.), as well as from novel sources, such as globe artichoke inflorescence (*Cynara cardunculus* L.) and its by-products [1]. Inulin is a linear polydisperse carbohydrate material consisting mainly of β-(1→2) fructosyl-fructose links. Because of the β configuration of the anomeric C2 in its fructose monomers, inulin resists hydrolysis by the digestive enzymes found inside the human small intestine, being classified as nondigestible food fiber [2–4]. Inulin reduces the risk of gastrointestinal diseases, decreases the levels of pathogenic bacteria in the intestine, and relieves constipation. A beneficial effect on bowel function is obtained with a daily intake of 12 g of inulin [2,5,6]. It exhibits many other health benefits; it stimulates the human body's immune system, decreases the risk of osteoporosis by increasing mineral absorption, and does not lead to a rise in serum glucose or stimulate insulin secretion, among other benefits [2,5,7,8].

Inulin may be widely used in the food industry as a prebiotic, a fat and sugar replacer, as well as dietary fiber [5]. It is stable in temperatures up to 140 °C and can, therefore, be processed easily in bread baking [9]. Inulin incorporation into baked goods can increase their nutritional quality as well as technological properties [10]. It is used to replace flour in bread at a rate of 3–10%. Inulin is not considered to be a food additive [11]. Its taste is neutral, being without any off-flavors or an aftertaste [12]. Since it exhibits many health benefits, it can be used ad libitum [9].

Approximately 93% of individuals with celiac disease consume bread daily [13]. Commercially produced breads are often prepared from various blends of starches and flours [14,15]. The absence of gluten presents a technological challenge, as wheat proteins play crucial roles in bread production and quality [16]. During dough preparation, proteins form a continuous matrix with viscoelastic behavior [17]. Wheat dough exhibits a high capacity to retain CO_2 and has low consistency. These properties result in high-quality bread with a large volume and good textural parameters, such as low hardness, high cohesiveness, and resilience [17]. In contrast, gluten-free doughs display different characteristics, which may be attributed to the molecular weight of the protein molecules and variations in chemical composition, primarily a lower content of the amino acid lysine [18]. Rice flour is frequently used in gluten-free bread baking because of its colorlessness, nutritional characteristics, bland taste, and low hypoallergenic properties. Flours with more distinctive colors, tastes, and flavors compared with wheat may not appeal to some consumers [19–21]. Although nutritional quality varies among products, gluten-free bread is usually low in fiber, proteins, micronutrients, vitamins, and minerals such as iron, zinc, magnesium, and calcium [14,19,20,22]. Gluten-free breads have a higher glycemic index than gluten-containing products because of the use of starches and sugars [23,24]. The texture and taste of bread are the most important characteristics and are often the main reasons why people dislike currently available gluten-free bread [13].

Inulin's ability to create a gel might be expected to improve the poor ability of gluten-free dough to trap leavening gas. However, the inulin's ability to form a gel is affected by the length of its chain. Short-chain inulin cannot form a gel, natural inulin forms a gel at concentrations above 30% w/w, and long-chain inulin forms a gel in the range of 20–40% w/w at room temperature due to its lower water solubility [10]. A positive impact of inulin on the crumb structure and volume of gluten-free bread prepared from a blend of rice flour, cassava starch, and soy flour, as well as a mixture of rice and acorn flours coupled with a mixture of corn starch and potato starch, has been previously described [25–27]. Due to its numerous health benefits, neutral taste, and the fact that it is not considered a food additive, inulin has great potential to increase the nutritional value of rice bread, which is a critical issue that needs to be addressed [14]. A higher inulin addition (up to 40%) than the previously published 10% was involved in this study. The aim of this paper is to describe the impact of inulin, ranging from 5% to 40%, on the rheological, textural, and sensory characteristics of rice dough and bread. The applicability of inulin in rice bread baking is also evaluated.

2. Materials and Methods

2.1. Material

Rice flour (89.7 g carbohydrates, 7.7 g protein, 1.3 g fat, and 1.3 g fiber per 100 g of dry flour) was kindly provided by Extrudo Bečice (s.r.o., Týn nad Vltavou, Czech Republic). The natural inulin from chicory roots in the form of white powder with an average particle size of 60–80 μm, inulin content of 90–99%, and degree of polymerization of 2–60 was kindly provided by Brenntag CR (spol. s r.o., Prague, Czech Republic). The substitution of 5%, 10%, 20%, 30%, and 40% inulin in rice flour was tested.

2.2. Dough Behavior during Uniaxial Deformation

The dough samples meant for studying the behavior under uniaxial deformation were prepared using flour or a blend of flour and inulin (10 g) mixed with water. Pure rice flour was mixed with 9 g of water. The amount of water used in the samples made from the blend of rice flour and inulin was determined by experimentation as the amount of water required to obtain a dough capable of holding together and not falling apart before testing. All ingredients were manually mixed inside a beaker. After mixing, the dough was given a rest period of around (40 ± 1) min at a temperature of (30 ± 1) °C. The sample was prepared, and the test was performed according to Smewing [28] using a TA.XT plus texture analyzer (Stable Micro Systems Ltd., Godalming, UK) equipped with an SMS/Kieffer Dough and Gluten Extensibility Rig. The dough was formed into 5 cm-long pieces with a trapezoidal cross-section (3 mm, 5 mm, and 4 mm). Every sample was stretched by the hook until it broke. The hook progressed at a speed of 3.30 mm/s during the test, with a trigger force of 0.5 g. The test measured both the force necessary to stretch the dough sample as well as the hook's displacement over time. The resistance to stretching, represented by R_m (N), was marked at its peak force. Correspondingly, the extensibility, noted as E (mm), was tracked at the point where the peak force was applied. Moreover, the *Area* under the curve was calculated. Each test was performed on dough samples prepared in at least seven replicates.

2.3. Rheological Characterization of Dough during Heating

The samples for testing the dough behavior during the heating test were prepared from flour or a flour/inulin blend (10 g) and water (10 g). All ingredients were mixed manually in a beaker. After the mixture was prepared, the dough was left to relax at an ambient temperature of (30 ± 1) °C for a period of approximately (5 ± 1) min in a beaker covered by a glass plate. The dough was placed between the 35 mm parallel P35 Ti L plates and compressed to a gap adjusted to 1.5 mm. The dough edges were trimmed with a spatula. To prevent the dough from drying out, the exposed side of the dough was coated with a methyl silicone polymer Lukopren N1000 (Lučební závody a.s. Kolín, Czech Republic). An oscillatory temperature ramp of 30–90 °C at 0.058 °C/s was performed using the HAAKE RheoStress 1 (Thermo Scientific, Prague, Czech Republic) to evaluate thermally induced changes in the dough's complex viscosity η^*. The testing procedure was conducted while maintaining a strain of 0.1% and a steady frequency of 1 Hz within the linear viscoelastic region. Each test was performed on dough samples prepared in at least five replicates.

2.4. Bread Preparation

The dough was prepared by mixing rice flour (100%), water (100%), sucrose (1.86%), salt (1.50%), and active dry yeast (1.80%). The part of flour (5%, 10%, 20%, 30%, and 40%) was replaced by inulin. The amounts of all ingredients were related to flour or flour/inulin dry matter.

Dry yeast was reactivated for 10 ± 1 min in a sugar solution (35 ± 1) °C. The ingredients were placed into an Eta Exclusive Gratus mixer bowl (Eta, a.s. Prague, Czech Republic) and mixed for 6 min. The dough (1000 g) was divided into 3 bread pans (12 cm × 26.5 cm × 7 cm) and placed into a proofer for (60 ± 2) min at (30 ± 1) °C and 85% relative air humidity. The loaves were baked for 40 ± 2 min at 180 ± 5 °C (MIWE cube, Pekass s.r.o. Plzeň, Czech Republic). The baked breads were removed from the pans and stored at room temperature (21 ± 3) °C for 2 h. The loaf volume was determined using plastic granulates of rape seed size. The loaf-specific volume (mL/g) was obtained by dividing the bread volume by the bread weight. The baking loss (%) was calculated as [(the weight of dough in pan before baking − the weight of bread after cooling)/(the weight of dough in pan before baking)] × 100. Loaf specific volume and baking loss were determined in at least six repetitions.

2.5. Properties of Breadcrumbs

For texture profile analysis (TPA) measurements, bread samples 35 mm in diameter and 10 mm in height were obtained from the center of each loaf. The sample was placed on the base of a TA.TX plus texture analyzer (Stable Micro Systems Ltd., UK) and squeezed twice to 4 mm with a 75.0 mm diameter P/75 cylinder probe. The probe test speed was 1.00 mm/s. The crumb parameters (hardness, springiness, cohesiveness, resilience, adhesiveness, and chewiness) were calculated. Hardness (N) is the peak force that occurs during the first compression. Springiness is the ability to spring back after the sample was deformed during the first compression and then allowed to rest for the target time. Cohesiveness is how well the sample withstands a second deformation relative to its resistance under the first deformation. Resilience is the sample's ability to regain its original height. Chewiness is the energy needed to chew the sample until it is ready to be swallowed [29]. At least five samples from each loaf were obtained and tested.

The pictures of the breadcrumbs were saved as bitmap files. Their resolution was 300 DPI in real-color format (RGB, 256 million colors). The images were then cropped to a resolution of 420 pixels. The cropped images were duplicated and converted into an 8 bit grayscale image. The grayscale images were thresholded using the software Paint Shop Pro XI (Corel Corporation, Ottawa, ON, Canada), which allowed conversion of the images into black and white colors. The pore number per image was calculated using the histogram tool in Paint Shop Pro. The porosity was determined in two replications.

2.6. Sensory Evaluation

A group of 30 highly motivated employees and students of the department, both male and female and between 19 and 65 years of age, were recruited to form the panel. The panelists were selected based on their availability, attitudes toward the products to be assessed, knowledge and skills, ability to communicate, and other aspects specified by ISO 8586 [30]. Sensory panel training was carried out according to Ellia [31] in sessions of 200 min divided into two parts: (1) training for the general aspects of sensory techniques and analysis and (2) training for the more specific characteristics of the bread. A panel of 20 members was involved in the sensory evaluation of the bread with added inulin. Six panel members were excluded from the evaluation due to disability or economic reasons.

The sensory evaluation was performed under standard conditions (ISO 8589) [32]. A nine-point hedonic scale (from 1 (dislike extremely) to 9 (like extremely)) was used to evaluate the crust appearance and color, crumb appearance and color, porosity, aroma, taste, and overall acceptability of the breads.

2.7. Statistical Analysis

The Shapiro–Wilk test was used to test the distribution of the obtained data sets. If the data set followed a normal distribution, then parametric analysis of variance (ANOVA) was used to test the significance of the differences among the samples. Differences were tested on $\alpha = 0.05$ significance level using the Tukey test. The results were expressed as mean values and a standard deviation.

If the data set did not follow a normal distribution, a non-parametric Kruskal–Wallis test, together with multiple comparison of the z' values and p values, was used to test the significant differences among samples. The results were expressed as median values.

Statistical analyses were performed using Statistica 13.0 (TIBCO Software s.r.o., Prague, Czech Republic).

3. Results and Discussion

3.1. The Effect of Inulin on Dough Characteristics

The addition of inulin had a notable impact on the dough behavior during uniaxial elongation tests. The presence of inulin weakened the rice dough, which is evident from the significant decrease in the dough's resistance to elongation (R_m) recorded in the samples with added inulin (Table 1). The weakening effect of the added inulin was also apparent in the values of the *Area* parameter, which relates to the energy required for dough deformation. The samples with added inulin required less energy for deformation (306–683 mN mm) than the samples made from pure rice flour (704 mN mm).

Conversely, the added inulin had the opposite effect on the wheat dough with 2–8% added inulin [33,34]. These results were explained by the interaction between inulin and gluten. The proteins in rice flour have a lower molecular weight than those in gluten, and they also differ in chemical composition [18], which may account for our observations. Inulin competed with starch for water in the dough and reduced the available water for starch hydration. Therefore, inulin's water binding ability was probably a key factor in modifying the dough properties [35], and this likely negated the differences between the samples with added inulin.

Table 1. Effect of inulin on rice dough resistance to extension R, area under curve Area, and extensibility E recorded during uniaxial deformation test [1].

Inulin (%)	R_m (mN)	Area (mN mm)	E (mm)
0	131 ± 13 a	704 ± 90 a	8.5 ± 0.4 b
5	57 ± 9 b	683 ± 90 a	10.2 ± 0.9 a
10	60 ± 7 b	472 ± 90 b	12.1 ± 0.9 a
20	64 ± 6 b	382 ± 95 bc	12.3 ± 0.9 a
30	67 ± 6 b	442 ± 80 b	11.4 ± 0.4 a
40	57 ± 2 b	306 ± 70 c	8.9 ± 0.3 b

[1] Mean values ± standard deviation (n = 7) followed by different letters in the column differ significantly ($p < 0.05$).

Extensibility E is another parameter that was recorded during the uniaxial elongation tests. The values of extensibility rose with the increasing amount of inulin and, after reaching a maximal extensibility in a sample with 20% inulin, the extensibility started to decrease. The differences between samples (5–30% inulin) were, however, not significant. The presence of inulin increased the polymerization of proteins present in the rice flour [33], which improved the doughs' ability to elongate. The 40% added inulin was probably higher than optimal, resulting in a negative impact on the dough characteristics. Since gluten-free doughs generally exhibit an insufficient ability to elongate and trap leavening gas, which is crucial for obtaining bread with the desired volume [36], the addition of up to 30% of inulin seems to be optimal to prepare dough with improved elongational characteristics.

The weakening effect of inulin on rice dough was also recorded during the heating tests (Figure 1). The complex viscosity η^* at the beginning of the heating tests was decreased by the presence of 10%, 20%, 30%, and 40% inulin. The thermally induced changes recorded in the dough with 5% added inulin was close to the dough prepared from pure rice flour. The presence of higher amounts of inulin (10–40%) resulted in a shift of the temperature of starch gelatinization toward higher values. This effect rose with a rising amount of inulin. Inulin is known to take part in the competition for water and may bind a part of water during dough mixing. Furthermore, the viscosity of an inulin solution is quite low [9], which may account for the decrease in complex viscosity observed in the samples containing inulin. When water was released from proteins denatured by temperature, inulin bound to a portion of this water, thereby reducing the dough viscosity. Furthermore, due to its hydrophilic nature, inulin competed with starch for the water necessary for starch gelatinization, resulting in an increase in the gelatinization temperature [37–39].

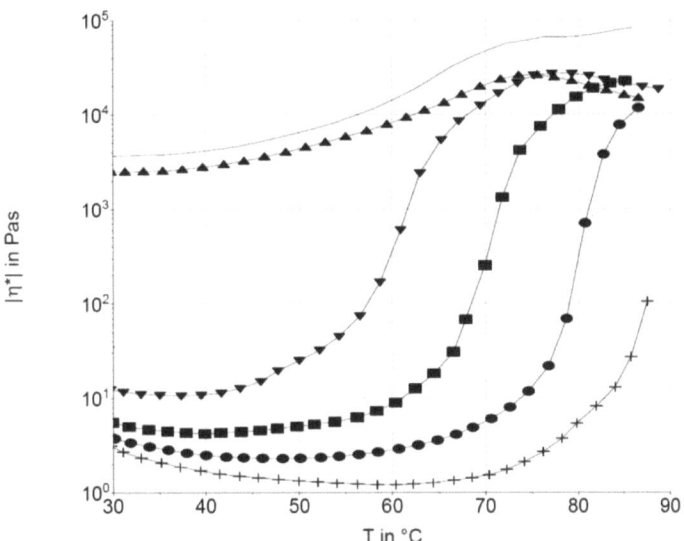

Figure 1. Thermally induced changes of complex viscosity η^* recorded in rice dough with added inulin (— 0%; ▲ 5%; ▼ 10%; ■ 20%; ● 30%; † 40%).

3.2. Effect of Inulin on Bread Characteristics

Baking losses represent the amount of water evaporating from dough during baking and cooling. The values of this parameter rose with an increasing amount of added inulin in samples with 0%, 5%, 10%, and 20% inulin, reaching the maximal value in bread containing 30% inulin (18.5%) (Table 2). The bread containing 40% inulin exhibited a lower value (17.1%). Water plays an important role in bread baking. It is used to hydrate proteins and starch granules during dough mixing. During baking, water is released from denatured proteins and is used for gelatinizing a part of the starch granules [17]. Since the flour was replaced by inulin in the tested samples, the content of starch was lower in these doughs than in the dough made from pure rice flour. Water released from denatured proteins might be used for starch gelatinization or might evaporate. Since the addition of inulin shifted the gelatinization temperature to higher values, a part of the water released from denatured proteins could not be used for starch gelatinization, evaporating from the dough, which was recorded as an increase in baking losses. Gelatinized starch plays a role in retaining gas in the dough and preventing bubbles from coalescing during the baking process [40]. This impacts the bread volume and breadcrumb porosity. The loaf's specific volume generally increased with an inulin content in the range of 0–30%, reaching a maximum in the bread with 30% added inulin (1.48 mL/g). A similar effect of inulin was observed in gluten-free breads prepared from blends of corn and potato starch, as well as in wheat bread. However, the addition of inulin did not exceed 12% in these studies [26,41,42]. The authors explained these observations as a competition between inulin and starch for water during baking. The decrease in water availability retards starch gelatinization, resulting in a delay in the formation of a viscous gel and solid-like behavior in the dough. Prolonged formation of the solid-like dough structure allowed for accumulation of the leavening gas in doughs, even at higher temperatures, until the yeast was inactivated. This effect increased with the addition of inulin. The considerable delay in gelatinization observed in the sample with 40% inulin (Figure 1) shifted the formation of solid-like dough structures to temperatures where the yeast was already inactivated, resulting in a significantly lower loaf-specific volume (1.16 mL/g). Even though the loaf-specific volume increased in the bread with 5–30% added inulin, this parameter remained lower than in wheat bread with added inulin [41].

Table 2. Effect of inulin on characteristics of rice bread and breadcrumbs [1].

Inulin (%)	Loaf-Specific Volume (mL/g)	Baking Losses (%)	Hardness (N)	Springiness (%)	Cohesiveness (%)	Resilience (%)	Adhesiveness (N s)	Chewiness (J)	Porosity (%)
0	1.16 ± 0.07 e	15.1 ± 0.2 c	24 ± 4 a	79 ± 6 ab	78 ± 5 a	47 ± 2 a	0.33 ± 0.09 a	15.1 ± 3.5 a	36
5	1.17 ± 0.02 e	15.6 ± 0.2 c	23 ± 3 a	77 ± 6 ab	77 ± 2 ab	45 ± 2 ab	0.16 ± 0.09 ab	13.5 ± 2.9 a	58
10	1.41 ± 0.02 b	16.8 ± 0.3 b	17 ± 2 b	77 ± 6 ab	79 ± 3 a	48 ± 3 a	0.22 ± 0.09 a	12.1 ± 1.7 a	55
20	1.35 ± 0.02 c	16.7 ± 0.2 b	16 ± 3 b	70 ± 8 ab	75 ± 3 ab	41 ± 4 bc	0.05 ± 0.02 b	10.4 ± 2.9 a	57
30	1.48 ± 0.02 a	18.5 ± 0.2 a	18 ± 4 ab	83 ± 2 a	80 ± 5 a	48 ± 3 a	0.02 ± 0.02 b	8.1 ± 0.9 b	55
40	1.29 ± 0.02 d	17.1 ± 0.5 b	20 ± 4 ab	63 ± 8 b	72 ± 4 b	39 ± 3 c	0.04 ± 0.02 b	8.1 ± 1.0 b	33

[1] Mean values ± standard deviation followed by different letters in the column differ significantly ($p < 0.05$).

The presence of up to 30% inulin also had a positive effect on the crumb porosity. This parameter increased with the increasing content of inulin, reaching a maximum value in the bread containing 30% inulin. A similar positive effect from inulin was also observed in breads with 4–12% added inulin [26,42]. The formation of pores may be related to changes in dough gelatinization initiated by inulin. The shift in gelatinization temperature and viscosity changes recorded in doughs with 5–30% added inulin resulted in a better ability of these doughs to accumulate leavening gas inside the pores than that recorded in dough made from pure rice and dough with 40% added inulin. The changes in dough characteristics initiated by the presence of 40% inulin were too extensive, rendering the dough unable to accumulate leavening gas and creating smaller pores (Figure 2f). The greatest difference between the size of the pores situated in the inner and outer parts of the crumbs was observed in the bread without added inulin. Larger-sized pores were situated mainly in the central part of the bread (presented in Figure 2a). The size of the pores decreased toward the outer parts, thereby reducing the average porosity value.

The texture characteristics of the bread were only marginally impacted by the presence of inulin. Nonetheless, the breadcrumb hardness, chewiness, and adhesiveness generally decreased with the inclusion of inulin. This is a positive result, as hard breadcrumbs are a common defect associated with gluten-free bread. The positive influence on the crumb hardness rose slightly with the increasing content of inulin until it reached a minimum in the bread made from a blend containing 20% inulin. In the breads prepared from blends containing a higher amount of inulin (30% and 40%), the crumb hardness began to rise. The presence of small pores surrounded by a thick dough layer might explain the hard crumbs in these breads. A similar effect of inulin on the crumb hardness was also recorded in bread prepared from a blend of rice and acorn flours [27]. However, the impact on wheat bread was the opposite [34,43].

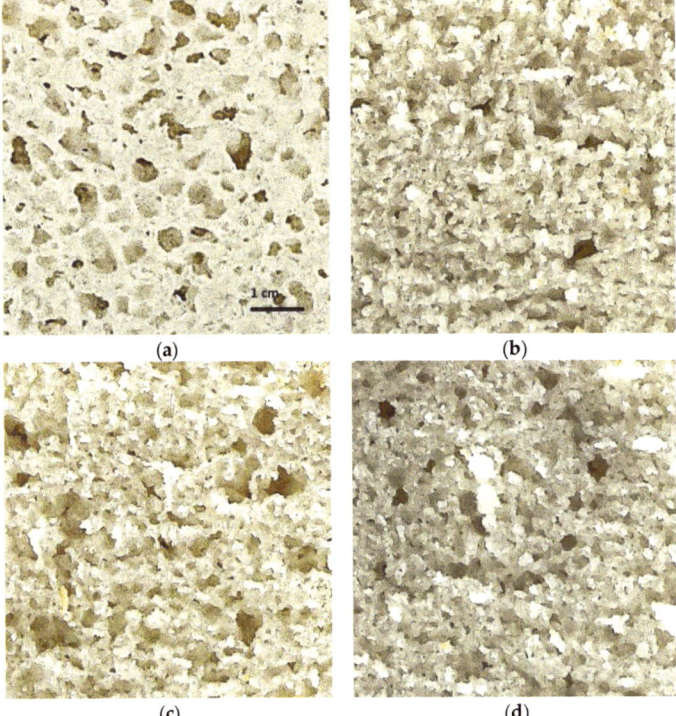

Figure 2. *Cont.*

Figure 2. Crumbs of bread prepared from rice flour with added inulin: (**a**) 0%; (**b**) 5%; (**c**) 10%; (**d**) 20%; (**e**) 30%; and (**f**) 40%.

The positive effect of inulin's addition on the crumb chewiness increased with the rising amount of added inulin. A significant impact on springiness, cohesiveness, and resilience was observed only in the bread prepared from the blend containing the highest amount of inulin (40%). Resilience and cohesiveness were decreased by inulin, suggesting a tendency for this bread to crumble when sliced or spread. A similar negative impact was not observed in the breads with 0%, 5%, 10%, 20%, and 30% added inulin. A similar effect was observed in steamed wheat bread [34], but other authors reported the opposite effect [27,43]. The observed discrepancies support the conclusion [7,10] that the effect of inulin on the textural characteristics is influenced by many factors affecting inulin function, including the degree of polymerization, the level of inulin replacement, type of fermentation, and protein characteristics. Moreover, these discrepancies highlight the need for further investigation into the effect of different types of inulin on the characteristics of bread prepared from various ingredients using different production technologies.

In our study, the addition of 30% inulin seemed to be optimal for producing bread with an acceptable loaf-specific volume, bread porosity, and other breadcrumb characteristics. However, it should be noted that higher baking losses should also be expected at the same time.

3.3. Effect of Inulin on Sensory Characteristics of Bread

Some of the sensory characteristics did not exhibit a normal distribution. Therefore, a Kruskal–Wallis test was applied to the sensory evaluation results, and the results were expressed as median values.

The crust and crumb color were similar in all breads (Figure 2a–f), and the evaluation of these parameters was not influenced by the content of inulin. Differences in crumb and crust color were not observed, as the content of short-chain inulin, which accelerates the Maillard reaction rate and forms a more appealing crust color [10], was not present in substantial amounts in the tested inulin. The panelists had divergent views on the color of the crust and crumb. One group found the pale color unattractive and tended to score it lower (1, 2, or 3 points). Conversely, other panelists found this color appealing and scored it with 7, 8, or 9 points. This resulted in a median value of 4–5 (Table 3). There was no tendency among the panelists to form separate groups with opposing views on any other parameter.

The evaluation of the other sensory characteristics generally rose with an increasing portion of inulin, reaching its maximum in the samples with 30% added inulin (Table 3). The panelists favored the bread with 30% added inulin. The overall acceptability of this sample lays between 7 (like moderately) and 8 (like very much). The panelists liked moderately (7) the crumb appearance and color, liked slightly (6) the crumb hardness and pore size and uniformity, and liked very much (8) the flavor intensity of this bread. Even if the presence of inulin was detected by the panelists in this bread, they found it pleasing and described its presence as "an evidence of healthy food". The panelists favored the bread containing 30% added inulin, which is in general agreement with the results of other tests, in which the samples with 30% added inulin were preferred as well. Even though the composition of the breads was not determined in this study, it can be assumed that the content of fiber in the bread with 30% added inulin was approximately 18 g/100 g. The average per capita bread consumption in Czech Republic is 136 g per day [44], which would equate to a daily intake of 23 g of inulin. This is close to the recommended intake of 25–30 g per day from food [45].

Table 3. Medians of the sensory parameters of breads with added inulin [1].

Inulin (%)	Crust Color	Crumb Color	Crumb Hardness	Pore (Size, Uniformity)	Flavor Intensity	Flavor Aftertaste	Overall Acceptability
0	5 a	4 a	5 ab	4 ab	3 b	3 b	3 ab
5	5 a	4 a	2 b	3 b	3 b	3 b	3 b
10	5 a	4 a	3 ab	6 a	3 b	4 ab	4 ab
20	5 a	4 a	3 ab	5 a	4 b	4 ab	4 b
30	5 a	4 a	6 a	6 a	8 a	5 a	8 a
40	5 a	4 a	2 b	2 b	2 b	3 b	2 b

[1] Score range: 1 = dislike extremely; 9 = like extremely. The median values (n = 20) followed by different letters in the column differ significantly.

The evaluation of the bread with 40% added inulin was even lower than that of the bread without added inulin. The panelists strongly disliked the hard crumb (2), small pores (2), and flavor intensity (2), and they moderately disliked the flavor's aftertaste (3). The small pores in this bread were surrounded by a thick dough layer (Figure 2f), which was perceived as hard crumbs. The characteristics of the breadcrumb can be explained by the low dough viscosity during baking and the delay in starch gelatinization (Figure 1). The dough viscosity required for the accumulation of an appropriate amount of leavening gas was probably reached when the yeast activity had already been retarded by high temperatures. Moreover, the intensity of flavor recognized in the bread with 40% inulin was too strong, thereby decreasing the evaluation of this bread.

4. Conclusions

The presence of inulin softened the dough and shifted the temperature of dough gelatinization toward higher temperatures. The added inulin positively decreased the crumb hardness, chewiness, and adhesiveness. A negative impact was recorded for the baking losses. This parameter, which is used to quantify the amount of water which evaporates from the dough during heating, was higher in the breads with added inulin. The added inulin had no significant effect on the springiness, cohesiveness, or resilience with up to 30% inulin, followed by a decrease in the values of these parameters in the bread with 40% added inulin. The addition of 30% inulin seemed to be optimal for obtaining rice bread with an acceptable loaf-specific volume, bread porosity, as well as other breadcrumb characteristics. The panelists favored this bread as well. It could be concluded that the addition of inulin should not exceed 30% to obtain rice bread with acceptable characteristics. The incorporation of inulin into commercially produced gluten-free bread could expand the range of nutritionally valuable bakery products. Consuming bread with 30% added inulin would equate to a daily intake of 23 g of inulin, which is close to the recommended value. Further research is required to test the applicability of inulin in the production of other types of bread. Given that inulin can replace fat and sugar, research focused on its applicability in pastry production may yield new results that can be applied in commercial bakeries.

Author Contributions: Conceptualization, I.B.; methodology, I.B.; software, I.B.; validation, I.B.; formal analysis, R.Š. and J.Š.; investigation, I.B. and R.Š.; resources, I.B. and J.M.; data curation, I.B.; writing—original draft preparation, I.B.; writing—review and editing, I.B., A.A., M.Z. and N.S.; visualization, I.B.; supervision, I.B. and J.M.; project administration, I.B.; funding acquisition, I.B. All authors have read and agreed to the published version of the manuscript.

Funding: This research was funded by IGA, grant numbers IGA/FT/2024/009 and IGA/FT/2024/006.

Institutional Review Board Statement: Not applicable.

Informed Consent Statement: Not applicable.

Data Availability Statement: The raw data supporting the conclusions of this article will be made available by the authors on request.

Acknowledgments: The authors sincerely thank David Bureš for the language help.

Conflicts of Interest: The authors declare no conflicts of interest.

References

1. Redondo-Cuenca, A.; Herrera-Vázquez, S.E.; Condezo-Hoyos, L.; Gómez-Ordóñez, E.; Rupérez, P. Inulin extraction from common inulin-containing plant sources. *Ind. Crops Prod.* **2021**, *170*, 113726. [CrossRef]
2. Kaur, N.; Gupta, A.K. Applications of inulin and oligofructose in health and nutrition. *J. Biosci.* **2002**, *27*, 703–714. [CrossRef] [PubMed]
3. Roberfroid, M.B. Introducing inulin-type fructans. *Br. J. Nutr.* **2005**, *93*, S13–S25. [CrossRef] [PubMed]
4. Roberfroid, M.B. Inulin-type fructans: Functional food ingredients. *J. Nutr.* **2007**, *137*, 2493S–2502S. [CrossRef] [PubMed]
5. Shoaib, M.; Shehzad, A.; Omar, M.; Rakha, A.; Raza, H.; Sharif, H.R.; Shakeel, A.; Ansari, A.; Niazi, S. Inulin: Properties, health benefits and food applications. *Carbohyd. Polym.* **2016**, *147*, 444–454. [CrossRef] [PubMed]
6. Commission Regulation (EU) 2015/2314 of 7 December 2015 Authorising a Health Claim Made on Foods, Other than Those Referring to the Reduction of Disease Risk and to Children's Development and Health and Amending Regulation (EU) No 432/2012 (Text with EEA Relevance). Available online: https://eur-lex.europa.eu/legal-content/en/ALL/?uri=CELEX:32015R2314 (accessed on 14 February 2024).
7. Morris, C.; Morris, G.A. The effect of inulin and fructo-oligosaccharide supplementation on the textural, rheological and sensory properties of bread and their role in weight management: A review. *Food Chem.* **2012**, *133*, 237–248. [CrossRef] [PubMed]
8. Niness, K.R. Inulin and oligofructose: What are they? *J. Nutr.* **1999**, *129*, 1402S–1406S. [CrossRef] [PubMed]
9. Meyer, D. Inulin. In *Handbook of Hydrocolloids*; Phillips, G.O., Williams, P.A., Eds.; CRC Press: Boca Raton, FL, USA, 2009; pp. 829–848.
10. Mohammadi, F.; Shiri, A.; Tahmouzi, S.; Mollakhalili-Meybodi, N.; Nematollahi, A. Application of inulin in bread: A review of technological properties and factors affecting its stability. *Food Sci. Nutr.* **2023**, *11*, 639–650. [CrossRef]
11. Regulation (EC) No 1333/2008 of The European Parliament and of The Council of 16 December 2008 on Food Additives (Text with EEA Relevance). Available online: https://eur-lex.europa.eu/legal-content/EN/TXT/HTML/?uri=CELEX:32008R1333 (accessed on 14 February 2024).
12. Wouters, R. Inulin. In *Stabilisers, Thickeners and Gelling Agents*; Imerson, A., Ed.; John Wiley and Sons, Ltd.: Chichester, UK, 2010; pp. 180–197.
13. Alencar, N.M.M.; de Araújo, V.A.; Faggian, L.; da Silveira Araújo, M.B.; Capriles, V.D. What about gluten-free products? An insight on celiac consumers' opinions and expectations. *J. Sens. Stud.* **2021**, *36*, e12664. [CrossRef]
14. Aguiar, E.V.; Santos, F.G.; Krupa-Kozak, U.; Capriles, V.D. Nutritional facts regarding commercially available gluten-free bread worldwide: Recent advances and future challenges. *Crit. Rev. Food Sci.* **2023**, *63*, 693–705. [CrossRef]
15. Roman, L.; Belorio, M.; Gomez, M. Gluten-free breads: The gap between research and commercial reality. *Compr. Rev. Food Sci. Food Saf.* **2019**, *18*, 690–702. [CrossRef] [PubMed]
16. Goesaert, H.; Brijs, K.; Veraverbeke, W.S.; Courtin, C.M.; Gebruers, K.; Delcour, J.A. Wheat flour constituents: How they impact bread quality, and how to impact their functionality. *Trends Food Sci. Technol.* **2005**, *16*, 12–30. [CrossRef]
17. Avramenko, N.A.; Tyler, R.T.; Scanlon, M.G.; Hucl, P.; Nickerson, M.T. The chemistry of bread making: The role of salt to ensure optimal functionality of its constituents. *Food Rev. Int.* **2018**, *34*, 204–225. [CrossRef]
18. Taylor, J.R.; Taylor, J.; Campanella, O.H.; Hamaker, B.R. Functionality of the storage proteins in gluten-free cereals and pseudocereals in dough systems. *J. Cereal Sci.* **2016**, *67*, 22–34. [CrossRef]
19. Arendt, E.K.; Dal Bello, F. Functional cereal products for those with gluten intolerance. In *Technology of Functional Cereal Products*; Hamaker, B.R., Ed.; Woodhead Publishing: Cambridge, UK, 2007; pp. 446–475.
20. Matos, M.E.; Rosell, C.M. Understanding gluten-free dough for reaching breads with physical quality and nutritional balance. *J. Sci. Food Agr.* **2015**, *95*, 653–661. [CrossRef] [PubMed]
21. Gujral, H.S.; Rosell, C.M. Improvement of the breadmaking quality of rice flour by glucose oxidase. *Food Res. Int.* **2004**, *37*, 75–81. [CrossRef]

22. Vici, G.; Belli, L.; Biondi, M.; Polzonetti, V. Gluten free diet and nutrient deficiencies: A review. *Clin. Nutr.* **2016**, *35*, 1236–1241. [CrossRef]
23. Matos Segura, M.E.; Rosell, C.M. Chemical composition and starch digestibility of different gluten-free breads. *Plant Foods Hum. Nutr.* **2011**, *66*, 224–230. [CrossRef]
24. Romão, B.; Botelho, R.B.A.; Alencar, E.R.; da Silva, V.S.N.; Pacheco, M.T.B.; Zandonadi, R.P. Chemical composition and glycemic index of gluten-free bread commercialized in Brazil. *Nutrients* **2020**, *12*, 2234. [CrossRef]
25. Sciarini, L.S.; Bustos, M.C.; Vignola, M.B.; Paesani, C.; Salinas, C.N.; Perez, G.T. A study on fibre addition to gluten free bread: Its effects on bread quality and in vitro digestibility. *J. Food Sci. Technol.* **2017**, *54*, 244–252. [CrossRef]
26. Ziobro, R.; Korus, J.; Juszczak, L.; Witczak, T. Influence of inulin on physical characteristics and staling rate of gluten-free bread. *J. Food Eng.* **2013**, *116*, 21–27. [CrossRef]
27. Shiri, A.; Ehrampoush, M.H.; Yasini Ardakani, S.A.; Shamsi, F.; Mollakhalili-Meybodi, N. Technological characteristics of inulin enriched gluten-free bread: Effect of acorn flour replacement and fermentation type. *Food Sci. Nutr.* **2021**, *9*, 6139–6151. [CrossRef]
28. Smewing, J. *Measurement of Dough and Gluten Extensibility Using the SMS/Kieffer Rig and the TA.XT2 Texture Analyser*; Stable Micro Systems Ltd.: Godalming, UK, 1995; 20p.
29. Trinh, K.T.; Glasgow, S. On the texture profile analysis test. In Proceedings of the Chemeca, Wellington, New Zealand, 23–26 September 2012.
30. *ISO 8586*; Sensory Analysis—General Guidelines for the Selection, Training and Monitoring of Selected Assessors and Expert Sensory Assessors. International Organization for Standardization: Geneva, Switzerland, 2012.
31. Elia, M. A procedure for sensory evaluation of bread: Protocol developed by a trained panel. *J. Sens. Stud.* **2011**, *26*, 269–277. [CrossRef]
32. *ISO 8589*; Sensory Analysis—General Guidance for the Design of Test Rooms. International Organization for Standardization: Geneva, Switzerland, 2007.
33. Liu, Y.; Leng, Y.; Xiao, S.; Zhang, Y.; Ding, W.; Ding, B.; Wu, Y.; Wang, X.; Fu, Y. Effect of inulin with different degrees of polymerization on dough rheology, gelatinization, texture and protein composition properties of extruded flour products. *LWT* **2022**, *159*, 113225. [CrossRef]
34. Luo, D.; Liang, X.; Xu, B.; Kou, X.; Li, P.; Han, S.; Liu, J.; Zhou, L. Effect of inulin with different degree of polymerization on plain wheat dough rheology and the quality of steamed bread. *J. Cereal Sci.* **2017**, *75*, 205–212. [CrossRef]
35. Juszczak, L.; Witczak, T.; Ziobro, R.; Korus, J.; Cieślik, E.; Witczak, M. Effect of inulin on rheological and thermal properties of gluten-free dough. *Carbohyd. Polym.* **2012**, *90*, 353–360. [CrossRef]
36. Burešová, I.; Kráčmar, S.; Dvořáková, P.; Středa, T. The relationship between rheological characteristics of gluten-free dough and the quality of biologically leavened bread. *J. Cereal Sci.* **2014**, *60*, 271–275. [CrossRef]
37. Hager, A.S.; Ryan, A.M.; Schwab, C.; Gänzle, M.G.; O'Doherty, J.V.; Arendt, E.K. Influence of the soluble fibres inulin and oat β-glucan on quality of dough and bread. *Eur. Food Res. Technol.* **2011**, *232*, 405–413. [CrossRef]
38. Tester, R.F.; Sommerville, M.D. The effects of non-starch polysaccharides on the extent of gelatinization, swelling and α-amylase hydrolysis of maize and wheat starches. *Food Hydrocoll.* **2003**, *17*, 41–54. [CrossRef]
39. Chen, Y.; Li, X.; Xu, F.; Yu, Q.; Zhang, Q. Effects of inulin with different polymerisation degrees on dough rheology and water distribution in the fresh noodles. *Int. J. Food Sci. Technol.* **2023**, *58*, 5418–5429. [CrossRef]
40. Hu, X.; Cheng, L.; Hong, Y.; Li, Z.; Li, C.; Gu, Z. An extensive review: How starch and gluten impact dough machinability and resultant bread qualities. *Crit. Rev. Food Sci.* **2023**, *63*, 1930–1941. [CrossRef] [PubMed]
41. Peressini, D.; Sensidoni, A. Effect of soluble dietary fibre addition on rheological and breadmaking properties of wheat doughs. *J. Cereal Sci.* **2009**, *49*, 190–201. [CrossRef]
42. Capriles, V.D.; Arêas, J.A. Effects of prebiotic inulin-type fructans on structure, quality, sensory acceptance and glycemic response of gluten-free breads. *Food Funct.* **2013**, *4*, 104–110. [CrossRef] [PubMed]
43. Rubel, I.A.; Pérez, E.E.; Manrique, G.D.; Genovese, D.B. Fibre enrichment of wheat bread with Jerusalem artichoke inulin: Effect on dough rheology and bread quality. *Food Struct.* **2015**, *3*, 21–29. [CrossRef]
44. Český Statistický Úřad. Available online: https://www.czso.cz/csu/xj/spotreba-potravin-1948-az-2022-v-grafech (accessed on 10 March 2024).
45. UCSF. Available online: https://www.ucsfhealth.org/education/increasing-fiber-intake (accessed on 10 March 2024).

Disclaimer/Publisher's Note: The statements, opinions and data contained in all publications are solely those of the individual author(s) and contributor(s) and not of MDPI and/or the editor(s). MDPI and/or the editor(s) disclaim responsibility for any injury to people or property resulting from any ideas, methods, instructions or products referred to in the content.

Article

The Influence of Arabinoxylan on the Properties of Sourdough Wheat Bread

Angelika Bieniek and Krzysztof Buksa *

Department of Carbohydrate Technology and Cereal Processing, University of Agriculture in Krakow, Balicka 122, 30-149 Krakow, Poland; angelika.bieniek@student.urk.edu.pl
* Correspondence: krzysztof.buksa@urk.edu.pl; Tel.: +48-12-6624748

Abstract: Sourdough bread is a traditional product made using lactic acid bacteria (LAB) and yeast. The influence of rye arabinoxylans (AXs) of different molar masses on sourdough wheat bread has not been studied to date. The aim of this study was to research the influence of arabinoxylans of different molar masses on the properties of sourdough wheat bread. The breads were baked using the sourdough method with wheat flour without and with 1% or 2% rye AX with different molar masses, which were unmodified, partially enzymatically hydrolyzed and cross-linked. The addition of all the AX preparations significantly increased the water absorption of the wheat flour. In particular, the addition of the preparation of cross-linked arabinoxylans at an amount of 2% caused the highest increase (by 9.8%) in the addition of water to the wheat flour dough. It was shown that a 2% addition of partially hydrolyzed AXs, with a low molar mass (190,440 g/mol), had the highest influence on increasing (by 23.7%) the volume of the bread and decreasing (by 41%) the crumb hardness of the sourdough bread, determined on the day of baking. The addition of the cross-linked AXs at an amount of 2% had the strongest influence on increasing the moisture content of the crumbs on the day of baking, both in the central (by 2.6%) and peripheral (by 5.1%) parts of the bread compared to the bread without the addition of AXs. The breads with all the AX preparations after the first and third days of storage had a higher crumb moisture content compared to the bread without the AXs.

Keywords: arabinoxylan; sourdough; wheat bread; molar mass

Citation: Bieniek, A.; Buksa, K. The Influence of Arabinoxylan on the Properties of Sourdough Wheat Bread. *Appl. Sci.* **2024**, *14*, 2649. https://doi.org/10.3390/app14062649

Academic Editor: Roberto Anedda

Received: 19 February 2024
Revised: 10 March 2024
Accepted: 19 March 2024
Published: 21 March 2024

Copyright: © 2024 by the authors. Licensee MDPI, Basel, Switzerland. This article is an open access article distributed under the terms and conditions of the Creative Commons Attribution (CC BY) license (https://creativecommons.org/licenses/by/4.0/).

1. Introduction

Sourdough bread is a traditional product that is made using lactic acid bacteria (LAB) and yeast [1]. Sourdough has a beneficial effect on bread quality characteristics, especially in baked products made from rye flours [2,3]. The acids produced by LAB influence the protein fraction. As a result of this action, gluten proteins have an increased ability to absorb water (swelling) and exhibit improved solubility [4–6]. Physicochemical changes in the protein fraction resulting from sourdough fermentation increase gas retention in the dough structure, which results in bread with a larger volume [6,7].

A reduction in the water absorption of flour and dough has been observed with the sourdough method [8–10], which is explained by the partial hydrolysis of proteins in an acidic environment [10]. The effect of hydrocolloid addition on the water absorption of sourdough has not been investigated.

The volume of sourdough wheat bread is larger compared to wheat bread baked without sourdough [11–13] due to the larger amount of gases produced during fermentation and retained in the dough structure [11,13]. It has also been shown that too much sourdough results in a weaker gluten structure and a consequently lower volume of bread [14]. The effect of hydrocolloid addition on the volume of sourdough bread has not been thoroughly investigated. The studies conducted so far have only shown that the addition of dextran has resulted in a lower volume of bread compared to bread without the addition of dextran, which has been explained by the influence of dextran on the interaction of starch and gluten in the dough [15]. It has also been shown that the amount of oat and rye fiber in sourdough wheat bread does not significantly affect its volume compared to sourdough wheat bread without the addition of fiber [16]. In addition, it has shown that the volume of sourdough wheat bread with water-insoluble arabinoxylans [11] as well as enrichment with oat fiber was higher compared to whole wheat bread [17].

In other studies, the effect of the addition of sourdough on the hardness of wheat bread crumb is ambiguous. It has been shown that the crumb hardness of sourdough wheat bread was either lower [12,18] or higher [13,14,19] compared to bread baked without sourdough. In the research conducted so far with dextran, there has not been a clear effect of hydrocolloid on the hardness of the crumb of sourdough wheat bread [15].

Other studies have shown that the increase in crumb hardness of sourdough wheat breads containing 0.1% dextran of different molar masses was lower compared to breads without added dextran [15]. The authors suggested that dextran delays the staling process of sourdough wheat bread due to its inhibitory effect on amylopectin retrogradation [15].

Studies have shown that the addition of sourdough either has no affect [14,18,20] or results in an increase in the moisture content of the crumb of sourdough wheat bread compared to bread baked using a method without sourdough [12,13,18]. The increased crumb moisture of sourdough bread has been explained by the higher addition of water to the dough for sourdough bread [18]. During sourdough fermentation, metabolites such as exopolysaccharides are produced that increase water retention in bread dough, which can result in a higher moisture content in the crumb of sourdough bread [12]. In the research published to date, information on the effect of hydrocolloids on the moisture content of sourdough wheat bread is scarce. It has been shown that 0.1% dextran, with a molar mass in the range of 9608–2,800,000 g/mol, does not significantly affect the crumb moisture content of sourdough wheat bread compared to bread without dextran [15].

Sourdough wheat breads exhibit less crumb moisture loss compared to bread without sourdough [13,14]. This is due to the addition of sourdough, which has a positive effect on the redistribution of moisture inside the bread, and thus causes less crumb moisture loss during storage. Moreover, sourdough metabolites such as organic acids, dextrins and exopolysaccharides, have affected the interaction between water molecules and bread components, such as starch, resulting in a lower crumb moisture loss of sourdough bread during storage compared to bread without sourdough [13,14].

Arabinoxylans (AXs) belong to the group of non-starch polysaccharides that are part of the dietary fiber of cereal grains [21]. The highest amount of total AXs is found in rye grain, at 8–12% [22–24]. However, the content of total AXs in wheat grain has been found to range from 0.8% to 9% [25,26]. The molar mass of natural AXs in rye grain is in the range of 197,800–2,000,000 g/mol [23,24,27–29], while in wheat grain it is 176,000–381,000 g/mol [28–31]. There are indications that the molar mass of water-insoluble AXs decreases as a consequence of acid hydrolysis, and thus their negative effect on bread quality has not been reported, but this mechanism has not been completely investigated [6,32,33].

The effect of AXs on the sourdough bread baking process has not been investigated in the studies conducted so far. On the other hand, it has been shown that AX significantly influences the process of wheat bread baking using the direct method and shapes its quality parameters. However, the amount of added preparation and the molar mass of AXs are crucial in this case [34,35]. The addition of AXs to wheat bread baked using the direct method improves its quality characteristics, such as the volume and porosity of the bread crumb. In addition, AXs support the retention of water in the bread crumb, which consequently causes its lower hardness [34,35].

According to the available knowledge, the influence of rye AXs significantly differing in molar mass, both natural and those with modified structures resulting from cross-linking and partial enzymatic hydrolysis, on the addition of water to the dough and the properties of sourdough wheat bread has not been studied so far. The aim of this study was to investigate the effect of AXs of different molar masses on the properties of sourdough wheat bread. Moreover, the effect of AXs on the aging of wheat bread baked with sourdough was studied.

2. Materials and Methods

The research material was wheat flour type 750 (PZZ Kraków, Podłęże, Poland). Arabinoxylans were isolated from rye flour of the Amilo variety (Danko, Choryń, Poland) produced by laboratory method. Starter cultures LV2 (SAF LEVAIN; Lesaffre, Marcq-en-Barœul, France), salt (POCh, Gliwice, Poland) and yeast (Lesaffre, France) were used for sourdough preparation.

2.1. Chemical Composition of Wheat Flour

Ash content was determined according to AOAC 930.05 [36]. Total protein was determined according to AOAC 950.36 [36]. Fat content was determined according to AOAC 930.05 [36]. Content of dietary fiber (total dietary fiber (TDF) as well as soluble (SDF) and insoluble (IDF) fractions) were determined according to AOAC 991.43 [36]. Starch and arabinoxylan contents were estimated after acid hydrolysis by HPLC/RI analysis according to Buksa et al. [24].

2.2. Isolation and Modification of Water-Soluble Rye Arabinoxylans

The water-soluble AXs were isolated from rye flour and modified according to the methods of Buksa et al. [24].

2.2.1. Isolation of Arabinoxylans

A total of 100 g of wholemeal rye flour was treated with 500 mL of 80% v/v EtOH at 90 °C for 2 h to inactivate cereal enzymes. The ethanol solution was removed, and the sediment was dried at 40 °C for 20 h, followed by extraction with 2 l of water at 25 °C for 6 h. The suspension was centrifuged, and the clear supernatant was boiled to coagulate soluble proteins, then the sample was cooled and incubated with α-amylase at 37 °C for 2 hr. The solution was boiled, then 20 g/L celite was added and filtered via a Buchner flask. The clear filtrate was transferred to a 4-fold solution of ethanol and acetone (1:1). The sediment was centrifuged, then frozen at −18 °C and stored for further modifications or washed twice with ethanol/acetone and twice with acetone alone. After the last centrifugation, the AX sediment was dried at 50 °C for 2 h. The yield of the unmodified AX preparation (designated AX_NM) was 2.7 g/100 g of whole wheat flour.

2.2.2. Modification of Isolated Rye Arabinoxylans by Cross-Linking

The frozen sediment of 15 g was thawed and dissolved in 40 mL of deionized water with intense stirring at 50 °C for 6 h. After this time, the solution was cooled to 25 °C, hydrogen peroxide H_2O_2 at a concentration of 1 μg/g of AXs and peroxidase at a concentration of 5 U/g of AXs were added, and again treated for 15 min. The process was stopped by flooding the solution with a 4-fold volume of ethanol and acetone solution (1:1). AX sediment was centrifuged and washed twice with ethanol/acetone and twice with acetone only to remove all water from the sample. After the last centrifugation, the sediment of AXs was dried at 50 °C for 2 h. The resulting preparation of cross-linked AXs was denoted as AX_CR.

2.2.3. Modification of Isolated Rye Arabinoxylans by Partial Enzymatic Hydrolysis

The frozen sediment of 15 g was thawed and dissolved in 40 mL of deionized water with intense stirring at 50 °C for 6 h. The obtained solution was cooled to 30 °C, then xylanase was added at 375 FXU/g arabinoxylan and incubated at 37 °C for 30 min. After boiling, the sample was centrifuged, and the resulting supernatant was transferred to a 4-fold volume of ethanol/acetone solution (1:1). The sediment AXs were centrifuged and washed twice with ethanol/acetone and twice with acetone only. After the last centrifugation, the sediment of AXs was dried at 50 °C for 2 h. The resulting preparation of partly hydrolyzed AX was denoted as AX_HYD.

2.3. Determination of the Monosaccharide Composition of Arabinoxylans, Arabinoxylan Content and Molecular Properties of Arabinoxylans

The monosaccharide composition of AXs and AX content in flour and AX preparations was determined by HPLC/RI method after acid hydrolysis according to Buksa et al. [24].

The distribution of molar mass of AXs was evaluated using HPSEC/RI according to Buksa et al. [37]. In short, the chromatographic system was composed of a Knauer chromatograph (Knauer, Berlin, Germany), equipped with a combination of OHpak SB-806HQ and SB-804HQ columns (Shodex, Tokyo, Japan) and a refractometric detector (Knauer, Germany). As eluent, 100 mM $NaNO_3$ was used at a flow rate of 0.6 mL/min. Separation was carried out at a column temperature of 60 °C. The calibration of the SEC system was carried out using pullulan standards (Shodex Standard, Macherey-Nagel, Düren, Germany) with known molar masses (P-5, 10, 100, 400 and 800) and arabinose (Sigma-Aldrich). The distribution of molar masses and apparent average molar mass Mw (related to pullulan standards) were calculated using Eurochrom (ver. 3.05, Knauer) and Clarity (ver. 4.0.1.700, DataApex, Prague, Czech Republic) software.

2.4. Baking Sourdough Wheat Bread with Arabinoxylans

2.4.1. Sourdough Preparation

To 25 g of wheat flour, 0.125 g of LV2 starter culture was added (i.e., 0.5% in relation to 100 g of flour used to prepare the sourdough) and 30 mL of water (obtaining a dough yield of 220%). After thoroughly mixing all the ingredients, the sourdough samples were incubated in a fermentation chamber at 30 °C for 24 h, with preliminary mixing for about an hour.

2.4.2. Preparation and Fermentation of Wheat Dough

In the case of the control dough, after sourdough preparation, a new portion of wheat flour (75 g) was added to the sourdough to obtain a 25% proportion of flour from the sourdough in the whole dough, yeast 2.5% (2.5 g), salt 1.8% (1.8 g) and water in the amount determined using the farinograph (dough with a consistency of 500 BU, determined according to ICC-Standard No. 115/1 [38]). In order to test the influence of AX on sourdough, wheat AX preparations of 1% and 2% by weight of flour were added in place of flour. All dough samples were mixed for 8 min and then 60 g of dough was kneaded, placed in a 3 cm × 3 cm × 4 cm baking pan and placed in the fermentation chamber for 40 min at 25–27 °C.

2.4.3. Baking Sourdough Wheat Bread and Analyzing the Properties of the Bread

After proofing, dough pieces were baked in a Viva-Meteor convection oven (Victus, Costa di Rovigo, Italy) at 230 °C for 20 min. After baking, loaves were cooled at room temperature for 30 min, and then, final analyses of the bread samples were performed and included the following:

- Bread volume measurement was performed using a three-dimensional laser-based scanner, Volscan Profiler (Stable Microsystems, Godalming, UK), according to the manufacturer's manual.
- Moisture of the bread crumb was measured by drying for 1 h at 130 °C, according to AOAC method 925.10 [39] in two places (central and peripheral part of bread).
- Texture parameters (hardness) of the bread crumb were measured using a texture analyzer TA.XT Plus (Stable Microsystems, Godalming, UK) according to the standard program, at the compression rate 5 mm/s. A sample of bread crumb, taken from the base of the loaf with a height 30 mm (the upper part of the bread was removed), was pressed to reach 10 mm maximum strain by a P/20 aluminum compression plate with a diameter of 15 mm, in two cycles with a 5 s delay. From the resulting parameters of

TPA, only the hardness of the crumb was used as an indicator of textural properties. The calculations were performed using the attached software Texture Exponent (ver. 3.0.5.0, Stable Microsystems, UK).

2.5. Statistical Analysis

All analyses were performed at least in triplicate. Statistical analysis of variance (ANOVA) was performed in order to determine statistical significance of the observed differences among mean values (Tukey's test at significance level 0.05). The statistical analysis was performed using Statistica v. 9.0 software (StatSoft, Inc., Tulsa, OK, USA).

3. Results and Discussion

The composition and properties of the flour were typical of wheat flour type 750 (Table 1). The content of ash, starch, protein and fat (Table 1) determined in the tested flour was typical for this type of flour [40–44]. The content of total dietary fiber in the wheat flour was also similar to other studies, as this component constitutes 3.0–3.6% for flours with a similar ash content [42,45,46]. The content of soluble fiber (SDF) in the tested flour was slightly higher, while insoluble fiber (IDF) was lower compared to the other studies regarding flour type 650, in which these values were 1.2% and 1.8%, respectively [46]. The content of AXs and the ratio of arabinose to xylose (Table 1) in the wheat flour studied corresponded to data presented in the literature [47–49].

Table 1. Chemical composition of flour.

Component	Wheat Flour Type 750
Starch [%]	75.3 ± 0.9
Protein [%]	12.2 ± 0.6
Fat [%]	1.7 ± 0.1
TDF *[%]	3.2 ± 0.1
SDF * [%]	1.5 ± 0.0
IDF * [%]	1.7 ± 0.0
AX [%] **	2.2 ± 0.2
A/X **	0.56 ± 0.04
Ash [%]	0.72 ± 0.01

* TDF—total dietary fiber, SDF—soluble dietary fiber, IDF—insoluble dietary fiber. ** AX—the sum of the content of arabinose and xylose after acid hydrolysis and multiplying the result by a factor of 0.88. A/X—the ratio of arabinose to xylose.

Table 2 presents the content and molecular properties of the AXs in the AX preparations isolated from rye grain. The AX preparations were determined as follows: unmodified (AX_NM), partially hydrolyzed (AX_HYD) and cross-linked (AX_CR). The AX content in the preparations at the level of approximately 78% indicated the high purity of the preparations and was typical compared to the content reported in other studies for rye AX preparations, ranging from 68 to 93% [50–52].

Table 2. Arabinoxylan content and molecular parameters of water-soluble arabinoxylan (AX) obtained from rye wholemeal.

Component	AX_NM	AX_HYD	AX_CR
AX [%]	78.2 ± 1.3 [a]	77.7 ± 1.0 [a]	77.6 ± 1.5 [a]
Molecular parameters of AX			
M_w [g/mol]	446,330 [b]	190,440 [a]	574,710 [c]
M_n [g/mol]	12,600 [b]	6290 [a]	13,400 [c]
Đ	35.4 [b]	30.3 [a]	42.9 [c]

AX_NM—non-modified AX preparation; AX_HYD—hydrolyzed AX preparation; AX_CR—cross-linked AX preparation. Mean values in rows marked with the same letters are not statistically significantly different at $p < 0.05$.

The molar mass of unmodified arabinoxylans (AX_NM) was typical of water-soluble rye AXs, which, according to data from other studies, have a molar mass in the range of 200,000–500,000 g/mol [27,52]. The AXs in the AX_HYD preparation modified using partial enzymatic hydrolysis were characterized by a low molar mass, which was similar to that determined as 219,000 g/mol in a study by Buksa [52], where the same method of AX modification was used. The AXs in the preparation of cross-linked arabinoxylans (AX_CR) had the highest molar mass, and this value was higher than the molar mass of 505,000 g/mol determined for AX obtained using the same method [52]. The determined molar masses of the AXs indicate that the process of isolation and modification (cross-linking and partial hydrolysis) of the AXs was carried out correctly.

Table 3 shows the water binding capacity (WBC) of wheat flour, and the dough yield (DY) and baking losses (BL, TBL) of the sourdough wheat bread without and with the AX preparations. The WBC of wheat flour without and with AX preparations was determined at the same dough consistency, specifically at 500 BU (Brabender Units). The WBC of wheat flour without AX addition (Table 3), was similar to data from other studies, where it ranged from 59% to 60% for wheat flour with an ash content of 0.46–0.63% [13,34]. The addition of AX_CR with the highest molar mass (574,710 g/mol) at a proportion of 2% led to the highest increase in the addition of water to wheat flour doughs of 9.8%, achieving a consistency of 500 BU. The addition of a 2% preparation of unmodified arabinoxylans (AX_NM) with a molar mass of 446,330 g/mol resulted in an 8.1% increase in water addition to the dough. A similar effect—an increase in water addition of about 6%—was observed by Koegelenberg and Chimphango [53] after using 1.2% unmodified AXs from wheat bran with a molar mass of 620,000 g/mol. The addition of the preparation of partially hydrolyzed arabinoxylans (AX_HYD) in an amount of 1%, with a molar mass of 190,440 g/mol, resulted in the lowest increase in the WBC of wheat flour (by 3.2%), which could be caused by the lower molar mass of AX.

Table 3. Properties of sourdough wheat bread with addition of AX preparations.

AX Preparation *	WBC [%] **			DY [g] **			BL ** [%]			TBL ** [%]		
	0%	1%	2%	0%	1%	2%	0%	1%	2%	0%	1%	2%
Control	56.2 ± 0.2 a			156.2 a			9.8 ± 1.6 a			13.6 ± 0.4 a		
AX_NM		60.6 ± 0.2 c	64.3 ± 0.2 f		160.6 c	164.3 f		11.0 ± 0.9 ab	12.4 ± 0.9 bc		14.6 ± 0.6 ab	16.1 ± 0.6 cd
AX_HYD		59.4 ± 0.5 b	61.2 ± 0.2 d		159.4 b	161.2 d		11.9 ± 0.8 ab	13.9 ± 1.1 c		15.4 ± 0.5 bc	16.9 ± 0.6 d
AX_CR		63.0 ± 0.3 e	66.0 ± 0.4 g		163.0 e	166.0 g		12.3 ± 0.8 bc	11.7 ± 0.7 ab		15.0 ± 0.5 bc	14.6 ± 0.7 ab

* Control—wheat bread without AXs; AX_NM—wheat bread with non-modified AX; AX_HYD—wheat bread with hydrolyzed AX; AX_CR—wheat bread with cross-linked AX. ** WBC—the water binding capacity, DY—the yield of dough obtained from 100 g of flour, BL—baking loss of hot bread, TBL—total baking loss after cooling. Mean values marked with the same letters are not statistically significantly different at $p < 0.05$.

The consequence of the increased water absorption of flour and the increased addition of water to the dough for the sourdough wheat bread was a higher dough yield. The addition of the AX_CR preparation, especially at 2%, had the highest effect on increasing the dough yield (Table 3), raising it by as much as 6.3% compared to the dough without AX addition. The addition of AX_NM in amounts of 1% and 2% also increased the dough yield by 2.8% and 5.2%, respectively. There was also an increase of 2.1% in the dough yield when AX_HYD was applied at 1%, but the effect of this preparation was the lowest. A higher dough yield is advantageous to the baking industry from an economic point of view because it allows for more bread to be baked from the same amount of flour [54].

During the bread baking process, there is a loss of weight due to the evaporation of water and other volatile substances, and this parameter is expressed as the baking loss (BL). However, after the bread has cooled, the total baking loss (TBL) is determined, which includes the evaporation of water during cooling [55,56]. The parameters influencing the baking loss of bread are the type, shape, size and volume of the bread, as well as the method of baking, the technological additives and the type of oven used [55]. The baking loss (BL) and total baking loss (TBL) are presented in Table 3. Baking loss measured immediately after removal from the oven in sourdough wheat bread without AXs accounted for 9.8%. The application of arabinoxylans AX_NM, AX_HYD at 1% and AX_CR at 2% did not significantly ($p < 0.05$) affect the baking loss of sourdough bread when compared to bread without sourdough. Similar results were reported in the other studies, where the addition of 0.1% dextran with a molar mass of 9608–750,000 g/mol to sourdough wheat bread did not significantly affect the parameter under investigation [15]. The AX_HYD preparation at 2% had the highest effect on increasing the baking loss of the sourdough wheat bread, increasing it by about 4.1% compared to the bread without AX addition. Probably, the partially hydrolyzed AX, due to its lowest molar mass, was not able to bind and retain as much water as the other AXs. In addition, the volume of bread with AX_HYD and the associated evaporation area of the breads was the highest (Table 4), which also contributed to the evaporation of larger amounts of water [57,58].

Table 4. Volume of sourdough wheat bread with addition of AX preparations.

AX Preparation *	BV ** [cm^3]			SBV ** (cm^3/100 g of Flour)		
	0%	1%	2%	0%	1%	2%
Control	121.7 ± 1.4 [a]			316.7 ± 3.6 [a]		
AX_NM		123.8 ± 1.5 [ab]	138.8 ± 1.3 [d]		331.2 ± 4.0 [b]	379.9 ± 3.4 [e]
AX_HYD		138.3 ± 1.5 [d]	145.8 ± 1.5 [e]		367.3 ± 4.0 [d]	391.6 ± 4.0 [f]
AX_CR		127.3 ± 0.5 [c]	125.5 ± 1.0 [abc]		345.7 ± 1.4 [c]	347.2 ± 2.8 [c]

* Abbreviations of sample names as in Table 3. ** BV—bread volume; SBV—specific bread volume. Mean values marked with the same letters are not statistically significantly different at $p < 0.05$.

The total baking losses measured for all the variants after the sourdough wheat bread cooled were higher compared to the losses measured immediately after removal from the oven. The addition of AX_NM at 1% and AX_CR at 2% had the lowest effect on increasing (by only 1% in both examples) the total baking loss of the sourdough wheat bread compared to the bread without AX addition (Table 3). The addition of the preparation of partially hydrolyzed arabinoxylans (AX_HYD) at 1% and 2% increased the total baking loss by 1.8% and 3.3%, respectively.

The volume of the breads (BV) and the specific volume of the breads (SBV) are shown in Table 4. The addition of 2% of the AX_HYD preparation had the highest effect on increasing (by 19.8%) the volume of sourdough wheat bread compared to the bread without AX addition. The 1% addition of AX_HYD also significantly increased the bread volume, by 14.1%, compared to the bread without AX addition, and a similar effect on this parameter was observed when a 2% addition of AX_NM was applied. This result is in agreement with data from the other studies, where a 1% addition of water-insoluble wheat pentosans also influenced the increase in the volume (BV) of sourdough bread [11], and a similar correlation was reported with the use of oat fiber [17]. The addition of the AX_CR preparation at 1% also increased (by 4.6%) the volume of the sourdough wheat bread compared to the bread without AXs. The addition of the AX_NM preparation at 1% and AX_CR at 2% did not significantly ($p < 0.05$) affect the volume (BV) of the sourdough wheat bread.

The specific volume (SBV) is the total volume of bread obtained from 100 g of flour, which takes into account not only the structure-forming properties, but also the water absorption of the flour and the associated dough yield [37]. The addition of the 2% AX_HYD preparation had the highest effect on increasing (by 23.7%) the specific volume of the sourdough wheat bread compared to the bread without AX addition (Table 4). The addition of AX_NM at both levels of substitution increased (by 4.6% and 20%, respectively) the volume of the sourdough wheat breads compared to the breads without AX addition. The addition of a preparation of cross-linked arabinoxylans (AX_CR) at both levels of substitution also increased (by 9.2% and 9.6%, respectively) the specific volume of the sourdough wheat breads. The observed correlation is not confirmed by other studies, where the addition of another hydrocolloid—dextran—affected the reduction in the specific volume of sourdough wheat breads compared to bread without dextran [15]. The differences In the results may have been due to the use of preparations with different molar masses. The molar mass of the AX preparations was 192,320–535,630 g/mol (Table 2), and their level of addition to the sourdough bread was 1% and 2%. In contrast, Zhang et al. [15] used dextran with a molar mass in the range of 9608–2,800,000 g/mol, and the level of addition to sourdough bread was 0.1%.

Table 5 shows the results regarding the hardness of the crumb of the wheat bread without and with AXs on the day of baking and after 1 and 3 days of storage. On the day of baking, the 1% and 2% addition of AX_HYD had the highest effect on reducing (by approximately 33% and 41%, respectively) the hardness of the crumb of the sourdough wheat bread compared to the bread without AX addition. The 2% share of AX_NM and 1% and 2% share of AX_CR also reduced the crumb hardness of the sourdough bread (by approximately 26%, 9% and 12%, respectively) on the day of baking compared to the bread without AXs. The AX_NM preparation at 1% did not significantly ($p < 0.05$) affect the hardness of the crumb of the sourdough wheat bread on the day of baking compared to the bread without AX addition (Table 5). In another study, a 0.1% share of a different hydrocolloid—dextran with a molar mass in the range of 9608–2,800,000 g/mol—also did not significantly influence the hardness of the bread crumb on the day of baking compared to bread without dextran [15].

Table 5. Hardness (N) of sourdough wheat bread with addition of AX preparations on the day of baking and after 1 and 3 days of storage.

AX Preparation *	Share [%]	Storage Time [Days]		
		0	1	3
Control	0%	9.7 ± 0.4 ^{cA}	17.5 ± 0.1 ^{eB}	28.9 ± 0.2 ^{deC}
AX_NM	1%	9.7 ± 0.4 ^{cA}	17.8 ± 1.7 ^{eB}	31.2 ± 2.2 ^{eC}
	2%	7.2 ± 0.3 ^{aA}	11.8 ± 0.1 ^{aB}	21.8 ± 0.8 ^{aC}
AX_HYD	1%	6.7 ± 0.3 ^{aA}	12.5 ± 0.1 ^{bB}	25.4 ± 2.3 ^{bcC}
	2%	6.5 ± 0.4 ^{aA}	11.8 ± 1.4 ^{abcB}	22.7 ± 1.2 ^{abC}
AX_CR	1%	8.8 ± 0.3 ^{bA}	14.3 ± 1.1 ^{cdB}	28.0 ± 0.7 ^{cdeC}
	2%	8.5 ± 0.4 ^{bA}	13.5 ± 0.1 ^{dB}	23.2 ± 1.4 ^{abC}

* Abbreviations of sample names as in Table 3. Capital letters indicate differences in results at day 0, 1 and 3 of analysis. Lowercase letters indicate differences in results with various arabinoxylan preparations. Mean values marked with the same letters are not statistically significantly different at $p < 0.05$.

The moisture content of the crumb of the breads was determined in the central (Table 6) and peripheral (Table 7) parts of the bread. This examination aimed to assess the effect of arabinoxylan preparations on reducing the moisture loss in the crumb and water migration in the bread. On the day of baking, the preparation of cross-linked arabinoxylans (AX_CR) at both levels had the strongest effect on increasing the crumb moisture in the central part of the sourdough wheat bread compared to the bread without AX addition (Table 6) and this parameter increased by 1.9% and 2.6%, respectively. This was due to the highest molar mass of the AXs of those used in the research and the highest amount of water added to the dough, as indicated by data from other studies [18]. On the day of baking, the addition of the AX_NM preparation at both levels also increased (by 1.5% and 1.9%, respectively) the moisture content of the crumb in the central part of the sourdough wheat bread (Table 6) compared to the bread without AX addition. On the day of baking, AX_HYD at 1% also had a significant ($p < 0.05$) effect on increasing the crumb moisture in the central part of the sourdough wheat bread compared to the bread without AX addition, but to the least extent. In another study, where a 0.1% share of dextran with a molar mass of 9608–2,800,000 g/mol was used, there was no significant effect on the crumb moisture of the sourdough wheat bread [15], which could be due to the different structure of the natural and modified AXs used. In addition, the AX substitution levels were 1% and 2%, while dextran was only added at a proportion of 0.1%.

Table 6. Moisture of the crumb in the central part of sourdough wheat bread with AX preparations on the day of baking and after 1 and 3 days of storage.

AX Preparation *	Share [%]	Storage Time [Days]		
		0	1	3
Control	0%	41.7 ± 0.3 ^{aC}	41.2 ± 0.1 ^{aB}	40.1 ± 0.0 ^{aA}
AX_NM	1%	43.2 ± 0.5 ^{bcB}	43.1 ± 0.4 ^{cdB}	40.9 ± 0.4 ^{bA}
	2%	43.6 ± 0.2 ^{cB}	43.5 ± 0.2 ^{dAB}	42.9 ± 0.5 ^{dA}
AX_HYD	1%	42.8 ± 0.2 ^{bC}	42.2 ± 0.2 ^{bB}	40.1 ± 0.0 ^{aA}
	2%	43.4 ± 0.5 ^{bcC}	42.4 ± 0.2 ^{bB}	41.3 ± 0.1 ^{bcA}
AX_CR	1%	43.6 ± 0.4 ^{cB}	43.5 ± 0.5 ^{dB}	41.8 ± 0.4 ^{cA}
	2%	44.3 ± 0.3 ^{dB}	44.1 ± 0.1 ^{eB}	43.2 ± 0.5 ^{eA}

* Abbreviations of sample names as in Table 3. Capital letters indicate differences in results at day 0, 1 and 3 of analysis. Lowercase letters indicate differences in results with various arabinoxylan preparations. Mean values marked with the same letters are not statistically significantly different at $p < 0.05$.

Table 7. Moisture of the crumb in the peripheral part of sourdough wheat bread with AX preparations on the day of baking and after 1 and 3 days of storage.

AX Preparation *	Share [%]	Storage Time [Days]		
		0	1	3
Control	0%	37.9 ± 0.6 ^{aC}	32.4 ± 0.6 ^{aB}	31.0 ± 0.5 ^{aA}
AX_NM	1%	40.9 ± 0.1 ^{cB}	34.2 ± 0.3 ^{bA}	34.0 ± 0.1 ^{cA}
	2%	42.8 ± 0.2 ^{eB}	36.4 ± 0.5 ^{dA}	35.7 ± 0.3 ^{dA}
AX_HYD	1%	39.8 ± 0.1 ^{bC}	34.0 ± 0.6 ^{bcB}	32.6 ± 0.4 ^{bA}
	2%	40.8 ± 0.2 ^{cC}	34.8 ± 0.2 ^{cB}	33.3 ± 0.7 ^{bA}
AX_CR	1%	42.6 ± 0.2 ^{deB}	36.4 ± 0.0 ^{dA}	36.1 ± 0.1 ^{dA}
	2%	43.0 ± 0.5 ^{eC}	37.3 ± 0.4 ^{eB}	36.7 ± 0.1 ^{eA}

* Abbreviations of sample names as in Table 3. Capital letters indicate differences in results at day 0, 1 and 3 of analysis. Lowercase letters indicate differences in results with various arabinoxylan preparations. Mean values marked with the same letters are not statistically significantly different at $p < 0.05$.

On the day of baking, the AX_CR preparation at the amount of 2% had the highest effect on increasing the moisture content of the peripheral part (crust) of the sourdough wheat bread, with an increase of 5.1% compared to the bread without AXs (Table 7). This could be due to the overall highest addition of water to the dough, as well as the low volume and surface area of the bread and the consequently lower intensity of water evaporation at the baking stage and immediately after it compared to the bread without AXs. On the day of baking, the AX_NM preparation in amounts of 1% and 2% also increased (by 3% and 4.9%, respectively) the crumb moisture in the peripheral part of the sourdough wheat bread compared to the bread without AXs. The 1% addition of AX_HYD also had a significant ($p < 0.05$) effect on increasing (by 1.9%) the crumb moisture in the peripheral part of the sourdough wheat bread.

This study, for the first time, examined the effect of the molar mass of AXs on the reduction in the hardness increase and moisture loss of sourdough wheat bread. The statistical analysis of the moisture content and crumb hardness of the sourdough breads without and with arabinoxylans showed ($p < 0.05$) that the hardness of the breads progressively increased with storage time, while the moisture content in the central and peripheral parts decreased.

After 1 and 3 days of storage (Table 5), the addition of all the AX preparations at the amount of 2% affected the increase in the hardness of the crumb of the sourdough wheat bread compared to the hardness of the control sample (bread without addition of AXs). A similar correlation was observed by Zhang et al. [15], where a 0.1% share of dextran with a molar mass of 9608–2,800,000 g/mol influenced the reduction in the increase in the crumb hardness of sourdough wheat bread compared to bread without the addition of dextran [15]. In general, the 1% addition of AX_HYD slightly reduced the increase in the bread crumb hardness, while the 1% addition of AX_NM and AX_CR had no significant effect ($p < 0.05$) on the reduction in the increase in the crumb hardness of the sourdough wheat bread after 1 and 3 days of storage compared to the hardness of the bread without AXs (Table 5). This may have been due to insufficient AXs in the bread to effectively affect the retrogradation of starch, which is responsible for the staling of the bread [15].

Tables 6 and 7 show the results of the moisture loss of the crumb during the storage of the sourdough breads without and with the AX preparations. On the first day of storage, the addition of 1% and 2% of the AX_NM and AX_CR preparations had an influence on reducing the moisture loss of the crumb in the central part of the sourdough bread compared to the breads with the AX preparations on the day of baking ($p < 0.05$), which was not observed for the bread with AX_HYD and the bread without AXs (Table 6). On the third day of storage, a significant loss of moisture in the central part of the bread crumb was observed in all the baked breads. In the peripheral part of the breads (crust), the moisture loss was observed on the first as well as the third day of storage in all the variants of the breads (Table 7). The crust drying occurred with crumb moisture retention in the central part of the AX sourdough bread. The water migration from the crumb to the crust did not occur or was delayed.

In general, the addition of all the preparations at both levels resulted in a higher moisture content of the crumb in the central (Table 6) and peripheral (Table 7) parts of the bread on the first and third days of storage compared to the bread without AXs. The most effective in reducing the crumb moisture loss was the addition of 2% of the cross-linked AX preparation, and, to a lower extent, the addition of 2% of AX_NM. The application of 1% AX_HYD resulted in a higher crumb moisture content in the central part of the bread after the first day of storage compared to the bread without AXs. However, after three days of storage, the moisture content of the crumb in the central part of bread with 1% AX_HYD was the same as the bread without AXs. The unmodified and cross-linked AXs had the strongest influence on reducing the moisture loss of the crumb in the central and peripheral parts of the bread, which was probably due to the high molar mass of AX (446,330–574,710 g/mol). In other studies, data have been reported on the influence of sourdough on reducing moisture loss in the crumb of wheat bread during storage [13,14]. However, the influence of hydrocolloids on reducing moisture loss in the crumb of sourdough wheat bread has not been studied to date.

4. Conclusions

The addition of AXs increased the water absorption of the wheat flour and dough yield proportionally to the amount and molar mass of the AXs. The addition of 2% of the AX_CR preparation, which contains AXs with the highest molar mass, caused the highest (by 9.8%) increase in the water absorption of the wheat flour dough. The addition of 2% of AX_NM increased the water absorption by 8.1%, while the addition of 2% of AX_HYD increased the water absorption of the wheat flour dough by 5%.

The partially hydrolyzed AXs in the AX_HYD preparation, with the lowest molar mass of 190,440 g/mol, was the most effective in increasing (by about 20%) the volume of the bread, especially the addition of 2% compared to the bread without added AXs. The addition of all the AX preparations had the effect of increasing the bread volume per 100 g of flour compared to the bread without AXs.

The addition of the partially hydrolyzed arabinoxylans (AX_HYD), especially at 2% most effectively reduced (by 41%) the hardness of the bread crumb on the day of baking compared to the bread without AXs. The reduction in the hardness of the bread crumb was observed as a consequence of the application of all the AX preparations, except for the addition of 1% of unmodified AXs.

On the day of baking, the AX_CR preparation at the amount of 2% had the strongest effect on increasing the moisture content of the crumb in the central (by 2.6%) and peripheral (by 5.1%) parts of the bread compared to the bread without AXs. Also, the other AX_NM and AX_HYD preparations at the amounts of 1% and 2% had an effect on increasing the moisture content of the bread crumb on the day of baking compared to the bread without AX addition.

On the first day of storage, the addition of the unmodified and cross-linked AX resulted in the inhibition of crumb moisture loss in the central part of the sourdough bread compared to the bread from the day of baking.

In general, the addition of all the preparations resulted in a higher moisture content of the crumb in the central and peripheral parts of the bread on the first and third days of storage compared to the bread without AXs.

Author Contributions: Conceptualization, K.B. and A.B.; methodology, K.B. and A.B.; software, K.B.; validation, K.B.; formal analysis, A.B.; investigation, A.B.; resources, A.B.; data curation, A.B.; writing—original draft preparation, A.B.; writing—review and editing, A.B. and K.B.; visualization, A.B.; supervision, K.B.; project administration, A.B. All authors have read and agreed to the published version of the manuscript.

Funding: This research received no external funding.

Institutional Review Board Statement: Not applicable.

Informed Consent Statement: Not applicable.

Data Availability Statement: Data are contained within the article.

Conflicts of Interest: The authors declare no conflicts of interest.

References

1. Gobbetti, M. The sourdough microflora: Interactions of lactic acid bacteria and yeasts. *Trends Food Sci. Technol.* **1998**, *9*, 267–274. [CrossRef]
2. Röcken, W. Applied aspects of sourdough fermentation. *Adv. Food Sci.* **1996**, *18*, 212–216.
3. Lorenz, K.; Brummer, J.M. Preferments and sourdoughs for German breads. In *Handbook of Dough Fermentations*; Kulp, K., Lorenz, K., Eds.; Marcel Dekker: New York, NY, USA, 2003; pp. 247–270.
4. Hoseney, R.C. Proteins of Cereals. In *Principles of Cereal Science and Technology*, 2nd ed.; American Association of Cereal Chemists (AACC): St. Paul, MN, USA, 1994; pp. 56–70.
5. Takeda, K.; Matsumura, Y.; Shimizu, M. Emulsifying and surface properties of wheat—Gluten under acidic conditions. *J. Food Sci.* **2001**, *66*, 393–399. [CrossRef]
6. Galle, S. Sourdough: A Tool to Improve Bread Structure. In *Handbook on Sourdough Biotechnology*; Gobbetti, M., Gänzle, M., Eds.; Springer: New York, NY, USA, 2012. [CrossRef]
7. Clarke, C.I.; Schober, T.J.; Arendt, E.K. Effect of Single Strain and Traditional Mixed Strain Starter Cultures on Rheological Properties of Wheat Dough and on Bread Quality. *Cereal Chem.* **2002**, *79*, 640–647. [CrossRef]
8. Gocmen, D.; Gurbuz, O.; Kumral, A.Y.; Dagdelen, A.F.; Sahin, I. The effects of wheat sourdough on glutenin patterns, dough rheology and bread properties. *Eur. Food Res. Technol.* **2007**, *225*, 821–830. [CrossRef]
9. Komlenić, D.K.; Ugarčić-Hardi, Ž.; Jukić, M.; Planinić, M.; Bucić-Kojić, A.; Strelec, I. Wheat dough rheology and bread quality effected by Lactobacillus brevis preferment, dry sourdough and lactic acid addition. *Int. J. Food Sci. Technol.* **2010**, *45*, 1417–1425. [CrossRef]
10. Chen, D.; Wang, J.; Jia, F.; Zhang, C. Effects of Sourdough Addition on the Quality and Shelf Life of Chinese Steamed Bread. *GOST* **2018**, *1*, 85–90. [CrossRef]
11. Corsetti, A.; Gobbetti, M.; De Marco, B.; Balestrieri, F.; Paoletti, F.; Russi, L.; Rossi, J. Combined Effect of Sourdough Lactic Acid Bacteria and Additives on Bread Firmness and Staling. *J. Agric. Food Chem.* **2000**, *48*, 3044–3051. [CrossRef]
12. Tamani, R.J.; Goh, K.K.T.; Brennan, C.S. Physico-Chemical Properties of Sourdough Bread Production Using Selected *Lactobacilli* Starter Cultures. *J. Food Qual.* **2013**, *36*, 245–252. [CrossRef]
13. Hayta, M.; Ertop, M.H. Physicochemical, textural and microbiological properties of optimised wheat bread formulations as affected by differently fermented sourdough. *Qual. Assur. Saf. Crops Foods* **2019**, *11*, 283–293. [CrossRef]

14. Rinaldi, M.; Paciulli, M.; Caligiani, A.; Sgarbi, E.; Cirlini, M.; Dall'Asta, C.; Chiavaro, E. Durum and soft wheat flours in sourdough and straight-dough bread-making. *J. Food Sci. Technol.* **2015**, *52*, 6254–6265. [CrossRef]
15. Zhang, Y.; Guo, L.; Xu, D.; Li, D.; Yang, N.; Chen, F.; Jin, Z.; Xu, X. Effects of dextran with different molecular weights on the quality of wheat sourdough breads. *Food Chem.* **2018**, *256*, 373–379. [CrossRef]
16. De Angelis, M.; Damiano, N.; Rizzello, C.G.; Cassone, A.; Di Cagno, R.; Gobbetti, M. Sourdough fermentation as a tool for the manufacture of low-glycemic index white wheat bread enriched in dietary fibre. *Eur. Food Res. Technol.* **2009**, *229*, 593–601. [CrossRef]
17. De Angelis, M.; Rizzello, C.G.; Alfonsi, G.; Arnault, P.; Cappelle, S.; Di Cagno, R.; Gobbetti, M. Use of sourdough lactobacilli and oat fibre to decrease the glycaemic index of white wheat bread. *Br. J. Nutr.* **2007**, *98*, 1196–1205. [CrossRef]
18. Jitrakbumrung, S.; Therdthai, N. Effect of Addition of Sourdough on Physicochemical Characteristics of Wheat and Rice Flour Bread. *Nat. Sci.* **2014**, *48*, 964–969.
19. Katsi, P.; Kosma, I.S.; Michailidou, S.; Argiriou, A.; Badeka, A.V.; Kontominas, M.G. Characterization of Artisanal Spontaneous Sourdough Wheat Bread from Central Greece: Evaluation of Physico-Chemical, Microbiological, and Sensory Properties in Relation to Conventional Yeast Leavened Wheat Bread. *Foods* **2021**, *10*, 635. [CrossRef]
20. Crowley, P.; Schober, T.J.; Clarke, C.I.; Arendt, E.K. The effect of storage time on textural and crumb grain characteristics of sourdough wheat bread. *Eur. Food Res. Technol.* **2002**, *214*, 489–496. [CrossRef]
21. Knudsen, K.E.B. Carbohydrate and lignin contents of plant materials used in animal feeding. *Anim. Feed Sci. Technol.* **1997**, *67*, 319–338. [CrossRef]
22. Bengtsson, S.; Aman, P. Isolation and chemical characterization of water-soluble arabinoxylans in rye grain. *Carbohydr. Polym.* **1990**, *12*, 267–277. [CrossRef]
23. Andersson, R.; Fransson, G.; Tietjen, M.; Åman, P. Content and Molecular-Weight Distribution of Dietary Fiber Components in Whole-Grain Rye Flour and Bread. *J. Agric. Food Chem.* **2009**, *57*, 2004–2008. [CrossRef]
24. Buksa, K.; Ziobro, R.; Nowotna, A.; Praznik, W.; Gambuś, H. Isolation, modification and characterization of soluble arabinoxylan fractions from rye grain. *Eur. Food Res. Technol.* **2012**, *235*, 385–395. [CrossRef]
25. Comino, P.; Shelat, K.; Collins, H.; Lahnstein, J.; Gidley, M.J. Separation and purification of soluble polymers and cell wall fractions from wheat, rye and hull less barley endosperm flours for structure-nutrition studies. *J. Agric. Food Chem.* **2013**, *61*, 12111–12122. [CrossRef]
26. Marcotuli, I.; Hsieh, Y.S.Y.; Lahnstein, J.; Yap, K.; Burton, R.A.; Blanco, A.; Fincher, G.B.; Gadaleta, A. Structural variation and content of arabinoxylans in endosperm and bran of durum wheat (*Triticum turgidum* L.). *J. Agric. Food Chem.* **2016**, *64*, 2883–2892. [CrossRef] [PubMed]
27. Ragaee, S.M.; Campbell, G.L.; Scoles, G.J.; McLeod, J.G.; Tyler, R.T. Studies on rye (*Secale cereale* L.) lines exhibiting a range of extract viscosities. 1. Composition, molecular weight distribution of water extracts, and biochemical characteristics of purified water-extractable arabinoxylan. *J. Agric. Food Chem.* **2001**, *49*, 2437–2445. [CrossRef]
28. Buksa, K.; Praznik, W.; Loeppert, R.; Nowotna, A. Characterization of water and alkali extractable arabinoxylan from wheat and rye under standardized conditions. *J. Food Sci. Technol.* **2016**, *53*, 1389–1398. [CrossRef] [PubMed]
29. Li, S.; Chen, H.; Cheng, W.; Yang, K.; Cai, L.; He, L.; Li, C. Impact of arabinoxylan on characteristics, stability and lipid oxidation of oil-in-water emulsions: Arabinoxylan from wheat bran, corn bran, rice bran, and rye bran. *Food Chem.* **2021**, *358*, 129813. [CrossRef] [PubMed]
30. Sun, Y.; Cui, S.W.; Gu, X.; Zhang, J. Isolation and structural characterization of water unextractable arabinoxylans from Chinese black-grained wheat bran. *Carbohydr. Polym.* **2011**, *85*, 615–621. [CrossRef]
31. Guo, X.N.; Yang, S.; Zhu, K.X. Impact of arabinoxylan with different molecular weight on the thermo-mechanical, rheological, water mobility and microstructural characteristics of wheat dough. *Int. J. Food Sci. Technol.* **2018**, *53*, 2150–2158. [CrossRef]
32. Vinkx, C.J.A.; Delcour, J.A. Rye (*Secale cereal* L.) Arabinoxylans: A Critical Review. *J. Cereal Sci.* **1996**, *24*, 1–14. [CrossRef]
33. Boskov Hansen, H.; Andreasen, M.; Nielsen, M.; Larsen, L.; Knudsen, B.K.; Meyer, A.; Christensen, L. Changes in dietary fibre, phenolic acids and activity of endogenous enzymes during rye bread-making. *Eur. Food Res. Technol.* **2002**, *214*, 33–42. [CrossRef]
34. Biliaderis, C.G.; Izydorczyk, M.S.; Rattan, O. Effect of arabinoxylans on bread-making quality of wheat flours. *Food Chem.* **1995**, *53*, 165–171. [CrossRef]
35. Saeed, F.; Arshad, M.U.; Pasha, I.; Suleria, H.A.R.; Arshad, M.S.; Qamar, A.; Ullah, A.; Sultan, S. Effect of arabinoxylan and arabinogalactan on textural attributes of bread: Arabinoxylan and arabinogalactan and textural study. *J. Food Process. Preserv.* **2015**, *39*, 1070–1088. [CrossRef]
36. AOAC. *Official Methods of Analysis*, 18th ed.; Association of Official Analytical Chemists International: Gaithersburg, MA, USA, 2006.
37. Buksa, K.; Nowotna, A.; Ziobro, R. Application of cross-linked and hydrolyzed arabinoxylans in baking of model rye bread. *Food Chem.* **2016**, *192*, 991–996. [CrossRef] [PubMed]
38. *ICC-Standard Method No. 115/1*; Method for Using the Brabender Farinograph. International Association for Cereal Science and Technology: Vienna, Austria, 1992.
39. Horwitz, W.; Latimer, G.W. *Official Methods of Analysis of AOAC International*, 18th ed.; Association of Official Analytical Chemistry International: Rockville, MD, USA, 2005.

40. Andersson, R.; Westerlund, E.; Tilly, A.C.; Åman, P. Natural Variations in the Chemical Composition of White Flour. *J. Cereal. Sci.* **1993**, *17*, 183–189. [CrossRef]
41. Goesaert, H.; Brijs, K.; Veraverbeke, W.S.; Courtin, C.M.; Gebruers, K.; Delcour, J.A. Wheat flour constituents: How they impact bread quality, and how to impact their functionality. *Trends Food Sci. Technol.* **2005**, *16*, 12–30. [CrossRef]
42. Oghbaei, M.; Prakash, J. Effect of Fractional Milling of Wheat on Nutritional Quality of Milled Fractions. *Trends Carbohydr. Res.* **2013**, *5*, 53–58.
43. Tharise, N.; Julianti, E.; Nurminah, M. Evaluation of physico-chemical and functional properties of composite flour from cassava, rice, potato, soybean and xanthan gum as alternative of wheat flour. *Int. Food Res. J.* **2014**, *21*, 1641–1649.
44. Kurek, M.A.; Wyrwisz, J.; Piwińska, M.; Wierzbicka, A. Influence of the wheat flour extraction degree in the quality of bread made with high proportions of β-glucan. *Food Sci. Technol.* **2015**, *35*, 273–278. [CrossRef]
45. Siljeström, M.; Westerlund, E.; Björck, I.; Holm, J.; Asp, N.G.; Theander, O. The effects of various thermal processes on dietary fibre and starch content of whole grain wheat and white flour. *J. Cereal Sci.* **1986**, *4*, 315–323. [CrossRef]
46. Pastuszka, D.; Gambuś, H.; Ziobro, R.; Mickowska, B.; Buksa, K.; Sabat, R. Quality and nutritional value of wheat bread with a preparation of oat proteins. *JMBFS J. Microbiol. Biotechnol. Food Sci.* **2012**, *1*, 980–987.
47. Izydorczyk, M.; Biliaderis, C.G.; Bushuk, W. Comparison of the Structure and Composition of Water-Soluble Pentosans from Different Wheat Varieties. *Cereal Chem.* **1991**, *68*, 139–144.
48. Saulnier, L.; Sado, P.E.; Branlard, G.; Charmet, G.; Guillon, F. Wheat arabinoxylans: Exploiting variation in amount and composi-tion to develop enhanced varieties. *J. Cereal Sci.* **2007**, *46*, 261–281. [CrossRef]
49. Izydorczyk, M.S.; Biliaderis, C.G. Cereal arabinoxylans: Advances in structure and physicochemical properties. *Carbhydr. Polym.* **1995**, *28*, 33–48. [CrossRef]
50. Delcour, J.A.; Rouseu, N.; Vanhaesendonck, I.P. Pilot-scale isolation of water-extractable arabinoxylans from rye. *Cereal Chem.* **1999**, *76*, 1–2. [CrossRef]
51. Hartmann, G.; Piber, M.; Koehler, P. Isolation and chemical characterization of water-extractable arabinoxylans from wheat and rye during breadmaking. *Eur. Food Res. Technol.* **2005**, *221*, 487–492. [CrossRef]
52. Buksa, K. Application of model bread baking in the examination of arabinoxylan—Protein complexes in rye bread. *Carbohydr. Polym.* **2016**, *148*, 281–289. [CrossRef] [PubMed]
53. Koegelenberg, D.; Chimphango, A.F.A. Effects of wheat-bran arabinoxylan as partial flour replacer on bread properties. *Food Chem.* **2017**, *221*, 1606–1613. [CrossRef] [PubMed]
54. Bieniek, A.; Buksa, K. Properties and Functionality of Cereal Non-Starch Polysaccharides in Breadmaking. *Appl. Sci.* **2023**, *13*, 2282. [CrossRef]
55. Kasprzak, M.; Rzedzicki, Z.; Sykut-Domńska, E. Wpływ dodatku razówki owsianej na cechy jakościowe chleba pszennego. *ŻYWNOŚĆ Nauka Technologia Jakość* **2011**, *1*, 124–139.
56. Cacak-Pietrzak, G.; Sujka, K.; Księżak, J.; Bojarszczuk, J.; Dziki, D. Sourdough Wheat Bread Enriched with Grass Pea and Lupine Seed Flour: Physicochemical and Sensory Properties. *Appl. Sci.* **2023**, *13*, 8664. [CrossRef]
57. Wagner, M.J.; Lucas, T.; Le Ray, D.; Trystram, G. Water transport in bread during baking. *J. Food Eng.* **2007**, *78*, 1167–1173. [CrossRef]
58. Buksa, K. Effect of pentoses, hexoses and hydrolysed arabinoxylan on the most abundant sugar, organic acid and alcohol contents during rye sourdough bread production. *Cereal Chem.* **2020**, *97*, 642–652. [CrossRef]

Disclaimer/Publisher's Note: The statements, opinions and data contained in all publications are solely those of the individual author(s) and contributor(s) and not of MDPI and/or the editor(s). MDPI and/or the editor(s) disclaim responsibility for any injury to people or property resulting from any ideas, methods, instructions or products referred to in the content.

Article

Physico-Chemical, Sensory, and Nutritional Properties of Shortbread Cookies Enriched with *Agaricus bisporus* and *Pleurotus ostreatus* Powders

Aneta Sławińska *, Ewa Jabłońska-Ryś and Waldemar Gustaw

Department of Fruits, Vegetables and Mushrooms Technology, Faculty of Food Sciences and Biotechnology, University of Life Sciences in Lublin, Skromna 8, 20-704 Lublin, Poland; ewa.jablonska-rys@up.lublin.pl (E.J.-R.); waldemar.gustaw@up.lublin.pl (W.G.)
* Correspondence: aneta.slawinska@up.lublin.pl; Tel.: +48-81-462-33-09

Abstract: Mushrooms, due to their basic composition and the presence of numerous mycochemicals, can be used to improve various food matrices. The objective of this study was to determine the impact of replacing wheat flour (2%, 4%, 6% w/w) with mushroom lyophilisates from cultivated mushrooms—*A. bisporus* and *P. ostreatus*—on the technological quality, basic nutritional and elemental composition, antioxidant activity (ABTS, FRAP), total polyphenol content (TPC), and sensory evaluation of shortbread cookies. The functional properties of blended flours were also determined, such as bulk density (BD), water- and oil-holding capacity (WHC, OHC), swelling capacity (SW), and water solubility index (WSI). The results show that the amounts of protein, fiber, and ash were higher in cookies enriched with mushrooms than in control cookies. The enriched products, depending on the amount of mushroom powder used and the mushroom species, had a higher content of zinc, iron, magnesium, potassium, and copper. The increase in the addition of mushroom powder resulted in a significant ($p < 0.05$) increase in the TPC content and antioxidant properties. The use of composite flours contributed to a significant increase in hardness (at 6% mushroom powder) and a change in color parameters, with lower whiteness and a greater ΔE recorded for cookies with *A. bisporus* lyophilisate. In the sensory evaluation, the samples enriched with *P. ostreatus* powder received higher scores compared with control samples, while the cookies with *A. bisporus* flour were evaluated lower than the control.

Keywords: mushroom powder; wheat flour replacement; shortbread cookies; basic composition; minerals; antioxidants; color; texture; sensory evaluation

Citation: Sławińska, A.; Jabłońska-Ryś, E.; Gustaw, W. Physico-Chemical, Sensory, and Nutritional Properties of Shortbread Cookies Enriched with *Agaricus bisporus* and *Pleurotus ostreatus* Powders. *Appl. Sci.* **2024**, *14*, 1938. https://doi.org/10.3390/app14051938

Academic Editor: António José Madeira Nogueira

Received: 1 February 2024
Revised: 22 February 2024
Accepted: 24 February 2024
Published: 27 February 2024

Copyright: © 2024 by the authors. Licensee MDPI, Basel, Switzerland. This article is an open access article distributed under the terms and conditions of the Creative Commons Attribution (CC BY) license (https://creativecommons.org/licenses/by/4.0/).

1. Introduction

Cookies as snacks are popular among consumers for many reasons. A wide selection of shapes and sizes, high digestibility, high energy value, relatively low production costs, convenience, and long shelf life contribute to their popularity [1]. As stated in the report "Production and distribution of confectionery. Bittersweet prospects for the industry" [2], regarding data from 2015–2021, confectionery production in the European Union is highly concentrated in six countries: Germany, Italy, France, the Netherlands, Belgium, and Spain, providing a total of 80% of the value of manufactured products. Poland is in seventh place in this ranking. This sector is quite an important part of the domestic food industry, accounting for almost 6% of its total production in 2021. In the Polish confectionery industry, cookies account for approximately 40% of the total production value.

Shortbread cookies are made from dough by combining flour, fat, and sugar. Additional ingredients that can be used include eggs or yolks, cream, flavors, potato flour, and chemical leavening agents. The best quality shortbread cookies are obtained by maintaining the weight proportions between flour, fat, and sugar of 3:2:1 [3]. The best choice for the production of cookies is soft white wheat flour, with weak gluten, which ensures a tender bite, a higher spread ratio, and a uniform surface structure [4]. However, white flour compared with whole grain flour has reduced content of ingredients such as fiber, lysine, B-group vitamins, and major and trace elements [5]. Partial or complete replacement of the base flour with another flour substitute (e.g., mushroom powders [6], pulse flour [7], fruit waste powders [8]) on the one hand improves the nutritional composition of blended flour, but on the other hand contributes to modifying the technological quality of flours and final products.

Consumer behavior stimulates food producers to design products with improved nutritional composition. The number of nutritional claims such as "source of", "rich in", "light", and health benefits is increasing [9,10]. Despite the availability of products with such claims, taste and cost of purchase are still the most important factors for consumers [10]. Modifying the composition of popular food products, e.g., cookies, in order to improve their nutritional or health-promoting value should not result in excessive increases in production costs and the final price. Mushrooms are cheap to produce because they can be grown indoors, they produce higher yields in a short time, and waste is often used for their cultivation [11,12]. The great advantage of cultivated mushrooms is their year-round availability. The popularity of mushrooms, their production, and consumption are constantly growing. Poland is a significant producer of this raw material in Europe. Cultivation is focused primarily on two species of mushrooms: *Agaricus bisporus* and *Pleurotus ostreatus*. The mentioned species are also the most frequently consumed and cultivated in the world, with *A. bisporus* taking first place [11,13].

Edible mushrooms are a raw material with a low fat content and at the same time a large amount of protein, fiber, ash, vitamins, sterols, and polyphenols [11,14–17]. The presence of a large group of mycochemicals contributes to the numerous health-promoting properties of mushrooms [18]. The appreciated taste and flavor of mushrooms as well as the chemical composition that determines their nutritional value and numerous health benefits encourage scientists to use this raw material as a functional food and for the design of functional foods. Mushrooms have been studied for their use as meat [19], fat [20], salt [19,20], or flour replacements [14,21,22]. Mushrooms have been used as a food additive in various forms, e.g., fresh or after thermal treatment [19], in the form of powders after drying and grinding [14,23,24], as water extracts [25], or polysaccharide fractions [26]. Preparing mushrooms as a flour substitute involves drying them using various methods [14,27,28] and then grinding the dried mushrooms into powder. Some aspects of using mushroom powder as a flour replacement are describe in an earlier article [14]. The base flour most often replaced with mushroom powder is wheat flour. Mushrooms have been studied as a substitute for flour in pasta production [29] and baked goods such as bread [14,30], cakes [31], cookies [22,24,27], and breadsticks [32]. Enriching these products with mushrooms contributed to obtaining products with an increased content of fiber [24,29], B vitamins, and vitamin D [14] or with a higher content of polyphenols [6,14,22]; however, the products were usually darker [14,21,22] and characterized by lower specific volume and higher hardness [14]. The presence of mushroom flour also resulted in a lower glycemic index of final products [29]. Mushroom powders have also been used in gluten-free formulas [33].

Mushrooms are a raw material rich in many major and trace elements [11] and may be an important source of these in the human diet. For adult Poles, the recommended dietary allowance (RDA) for various major elements is for calcium (Ca), 1000 mg/day; for magnesium (Mg), 310–400 mg/day; for iron (Fe), 10–18 mg/day. In turn, the RDA for trace elements is in the case of zinc (Zn), 8–11 mg/day; copper (Cu), 0.9 mg/day; selenium (Se), 55 mg/day; and manganese (Mn), 1.8–2.3 mg/day [34]. In the European population, the average dietary intakes of selected elements in adults during the day are Ca from 598 mg [35] to 1374 mg [36], Mg from 232 mg to 439 mg [37], Fe from 9.4 mg to 17.9 mg [38], Zn from 8–14 mg [39], Cu from 1.15–2.07 mg [40], Se from 31–65.6 μg [41], and Mn from 2 mg to 6 mg [42]. Mushrooms, compared with most vegetables, contain a larger amount of phosphorus (P) and potassium (K), and a relatively high content of Mg and Se [43]. However, mushrooms also can bind lead (Pb) or cadmium (Cd) and may constitute nutritional hazards [44]. Therefore, it is important to monitor the amount of these heavy metals in the mushroom biomass. The maximum permitted content of Cd and Pb in three species of mushrooms cultivated by producers, i.e., button mushrooms, oyster mushrooms, and shiitake (*Lentinula edodes*) is 0.15–0.2 mg Cd and 0.3 mg Pb per 1 kg of fresh weight [45]. With an average 90% water content in mushrooms, the amounts of these elements in dry weight should not exceed 1.5–2 mg Cd and 3 mg Pb on a dry weight basis [44].

The aim of the present research was to estimate the impact of using lyophilisates from white button mushrooms and oyster mushrooms as partial wheat flour substitutes (2%, 4%, 6% w/w) on the functional properties of the obtained blended flours as well as on physical parameters, basic nutritional composition, mineral content, selected health-promoting properties, and sensory evaluation of shortbread cookies prepared from these composite flours.

2. Materials and Methods

2.1. Mushroom Powder Preparation

Two mushroom species, white button mushrooms (*Agaricus bisporus* (Lange) Sing.) and oyster mushrooms (*Pleurotus ostreatus* (Jacq.) P. Kumm.), were obtained directly from the mushroom producer and processed within 24 h of harvesting. The raw materials were stored under refrigerated conditions prior to the treatments. The moisture content was 92.19% and 90.51% on a wet weight basis for button mushrooms and oyster mushrooms, respectively. The first stages of mushroom processing included washing and cutting into slices (3–4 mm). After freezing (-80 °C; 24 h), the raw material was dried (72 h) in a lyophilizer (Christ Alpha 1-2 LD plus, Germany). The obtained lyophilisates were ground (8000 rpm, 4 min) into flour in a laboratory mill (Retsch GM200, Retsch GmbH, Haan, Germany). Subsequently, the powders were sifted with a 0.25 mm sieve. The obtained powders were applied as a partial substitute for base flour in shortbread cookies.

2.2. Making the Shortbread Cookies

The ingredients from which the shortbread cookies (control samples) were prepared were as follows: 360 g of wheat flour (GoodMills Polska Sp. z o.o., Plony Natury, type 450), 240 g of butter (Mlekovita, 82% fat), 100 g of powdered sugar (Pfeifer & Langen Marketing Sp. z o.o., Diamant), and 40 g of yolk (Agrowita Sp. z o.o., Moja Kurka). To obtain other versions of cookies, the wheat flour was partially substituted for powdered lyophilisates (2%, 4%, 6% w/w). The dough was prepared using a Thermomix TM6 device (Vorwerk Elektrowerke GmbH & Co. KG, Wuppertal, Germany). First, the flour and sugar were mixed for 2 min. Then, the dough was mixed for another 3 min after adding the butter and next the yolk. The dough was left for 1 h at 4 °C to rest. Next, 5 mm thick sheets of dough were formed, from which round cookies were cut using stainless steel molds (Ø 70 mm). The shortbread cookies were baked (190 °C; 9 min) in a ChefTop oven (Unox, Cadoneghe, Italy). Before further analyses, the cookies were left to cool at a temperature of 20 ± 2 °C and then stored in a plastic container.

The samples of obtained cookies (Figure 1) were marked as follows: control—cookies with 100% wheat flour; Ab2—cookies with 2% *A. bisporus* lyophilisate as a flour substitute; Ab4—cookies with 4% *A. bisporus* lyophilisate as a flour substitute; Ab6—cookies with 6% *A. bisporus* lyophilisate as a flour substitute; Po2—cookies with 2% *P. ostreatus* lyophilisate as a flour substitute; Po4—cookies with 4% *P. ostreatus* lyophilisate as a flour substitute; Po6—cookies with 6% *P. ostreatus* lyophilisate as a flour substitute.

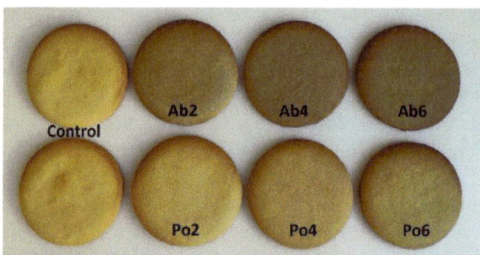

Figure 1. Shortbread cookies enriched with different levels of mushroom powder. Control—cookies with 100% wheat flour; Ab2—cookies with 2% *A. bisporus* lyophilisate as a flour substitute; Ab4—cookies with 4% *A. bisporus* lyophilisate as a flour substitute; Ab6—cookies with 6% *A. bisporus* lyophilisate as a flour substitute; Po2—cookies with 2% *P. ostreatus* lyophilisate as a flour substitute; Po4—cookies with 4% *P. ostreatus* lyphilisate as a flour substitute; Po6—cookies with 6% *P. ostreatus* lyophilisate as a flour substitute.

2.3. Basic Composition of Mushroom Powders, Wheat Flour and Shortbread Cookies

The basic components such as moisture, protein, fat, ash, and total dietary fiber of mushroom powders, wheat flour, and cookies were determined in accordance with American Association of Cereal Chemists (AACC) methods [46]. After subtracting the sum of these basic ingredients from 100, the amount of digestible carbohydrates was obtained. The factor 6.25 was used to estimate the amount of raw protein in flour and cookies [24], while in the case of mushrooms the factor 4.38 [43] was used due to the significant chitin content. Based on the amount of the basic components, the energy value was determined using following conversion factors per 1 g of nutrient: fat—9 kcal; protein and carbohydrates—4 kcal; dietary fiber—2 kcal [47].

2.4. Mineral Composition of Mushroom Powders, Flour and Shortbread Cookies

The content of 13 elements in wheat flour, mushroom powders, and shortbread cookies was determined. Three groups of elements were analyzed: (i) major essential elements (Ca, K, Mg, Na); (ii) essential trace elements (Cu, Fe, Mn, Ni, Zn, Se, Co); (iii) trace toxic elements (Pb, Cd), in accordance with the protocol by Kasprzyk et al. [48] with modifications. Before determining the elements, samples (0.5 g) were poured with 5 mL of HNO_3 and subjected to mineralization in a microwave oven (210 °C; 7 atmospheres). The obtained samples were diluted with demineralized water to 50 mL and then analyzed using flame atomic absorption spectrometry (AAS—Varian SpectrAA 280FS, Australia) for the amounts of the following elements: K, Na, Ca, Mg, Fe, Zn, Mn, Cu, or by inductively coupled plasma mass spectrometer (ICP Mass Spectrometer Varian MS-820 Belrose, Australia) for the amounts of such elements as Cd, Pb, Se, Co and Ni. The element content was expressed as mean values in mg/kg dw ($n = 3$).

2.5. Colour Measurement

The L*(brightness), a* (red/green value), and b* (blue/yellow value) color parameters of cookies, wheat flour, and mushroom powders were determined using a 3Color K9000Neo colorimeter (3Color, Narama, Poland). The measurement conditions used were as follows: D65 light source, observer—10° field of view; diaphragm measuring diameter—11 mm. In total, 15 measurements of color parameters were performed. Moreover, the browning index (BI) [49] was determined for all versions of the cookies, along with total color change (ΔE) [50] between cookies supplemented with mushroom powders and control cookies. The parameters ΔE and BI were calculated based on the equations below (Equations (1) and (2), respectively):

$$\Delta E = [(L^*_{sample} - L^*_{control})^2 + (a^*_{sample} - a^*_{control})^2 + (b^*_{sample} - b^*_{control})^2]^{\frac{1}{2}} \quad (1)$$

$$BI = 100 - L^* \qquad (2)$$

2.6. Functional Properties of Mushroom Powder, Base Flour and Blended Flour

The bulk density (BD) was measured in accordance with the protocol by Okezie and Bello [51] with some modifications. A 50 mL cylinder was filled with 10 g of wheat flour and blended flour or 3 g of mushroom powders and then the volume was read. The BD value was expressed as the ratio of the mass of a given flour or lyophilisate to its volume (g/mL).

Swelling capacity (SC) was measured in accordance with the methodology given by Tosh and Yada [52] with minor modifications. In a 50 mL cylinder, 3 g of wheat flour and blended flour or 1 g of mushroom powder were mixed with distilled water, which was topped up to 30 mL. The mixture was vortexed for 1 min and left for 24 h at a temperature of 20 ± 2 °C. Then, the final volume (Vf) was read and SC was calculated according to Equation (3):

$$SC = Vf \text{ (mL)}/\text{Sample weight (g)} \qquad (3)$$

The water solubility index (WSI) was measured in accordance with the protocol by Zhang et al. [53] with modifications. A mixture of 0.5 g of wheat flour, mushroom powder, or blended flour (W1) and 25 mL of distilled water in a 50 mL falcon tube was incubated in a water bath (30 min, 80 °C). After cooling, the samples were centrifuged (5000× g; 20 min) (MPW-350R, Warsaw, Poland). The supernatant from the sediment was poured into a previously weighed vessel (W2) and dried (105 °C; 24 h). The mass of the obtained residue (W3) was weighed. The water solubility index was calculated according to Equation (4):

$$WSI\ (\%) = (W3\ (g) - W2\ (g))/(W1\ (g) \times 100) \qquad (4)$$

The WHC and OHC were determined in accordance with the method described by Tan et al. [54] with modifications. For this purpose, 100 mg of wheat flour and blended flour or 33 mg of mushroom powder (W1) was blended with 1.5 mL of distilled water or rapeseed oil in previously weighed 2 mL Eppendorf tubes (W2). The mixture was thoroughly vortexed for 1 min and left for 0.5 h at 20 ± 2 °C. Then, the samples were centrifuged for 20 min at 10,000× g (MPW-350R, Warsaw, Poland). The supernatant was carefully removed and the tubes with the contents were left upside down for 30 min to allow the remaining water and oil to drain and the obtained residue was weighed (W3). WHC and OHC were presented as the weight of water or oil bound by 1 g of sample. WHC and OHC were calculated according to Equation (5):

$$WHC\ (g^{water}/g)\ \text{or}\ OHC\ (g^{oil}/g) = (W3\ (g) - W2\ (g) - W1(g))/W1\ (g) \qquad (5)$$

2.7. Basic Properties of Cookies

The water activity (a_w) was determined at 25 °C using LabSwift-aw equipment (Novasina AG, Lachen, Switzerland). The measurements were taken 24 h after baking and keeping the cookies at room temperature. Prior to determination, the samples were stored in a plastic container. Measurements were taken three times for each version of the cookies, and a 3 g sample was used each time for a_w measurement.

For each version of the cookies, the average weight (g) was estimated, and the diameter (D) (mm) and thickness (T) (mm) were also evaluated using an electronic caliper. Based on these two parameters, the spread ratio (D/T) was calculated [55]. In total, 12 measurements were performed for each batch of cookies.

2.8. Cookies Texture

The texture of samples was analyzed with a TA.XTplusC Texture Analyser (Stable Micro Systems, Godalming, UK) within 24 h after baking. Before the measurements were taken, fragments with a diameter of 50 mm were cut out from the middle part of the cookies. Cookies was measured using a sharp cutting blade probe (type HDP/BS) at a pre-test speed of 1 mm/s, test speed of 3 mm/s, post-test speed of 10 mm/s. The data were analyzed using Exponent Connect 8.0 software (Stable Micro System Ltd., Surrey, UK). The cutting force was used as an indicator of cookies' hardness (g). In total, 12 measurements were performed for each batch of cookies.

2.9. Total Phenolic Content (TPC) and Antioxidant Properties

2.9.1. Extraction Procedure

The extraction procedure was carried out in accordance with the protocol presented by Radzki et al. [15] with modifications. A laboratory mill (Retsch GM200, Retsch GmbH, Haan, Germany) was used for grinding the cookie samples. The obtained fine powders were sifted through a sieve (0.25 mm). Ten mL of ethanol (80% v/v) was mixed with samples of wheat flour and ground cookies (500 mg each) and 100 mg of mushroom powder. Extraction was performed in a water bath (80 °C; 180 rpm; 1 h). Next, the mixture was cooled and centrifuged (4200× g; 20 min) (MPW-350R, Warsaw, Poland). Extracts were prepared in triplicate for all samples.

2.9.2. Total Phenolic Content (TPC)

The TPC was quantified in accordance with the method described by Singleton and Rossi [9] and Dubost et al. [56] with some modifications. The ethanolic extracts (200 µL) were mixed with diluted (10:1) Folin and Ciocalteu reagent (800 µL). After 3 min, 1250 µL of 7% Na_2CO_3 was added, and the mixtures were left to stand for 0.5 h in the dark at 20 ± 2 °C. The absorbance was read at 725 nm (Helios Gamma, Thermo Fisher Scientific, Waltham, MA, USA) against a blank sample. The TPC was presented as gallic acid equivalent (GAE) per 1 g of dry weight (dw).

2.9.3. Antioxidant Activity

Measurement of ABTS (2,2'-azino-bis(3-ethylbenzothiazoline-6-sulfonic acid)) radical scavenging activity was conducted in accordance with the protocol by Re et al. [57]. Ethanolic extracts (100 µL) after mixing with ABTS + solution (1000 µL) were measured at 734 nm after 15 min of incubation. In turn, the ferric reducing antioxidant power (FRAP) measurement was carried out in accordance with the methodology presented by Benzie and Strain [58]. FRAP solution (1900 µL) was mixed with ethanolic extracts (100 µL) and, after incubation (37 °C; 15 min), the absorbance measurements were conducted at 593 nm. Antioxidant activity measured by ABTS and FRAP methods was expressed in µmol of trolox equivalent (TE) per 1 g of dw.

2.10. Dry Weight

The oven-drying method was used to determine the water content of samples by drying them at 105 °C for at least 24 h. Based on the water content, the dry weight was calculated (dw) [15].

2.11. Sensory Evaluation

Shortbread cookies were subjected to sensory evaluation by a panel of 25 untrained consumers aged 20 to 56 (14 women and 11 men). The assessment was conducted among employees and students at Life Sciences University in Lublin. Cookies (coded with a random 3-digit number) were served on white plates one day after production. A 9-point hedonic scale was used to estimate the degree of overall liking or disliking of different types of cookie, where 1 = dislike extremely, 5 = neither like nor dislike, 9 = like extremely). The following cookie attributes were assessed: appearance, color, aroma, taste, texture, and overall acceptability [59].

2.12. Statistical Analysis

The results were statistically analyzed (one-way ANOVA), comparing means via the Tukey test ($p < 0.05$). STATISTICA13.3 software (StatSoft, Cracow, Poland) was used for analyses. The results were expressed as mean values ± standard deviation (SD).

3. Results and Discussion

3.1. Basic Composition of Wheat Flour, Mushroom Powders, and Shortbread Cookies

Table 1 presents the results for the basic composition of raw materials (mushroom powders and wheat flour) and shortbread cookies. Compared with wheat flour, mushroom lyophilisates contained significantly ($p < 0.05$) higher protein content (from 26.89% to 33.61%) and fat content (from 2.75% to 3.20%), 16–20 times more ash, and 10–15 times more fiber. The basic composition of mushroom powders used as a substitute for base flour translates into the composition of baked goods. The increasing content of mushroom flour from 0% to 6% contributed to a significant ($p < 0.05$) increase in the amount of protein, ash, and fiber in the cookies. The highest protein content was recorded in cookies with 6% button mushroom (7.20%) compared with the control cookies (6.21%). With 6% replacement of wheat flour, the amount of ash compared with the control cookies increased to more than double in the case of cookies supplemented with oyster mushrooms (0.5%) and to more than three times in the case of cookies with *A. bisporus* (0.64%). Cookies enriched with mushroom lyophilisates had a higher fiber content of from 5.67% (Ab2 cookies) to 8.02% (Po6 cookies) compared with control cookies (2.8%). A slight decrease in the amount of carbohydrates in products with mushrooms was recorded, and no significant differences were noticed in the amount of fat between the different versions of the cookies. The results presented in this work show that the highest moisture content was recorded in cookies with 100% wheat flour (5.34%) and cookies with 2% button mushroom powder (5.09%). The remaining versions of the cookies had significantly lower moisture content, from 4.10% to 4.57%.

Table 1. Basic composition of raw materials and shortbread cookies.

Sample	Protein %	Fat %	Ash %	Carbohydrates %	Fiber %	Moisture %	Energy Value kcal/100 g
Raw materials							
Ab powder	33.61 ± 0.31 [C]	3.20 ± 0.04 [C]	9.68 ± 0.02 [C]	15.82 ± 0.57 [B]	31.15 ± 0.14 [B]	6.54 ± 0.11 [A]	289 ± 1.27 [B]
Po powder	26.89 ± 1.06 [B]	2.75 ± 0.09 [B]	8.36 ± 0.08 [B]	7.86 ± 0.54 [A]	45.77 ± 0.7 [C]	8.37 ± 0.04 [B]	255 ± 0.35 [A]
Wheat flour	11 ± 0.2 [A]	1.2 ± 0.08 [A]	0.5 ± 0.02 [A]	71 ± 1.2 [C]	3.0 ± 0.2 [A]	13.3 ± 0.11 [C]	345 ± 2.71 [C]
Cookies							
Control	6.21 ± 0.04 [a]	29.23 ± 0.13 [a]	0.21 ± 0.03 [a]	56.21 ± 0.29 [d]	2.80 ± 0.09 [a]	5.34 ± 0.07 [b]	518 ± 2.10 [b]
Ab2	6.67 ± 0.04 [c]	29.31 ± 0.07 [a]	0.34 ± 0.02 [b]	52.93 ± 0.07 [b]	5.67 ± 0.10 [b]	5.09 ± 0.00 [b]	513 ± 0.70 [ab]
Ab4	6.76 ± 0.03 [c]	29.46 ± 0.18 [a]	0.52 ± 0.03 [b]	53.23 ± 0.33 [bc]	5.91 ± 0.12 [b]	4.12 ± 0.03 [a]	517 ± 0.57 [b]
Ab6	7.20 ± 0.10 [d]	29.57 ± 0.17 [a]	0.64 ± 0.02 [d]	51.15 ± 0.33 [a]	6.87 ± 0.14 [d]	4.57 ± 0.02 [a]	513 ± 1.52 [ab]
Po2	6.45 ± 0.02 [b]	29.30 ± 0.20 [a]	0.28 ± 0.01 [b]	53.69 ± 0.26 [c]	5.91 ± 0.15 [b]	4.37 ± 0.09 [a]	516 ± 1.60 [ab]
Po4	6.75 ± 0.02 [c]	29.44 ± 0.32 [a]	0.38 ± 0.02 [c]	52.90 ± 0.26 [b]	6.43 ± 0.14 [c]	4.10 ± 0.16 [a]	516 ± 4.28 [ab]
Po6	6.78 ± 0.05 [c]	29.38 ± 0.13 [a]	0.50 ± 0.01 [e]	50.87 ± 0.19 [a]	8.02 ± 0.15 [e]	4.45 ± 0.22 [a]	511 ± 0.91 [a]

A–C or a–e—the different letters in columns mean that there are significant differences between mean values (HSD Tukey's test, $p < 0.05$, $n = 3$); Ab powder—*A. bisporus* powder; Po powder—*P. ostreatus* powder; control—cookies with 100% wheat flour; Ab2—cookies with 2% *A. bisporus* lyophilisate as a flour substitute; Ab4—cookies with 4% *A. bisporus* lyophilisate as a flour substitute; Ab6—cookies with 6% *A. bisporus* lyophilisate as a flour substitute; Po2—cookies with 2% *P. ostreatus* lyophilisate as a flour substitute; Po4—cookies with 4% *P. ostreatus* lyophilisate as a flour substitute; Po6—cookies with 6% *P. ostreatus* lyophilisate as a flour substitute.

The mushroom powders used for this research can be considered high-protein and high-fiber foods. According to European Union law [60], food that contains at least 3 g of fiber per 100 g or at least 1.5 g of fiber per 100 kcal may be called a "source of fiber", while food containing at least 6 g of fiber per 100 g or at least at least 3 g of fiber per 100 kcal can be considered "high in fiber". The same document specifies the possibility of using the claims "source of protein" and "high protein" in the cases of foods where at least 12% or 20% of the energy value of the food comes from protein.

Mushrooms are a raw material with a significant amount of fiber, minerals, and protein containing all essential amino acids, while being low in fat [43]. The amount of protein reported in *A. bisporus* ranges from 7% to 40.5% of dry weight, while in *Pleurotus* spp. it ranges from 7.6% to 37.04% [61,62]. The main component of mushrooms, apart from water, is carbohydrates, which include mono- and disaccharides, polyols, polysaccharides such as β-glucans, glycogen, and chitin [63]. The data for total carbohydrate content vary in the range from 50.9 to 74.0% in white button mushrooms and from 51.9% to 85.2% in oyster mushrooms [64]. Thanks to the significant presence of non-starch polysaccharides, mushrooms are a very good source of dietary fiber, i.e., carbohydrate polymers, which are not hydrolyzed by the endogenous enzymes in humans. Mushroom fiber is primarily the insoluble fraction of glucans and chitin and the fraction soluble in water, usually constituting less than 10% of dry matter [65]. The amount of total dietary fiber (TDF) in mushroom species and fruiting body parts varies. Synytsya et al. [66] reported that the TDF content in *Pleurotus* species was 34.5–63.1% in pilei and 38.9–64.8% in stems. Authors Nile and Park [67] reported that the TDF content of the 20 tested mushrooms ranged from 24% to 36% of dry matter, with *A. bisporus* containing 31% total dietary fiber. Mushrooms are low in fats, with linoleic acid making up 75% of the total fatty acids [68]. Kirbağ and Akyüz [69] reported that the fat content in *A. bisporus* and *Pleurotus* spp ranged from 0.5% to 1.3%, while Shbeeb et al. [68] reported fat content ranging from 2.5% in *P. ostreatus* to 3.1% in *A. bisporus*. The ash content in mushrooms is relatively high and ranges from 52.7 to 120 g/kg dw in selected cultivated species and from 55.3 to 232.8 g/kg dw in some wild-grown mushrooms [43].

The results presented by other authors show that partial replacement of wheat flour with powder from *Pleurotus ostreatus* [23], *P. sajor-caju* [27], *P. albidus* [21], *Termitomyces robustus* [70], *Lentinula edodes* [71], *Calocybe indica* [6], or *Cordyceps militaris* [22] results in an increase in the content of protein, dietary fiber, and ash and a decrease in fat and carbohydrates in cookies enriched with mushroom flour. Shams et al. [72] reported that replacing barley flour with *Agaricus bisporus* powder at an amount of 10–50% contributed to a decrease in the content of fiber and carbohydrates, which was due to the fact that barley flour is a better source of fiber than mushrooms. However, these samples had a higher protein and ash content than the control. Replacing sorghum flour with from 5% to 15% shiitake, black, and silver ear mushroom powder contributed to an increase in protein content only in the case of shiitake mushroom biscuits [24]. The protein content showed a decrease in the following order: shiitake mushroom flour (24.68 g/100 g) > sorghum flour (11.74 g/100 g) > black ear mushroom flour (10.92 g/100 g) > silver ear mushroom flour (10.88 g/100 g). However, mushroom flours had higher fiber content (from 38.46 to 76.78 g/100 g) than the base flour (11.50 g/100 g), which contributed to obtaining high-fiber biscuits.

3.2. Mineral Composition

The mineral composition of mushroom powders and base flour is summarized in Table 2. In turn, Table 3 presents the mineral content of cookies enriched with mushroom flour. Compared with wheat flour, mushroom lyophilisates are characterized by significantly ($p < 0.05$) higher amounts of most of the analyzed elements: Mg, K, Na, Fe, Zn, Cu, Mn, and Ni. The content of toxic elements (Cd, Pb) in the mushroom powders is within the standards set by European Union regulations [45]. Similarly, Pb and Cd in the cookies were not recorded, nor was sodium (Na). There were no significant ($p < 0.05$) differences in the content of elements such as Ca, Mn, Se, Co, or Ni between the variants of the obtained cookies. Higher levels of Zn were recorded in all cookies with the addition of mushroom powders (from 7.97 to 10.73 mg/kg dw) compared with the control cookies (6.99 mg/kg dw). The use of lyophilisate from *A. bisporus* in amounts of 2–6% contributed to a significant increase in the Cu content in baked goods, in the range from 1.83 to 2.83 mg/kg dw, compared with the control (1.36 mg/kg dw). Inclusion of at least 2% dried oyster mushroom contributed to a more than twofold higher K content in the supplemented cookies (203.14 mg/kg dw) compared with the content of this element in the control samples (81.52 mg/kg dw). In cookies where part of the base flour was substituted with button and oyster mushroom powder from 4% to 6%, higher amounts of iron or magnesium were recorded.

Table 2. Mineral composition of wheat flour and mushroom powders.

Element mg/kg dw	A. bisporus Powder	P. ostreatus Powder	Wheat Flour
Ca	320.14 ± 6.97 [c]	114.44 ± 4.15 [a]	234.91 ± 3.52 [b]
Mg	1044.99 ± 22.84 [b]	1062.48 ± 17.63 [b]	155.32 ± 8.73 [a]
K	1962.06 ± 54.20 [b]	15,758.11 ± 126.65 [c]	231.06 ± 10.47 [a]
Na	441.55 ± 10.07 [b]	85.37 ± 4.12 [a]	nd
Fe	34.58 ± 2.84 [b]	53.34 ± 2.29 [c]	6.86 ± 0.32 [a]
Zn	56.44 ± 1.91 [b]	51.44 ± 2.58 [b]	5.57 ± 0.25 [a]
Cu	36.13 ± 2.39 [c]	7.13 ± 0.09 [b]	1.89 ± 0.14 [a]
Mn	5.08 ± 0.03 [c]	4.42 ± 0.14 [b]	3.18 ± 0.07 [a]
Se	0.414 ± 0.007 [b]	0.115 ± 0.004 [a]	0.116 ± 0.005 [a]
Co	0.061 ± 0.003 [a]	0.059 ± 0.004 [a]	0.060 ± 0.001 [a]
Ni	0.184 ± 0.008 [c]	0.161 ± 0.007 [b]	0.127 ± 0.003 [a]
Pb	0.029 ± 0.006 [a]	0.042 ± 0.003 [b]	nd
Cd	0.038 ± 0.004 [b]	0.176 ± 0.002 [c]	0.017 ± 0.002 [a]

[a–c]—different letters in a row mean that there are significant differences between mean values (HSD Tukey's test, $p < 0.05$, $n = 3$); nd—not detected.

Table 3. Mineral composition of shortbread cookies.

Element mg/kg dw	Cookies						
	Control	Ab2	Ab4	Ab6	Po2	Po4	Po6
Ca	371.15 ± 13.79 [a]	373.52 ± 14.13 [a]	370.11 ± 10.12 [a]	378.13 ± 14.83 [a]	363.81 ± 13.64 [a]	363.11 ± 19.88 [a]	356.95 ± 13.66 [a]
Mg	112.09 ± 6.78 [a]	123.77 ± 3.73 [ab]	137.97 ± 6.96 [bc]	152.78 ± 8.04 [c]	119.78 ± 9.85 [ab]	127.65 ± 10.54 [ab]	142.00 ± 9.87 [bc]
K	81.52 ± 4.40 [a]	94.89 ± 5.60 [a]	100.46 ± 6.83 [a]	123.66 ± 11.68 [a]	203.14 ± 18.10 [b]	322.25 ± 28.04 [c]	408.79 ± 22.85 [d]
Na	nd	nd	nd	nd	nd	nd	nd
Fe	6.99 ± 0.13 [a]	7.37 ± 0.51 [a]	7.95 ± 0.46 [abc]	8.75 ± 0.34 [bcd]	7.82 ± 0.29 [ab]	8.88 ± 0.19 [cd]	9.69 ± 0.53 [d]
Zn	6.99 ± 0.08 [a]	8.33 ± 0.06 [bc]	9.40 ± 0.32 [de]	10.73 ± 0.46 [f]	7.97 ± 0.18 [b]	9.00 ± 0.43 [cd]	10.21 ± 0.49 [ef]
Cu	1.36 ± 0.05 [a]	1.83 ± 0.03 [b]	2.39 ± 0.10 [c]	2.83 ± 0.08 [d]	1.41 ± 0.03 [a]	1.46 ± 0.02 [a]	1.51 ± 0.09 [a]
Mn	1.64 ± 0.02 [a]	1.64 ± 0.05 [a]	1.63 ± 0.07 [a]	1.67 ± 0.07 [a]	1.60 ± 0.07 [a]	1.63 ± 0.04 [a]	1.67 ± 0.07 [a]
Se	0.103 ± 0.006 [a]	0.108 ± 0.007 [a]	0.111 ± 0.010 [a]	0.116 ± 0.014 [a]	0.102 ± 0.006 [a]	0.105 ± 0.005 [a]	0.114 ± 0.014 [a]
Co	0.051 ± 0.002 [a]	0.050 ± 0.004 [a]	0.052 ± 0.001 [a]	0.057 ± 0.005 [a]	0.053 ± 0.001 [a]	0.053 ± 0.003 [a]	0.055 ± 0.005 [a]
Ni	0.158 ± 0.006 [a]	0.160 ± 0.006 [a]	0.161 ± 0.008 [a]	0.163 ± 0.006 [a]	0.158 ± 0.006 [a]	0.155 ± 0.002 [a]	0.161 ± 0.007 [a]
Pb	nd	nd	nd	nd	nd	nd	nd
Cd	nd	nd	nd	nd	nd	nd	nd

[a–f]—different letters in a row mean that there are significant differences between mean values (HSD Tukey's test, $p < 0.05$, $n = 3$); nd—not detected; control—cookies with 100% wheat flour; Ab2—cookies with 2% A. bisporus lyophilisate as a flour substitute; Ab4—cookies with 4% A. bisporus lyophilisate as a flour substitute; Ab6—cookies with 6% A. bisporus lyophilisate as a flour substitute; Po2—cookies with 2% P. ostreatus lyophilisate as a flour substitute; Po4—cookies with 4% P. ostreatus lyophilisate as a flour substitute; Po6—cookies with 6% P. ostreatus lyophilisate as a flour substitute.

The increase in most minerals in mushroom-enriched cookies was the result of the higher amounts of ash in the mushroom powders (Table 1). As shown by the results presented in other works, the addition of mushroom powder leads to an increase in the ash and element content in composite flours where the base is sweet potato and rice flour [73] or maize flour [74]. Rathore et al. [6] observed an increase in the amounts of ash and elements (Zn, Fe, K) in cookies where part of the wheat flour was replaced with *Calocybe indica* flour. Owheruo et al. [23] recorded a significant ($p < 0.05$) increase in the amounts of ash and elements such as Na, Ca, K, and Zn in cookies prepared from wheat flour with the addition of oyster mushroom flour. The authors suggested that the biscuits they obtained would be suitable for people on a low salt diet, because the biscuits had a low sodium to potassium ratio (below 1).

The amounts of individual elements in mushrooms are the result of many factors, including species, part of the fruiting body (e.g., cap, stipe), fungal lifestyle (e.g., saprotrophs), and type of growing medium [43,75]. According to the literature data [11,13,76], the amounts of major essential elements in cultivated mushrooms varied; in the case of

Ca it was 860–1400 mg/kg dw and 190–1500 mg/kg dw; for K it was from 18,321–49,000 mg/kg dw and 21,840–51,000 mg/kg dw; for Mg it was from 1099–1480 mg/kg dw and 165–2300 mg/kg dw; and for Na it was from 240–957 mg/kg dw and 250–1440 mg/kg dw, for *A. bisporus* and *P. ostreatus*, respectively.

According to EU regulations [60,77], the condition for using the "source of mineral/s" nutritional claim is a content of at least 15% of the RDA of a given ingredient. In turn, the nutritional claim "high mineral/s" can only be used if the product contains at least twice the value of products marked as a "source of mineral/s". Taking into account the moisture content of the mushroom powders used in our tests, it can be concluded that in the case of *A. bisporus* flour, the nutritional claims "source of Mg, Mn, and Se" and "high Fe, Zn, Cu" can be used, and in the case of oyster mushroom flour, the nutritional claims "source of Mg, Mn, Se, and K" and "high Fe, Zn, Cu" can be used.

3.3. Colour Measurements

Table 4 presents the L^*, a^*, b^*, ΔE, and BI for the cookies and L^*, a^*, b^* for wheat flour and mushroom lyophilisates. Color is one of the most important features influencing consumer acceptance of a product. In turn, the type of flour or substitute used has a significant impact on the color of the cookies. The values of all color parameters for raw materials (wheat flour and mushroom powders) were different. The lightness (L^*) was the highest for wheat flour, and among the mushroom powders, the powder from freeze-dried oyster mushrooms ($L^* = 87.25$) was much lighter than that from button mushrooms ($L^* = 82.91$). In turn, regarding chromatic values, a higher share of green color was recorded for oyster mushroom powder ($a^* = -0.86$), a higher share of red color ($a^* = 1.47$) for button mushroom powder, and higher values of the b^* parameter (from 14.39 to 15.18) for mushroom powders compared with wheat flour ($b^* = 9.34$).

Table 4. Color parameters of mushroom powders, wheat flour, and shortbread cookies.

Sample	Parameter				
	L^*	a^*	b^*	ΔE	BI
Raw materials					
A. bisporus powder	82.91 ± 0.21 [A]	1.47 ± 0.07 [C]	14.39 ± 0.22 [B]	-	-
P. ostreatus powder	87.25 ± 0.23 [B]	-0.86 ± 0.06 [A]	15.18 ± 0.34 [C]	-	-
Wheat flour	93.47 ± 0.18 [C]	0.36 ± 0.03 [B]	9.34 ± 0.17 [A]	-	-
Cookies					
Control	77.39 ± 1.00 [f]	3.10 ± 0.47 [a]	26.50 ± 1.31 [b]	-	22.61 ± 1.00 [a]
Ab2	66.04 ± 1.00 [c]	5.25 ± 0.71 [b]	21.07 ± 1.00 [a]	12.92 ± 1.30 [c]	33.96 ± 1.00 [d]
Ab4	62.61 ± 0.71 [b]	6.19 ± 0.54 [bc]	21.73 ± 0.66 [a]	15.95 ± 1.01 [d]	37.39 ± 0.71 [e]
Ab6	60.97 ± 1.33 [a]	7.11 ± 0.75 [d]	21.88 ± 0.72 [a]	17.33 ± 1.71 [d]	39.03 ± 1.33 [f]
Po2	75.30 ± 1.27 [e]	5.37 ± 1.26 [b]	29.17 ± 1.41 [c]	4.63 ± 1.59 [a]	24.70 ± 1.27 [b]
Po4	74.66 ± 1.39 [e]	6.12 ± 1.17 [bc]	29.00 ± 1.30 [c]	5.15 ± 1.18 [a]	25.34 ± 1.39 [b]
Po6	72.11 ± 1.14 [d]	6.67 ± 1.09 [cd]	28.96 ± 1.06 [c]	7.05 ± 1.30 [b]	27.89 ± 1.14 [c]

L^*—brightness; a^*—red/green value; b^*—blue/yellow value; [A–C] or [a–f]—the different letters in columns mean that there are significant differences between mean values (HSD Tukey's test, $p < 0.05$, $n = 15$); ΔE—total colour change; BI—browning index; control—cookies with 100% wheat flour; Ab2—cookies with 2% *A. bisporus* lyophilisate as a flour substitute; Ab4—cookies with 4% *A. bisporus* lyophilisate as a flour substitute; Ab6—cookies with 6% *A. bisporus* lyophilisate as a flour substitute; Po2—cookies with 2% *P. ostreatus* lyophilisate as a flour substitute; Po4—cookies with 4% *P. ostreatus* lyophilisate as a flour substitute; Po6—cookies with 6% *P. ostreatus* lyophilisate as a flour substitute.

Traditional shortbread cookies are characterized by color ranging from yellow through golden to slightly brown. Control cookies were characterized by the highest value of the L^* parameter (77.39). With the increase in the addition of mushroom lyophilisate, the value of this parameter was significantly lower, from 75.30 to 72.11 for cookies with *P. ostreatus* powder and from 66.04 to 60.97 for cookies with the addition of *A. bisporus*. An inverse relationship was noted for the a^* parameter of enriched cookies, for which the value was significantly higher (from 5.25 to 6.67), while the value of the a* parameter of control cookies was 3.10. In turn, the highest yellowness (b* parameter) was recorded for cookies with the addition of oyster mushrooms, then for control cookies, and the lowest for cookies with button mushrooms.

Higher ΔE was noted for the cookies with *A. bisporus* (from 12.92 to 17.33) than those with *P. ostreatus* (from 4.63 to 7.05). A similar relationship was noted for the browning index. The lowest BI value was observed for cookies without mushrooms (22.61), cookies enriched with oyster mushrooms had a BI of 24.70 to 27.89, and the browning index of the cookies with *A. bisporus* ranged from 33.96 to 39.03.

The results presented in this article show that freeze-dried button mushrooms are darker than freeze-dried oyster mushrooms, even though fresh mushroom caps of the white variety are characterized by higher values of the L* parameter. The results presented by other researchers also confirm this. Examples of color parameter values for the caps of fresh white button mushrooms given in other reports include parameter L* ranging from 89.02 to 93.23, parameter a* ranging from 0.57 to 0.73, and parameter b* equal to 12.75 or 12.8 [78,79]. In turn, according to Kic [80], the caps of fresh oyster mushroom fruiting bodies are darker (L* = 75.94 and 78.09), while the other parameters range from −0.04 to −0.21 and from 12.29 to 13.05 for parameter a* and b*, respectively. According to other researchers, the color parameters of freeze-dried button mushrooms are as follows: parameter L* from 73.39 to 86.19, parameter a* from 0.89 to 1.66, and parameter b* from 10.22 to 15.29 [14,81]. In the case of freeze dried oyster mushrooms, the whiteness parameter L* ranged from 82.42 to 84.72, while the value of the chromatic coordinate a* ranged from −0.58 to 1.49, and for the chromatic coordinate b* it was 12.42 and 15.47 [82,83].

The color of dried mushrooms is influenced by many factors, including preliminary processing (e.g., washing, cutting) [84] and the drying method [85], as well as the parameters used [86]. During pre-treatment, the chemical composition (phenolic compounds, free amino acids) and the activity of oxidizing enzymes (e.g., peroxidase, polyphenol oxidase) contributes significantly to changing the color of the raw material [87]. *A. bisporus* are mushrooms with a high polyphenol content and high enzymatic activity [88]. The drying method also determines the color of the raw materials. When convective drying is used, the main role in the darkening of dried products is played primarily by Maillarad reactions [89], while in freeze drying, the enzymatic activity of raw materials [90] has a significant impact. According to Ucar and Karadag [83], the L* value of *P. ostreatus* increased after freeze-drying. This is confirmed by the results obtained, where the mushroom powder from white button mushrooms is clearly darker than that obtained from oyster mushrooms.

The effects of partial replacement of wheat [21,22], whole grain [91], barley [72] and sorghum [24] flour with mushroom powder on the color change of cookies have been observed by other researchers. Regardless of whether the basic flour was replaced by an amount of 1–5% [22] or even up to 100% [21] mushroom powder, the value of the L* parameter was lower compared with control cookies. Only cookies made from whole grain flour where 10% and 30% of the flour was replaced with dried oyster mushrooms showed a similar L* value [91], and cookies in which sorghum flour was replaced by 5%, 10%, or 15% silver ear mushroom powder had L* values that were significantly higher [24]. In the case of the chromatic coordinate a*, there was no significant effect of supplementation with dried *Pleurotus albidus* [21], and there was increase in the value of this parameter for cookies supplemented with *Cordyceps militaris* powder [22], while there was a decrease in the redness of cookies with the addition of *P. ostreatus* [91], shiitake, or black ear mushrooms [24] compared with the control. For the chromatic b* coordinate, an increase in the value was observed in the case of cookies supplemented with *C. militaris* [22], *A. bisporus* [72], or silver ear mushrooms [24] and a decrease in the yellowness of cookies supplemented with *P. albidus* [21], *P. ostreatus* [91], shiitake, or black ear mushrooms [24].

The change in the color of the surface of bakery products is the result of non-enzymatic browning reactions. i.e., Maillard reactions and caramelization, which result in the formation of colorful high-molecular compounds, caramels, and melanoidins [92]. Maillard reactions depend on the presence of reducing sugars, free amino acids, proteins, and nitrogen-containing compounds, while caramelization occurs as a result of the reaction of reducing sugars at appropriately high temperatures. These reactions occur more intensively with lower water content, i.e., mainly on the surface of bakery products, where water evaporates intensively [49].

3.4. Functional Properties of Mushroom Powder, Wheat Flour, and Blended Flours

Data regarding functional properties of mushroom powders, base flour, and blended flours are presented in Table 5. Functional properties reflect the complex interactions between compounds and the structure and physico-chemical properties of food ingredients in a given environment [59].

Table 5. Functional properties of mushroom powders, wheat flour, and blended flours.

Sample	Parameter				
	BD (g/mL)	WHC (g^{water}/g)	OHC (g^{oil}/g)	SC (mL/g)	WSI (%)
Ab powder	0.10 ± 0.00 [B]	5.17 ± 0.26 [A]	5.44 ± 0.32 [A]	20.51 ± 0.48 [B]	42.13 ± 0.22 [A]
Po powder	0.08 ± 0.01 [A]	7.32 ± 0.36 [B]	7.29 ± 0.10 [B]	16.51 ± 0.41 [A]	54.06 ± 0.41 [B]
Wheat flour	0.76 ± 0.01 [f]	0.77 ± 0.02 [a]	0.68 ± 0.01 [a]	2.59 ± 0.08 [ab]	7.30 ± 0.17 [a]
WFAb2	0.70 ± 0.01 [e]	0.80 ± 0.01 [a]	0.76 ± 0.02 [b]	2.61 ± 0.04 [ab]	7.94 ± 0.26 [ab]
WFAb4	0.66 ± 0.01 [d]	0.83 ± 0.02 [a]	0.85 ± 0.02 [c]	2.70 ± 0.03 [b]	8.47 ± 0.13 [b]
WFAb6	0.63 ± 0.01 [bc]	0.87 ± 0.03 [ab]	0.95 ± 0.00 [d]	2.88 ± 0.04 [c]	9.80 ± 0.42 [c]
WFPo2	0.65 ± 0.02 [cd]	0.90 ± 0.06 [ab]	0.80 ± 0.03 [bc]	2.56 ± 0.04 [a]	7.91 ± 0.04 [ab]
WFPo4	0.62 ± 0.01 [b]	0.99 ± 0.10 [bc]	0.91 ± 0.02 [d]	2.61 ± 0.02 [ab]	10.10 ± 0.20 [c]
WFPo6	0.58 ± 0.01 [a]	1.07 ± 0.03 [c]	1.03 ± 0.03 [e]	2.98 ± 0.05 [c]	11.15 ± 0.32 [d]

BD—bulk density; WHC or OHC—water- or oil-holding capacity; SW—swelling capacity; WSI—water solubility index; [A,B] or [a–f]—different letters in columns mean that there are significant differences between mean values (HSD Tukey's test; $p < 0.05$; $n = 3$); Ab—*A. bisporus*; Po—*P. ostreatus*; WFAb2—wheat flour with 2% addition of *A. bisporus*; WAb4—wheat flour with 4% addition of *A. bisporus*; WAb6—wheat flour with 6% addition of *A. bisporus*; WPo2—wheat flour with 2% addition of *P. ostreatus*; WPo4—wheat flour with 4% addition of *P. ostreatus*; WPo6—wheat flour with 6% addition of *P. ostreatus*.

The BD is a parameter describing the expansion and porosity of flours [93]. Bulk density was significantly lower for mushroom powders (0.08–0.10 g/mL) than for wheat flour (0.76 g/mL). It is clear that replacing part of the wheat flour with mushroom lyophilisate results in a reduction in the BD value of composite flours (0.58–0.70 g/mL). Flour blends containing oyster mushroom powder had lower BD values than flours with button mushroom. BD value is affected by practical size [7] and moisture content [59]. Van Toan and Thu [71] obtained similar BD results for wheat flour (0.72 g/mL). In turn, the powder from shiitake mushrooms dried at 65 °C had a BD of 0.372 g/mL. In another publication, the authors reported that the bulk densities of mushroom powders were 0.22 g/mL and 0.28 g/mL for *A. bisporus* and *P. ostreatus*, respectively [17].

The highest water-holding capacity (WHC) was recorded for oyster mushroom (7.32 g/g) and *A. bisporus* lyophilisate (5.17 g/g). The high WHC values of mushroom powders also resulted in an increase in WHC for blended flours. However, significantly ($p < 0.05$) higher values were recorded for flour with 4% and 6% *P. ostreatus* (0.99 and 1.07 g/g, respectively) compared with wheat flour (0.77 g/g). Similar relationships are presented by other authors. Rathore et al. [6] reported that replacing wheat flour (WHC = 37.78%) with *C. indica* powder from 5% to 20% resulted in an increase in WHC from 41.74% to 54.69%. Tu et al. [24] reported that compared with sorghum flour, for which WHC was 2.04 g/g, powders from three mushroom species had higher WHC (11.63 g/g for black ear, 9.65 g/g for silver ear, and 3.76 g/g for shiitake mushroom). The water-holding capacity of composite flours with mushroom powders (5–15%) was significantly ($p < 0.05$) higher than that of the base flour. The authors noticed a positive correlation ($p < 0.001$) of WHC and the amount of soluble and insoluble fiber in mushroom powders. Higher water-holding capacity may be related to a higher polysaccharide content. This is confirmed by our research (Table 1), where a significantly higher fiber content was found in oyster mushrooms. Cornelia and Chandra [28] explain that the lower water-absorption properties of oven-dried oyster mushroom powder compared with sun and cabinet drying are the result of greater degradation of the fiber due to high temperature and too long a water-removal process. In addition to the high content of water-soluble polysaccharides [16], mushrooms are characterized by a high proportion of polar amino acids influencing hydrophilic interactions in the food matrix [17,94]. Rathore et al. [6] indicate that the increase in the water absorption of composite flour may result from the increase in the leaching and solubility of amylose and the destruction of the crystalline structure of starch. In addition to the chemical composition (amounts of polysaccharides and hydrophilic proteins) of the mushroom powder, the practical size of the powder also influences its water-holding capacity. The results of research by Heo et al. [95] show that the water-holding capacity of freeze-dried button mushroom powder decreases significantly ($p < 0.05$) with decreasing practical size.

The OHC of mushroom lyophilisates was significantly higher (5.44 g/g for button and 7.29 g/g for oyster mushrooms) than that of wheat flour (0.68 g/g). The increase in the content of mushroom lyophilisate in composite flours also contributed to an increase in the oil-holding capacity. The OHC of flours enriched with lyophilized mushrooms ranged from 0.76 g/g for flour with 2% *A. bisporus* to 1.03 for flour with 6% *P. ostreatus*. These results are similar to those presented in other articles. In the paper by Van Toan and Thu [71] the authors report that the OHC for wheat flour is 0.91 g/g, and replacing wheat flour in an amount from 5% to 15% with shitake mushroom flour contributed to an increase in the ability to retain oil from 0.925 g/g to 1.575 g/g. In another study [17], it was reported that *A. bisporus* and *P. ostreatus* powders had higher oil-holding capacity (548.3% and 462.6% respectively) compared with maize flour (297.2%), and replacing the base flour with mushroom powders by 10% up to 50% resulted in an increase in fat binding in composite flours (from 302.2% to 433.2%). The OHC is an important feature that can improve flavor and mouthfeel and enhance texture and product yield [96]. The main ingredients that contribute to fat-holding capacity are hydrophobic proteins [97]. Thermal processing of food leads to the exposure of a larger amount of non-polar amino acids in the protein side chains, which in turn results in a stronger bond of proteins with fats [98]. These protein–lipid interactions are attributed to the physical binding of fat molecules between proteins and non-covalent bonds, including hydrophobic, hydrogen, and electrostatic bonds [99]. OHC is particularly desirable in products with minced meat, in meat substitutes, gravies, and soups, and allows the storage time of bakery and confectionery products to be extended [96].

The swelling capacity (SC) describes the ability of the matrix to expand due to water absorption [95]. Data regarding swelling capacity (SC) are presented in Table 5. Higher values for the discussed parameter were found for freeze-dried *A. bisporus* (20.51 mL/g) and *P. ostreatus* (16.51 mL/g), while the SC for wheat flour was 2.59 mL/g. However, significantly ($p < 0.05$) higher SC values of blended flours were recorded only for the versions in which the base flour was replaced by 6% mushroom powder. According to Ishara et al. [17], SC for mushroom powder is 14.47 mL/g and 13.71 mL/g for button and oyster mushrooms, respectively. In turn, the SC for composite flours where 10 to 50% of maize flour was replaced with mushroom powder ranged from 12.3 mL/g to 12.97 mL/g, while the SC for 100% maize flour was 12.81 mL/g. The results presented in the next paper [95] show that the SC of freeze-dried *A. bisporus* depends on the practical size of the mushroom powder. The data show that coarse mushroom powder has a significantly ($p < 0.05$) higher SC (10.92 mL/g) compared with fine (SC = 8.20 mL/g) and superfine (SC = 3.13 mL/g) mushroom powders. The SC of flour is influenced by the amounts of proteins, starch, and fiber [100]. Ishara et al. [17] suggest that hydrating properties, including WHC and SC, are probably caused by the presence of fiber and a porous structure favoring the absorption, retention, and swelling of flour particles in water. This is confirmed by our research showing that mushroom powders have higher content of these compounds than wheat flour (Table 1).

The results of the WSI measurements of the samples are presented in Table 5. This parameter was higher for mushroom powders (42.13% for *A. bisporus* and 54.06% for *P. ostreatus*) compared with wheat flour (7.30%). For composite flours, WSI was significantly ($p < 0.05$) higher for flours with 4% or 6% addition of mushroom lyophilisates compared with the WSI of base flour, and the highest value for this parameter was recorded for blended flour with 6% addition of oyster mushrooms (11.15%). Determining the WSI values of mushroom powders and composite flours with the addition of mushrooms has been the subject of research by other authors. Ishara et al. [17] reported that the solubility index of button mushroom flour was 60.25% and that for oyster mushroom flour was 50.99%, and the WSI for mushroom-enriched flours increased with the increase in the amount of mushroom powder. Another work reported the solubility index values for mushroom powders to be 26.55 g/g, 5.26 g/g, and 8.39 g/g for *Lentinula edodes*, black, and silver ear mushrooms, respectively [71].

The presence of proteins and soluble dietary fiber is largely responsible for the hydrating properties of mushrooms, and a higher amount of these compounds results in a higher solubility index [101]. Mushrooms are an abundant source of complex carbohydrates, including chitin and the water-soluble polysaccharide fraction (WSP). The literature data indicate that the WSP content in fresh fruiting bodies of the oyster mushroom was 78.7 mg/g dw [16], while the amount of WSP in non-processed fruiting bodies of *A. bisporus* was 96.9 mg/d dw [102]. Moreover, *A. bisporus* lyophilisate had a higher protein content than oyster mushroom (Table 1). These data could explain the higher WSI value of the *A. bisporus* powder in our study. Kraithong et al. [93] indicate that a high solubility index suggests a large content of water-soluble ingredients that can form a suspension during hydrothermal treatment. In turn, the lowest WSI may indicate a high capacity to maintain food structures during such treatments.

The water solubility index (WSI) and other indicators, e.g., water-holding capacity (WHC), allow assessment of the material's behavior in food matrices as a binder, stabilizer, and emulsifier, as well as a source of protein in dairy and baked goods, drinks, and meat products [103].

3.5. Basic Properties of Cookies

The effect of button and oyster mushroom powders on weight, thickness, diameter, and spread ratio of the shortbread cookies is given in Table 6.

Table 6. Basic properties of shortbread cookies.

Sample	Parameter					
	Weight (g)	Diameter (D) (mm)	Thickness (T) (mm)	Spread Ratio D/T	a_w	Hardness (g)
Control	26.25 ± 0.96 [a]	73.27 ± 0.30 [ab]	7.92 ± 0.41 [a]	9.27 ± 0.47 [ab]	0.513 ± 0.01 [e]	569.78 ± 112.83 [a]
Ab2	26.46 ± 1.00 [a]	74.30 ± 0.99 [bc]	8.06 ± 0.35 [a]	9.24 ± 0.45 [ab]	0.482 ± 0.01 [d]	564.94 ± 120.02 [a]
Ab4	25.60 ± 0.79 [a]	74.32 ± 0.75 [bc]	7.78 ± 0.41 [a]	9.58 ± 0.43 [b]	0.445 ± 0.01 [bc]	613.04 ± 122.59 [a]
Ab6	25.93 ± 0.90 [a]	74.31 ± 0.74 [bc]	8.21 ± 0.28 [a]	9.06 ± 0.29 [ab]	0.463 ± 0.01 [cd]	797.24 ± 123.94 [bc]
Po2	25.44 ± 0.75 [a]	75.05 ± 0.78 [c]	7.83 ± 0.20 [a]	9.59 ± 0.31 [b]	0.437 ± 0.00 [b]	526.13 ± 79.35 [a]
Po4	25.43 ± 0.70 [a]	74.62 ± 1.24 [bc]	8.32 ± 0.12 [a]	8.97 ± 0.18 [ab]	0.404 ± 0.01 [a]	659.21 ± 116.87 [ab]
Po6	25.53 ± 0.87 [a]	72.76 ± 0.36 [a]	8.29 ± 0.44 [a]	8.80 ± 0.44 [a]	0.442 ± 0.01 [bc]	894.01 ± 138.43 [c]

[a–e] the different letters in columns mean that there are significant differences between mean values (HSD Tukey's test; $p < 0.05$); a_w—water activity; control—cookies with 100% wheat flour; Ab2—cookies with 2% *A. bisporus* lyophilisate as a flour substitute; Ab4—cookies with 4% *A. bisporus* lyophilisate as a flour substitute; Ab6—cookies with 6% *A. bisporus* lyophilisate as a flour substitute; Po2—cookies with 2% *P. ostreatus* lyophilisate as a flour substitute; Po4—cookies with 4% *P. ostreatus* lyophilisate as a flour substitute; Po6—cookies with 6% *P. ostreatus* lyophilisate as a flour substitute.

Differences in the values of parameters such as weight and thickness were not significant ($p < 0.05$). In the case of the next parameter, diameter, it was found that replacing wheat flour with button mushroom powder slightly increased the diameter of the cookies, but the use of *A. bisporus* lyophilisate in an amount from 2% to 6% had no significant effect. In turn, substituting wheat flour with freeze-dried oyster mushroom contributed to a significant change in the diameter of the cookies. It was observed that with a larger amount of oyster mushroom lyophilisate, the diameter of the supplemented cookies decreased; however, the addition of 2% freeze-dried oyster mushroom resulted in a larger diameter of the cookies (75.05 mm), and the addition of 6% oyster mushroom lyophilisate caused a decrease in diameter (72.76 mm) compared with cookies without mushrooms (D = 73.27 mm).

The spread ratio parameter describes the shape and quality of cookies [72]. The discussed parameter of the samples ranged from 8.80 (for the Po6 sample) to 9.59 (for the Po2 sample), however, no significant ($p < 0.05$) differences were noted between the results.

Chen et al. [22] reported that using dried *C. militaris* in amounts of 1%, 3%, and 5% instead of wheat flour, the supplemented cookies had similar diameter, thickness, and spread ratio compared with the control cookies, but the weights of cookies with 3% or 5% mushrooms were significantly lower than the control cookies. Rathore et al. [6] write that the addition of *Calocybe indica* in an amount of 5–20% to the cookies had no significant effect on the weight. However, it was found that with the increase in the mushroom powder content, the thickness increased significantly, while opposite tendencies were observed for the diameter and spread factor. The addition of *A. bisporus* to barley flour cookies in an amount from 10% to 50% resulted in significant increases in diameter and weight of samples, with 20% or more addition of mushroom flour producing a decrease in the thickness value and spread ratio; however, no significant difference was found for these two parameters ($p \leq 0.05$) [72].

The results regarding water activity (a_w) are presented in Table 6. This parameter corresponded to moisture content (Table 1). The highest a_w values were noted for the control sample (a_w = 0.513) and cookies with 2% *A. bisporus* (a_w = 0.482), and the lowest for cookies with 4% *P. ostreatus* powder (a_w = 0.404); however, an increasing tendency was observed for cookies with 4% and 6% mushroom. Water activity and moisture content are crucial in the determination of the quality, acceptability, and storage stability of bakery products with high content of sugar and fat. Typical cookies have low water activity and low final moisture content (1–5%), which guarantees a long shelf life [27,104]. Food with a_w below 0.6 is considered microbiologically stable. However, a drop in a_w below 0.2 results in accelerated fat oxidation reactions [104].

Shams et al. [72] reported that cookies based on barley flour were characterized by comparatively low a_w value (0.402) and moisture content (3.81%), while cookies in which 10% to 50% of barley flour was replaced with *A. bisporus* powder were characterized by significantly higher water activity and moisture content. Substitution of wheat flour with *C. militaris* powder from 1% to 5% resulted in a slight increase in moisture content, from 6.45% for control cookies to 6.70% for cookies with 5% *C. militaris* flour, but no significant differences were found for this parameter [22]. In turn, Rathore et al. [6] reported that wheat cookies supplemented with *C. indica* (from 5% to 20%) had moisture content ranging from 5.5% to 4.8%, with the highest moisture content in control cookies (5.5%).

The hardness of the control samples was 569.78 g (Table 6). In turn, the value of this parameter for cookies enriched with mushrooms ranged from 564.94 g for cookies with the addition of 2% button mushroom lyophilisate to 894.01 g for cookies with the addition of 6% *P. ostreatus* powder. Replacing 4% or 6% base flour with mushroom lyophilisate resulted in an increase in the hardness of the cookies, but significantly ($p < 0.05$) higher values compared with the control sample were recorded only for cookies with 6% addition of mushroom lyophilisates. The influence of the addition of mushroom flours to base flours on the hardness of cookies has been analyzed by other researchers. Shams et al. [72] reported that a decrease was recorded in the hardness of barley cookies enriched with *A. bisporus* lyophilisate in an amount of 10–50%. Control cookies exhibited the maximum peak force (24.75 N), while for cookies enriched with mushroom powder, a decreasing trend was found for hardness, from 21.35 N to 14.31 N. Cornelia and Chandra [28] report that the increase in the hardness of cookies with the addition of *P. ostreatus* in an amount of 25–35% was the result of the increase in the protein content. However, this parameter also depended on the kind of fat used and on the method of drying mushrooms in the procedure of preparing the mushroom flour. In another work [22], when replacing wheat flour in cookies with *C. militaris* powder in amounts of 1%, 3%, or 5%, a slight decrease in hardness was observed. The hardness of the basic cookies was 3.75 N, and for the supplemented cookies from 3.24 N to 3.17 N, but the differences were not significant ($p < 0.05$). Chen et al. [22] suggest that the lower hardness values may be a result of disruption of the gluten network by the addition of *C. militaris* powder. Rathore et al. [6] noted an increasing trend in the hardness of wheat cookies with the addition of *C. indica* powder. The hardness increased from 23.14 N for the control cookies to 43.18 N for the cookies with the highest content (20%) of mushroom powder. However, there was no significant ($p < 0.05$) difference between the hardness of control cookies and those containing 5% mushroom powder. The authors explain the increase in this parameter by the presence of a larger amount of fiber in the *C. indica* powder, which could have disturbed the protein–starch interaction and changed the texture of the cookies. Tu et al. [24] reported that the change in the hardness of sorghum cookies, in which the flour was partially replaced by black ear, silver ear, and shiitake mushroom powder, was the result of a change in fiber, protein, and water content. Replacing 5% to 15% of sorghum flour with *L. edodes* or black ear mushroom powder significantly ($p < 0.05$) increased the hardness of the cookies, while no such effect was found in the case of silver ear mushroom powder. The authors emphasize the occurrence of positive correlations ($p < 0.01$) between hardness and insoluble dietary fiber, protein, and moisture content. Research shows that the hardness of biscuits increases gradually with increasing protein and gluten content [105]. However, gluten may play a secondary role in determining the texture of cookies [106]. It is possible to obtain gluten-free cookies, e.g., based on sorghum [24] or legume flour [101]. It is suggested that the texture of cookies depends mainly on starch gelatinization and sugar crystallization and not on the protein/starch structure [107]. Dietary fiber interacts physically with starch, acting as a coating or capsule that protects the starch granules from gelatinization and digestion [108]. This confirms the results presented in this paper. The significantly higher hardness of Ab6 and Po6 samples may be the result of a higher amount of fiber compared with cookies made from 100% wheat flour (Table 1). The hardness of cookies is influenced by interaction of many components of the food matrix, including primarily starch granules and other compounds: proteins/gluten, fiber, sugar, fat, and water [109].

3.6. Total Phenolic Content (TPC) and Antioxidant Properties

The TPC and antioxidant activities of the wheat flour, mushroom lyophilisates, and shortbread cookies enriched with button and oyster mushroom powders are presented in Figure 2.

Wheat flour and bakery products based on it are characterized by a low content of total polyphenols and low antioxidant properties [110–112]. The results presented in this work also confirm this. Wheat flour was characterized by the lowest content of TPC (0.47 mg GAE/g dw) as well as the lowest antioxidant properties compared with mushroom powders, with an almost four-fold higher content of polyphenols and higher antioxidant properties recorded for freeze-dried *A. bisporus* than in *P. ostreatus*. As expected, the increase in the addition of mushroom flour contributed to a significant ($p < 0.05$) increase in the TPC and antioxidant properties of shortbread cookies; however, no significant difference was observed between the amount of TPC in control cookies (0.21 mg GAE/g dw) and that in cookies with 2% addition of *P. ostreatus* (0.26 mg GAE/g dw), nor between levels of antioxidant properties measured via the ABTS method for control cookies and cookies with 2% addition of button or oyster mushroom powders.

A. bisporus and *P. ostreatus* are good sources of phenolic compounds and other antioxidants [76,102,113]. In a previous study [14], the content of total polyphenols in ethanolic extracts from *A. bisporus* was recorded at the level of 10.44 mg GAE/g dw. Smolskaitė et al. [114] reported that, depending on the type of solvent, the TPC values in extracts of button and oyster mushrooms were in the ranges of 4.21–4.64 and 4.26–5.67 mg GAE/g, respectively. Palacios et al. [115] reported that in methanol extracts of several tested mushroom species, the button mushroom, after *Boletus edulis*, had the highest polyphenol content, while the oyster mushroom had lower phenolic concentrations.

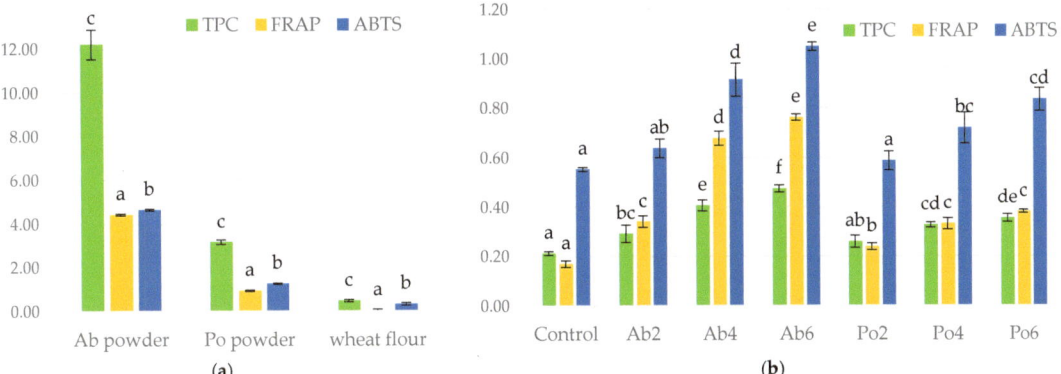

Figure 2. Total polyphenol content (TPC) (in mg GAE/g dw) and antioxidant properties (FRAP, DPPH) (in µmol TE/g dw) of (**a**) mushroom powders, wheat flour, and (**b**) shortbread cookies. a–f—different letters between bars of the same color mean that there are significant differences between mean values (HSD Tukey's test; $p < 0.05$; $n = 3$); Ab—*A. bisporus*; Po—*P. ostreatus*; control—cookies with 100% wheat flour; Ab2—cookies with 2% *A. bisporus* lyophilisate as a flour substitute; Ab4—cookies with 4% *A. bisporus* lyophilisate as a flour substitute; Ab6—cookies with 6% *A. bisporus* lyophilisate as a flour substitute; Po2—cookies with 2% *P. ostreatus* lyphilisate as a flour substitute; Po4—cookies with 4% *P. ostreatus* lyophilisate as a flour substitute; Po6—cookies with 6% *P. ostreatus* lyophilisate as a flour substitute.

Our results regarding the increase in TPC and the antioxidant properties of cookies enriched with mushroom powders are in agreement with the results presented in other articles. Enrichment with *C. militaris* powder positively affected the TPC and antioxidant activity (FRAP, DPPH and ABTS assay) of cookies with 1%, 3%, and 5% mushroom powder but there was no significant difference between the control and cookies with 1% *C. militaris* [22]. Rathore et al. [6] reported that in cookies in which wheat flour was replaced with *C. indica* powder in amounts from 5% to 20%, significantly ($p < 0.05$) higher content of polyphenols and flavonoids was noted, and the highest values observed were 17.53 mg GAE/g dw and 0.42 µg quercetin/g dw for cookies with 20% *C. indica*, while for the control sample, 6.26 mg GAE/g dw and 0.14 µg quercetin/g dw were recorded, respectively. The authors also observed an increasing trend in the level of antioxidant activity according to DPPH and FRAP assays for cookies with increasing content of *C. indica* powder. In another study [31], replacing barley flour with *A. bisporus* flour (from 10% to 50%) significantly increased the amount of TPC (from 53.36 to 71.12 mg GAE/g, respectively) compared with control cookies (49.23 mg GAE/g). In the same work, it was reported that cookies with a higher content of mushroom powder were characterized by higher DPPH scavenging activity and reducing power.

The increase in the TPC of mushroom-enriched cookies may be the result of the presence of the mushroom fiber, which limits the release of bound phenolic compounds [72]. Polyphenolic compounds tend to bind with polysaccharides, which largely affects the antioxidant properties of the polysaccharide fraction of mushrooms [116]. In turn, Han and Koh [117] write that thermal processing of food results in both the release of insoluble bound polyphenols and the breakdown of polyphenols under the influence of high temperature. The rise in antioxidant activity in bakery products enriched with mushroom powder may be the result not only of larger amounts of antioxidant compounds such as polyphenols or flavonoids present in greater amounts in mushrooms than in the base flour but also the presence other antioxidants like high-molecular brown pigments—melnoidins—formed in the Maillard reaction during the baking process [72].

3.7. Sensory Evaluation

The results of the sensory evaluation of shortbread cookies are presented in Figure 3.

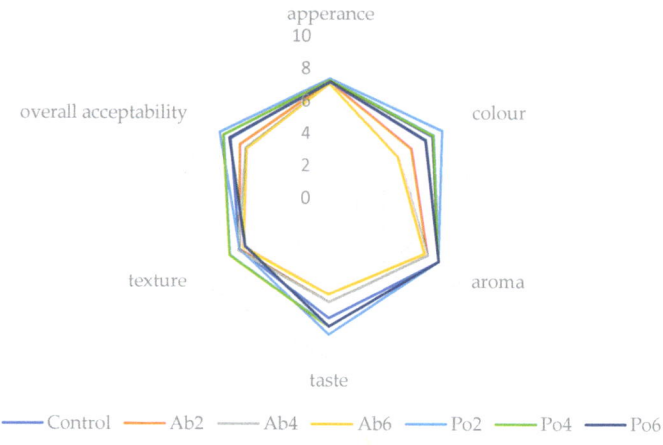

Figure 3. Sensory evaluation of shortbread cookies. Control—cookies with 100% wheat flour; Ab2—cookies with 2% *A. bisporus* lyophilisate as a flour substitute; Ab4—cookies with 4% *A. bisporus* lyophilisate as a flour substitute; Ab6—cookies with 6% *A. bisporus* lyophilisate as a flour substitute; Po2—cookies with 2% *P. ostreatus* lyophilisate as a flour substitute; Po4—cookies with 4% *P. ostreatus* lyophilisate as a flour substitute; Po6—cookies with 6% *P. ostreatus* lyophilisate as a flour substitute.

Appearance was the least differentiated parameter according to the panelists (Figures 1 and 3). The average number of points for the appearance of shortbread cookies ranged from 7.0 (for Ab4 and Ab6 cookies) to 7.3 (for Po2 cookies). This is confirmed by the results for basic cookie parameters such as weight, thickness, and spread ratio, which also varied only slightly (Table 6). Modification of the basic recipe consisting of replacing part of the wheat flour with freeze-dried mushrooms had a greater impact on other attributes in the sensory evaluation of cookies. The base cookies had an average value of 7.5 for the color attribute. Lower scores for color were recorded for all versions of the cookies with button mushrooms (6.0 for Ab2, 5.0 for Ab4 and Ab6) and cookies with 6% oyster mushrooms (7.0). In turn, the colors of cookies with 2% or 4% freeze-dried oyster mushrooms were rated the highest (8.2 and 7.6, respectively). Taking into account the results of color parameters (Table 4), it can be seen that the cookies with *A. bisporus*, rated lowest by the panelists in terms of color, were also characterized by the lowest values of the L* parameter and the highest ΔE and BI. In turn, the highest-rated cookies with 2% *P. ostreatus* were characterized by the lowest ΔE, a slightly lower value of the L* parameter, and a slightly higher BI value, and were more yellow and red in comparison with the control samples. The aroma of the control cookies and all versions of the cookies with *P. ostreatus* powder were evaluated similarly (8.0). In turn, the aroma of cookies with button mushrooms was assessed in the range from 7.0 (Ab6) to 7.2 (Ab2, Ab4). Cookies with oyster mushroom obtained higher taste scores, from 8.0 (for Po4 and Po6) to 8.5 (for Po2) compared with the control cookies (7.5). The texture of the shortbread cookies was rated as follows: Po2 (7.2) > Ab4 (6.6) > control, Ab2, Po2 (6.5) > Ab6 (6.2) > Po6 (6.1) samples. Taking into account the hardness results (Table 6), the lowest texture scores in the sensory evaluation are consistent with the highest averages for hardness in the case of cookies with 6% mushroom powder. Higher notes for overall acceptability were recorded for cookies with the addition of oyster mushrooms (from 7.3 for

Po6 to 8.0 for Po2) compared with the notes for control cookies (7.2). In turn, cookies with button mushroom powder had the lowest scores, from 6.0 (Ab6) to 6.5 (Ab2).

The results presented by other authors regarding sensory evaluation show that the degree of acceptance of cookies enriched with mushroom powders depends on the species of mushrooms and the amount of added mushroom flour. According to Chen et al. [22], replacing base flour with *C. militaris* powder at an amount of 1% had no significant effect on all analyzed attributes relative to the control. A larger addition of mushroom powder (3% and 5%) lowered the color assessment by the panel. The odor and taste of samples with 1% and 3% *C. militaris* were rated higher than those of the control cookies. In turn, cookies with 5% mushroom powder added had too strong a taste and odor, which resulted in lower scores for these attributes. Cookies with 3% *C. militaris* received the highest notes for the following attributes: overall acceptability, taste, odor, and texture. Another study [27] analyzed the results of sensory evaluation on a 7-point scale for biscuits enriched with *Pleurotus sajor-caju* powder in amounts of 4%, 8%, and 12%. Biscuits with 4% mushroom flour received the highest marks for aroma, color, flavor and overall acceptance. The authors reported that biscuits with 4% *P. sajor-caju* had a milder flavour, lighter color, finer texture, and were comparable to the control biscuits. In turn, cookies with 12% *P. sajor-caju*, according to the evaluators, had an unattractive texture, color that was too dark, and flavor that was too intense. The authors emphasized that despite the highest scores being achieved by cookies with 4% mushroom powder, cookies with 8% *P. saju-caju* were also acceptable in terms of appearance, crispiness, flavor, and overall acceptance. The results of the sensory evaluation on a 9-point scale presented by Van Toan and Thu [71] show that the addition of 5% shiitake flour can positively affect the improvement of the attributes (color, taste, aroma, crispiness, and overall impression) of cookies compared with basic cookies. The lowest scores were given to cookies with a maximum of 15% mushroom flour. Although addition of 5%, 10%, or 15% *L. edodes* flour was acceptable to consumers, the authors recommended the addition of 5%. Replacing the basic flour with a larger amount of mushroom flour may also have a positive impact on significantly higher scores for selected attributes in the 9-point assessment, as presented by Baltacıoğlu et al. [91] in their work. Among biscuits enriched with 10%, 20% or 30% *P. ostreatus* powder, biscuits with 10% mushroom flour were characterized by the highest scores for color, homogeneity and size of pores, odor, and overall acceptability. The versions of cookies with 20% or 30% added *P. ostreatus* powder received lower scores.

In sensory evaluation, attributes such as taste or aroma are determined by the presence of compounds such as free and soluble sugars, sugar alcohols, organic acids, free amino acids, and 5′-nucleotides [63,118]. For example, the high content of free sugars and sugar alcohols may increase the perception of the moderately sweet taste of mushrooms [119]. As Mau writes [118], mannitol contributes most to the sweet taste, but the predominant taste and flavor of mushrooms is umami. According to the data collected and described by Jiang et al. [120], the button mushroom is characterized by a sweet, umami, and typical mushroom flavor, while a sour, astringent, and bitter flavor is typical of oyster mushrooms. Mau [118] suggests that due to the presence of monosodium glutamate-like (MSG-like) components, mushrooms go well with meat, seafood, soups, and cooked vegetables, but they cannot improve the taste of fruit, juices, desserts, or cooked cereals. According to the same publication, the level of monosodium glutamate equivalent was higher in *A. bisporus* (114%) than in *P. ostreatus* (48.0%), taking into account dry weight. Selli et al. [121] reported that thermal treatment is an important factor for odorants in mushrooms. High temperature contributes to the evaporation of compounds and the formation of aroma precursors, mainly through non-enzymatic browning reactions.

4. Conclusions

A. bisporus and *P. ostreatus* lyophilisates were characterized by higher amounts of basic nutrients, polyphenol compounds, elements (K, Mg, Na, Fe, Zn, Cu, Ni) compared with wheat flour. At the same time, the content of Pb and Cd was below the maximum safe limits set by EU regulations. The use of the lyophilisates as a partial substitute (2–6%) for wheat flour in shortbread cookies contributed to a significant ($p < 0.05$) increase in the amounts of selected elements, protein, and ash in all versions of the cookies. Moreover, samples with fiber above 3 g/100 g (Ab2, Ab4, Po2) and above 6 g/100 g (Ab6, Po4, Po6) were obtained, which would allow the use of "source of/high in fiber" nutrition claims.

The results presented in this study show that substituting a small amount (2–6%) of wheat flour with mushroom lyophilisates affects the functional properties of composite flours as well as the finished products. The values of the functional parameters of blended flours compared with the base flour were significantly ($p < 0.05$) lower for BD and higher for OHC for all blended flour versions, higher for WSI for flours with the addition of 4–6% mushroom powders, and higher for WHC for flours with 4% and 6% addition of oyster mushroom lyophilisate. The values of basic parameters of cookies such as weight, thickness, and spread ratio of enriched cookies did not differ statistically ($p < 0.05$) from the control samples. In turn, the values of the a_w parameter were lower. With the increase in the addition of mushroom lyophilisate, the L* value was significantly lower, while the value of the parameter a* (redness) increased. Higher ΔE and BI were recorded for the cookies with *A. bisporus*. Cookies with 6% mushroom powders (Ab6, Po6) were characterized by significantly higher hardness. The results of the sensory evaluation clearly indicate that among the analyzed versions of the cookies, the highest scores were given to samples with the addition of oyster mushroom, while the lowest scores were given to cookies with the addition of button mushrooms.

To sum up, the blending of wheat flour with oyster mushroom lyophilisate up to 6% seems to be a compromise between obtaining products with improved nutritional composition and maintaining sensory quality and acceptance by consumers.

Author Contributions: Conceptualization, A.S.; methodology, A.S., E.J.-R. and W.G.; software, A.S. and W.G.; validation, A.S., E.J.-R. and W.G.; formal analysis, A.S., E.J.-R. and W.G.; investigation, A.S., E.J.-R. and W.G.; resources, A.S. and E.J.-R.; data curation, A.S. and W.G.; writing—original draft preparation, A.S.; writing—review and editing, A.S.; visualization, A.S. and E.J.-R.; supervision, A.S.; project administration, A.S.; funding acquisition, E.J.-R. All authors have read and agreed to the published version of the manuscript.

Funding: Project financed under the program of the Minister of Education and Science under the name "Regional Initiative of Excellence" in 2019–2023, project number 029/RID/2018/19, funding amount PLN 11.927.330.00.

Institutional Review Board Statement: Not applicable.

Informed Consent Statement: Not applicable.

Data Availability Statement: The data used to support the findings of this study can be made available by the corresponding author upon request.

Conflicts of Interest: The authors declare no conflicts of interest.

References

1. Sadowska-Rociek, A.; Cieślik, E. Carbohydrate-Based Fat Mimetics Can Affect the Levels of 3-Monochloropropane-1,2-Diol Esters and Glycidyl Esters in Shortbread Biscuits. *Plant Foods Hum. Nutr.* **2019**, *74*, 216–222. [CrossRef]
2. Production and Distribution of Confectionery. Bittersweet Prospects for the Industr (in Polish: "Produkcja i Dystrybucja Słodyczy. Słodko-Gorzkie Perspektywy Branży). Available online: https://www.pekao.com.pl/dam/jcr:a82e0025-8cf7-4726-bbc9-c16caa3 5cc53/Produkcja%20i%20dystrybucja%20s%C5%82odyczy_kwiecien2023.pdf (accessed on 19 April 2023).
3. Kruszewski, B.; Sujka, K. The influence of addition of beetroot pomace on shortbread cookies quality (in Polish: Wpływ dodatku wytłoków z buraka ćwikłowego na wybrane cechy ciastek kruchych). *Prz. Zboż. Młyn.* **2022**, *4*, 26–31.
4. Pareyt, B.; Wilderjans, E.; Goesaert, H.; Brijs, K.; Delcour, J.A. The Role of Gluten in a Sugar-Snap Cookie System: A Model Approach Based on Gluten–Starch Blends. *J. Cereal Sci.* **2008**, *48*, 863–869. [CrossRef]
5. Li, Y.; Wang, H.; Wang, L.; Qiu, J.; Li, Z.; Wang, L. Milling of Wheat Bran: Influence on Digestibility, Hydrolysis and Nutritional Properties of Bran Protein during in Vitro Digestion. *Food Chem.* **2023**, *404*, 134559. [CrossRef]
6. Rathore, H.; Sehwag, S.; Prasad, S.; Sharma, S. Technological, Nutritional, Functional and Sensorial Attributes of the Cookies Fortified with Calocybe Indica Mushroom. *J. Food Meas. Charact.* **2019**, *13*, 976–987. [CrossRef]

7. Nkurikiye, E.; Pulivarthi, M.K.; Bhatt, A.; Siliveru, K.; Li, Y. Bulk and Flow Characteristics of Pulse Flours: A Comparative Study of Yellow Pea, Lentil, and Chickpea Flours of Varying Particle Sizes. *J. Food Eng.* **2023**, *357*, 111647. [CrossRef]
8. Zlatanović, S.; Kalušević, A.; Micić, D.; Laličić-Petronijević, J.; Tomić, N.; Ostojić, S.; Gorjanović, S. Functionality and Storability of Cookies Fortified at the Industrial Scale with up to 75% of Apple Pomace Flour Produced by Dehydration. *Foods* **2019**, *8*, 561. [CrossRef]
9. Verhagen, H.; Vos, E.; Francl, S.; Heinonen, M.; Van Loveren, H. Status of Nutrition and Health Claims in Europe. *Arch. Biochem. Biophys.* **2010**, *501*, 6–15. [CrossRef]
10. Duarte, P.; Teixeira, M.; Costa E Silva, S. Healthy Eating as a Trend: Consumers' Perceptions towards Products with Nutrition and Health Claims. *RBGN* **2021**, *23*, 405–421. [CrossRef]
11. Siwulski, M.; Niedzielski, P.; Budka, A.; Budzyńska, S.; Kuczyńska-Kippen, N.; Kalač, P.; Sobieralski, K.; Mleczek, M. Patterns of Changes in the Mineral Composition of Agaricus Bisporus Cultivated in Poland between 1977 and 2020. *J. Food Compos. Anal.* **2022**, *112*, 104660. [CrossRef]
12. Oyedele, O.A.; Adeosun, M.V.; Koyenikan, O.O. Low Cost Production of Mushroom Using Agricultural Waste in a Controlled Environment for Economic Advancement. *Int. J. Waste Resour.* **2018**, *8*, 1–5. [CrossRef]
13. Mleczek, M.; Rzymski, P.; Budka, A.; Siwulski, M.; Jasińska, A.; Kalač, P.; Poniedziałek, B.; Gąsecka, M.; Niedzielski, P. Elemental Characteristics of Mushroom Species Cultivated in China and Poland. *J. Food Compos. Anal.* **2018**, *66*, 168–178. [CrossRef]
14. Sławińska, A.; Sołowiej, B.G.; Radzki, W.; Fornal, E. Wheat Bread Supplemented with Agaricus Bisporus Powder: Effect on Bioactive Substances Content and Technological Quality. *Foods* **2022**, *11*, 3786. [CrossRef] [PubMed]
15. Radzki, W.; Slawinska, A.; Jablonska-Rys, E.; Gustaw, W. Antioxidant Capacity and Polyphenolic Content of Dried Wild Edible Mushrooms from Poland. *Int. J. Med. Mushr.* **2014**, *16*, 65–75. [CrossRef]
16. Radzki, W.; Ziaja-Sołtys, M.; Nowak, J.; Rzymowska, J.; Topolska, J.; Sławińska, A.; Michalak-Majewska, M.; Zalewska-Korona, M.; Kuczumow, A. Effect of Processing on the Content and Biological Activity of Polysaccharides from Pleurotus Ostreatus Mushroom. *LWT—Food Sci. Techol.* **2016**, *66*, 27–33. [CrossRef]
17. Ishara, J.R.; Sila, D.N.; Kenji, G.M.; Buzera, A.K. Nutritional and Functional Properties of Mushroom (*Agaricus Bisporus* & *Pleurotus Ostreatus*) and Their Blends with Maize Flour. *AJFST* **2018**, *6*, 33–41. [CrossRef]
18. Carrasco-González, J.A.; Serna-Saldívar, S.O.; Gutiérrez-Uribe, J.A. Nutritional Composition and Nutraceutical Properties of the Pleurotus Fruiting Bodies: Potential Use as Food Ingredient. *J. Food Compos. Anal.* **2017**, *58*, 69–81. [CrossRef]
19. Wong, K.M.; Decker, E.A.; Autio, W.R.; Toong, K.; DiStefano, G.; Kinchla, A.J. Utilizing Mushrooms to Reduce Overall Sodium in Taco Filling Using Physical and Sensory Evaluation. *J. Food Sci.* **2017**, *82*, 2379–2386. [CrossRef] [PubMed]
20. Cerón-Guevara, M.I.; Rangel-Vargas, E.; Lorenzo, J.M.; Bermúdez, R.; Pateiro, M.; Rodríguez, J.A.; Sánchez-Ortega, I.; Santos, E.M. Reduction of Salt and Fat in Frankfurter Sausages by Addition of Agaricus Bisporus and Pleurotus Ostreatus Flour. *Foods* **2020**, *9*, 760. [CrossRef]
21. Stoffel, F.; Santana, W.D.O.; Fontana, R.C.; Camassola, M. Use of Pleurotus Albidus Mycoprotein Flour to Produce Cookies: Evaluation of Nutritional Enrichment and Biological Activity. *Innov. Food Sci. Emerg.* **2021**, *68*, 102642. [CrossRef]
22. Chen, C.; Han, Y.; Li, S.; Wang, R.; Tao, C. Nutritional, Antioxidant, and Quality Characteristics of Novel Cookies Enriched with Mushroom (*Cordyceps militaris*) Flour. *CyTA—J. Food* **2021**, *19*, 137–145. [CrossRef]
23. Owheruo, J.O.; Edo, G.I.; Oluwajuyitan, D.T.; Faturoti, A.O.; Martins, I.E.; Akpoghelie, P.O.; Agbo, J.J. Quality Evaluation of Value-Added Nutritious Biscuit with High Antidiabetic Properties from Blends of Wheat Flour and Oyster Mushroom. *Food Chem. Adv.* **2023**, *3*, 100375. [CrossRef]
24. Tu, J.; Brennan, M.A.; Hui, X.; Wang, R.; Peressini, D.; Bai, W.; Cheng, P.; Brennan, C.S. Utilisation of Dried Shiitake, Black Ear and Silver Ear Mushrooms into Sorghum Biscuits Manipulates the Predictive Glycaemic Response in Relation to Variations in Biscuit Physical Characteristics. *Int. J. Food Sci. Technol.* **2022**, *57*, 2715–2728. [CrossRef]
25. Pelaes Vital, A.C.; Goto, P.A.; Hanai, L.N.; Gomes-da-Costa, S.M.; De Abreu Filho, B.A.; Nakamura, C.V.; Matumoto-Pintro, P.T. Microbiological, Functional and Rheological Properties of Low Fat Yogurt Supplemented with Pleurotus Ostreatus Aqueous Extract. *LWT—Food Sci. Techol.* **2015**, *64*, 1028–1035. [CrossRef]
26. Radzki, W.; Skrzypczak, K.; Sołowiej, B.; Jabłońska-Ryś, E.; Gustaw, W. Properties of Yogurts Enriched with Crude Polysaccharides Extracted from Pleurotus Ostreatus Cultivated Mushroom. *Foods* **2023**, *12*, 4033. [CrossRef]
27. Ng, S.H.; Robert, S.D.; Wan Ahmad, W.A.N.; Wan Ishak, W.R. Incorporation of Dietary Fibre-Rich Oyster Mushroom (Pleurotus Sajor-Caju) Powder Improves Postprandial Glycaemic Response by Interfering with Starch Granule Structure and Starch Digestibility of Biscuit. *Food Chem.* **2017**, *227*, 358–368. [CrossRef]
28. Cornelia, M.; Chandra, J. Utilization of White Oyster Mushroom Powder (Pleurotus Ostreatus (Jacq.) P. Kumm.) in the Making of Biscuit as Emergency Food Product. *EurAsian J. BioSciences* **2019**, *13*, 1859–1866.
29. Lu, X.; Brennan, M.A.; Serventi, L.; Liu, J.; Guan, W.; Brennan, C.S. Addition of Mushroom Powder to Pasta Enhances the Antioxidant Content and Modulates the Predictive Glycaemic Response of Pasta. *Food Chem.* **2018**, *264*, 199–209. [CrossRef]
30. Gaglio, R.; Guarcello, R.; Venturella, G.; Palazzolo, E.; Francesca, N.; Moschetti, G.; Settanni, L.; Saporita, P.; Gargano, M.L. Microbiological, Chemical and Sensory Aspects of Bread Supplemented with Different Percentages of the Culinary Mushroom *Pleurotus Eryngii* in Powder Form. *Int. J. Food Sci. Technol.* **2019**, *54*, 1197–1205. [CrossRef]
31. Salehi, F.; Kashaninejad, M.; Asadi, F.; Najafi, A. Improvement of Quality Attributes of Sponge Cake Using Infrared Dried Button Mushroom. *J. Food Sci. Technol.* **2016**, *53*, 1418–1423. [CrossRef]

32. Proserpio, C.; Lavelli, V.; Gallotti, F.; Laureati, M.; Pagliarini, E. Effect of Vitamin D2 Fortification Using Pleurotus Ostreatus in a Whole-Grain Cereal Product on Child Acceptability. *Nutrients* **2019**, *11*, 2441. [CrossRef]
33. Olawuyi, I.F.; Lee, W.Y. Quality and Antioxidant Properties of Functional Rice Muffins Enriched with Shiitake Mushroom and Carrot Pomace. *Int. J. Food Sci. Technol.* **2019**, *54*, 2321–2328. [CrossRef]
34. Jarosz, M.; Rychlik, E.; Stoś, K.; Charzewska, J. *Normy Żywienia dla Populacji Polski i Ich Zastosowanie*; Narodowy Instytut Zdrowia Publicznego—Państwowy Zakład Higieny: Warszawa, Poland, 2020; ISBN 978-83-65870-28-5.
35. Szponar, L.; Sekuła, W.; Rychlik, E.; Ołtarzewski, M.; Figurska, K. *Badania Indywidualnego Spożycia Żywności i Stanu Odżywienia w Gospodarstwach Domowych*, 1st ed.; Instytut Żywności i Żywienia: Warszawa, Poland, 2003; ISBN 83-86060-60-3.
36. EFSA Panel on Dietetic Products, Nutrition and Allergies (NDA). Scientific Opinion on the Tolerable Upper Intake Level of Calcium. *EFSA J.* **2012**, *10*, 2814. [CrossRef]
37. EFSA Panel on Dietetic Products, Nutrition and Allergies (NDA). Scientific Opinion on Dietary Reference Values for Magnesium. *EFSA J.* **2015**, *13*, 4186. [CrossRef]
38. EFSA Panel on Dietetic Products, Nutrition and Allergies (NDA). Scientific Opinion on Dietary Reference Values for Iron. *EFSA J.* **2015**, *13*, 4254. [CrossRef]
39. EFSA Panel on Dietetic Products, Nutrition and Allergies (NDA). Scientific Opinion on Dietary Reference Values for Zinc. *EFSA J.* **2014**, *12*, 3844. [CrossRef]
40. EFSA Panel on Dietetic Products, Nutrition and Allergies (NDA). Scientific Opinion on Dietary Reference Values for Copper. *EFSA J.* **2015**, *13*, 4253. [CrossRef]
41. EFSA Panel on Dietetic Products, Nutrition and Allergies (NDA). Scientific Opinion on Dietary Reference Values for Selenium. *EFSA J.* **2014**, *12*, 3846. [CrossRef]
42. EFSA Panel on Dietetic Products, Nutrition and Allergies (NDA). Scientific Opinion on Dietary Reference Values for Manganese. *EFSA J.* **2013**, *11*, 3419. [CrossRef]
43. Kalač, P. A Review of Chemical Composition and Nutritional Value of Wild-growing and Cultivated Mushrooms. *J. Sci. Food Agric.* **2013**, *93*, 209–218. [CrossRef] [PubMed]
44. Falandysz, J.; Borovička, J. Macro and Trace Mineral Constituents and Radionuclides in Mushrooms: Health Benefits and Risks. *Appl. Microbiol. Biotechnol.* **2013**, *97*, 477–501. [CrossRef] [PubMed]
45. Commission Regulation (EU) 2023/915 of 25 April 2023 on Maximum Levels for Certain Contaminants in Food and Repealing Regulation (EC) No 1881/2006 (Text with EEA Relevance). *OJ* **2023**, L 119, 103–157.
46. American Association of Cereal Chemistry (AACC). AACC Approved Methods of Analysis, 11th Ed. Available online: https://www.cerealsgrains.org/resources/methods/Pages/default.aspx (accessed on 1 October 2023).
47. European Commision (EC). Consolidated Text: Regulation (EU) No 1169/2011 of the European Parliament and of the Council of 25 October 2011 on the Provision of Food Information to Consumers, Amending Regulations (EC) No 1924/2006 and (EC) No 1925/2006 of the European Parliament and of the Council, and Repealing Commission Directive 87/250/EEC, Council Directive 90/496/EEC, Commission Directive 1999/10/EC, Directive 2000/13/EC of the European Parliament and of the Council, Commission Directives 2002/67/EC and 2008/5/EC and Commission Regulation (EC) No 608/2004 (Text with EEA Relevance). *OJ* **2011**, L 304, 18.
48. Kasprzyk, A.; Kilar, J.; Chwil, S.; Rudaś, M. Content of Selected Macro- and Microelements in the Liver of Free-Living Wild Boars (Sus Scrofa L.) from Agricultural Areas and Health Risks Associated with Consumption of Liver. *Animals* **2020**, *10*, 1519. [CrossRef] [PubMed]
49. Ramírez-Jiménez, A.; Guerra-Hernández, E.; García-Villanova, B. Browning Indicators in Bread. *J. Agric. Food Chem.* **2000**, *48*, 4176–4181. [CrossRef] [PubMed]
50. Carini, E.; Vittadini, E.; Curti, E.; Antoniazzi, F.; Viazzani, P. Effect of Different Mixers on Physicochemical Properties and Water Status of Extruded and Laminated Fresh Pasta. *Food Chem.* **2010**, *122*, 462–469. [CrossRef]
51. Okezie, B.O.; Bello, A.B. Physicochemical and Functional Properties of Winged Bean Flour and Isolate Compared with Soy Isolate. *J. Food Sci.* **1988**, *53*, 450–454. [CrossRef]
52. Tosh, S.M.; Yada, S. Dietary Fibres in Pulse Seeds and Fractions: Characterization, Functional Attributes, and Applications. *Food Res. Int.* **2010**, *43*, 450–460. [CrossRef]
53. Zhang, Z.; Song, H.; Peng, Z.; Luo, Q.; Ming, J.; Zhao, G. Characterization of Stipe and Cap Powders of Mushroom (Lentinus Edodes) Prepared by Different Grinding Methods. *J. Food Eng.* **2012**, *109*, 406–413. [CrossRef]
54. Tan, E.-S.; Ying-Yuan, N.; Gan, C.-Y. A Comparative Study of Physicochemical Characteristics and Functionalities of Pinto Bean Protein Isolate (PBPI) against the Soybean Protein Isolate (SPI) after the Extraction Optimisation. *Food Chem.* **2014**, *152*, 447–455. [CrossRef]
55. Öztürk, S.; Cerit, İ.; Mutlu, S.; Demirkol, O. Enrichment of Cookies with Glutathione by Inactive Yeast Cells (Saccharomyces Cerevisiae): Physicochemical and Functional Properties. *J. Cereal Sci.* **2017**, *78*, 19–24. [CrossRef]
56. Dubost, N.; Ou, B.; Beelman, R. Quantification of Polyphenols and Ergothioneine in Cultivated Mushrooms and Correlation to Total Antioxidant Capacity. *Food Chem.* **2007**, *105*, 727–735. [CrossRef]
57. Re, R.; Pellegrini, N.; Proteggente, A.; Pannala, A.; Yang, M.; Rice-Evans, C. Antioxidant Activity Applying an Improved ABTS Radical Cation Decolorization Assay. *Free Radical. Bio Med.* **1999**, *26*, 1231–1237. [CrossRef] [PubMed]

58. Benzie, I.F.F.; Strain, J.J. The Ferric Reducing Ability of Plasma (FRAP) as a Measure of "Antioxidant Power": The FRAP Assay. *Anal. Biochem.* **1996**, *239*, 70–76. [CrossRef] [PubMed]
59. Chandra, S.; Singh, S.; Kumari, D. Evaluation of Functional Properties of Composite Flours and Sensorial Attributes of Composite Flour Biscuits. *J. Food Sci. Technol.* **2015**, *52*, 3681–3688. [CrossRef]
60. Commission Regulation (EU) No 1047/2012 Regulation (EC) No 1924/2006 of the European Parliament and of the Council of 20 December 2006 on Nutrition and Health Claims Made on Foods. *OJ 2006, L 404*, 1–31.
61. Bernaś, E.; Jaworska, G.; Lisiewska, Z. Edible Mushrooms as a Source of Valuable Nutritive Constituents. *Acta Sci. Pol.—Technol. Aliment.* **2006**, *5*, 5–20.
62. Diamantopoulou, P.; Fourtaka, K.; Melanouri, E.M.; Dedousi, M.; Diamantis, I.; Gardeli, C.; Papanikolaou, S. Examining the Impact of Substrate Composition on the Biochemical Properties and Antioxidant Activity of Pleurotus and Agaricus Mushrooms. *Fermentation* **2023**, *9*, 689. [CrossRef]
63. Sławińska, A.; Jabłońska-Ryś, E.; Stachniuk, A. High-Performance Liquid Chromatography Determination of Free Sugars and Mannitol in Mushrooms Using Corona Charged Aerosol Detection. *Food Anal. Methods* **2021**, *14*, 209–216. [CrossRef]
64. Vetter, J. The Mushroom Glucans: Molecules of High Biological and Medicinal Importance. *Foods* **2023**, *12*, 1009. [CrossRef]
65. Cheung, P.C.K. Mini-Review on Edible Mushrooms as Source of Dietary Fiber: Preparation and Health Benefits. *Food Sci. Hum. Wellness* **2013**, *2*, 162–166. [CrossRef]
66. Synytsya, A.; Míčková, K.; Jablonský, I.; Sluková, M.; Čopíková, J. Mushrooms of Genus Pleurotus as a Source of Dietary Fibres and Glucans for Food Supplements. *Czech J. Food Sci.* **2008**, *26*, 441–446. [CrossRef]
67. Nile, S.; Park, S.W. Total, Soluble, and Insoluble Dietary Fibre Contents of Wild Growing Edible Mushrooms. *Chech J. Food Sci.* **2014**, *32*, 302–307. [CrossRef]
68. Shbeeb, D.A.; Farahat, M.F.; Ismail, H.M. Macronutrients Analysis of Fresh and Canned Agaricus Bisporus and Pleurotus Ostreatus Mushroom Species Sold in Alexandria Markets, Egypt. *Prog. Nutr.* **2020**, *21*, 203–209. [CrossRef]
69. Kirbağ, S.; Akyüz, M. Nutritive Value of Edible Wild and Cultured Mushrooms. *Turk. J. Biol.* **2010**, *34*, 97–102. [CrossRef]
70. Ogidi, C.O.; Ogunlade, A.O.; Bodunde, R.S.; Aladejana, O.M. Evaluation of Nutrient Contents and Antioxidant Activity of Wheat Cookies Fortified with Mushroom (*Termitomyces robustus*) and Edible Insects. *J. Culin. Sci. Technol.* **2023**, 1–19. [CrossRef]
71. Van Toan, N.; Thu, L.N.M. Preparation and Improved Quality Production of Flour and the Made Biscuits from Shitake Mushroom (*Lentinus edodes*). *J. Nutr. Diet.* **2018**, *1*, 1–9.
72. Shams, R.; Singh, J.; Dash, K.K.; Dar, A.H.; Pandiselvam, R. Utilization of Button Mushroom (*Agaricus Bisporus*) Powder to Improve the Physiochemical and Functional Properties of Cookies. *Sustain. Food Technol.* **2023**, *1*, 306–318. [CrossRef]
73. Sulieman, A.; Zhu, K.-X.; Peng, W.; Shoaib, M.; Hassan, H.; Zhou, H.-M. Compositional, Functional and Pasting Properties of Composite Flour Fortified with Button Mushroom (*Agaricus bisporus*) Powder and Inulin. *J. Food Nutr. Res.* **2017**, *5*, 614–621. [CrossRef]
74. Bamidele, O.P.; Fasogbon, B.M. Nutritional and Functional Properties of Maize-Oyster Mushroom (*Zea mays-Pleurotus ostreatus*) Based Composite Flour and Its Storage Stability. *Open Agric.* **2020**, *5*, 40–49. [CrossRef]
75. Falandysz, J.; Frankowska, A.; Jarzynska, G.; Dryzałowska, A.; Kojta, A.; Zhang, D. Survey on Composition and Bioconcentration Potential of 12 Metallic Elements in King Bolete (Boletus Edulis) Mushroom That Emerged at 11 Spatially Distant Sites. *J. Environ. Sci. Health B* **2011**, *46*, 231–246. [CrossRef]
76. Wickramasinghe, M.A.; Nadeeshani, H.; Sewwandi, S.M.; Rathnayake, I.; Kananke, T.C.; Liyanage, R. Comparison of Nutritional Composition, Bioactivities, and FTIR- ATR Microstructural Properties of Commercially Grown Four Mushroom Species in Sri Lanka; Agaricus Bisporus, Pleurotus Ostreatus, Calocybe Sp. (MK-White), Ganoderma Lucidum. *Food Prod. Process. Nutr.* **2023**, *5*, 43. [CrossRef]
77. Commission Directive 2008/100/EC of 28 October 2008 Amending Council Directive 90/496/EEC on Nutrition Labelling for Foodstuffs as Regards Recommended Daily Allowances, Energy Conversion Factors and Definitions. *OJ 2008, L 285*, 9–12.
78. Jabłońska-Ryś, E.; Sławińska, A.; Skrzypczak, K.; Kowalczyk, D.; Stadnik, J. Content of Biogenic Amines and Physical Properties of Lacto-Fermented Button Mushrooms. *Appl. Sci.* **2022**, *12*, 8957. [CrossRef]
79. Jabłońska-Ryś, E.; Sławińska, A.; Radzki, W.; Gustaw, W. Evaluation of the Potential Use of Probiotic Strain Lactobacillus Plantarum 299v in Lactic Fermentation of Button Mushroom Fruiting Bodies. *Acta Sci. Pol. Technol. Aliment.* **2016**, *15*, 399–407. [CrossRef] [PubMed]
80. Kic, P. Mushroom Drying Characteristics and Changes of Colour. In Proceedings of the 17th International Scientific Conference: Engineering for Rural Development, Jelgava, Lithuania, 23 May 2018; pp. 432–438.
81. Shams, R.; Singh, J.; Dash, K.K.; Dar, A.H. Comparative Study of Freeze Drying and Cabinet Drying of Button Mushroom. *Appl. Food Res.* **2022**, *2*, 100084. [CrossRef]
82. Sajad, S.; Singh, J.; Gupta, N.; Sharma, S.; Sharma, M.; Sharma, V.; Shankar, U. Physico-Chemical, Color Profile and Total Phenol Content of Freeze Dried (*Oyster mushroom*) Pleurotus Ostreatus. *Pharma Innov. J.* **2023**, *12*, 2076–2078.
83. Ucar, T.M.; Karadag, A. The Effects of Vacuum and Freeze-Drying on the Physicochemical Properties and in Vitro Digestibility of Phenolics in Oyster Mushroom (*Pleurotus ostreatus*). *J. Food Meas. Charact.* **2019**, *13*, 2298–2309. [CrossRef]
84. Lagnika, C.; Zhang, M.; Nsor-Atindana, J.; Bashari, M. Effects of Ultrasound and Chemical Treatments on White Mushroom (Agaricus Bisporus) Prior to Modified Atmosphere Packaging in Extending Shelf-Life. *J. Food Sci. Technol.* **2014**, *51*, 3749–3757. [CrossRef]

85. Wang, H.; Zhang, M.; Mujumdar, A.S. Comparison of Three New Drying Methods for Drying Characteristics and Quality of Shiitake Mushroom (*Lentinus edodes*). *Dry Technol.* **2014**, *32*, 1791–1802. [CrossRef]
86. Engin, D. Effect of Drying Temperature on Color and Desorption Characteristics of Oyster Mushroom. *Food Sci. Technol.* **2020**, *40*, 187–193. [CrossRef]
87. Wu, S.; Nie, Y.; Zhao, J.; Fan, B.; Huang, X.; Li, X.; Sheng, J.; Meng, D.; Ding, Y.; Tang, X. The Synergistic Effects of Low-Concentration Acidic Electrolyzed Water and Ultrasound on the Storage Quality of Fresh-Sliced Button Mushrooms. *Food Bioprocess Technol.* **2018**, *11*, 314–323. [CrossRef]
88. Bernaś, E. Comparison of the Mechanism of Enzymatic Browning in Frozen White and Brown A. Bisporus. *Eur. Food Res. Technol.* **2018**, *244*, 1239–1248. [CrossRef]
89. Yang, X.; Zhang, Y.; Kong, Y.; Zhao, J.; Sun, Y.; Huang, M. Comparative Analysis of Taste Compounds in Shiitake Mushrooms Processed by Hot-Air Drying and Freeze Drying. *Int. J. Food Prop.* **2019**, *22*, 1100–1111. [CrossRef]
90. Arumuganathan, T.; Manikantan, M.R.; Indurani, C.; Rai, R.D.; Kamal, S. Texture and Quality Parameters of Oyster Mushroom as Influenced by Drying Methods. *Int. Agrophys* **2010**, *24*, 339–342.
91. Baltacıoğlu, C.; Baltacıoğlu, H.; Seyhan, R.; Uğur, Ö.; Avcu, O. Investigation of the Effect of Oyster Mushroom (*Pleurotus ostreatus*) Powder on Biscuit Production and Effect on Quality Criteria by Fourier-transform Infrared Spectroscopy. *J. Food Process. Preserv.* **2021**, *45*, e15174. [CrossRef]
92. Purlis, E. Browning Development in Bakery Products—A Review. *J. Food Eng.* **2010**, *99*, 239–249. [CrossRef]
93. Kraithong, S.; Lee, S.; Rawdkuen, S. Physicochemical and Functional Properties of Thai Organic Rice Flour. *J. Cereal Sci.* **2018**, *79*, 259–266. [CrossRef]
94. Mattila, P.; Salo-Väänänen, P.; Könkö, K.; Aro, H.; Jalava, T. Basic Composition and Amino Acid Contents of Mushrooms Cultivated in Finland. *J. Agric. Food Chem.* **2002**, *50*, 6419–6422. [CrossRef]
95. Heo, T.-Y.; Kim, Y.-N.; Park, I.B.; Lee, D.-U. Amplification of Vitamin D2 in the White Button Mushroom (Agaricus Bisporus) by UV-B Irradiation and Jet-Milling for Its Potential Use as a Functional Ingredient. *Foods* **2020**, *9*, 1713. [CrossRef]
96. Wang, N.; Maximiuk, L.; Fenn, D.; Nickerson, M.T.; Hou, A. Development of a Method for Determining Oil Absorption Capacity in Pulse Flours and Protein Materials. *Cereal Chem.* **2020**, *97*, 1111–1117. [CrossRef]
97. Ohizua, E.R.; Adeola, A.A.; Idowu, M.A.; Sobukola, O.P.; Afolabi, T.A.; Ishola, R.O.; Ayansina, S.O.; Oyekale, T.O.; Falomo, A. Nutrient Composition, Functional, and Pasting Properties of Unripe Cooking Banana, Pigeon Pea, and Sweetpotato Flour Blends. *Food Sci. Nutr.* **2017**, *5*, 750–762. [CrossRef] [PubMed]
98. Khan, S.H.; Butt, M.S.; Sharif, M.K.; Sameen, A.; Mumtaz, S.; Sultan, M.T. Functional Properties of Protein Isolates Extracted from Stabilized Rice Bran by Microwave, Dry Heat, and Parboiling. *J. Agric. Food Chem.* **2011**, *59*, 2416–2420. [CrossRef] [PubMed]
99. Zhang, Y.; Sharan, S.; Rinnan, Å.; Orlien, V. Survey on Methods for Investigating Protein Functionality and Related Molecular Characteristics. *Foods* **2021**, *10*, 2848. [CrossRef] [PubMed]
100. Farooq, Z.; Boye, J.I. Novel Food and Industrial Applications of Pulse Flours and Fractions. In *Pulse Foods Processing, Quality and Nutraceutical Applications*; Tiwari, B.K., Gowen, A., McKenna, B., Eds.; Elsevier: Burlington, VT, USA, 2011; pp. 283–323, ISBN 978-0-12-382018-1.
101. Sulieman, A.A.; Zhu, K.-X.; Peng, W.; Hassan, H.A.; Obadi, M.; Siddeeg, A.; Zhou, H.-M. Rheological and Quality Characteristics of Composite Gluten-Free Dough and Biscuits Supplemented with Fermented and Unfermented Agaricus Bisporus Polysaccharide Flour. *Food Chem.* **2019**, *271*, 193–203. [CrossRef]
102. Radzki, W.; Ziaja-Sołtys, M.; Nowak, J.; Topolska, J.; Bogucka-Kocka, A.; Sławińska, A.; Michalak-Majewska, M.; Jabłońska-Ryś, E.; Kuczumow, A. Impact of Processing on Polysaccharides Obtained from Button Mushroom (*Agaricus bisporus*). *Int. J. Food Sci. Technol.* **2019**, *54*, 1405–1412. [CrossRef]
103. Oikonomou, N.A.; Krokida, M.K. Water Absorption Index and Water Solubility Index Prediction for Extruded Food Products. *Int. J. Food Prop.* **2012**, *15*, 157–168. [CrossRef]
104. Cervenka, L.; Brožková, I.; Vytřasová, J. Effects of the Principal Ingredients of Biscuits upon Water Activity. *J. Food Nutr. Res.* **2006**, *45*, 39–43.
105. Pauly, A.; Pareyt, B.; Lambrecht, M.A.; Fierens, E.; Delcour, J.A. Flour from Wheat Cultivars of Varying Hardness Produces Semi-Sweet Biscuits with Varying Textural and Structural Properties. *LWT—Food Sci. Techol.* **2013**, *53*, 452–457. [CrossRef]
106. Liu, L.; Yang, T.; Yang, J.; Zhou, Q.; Wang, X.; Cai, J.; Huang, M.; Dai, T.; Cao, W.; Jiang, D. Relationship of Starch Pasting Properties and Dough Rheology, and the Role of Starch in Determining Quality of Short Biscuit. *Front. Plant Sci.* **2022**, *13*, 829229. [CrossRef]
107. Thejasri, V.; Hymavathi, T.V.; Roberts, T.P.P.; Anusha, B.; Devi, S.S. Sensory, Physico-Chemical and Nutritional Properties of Gluten Free Biscuits Formulated with Quinoa (*Chenopodium quinoa Willd.*), Foxtail Millet (*Setaria italica*) and Hydrocolloids. *Int. J. Curr. Microbiol. Appl. Sci.* **2017**, *6*, 1710–1721. [CrossRef]
108. Zhang, H.; Sun, S.; Ai, L. Physical Barrier Effects of Dietary Fibers on Lowering Starch Digestibility. *Curr. Opin. Food Sci.* **2022**, *48*, 100940. [CrossRef]
109. Adedara, O.A.; Taylor, J.R.N. Roles of Protein, Starch and Sugar in the Texture of Sorghum Biscuits. *LWT—Food Sci. Techol.* **2021**, *136*, 110323. [CrossRef]
110. Sharma, P.; Gujral, H.S. Antioxidant Potential of Wheat Flour Chapattis as Affected by Incorporating Barley Flour. *LWT—Food Sci. Techol.* **2014**, *56*, 118–123. [CrossRef]

111. Irakli, M.; Katsantonis, D.; Kleisiaris, F. Evaluation of Quality Attributes, Nutraceutical Components and Antioxidant Potential of Wheat Bread Substituted with Rice Bran. *J. Cereal Sci.* **2015**, *65*, 74–80. [CrossRef]
112. Dziki, D.; Lisiecka, K.; Gawlik-Dziki, U.; Różyło, R.; Krajewska, A.; Cacak-Pietrzak, G. Shortbread Cookies Enriched with Micronized Oat Husk: Physicochemical and Sensory Properties. *Appl. Sci.* **2022**, *12*, 12512. [CrossRef]
113. Jabłońska-Ryś, E.; Sławińska, A.; Szwajgier, D. Effect of Lactic Acid Fermentation on Antioxidant Properties and Phenolic Acid Contents of Oyster (*Pleurotus ostreatus*) and Chanterelle (*Cantharellus cibarius*) Mushrooms. *Food Sci. Biotechnol.* **2016**, *25*, 439–444. [CrossRef] [PubMed]
114. Smolskaitė, L.; Venskutonis, P.R.; Talou, T. Comprehensive Evaluation of Antioxidant and Antimicrobial Properties of Different Mushroom Species. *LWT—Food Sci. Techol.* **2015**, *60*, 462–471. [CrossRef]
115. Palacios, I.; Lozano, M.; Moro, C.; D'Arrigo, M.; Rostagno, M.A.; Martínez, J.A.; García-Lafuente, A.; Guillamón, E.; Villares, A. Antioxidant Properties of Phenolic Compounds Occurring in Edible Mushrooms. *Food Chem.* **2011**, *128*, 674–678. [CrossRef]
116. Radzki, W.; Sławińska, A.; Skrzypczak, K.; Michalak-Majewska, M. The Impact of Drying of Wild-Growing Mushrooms on the Content and Antioxidant Capacity of Water-Soluble Polysaccharides. *Int. J. Med. Mushrooms* **2019**, *21*, 393–400. [CrossRef]
117. Han, H.-M.; Koh, B.-K. Antioxidant Activity of Hard Wheat Flour, Dough and Bread Prepared Using Various Processes with the Addition of Different Phenolic Acids. *J. Sci. Food Agric.* **2011**, *91*, 604–608. [CrossRef] [PubMed]
118. Mau, J.-L. The Umami Taste of Edible and Medicinal Mushrooms. *Int. J. Med. Mushrooms* **2005**, *7*, 119–126. [CrossRef]
119. Beluhan, S.; Ranogajec, A. Chemical Composition and Non-Volatile Components of Croatian Wild Edible Mushrooms. *Food Chem.* **2011**, *124*, 1076–1082. [CrossRef]
120. Jiang, C.; Duan, X.; Lin, L.; Wu, W.; Li, X.; Zeng, Z.; Luo, Q.; Liu, Y. A Review on the Edible Mushroom as a Source of Special Flavor: Flavor Categories, Influencing Factors, and Challenges. *Food Front* **2023**, *4*, 1561–1577. [CrossRef]
121. Selli, S.; Guclu, G.; Sevindik, O.; Kelebek, H. Variations in the Key Aroma and Phenolic Compounds of Champignon (Agaricus Bisporus) and Oyster (Pleurotus Ostreatus) Mushrooms after Two Cooking Treatments as Elucidated by GC–MS-O and LC-DAD-ESI-MS/MS. *Food Chem.* **2021**, *354*, 129576. [CrossRef]

Disclaimer/Publisher's Note: The statements, opinions and data contained in all publications are solely those of the individual author(s) and contributor(s) and not of MDPI and/or the editor(s). MDPI and/or the editor(s) disclaim responsibility for any injury to people or property resulting from any ideas, methods, instructions or products referred to in the content.

Article

Nutritional Value, Physical Properties, and Sensory Quality of Sugar-Free Cereal Bars Fortified with Grape and Apple Pomace

Agata Blicharz-Kania, Kostiantyn Vasiukov *, Agnieszka Sagan, Dariusz Andrejko, Weronika Fifowska and Marek Domin

Department of Biological Bases of Food and Feed Technologies, University of Life Sciences in Lublin, Głęboka Str. 28, 20-612 Lublin, Poland; agata.kania@up.lublin.pl (A.B.-K.)
* Correspondence: kostiantyn.vasiukov@up.lublin.pl

Abstract: Cereal bars are so-called convenience foods. Consumers value these products as a healthier alternative to traditional chocolate bars. Since these snacks usually contain added dried fruit, they have high potential for the utilisation of waste materials from the fruit industry. The study aimed to determine the effect of fortification of cereal bars with grape and apple pomace on their nutritional value, physical properties, and sensory quality. The control recipe was modified by replacing 10 or 20 g of sultanas with apple or grape pomace. The fortification with these food by-products resulted in a significant increase in the moisture content of the products, an increase in soluble fibre content, and a decrease in the level of antioxidant compounds. The strength of the cereal bars supplemented with grape and apple pomace increased. In addition, the panellists noticed a colour difference compared to the unmodified product ($2 < \Delta E < 5$). A positive effect of the addition of the fruit pomace on the visual characteristics of the cereal bars was also observed. No changes were observed in the tastiness of the product. On the other hand, the aroma of the modified products and the texture of the bars containing the apple residue were less acceptable. In conclusion, cereal bars containing grape pomace and up to 10 g of apple pomace are characterised by high soluble dietary fibre content and desirable sensory and mechanical properties and are therefore recommended for industrial production.

Keywords: conventional food; cereal bars; fruit industry; food by-products

Citation: Blicharz-Kania, A.; Vasiukov, K.; Sagan, A.; Andrejko, D.; Fifowska, W.; Domin, M. Nutritional Value, Physical Properties, and Sensory Quality of Sugar-Free Cereal Bars Fortified with Grape and Apple Pomace. *Appl. Sci.* **2023**, *13*, 10531. https://doi.org/10.3390/app131810531

Academic Editor: Monica Gallo

Received: 31 July 2023
Revised: 13 September 2023
Accepted: 15 September 2023
Published: 21 September 2023

Copyright: © 2023 by the authors. Licensee MDPI, Basel, Switzerland. This article is an open access article distributed under the terms and conditions of the Creative Commons Attribution (CC BY) license (https:// creativecommons.org/licenses/by/ 4.0/).

1. Introduction

A diet rich in fruit and vegetables plays an important role in the prevention of oxidative stress-related diseases. Such disorders are most often caused by a poor diet consisting of processed foods, alcohol consumption, or smoking. This leads to an overproduction of free radicals in the body, resulting in accelerated ageing processes and the development of cancer, atherosclerosis, stroke, and Parkinson's or Alzheimer's disease. The likelihood of these diseases can be significantly reduced by consuming fruit containing antioxidant compounds, such as polyphenols, carotenoids, or ascorbic acid. Introducing fresh fruit into the diet may be the most effective way of supplying the aforementioned components to the body [1,2]. However, today's lifestyle of the typical consumer makes the use of unprocessed foods quite problematic. Thus, there is a growing interest in foods that are convenient, yet healthy and minimally processed. Consumers are increasingly turning to natural juices (NFC—Not From Concentrate). The scale of their production is also increasing, which in turn results in an increasing amount of post-production waste, i.e., pomace [3,4].

Fruit residues contain large amounts of valuable nutrients. For example, grape residues have been shown to contain 55.6 g of total dietary fibre per 100 g of dry mass and almost 13% of protein in dry mass [5]. They are also an important source of polyphenols [6]. The main phenolic constituents of grape pomace are anthocyanins, flavanols, and stilbenes. The total polyphenol content ranges from 0.68 to 0.75 mg GAE/100 g of dry mass and the anthocyanin content varies from 84.4 to 131 mg/100 g of dry mass [7]. Similarly, apple pomace has high content of antioxidant substances. Schieber et al. (2003) [8] showed that freeze-dried apple pomace extract contained 117.6 mg/kg phenolic compounds. In addition, apple residue is a source of pectin (0.66 g per 100 g fresh weight) and dietary fibre (2.33 g per 100 g fresh weight) [9,10].

Besides the high level of active ingredients, the fruit pomace by-product still contains a high amount of water and is a perishable material. Therefore, it must be processed to be protected from microorganism growth and prepared for storage and subsequent consumption. Properly processed fruit residues can serve as a raw material for the extraction of specific active substances [6] or can be used as an additive in various types of products. The addition of by-products to food can increase its nutritional value. However, unfavourable changes in the physical and organoleptic properties of the products may pose a problem. Numerous studies on the extraction of active ingredients from expeller or fortification of food with residues from the food industry have recently been conducted [11–16]. So far, the research has mainly been focused on the possibility of using plant residues for the fortification of basic products, such as pasta or bread. However, there is not enough information on the possibility of using by-products to produce convenience foods, including cereal snacks. Cereal bars are an interesting alternative for the management of fruit pomace. They are valued by consumers for their simple natural composition. Among cereals, oats are the most widely used to prepare cereal bars due to the high quality and content of protein, predominance of unsaturated fatty acids, and dietary fibre composition. Oat grain also contains significant amounts of soluble phenolic compounds, β-glucans, minerals, and vitamins, including fat-soluble vitamin E. The high dietary value of oat grain is reflected in its suitability for the production of functional foods [17,18]. However, the use of oats increases the water absorption of the dough and increases its softening. Additional incorporation of by-products of the fruit industry may result in a significant change in the structure and strength of the products obtained.

The aim of this study was to determine the effect of fortification of cereal bars with grape and apple pomace on their nutritional value, physical properties, and sensory quality.

2. Materials and Methods

2.1. Material

The basic raw materials used for the study were apples (Jonagold variety) and dark stone grapes (Attila variety) purchased from a local supermarket. In order to obtain pomace, the fresh fruit was subjected to pressing using a Sana Juicer by Omega EUJ-707 slow-speed juicer. The leftover apples and grapes were dried in a POL-EKO, SLN 15 STD laboratory dryer at 60 °C (until the desired moisture content of $12 \pm 1\%$ was achieved) and then crushed in a Chemland FW100 laboratory grinder.

The recipe composition of the sugar-free cereal bars is shown in Table 1. The control recipe was modified by replacing 10 or 20 g of sultanas with apple and grape pomace.

2.2. Preparation of Dough and Baking Bars

Before preparing the dough, the oatmeal, barley, rye, seeds, and coconut chips were ground in a Chemland FW100 laboratory grinder. The bananas were ground in a KENWOOD MAJOR classic blender. The dry ingredients were combined and mixed thoroughly, and the remaining food by-products were incorporated. The dough was kneaded for 5 min using the KENWOOD food processor. The prepared dough was placed in 100×25 mm silicone moulds. The bars were baked in a Hounö KD 8940 Randers oven at 180 °C for 20 min. After the heat treatment, the bars were left to cool. Next, they were placed in sealed plastic containers and stored at ambient temperature (23 ± 1 °C) before further testing.

Table 1. Recipe composition of the cereal bars.

Sample	Component [g]												
	Oatmeal Flakes	Barley Flakes	Rye Flakes	Sesame Seeds	Sunflower Seeds	Almonds	Pumpkin Seeds	Coconut Chips	Peanut Cream	Fresh Bananas	Sultanas	Grape Pomace	Apple Pomace
CB	140	20	20	10	10	10	10	10	70	180	50	-	-
G1	140	20	20	10	10	10	10	10	70	180	40	10	-
G2	140	20	20	10	10	10	10	10	70	180	30	20	-
A1	140	20	20	10	10	10	10	10	70	180	40	-	10
A2	140	20	20	10	10	10	10	10	70	180	30	-	20

CB-control bars; G1-bars with 10 g grape pomace addition; G2-bars with 20 g grape pomace addition; A1-bars with 10 g apple pomace addition; A2-bars with 20 g apple pomace addition.

2.3. Determination of Moisture

The moisture content was determined according to the standard method [19]. The bars were crushed before measurement. An approximately 2 g sample of the material was dried at 130 °C until no weight loss was observed. The process was carried out using a laboratory dryer (POL-EKO Aparatura, type SLN 15 STD, Wodzisław, Poland). The test was performed in triplicate.

2.4. Determination of Polyphenol Content

To determine the polyphenol content, crushed bar samples were extracted with 80% methanol [12] and then centrifuged for 15 min at 5800 RPM. Total polyphenol content was determined using the Folin-Ciocalteau method [20]. Absorbance was read at 765 nm on a Helios Omega UV-Vis spectrophotometer (Thermo Scientific, Waltham, MA, USA). A calibration curve was performed using gallic acid. Results were expressed as mg gallic acid per 1 g dry weight of the sample. The determinations were performed in triplicate.

2.5. Determination of Dietary Fibre Content

The determination of dietary fibre was carried out using the weight method (AACC 32-05, AACC 32-21, AOAC 991.43, AOAC 985.29) [19,21]. The test sample was digested with the thermostable α-amylase, pepsin, and pancreatin enzymes. Next, the undigested residue of insoluble dietary fibre (IDF) and, after precipitation from the supernatant solution, soluble dietary fibre (SDF) was determined by weight. Total dietary fibre (TDF) was calculated as the sum of the three above. The test was performed in triplicate.

2.6. Determination of Mechanical Strength

The mechanical strength of the bars was determined using a Zwick/Roel Z0.5 testing machine. Inches of the product were placed on stationary wedge supports (40 mm spacing). Three-point breaking tests were carried out at a speed of 5 mm·min^{-1} using a wedge-breaking element. The test was conducted until complete failure of the material, i.e., a 40% decrease in the maximum force recorded during the test. The tests were performed in five repetitions. The maximum force recorded by the testXpert II v3.5 software was taken as the final result.

2.7. Determination of Colour

A 3Color SF80 spectrophotometer (light source D65, observer 10°, measuring head aperture 8 mm) was used to analyse the colour parameters. The parameters measured were: L^*—describing the brightness (0 = white and 100 = black), a^*—describing the colour change from green (−) to red (+), and b^*—describing the colour change from blue (−) to yellow (+).

The total colour change ΔE was also calculated. The determinations were performed in five replicates.

2.8. Sensory Analysis

The bar samples were assessed by a panel of 52 semi-trained team members. They were trained in the descriptive aspects of the test. The consumers assessed the appearance, aroma, consistency, and palatability of the bars. The participants were also asked to rate the product overall. The results were presented in a 5-point structural scale (from 1—"dislike very much" to 5—"like very much"). The following criteria were taken into account when selecting the panellists: good health, non-smoker, not allergic to peanuts and almonds, and consenting to participate in the study. The evaluation was carried out 24 h after baking in a laboratory with LED lighting and room temperature. The panellists were served mineral water as a neutralising agent. A random order of serving the samples was adopted.

2.9. Statistical Analysis

The results were statistically analysed using Statistica 12 software (StatSoft Inc., Tulsa, OK, USA). The distribution of the data was checked for normality by performing the Shapiro–Wilk normality test at an alpha level of 0.05. A significance level of $\alpha = 0.05$ was used for inference. ANOVA extended post hoc analysis based on the Tukey test was used to determine the significance of differences.

3. Results and Discussion

The photograph (Figure 1) presents cereal bars with the addition of fruit pomace. The products obtained were characterised by different nutritional compositions and different physical and sensory properties.

Figure 1. Pictures of the experimental products: CB—control bars; G1—bars with 10 g grape pomace addition; G2—bars with 20 g grape pomace addition; A1—bars with 10 g apple pomace addition; A2—bars with 20 g apple pomace addition.

3.1. Chemical Analysis

The moisture content in the cereal bars from the control sample (Table 2) was at a level typical of this type of product and was approximately 16.3%. The addition of the fruit pomace resulted in a significant increase in the moisture content of the products. The increase in the moisture content of products containing dried/powdered fruit pomace is probably related to the high pectin content. These substances are responsible for the ability of products to retain water [22,23]. Low-moisture bakery products, such as cereal bars and biscuits, are generally characterized by long life due to their low water activity. However, during storage, quality decay occurs due to moisture adsorption or the development of lipid oxidation. Oxidation is a complex set of reactions, which can be prevented by the addition of antioxidants in the formulation [24]. Therefore, moisture control plays a critical role in determining the quality and shelf life of cereal snacks. Additional protective measures are necessary for products with higher water content. Appropriate storage conditions, new aseptic technologies, and controlled atmosphere/modified atmosphere packaging can extend the product shelf life [25].

Table 2. Chemical compositions of cereal bars fortified with grape and apple pomace.

Sample	Moisture [%]	TPC [mg/g]	IDF [%]	SDF [%]	TDF [%]
CB	16.28 ± 0.62 [e]	1.21 ± 0.02 [b]	12.23 ± 0.11 [a]	5.11 ± 0.08 [c]	17.34 ± 0.19 [ab]
G1	18.13 ± 0.07 [d]	1.00 ± 0.03 [a]	11.60 ± 0.07 [b]	5.44 ± 0.06 [b]	17.04 ± 0.13 [b]
G2	19.50 ± 0.36 [c]	1.04 ± 0.05 [a]	10.84 ± 0.11 [c]	5.45 ± 0.04 [b]	16.29 ± 0.15 [c]
A1	21.17 ± 0.37 [b]	1.03 ± 0.01 [a]	12.26 ± 0.12 [a]	5.36 ± 0.04 [b]	17.62 ± 0.17 [a]
A2	23.64 ± 0.23 [a]	0.94 ± 0.05 [a]	11.54 ± 0.05 [b]	5.75 ± 0.07 [a]	17.30 ± 0.11 [ab]

CB—control bars; G1—bars with 10 g grape pomace addition; G2—bars with 20 g grape pomace addition; A1—bars with 10 g apple pomace addition; A2—bars with 20 g apple pomace addition. Data are presented as mean (n = 3) ± standard deviation; values of each parameter with different superscript letter in the rows are significantly different (Tukey test $p \leq 0.05$).

The highest average polyphenol content was recorded in the sample of bars with the unmodified recipe. The addition of grape and apple pomace reduced the content of antioxidant compounds. It was further observed that the increase in the proportion of fruit residues from 10 to 20 g had no significant effect on changes in the number of polyphenols in the cereal bars. It should be noted that sultanas, or dried grapes, were substituted with the fruit residue, i.e., raw materials with very high polyphenol content (10.7 mg of GAE/g wet weight) [26]. In studies conducted by other authors, where pomace was used to substitute cereal raw materials, the polyphenol content increased significantly in the fortified products [27–29].

The addition of the apple and grape pomace resulted in a significant increase in soluble dietary fibre (SDF). The relatively high SDF content in the fruit residue-supplemented bars was probably related to the high pectin content, i.e., over 14 g/100 g of dried apple pomace [30]. The average insoluble fibre and total fibre content also increased after the addition of 10 g of the apple residue. However, the statistical analysis did not confirm the significance of these changes. In contrast, it was observed that the introduction of 20 g of the grape residue into the recipe reduced the amount of total dietary fibre (TDF).

3.2. Analysis of Physical Properties

The strength of the cereal bars changed significantly when the fruit pomace was introduced into the recipe (Figure 2). The use of the grape residues had a positive effect on the mechanical properties of the products. The force required to break down the bars increased by almost 20%. In contrast, the addition of the apple pomace resulted in a decrease in the breaking strength of the cereal bars, but the changes were only significant when the proportion of the apple residue was increased from 10 to 20 g per dough portion. The increased strength of the cereal bars may be related to an increase in adhesiveness, i.e., the strength of the internal bonds holding the product together. The parameters described are closely related to the technological properties and composition of the food raw materials. Higher moisture content, water binding capacity, and the presence of structure-forming substances, such as cellulose or pectin, have a positive effect on the compactness of the product, thereby increasing its resistance to pressure damage [31].

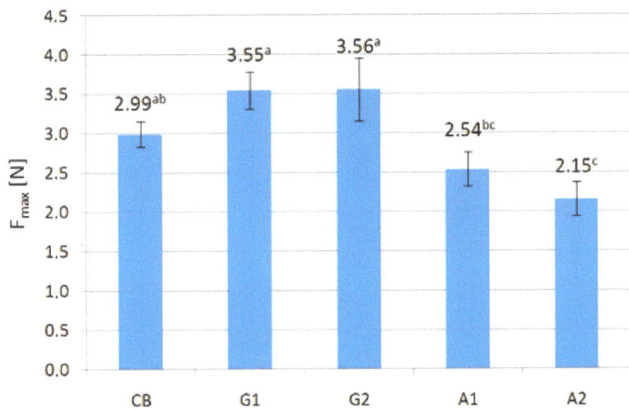

Figure 2. Strength of cereal bars fortified with grape and apple pomace: CB—control bars; G1—bars with 10 g grape pomace addition; G2—bars with 20 g grape pomace addition; A1—bars with 10 g apple pomace addition; A2—bars with 20 g apple pomace addition. Data are presented as mean ($n = 5$). Error bars indicate standard deviations; values of each parameter with different superscript letters in the rows are significantly different (Tukey test $p \leq 0.05$).

3.3. Colour Parameters

The L^* colour brightness of the cereal bars did not change significantly ($p > 0.05$) after the modification of their recipe (Table 3). The values of the parameter a^* increased slightly after the addition of the tested food by-products, but the statistical analysis showed that these changes were not significant ($p > 0.05$). On the other hand, it was observed that the introduction of the apple pomace had an impact on the mean values of the parameter b^*. This parameter of cereal bars fortified with the apple residues significantly decreased, which indicates that the colour of the A1 and A2 bars was less chromatic towards yellow than that of the CB bars. Regardless of the amount and type of the fruit pomace used, the colour difference $2 < \Delta E < 5$, in comparison with the unmodified product, was noticeable to the panellists [32]. Similar trends in the colour change in cereal bars were observed in an experiment conducted by Sandini et al. (2020) [33]. Likewise in the present study, the authors modified the bar recipe by replacing sultanas with biomass from grape wine fermentation. The colour analysis showed no significant differences in the L^* and a^* parameters. However, the introduction of the by-product was found to result in a reduction in the b^* and C^* parameters. It was therefore concluded that a lower saturation value (C^*) was indicative of a darkening of the sample following the introduction of the winemaking residue.

Table 3. Colour parameters of cereal bars fortified with grape and apple pomace.

Sample	L^*	a^*	b^*	ΔE
CB	33.98 ± 6.57	7.49 ± 2.00	18.61 ± 2.65 [a]	
G1	36.10 ± 2.77	8.67 ± 0.57	17.78 ± 1.58 [abc]	2.56
G2	37.40 ± 0.82	9.22 ± 0.81	16.28 ± 0.73 [ab]	4.48
A1	35.78 ± 0.76	8.20 ± 0.30	15.17 ± 0.75 [c]	3.95
A2	36.96 ± 0.65	8.32 ± 0.33	14.82 ± 0.98 [bc]	4.89

CB—control bars; G1—bars with 10 g grape pomace addition; G2—bars with 20 g grape pomace addition; A1—bars with 10 g apple pomace addition; A2—bars with 20 g apple pomace addition. Data are presented as mean ($n = 5$) ± standard deviation; values of each parameter with different superscript letter in the rows are significantly different (Tukey test $p \leq 0.05$). For parameters L^* and a^* $p > 0.05$.

3.4. Sensory Evaluation

The introduction of the grape and apple residues into the recipe of the cereal bars contributed to significant changes in sensory properties. The results of the sensory evaluation are shown in Figure 3. The data obtained demonstrate a positive effect of the addition of the apple pomace on the visual characteristics of the cereal bars. The introduction of the apple and grape residue into the bar recipe resulted in deterioration of the aroma. Probably, the use of a higher dose of the apple and grape residues would have facilitated identification of the aroma by the panelists [34].

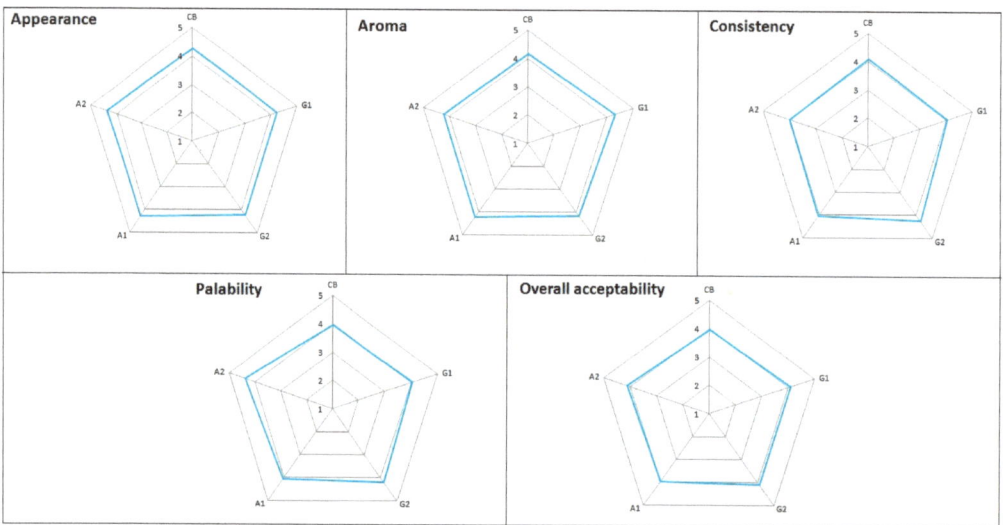

Figure 3. Sensory evaluation of cereal bars fortified with grape and apple pomace: CB—control bars; G1—bars with 10 g grape pomace addition; G2—bars with 20 g grape pomace addition; A1—bars with 10 g apple pomace addition; A2—bars with 20 g apple pomace addition.

The consistency of the bars containing the fruit pomace did change according to the tasters. The use of 20 g of the grape pomace (G2) had a positive effect on the texture of the products. However, the introduction of the same amount of the apple pomace into the recipe resulted in a deterioration of the consistency of the bars. The textural properties of this type of snack are highly dependent on the moisture content and composition of the product. The apple pomace-fortified cereal bars were characterised by higher moisture content. This parameter increased with the increasing proportion of the fruit residue, which probably resulted in a deterioration of the textural properties of the products [35].

The modification of the recipe with 20 g of the fruit pomace resulted in favourable changes in the palatability of the bars but did not affect their flavour. Palatability is a characteristic that largely determines the acceptability of a food product. The introduction of fruit processing by-products into cereal snacks usually does not result in adverse changes in their taste. However, it may have a negative impact on their texture [36,37].

The sugar-free cereal bars containing the fruit pomace were better accepted by the panellists, especially those supplemented with a higher amount of the by-products.

4. Conclusions

The results of the experiment show that cereal bars can be enriched with waste products from the fruit industry. Products fortified with grape and apple pomace have partially different properties than traditional cereal bars. The introduction of fruit residues increases product moisture and soluble dietary fibre content. These changes probably contribute

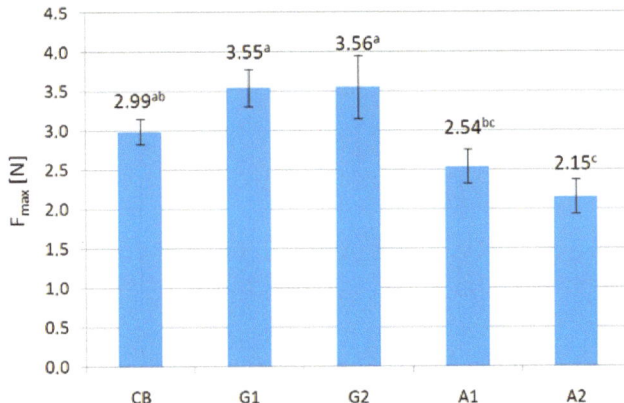

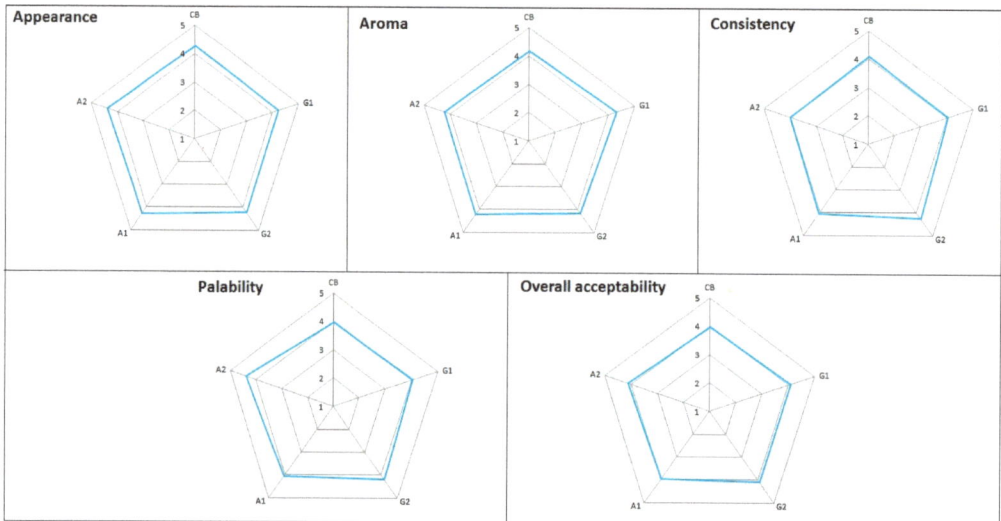

to an increase in the mechanical strength of the bars, with concomitant deterioration in texture assessed sensorially (in products fortified with 20 g of apple pomace). As shown in the study, the introduction of fruit residues does not affect the palatability of the product. However, the colour of the cereal bars changes. It is presumed that consumers will notice a colour difference compared to the unmodified product ($2 < \Delta E < 5$), while the results of the sensory evaluation show a positive effect of the addition of fruit pomace on the visual characteristics of the cereal bars.

In conclusion, cereal bars are products with great potential for sustainable food production, contributing to the generation of as little waste as possible. Cereal bars containing grape pomace and up to 10 g of apple pomace are characterised by high soluble dietary fibre content and desirable sensory and mechanical properties. Therefore, they are recommended for industrial production. Importantly, these fortified products are characterised by high moisture content. In further studies, it will be necessary to evaluate the quality of the product during storage to determine the shelf life and appropriate storage temperature. It is also recommended to conduct further research on the colour change in fortified products stored for a longer time.

Low mechanical strength and very high moisture content of bars containing 20 g of apple pomace may have a disadvantageous effect on the shelf life and preservation of the structure of the products during transport and storage. Therefore, it is not recommended to use bars made according to recipe A2 for industrial production.

Author Contributions: Conceptualization, A.B.-K., W.F. and D.A.; methodology, A.B.-K. and A.S.; formal analysis, K.V.; investigation, A.B.-K., A.S., W.F. and M.D.; resources, A.B.-K. and K.V.; data curation, A.B.-K.; writing—original draft preparation, A.B.-K. and K.V.; writing—review and editing, A.B.-K. and K.V.; project administration, D.A. All authors have read and agreed to the published version of the manuscript.

Funding: This research received no external funding.

Institutional Review Board Statement: Approval was obtained from the University Ethics Committee for Research with Human Participation. Number of the issued resolution UKE/06/2023.

Informed Consent Statement: Informed consent was obtained from all subjects involved in the study.

Data Availability Statement: The data presented in this study are available upon request from the corresponding author.

Conflicts of Interest: The authors declare no conflict of interest.

References

1. Bacchetti, T.; Turco, I.; Urbano, A.; Morresi, C.; Ferretti, G. Relationship of fruit and vegetable intake to dietary antioxidant capacity and markers of oxidative stress: A sex-related study. *Nutrition* **2019**, *61*, 164–172. [CrossRef] [PubMed]
2. Li, Y.; Ambrosone, C.B.; McCullough, M.J.; Ahn, J.; Stevens, V.L.; Thun, M.J.; Hong, C.C. Oxidative stress-related genotypes, fruit and vegetable consumption and breast cancer risk. *Carcinogenesis* **2009**, *30*, 777–784. [CrossRef] [PubMed]
3. Tian, Y.; Sun, L.; Yang, Y.; Gou, X.; Niu, P.; Guo, Y. Changes in the physicochemical properties, aromas and polyphenols of not from concentrate (NFC) apple juice during production. *CYTA J. Food* **2018**, *16*, 755–764. [CrossRef]
4. Zhang, J.; Liu, H.; Sun, R.; Zhao, Y.; Xing, R.; Yu, N.; Deng, T.; Ni, X.; Chen, Y. Volatolomics approach for authentication of not-from-concentrate (NFC) orange juice based on characteristic volatile markers using headspace solid phase microextraction (HS-SPME) combined with GC-MS. *Food Control* **2022**, *136*, 108856. [CrossRef]
5. Bianchi, F.; Cervini, M.; Giuberti, G.; Rocchetti, G.; Lucini, L.; Simonato, B. Distilled grape pomace as a functional ingredient in vegan muffins: Effect on physicochemical, nutritional, rheological and sensory aspects. *Int. J. Food Sci. Technol.* **2022**, *57*, 4847–4858. [CrossRef]
6. Monrad, J.K.; Suárez, M.; Motilva, M.J.; King, J.W.; Srinivas, K.; Howard, L.R. Extraction of anthocyanins and flavan-3-ols from red grape pomace continuously by coupling hot water extraction with a modified expeller. *Food Res. Int.* **2014**, *65*, 77–87. [CrossRef]
7. Castellanos-Gallo, L.; Ballinas-Casarrubias, L.; Espinoza-Hicks, J.C.; Hernández-Ochoa, L.R.; Muñoz-Castellanos, L.N.; Zermeño-Ortega, M.R.; Borrego-Loya, A.; Salas, E. Grape pomace valorization by extraction of phenolic polymeric pigments: A review. *Processes* **2022**, *10*, 469. [CrossRef]

8. Schieber, A.; Hilt, P.; Streker, P.; Endreß, H.U.; Rentschler, C.; Carle, R. A new process for the combined recovery of pectin and phenolic compounds from apple pomace. *IFSET* **2003**, *4*, 99–107. [CrossRef]
9. Colin-Henrion, M.; Mehinagic, E.; Renard, C.M.; Richomme, P.; Jourjon, F. From apple to applesauce: Processing effects on dietary fibres and cell wall polysaccharides. *Food Chem.* **2009**, *117*, 254–260. [CrossRef]
10. Tarko, T.; Duda-Chodak, A.; Bebak, A. Biological activity of selected fruit and vegetable pomaces. *Food Sci. Technol. Qual.* **2012**, *19*, 55–65. [CrossRef]
11. Peričin, D.; Radulović-Popović, L.; Vaštag, Ž.; Mađarev-Popović, S.; Trivić, S. Enzymatic hydrolysis of protein isolate from hull-less pumpkin oil cake: Application of response surface methodology. *Food Chem.* **2009**, *115*, 753–757. [CrossRef]
12. Hayta, M.; Özugur, G.; Etgü, H.; Seker, I.T. Effect of grape (*Vitis vinifera* L.) pomace on the quality, total phenolic content and anti-radical activity of bread. *J. Food Process. Preserv.* **2014**, *38*, 980–986. [CrossRef]
13. Sarkis, J.R.; Michel, I.; Tessaro, I.C.; Marczak, L.D.F. Optimization of phenolics extraction from sesame seed cake. *Sep. Purif.* **2014**, *122*, 506–514. [CrossRef]
14. Zardo, I.; de Espíndola Sobczyk, A.; Marczak, L.D.F.; Sarkis, J. Optimization of ultrasound assisted extraction of phenolic compounds from sunflower seed cake using response surface methodology. *Waste Biomass Valorization* **2019**, *10*, 33–44. [CrossRef]
15. de Oliveira Filho, J.G.; Egea, M.B. Sunflower seed byproduct and its fractions for food application: An attempt to improve the sustainability of the oil process. *J. Food Sci.* **2021**, *86*, 1497–1510. [CrossRef]
16. Ahlström, C.; Thuvander, J.; Rayner, M.; Mayer Labba, I.C.; Sandberg, A.S.; Östbring, K. Pilot-Scale Protein Recovery from Cold-Pressed Rapeseed Press Cake: Influence of Solids Recirculation. *Processes* **2022**, *10*, 557. [CrossRef]
17. Rasane, P.; Jha, A.; Sabikhi, L.; Kumar, A.; Unnikrishnan, V.S. Nutritional advantages of oats and opportunities for its processing as value added foods-a review. *J. Food Sci. Technol.* **2015**, *52*, 662–675. [CrossRef]
18. Sterna, V.; Zute, S.; Brunava, L. Oat grain composition and its nutrition benefice. *Agric. Agric. Sci. Procedia* **2016**, *8*, 252–256. [CrossRef]
19. AACC (American Association of Cereal Chemistry). *Approved Methods*, 10th ed.; AACC: St. Paul, MN, USA, 2000. Available online: http://methods.aaccnet.org/toc.aspx (accessed on 14 April 2022).
20. Lachowicz, S.; Bieniek, A.; Gil, Z.; Bielska, N.; Markuszewski, B. Phytochemical parameters and antioxidant activity of new cherry silverberry biotypes (*Elaeagnus multiflora* Thunb.). *Eur. Food Res. Technol.* **2019**, *245*, 1997–2005. [CrossRef]
21. AOAC (Association of Official Analytical Chemists International). *Official Methods*, 21st ed.; AOAC: Rockville, MD, USA, 2019. Available online: https://www.aoac.org/official-methods-of-analysis-21st-edition-2019/ (accessed on 14 April 2022).
22. Quiles, A.; Campbell, G.M.; Struck, S.; Rohm, H.; Hernando, I. Fiber from fruit pomace: A review of applications in cereal-based products. *Food Rev. Int.* **2018**, *34*, 162–181. [CrossRef]
23. Znamirowska, A.; Kalicka, D.; Buniowska, M.; Rozek, P. Effect of dried apple powder additive on physical-chemical and sensory properties of yoghurt. *Food Sci. Technol. Qual.* **2018**, *25*, 71–80.
24. Manzocco, L.; Romano, G.; Calligaris, S.; Nicoli, M.C. Modeling the effect of the oxidation status of the ingredient oil on stability and shelf life of low-moisture bakery products: The case study of crackers. *Foods* **2020**, *9*, 749. [CrossRef] [PubMed]
25. Galić, K.; Ćurić, D.; Gabrić, D. Shelf life of packaged bakery goods—A review. *Crit. Rev. Food Sci. Nutr.* **2009**, *49*, 405–426. [CrossRef] [PubMed]
26. Williamson, G.; Carughi, A. Polyphenol content and health benefits of raisins. *Nutr. Res.* **2010**, *30*, 511–519. [CrossRef] [PubMed]
27. León, E.A.V.; Aldapa, C.A.G.; Rojas, J.A.; Torres, A.V.; Uribe, J.P.H.; Rodríguez, H.M.P.; Cortez, R.O.N. Phytochemical content and antioxidant activity of extruded products made from yellow corn supplemented with apple pomace powder. *Food Sci. Technol.* **2022**, *42*, e91221. [CrossRef]
28. Valková, V.; Ďúranová, H.; Havrlentová, M.; Ivanišová, E.; Mezey, J.; Tóthová, Z.; Gabríny, L.; Kačániová, M. Selected physico-chemical, nutritional, antioxidant and sensory properties of wheat bread supplemented with apple pomace powder as a by-product from juice production. *Plants* **2022**, *11*, 1256. [CrossRef]
29. Gumul, D.; Kruczek, M.; Ivanišová, E.; Słupski, J.; Kowalski, S. Apple pomace as an ingredient enriching wheat pasta with health-promoting compounds. *Foods* **2023**, *12*, 804. [CrossRef]
30. Sobczak, P.; Nadulski, R.; Kobus, Z.; Zawiślak, K. Technology for apple pomace utilization within a sustainable development policy framework. *Sustainability* **2022**, *14*, 5470. [CrossRef]
31. Vildan, E.Y.İ.Z.; Tontul, İ.; Türker, S. Edible coating of cereal bars using different biopolymers: Effect on physical and chemical properties during storage. *GIDA* **2020**, *45*, 1019–1029.
32. Wiedemair, V.; Gruber, K.; Knöpfle, N.; Bach, K.E. Technological changes in wheat-based breads enriched with hemp seed press cakes and hemp seed grit. *Molecules* **2022**, *27*, 1840. [CrossRef]
33. Sandini, M.B.; Biz, A.P.; Bertolo, A.P.; Bagatini, L.; Riego, E.; Cavalheiro, D. Enriched cereal bars with wine fermentation biomass. *J. Sci. Food Agric.* **2020**, *101*, 542–547.
34. Carvalho, V.S.; Conti-Silva, A.C. Cereal bars produced with banana peel flour: Evaluation of acceptability and sensory profile. *J. Sci. Food Agric.* **2018**, *98*, 134–139. [CrossRef]
35. Eyiz, V.; Tontul, İ.; Türker, S. The effect of edible coatings on physical and chemical characteristics of fruit bars. *J. Food Meas. Charact.* **2020**, *14*, 1775–1783. [CrossRef]

36. Usman, M.; Ahmed, S.; Mehmood, A.; Bilal, M.; Patil, P.J.; Akram, K.; Farooq, U. Effect of apple pomace on nutrition, rheology of dough and cookies quality. *J. Food Sci. Technol.* **2020**, *57*, 3244–3251. [CrossRef] [PubMed]
37. Acun, S.; Gül, H. Effects of grape pomace and grape seed flours on cookie quality. *Qual. Assur. Saf.* **2014**, *6*, 81–88. [CrossRef]

Disclaimer/Publisher's Note: The statements, opinions and data contained in all publications are solely those of the individual author(s) and contributor(s) and not of MDPI and/or the editor(s). MDPI and/or the editor(s) disclaim responsibility for any injury to people or property resulting from any ideas, methods, instructions or products referred to in the content.

Article

Effect of Plant Extracts Addition on the Physico-Chemical and Sensory Properties of Biscuits

Salih Salihu [1], Njomza Gashi [1] and Endrit Hasani [1,2,*]

[1] Department of Food Technology with Biotechnology, Faculty of Agriculture and Veterinary, University of Prishtina, 10000 Prishtina, Kosovo; salih.salihu@uni-pr.edu (S.S.); njomza.gashi5@student.uni-pr.edu (N.G.)
[2] Department of Livestock Products and Food Preservation Technology, Institute of Food Science and Technology, Hungarian University of Agriculture and Life Sciences, Ménesi út 43-45, 1118 Budapest, Hungary
* Correspondence: endrithasani96@gmail.com

Abstract: Biscuits are one of the most consumed bakery products that contain a high content of fat, sugar, and different additives that may cause various health problems. This has led to an increased focus on enriching bakery products with plant extracts to improve their nutritional and sensory properties. The objective of the current work was to investigate the effect of replacing wheat flour with plant extracts such as blueberry and cranberry (at concentrations of 3%, 6%, and 9%) and compare with control biscuits regarding the physico-chemical and color parameters. In addition, sensory analysis was conducted to determine the consumer acceptability of the enriched biscuits. The enrichment of biscuits with blueberry powder significantly increased the moisture content and decreased pH values ($p < 0.05$). Similarly, cranberry-enriched biscuits had a significantly higher moisture content, water activity, and decreased pH values compared to control samples ($p < 0.05$). On the other hand, enrichment of biscuits with either blueberry or cranberry powder significantly decreased lightness (L^*), yellowness (b^*), chroma value (C^*), and h-value (h) but increased the redness values (a^* value) of samples ($p < 0.05$). Our results showed that with increasing concentrations of plant extract addition in biscuits, the sensory attributes such as odor and taste were significantly improved. The results of the study suggest that the addition of plant extracts to biscuits improved their physico-chemical and sensory properties.

Keywords: biscuits; blueberry; cranberry; color; sensory; physico-chemical parameters

Citation: Salihu, S.; Gashi, N.; Hasani, E. Effect of Plant Extracts Addition on the Physico-Chemical and Sensory Properties of Biscuits. *Appl. Sci.* 2023, *13*, 9674. https://doi.org/10.3390/app13179674

Academic Editors: Anna Wirkijowska, Piotr Zarzycki, Agata Blicharz-Kania and Urszula Pankiewicz

Received: 31 July 2023
Revised: 20 August 2023
Accepted: 25 August 2023
Published: 27 August 2023

Copyright: © 2023 by the authors. Licensee MDPI, Basel, Switzerland. This article is an open access article distributed under the terms and conditions of the Creative Commons Attribution (CC BY) license (https:// creativecommons.org/licenses/by/ 4.0/).

1. Introduction

Biscuits are important items of the confectionary industry which are rich in carbohydrates, fats, proteins, salts, and minerals. Traditional ingredients of biscuits such as oil, eggs, different additives, and flour, do not provide much nutritional value for the body. Their current great popularity has come as a result of the convenience they offer for consumption as a ready-made product, the long term of storage, and availability in different shapes, sizes, and compositions in the market. In recent years, improving the nutritional and sensory values of confectionary products is one of the main goals of this industry, which is developing rapidly [1]. Modification of traditional biscuit recipes by adding healthy ingredients has proven to have a positive effect on the production of a product which has functional properties and is acceptable for consumption. Enriching bakery products with natural antioxidants provides health benefits to consumers [2,3]. This affects the increase in the consumer intake of bioactive substances from bakery products that traditionally do not contain these compounds [4]. Such enrichment may also affect the rheological properties, physico-chemical characteristics, and consumer acceptability of bakery products. However, a less desirable aspect of adding plant ingredients to biscuits can be considered to be the possible negative impact on taste [5].

Plant ingredients provide a good solution to improve the nutritional content of biscuits because of their high concentrations of vitamins, minerals, prebiotics, probiotics, and fibers.

Therefore, it is in the interest of the bakery industry to incorporate such ingredients and their extracts in the development of biscuits with improved physico-chemical and sensory properties [6]. In this regard, there are many plant extracts that have been proven to be beneficial when added to biscuits such as lemon peel and its pomace [7] grapes seeds [8], apple powder [9], watermelon, orange pomace [10], horseradish [11], moringa flower powder, and leaf powder [12]. According to Kozlowska et al. [2] the addition of plant extracts to biscuit recipes can improve their sensory properties and extend shelf life by preventing oxidation.

Among various plant ingredients, berry fruits extracts are known for their excellent health properties, but also for their aroma, taste, and color. Blueberry powder addition is a simple way to improve the antioxidant content and the shelf life of biscuits [13]. Blueberries have multiple health properties due to their ingredients such as phenolic acids (caffeic, chlorogenic, ferulic, p-coumaric, and cinnamic acids) and flavonoids (anthocyanidins). In fact, studies show that berries, as fruits, ease problems with diabetes, heart disease, obesity, osteoporosis, and prevent bone loss [14]. The number of food products enriched with blueberries is expected to rise significantly as a result of all these functional advantages. Biscuits enriched with blueberries show a higher content of polyphenols, thus also a higher antioxidant activity that comes from the presence of blueberries [15]. According to Šarić et al. (2016) the addition of blueberry pomace in different concentrations up to 30% in the preparation of biscuits affects the reduction of fat content and the increase of beneficial ingredients such as fibers, vitamins, and phenolic compounds [16]. However, even the application of lower amounts of blueberry extract has shown positive effects on the characteristics of biscuits, where, according to Aksoylu et al. [17], biscuits enriched with only 5% blueberry extracts showed high antioxidant activity.

In the same way, cranberries are known for containing many bioactive components. Vitamins such as anthocyanins, procyanidins, and flavanols in cranberries have been documented to have potential effects in cancer prevention. Being a source of these bioactive ingredients, cranberries have proven to be effective in reducing the recurrence of urinary tract infections, thus reducing the need for taking antibiotics in such cases [18]. Also, cranberries positively affect atherosclerotic cholesterol profiles and reduce some cardiometabolic risk factors. Cranberry juice or cranberries themselves have been shown to protect against intestinal inflammation and inhibit bacterial colonization in the stomach [19]. They also have a high content of flavonoids and their antioxidant effect, due to the flavonoids they contain, protects the body from free radicals [20]. In general, consumers choose the processed forms of cranberry for consumption in their juice, sauces, supplements, and sweetened dried fruits, while few prefer their consumption to be in fresh form [21], therefore their incorporation in biscuits would bring innovation for consumers in the market. Similar to blueberries, the application of cranberries in the production of biscuits results in higher values of antioxidant activity and polyphenolic content compared to samples without cranberry extract [22]. Cranberry powder can also be used to give color to different foods instead of using synthetic additives.

Based on these health benefits, the formulation of biscuits fortified with different herbal ingredients can help improve the general nutritional status of the population. This technology can also be an encouragement for the food industry to develop new products through the principle of enriching them with different ingredients with functional properties [23]. The formulation of the biscuit's recipe with a certain percentage of blueberry and cranberry powder affects the increase in the nutritional value of the biscuits and their functional properties. Moreover, such components when incorporated into biscuits enable easier intake of these ingredients by consumers, thus offering new healthy options for obtaining plant ingredients in addition to their fresh form. The aim of this work was to produce biscuits enriched with blueberry and cranberry powder and to analyze the effect of these bioactive compounds in the physico-chemical and sensory attributes of biscuits.

2. Materials and Methods

2.1. Preparation of Biscuits

Raw materials used for biscuit preparation include: wheat flour, egg, butter, vanilla pudding, sugar powder, baking powder, and vanilla sugar (Table 1). All these ingredients were placed into a container and mixed by hand (3–5 min) until a compact mass was reached. The biscuit dough was kept at a temperature of 5 °C for two hours and then it was shaped. Baking was carried out for 10–15 min at 150 °C in the baking oven. The same recipe was used for all the biscuits, except for the biscuits enriched with blueberry and cranberry powder, where the corresponding extracts with 3%, 6%, and 9% have been added, replacing the wheat flour. Blueberry powder was purchased from Arctic Flavors, Espoo, Finland, and cranberry powder from LOOV, Tallinn, Estonia. Nutritional facts for blueberry powder per 100 g include: fat content of 6.5 g, carbohydrates 60.4 g, protein 4.7 g, fiber 19.5 g, salt 30.2 mg, vitamin C 42.6 mg, vitamin E 11.2 mg, and vitamin K 53.3 mg. Cranberries also have a very rich content with fat 0.2 g/100 g, carbohydrates 2 g, dietary fiber 6 g, potassium 28.23 mg, calcium 4.46 mg, vitamin E 0.23 mg, vitamin C 5.71 mg, manganese 1.56 mg, anthocyanin 34.8 mg, polyphenols 34.8 mg, and benzoic acid 5.04 mg. All biscuit samples were prepared in triplicate according to the recipe described in Table 1.

Table 1. Formulations for biscuit preparation.

Ingredients	Biscuits Composition (g)			
	C	B1	B2	B3
Wheat flour	100	97	94	91
Blueberry/cranberry powder	0	3	6	9
Egg	21.16	21.16	21.16	21.16
Butter	49.87	49.87	49.87	49.87
Sugar powder	59.89	59.89	59.89	59.89
Vanilla sugar	3.96	3.96	3.96	3.96
Vanilla pudding	15.30	15.30	15.30	15.30
Baking powder	1.31	1.31	1.31	1.31

C—biscuits without blueberry/cranberry powder, B1—biscuits with 3% blueberry/cranberry powder, B2—biscuits with 6% blueberry/cranberry powder, and B3—biscuits with 9% blueberry/cranberry powder.

2.2. Physico-chemical Evaluation of the Biscuits

The weight, height, and specific gravity of biscuits were determined for physical evaluation. Weight was determined using an analytical scale, height using a ruler, and specific gravity was determined using a pycnometer. Specific gravity results were obtained by dividing the weight of the dough mass of the sample with the equal volume of water [24].

From the chemical measurements, moisture content, acidity, pH value, and water activity were determined. Moisture content was determined by applying the temperature of 130 °C until reaching the constant weight of the samples [25]. A pH meter was used to measure the pH of the samples after calibration. Meanwhile, the acidity was determined by the titration method using sodium hydroxide 0.1 mol/dm^3 as a titrant [25]. A Novasina LabMaster-aw neo type instrument (Novasina, Zurich, Switzerland) was used to measure the water activity of the biscuit samples. All measurements were conducted in triplicates.

2.3. Color Attributes

Color attributes, such as lightness (L^*), redness (a^*), and yellowness (b^*) were measured using a CR-410-type colorimeter (Konica Minolta Sensing Inc., Tokyo, Japan) after white calibration of the instrument. Five parallel readings L^*, a^*, and b^* values were recorded for each sample and from the measured values chroma value (C^*) and hue angle (h^*) were calculated using the following equations:

$$\text{Chroma: } C^* = [(a^*)^2 + (b^*)^2]^{1/2} \tag{1}$$

$$\text{Hue angle: } h^* = \tan^{-1}(b^*/a^*) \tag{2}$$

Total color difference (ΔE) between biscuits samples was calculated using the method described by Knispel [26].

2.4. Sensory Analysis

Sensory parameters, including shape, color, odor, taste, texture, and mouthfeel, were evaluated through a 9-point hedonic evaluation scale, where 1 = dislike extremely and 9 = like extremely. For this study, 60 sensory non-trained panelists from the Food Technology with Biotechnology Department, Faculty of Agriculture and Veterinary, University of Pristina, were asked to evaluate the samples. Water and salt crackers were used during sensory evaluation to neutralize the mouths of the panelists.

2.5. Statistical Analysis

The experimental data were analyzed using IBM SPSS (Version 26.0, Armnouk, NY, USA, 2020). Data were analyzed using the analysis of variance (ANOVA) and General Linear Model (GLM). The Kolmogorov–Smirnov test was used to test the normality of residuals ($p > 0.05$). Levene's test was performed to check the homogeneity of variances ($p > 0.05$). The differences between groups were analyzed using Tukey's post hoc tests if homogeneity of variances was not violated. Meanwhile, if this assumption was violated then the Games–Howell test was performed.

3. Results

3.1. Physico-chemical Analysis of Biscuits

The physico-chemical parameters of the biscuits are presented in Table 2. The results showed that there was a significant difference ($p < 0.05$) in water activity between biscuits enriched with cranberry powder (6 and 9%) and control samples. Moreover, biscuits enriched with 9% cranberry powder had significantly higher water activity compared to biscuits with 3 and 6% cranberry powder. On the one hand, water activity of biscuits enriched with 3 to 9% of blueberry powder was not significantly different compared to control samples. On the other hand, significant differences were shown in moisture content ($p < 0.05$), where biscuits enriched with 9% blueberry and those with 9% cranberry differed from the control sample. Similarly, Mehta et al. [27] reported an increase in moisture content in samples enriched with tomato pomace, which can be explained by the fact that powdered cranberry and blueberry extracts may have greater water holding capacity than wheat flour. Similarly, Kolesárová et al. [28] reported a significant increase in moisture content with the addition of 5 and 15% of Saskatoon berry in biscuit composition.

Table 2. Physico-chemical parameters of biscuits enriched with plant extracts.

Sample	PE (%)	Weight (g)	Height (cm)	Specific Gravity (g/cm³)	Moisture (%)	Water Activity	pH	Acidity
Control	0	8.76 ± 1.01 [a]	0.43 ± 0.06 [a]	0.73 ± 0.01 [a]	4.48 ± 0.24 [b]	0.32 ± 0.01 [c]	6.87 ± 0.08 [a]	7.36 ± 1.21 [b]
Blueberry-enriched biscuits	3	8.21 ± 0.47 [a]	0.55 ± 0.09 [a]	0.73 ± 0.02 [a]	5.26 ± 0.19 [ab]	0.32 ± 0.0 [c]	6.49 ± 0.04 [b]	8.99 ± 0.85 [ab]
	6	9.68 ± 0.23 [a]	0.43 ± 0.06 [a]	0.73 ± 0.01 [a]	5.63 ± 0.66 [ab]	0.34 ± 0.01 [bc]	6.25 ± 0.04 [c]	9.91 ± 1.68 [ab]
	9	9.52 ± 0.61 [a]	0.47 ± 0.06 [a]	0.74 ± 0.01 [a]	5.98 ± 0.35 [a]	0.35 ± 0.03 [bc]	6.10 ± 0.05 [cd]	11.22 ± 2.36 [ab]
Cranberry-enriched biscuits	3	8.81 ± 0.66 [a]	0.47 ± 0.06 [a]	0.74 ± 0.02 [a]	5.73 ± 0.48 [ab]	0.33 ± 0.01 [bc]	6.04 ± 0.04 [d]	11.68 ± 0.38 [ab]
	6	9.63 ± 0.72 [a]	0.40 ± 0.00 [a]	0.76 ± 0.03 [a]	5.75 ± 0.75 [ab]	0.39 ± 0.01 [b]	5.26 ± 0.04 [e]	13.74 ± 2.76 [a]
	9	9.42 ± 0.31 [a]	0.40 ± 0.00 [a]	0.78 ± 0.04 [a]	6.60 ± 0.64 [a]	0.49 ± 0.05 [a]	4.38 ± 0.08 [f]	14.16 ± 2.83 [a]

PE—Plant extract. Data are expressed as mean ± standard deviation. Means with different superscripts in same column are significantly different ($p < 0.05$).

The enrichment of biscuits with blueberry and cranberry powder also had an impact on the acidity and pH values of biscuits, where significant differences were recorded. Both enriched biscuits samples with either cranberry or blueberry powder showed significant differences on pH values compared to the control biscuits samples (without plant extract) (Table 2). It can be emphasized that cranberry powder's addition of 3 to 9% had a significantly higher effect on decreasing pH values of biscuits compared with blueberry powder. Meanwhile, in terms of acidity, only the biscuit samples with 6% and 9% cranberry powder showed significant differences from the control biscuit samples. This can be explained by the fact that berries, including blueberry and cranberry, have a high content of organic acids, which has influenced the increase in the overall acidity of the biscuits [12]. On the other hand, there was no significant difference ($p > 0.05$) between analyzed samples in weight, height, and specific gravity parameters.

3.2. Color Attributes

Color is one of the key factors affecting the initial consumer acceptability of the food product. Nowadays, consumers are aiming for a healthy diet which includes natural dye compounds in foods instead of artificial ones. In this sense, the enrichment of biscuits with plant extracts that contain natural dyes such as anthocyanins could potentially have a positive influence on consumers' choice priorities. Color attributes of biscuits enriched with different concentrations of cranberry and blueberry extracts are presented in Table 3. Lightness values (L^*) were significantly decreased with increasing the blueberry powder from 0 to 6% in biscuits ($p < 0.05$). However, no significant differences were observed in lightness values between 6 and 9% blueberry-enriched biscuits ($p > 0.05$). A similar decreasing trend on lightness values was observed with increasing the cranberry powder from 0 to 9% in enriched biscuit samples. Lower lightness in enriched biscuits can be explained by the dark color derived from natural dye compounds of berries such as anthocyanins and by Maillard reactions during baking [17]. Similarly, Aksoylo et al. [17] reported that enriched biscuits with approximately 5% blueberry powder provided lower lightness compared to the control samples. Tarasevičienė et al. [29] also reported that the addition of 10% raspberry, red currant, and strawberry pomace significantly decreased the lightness of the enriched cookies.

On the other hand, redness values (a^*) were significantly increased with increasing the blueberry plant extract addition from 0 to 9% in biscuit composition. Similarly, redness values of the biscuits were increased with increasing cranberry powder addition from 0 to 3% and from 3 to 9% ($p < 0.05$). The increase in redness value in enriched biscuits can be attributed to high anthocyanin content known as red pigment present in berries [30]. Pasqualone et al. [31] reported a strong significant correlation between redness and anthocyanin content in anthocyanin-enriched biscuits. A previous study also reported that redness values were increased with increasing the blueberry content in biscuits [17].

Yellowness (b^*) values of biscuits were significantly reduced after 3% of cranberry powder addition ($p < 0.05$). Meanwhile, no significant change on yellowness was observed between 3, 6, and 9% cranberry-enriched biscuits ($p > 0.05$). On contrary, yellowness values of the biscuits were significantly reduced after 3% and after 6% blueberry powder addition ($p < 0.05$). The yellowness decrease in enriched biscuit samples can be explained by the lower amount of wheat flour in biscuit formulation (Table 1), and consequently lower carotenoid content, compared to control biscuit samples [31]. Tarasevičienė et al. [29] also reported that cookies enriched with addition of 10 to 20% raspberry, red currant, or strawberry pomace had significantly lower yellowness values compared to control samples. Chroma or saturation values (C^* value) of control samples (without plant extract) were significantly higher than both blueberry- and cranberry-enriched biscuits ($p < 0.05$). Similarly, Molnar et al. [32] reported that chroma values of biscuits were significantly reduced with addition of either black currant or jostaberry powders. The h-value of the biscuits was significantly decreased with increasing the concentration of blueberry powder from 0 to 9% ($p < 0.05$). Similarly, the h value of cranberry-enriched biscuits decreased with increasing the powder concentration from 0 to 3 % and from 6 to 9 % ($p < 0.05$). Previous authors reported similar results of the h-value decreasing with the addition of plant extract powder in biscuits [17,32].

Table 3. Color attributes of biscuits enriched with plant extracts.

Attribute	Sample	Type of Plant Extract		p-Value
		Blueberry	Cranberry	
Lightness (L^*)	Control	76.89 [c]	76.89 [c]	
	3%	67.77 [bB]	63.28 [bA]	<0.001
	6%	65.06 [bB]	56.08 [aA]	<0.001
	9%	62.28 [aB]	54.86 [aA]	<0.001
Redness (a^*)	Control	0.08 [a]	0.08 [a]	
	3%	5.49 [bB]	3.43 [bA]	<0.001
	6%	6.35 [bB]	4.69 [cA]	<0.001
	9%	7.82 [cB]	6.76 [dA]	<0.05
Yellowness (b^*)	Control	34.52 [b]	34.52 [c]	
	3%	22.74 [aB]	15.55 [bA]	<0.001
	6%	22.62 [aB]	11.98 [aA]	<0.001
	9%	22.46 [aB]	9.56 [aA]	<0.001
Chroma (C^*)	Control	34.53 [b]	34.53 [c]	
	3%	23.40 [aB]	15.93 [bA]	<0.001
	6%	23.50 [aB]	12.88 [aA]	<0.001
	9%	23.80 [aB]	11.77 [aA]	<0.001
h-value (h)	Control	89.89 [c]	89.89 [d]	
	3%	76.42 [bA]	77.58 [cA]	0.193
	6%	74.33 [bB]	68.38 [bA]	<0.001
	9%	70.83 [aB]	53.80 [aA]	<0.001

a–d means with different letters in the same column are significantly different for percentage of plant extract ($p < 0.05$). A, B means with different letters in the same row are significantly different for plant extract type ($p > 0.05$; $p < 0.05$; $p < 0.001$).

Blueberry-enriched biscuits (3 to 9%) had significantly lower lightness, yellowness, and chroma values compared to cranberry-enriched biscuits ($p < 0.001$). Similarly, blueberry-enriched biscuits (3 to 9%) had significantly lower redness values compared to cranberry-enriched biscuits. h-values were significantly lower in blueberry-enriched biscuits compared to cranberry-enriched biscuits, with the exception of 3% enrichment. This shows that the addition of blueberry plant extract had a higher effect on changing the main color attributes of the biscuits compared to cranberry powder within the same concentrations.

However, for a better understanding of changes in color attributes of the enriched biscuits, authors believe that the total color difference can be evaluated between the studied treatments. The results of total color difference (ΔE) between biscuits enriched with different concentration of plant extracts are presented in Tables 4 and 5. According to Mokrzycki and Tatol [33], an observer notices two different colors when the ΔE is higher than 5. Our results showed that two distinct colors are perceived when the observer compares control biscuit samples (without plant extract) and enriched biscuits with either blueberry or cranberry powder (ΔE > 5) (Tables 4 and 5). Meanwhile, color differences can also be perceived by an inexperienced observer when 3 and 6% enriched blueberry biscuits samples are compared (2 < ΔE < 3.5) (Table 4). A similar result was observed when comparing color properties (lightness, redness, and yellowness) of 6 and 9% blueberry and cranberry biscuits samples (Table 5).

Table 4. Total color difference between biscuits enriched with blueberry extracts.

	Total Color Difference (ΔE)			
Treatment	C	BB 3%	BB 6%	BB 9%
C	-	V	V	V
BB 3%	15.86	-	III	V
BB 6%	17.92	2.84	-	III
BB 9%	20.47	5.97	3.15	-

BB—Blueberry plant extract. Latin numbers in the table indicate the total color difference (ΔE) categories: Category I: $0 < \Delta E < 1$, observer perceives no difference; category II: $1 < \Delta E < 2$, only the experienced observer perceives the difference; category III: $2 < \Delta E < 3.5$, the color difference is perceived also by an inexperienced observer; category IV: $3.5 < \Delta E < 5$, a clear color difference is perceived; and category V: $\Delta E > 5$, observer notices two distinct colors.

Table 5. Total color difference between biscuits enriched with cranberry extracts.

	Total Color Difference (ΔE)			
Treatment	C	CB 3%	CB 6%	CB 9%
C	-	V	V	V
CB 3%	23.59	-	V	V
CB 6%	31.02	8.13	-	III
CB 9%	33.96	10.85	3.41	-

CB—Cranberry plant extract. Latin numbers in the table indicate the total color difference (ΔE) categories: Category I: $0 < \Delta E < 1$, observer perceives no difference; category II: $1 < \Delta E < 2$, only the experienced observer perceives the difference; category III: $2 < \Delta E < 3.5$, the color difference is perceived also by an inexperienced observer; category IV: $3.5 < \Delta E < 5$, a clear color difference is perceived; and category V: $\Delta E > 5$, observer notices two distinct colors.

3.3. Sensory Analysis

The main attributes on which consumers base the purchase and acceptability of a food or novel product are taste, nutritional values, and its impact on health. The addition of plant extracts to bakery products is seen as a future solution to improve their nutritional and functional properties due to the bioactivity derived from the phytochemicals of the plant ingredients [34]. However, the sensory attributes are those that are evaluated first by the consumer and influence the selection of a food product for consumption. Results of sensory attributes of biscuits enriched with different concentrations of blueberry and cranberry extracts are presented in Figures 1 and 2.

According to our results, there were significant differences in all the parameters included in the sensory evaluation of biscuits enriched with blueberry powder (Figure 1). The highest score for all parameters was obtained for biscuits enriched with 9% blueberry. Increasing the concentration of blueberry powder resulted in increasing the acceptability of consumers for all the attributes, especially taste and mouthfeel. Similarly, Kolesárová et al. [28] reported a significant increase on taste scores of biscuits enriched with 10 and 15% of Saskatoon berries. Contrary to this, another study has shown that there were no significant differences in aroma, taste, color, and overall acceptability of cookies with 10 and 20% red beetroot powder from the control samples [35]. This shows that consumers positively expect such formulations but differences in preferences vary depending on the amount of added extract and the extract used.

Compared to the control sample, slightly lower values were recorded by the samples of biscuits with 3% and 6% blueberry, which can be explained by the fact that the color of these biscuits was not as intense as that of biscuits with 9% blueberry which turned out to be the most liked. Ahmed and Ashraf [36] also reported an increase in liking for the appearance of the biscuits supplemented with different levels of whey protein concentrate, where the increase in the amount of whey protein concentrate was accompanied by an increase in the evaluation by consumers for the appearance and the aroma of the product. Consumers preferred biscuits with the darkest color and this result agrees with the results of a study for biscuits with buckwheat flour. Mouthfeel values were mostly affected by samples with 9% blueberry extract which is in accordance with Anselm et al.'s [37] results for biscuits with African pear and orange flesh sweet potato flour blends. Generally, biscuits enriched with 9% blueberry powder were the most acceptable sample among panelists (48.3%), while biscuits without blueberry powder were the least liked (13.3%).

Similarly, results showed there were significant differences in the color, shape, texture, odor, and taste of biscuits with cranberry powder. The addition of cranberry powder significantly enhanced the scores for shape, texture, odor, and taste (Figure 2). Biscuits enriched with 6% and those with 9% cranberry were evaluated with the highest scores compared to samples with 3% cranberry and the control sample, which were evaluated with the lowest scores. The panelists considered that biscuits enriched with 6% cranberry had the best taste and had the most attractive sensory attributes (40%), while biscuits enriched with 3% cranberry received the lowest score of overall acceptance (10%). This may have happened since with 6% addition of cranberry powder the change in the biscuits' taste was clearly observed. These results agreed with the findings of Al-Marazeeq and Angor [38], who concluded that the taste of biscuits was enhanced by the addition of wheat germ at a level of 20%. In terms of texture and shape, the consumer acceptability was higher for biscuit samples with more cranberry extract which may be because of the greater softness of the product when a larger amount of plant extract was incorporated. Similar results were also achieved by Najjar et al. [39] in the study completed with cookies formulated with date seed powder.

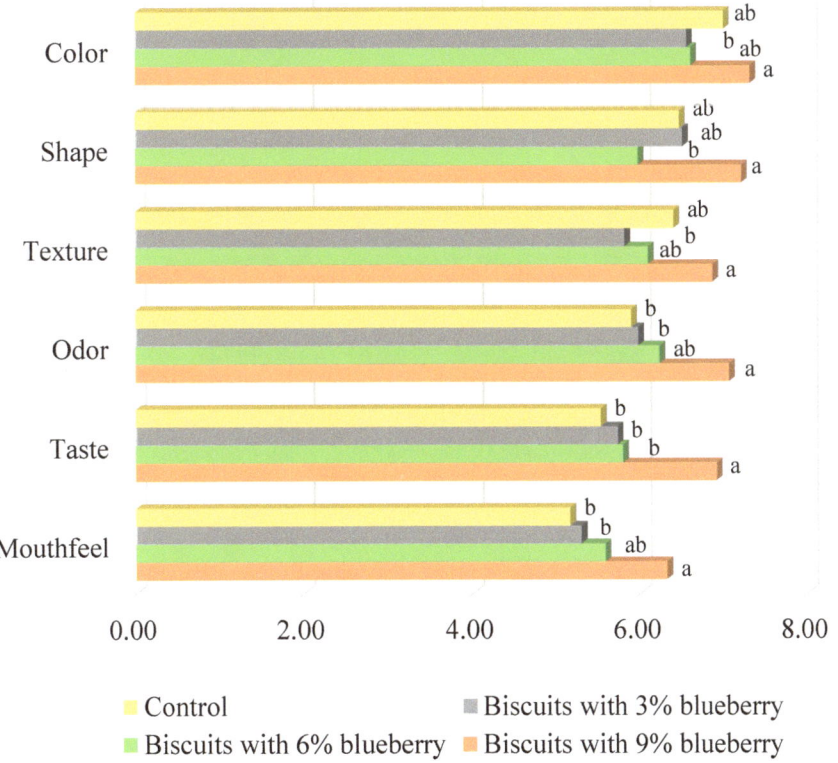

Figure 1. Sensory attributes of enriched biscuits with blueberry powder. a, b means with different letters next to the bars are significantly different for percentage of plant extract ($p < 0.05$).

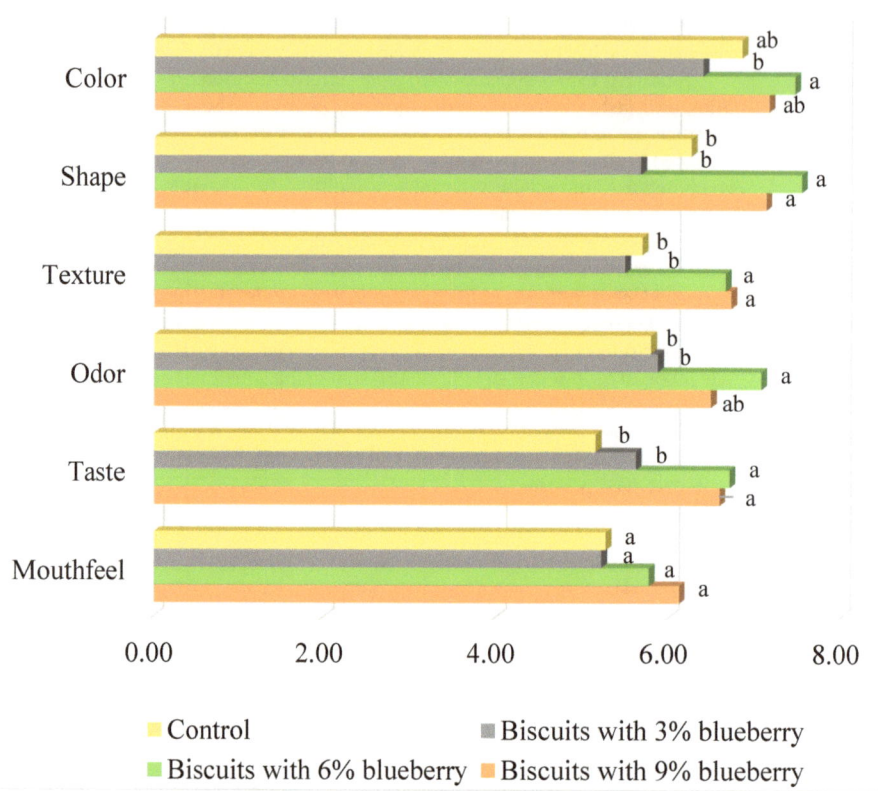

Figure 2. Sensory attributes of enriched biscuits with cranberry powder. a, b means with different letters next to the bars are significantly different for percentage of plant extract ($p < 0.05$).

Generally, biscuits enriched with blueberry and cranberry powder showed acceptable sensory attributes among panelists. These results agreed with Tarasevičienė et al. [29], who reported that the enrichment of cookies with berries' powder enhanced the acceptance of consumers for these products, since they had better color and taste characteristics. Based on our results, biscuits containing a higher amount of blueberry powder had better sensory properties including taste, mouthfeel, and texture. Similarly, Kolesárová et al. [28] reported that with higher addition of Saskatoon berry powder instead of flour the sensory properties of the biscuits were highly improved.

4. Conclusions

The present study demonstrated that the addition of plant extracts such as blueberry and cranberry had a positive effect on some of the physico-chemical and sensory properties of biscuits. The addition of blueberry extract increased the moisture content and decreased the pH values of biscuits. Meanwhile, cranberry-enriched biscuits had lower pH values, higher moisture content, water activity, and acidity compared to control biscuits. On the other hand, color attributes of biscuits such as lightness, yellowness, chroma, and hue values decreased with the addition of blueberry or cranberry extract. Meanwhile, redness values were higher in plant extract-enriched biscuits compared to control samples (without plant extract). Based on the overall acceptability results, biscuits enriched with 9% blueberry powder were the most favored regarding odor, taste, and mouthfeel. On the other hand, from cranberry-enriched biscuits 6 and 9% additions were the most favored among consumers regarding shape, texture, and taste compared with 3% cranberry-enriched biscuits and control samples. This lead to the conclusion that berries' extracts can be applied in the food industry to develop bakery products with improved quality and sensory properties. However, future studies need to be conducted to examine the effect of berries' extracts on functional properties of biscuits such as antioxidant activity and polyphenolic content.

Author Contributions: Conceptualization, S.S. and E.H.; methodology, E.H.; software, E.H.; validation, S.S. and E.H.; formal analysis, N.G.; investigation, E.H. and N.G.; resources, S.S.; data curation, E.H.; writing—original draft preparation, E.H., S.S. and N.G.; writing—review and editing, E.H. and S.S.; visualization, E.H. and N.G.; supervision, S.S. and E.H.; project administration, S.S. and E.H.; funding acquisition, S.S. All authors have read and agreed to the published version of the manuscript.

Funding: This research received no external funding.

Institutional Review Board Statement: Not applicable.

Informed Consent Statement: Not applicable.

Data Availability Statement: The data presented in this study are available on request from the corresponding author.

Acknowledgments: The authors want to thank the sensory panelists from the Department of Food Technology and Biotechnology, University of Prishtina for their participation in the sensory evaluation.

Conflicts of Interest: The authors declare no conflict of interest.

References

1. Goubgou, M.; Songré-Ouattara, L.T.; Bationo, F.; Lingani-Sawadogo, H.; Traoré, Y.; Savadogo, A. Biscuits: A systematic review and metaanalysis of improving the nutritional quality and health benefits. *Food Prod. Process. Nutr.* **2022**, *3*, 26. [CrossRef]
2. Kozlowska, M.; Zbikowska, A.; Marciniak-Lukasiak, K.; Kowalska, M. Herbal Extracts Incorporated into Shortbread Cookies: Impact on Color and Fat Quality of the Cookies. *Biomolecules* **2019**, *9*, 858. [CrossRef]
3. Reddy, V.; Urooj, A.; Kumar, A. Evaluation of antioxidant activity of some plant extracts and their application in biscuits. *Food Chem.* **2004**, *90*, 317–321. [CrossRef]
4. Krajewska, A.; Dziki, D. Enrichment of Cookies with Fruits and Their By-Products: Chemical Composition, Antioxidant Properties, and Sensory Changes. *Molecules* **2023**, *28*, 4005. [CrossRef]
5. Torbica, A.; Škrobot, D.; Hajnal, E.J.; Belović, M.; Zhang, N. Sensory and physico-chemical properties of wholegrain wheat bread prepared with selected food by-products. *LWT* **2019**, *114*, 108414. [CrossRef]
6. Mironeasa, S. Current Approaches in Using Plant Ingredients to Diversify Range of Bakery and Pasta Products. *Appl. Sci.* **2022**, *12*, 2794. [CrossRef]
7. Imeneo, V.; Romeo, R.; Gattuso, A.; De Bruno, A.; Piscopo, A. Functionalized Biscuits with Bioactive Ingredients Obtained by Citrus Lemon Pomace. *Foods* **2021**, *10*, 2460. [CrossRef] [PubMed]
8. Acun, S.; Gül, H. Effects of grape pomace and grape seed flours on cookie quality. *Qual. Assur. Saf. Crops Foods* **2013**, *6*, 81–88. [CrossRef]
9. Alsuhaibani, A.M. Biochemical and Biological Study of Biscuit Fortified with Apple Powder. *Middle East J. Agric. Res.* **2015**, *4*, 984–990.
10. Ogo, A.O.; Ajekwe, D.J.; Enenche, D.E.; Obochi, G.O. Quality Evaluation of Novel Biscuits Made from Wheat Supplemented with Watermelon Rinds and Orange Pomace Flour Blends. *Food Nutr. Sci.* **2021**, *12*, 332–341. [CrossRef]
11. Tomsone, L.; Galoburda, R.; Kruma, Z.; Majore, K. Physicochemical Properties of Biscuits Enriched with Horseradish (*Armoracia rusticana* L.) Products and Bioaccessibility of Phenolics after Simulated Human Digestion. *Polish J. Food Nutr. Sci.* **2020**, *70*, 419–428. [CrossRef]
12. Yadav, K.C.; Bhattarai, S.; Shiwakoti, L.D.; Paudel, S.; Subedi, M.; Pant, B.R.; Paudel, M.; Dhugana, S.; Bhattarai, S.; Tiwari, T.; et al. Sensorial and chemical analysis of biscuits prepared by incorporating Moringa flower powder and leaf powder. *Int. J. Food Propert.* **2022**, *25*, 894–906. [CrossRef]
13. Bhaduri, S.; Navder, K.P. Freeze Dried Blueberry Powder Fortification Improves the Quality of Gluten Free Snacks. *J. Food Process. Technol.* **2014**, *5*, 12. [CrossRef]
14. Patel, S. Blueberry as functional food and dietarysupplement: The natural way to ensureholistic health. *Medit. J. Nutr. Metab.* **2004**, *7*, 133–143. [CrossRef]
15. Perez, C.; Tagliani, C.; Arcia, P.; Cozzano, S.; Curutchet, A. Blueberry by-product used as an ingredient in the development of functional cookies. *Food Sci. Technol. Int.* **2018**, *24*, 301–308. [CrossRef]

16. Šarić, B.; Mišan, A.; Mandić, A.; Nedeljković, N.; Pojić, M.; Pestorić, M.; Đilas, S. Valorisation of raspberry and blueberry pomace through the formulation of value-added gluten-free cookies. *J. Food Sci. Technol.* **2016**, *53*, 1140–1150. [CrossRef]
17. Aksoylu, Z.; Çağindi, Ö.; Köse, E. Effects of blueberry, grape seed powder and poppy seed incorporation on physicochemical and sensory properties of biscuit. *J. Food Qual.* **2015**, *38*, 164–174.
18. Jeffrey, B.B.; Terri, C.A.; Aedin, C.; Penny, K.E.; Amy, H.; Claudine, M.; Luisa, O.M.; Helmut, S.; Ann, S.R.; Joseph, V.A. Cranberries and Their Bioactive Constituents in Human Health. *Adv. Nutr.* **2013**, *4*, 618–632. [CrossRef]
19. Zhao, S.; Liu, H.; Gu, L. American cranberries and health benefits—An evolving story of 25 years. *J. Sci. Food Agric.* **2020**, *100*, 5111–5116. [CrossRef]
20. Amin, R.; ThallurI, C.; Docea, A.O.; Sharifi-Rad, J.; Calina, D. Therapeutic potential of cranberry for kidney health and diseases. *eFood* **2022**, *3*, e33. [CrossRef]
21. Grace, M.H.; Massey, A.R.; Mbeunkui, F.; Yousef, G.G.; Lila, M.A. Comparison of Health-Relevant Flavonoids in Commonly Consumed Cranberry Products. *J. Food Sci.* **2012**, *77*, H176–H183. [CrossRef]
22. Mureşan, C.; Romina, V. The Effect of Cranberry and Grape Seed Addition on Quality Characteristics of Cookies. *J. Agroaliment. Process. Technol.* **2018**, *24*, 236–241.
23. Farzana, T.; Hossai, F.B.; Abedin, M.J.; Afrin, S.; Rahman, S.S. Nutritional and sensory attributes of biscuits enriched with buckwheat. *J. Agric. Food Res.* **2022**, *10*, 100394. [CrossRef]
24. Bhaduri, S.; Mukherjee, A.K. Rheology of Muffin Batters by Line Spread Test and Viscosity Measurements. *Int. J. Food Sci. Nutr. Diet.* **2016**, *5*, 325–329. [CrossRef]
25. Sapozhnikov, A.N.; Rozhdestvenskaya, L.N.; Kopylova, A.V. Quality Evaluation of Bakery Products Enriched with Spinach. *IOP Conf. Ser. Earth Environ. Sci.* **2019**, *346*, 012062. [CrossRef]
26. Knispel, G. Factors affecting the process of color matching restorative materials to natural teeth. *Quint. Int.* **1991**, *22*, 525–531.
27. Mehta, D.; Prasad, P.; Sangwan, R.S.; Yadav, S.K. Tomato processing byproduct valorization in bread and muffin: Improvement in physicochemical properties and shelf-life stability. *J. Food Sci. Technol.* **2018**, *55*, 2560–2568. [CrossRef] [PubMed]
28. Kolesárová, A.; Solgajová, M.; Bojňanská, T.; Kopčeková, J.; Zeleňáková, L.; Mrázová, J. The Effect of Saskatoon Berry (*Amelanchier alnifolia* Nutt.) Addition on the technological properties of wheat flour and the quality of biscuits. *J. Microbiol. Biotechnol. Food Sci.* **2022**, *12*, e9251. [CrossRef]
29. Tarasevičienė, Ž.; Čechovičienė, I.; Jukniūtė, K.; Šlepetienė, A.; Aurelija, P. Qualitative properties of cookies enriched with berries pomace. *Food Sci. Technol.* **2021**, *41*, 474–481. [CrossRef]
30. Bechtold, T.; Mahmud-Ali, A.; Mussak, R. Anthocyanin dyes extracted from grape pomace for the purpose of textile dyeing. *J. Sci. Food Agric.* **2007**, *87*, 2589–2595. [CrossRef]
31. Pasqualone, A.; Bianco, A.M.; Paradiso, V.M. Production trials to improve the nutritional quality of biscuits and to enrich them with natural anthocyanins. *CyTA J. Food* **2013**, *11*, 301–308. [CrossRef]
32. Molnar, D.; Rimac Brnčić, S.; Vujić, L.; Gyimes, E.; Krisch, J. Characterization of biscuits enriched with black currant and jostaberry powder. *Hrvat. Časopis Prehrambenu Tehnol. Biotehnol. Nutr.* **2015**, *10*, 31–36.
33. Mokrzycki, W.S.; Tatol, M. Colour difference∆ E-A survey. *Mach. Graph. Vis.* **2011**, *20*, 383–411.
34. Gao, J.; Koh, A.H.; Zhou, W. Enhancing health benefits of bakery products using phytochemicals. *Adv. Food Nutr. Res.* **2022**, *99*, 239–281. [CrossRef]
35. Rabie, M.M.; Ghoneim, G. Physico-chemical and Sensory Properties of Biscuits Fortified by with Red Table Beetroot (Beta Vulgaris) Powder. *Curr. Sci. Int.* **2022**, *11*, 174–183.
36. Ahmed, H.A.M.; Ashraf, S.A. Physico-chemical, textural and sensory characteristics of wheat flour biscuits supplemented with different levels of whey protein concentrate. *Curr. Res. Nutr. Food Sci. J.* **2019**, *7*, 761–771. [CrossRef]
37. Anselm, O.U.; Dixon, O.N.; Ugochi, U. Nutrient assessment of gluten free biscuit from African pear and orange flesh sweet potato flour blends. *J. Agric. Food Sci. Biotechnol.* **2023**, *1*, 83–94. [CrossRef]
38. Al-Marazeeq, K.M.; Angor, M.M. Chemical characteristic and sensory evaluation of biscuit enriched with wheat germ and the effect of storage time on the sensory properties for this product. *Food Nutr. Sci.* **2017**, *8*, 189–195. [CrossRef]
39. Najjar, Z.; Alkaabi, M.; Alketbi, K.; Stathopoulos, C.; Ranasinghe, M. Physical chemical and textural characteristics and sensory evaluation of cookies formulated with date seed powder. *Foods* **2022**, *11*, 305. [CrossRef] [PubMed]

Disclaimer/Publisher's Note: The statements, opinions and data contained in all publications are solely those of the individual author(s) and contributor(s) and not of MDPI and/or the editor(s). MDPI and/or the editor(s) disclaim responsibility for any injury to people or property resulting from any ideas, methods, instructions or products referred to in the content.

Article

The Influence of Tomato and Pepper Processing Waste on Bread Quality

Anna Wirkijowska [1], Piotr Zarzycki [1,*], Dorota Teterycz [1], Agnieszka Nawrocka [2], Agata Blicharz-Kania [3] and Paulina Łysakowska [1]

[1] Division of Engineering and Cereals Technology, Department of Plant Food Technology and Gastronomy, University of Life Sciences in Lublin, Skromna 8, 20-704 Lublin, Poland; anna.wirkijowska@up.lublin.pl (A.W.); dorota.teterycz@up.lublin.pl (D.T.); paulina.lysakowska@up.lublin.pl (P.Ł.)
[2] Institute of Agrophysics Polish Academy of Sciences, Doświadczalna 4, 20-290 Lublin, Poland; a.nawrocka@ipan.lublin.pl
[3] Department of Biological Bases of Food and Feed Technologies, Faculty of Production Engineering, University of Life Sciences in Lublin, Głęboka 28, 20-612 Lublin, Poland; agata.kania@up.lublin.pl
* Correspondence: piotr.zarzycki@up.lublin.pl

Abstract: Worldwide, there is a significant amount of food waste, highlighting the need to reduce waste throughout the production process. This study investigated the impact of incorporating vegetable processing waste from tomatoes (TP) and bell peppers (PB) on dough characteristics and bread quality, with concentrations of TP and PB ranging from 3% to 12% based on flour weight. The addition of TP and PB influenced the farinograph characteristics, increasing water absorption, dough development, and softening while reducing stability time. However, the changes in bread quality, including baking yield, loss, volume, and crumb porosity, were not significant. The texture properties, such as hardness, chewiness, and cohesiveness of the crumb, showed no significant changes within the supplemented levels up to 9%. Additionally, the TP and PB had a significant impact on the color of the bread crumb, increasing redness and yellowness, particularly with PB. Fortification with TP and PB up to 9% resulted in baking characteristics comparable to 100% wheat bread. The addition of TP and PB changed nutrient content, particularly dietary fiber, without significantly altering the caloric value of the bread. However, semi-consumer sensory evaluation indicated a decrease in aroma and taste when PB exceeded 9%, and a similar effect on taste was indicated when TP exceeded 9%. In conclusion, TP and PB at supplementation levels up to 9% can enhance the nutritional profile of bread and maintain its baking quality.

Keywords: bread fortification; by-product; dough rheology; physical and functional properties; wheat flour replacement; zero waste

1. Introduction

One of the major challenges facing the agri-food industry today is the elimination, reduction, or reuse of significant amounts of waste and by-products generated at various stages of the food production process [1]. These efforts align with the European Union's (EU) plan for a circular economy, which aims to reduce food waste, increase the value and longevity of products, and promote more efficient use of materials and resources in the economy [2]. According to data from the Food and Agriculture Organization (FAO), in the processing of oilseeds, approximately 20% of oilseeds are wasted, while for meat and dairy products, this figure is 20%; for grains, this figure is 30%; for fish, this figure is 35%; and for fruits and vegetables, it ranges from 40% to 50% [3]. Regarding total global food production, the amount of food wasted is estimated to be around 1.3 billion tons. Utilizing by-products from food processing that are rich in nutrients in new product development is a recommended approach for alleviating this [3–6].

One potential source of by-products that can be used to modify food product recipes is vegetable processing waste, specifically tomato by-products (TP) and bell pepper by-products (PB). These by-products have been studied for their potential applications in various food products, contributing to reducing food waste and enhancing the nutritional value of food [7–9]. Previous research has shown that TP can be a good source of dietary fiber, with an approximate content of 61% on a dry basis, while PB has a dietary fiber content of approximately 33% on a dry matter basis [9]. Additionally, dried tomato waste, including seeds and skin, contains approximately 17–23% protein, and the placenta of bell peppers has a protein content of about 28% [8,10]. Furthermore, both TP and PB are rich sources of lysine and sulfur amino acids such as methionine and cysteine, which can improve the overall protein quality of wheat-based food products [8,9]. TP, which contain a large amount of seeds, are a rich source of bioactive compounds that have been shown to exhibit strong antioxidant, anticancer, and antimicrobial activity in numerous studies. Tomato seeds contain no antinutritive agents or toxic elements [11,12]. The consumption of tomatoes is generally recognized as healthy, but as with all foods, there are limits and concerns to be mindful of. The vast consumption of tomato skin and seeds by humans may lead to irritable bowel syndrome, causing bloating and diarrhea [12]. Some research suggests that seed protein may be a relevant allergen, although whether it is predictive of systemic reactions remains to be determined [13]. Research also indicates that bell peppers are rich in phenolic compounds and flavonoids, which may offer benefits to human health. Diets rich in phytochemicals have been associated with a reduced risk of chronic non-communicable diseases, including diabetes, osteoporosis, and cancer. These beneficial effects are often attributed to the antioxidant capacity of polyphenols and flavonoids, which can help mitigate oxidative stress. The regular consumption of bell peppers can improve one's health and prevent degenerative diseases [14].

Bread is a widely consumed staple food globally, with an average per capita consumption of around 250 g per day [15]. It primarily provides carbohydrates (70–80% dry matter), proteins (10–14% dry matter), minerals (0.5–0.8% dry matter), and fats (0.7–1.35% dry matter). However, the dietary fiber content in bread is relatively low, typically around 2–3% [6,16]. To enhance the nutritional value of bread, there is a growing trend of incorporating non-traditional raw materials, including high-protein waste products from the plant food industry [17,18]. The introduction of additional ingredients, including by-products, into bread recipes not only affects the health-promoting properties of the resulting products but also the rheological characteristics of the dough. These changes can significantly impact the quality attributes of bread. For instance, the incorporation of high-fiber ingredients into the dough can disrupt the formation of the gluten network by creating new hydrogen bonds or altering the conformation of disulfide bridges. Such changes can influence the rheological properties of the dough by improper folding of polypeptide chains or aggregation of protein complexes [19]. The addition of fiber-rich ingredients, due to the presence of hydroxyl groups in their structure that can form hydrogen bonds with water, can increase the water absorption capacity [20]. While the high water absorption capacity of fiber can have a positive effect on the baking properties of the mixture [21], it can lead to dehydration of the gluten network, resulting in reduced elasticity and decreased resistance to mixing [22]. The weakening of the gluten network structure by vegetable by-products such as TP and PB has also been confirmed in previous studies examining changes in the secondary structure of the gluten network [23]. These findings further support the notion that the addition of fiber-rich ingredients can have a significant impact on the rheological properties of dough and the overall quality of bread.

Therefore, the objective of this study was to examine the effects on the rheological properties of dough and the quality of bread after incorporating vegetable processing waste from tomatoes (TP) and bell peppers (PB) into a recipe for wheat bread. Additionally, the physicochemical features and nutrient composition of the bread were analyzed to assess the potential for producing bread with increased nutritional value, particularly in terms of dietary fiber, while maintaining the desired quality characteristics preferred by consumers.

This research aimed to contribute to both diversifying the range of bread products and reducing food waste by utilizing vegetable processing waste.

2. Materials and Methods

2.1. Materials

The wheat flour (type 750) used as the primary raw material in this study was obtained from a local supermarket in Lublin, Poland. The flour had an ash content of 0.72% d.b., a wet gluten content of 27.2% ± 1.1, a gluten index of 98.3 ± 0.5, a falling number of 301 s ± 8, and an equivalent diameter of 0.12 mm. By-products from red bell pepper processing, namely pepper placenta (PB) without seeds, and by-products from tomato processing, specifically tomato waste (TP) containing seeds and skin, were also used. These by-products were sourced from Krokus, Pająków, Poland.

Before usage, TP and PB were prepared according to the procedure described previously by Teterycz and Sobota [9]. The vegetable by-products were dried for 17 h in static dryers (EAC 30-Lab, ItalPast, Fidenza, Italy) using a low temperature profile (30–40 °C; 72–25% RH—relative humidity). Subsequently, the by-products were ground using a laboratory knife mill (Grindomix GM 200, Retsch, GmbH, Haan, Germany) to obtain flour with a particle size below 0.250 mm (>95%). The resulting flour was stored in dark sealed containers prior to bread making and chemical analysis. The equivalent diameter was determined based on the conducted sieve analysis of the used raw materials. Each time, a 100 g sample of the material was taken and sieved through a set of sieves (315, 250, 200, 180, 160, 125, 80, and 60 μm) for 10 min using a sieve shaker (CISA BA 200N, Barcelona, Spain). The equivalent diameter for TP was 0.240 mm, and for PB, it was 0.180 mm.

2.2. Bread Making Procedure

A total of nine bread formulas were prepared, each utilizing different ratios of wheat flour to TP and PB. The control bread formula (CON) consisted of 100% wheat flour. Additionally, four bread formulas enriched with TP and four with PB were created, where wheat flour was substituted with TP or PB at varying levels: 3, 6, 9, and 12 g per 100 g. The samples were labeled as TP3, TP6, TP9, TP12, PB3, PB6, PB9, and PB12, respectively. The complete bread formula consisted of 600 g of flour, which could be either wheat flour or a mixture of wheat flour with PB or TP. Other ingredients included 9 g of salt, 18 g of compressed yeast (*Saccharomyces cerevisiae*), and an appropriate amount of water. The water content for each formula was determined based on the previously established farinographic water absorption (WA) measured at 500 Brabender units consistency.

The bread making procedure used in this study followed the methodology described by Zarzycki et al. [18]. The bread dough was prepared using the straight dough method. All the dough ingredients were mixed in a BEAR Varimixer Teddy 5 L (Verimixer A/S, Copenhagen, Denmark) at level one (low speed) for 3 min and then at high speed until complete gluten development was achieved, as indicated by the farinograph. The dough was then fermented in a proofing chamber (Tefi Klima pro 100, Debag, Germany) at a temperature of 30 °C and a RH of 85 ± 2% for 90 min. At the 60 min mark, an intermediate punching step involving mixing at low speed was performed for 30s. Following the intermediate punching step, the dough was divided by hand into portions weighing 290 g ± 5 g. These portions were then molded and placed into baking pans measuring 18 × 7.5 × 7.0 cm. The dough was allowed to rest for an additional 30 min in the proofing chamber at a temperature of 30 °C and a RH of 85 ± 2%. The fermentation time was monitored for each formulation. Subsequently, the fermented dough samples were baked in a bakery oven (Helios pro 100, Debag, Germany) at a temperature of 230 °C for 30 min. Three loaves of bread prepared with each formula were baked in three separate baking tests, yielding a total of nine loaves of bread for each formula. After baking and cooling for 1 h outside the oven, the bread loaves were weighed, placed in individual plastic bags (one loaf per bag), sealed, and stored at room conditions (20 °C, 50% RH) until further analysis.

2.3. Farinograph Properties of Dough

Farinograph parameters, including water absorption (WA), dough development time (DDT), stability time (ST), dough softening (DS), and Farinograph Quality Number (FQN), were analyzed for both wheat flour and mixed wheat flour with vegetable raw materials (TP and PB) at different levels. The measurements were taken using a Farinograph-E (Brabender, model 8110142, Duisburg, Germany) following the AACC method 54-21 [24]. The determinations of farinograph parameters were performed in triplicate for each sample.

2.4. Evaluation of Bread Quality Characteristics

Bread quality parameters were evaluated in this study, including bread yield (BY), which was calculated using Equation (1); baking loss (BL), which was calculated using Equation (2); bread volume, which was determined using the rapeseed displacement method [AACC Method 10-05.01]; specific volume ($cm^3 \cdot g^{-1}$), which was calculated as the ratio of bread volume to bread mass; crumb porosity, which was assessed on a scale from 1 to 8 (8 = only small alveoli and 1 = mix of large and small alveoli) using Dallmann's classification reported by Bot et al. [25]; and crumb moisture content, which was determined according to AACC Method 44-15.02. All these assessments were conducted 24 h after baking and repeated three times.

$$BY = \frac{W_1}{W_2} \cdot 100\% \tag{1}$$

$$BL = \frac{W_3 - W_1}{W_3} \cdot 100\% \tag{2}$$

where W_1 represents the weight of the baked bread (measured 1 h after removal from the oven), W_2 represents the weight of the flour used for a specific loaf of bread, and W_3 represents the weight of the dough (proofed doughs were weighed immediately prior to being placed in the oven).

2.5. Evaluation of Color Parameters of Bread Crumbs

The color of the bread crumbs, expressed as L*, a*, b* values in the CIE Lab color system, was measured using a spherical spectrophotometer (Chroma Meter CR 5, Konica Minolta, Sakai Osaka, Japan). The measurements were taken with a standard light source (D65), a standard visual field (10 degrees), and an 8 mm diameter aperture. The spectrophotometer was calibrated using white and black standard plates. The measurements were carried out 10 times for each sample.

The total color difference (ΔE^*) between the control sample (L_c^*, a_c^*, b_c^*—taken as a reference sample) and the bread loaves supplemented with TP or PB (L_i^*, a_i^*, b_i^*) was calculated using Equation (3). The whiteness index (WI) and yellowness index (YI) of each bread sample were calculated from the acquired L*, a*, and b* data using Equations (4) and (5), respectively.

$$\Delta E^* = \sqrt{(L_c^* - L_i^*)^2 + (a_c^* - a_i^*)^2 + (b_c^* - b_i^*)^2} \tag{3}$$

$$WI = 100 - \sqrt{((100 - L^*)^2 + a^2 + b^2)} \tag{4}$$

$$YI = 142.83 \cdot \frac{b^*}{L^*} \tag{5}$$

2.6. Texture Profile Analysis (TPA) of Bread

A TPA analysis of the bread crumbs was conducted following the procedure described by Wirkijowska et al. [17]. In summary, the bread loaves were sliced into 20 mm wide slices, and the outer parts were removed. From these slices, samples in the form of cuboids measuring 30 × 30 × 20 mm were cut for assessment. The double compression test was performed using a testing machine Zwick/Roell Z0.5, (BT1-FR0.5TN.D14, Ulm, Germany) with a maximum force of 500 N. The following parameters were applied: compression to 50% of the initial height, a constant head speed of 1 mm/s, and a flat cylindrical disk with a diameter of 100 mm. Based on the conducted analysis, force–deformation curves were obtained. Using the testXpert II software, properties such as hardness [N] (maximum force during the first compression), springiness [-] (ratio of deformation in the second cycle to deformation in the first cycle), cohesiveness [-] (ratio of the area under the force curve in the second cycle to the area under the force curve in the first cycle), and chewiness [N] (product of hardness, springiness, and cohesiveness) were calculated. The TPA analysis was conducted 24 h and 72 h after baking, and each sample was measured 7 times.

2.7. Semi-Consumer Sensory Evaluation of Bread

Semi-consumer sensory evaluation of bread was conducted using a five-point hedonic scale, where 1 represented "dislike extremely", 3 represented "neither like nor dislike", and 5 represented "like extremely". The evaluation involved 30 panelists (male/female ratio of 70:30, and an age range of 19 to 55 years) consisting of students and staff from the Faculty of Food Science and Biotechnology at the University of Life Sciences in Lublin (participation in the research was voluntary). The panelists were selected based on the following criteria: regular consumption of bread (at least four times per week), good health, and no allergic reactions to gluten/wheat products. The panelists assessed the sensory attributes of the bread, including appearance, aroma, taste, color, texture (elasticity and porosity), and overall acceptance. The bread samples were mechanically sliced into 1 cm thick slices, coded, and served in a randomized order.

2.8. Chemical Composition of Raw Materials and Bread

The chemical composition of the raw materials and bread baked with different formulas was assessed using the AACC and AOAC methods [24,26]. The following parameters were determined: moisture content [AACC Method 44-15A]; ash content [AACC Method 08-01]; protein content using the Kjeldahl method [AACC Method 46-08] with a conversion factor of N × 5.7, fat content [AACC Method 30-26]; and total, soluble, and insoluble dietary fiber (TDF, SDF and IDF, respectively) according to AOAC 991.43, AACC 32-07, AACC 32-21, AOAC 985.29, and AACC 32-05. Available carbohydrate were calculated by subtracting the sum of protein, fat, water, ash, and total dietary fiber from the total weight of the wet sample. The energy value was determined in kilocalories (kcal) per 100 g of wet bread using Atwater factors, where protein and carbohydrate contribute 4 kcal/g, fat contributes 9 kcal/g, and total dietary fiber contributes 2 kcal/g. All chemical tests were conducted in three replications.

2.9. Statistical Analysis

Analytical results were processed using one-way analysis of variance (ANOVA), followed by the post hoc multiple comparison Tukey test to highlight significant differences ($p \leq 0.05$) among samples. All data were analyzed using Statistica software (ver.13.3, StatSoft Polska, Kraków, Poland). The data are expressed as mean values ± standard deviations.

3. Results and Discussion

3.1. Farinograph Properties of Dough

The farinographic characteristics facilitate the management of production process parameters and provide insights into the effect of specific additives on the water absorption of flour and dough consistency. The basic farinographic characteristics of wheat flour and wheat flour with the vegetable component (TP and PB) are provided in Table 1. The results indicate that the water absorption of the dough increased from 57.7% to 58.2% and to 61.6% by increasing the levels up to 12% of PB and TP, respectively. However, the changes in the dough fortified with PB were slight, and no significant differences ($p \geq 0.05$) were found compared to the control sample. The higher water absorption observed in the dough fortified with TP compared to PB may be attributed to the higher content of TDF in TP, as shown in Table 2. Typically, increasing the content of dietary fiber in dough (through various types of additional ingredients) leads to an increase in water absorption (WA) [17,27]. This phenomenon can be explained by the presence of a large number of hydrophilic groups in the structure of dietary fiber, allowing for more water interaction through hydrogen bonding. Consequently, the dough can absorb a higher amount of water. In general, high water absorption is an indicator of good baking performance [21]. However, the higher water absorption of fiber compared to gluten proteins can lead to dehydration of gluten matrix during the mixing process. As a result, there is an increased resistance to mixing and, at the same time, a reduced elasticity of the gluten network [22].

Table 1. Farinograph analysis of wheat dough with progressive addition of tomato waste (TP) and pepper placenta (PB) from 3 to 12 g/100 g.

Sample	WA [%]	DDT [min]	ST [min]	DS [FU]	FQN
CON	57.7 ± 0.5 [f]	2.3 ± 0.3 [c]	12.7 ± 0.3 [a]	28.3 ± 2.1 [d]	108.3 ± 37.2 [a]
TP3	59.3 ± 0.5 [ed]	2.7 ± 1.1 [c]	6.1 ± 0.3 [cb]	79.7 ± 15.6 [c]	71.0 ± 3.0 [ba]
TP6	60.0 ± 0.5 [dc]	3.3 ± 1.8 [bc]	6.7 ± 2.1 [b]	112.7 ± 14.8 [b]	69.0 ± 10.6 [b]
TP9	61.2 ± 0.4 [cb]	4.0 ± 0.4 [b]	5.3 ± 0.3 [cb]	140.7 ± 6.4 [b]	57.3 ± 3.2 [b]
TP12	61.6 ± 0.2 [b]	3.5 ± 0.4 [b]	4.3 ± 0.3 [c]	133.3 ± 8.7 [b]	54.0 ± 5.2 [b]
PB3	59.0 ± 0.1 [fed]	6.6 ± 0.3 [a]	6.3 ± 0.7 [cb]	210.3 ± 9.3 [a]	83.3 ± 1.2 [ba]
PB6	62.1 ± 0.6 [abc]	5.2 ± 0.3 [ba]	4.9 ± 0.2 [cb]	236.7 ± 11.0 [a]	70.0 ± 3.0 [b]
PB9	57.7 ± 0.1 [f]	5.3 ± 0.2 [ba]	4.6 ± 0.2 [cb]	221.7 ± 4.9 [a]	72.0 ± 1.0 [ba]
PB12	58.2 ± 0.7 [fe]	5.3 ± 0.2 [ba]	4.8 ± 0.6 [cb]	232.0 ± 8.7 [a]	66.3 ± 2.5 [b]

CON—control sample (100% wheat flour); mean value ($n = 3$) ± SD; means in the same column with different letters ([a–f]) are significantly different (Tukey test, $p \leq 0.05$); WA—water adsorption; DDT—dough development time; ST—Stability time; DS—Dough softening; FQN—Farinograph Quality Number.

The significant indicators used to determine the strength of flour included DDT, ST, and DS. Increased dough development time and stability time, along with a decreased degree of softening, indicate flour with strong gluten, which demonstrates resistance to changes in consistency during mixing [28]. The conducted research has shown that both the addition of PB and TP not only results in an increase in DDT but also yields a simultaneous decrease in ST and an increase in DS compared to the control sample (Table 1). The obtained results indicate a weakening of the dough structure caused by the aforementioned additives, which was also confirmed by a significant ($p \leq 0.05$) decrease in FQN values (Table 1). The observed relationships can be partially explained by interactions between fiber and gluten, which hinder the complete hydration of proteins, thereby impeding the proper formation of the gluten matrix during dough mixing [29]. Moreover, the observed higher impact of adding PB on DDT and DS compared to adding TP may be due to the significantly higher ash content in PB (Table 2). This leads, among other things, to a significant increase in magnesium, potassium, and sodium levels, which, as previous studies have shown, can result in increased dough resistance to mixing and soften the dough further [9]. An important influence is also exerted by the reduction in gluten protein content, which is caused by the addition of gluten-free ingredients, as well as the physical disorganization of the gluten matrix, leading to a decrease in the strength of the gluten network [30,31]. The weakening of the gluten network structure by vegetable by-products such as TP and PB has also been confirmed in previous studies examining changes in the secondary structure of the gluten network [23].

Table 2. Chemical composition of raw materials: wheat flour (WF), tomato waste (TP), and pepper placenta (PB), and bread with progressive addition of TP and PB from 3 to 12 g/100 g.

Sample	Raw Materials and Bread Compositions [% d.b.]								
	Moisture [%]	Ash	Protein	Fat	TDF	IDF	SDF	CHO	Energy [kcal/100 g]
Raw materials									
WF	9.4 ± 0.0 [b]	0.72 ± 0.01 [c]	13.16 ± 0.07 [c]	0.49 ± 0.00 [c]	5.36 ± 0.04 [c]	2.43 ± 0.18 [c]	2.93 ± 0.22 [c]	80.3 ± 0.1 [a]	352.3 ± 0.1 [a]
TP	6.5 ± 0.0 [c]	3.81 ± 0.06 [b]	20.53 ± 0.20 [b]	11.53 ± 0.42 [a]	60.9 ± 0.27 [a]	49.61 ± 0.38 [a]	11.29 ± 0.11 [b]	3.2 ± 0.1 [c]	299.9 ± 2.7 [b]
PB	11.7 ± 0.6 [a]	13.28 ± 0.19 [a]	28.47 ± 0.44 [a]	3.17 ± 0.04 [b]	33.47 ± 0.58 [b]	16.34 ± 0.89 [b]	17.13 ± 0.31 [a]	21.6 ± 0.9 [b]	261.1 ± 0.2 [c]
Bread									
CON	43.1 ± 0.6 [ba]	2.48 ± 0.05 [e]	13.35 ± 0.03 [f]	0.27 ± 0.07 [e]	6.77 ± 0.36 [f]	3.14 ± 0.26 [e]	3.64 ± 0.62 [c]	69.5 ± 0.4 [a]	197.9 ± 0.9 [ab]
TP3	42.0 ± 0.2 [b]	2.53 ± 0.06 [de]	13.72 ± 0.03 [e]	0.64 ± 0.03 [dc]	8.49 ± 0.22 [e]	4.19 ± 0.1 [ed]	4.30 ± 0.12 [bc]	67.0 ± 0.3 [cba]	200.3 ± 0.6 [a]
TP6	42.7 ± 0.7 [ba]	2.58 ± 0.04 [de]	13.82 ± 0.01 [ed]	0.97 ± 0.04 [b]	10.69 ± 0.63 [c]	5.99 ± 0.43 [cb]	4.70 ± 0.2 [bac]	65.9 ± 1.2 [dcb]	200.0 ± 3.3 [a]
TP9	41.9 ± 0.2 [b]	2.56 ± 0.04 [e]	14.01 ± 0.19 [dc]	1.33 ± 0.08 [a]	12.42 ± 0.41 [b]	7.28 ± 0.49 [b]	5.14 ± 0.08 [ba]	63.7 ± 1.1 [d]	201.9 ± 3 [a]
TP12	43 ± 0.3 [ba]	2.87 ± 0.01 [c]	14.24 ± 0.03 [cb]	1.41 ± 0.02 [a]	15.52 ± 0.1 [a]	10.1 ± 0.26 [a]	5.42 ± 0.36 [ba]	58.7 ± 0.0 [e]	191.2 ± 0.0 [c]
PB3	43.1 ± 0.2 [ba]	2.84 ± 0.01 [dc]	13.57 ± 0.04 [ef]	0.37 ± 0.07 [e]	8.43 ± 0.6 [e]	3.59 ± 0.42 [ed]	4.84 ± 0.18 [ba]	67.5 ± 0.4 [ba]	196.2 ± 0.7 [abc]
PB6	43.8 ± 0.3 [a]	2.84 ± 0.04 [dc]	14.01 ± 0.0 [dc]	0.47 ± 0.07 [ed]	9.02 ± 0.06 [ed]	3.76 ± 0.22 [ed]	5.27 ± 0.17 [ba]	66.5 ± 0.0 [cb]	193.4 ± 0.3 [bc]
PB9	42.4 ± 0.1 [ba]	3.26 ± 0.16 [b]	14.51 ± 0.04 [b]	0.61 ± 0.07 [dc]	9.97 ± 0.03 [edc]	4.56 ± 0.4 [edc]	5.41 ± 0.42 [ba]	64.8 ± 0.5 [dc]	197.4 ± 0.7 [ab]
PB12	42.7 ± 0.2 [ba]	3.58 ± 0.02 [a]	14.92 ± 0.01 [a]	0.73 ± 0.01 [c]	10.33 ± 0.62 [dc]	4.78 ± 0.54 [dc]	5.56 ± 0.08 [a]	63.7 ± 0.7 [d]	195.9 ± 0.9 [abc]

CON—control sample (100% wheat flour); CHO—digestible carbohydrates; mean value (n = 3) ± SD; different letters ([a-f]) within a column indicate statistically significant differences (Tukey test, $p \leq 0.05$).

3.2. Evaluation of Bread Quality Characteristics

Table 3 presents the results of the basic physical properties of the control and supplemented bread loaves. All the fortified bread samples exhibited good physical parameters (BY, BL, SV, and crumb porosity) that were comparable to the control. The BY value ranged from 135.4% to 142.3%. In the case of the bread fortified with TP, a slight decrease in BY was observed, but these changes were not statistically significant ($p \geq 0.05$). Regarding the bread fortified with PB, a slight increase in BY was observed, which was statistically significant ($p \leq 0.05$) for supplementation above 9%. The addition of the TP and PB also did not significantly affect the total baking loss ($p \geq 0.05$). The BL values for the tested bread samples ranged from 8.4% to 11.0%, which were slightly lower than the values reported by other authors for wheat bread and bread with the addition of dietary fiber components (ranging from 11.0% to 15.8%) [17,18,32,33].

Table 3. The physical properties of bread with progressive addition of tomato waste (TP) and pepper placenta (PB) from 3 to 12 g/100 g.

Sample	Bread Yield [%]	Baking Loss [%]	Specific Volume [cm^3 g^{-1}]	Crumb Moisture [%]	Crumb Porosity [-]
CON	138.0 ± 1.3 [cb]	9.5 ± 0.9 [ab]	2.82 ± 0.15 [a]	43.08 ± 0.41 [ba]	8.0 ± 0.0 [a]
TP3	135.7 ± 0.3 [c]	11.0 ± 0.2 [a]	2.85 ± 0.10 [a]	42.08 ± 0.16 [dc]	7.7 ± 0.6 [ab]
TP6	135.4 ± 0.3 [c]	10.9 ± 0.2 [a]	2.29 ± 0.22 [b]	42.70 ± 0.71 [bdc]	8.0 ± 0.6 [a]
TP9	136.1 ± 0.8 [c]	10.6 ± 0.5 [a]	2.74 ± 0.09 [a]	41.89 ± 0.13 [d]	7.3 ± 0.6 [ab]
TP12	137.1 ± 0.5 [c]	10.2 ± 0.3 [a]	2.54 ± 0.01 [b]	43.05 ± 0.25 [ba]	7.3 ± 0.6 [ab]
PB3	140.4 ± 0.5 [ab]	9.3 ± 0.3 [ab]	2.37 ± 0.06 [b]	43.06 ± 0.22 [ba]	7.0 ± 0.0 [ab]
PB6	140.5 ± 0.9 [ab]	9.5 ± 0.6 [ab]	2.78 ± 0.13 [a]	43.81 ± 0.22 [a]	6.7 ± 0.6 [ab]
PB9	140.9 ± 1.3 [a]	9.3 ± 0.9 [ab]	2.69 ± 0.22 [a]	42.43 ± 0.11 [bdc]	6.7 ± 0.6 [ab]
PB12	142.3 ± 1.1 [a]	8.4 ± 0.7 [b]	2.55 ± 0.36 [ab]	42.71 ± 0.11 [bc]	6.3 ± 0.6 [b]

CON—control sample (100% wheat flour); mean value (n = 3) ± SD; means in the same column with different letters ([a–d]) are significantly different (Tukey test, $p \leq 0.05$).

One of the key factors determining bread quality is the loaf volume. Loaves with a larger volume are generally more appealing to consumers [6]. SV ranged from 2.82 cm^3·g^{-1} to 2.29 cm^3·g^{-1}, with the maximum value observed in the control sample, and it decreased with the incorporation of vegetable by-products. However, a clear trend cannot be identified. With the addition of 6% TP, the specific volume decreased by 19%, which was the largest observed reduction. The effect of dry tomato waste addition on the volume of bread was also studied by Nour et al. [8]. They found a significant decrease in the volume of bread with tomato waste addition compared to the control bread. The volume of bread generally depends on gas formation and gas retention, both of which can be affected by the fiber content. The dilution effect, which restricts the water available for gluten hydration and development, as well as the physical disruption of gluten matrix formation, can be responsible for the reduction in bread volume [6]. The obtained results are consistent with the previously demonstrated weakening of the gluten network caused by the addition of TP and PB. A similar impact on SV was also observed in a study by Sogi et al. [34], who utilized the addition of tomato seed flour. On the contrary, in their study on the influence of tomato seed flour addition, Mironeasa et al. [35] demonstrated an increase in bread volume, particularly when the addition did not exceed 10%.

The enhanced addition of vegetable by-products correlates with a lower bread crumb porosity. These differences can also be observed in the digital images of the bread slices (Figure 1). Bread fortified with TP exhibits slightly higher porosity compared to bread fortified with PB; however, the differences are not statistically significant ($p \geq 0.05$). The crumb moisture ranged from 41.89% to 43.81%. The changes in moisture caused by the addition of TP and PB did not exceed 3%.

Although there were differences in BY, BL, SV, and crumb porosity between the control and supplemented samples, they were not substantial. Therefore, we can conclude that fortification with TP and PB resulted in baking characteristics comparable to 100% wheat bread.

3.3. Evaluation of Color Parameters of Bread Crumbs

In addition to taste and texture, color is an important sensory indicator of baked goods, and it plays a significant role in meeting consumer expectations. The color of bread is influenced by various factors, including baking parameters, the recipe, and dough characteristics [33,36]. In the present study, the color analysis of the bread was conducted using the CIELab color space, also known as the Lab* color space, developed by the International Commission on Illumination (CIE). The color coordinates of the CIELab color space (L*, a*, and b*) were used to calculate derived parameters, including the total color difference (ΔE^*), whiteness index (WI), and the yellowness index (YI) (Table 4). The addition of TP and PB significantly impacts the color of the bread, as indicated by ΔE* values ranging from 4.8 to 14.8 for TP and from 7.1 to 20.2 for PB (Table 4), corresponding to low (3%) and high (12%) levels of incorporation, respectively. ΔE* values exceeding 3 suggest that the color difference is noticeable, even to an untrained observer [37].

Table 4. The color coordinates (L*, a*, b*) of bread crumbs with progressive addition of tomato waste (TP) and pepper placenta (PB) from 3 to 12 g/100 g.

Sample	L*	a*	b*	ΔE*	WI	YI
CON	61.0 ± 2.1 [a]	1.6 ± 0.3 [i]	15.0 ± 0.7 [g]	-	58.2 ± 2.1 [a]	35.2 ± 2.4 [h]
TP3	62.5 ± 1.6 [a]	2.6 ± 0.2 [h]	19.2 ± 0.5 [f]	4.8 ± 0.7 [h]	57.8 ± 1.4 [a]	43.9 ± 1.5 [g]
TP6	60.7 ± 1.4 [a]	4.3 ± 0.2 [f]	22.8 ± 0.8 [d]	8.4 ± 0.4 [f]	54.4 ± 0.9 [b]	53.6 ± 1.3 [f]
TP9	61.0 ± 1.1 [a]	5.0 ± 0.5 [e]	24.6 ± 1.2 [c]	10.2 ± 1.2 [e]	53.6 ± 1.2 [b]	57.6 ± 3.1 [e]
TP12	56.0 ± 0.7 [c]	6.9 ± 0.4 [c]	27.8 ± 0.4 [b]	14.8 ± 0.6 [c]	47.5 ± 0.7 [c]	71.1 ± 1.6 [c]
PB3	58.5 ± 1.0 [b]	3.7 ± 0.3 [g]	21.2 ± 0.5 [e]	7.1 ± 0.9 [g]	53.2 ± 1.1 [b]	51.9 ± 2.1 [f]
PB6	54.3 ± 1.0 [dc]	6.0 ± 0.2 [d]	25.4 ± 0.6 [c]	13.1 ± 0.7 [d]	47.4 ± 0.9 [c]	66.7 ± 1.8 [d]
PB9	53.5 ± 0.7 [d]	7.7 ± 0.3 [b]	27.9 ± 0.5 [b]	16.1 ± 0.6 [b]	45.2 ± 0.6 [d]	74.5 ± 1.6 [b]
PB12	49.6 ± 1.4 [e]	9.5 ± 0.4 [a]	29.6 ± 0.9 [a]	20.2 ± 0.8 [a]	40.8 ± 1.1 [e]	85.2 ± 2.6 [a]

CON—control sample (100% wheat flour); ΔE*—the total color difference; WI—whiteness index; YI—yellowness index. Data are presented as mean ($n = 15$) ± standard deviation; means in the same column with different letters ([a–i]) are significantly different (Tukey test, $p \leq 0.05$).

The L* values of the bread fortified with PB significantly decreased (from 61 to 49.6) as the proportion of PB increased. However, for the bread fortified with TP, the changes were not statistically significant ($p \geq 0.05$) until the inclusion level of TP reached 12%, where a significant ($p \leq 0.05$) decrease was observed. The observed darkening of the bread color was confirmed by the significant decrease in the WI for both TP- and PB-fortified bread. In the study conducted by Majzoobi et al. [38], a significant decrease in bread color was observed with the addition of tomato waste, even at low levels. This could be attributed to the use of higher drying temperatures (60 °C) for the by-products, resulting in the raw material having a darker color. The negative correlation between L* and the increasing proportions of TP and PB aligns with a previous study by Teterycz and Sobota [9], who examined the impact of adding various proportions of TP and PB to pasta. Tomato waste and pepper placenta are rich sources of carotenoids, specifically capsanthin in peppers [39] and lycopene in tomatoes [40]. These carotenoids are responsible for both the darker color and increased redness observed in the product [9,38]. The values of parameters a* and b* significantly increased ($p \leq 0.05$) with an increasing percentage of both TP and PB. This suggests that the addition of TP and PB increased the red and yellow components within the bread samples. The changes in the YI also clearly indicate a shift in color towards yellow. The changes were more prominent in the case of PB, as shown in Table 3.

3.4. Texture Profile Analysis (TPA) of Bread

The results of the bread crumb texture analysis, including four crucial parameters (hardness, springiness, cohesiveness, and chewiness), are presented in Table 5. Hardness, which measures the force required to deform the product, is commonly used in the analysis of bakery products and serves as an indicator of staling [33,38]. The hardness of the fresh bread crumb, measured 24 h after baking, ranged from 4.8 N to 7.5 N and varied depending on the amount of supplementation and recipe variation. Increasing the dosage of both by-products, TP and PB, in the bread formulations resulted in higher values of hardness. Generally, the crumb hardness of the breads containing PB was lower than that of the samples with TP. However, statistically significant ($p \leq 0.05$) changes were observed only in the samples supplemented with 12% tomato waste (TP). Therefore, it can be concluded that the addition of pepper placenta (PB) up to 12% and TP up to 9% did not have a significant ($p \geq 0.05$) impact on the hardness of the bread crumbs after 24 h. In contrast, a significant reduction ($p \leq 0.05$) in springiness, which measures the degree of shape recovery after deformation, was observed even with the addition of 3% PB or TP. However, no statistical differences were observed between the breads supplemented with vegetable by-products, regardless of the proportion used. The addition of TP to the bread recipe slightly increased the chewiness of the product, which refers to the strength required to chew a piece of food. However, significant changes ($p \leq 0.05$) in this parameter were only observed in the samples containing 12% TP. On the other hand, the addition of PB did not have a significant effect on the chewiness of the bread. The statistical analysis did not identify any significant changes in the cohesiveness of the bread crumbs based on the type of supplementation and the interactions between the variables (supplementation type and amount).

Table 5. Texture profile analysis of the bread samples with the progressive addition of tomato waste (TP) and pepper placenta (PB) from 3 to 12 g/100 g after 24 and 72 h of storage.

Sample	Hardness [N]		Cohesiveness [-]		Chewiness [N]		Springiness [-]	
	24 h	72 h	24 h	72 h	24 h	72 h	24 h	72 h
CON	4.8 ± 0.4 [bB]	9.83 ± 1.69 [eA]	0.62 ± 0.02 [baA]	0.4 ± 0.03 [bB]	2.8 ± 0.1 [bB]	3.5 ± 0.6 [dA]	0.96 ± 0.03 [aA]	0.88 ± 0.06 [aB]
TP3	5.0 ± 1.2 [bB]	12.8 ± 1.46 [dcbA]	0.61 ± 0.01 [baA]	0.4 ± 0.01 [bB]	2.7 ± 0.6 [bB]	4.5 ± 0.7 [cbaA]	0.89 ± 0.04 [bA]	0.86 ± 0.04 [aA]
TP6	6.0 ± 1.0 [baB]	12.92 ± 1.63 [dcbeA]	0.61 ± 0.01 [baA]	0.38 ± 0.02 [bcB]	3.2 ± 0.5 [baA]	3.9 ± 0.5 [dcbA]	0.87 ± 0.03 [bA]	0.81 ± 0.02 [abB]
TP9	6.2 ± 1.3 [baB]	13.4 ± 1.37 [cbA]	0.6 ± 0.03 [baA]	0.36 ± 0.01 [cdB]	3.3 ± 0.8 [baA]	3.9 ± 0.4 [dcbA]	0.89 ± 0.05 [bA]	0.81 ± 0.05 [abA]
TP12	7.5 ± 0.9 [aB]	19.69 ± 2.46 [aA]	0.59 ± 0.02 [bA]	0.34 ± 0.02 [dB]	3.9 ± 0.4 [aB]	5.2 ± 0.5 [aA]	0.88 ± 0.04 [bA]	0.77 ± 0.04 [bB]
PB3	4.8 ± 0.6 [bB]	10.2 ± 1.25 [deA]	0.63 ± 0.04 [aA]	0.44 ± 0.02 [aB]	2.7 ± 0.3 [bB]	3.7 ± 0.4 [dcA]	0.87 ± 0.04 [bA]	0.83 ± 0.04 [abA]
PB6	5.0 ± 1.0 [bB]	10.77 ± 0.84 [dceA]	0.62 ± 0.03 [baA]	0.38 ± 0.01 [bcB]	2.7 ± 0.5 [bB]	3.4 ± 0.2 [dA]	0.87 ± 0.03 [bA]	0.82 ± 0.07 [abA]
PB9	5.3 ± 0.5 [bB]	12.12 ± 1.88 [dcbeA]	0.6 ± 0.04 [baA]	0.37 ± 0.01 [bcdB]	2.6 ± 0.3 [bB]	3.6 ± 0.4 [dcA]	0.85 ± 0.03 [bA]	0.81 ± 0.06 [abA]
PB12	5.5 ± 0.6 [bB]	14.86 ± 1.24 [bA]	0.58 ± 0.02 [bA]	0.37 ± 0.03 [bcdB]	2.7 ± 0.3 [bB]	4.8 ± 0.9 [baA]	0.83 ± 0.02 [bA]	0.82 ± 0.06 [abA]

CON—control sample (100% wheat flour); mean value ($n = 7$) ± SD; different lowercase letters ([a–e]) within a column and different uppercase letters ([A,B]) within a row indicate statistically significant differences (Tukey test, $p \leq 0.05$).

Previous studies [7,34,35,38] have reported on the transformative effects adding tomato (seeds and residue) and paprika powder has on crumb texture parameters. Sogi et al. [34] observed that an increase in the addition of tomato seed pomace resulted in a significant increase in wheat bread firmness. Mironeasa et al. [35] found that supplementation with powdered tomato seeds increased the hardness and chewiness of wheat bread crumbs while negatively affecting its cohesiveness. Interestingly, Majzoobi et al. [38], who used whole tomato powder for bread fortification, demonstrated that the hardness of enriched bread crumbs was lower than in their control sample, especially at higher levels of tomato powder supplementation. Choi et al. [7], in their analysis of wheat bread fortified with whole pepper powder, showed that hardness, springiness, cohesiveness, and chewiness increased with the addition of paprika powder.

During storage (72 h versus 24 h), there was an increase in the hardness and chewiness of the bread crumbs, while the cohesiveness values decreased in all recipe variants. In terms of springiness, the changes were minimal. In both the TP-fortified bread and the PB-fortified bread, the largest changes observed pertained to hardness, with slightly greater changes being observed in the bread fortified with TP. However, the values of this parameter significantly differed from the control in the TP-fortified bread (above 9%) and in the bread fortified with PB only in samples supplemented with 12% of these ingredients. The changes in the textural properties observed while the bread was stored were generally consistent with the results reported by other researchers. Choi et al. [7] analyzed bread fortified with whole pepper powder and found that the hardness and chewiness of the bread crumb increased with storage time, while the springiness and cohesiveness values decreased. Similarly, Majzoobi et al. [38] reported an increase in hardness during storage for bread fortified with tomato pomace. However, our study did not indicate a significant effect of adding TP or PB on reducing the rate of bread staling during storage, as concluded by assessing bread texture. This is contrary to the findings of Majzoobi et al. [38], which demonstrated the potential for delaying the staling process of flatbread (Barbari bread) by adding tomato pomace.

3.5. Consumer Sensory Evaluation of Bread

Sensory acceptance and consumer preference are crucial factors in determining the success of a new product or formula. Therefore, alongside assessing other quality features of the bread, a sensory evaluation was conducted to determine consumer acceptance and identify any inadequate sensory attributes (Figure 2a,b). Moreover, the surface and cross-sections of the bread samples are illustrated in Figure 2, providing a visual representation of the bread's appearance. The results of the sensory evaluation, as depicted in Figure 1, revealed that an increase in the addition level of TP or PB from 3 to 12 g/100 g resulted in a decrease in the overall acceptability score for both cases. Specifically, the overall acceptability score decreased from 4.87 to 4.17 with higher levels of TP or PB (Figure 2a,b). These findings are consistent with the observations made by Majzoobi et al. [38] in relation to the use of tomato pomace, which also demonstrated an impact on taste. In the case of PB, taste and smell were the sensory attributes that were found to be inadequate. These findings highlight the importance of sensory attributes in determining consumer acceptability towards bread fortified with TP or PB.

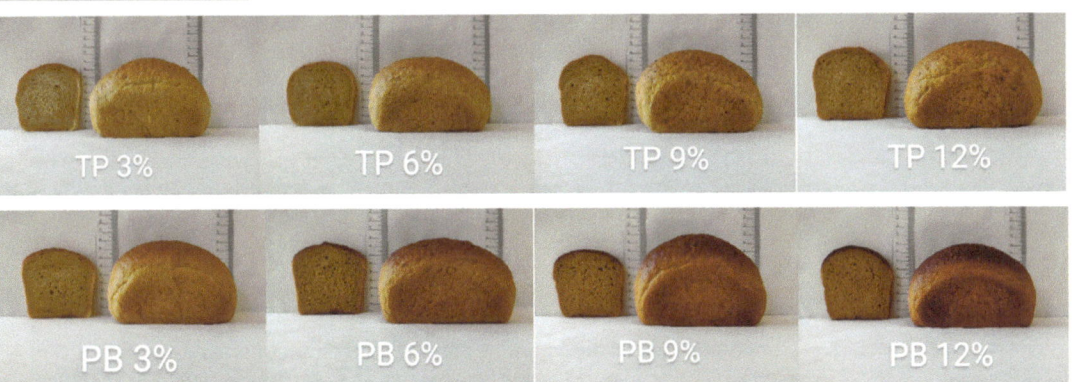

Figure 1. Surface and cross-sections of bread with progressive addition of tomato waste (TP) and pepper placenta (PB) from 3 to 12 g/100 g.

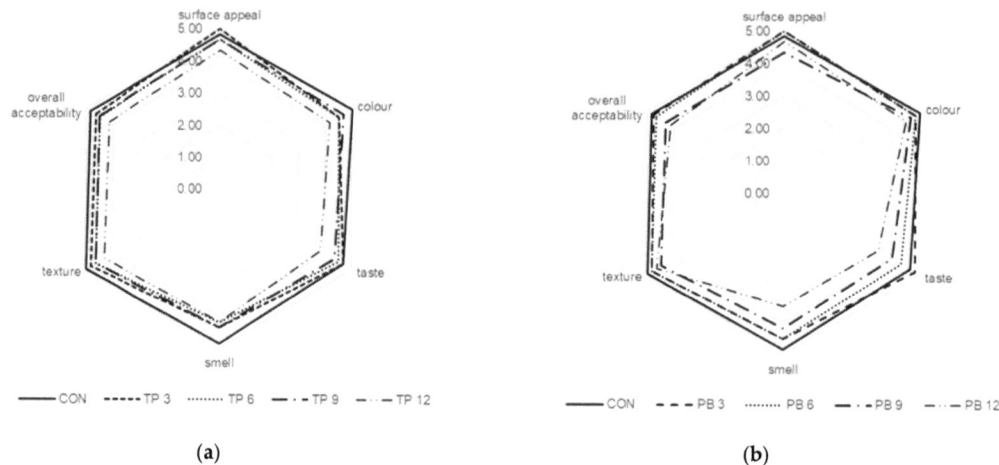

Figure 2. Sensory characteristics of bread samples at different levels of (**a**) tomato waste (TP) and (**b**) pepper placenta (PB) addition.

3.6. Chemical Composition of Raw Materials and Bread

Table 2 presents the chemical composition of wheat flour, TP, and PB. The results demonstrate that TP and PB have significantly higher amounts of fiber (TDF, SDF, and IDF), protein, fat, and ash content compared to wheat flour. Additionally, it can be observed that TP has nearly twice the amount of total fiber compared to PB (60.9% d.b. and 33.47% d.b., respectively), and this is primarily due to its high insoluble fiber content. Despite having a lower total fiber content, PB is a better source of soluble fiber (17.13% d.b.), as evidenced by the fact that it has a soluble fiber content that is approximately 50% higher than that of TP (11.29% d.b.).

As expected, the partial substitution of wheat flour with TP or PB resulted in a significant increase ($p \leq 0.05$) in the protein, lipid, and dietary fiber content (in all fractions), while the carbohydrates content decreased in the fortified bread compared to the control. We found that the addition of 12 g/100 g of TP to the bread formula resulted in a 129% increase in total dietary fiber, a 422% increase in fat, and a 16% increase in minerals, with a 16% reduction in carbohydrate content (compared to control sample). In the case of PB, with the same inclusion level, it increased the TDF content by 53%, fat content by 170%, and ash content by approximately 44% while reducing the carbohydrate content by about 8%. It is worth noting that, despite higher fat and protein contents and a lower carbohydrate content, the bread fortified with TP or PB had an energy value comparable to that of the control sample. Except for the 12% addition of TP, no statistically significant differences ($p \geq 0.05$) were observed. The application of both vegetable by-products additives made it possible to improve the chemical composition of the bread while maintaining consumer acceptability. These findings confirm the potential of vegetable by-products such as TP and PB as promising food additives that enhance the nutritional properties of foods, particularly by increasing their dietary fiber content [9].

4. Conclusions

In conclusion, incorporating vegetable processing waste from bell peppers (PB) and tomatoes (TP) into a bread recipe resulted in significant improvements in the nutritional composition of the bread. The fortified bread showed higher protein, lipid, and dietary fiber content, while the carbohydrate content was reduced compared to the control sample. The addition of 12 g/100 g of TP increased the total dietary fiber by 129%, fat by 422%, and minerals by 16%, with a 16% decrease in carbohydrates. Similarly, the addition of PB at the same inclusion level increased the TDF content by 53%, fat content by 170%, and ash content by approximately 44% while reducing carbohydrates by about 8%. Furthermore, the fortified bread exhibited an energy value comparable to that of the control sample, despite the higher fat and protein content and lower carbohydrate content. The sensory attributes and textural properties of the bread were also maintained within acceptable levels. The sensory evaluation revealed that higher levels of TP negatively affected taste, while PB supplementation primarily affected taste and smell. These findings underscore the potential of vegetable by-products, namely TP and PB, as valuable food additives for enhancing the nutritional profile of bread. Incorporating these waste materials into food production not only promotes sustainability but also helps reduce food waste. Furthermore, future research should delve into exploring additional applications and optimizing the utilization of these vegetable processing waste in various food products. It is important to focus on finding the optimal levels of supplementation to improve the sensory characteristics of the fortified bread while preserving the desired nutritional benefits. Such efforts will contribute to expanding the use of vegetable by-products in the food industry and promoting a more sustainable and resource-efficient approach to food production. However, further research should aim to investigate the content of substances that may act as contraindications for consuming fortified bread by individuals with health disorders, including people with food sensitivity, allergies, autoimmune diseases, and a predisposition for inflammatory issues.

Author Contributions: Conceptualization, A.W. and P.Z.; methodology, A.W. and P.Z.; formal analysis, A.W.; investigation, A.W., P.Z., A.N., D.T., A.B.-K. and P.Ł.; resources, P.Z.; data curation, P.Z. and A.W.; writing—original draft preparation, A.W. and P.Z.; writing—review and editing, A.W. and P.Z.; visualization, A.W. and P.Z.; supervision, A.W. All authors have read and agreed to the published version of the manuscript.

Funding: The authors declare that no funds, grants, or other support were received during the preparation of this manuscript.

Institutional Review Board Statement: Not applicable. According to the Bioethics Commission (UP Lublin, Poland), the study did not require the consent of the Commission.

Informed Consent Statement: Informed consent was obtained from all volunteers involved in the sensory study.

Data Availability Statement: The data presented in this study are available on request from the corresponding author.

Conflicts of Interest: The authors declare no conflict of interest.

References

1. Corrado, S.; Caldeira, C.; Eriksson, M.; Hanssen, O.J.; Hauser, H.E.; van Holsteijn, F.; Liu, G.; Ostergren, K.; Parry, A.; Secondi, L.; et al. Food waste accounting methodologies: Challenges, opportunities, and further advancements. *Glob. Food Sec.* **2019**, *20*, 93–100. [CrossRef] [PubMed]
2. Faustino, M.; Veiga, M.; Sousa, P.; Costa, E.M.; Silva, S.; Pintado, M. Agro-Food Byproducts as a New Source of Natural Food Additives. *Molecules* **2019**, *24*, 1056. [CrossRef]
3. Ancuţa, P.; Sonia, A. Oil press-cakes and meals valorization through circular economy approaches: A review. *Appl. Sci.* **2020**, *10*, 7432. [CrossRef]
4. Jimenez-Moreno, N.; Esparza, I.; Bimbela, F.; Gandia, L.M.; Ancin-Azpilicueta, C. Valorization of selected fruit and vegetable wastes as bioactive compounds: Opportunities and challenges. *Crit. Rev. Environ. Sci. Technol.* **2020**, *50*, 2061–2108. [CrossRef]
5. Machado, A.; Gerald, M.V.; do Nascimento, R.P.; Moya, A.; Vezza, T.; Diez-Echave, P.; Galvez, J.J.; Cazarin, C.B.B.; Junior, M.R.M. Polyphenols from food by-products: An alternative or complementary therapy to IBD conventional treatments. *Food Res. Int.* **2021**, *140*, 110018. [CrossRef]
6. Makowska, A.; Zielińska-Dawidziak, M.; Waszkowiak, K.; Myszka, K. Effect of Flax Cake and Lupine Flour Addition on the Physicochemical, Sensory Properties, and Composition of Wheat Bread. *Appl. Sci.* **2023**, *13*, 7840. [CrossRef]
7. Choi, S.N.; Kim, H.J.; Chung, N.Y. Quality characteristics of bread added with paprika powder. *Korean J. Food Cook Sci.* **2012**, *28*, 839–846. [CrossRef]
8. Nour, V.; Ionica, M.E.; Trandafir, I. Bread enriched in lycopene and other bioactive compounds by addition of dry tomato waste. *J. Food Sci. Technol.* **2015**, *52*, 8260–8267. [CrossRef]

9. Teterycz, D.; Sobota, A. Use of High-Protein and High-Dietary-Fibre Vegetable Processing Waste from Bell Pepper and Tomato for Pasta Fortification. *Foods* **2023**, *12*, 2567. [CrossRef] [PubMed]
10. Adeyeye, E.I. The contribution of flesh, placenta and seeds to the nutritional attributes of a variety of Capsicum annum (Bell pepper). *Elixir Food Sci.* **2014**, *68*, 22587–22594.
11. Kumar, M.; Chandran, D.; Tomar, M.; Bhuyan, D.J.; Grasso, S.; Sá, A.G.A.; Carciofi, B.A.M.; Radha; Dhumal, S.; Singh, S.; et al. Valorization Potential of Tomato (*Solanum lycopersicum* L.) Seed: Nutraceutical Quality, Food Properties, Safety Aspects, and Application as a Health-Promoting Ingredient in Foods. *Horticulturae* **2022**, *8*, 265. [CrossRef]
12. Kumar, M.; Tomar, M.; Bhuyan, D.J.; Punia, S.; Grasso, S.; Sa, A.G.A.; Mekhemar, M. Tomato (*Solanum lycopersicum* L.) seed: A review on bioactives and biomedical activities. *Biomed. Pharmacother.* **2021**, *142*, 112018. [CrossRef]
13. Gonzalez, M.; Martín-Pedraza, L.; Somoza, M.L.; Blanca-López, N.; Macías, M.L.; Perez, D. Sensitisation patterns to tomato seed. *Clin. Transl. Allergy* **2015**, *5*, 120. [CrossRef]
14. Anaya-Esparza, L.M.; Mora, Z.V.-D.L.; Vázquez-Paulino, O.; Ascencio, F.; Villarruel-López, A. Bell Peppers (*Capsicum annum* L.) Losses and Wastes: Source for Food and Pharmaceutical Applications. *Molecules* **2021**, *26*, 5341. [CrossRef] [PubMed]
15. Mollakhalili-Meybodi, N.; Ehrampoush, M.H.; Hajimohammadi, B.; Mosaddeg, M.H. Formulation optimization of functional wheat bread with low glycemic index from technological and nutritional perspective. *Food Sci. Nutr.* **2023**, *11*, 284–294. [CrossRef]
16. Almeida, E.L.; Chang, Y.K.; Steel, C.J. Dietary fibre sources in bread: Influence on technological quality. *LWT* **2013**, *50*, 545–553. [CrossRef]
17. Wirkijowska, A.; Zarzycki, P.; Sobota, A.; Nawrocka, A.; Blicharz-Kania, A.; Andrejko, D. The possibility of using by-products from the flaxseed industry for functional bread production. *LWT* **2020**, *118*, 108860. [CrossRef]
18. Zarzycki, P.; Wirkijowska, A.; Nawrocka, A.; Kozłowicz, K.; Krajewska, M.; Kłosok, K.; Krawęcka, A. Effect of Moldavian dragonhead seed residue on the baking properties of wheat flour and bread quality. *LWT* **2022**, *155*, 112967. [CrossRef]
19. Miś, A.; Dziki, D. Extensograph curve profile model used for characterising the impact of dietary fibre on wheat dough. *J. Cereal Sci.* **2013**, *57*, 471–479. [CrossRef]
20. Chouaibi, M.; Rezig, L.; Boussaid, A.; Hamdi, S. Insoluble tomato-fiber effect on wheat dough rheology and cookies' quality. *Ital. J. Food Sci.* **2019**, *31*, 1–18. [CrossRef]
21. Zecevic, V.; Boskovic, J.; Knezevic, D.; Micanovic, D.; Milenkovic, S. Influence of cultivar and growing season on quality properties of winter wheat (*Triticum aestivum* L.). *Afr. J. Agric. Res.* **2013**, *8*, 2545–2550.
22. Miś, A.; Nawrocka, A.; Dziki, D. Behaviour of dietary fibre supplements during bread dough development evaluated using novel farinograph curve analysis. *Food Bioproc. Technol.* **2017**, *10*, 1031–1041. [CrossRef]
23. Nawrocka, A.; Zarzycki, P.; Kłosok, K.; Welc, R.; Wirkijowska, A.; Teterycz, D. Effect of dietary fibre waste originating from food production on the gluten structure in common wheat dough. *Int. Agrophys.* **2023**, *37*, 101–109. [CrossRef]
24. AACC (American Association of Cereal Chemists). *AACC Approved Methods of Analysis*, 11th ed.; AACC (American Association of Cereal Chemists): St. Paul, MN, USA, 2010.
25. Bot, B.; Sanchez, H.; De la Torre, M.; Osella, C. Mother dough in bread making. *J. Food Nutr. Sci.* **2014**, *2*, 24–29. [CrossRef]
26. AOAC (Association of Official Analytical Chemists International). *AOAC Official Methods*, 20th ed.; AOAC (Association of Official Analytical Chemists International): Rockville, MD, USA, 2016.
27. Dziki, D.; Cacak-Pietrzak, G.; Gawlik-Dziki, U.; Sułek, A.; Kocira, S.; Biernacka, B. Effect of Moldavian dragonhead (*Dracocephalum moldavica* L.) leaves on the baking properties of wheat flour and quality of bread. *CYTA J. Food* **2019**, *17*, 536–543. [CrossRef]
28. Wang, J.; Rosell, C.M.; de Barber, C.B. Effect of the addition of different fibres on wheat dough performance and bread quality. *Food Chem.* **2002**, *79*, 221–226. [CrossRef]
29. Liu, J.; Shim, Y.Y.; Timothy, J.T.; Wang, Y.; Reaney, M.J. Flaxseed gum a versatile natural hydrocolloid for food and non-food applications. *Trends Food Sci. Technol.* **2018**, *75*, 146–157. [CrossRef]
30. Marpalle, P.; Sonawane, S.K.; Arya, S.S. Effect of flaxseed flour addition on physicochemical and sensory properties of functional bread. *LWT* **2014**, *58*, 614–619. [CrossRef]
31. Codina, G.G.; Istrate, A.M.; Gontariu, I.; Mironeasa, S. Rheological properties of wheat–flaxseed composite flours assessed by mixolab and their relation to quality features. *Foods* **2019**, *8*, 333. [CrossRef]
32. Kasprzak, M.; Rzedzicki, Z. Application of grasspea wholemeal in the technology of white bread production. *Pol. J. Food Nutr. Sci.* **2012**, *62*, 207–213. [CrossRef]
33. Blicharz-Kania, A.; Pecyna, A.; Zdybel, B.; Andrejko, D.; Marczuk, A. Sunflower seed cake as a source of nutrients in gluten-free bread. *Sci. Rep.* **2023**, *13*, 10864. [CrossRef] [PubMed]
34. Sogi, D.S.; Sidhu, J.S.; Arora, M.S.; Garg, S.K.; Bawa, A.S. Effect of tomato seed meal supplementation on the dough and bread characteristics of wheat (PBW 343) flour. *Int. J. Food Prop.* **2002**, *5*, 563–571. [CrossRef]
35. Mironeasa, S.; Codină, G.G.; Mironeasa, C. Effect of composite flour made from tomato seed and wheat of 650 type of a strong quality for bread making on bread quality and alveograph rheological properties. *Int. J. Food Eng.* **2018**, *4*, 22–26. [CrossRef]
36. Lukas, B.F.; Morais, M.G.; Santos, T.D.; Costa, J.A.V. Spirulina for snack enrichment: Nutritional, physical and sensory evaluations. *LWT* **2018**, *90*, 270–276. [CrossRef]
37. Pathare, P.B.; Opara, U.L.; Al-Said, F.A.J. Colour measurement and analysis in fresh and processed foods: A review. *Food Bioproc. Technol.* **2013**, *6*, 36–60. [CrossRef]

38. Majzoobi, M.; Ghavi, F.S.; Farahnaky, A.; Jamalian, J.; Mesbahi, G. Effect of tomato pomace powder on the physicochemical properties of flat bread (*Barbari bread*). *J. Food Process. Preserv.* **2011**, *35*, 247–256. [CrossRef]
39. Saini, R.K.; Prasad, P.; Lokesh, V.; Shang, X.; Shin, J.; Keum, Y.S.; Lee, J.H. Carotenoids: Dietary sources, extraction, encapsulation, bioavailability, and health benefits-A review of recent advancements. *Antioxidants* **2022**, *11*, 795. [CrossRef]
40. Madia, V.N.; De Vita, D.; Ialongo, D.; Tudino, V.; De Leo, A.; Scipione, L.; Di Santo, R.; Costi, R.; Messore, A. Recent advances in recovery of lycopene from tomato waste: A potent antioxidant with endless benefits. *Molecules* **2021**, *26*, 4495. [CrossRef] [PubMed]

Disclaimer/Publisher's Note: The statements, opinions and data contained in all publications are solely those of the individual author(s) and contributor(s) and not of MDPI and/or the editor(s). MDPI and/or the editor(s) disclaim responsibility for any injury to people or property resulting from any ideas, methods, instructions or products referred to in the content.

Article

Sourdough Wheat Bread Enriched with Grass Pea and Lupine Seed Flour: Physicochemical and Sensory Properties

Grażyna Cacak-Pietrzak [1], Katarzyna Sujka [1], Jerzy Księżak [2], Jolanta Bojarszczuk [2] and Dariusz Dziki [3],*

[1] Department of Food Technology and Assessment, Institute of Food Sciences, Warsaw University of Life Sciences, 159C Nowoursynowska Street, 02-776 Warsaw, Poland; grazyna_cacak_pietrzak@sggw.edu.pl (G.C.-P.); katarzyna_sujka@sggw.edu.pl (K.S.)

[2] Department of Forage Crop Production, Institute of Soil Sciences and Plant Cultivation—State Research Institute, 8 Czartoryskich Street, 24-100 Pulawy, Poland; jksiezak@iung.pulawy.pl (J.K.); jbojarszczuk@iung.pulawy.pl (J.B.)

[3] Department of Thermal Technology and Food Process Engineering, University of Life Sciences in Lublin, 31 Głęboka Street, 20-612 Lublin, Poland

* Correspondence: dariusz.dziki@up.lublin.pl

Citation: Cacak-Pietrzak, G.; Sujka, K.; Księżak, J.; Bojarszczuk, J.; Dziki, D. Sourdough Wheat Bread Enriched with Grass Pea and Lupine Seed Flour: Physicochemical and Sensory Properties. *Appl. Sci.* **2023**, *13*, 8664. https://doi.org/10.3390/app13158664

Academic Editor: Anna Lante

Received: 4 July 2023
Revised: 23 July 2023
Accepted: 25 July 2023
Published: 27 July 2023

Copyright: © 2023 by the authors. Licensee MDPI, Basel, Switzerland. This article is an open access article distributed under the terms and conditions of the Creative Commons Attribution (CC BY) license (https://creativecommons.org/licenses/by/4.0/).

Abstract: Legume seeds, such as grass pea, yellow lupine, and narrow-leaf lupine, are highly nutritious and offer a wide range of health benefits. The objective of this research was to explore the possibility of partially replacing wheat flour (at levels of 10, 15, 20, and 25%) with flour derived from these legume seeds in sourdough wheat bread and examine its impact on the physicochemical and sensory properties of the bread. The physical properties of the dough were also assessed. The substitution of wheat flour with ground legume seeds resulted in increased water absorption (from 54.1 to 63.5%) and prolonged dough development time (from 2.0 to 13.5 min). Ground lupine seeds reduced the volume of the bread and increased its crumb density, consequently making the bread harder. The most significant increase in hardness was observed when narrow-leaf lupine flour was added to the wheat flour (from 8.4 to 22.5 N). Narrow-leaf lupine had the greatest impact on enhancing the protein content in the enriched bread (from 11.5 to 20%), while yellow lupine caused the highest increase in fiber content (from 1.9 to 6.9%). The proposed additives slightly but significantly ($p < 0.05$) increased the antioxidant activity and phenolic content in the bread samples. Importantly, for all legume seeds, replacing up to 15% of the wheat flour allowed the production of bread with high consumer acceptability.

Keywords: legume seeds; antioxidant properties; color; texture; sensory analysis

1. Introduction

Bread, a widely consumed grain product worldwide, is predominantly made from wheat flour [1,2] which primarily contains starch (60–85%) and proteins (9–12%) [3,4]. The content of nutrients varies depending on the extraction rate [4]. The production of wheat bread typically involves the use of refined flours, also known as low-extraction flours, which are characterized by low levels of dietary fiber, proteins, mineral components, and bioactive compounds [2,3]. Furthermore, the proteins present in wheat flour are incomplete, lacking certain essential amino acids (mainly lysine, which limits their digestibility) [3,5,6].

Enhancing the nutritional quality of wheat bread can be achieved by incorporating natural plant-based ingredients into the recipe. Research has validated the positive nutritional impacts of adding herbs and spices to the bread [2,7–10], pomace [11–15], and pseudocereal flours [16,17]. Valuable recipe additions can also include flours made from legume seeds [4,18–21].

Leguminous plants belong to the family *Leguminosae* (or *Fabaceae*), which encompasses over 18,000 different species. Their cultivation accounts for approximately 15% of the world's agricultural land [22]. In 2021, the production of legume seeds reached 88.97 million tons [23]. Legume seeds are a valuable source of food for people worldwide [24–29]. They are a good source of protein, dietary fiber, minerals, vitamins, and bioactive phenolic compounds [30–34]. Legume seeds contain anywhere from 17% to even 50% protein [34–36] that has a significantly higher biological value compared to grain protein [26,32,34]. They also have a lower glycemic index compared to grains [30,33,37,38]. Consuming legume seeds is recommended for the prevention of type 2 diabetes and can help better control glycemia in individuals with diabetes [39]. Regular consumption of legume seeds can also contribute to the prevention of other chronic diseases, such as obesity, cardiovascular diseases, and certain cancers [30,33,40]. Some of the most popular and commonly consumed legume seeds include peas, beans, broad beans, chickpeas, and lentils. Others, such as cowpeas, lupines, vetches, lentil vetches, or white lupines, are still underappreciated [27,29].

Grass pea, which has been grown since ancient times, is used in human nutrition and as animal feed is likely the oldest plant in Europe [41]. Currently, interest in this plant is limited to a few species, including *Lathyrus sativus* [42,43] and *Lathyrus maritimus* [44–46], mainly cultivated in India, Bangladesh, Pakistan, Nepal, Ethiopia, and China [47]. Grass pea contains 20–36% high-quality protein [48]. Its positive effects in treating cardiovascular diseases, hypoxia, and hypertension have been demonstrated [47,49–51].

Lupine has been cultivated for over 2000 years in Europe and South America [52,53]. Three main species of lupine are primarily grown: narrow-leafed lupine (*Lupinus angustifolius*), yellow lupine (*Lupinus luteus*), and white lupine (*Lupinus albus*). Lupine seeds have the highest protein content among all legume species (29–52% dry weight) [54]. The main protein groups in lupine are albumins and globulins, which are characterized by their high biological value due to a significant amount of essential amino acids, particularly lysine [1,54]. Lupine seeds are also a valuable source of carotenoids, tocopherols, and lecithin [4,55]. Consuming lupine seeds is recommended for the prevention of conditions such as hypercholesterolemia, diabetes, and arterial hypertension [4,19,56].

Due to their high nutritional value and sensory qualities, both grass pea and lupine seeds can be used as ingredients in functional food products [20,55,57,58]. This study aimed to assess the suitability of grass pea and lupine seed flour as a component in sourdough bread recipes using organic wheat flour as a base.

2. Materials and Methods

2.1. Raw Materials

To prepare the bread dough, the following ingredients were utilized: commercially available white wheat flour (type 550, BIO from BioLife Sp. z o.o. located in Bielsk Podlaski, Poland); fresh pressed yeast sourced from Lesaffre Polska S.A. in Wołczyn, Poland; and salt supplied by Cenos Sp. z o.o. in Września, Poland. Additionally, flours obtained from grass pea (GP) of the Derek variety, narrow-leaved lupine (NL) of the Roland variety, and yellow lupine (YL) of the Salut variety were used. The legume seeds were obtained from an organic cultivation experiment carried out at the Institute of Soil Science and Plant Cultivation—State Research Institute in Puławy. These seeds were harvested in 2022, cleaned, and subsequently ground into particles measuring less than 1.0 mm using an A11 analytical mill (IKA Works GmbH & Co., Staufen, Germany).

2.2. Baking Properties of Wheat Flour and Physical Properties of Dough

The baking properties of the wheat flour such as the yield and quality of gluten (AACC, Method 38.12), the falling number (AACC, Method 56–81B), and the physical properties of the dough were determined using a Farinograph-E model 810114 (Brabender GmbH & Co. KG, Duisburg, Germany (AACC Method 54–21) according to the approved methods of the American Association of Cereal Chemistry (AACC) [59]. Prior to the analysis, blends were prepared by replacing wheat flour with legume seed flours (GP, NL, and YL) in amounts of 10, 15, 20, and 25% by weight of the flour. The control sample consisted of wheat flour dough.

2.3. Baking Procedure

The bread dough was prepared using a two-phase method with wheat sourdough. The sourdough was inoculated with cultures of *Lactiplantibacillus plantarum* and *Levilactobacillus brevis* bacteria obtained from the collection of pure cultures of the Department of Food Technology and Assessment, Warsaw University of Life Sciences, Warsaw, Poland. The sourdough had a yield of 200%. Fermentation of the sourdough took place for 7 days at a temperature of 25 °C. The sourdough was added in an amount equivalent to 10% of the total weight of the wheat flour. The basic recipe for the bread dough (control sample) included 700 g of wheat flour, 70 g of wheat sourdough, 21 g of fresh pressed yeast, 10.5 g of salt, and water added as necessary to achieve a dough consistency of 350 BU. The amount of water added was determined based on the calculated water absorption capacity of the farinographic flour/blends. In the blends, wheat flour was substituted with legume seed flours, GP, NL, and annual yellow lupine (YL) in varying proportions of 10, 15, 20, and 25%. The bread was prepared according to the protocol described by Cacak-Pietrzak et al. [2]. In Table 1, an explanation of the description of the abbreviations used for the bread sample analysis is presented.

Table 1. List of codes for analyzed bread samples.

Sample Code	Wheat Flour (%)	Grass Pea Flour (%)	Yellow Lupine Flour (%)	Narrow-Leaf Lupine Flour (%)
CD	100	-	-	-
GPD10	90	10	-	-
GPD15	85	15	-	-
GPD20	80	20	-	-
GPD25	75	25	-	-
YLD10	90	-	10	-
YLD15	85	-	15	-
YLD20	80	-	20	-
YLD25	75	-	25	-
NLD10	90	-	-	10
NLD15	85	-	-	15
NLD20	80	-	-	20
NLD25	75	-	-	25

2.4. Basic Composition of Raw Materials

The basic chemical composition (moisture (Method 44–15.02), ash (Method 08–01.01), protein (Method 46–10.01), and fat (Method 30–10.01)) of the wheat flour (WF), GP, NL, YL, and bread was determined using AACC methods [2,59]. Additionally, the amount of digestible carbohydrates was computed according to the difference [2].

2.5. Bread Yield, Volume, and Density

The bread loaves were weighed, and the bread volume, yield, and density were calculated [14,60]. The volume of the bread was measured using a 3D scanner (NextEngine, West Los Angeles, CA, USA) and calculated using computer software (MeshlLab, ISTI-CNR Research Centre, Rome, Italy). It was then converted to represent 100 g of bread. Additionally, the density of the bread's crumb was also determined along with the ratio of the bread sample's mass to its volume. The yield of bread (Y) was calculated as follows:

$$Y = \frac{a \times w}{b} \quad (1)$$

where b represents the weight of the dough portion before baking, c is the mass of the bread after cooling (in grams), and w is the dough yield. In addition, the baking losses were calculated [2].

2.6. Crumb Texture

The texture parameters of the crumb were determined using a TA.XT2i texture analyzer (Stable Microsystem, Surrey, UK). The analysis was conducted according to the methodology described by Romankiewicz et al. [60]. Briefly, circular samples with a diameter of 30 mm were obtained by cutting bread slices that were 20 mm thick. These samples were then compressed using a 25 mm diameter probe. The compression was set at 40% penetration with a 45 s delay between the first and second compressions. The probe speed was set at 1 mm/s. The texture parameters of the bread crumb were determined by analyzing the resulting curve using the Texture Expert Exceed v. 1.00 computer software.

2.7. Color of Raw Materials and Bread Samples

The color parameters of the raw materials and crumb samples (L*—lightness, a*—redness or greenness, and b*—yellowness or blueness) were determined using the reflectance method in the CIE-Lab* color space. The absolute color difference (ΔE) was also calculated [61].

2.8. Total Phenolic Content and Antioxidant Capacity

2.8.1. Extract Preparation

The hydroalcoholic extracts were prepared to determine the total phenolic content and antioxidant capacity of both the raw materials and bread samples. A total of 1 g of each type of raw material and bread was mixed with 50 mL of 50% (v/v) methanol. The mixture was allowed to extract for 30 min at room temperature and subsequently subjected to centrifugation at $9000 \times g$ for 15 min. The procedure was repeated three times, and the supernatants were collected for the analysis and stored at $-20\ ^\circ C$ until further analyses.

2.8.2. Total Phenolic Content

The total polyphenol content was determined using the Folin–Ciocalteu spectrophotometric method following the procedure described by Romankiewicz et al. [60]. The concentration of phenolic compounds was read from the standard curve determined for gallic acid (the linearity range was 10 µg/mL to 2000 µg/mL; $R^2 = 0.999$) and expressed as the gallic acid equivalent (GAE) in mg/g DW.

2.8.3. Antiradical Activity against DPPH Free Radicals

The ability to quench free radicals of DPPH was determined using the spectrophotometric method [2,62]. The inhibition percentage of DPPH discoloration was calculated as in (1):

$$AA = (Ac - Ap)/(Ac) \cdot 100\%, \qquad (2)$$

where Ac—the absorbance of control and Ap—the absorbance of extract.

The antiradical activity was expressed as EC50 (efficient concentration), i.e., the concentration of sample (mg DW/mL) needed to obtain 50% of initial activity.

2.8.4. Antiradical Activity against ABTS•+ Free Radicals

The ability to quench cationic radicals ABTS•+ was determined according to the procedure described by Romankiewicz et al. [60] and Re et al. [63].

The results of antioxidant activity were expressed as the EC_{50} index (mg DM/mL) [2].

2.9. Sensory Evaluation of Bread

The sensory evaluation of the bread was conducted according to the methodology provided by Garcia-Gómez et al. [64] using a 9-point hedonic scale one day after baking. The evaluation team consisted of 52 panelists (employees and students of Warsaw University of Life Sciences, Warsaw, Poland) aged 20 to 58 years. The participants selected for the study were required to be regular bread consumers. Consumer evaluations were conducted in individual sensory booths within a sensory laboratory by utilizing a hedonic taste sheet.

The bread samples were assessed at room temperature. Participants were instructed to rinse their mouths with water between samples to ensure a clean palate. The evaluations followed a sequential monadic test design employing a complete block design. The consumers were not provided any information about the samples and did not receive any monetary incentives to avoid bias in their participation.

2.10. Statistical Analysis of Results

The measurements were carried out at least three times, and the statistical analysis was conducted using Statistica 13.3 software from TIBCO Software (Palo Alto, CA, USA). The analysis involved performing an analysis of variance (ANOVA) and determining homogeneous groups using Tukey's test with a significance level set at $\alpha = 0.05$.

3. Results and Discussion

3.1. Water Absorption and Physical Properties of Dough

Conducting farinographic assessment is helpful in developing bread recipes and determining optimal parameters for the dough fermentation process [65]. The water absorption of the tested wheat flour was relatively low (54.1%) (Table 2) but typical for light wheat flours obtained from organic wheat grains [66]. The addition of flour made from legume seeds significantly increased the water absorption of the mixtures. The greatest changes in water absorption (increase up to 63.5%) occurred after adding YL at a 25% level (YLD25). This means that the dough with this additive could absorb more water, resulting in higher dough and bread yield in practice. The increased water absorption of the mixtures was probably due to the high protein and fiber content in the legume seed flours, as indicated by the research results of other authors [21,67,68]. The addition of flour made from legume seeds had a statistically significant effect on prolonging the dough development time from 2.0 min (CD) to 13.7 min (YLD15). The greatest increase in this parameter was observed with the addition of legume seed flour at a level of 10–15%, while further increasing the level of addition resulted in its decrease. Interestingly, the dough stability varied depending on the type and level of the additive, either increasing or decreasing. The dough stability of the control sample (CD) was 9.1 min. Significant prolongation of the dough stability was observed when adding YL at 10% and 15% levels (YLD10 and YLD15). On the other hand, a decrease in dough stability, indicating weakening of its structure, occurred when adding GP and NL at levels of 15% and above. The softening of the control dough (CD) was 35 BU. Changes in this parameter also depended on the type and level of the additive. The dough with GP and NL additives up to 15% (GPD10, GPD15, NLD10, and NLD15), as well as all dough with YL additives exhibited significantly less softening compared to the control sample (CD).

Table 2. Water absorption and physical properties of dough and enriched dough samples.

Sample	Water Absorption (%)	Development Time (min)	Stability of Dough (min)	Degree of Softening (BU)
CD	54.1 ± 0.1 [g]	2.0 ± 0.1 [h]	9.1 ± 0.7 [c]	35 ± 4.6 [bc]
GPD10	55.1 ± 0.1 [f]	6.8 ± 0.2 [e]	9.7 ± 0.1 [c]	19 ± 1 [fg]
GPD15	55.0 ± 0.1 [f]	6.2 ± 0.3 [efg]	7.7 ± 0.3 [d]	28 ± 5 [de]
GPD20	55.1 ± 0.1 [f]	5.6 ± 0.2 [fg]	6.1 ± 0.1 [ef]	35 ± 0 [bc]
GPD25	55.0 ± 0.1 [f]	5.7 ± 0.0 [fg]	4.0 ± 0.1 [g]	51 ± 2 [a]
YLD10	56.9 ± 0.1 [d]	10.7 ± 0.1 [c]	14.0 ± 0.1 [a]	4 ± 1 [i]
YLD15	59.2 ± 0.2 [c]	13.7 ± 0.1 [a]	12.5 ± 0.1 [b]	12 ± 2 [gh]
YLD20	62.0 ± 0.2 [b]	12.6 ± 0.1 [b]	9.5 ± 0.2 [c]	8 ± 1 [hi]
YLD25	63.5 ± 0.1 [a]	8.6 ± 0.6 [d]	9.0 ± 0.1 [c]	3 ± 0 [i]

Table 2. Cont.

Sample	Water Absorption (%)	Development Time (min)	Stability of Dough (min)	Degree of Softening (BU)
NLD10	56.1 ± 0.1 [e]	6.4 ± 0.1 [de]	9.6 ± 0.3 [c]	7 ± 0 [hi]
NLD15	55.9 ± 0.1 [e]	6.4 ± 0.1 [de]	6.9 ± 0.1 [e]	22 ± 2 [ef]
NLD20	55.9 ± 0.1 [e]	5.5 ± 0.1 [g]	5.8 ± 0.1 [f]	32 ± 2 [cd]
NLD25	55.9 ± 0.1 [e]	5.6 ± 0.2 [g]	3.8 ± 0.2 [g]	41 ± 2 [b]

CD—control dough; GPD10-GPD25—dough with 10, 15, 20, and 25% of grass pea flour; YLD10-YLD25—dough with 10, 15, 20, and 25% of yellow lupine flour; NLD10-NLD25—dough with 10, 15, 20, and 25% of narrow-leaf lupine flour. The values designated by the letters [a–i] were significantly different ($p < 0.05$).

3.2. Basic Properties of Bread Samples

During the baking and cooling process of bread, there is a loss in its mass caused by the evaporation of water and other volatile substances, such as carbon dioxide, alcohol, and volatile acids. As a result, in addition to the decrease in mass, there is also a loss in bread aroma [69]. Substituting a portion of wheat flour with YL and NL wheat flour resulted in a statistically significant reduction in bread baking loss from 11.6% (CB) to 10.1% (YLB25) (Table 3). However, the addition of GP increased the baking loss of the bread, but only when used in quantities of 15% and 20% (GPB15 and GPB20). The bread yield of the control (CB) was 139.0%. There was a statistically significant increase in the bread yield after adding YL at 15% and above, and at a 25% level of this additive, the bread yield increased up to 147.1% (YLB25). This can be attributed to the high content of fiber and protein in the added ingredient. These substances had a high capacity for absorbing and retaining water in the dough, resulting in better dough consistency and reduced water loss during the baking process [1,19]. The bread volume made from wheat flour (CB) was 365 cm^3 per 100 g, and the crumb's specific mass was 0.26 g·cm^{-3}. The addition of legume flour significantly reduced the bread volume, which led to an increase in the crumb's specific mass. The values of these parameters changed linearly with the increasing level of substitution of wheat flour with legume flours. The reduction in bread volume after introducing ingredients with high fiber content into the recipe can be explained by the phenomenon of interrupting the continuity of the gluten network by these components. Additionally, the formation of the gluten network may have been hindered due to the presence of additional non-gluten proteins [60,65,70]. The formation of a weaker gluten network resulted in the loss of part of the generated carbon dioxide during fermentation and, consequently, the production of bread with a smaller volume [71].

Table 3. Basic properties of control and enriched bread samples.

Sample	Baking Loss (%)	Bread Yield (%)	Volume (cm^3 100^{-1} g)	Crumb Density (g cm^{-3})
CB	11.6 ± 0.1 [bc]	139.0 ± 0.7 [de]	365 ± 3.7 [a]	0.26 ± 0.01 [f]
GPB10	11.9 ± 1.3 [ab]	138.4 ± 0.5 [de]	312 ± 2.1 [b]	0.32 ± 0.00 [e]
GPB15	12.2 ± 0.1 [a]	139.3 ± 0.4 [d]	289 ± 5.8 [c]	0.34 ± 0.01 [de]
GPB20	12.1 ± 1.3 [a]	139.1 ± 0.3 [de]	272 ± 0.9 [d]	0.37 ± 0.01 [d]
GPB25	11.3 ± 0.2 [cd]	140.1 ± 0.8 [cd]	262 ± 0.8 [ef]	0.41 ± 0.01 [c]
YLB10	10.9 ± 0.2 [def]	139.7 ± 0.5 [d]	292 ± 2.6 [c]	0.35 ± 0.01 [e]
YLB15	10.8 ± 0.1 [ef]	142.0 ± 0.5 [c]	273 ± 2.2 [d]	0.37 ± 0.00 [d]
YLB20	11.1 ± 0.1 [de]	144.0 ± 0.2 [b]	257 ± 2.9 [f]	0.42 ± 0.00 [bc]
YLB25	10.1 ± 0.2 [e]	147.1 ± 0.3 [a]	228 ± 1.7 [h]	0.48 ± 0.01 [a]

Table 3. Cont.

Sample	Baking Loss (%)	Bread Yield (%)	Volume (cm^3 100^{-1} g)	Crumb Density (g cm^{-3})
NLB10	10.8 ± 0.1 [ef]	137.3 ± 0.6 [e]	311 ± 1.3 [b]	0.33 ± 0.01 [e]
NLB15	10.6 ± 0.1 [gh]	139.1 ± 0.3 [de]	285 ± 0.5 [c]	0.38 ± 0.01 [d]
NLB20	10.5 ± 0.2 [gh]	139.5 ± 0.9 [d]	270 ± 2.5 [de]	0.39 ± 0.01 [d]
NLB25	10.3 ± 0.1 [h]	139.8 ± 0.3 [d]	245 ± 1.3 [g]	0.44 ± 0.01 [b]

CB—control bread; GPB10-GPB25—bread with 10, 15, 20, and 25% of grass pea flour; YLB10-YLB25—bread with 10, 15, 20, and 25% of yellow lupine flour; NLB10-NLB25—bread with 10, 15, 20, and 25% of narrow-leaf lupine flour. The values designated by the letters [a–h] were significantly different ($p < 0.05$).

3.3. Crumb Texture

The addition of flour made from legume seeds had a statistically significant impact on the increase in the hardness of bread compared to the control sample. The hardness of the control sample (CB) was 8.37 N (Table 4). As the level of legume flour addition increased, the values of this parameter increased linearly. The addition of GP at a level of 25% resulted in an almost twofold increase in bread hardness (13.04 N) compared to the control sample, while in the case of a 25% addition of YL and NL, the hardness of the bread increased almost threefold (21.19 N and 22.54 N, respectively). These changes were due to a decrease in loaf volume and an increase in crumb density, which made the crumb more compact and dense. Other texture parameters such as elasticity, springiness, and cohesiveness of the crumb gradually decreased with increasing levels of legume flour addition. These changes were generally statistically significant compared to the control sample except for bread enriched with up to 20% GP. Many studies [1,10,12,71] indicated that the addition of plant-based ingredients such as legume flour negatively affected the texture of wheat bread. These changes resulted from a weaker gluten network structure and reduced retention of carbon dioxide generated during dough fermentation.

Table 4. Crumb texture of control and enriched bread samples.

Sample	Hardness (N)	Elasticity (-)	Springiness (-)	Cohesiveness (-)
CB	8.37 ± 0.15 [h]	0.23 ± 0.01 [a]	0.87 ± 0.01 [a]	0.65 ± 0.01 [a]
GPB10	11.35 ± 0.41 [g]	0.22 ± 0.02 [ab]	0.84 ± 0.01 [ab]	0.56 ± 0.01 [bc]
GPB15	11.73 ± 1.10 [g]	0.19 ± 0.01 [cde]	0.82 ± 0.02 [abc]	0.48 ± 0.02 [def]
GPB20	12.08 ± 0.44 [fg]	0.17 ± 0.01 [efg]	0.82 ± 0.04 [abc]	0.45 ± 0.02 [ef]
GPB25	13.04 ± 0.28 [f]	0.14 ± 0.00 [h]	0.79 ± 0.01 [bcd]	0.41 ± 0.04 [f]
YLB10	15.38 ± 0.31 [e]	0.18 ± 0.00 [def]	0.82 ± 0.01 [abc]	0.49 ± 0.01 [cde]
YLB15	17.21 ± 0.42 [d]	0.18 ± 0.01 [def]	0.81 ± 0.01 [bcd]	0.51 ± 0.02 [cde]
YLB20	19.42 ± 0.40 [c]	0.17 ± 0.01 [efg]	0.81 ± 0.02 [bcd]	0.52 ± 0.02 [bcd]
YLB25	21.19 ± 0.72 [b]	0.15 ± 0.02 [gh]	0.78 ± 0.02 [cd]	0.49 ± 0.03 [cde]
NLB10	11.69 ± 0.07 [g]	0.21 ± 0.01 [bc]	0.84 ± 0.02 [ab]	0.59 ± 0.07 [ab]
NLB15	15.77 ± 0.39 [e]	0.20 ± 0.00 [bcd]	0.78 ± 0.03 [cd]	0.55 ± 0.02 [bc]
NLB20	17.97 ± 0.52 [d]	0.19 ± 0.01 [cde]	0.75 ± 0.02 [d]	0.54 ± 0.04 [bcd]
NLB25	22.54 ± 0.27 [a]	0.16 ± 0.01 [fgh]	0.69 ± 0.01 [e]	0.49 ± 0.00 [cde]

CB—control bread; GPB10-GPB25—bread with 10, 15, 20, and 25% of grass pea flour; YLB10-YLB25—bread with 10, 15, 20, and 25% of yellow lupine flour; NLB10-NLB25—bread with 10, 15, 20, and 25% of narrow-leaf lupine flour. The values designated by the letters [a–h] were significantly different ($p < 0.05$).

3.4. Color of Raw Materials and Bread

Color is one of the key indicators of bread quality and plays a significant role in consumer acceptance [14,60]. The lightness values (L*) were significantly highest for the control sample (CB) and bread with 10% YL (YLB10) (Table 5). As the level of legume flour addition increased, the lightness of the bread crumb decreased linearly, which was due to the darker color of these added ingredients compared to wheat flour. Similarly, the values of the color parameters a* and b* changed with the increasing inclusion of legume flour in the bread formulation. Bread with a YL addition particularly exhibited high intensities of red and yellow colors, which corresponded to the color of this ingredient. The absolute color difference (ΔE) between the control bread and the bread enriched with legume flour ranged from 8.0 to 21.3. This indicated that even a 10% addition of legume flour had a significant impact on the color of the bread crumb, and the observed changes in terms of darkening were noticeable even to an inexperienced observer. Many studies [1,7,9,10,12,14,65] indicated changes in bread color resulting from enriching the composition with natural plant-based additives. These changes were caused by the presence of natural pigments in plant-based raw materials. Legume seeds, for example, contain carotenoids characterized by intense yellow-orange color. Lupine seeds, in particular, are rich in these compounds [4,55].

Table 5. Color of raw materials, control, and enriched bread samples.

Sample	Lightness	Redness	Yellowness	ΔE
WF	90.91 ± 0.11 [A]	0.46 ± 0.03 [D]	10.23 ± 0.25 [D]	-
GP	86.68 ± 0.04 [B]	0.76 ± 0.03 [C]	17.18 ± 0.06 [C]	-
YL	82.84 ± 0.21 [D]	3.77 ± 0.12 [A]	27.45 ± 0.17 [A]	-
NL	83.80 ± 0.21 [C]	1.86 ± 0.04 [B]	24.25 ± 0.07 [B]	-
CB	70.38 ± 0.78 [a]	0.14 ± 0.02 [h]	14.22 ± 0.24 [f]	-
GPB10	63.77 ± 0.42 [e]	0.28 ± 0.04 [gh]	18.73 ± 0.68 [e]	8.0
GPB15	62.90 ± 0.23 [ef]	0.40 ± 0.02 [g]	18.98 ± 0.09 [e]	8.9
GPB20	61.73 ± 0.15 [gh]	0.65 ± 0.04 [f]	22.28 ± 0.83 [cd]	11.8
GPB25	60.71 ± 0.17 [hi]	0.98 ± 0.08 [e]	23.46 ± 0.32 [c]	13.4
YLB10	69.44 ± 0.46 [a]	1.30 ± 0.02 [d]	23.20 ± 0.20 [c]	9.1
YLB15	67.78 ± 0.22 [b]	1.73 ± 0.04 [c]	26.13 ± 0.59 [b]	12.3
YLB20	66.68 ± 0.39 [c]	2.17 ± 0.05 [b]	26.78 ± 0.27 [b]	13.3
YLB25	65.23 ± 0.24 [d]	3.07 ± 0.05 [a]	29.17 ± 0.11 [a]	21.3
NLB10	65.62 ± 0.05 [cd]	0.79 ± 0.06 [ef]	21.52 ± 0.29 [d]	8.7
NLB15	62.62 ± 0.31 [fg]	1.28 ± 0.03 [d]	25.98 ± 0.19 [b]	14.2
NLB20	60.90 ± 0.06 [hi]	1.62 ± 0.03 [c]	26.78 ± 0.76 [b]	15.9
NLB25	60.23 ± 0.17 [i]	2.32 ± 0.15 [b]	29.36 ± 0.50 [a]	18.4

WF—wheat flour; GP—grass pea flour; YL—yellow lupine flour; NL—narrow-leaf lupine flour; CB—control bread; GPB10-GPB25—bread with 10, 15, 20, and 25% of grass pea flour; YLB10-YLB25—bread with 10, 15, 20, and 25% of yellow lupine flour; NLB10-NLB25—bread with 10, 15, 20, and 25% of narrow-leaf lupine flour. The values designated by the different letters [A-D], or [a-i] were significantly different ($p < 0.05$).

3.5. Basic Chemical Composition of Raw Materials and Bread

The parameters of wheat flour (WF) were as follows: total protein content—11.13% dry matter (DM), total ash content—0.59% DM, fiber content—1.83% DM, fat content—1.22% DM, and carbohydrate content—85.24% DM (Table 6). The wheat flour exhibited low enzymatic activity of amylolytic enzymes (falling number—310 s) and a low wet gluten yield of 23.3%, typical for light wheat flours obtained from organic grain milling [66]. It should be emphasized that the gluten showed good quality (gluten index 93). Flour from legume seeds contained significantly more total protein than wheat flour. The content of this component in the GP flour was 31.99% DM, while in the YL and NL flours, it was 34.01% and 48.0% DM, respectively. The high protein content in legume seeds has been indicated by the results of studies by many authors [18,21,22,41,58,68]. Flours from legume seeds also proved to be much better sources of fiber and, in the case of lupine flours, fat as well. The highest amounts of these components were found in the YL flour, namely 19.31% and 6.42% DM, respectively. The total ash content in the legume seed flours ranged from 3.31% to 3.83% DM, which means they contained 5.6 to 6.5 times more mineral components compared to the wheat flour.

Table 6. Basic chemical composition of raw materials, control, and enriched bread samples.

Sample	Protein (% DM)	Ash (% DM)	Fiber (% DM)	Fat (% DM)	Carbohydrates (% DM)
WF	11.13 ± 0.13 [D]	0.59 ± 0.02 [D]	1.83 ± 0.01 [D]	1.22 ± 0.02 [C]	85.24 ± 0.08 [A]
GP	31.99 ± 0.04 [C]	3.31 ± 0.02 [C]	6.09 ± 0.02 [C]	0.32 ± 0.02 [D]	58.29 ± 0.05 [B]
YL	34.01 ± 0.03 [B]	3.66 ± 0.00 [B]	19.31 ± 0.02 [A]	6.42 ± 0.03 [A]	36.60 ± 0.05 [C]
NL	48.18 ± 0.12 [A]	3.83 ± 0.01 [A]	16.68 ± 0.04 [B]	4.73 ± 0.01 [B]	26.58 ± 0.13 [D]
CB	11.45 ± 0.02 [k]	0.87 ± 0.02 [h]	1.90 ± 0.01 [l]	1.29 ± 0.02 [h]	84.49 ± 0.08 [a]
GPB10	13.70 ± 0.04 [i]	1.41 ± 0.01 [f]	2.21 ± 0.02 [l]	1.20 ± 0,02 [i]	81.48 ± 0.04 [b]
GPB15	14.42 ± 0.00 [h]	1.49 ± 0.01 [d]	2.50 ± 0.00 [k]	1.10 ± 0.01 [j]	80.59 ± 0.08 [c]
GPB20	15.12 ± 0.08 [f]	1.53 ± 0.00 [c]	2.72 ± 0.04 [j]	1.08 ± 0.04 [j]	79.55 ± 0.12 [e]
GPB25	16.04 ± 0.02 [d]	1.60 ± 0.02 [b]	3.59 ± 0.02 [g]	0.99 ± 0.01 [k]	77.78 ± 0.03 [g]
YLB10	13.42 ± 0.04 [j]	1.34 ± 0.01 [g]	3.41 ± 0.01 [h]	1.82 ± 0.04 [e]	80.01 ± 0.04 [d]
YLB15	14.95 ± 0.03 [fg]	1.45 ± 0.02 [e]	4.20 ± 0.02 [e]	2.11 ± 0.02 [c]	77.24 ± 0.02 [h]
YLB20	15.52 ± 0.04 [e]	1.50 ± 0.01 [d]	5.30 ± 0.04 [b]	2.31 ± 0.04 [b]	75.37 ± 0.04 [i]
YLB25	16.89 ± 0.12 [c]	1.63 ± 0.00 [b]	6.10 ± 0,00 [a]	2.51 ± 0.02 [a]	72.87 ± 0.04 [k]
NLB10	14.86 ± 0.06 [g]	1.41 ± 0.02 [f]	3.09 ± 0.06 [i]	1.50 ± 0.05 [g]	79.14 ± 0.05 [f]
NLB15	16.72 ± 0.02 [c]	1.48 ± 0.01 [d]	4.01 ± 0.00 [f]	1.70 ± 0.02 [f]	76.00 ± 0.01 [h]
NLB20	18.20 ± 0.03 [b]	1.54 ± 0.02 [c]	4.90 ± 0.05 [d]	2.02 ± 0.04 [d]	73.34 ± 0.04 [j]
NLB25	20.00 ± 0.08 [a]	1.72 ± 0.00 [a]	5.08 ± 0.02 [c]	2.11 ± 0.05 [c]	71.09 ± 0.05 [l]

WF—wheat flour; GP—grass pea flour; YL—yellow lupine flour; NL—narrow-leaf lupine flour; CB—control bread; GPB10-GPB25—bread with 10, 15, 20, and 25% of grass pea flour; YLB10-YLB25—bread with 10, 15, 20, and 25% of yellow lupine flour; NLB10-NLB25—bread with 10, 15, 20, and 25% of narrow-leaf lupine flour. The values designated by the different letters [A-D] or [a-k] were significantly different ($p < 0.05$).

The chemical composition of the control bread (CB) was as follows: total protein content of 11.45% DM, total ash content of 0.87% DM, fiber content of 1.90% DM, fat content of 1.29% DM, and carbohydrate content of 84.49% DM (Table 5). The moisture of the bread samples was between 37.1 and 38.2%. With an increase in the level of addition of flours from legume seeds, the total protein content, total ash content, crude fiber, and fat content increased significantly, while the carbohydrate content decreased compared to the control sample. This resulted in an increase in the nutritional value of the bread. Bread with the addition of flours from legume seeds can be a good source of complete protein mainly composed of albumins and globulins [41,54]. The protein content in the bread with 25% levels of GP, YL, and NL was as follows: 16.04% DM (GPB25), 16.89% DM (YLB25), and 20.00% DM (NLB25). Importantly, protein from lentils and lupines contains significant amounts of lysine [1,41,54], which is a limiting amino acid for the biological value of wheat protein [6]. Additionally, it is a good source of amino acids such as leucine and arginine [1,41,54]. The fiber content and mineral components increased when compared to the CB sample. The bread with 25% legume flour contained about twice as much dietary fiber (LSB25) or three times as much dietary fiber (LAB25 and LLB25) and about twice as many minerals.

3.6. Phenolic Content and Antioxidant Capacity

The total content of phenolic compounds in the raw materials ranged from 0.86 mg GAE g DM^{-1} in the wheat flour to 2.15 mg GAE g DM^{-1} in the YL flour. The extracts from these raw materials also exhibited the lowest and highest antioxidant activity, respectively (Table 7). Enriching bread with flour from legume seeds resulted in a slight but statistically significant increase in the phenolic content in the bread. The highest increase was observed in the bread enriched with NL (from 0.72 mg GAE g DM^{-1} (CB) to 1.12 mg GAE g DM^{-1} (NLB25)), while the smallest increase was observed in the bread with GP (from 0.72 mg GAE g DM^{-1} (CB) to 0.99 mg GAE g DM^{-1} (GLB25)). The values of the EC$_{50}$ index were also significantly lower for the bread enriched with legume seed flour. This indicated higher antioxidant activity of the enriched bread. These relationships were observed for both antioxidant activities against DPPH and ABTS. The bread enriched with NL flour exhibited the highest activity against DPPH and consequently the lowest EC$_{50}$ values, while the bread with GP flour showed the highest activity against ABTS. On the other hand, the bread enriched with YL flour had the lowest antioxidant activity against ABTS, and the bread with GP flour had the lowest antioxidant capacity against DPPH. The increase in the content of phenolic compounds and antioxidant activity in the enriched bread resulted from the use of whole grain legume seed flour as an additive. Most of the bioactive substances were present in the fruit-seed coat of seeds [31]. Many authors observed that flour enrichment with different additives plant additives increased the antioxidant activity of bread. This effect was especially visible when raw materials that were rich in fiber were incorporated into wheat flour [10,13,14].

Table 7. Phenolic content and antioxidant capacity of raw materials, control, and enriched bread samples.

Sample	TPC (mg GAE g DM^{-1})	EC$_{50\ DPPH}$ (mg DM mL^{-1})	EC$_{50\ ABTS}$ (mg DM mL^{-1})
WF	0.86 ± 0.02 [A]	217 ± 5 [C]	188 ± 2 [B]
GP	1.72 ± 0.04 [B]	169 ± 4 [B]	178 ± 2 [AB]
YL	1.88 ± 0.04 [C]	160 ± 9 [AB]	169 ± 4 [AB]
NL	2.15 ± 0.05 [D]	148 ± 4 [A]	164 ± 5 [A]
CB	0.72 ± 0.02 [g]	275 ± 5 [k]	213 ± 18 [f]
GPB10	0.81 ± 0.02 [ef]	241 ± 3 [j]	186 ± 1 [ac]
GPB15	0.85 ± 0.01 [e]	230 ± 2 [i]	163 ± 2 [e]
GPB20	0.89 ± 0.03 [bf]	218 ± 2 [h]	148 ± 3 [d]
GPB25	0.99 ± 0.02 [ad]	204 ± 3 [g]	139 ± 3 [d]
YLB10	0.92 ± 0.02 [bc]	186 ± 4 [f]	199 ± 4 [b]
YLB15	1.00 ± 0.03 [ad]	174 ± 2 [e]	192 ± 3 [ab]
YLB20	1.03 ± 0.03 [ag]	165 ± 4 [d]	193 ± 3 [ab]
YLB25	1.09 ± 0.03 [h]	154 ± 4 [c]	191 ± 5 [ab]
NLB10	0.93 ± 0.02 [bc]	158 ± 1 [cd]	183 ± 7 [ac]
NLB15	0.97 ± 0.01 [cd]	145 ± 3 [b]	181 ± 3 [c]
NLB20	1.04 ± 0.01 [ag]	140 ± 2 [ab]	189 ± 2 [abc]
NLB25	1.12 ± 0.02 [h]	136 ± 2 [a]	168 ± 3 [e]

WF—wheat flour; GP—grass pea flour; YL—yellow lupine flour; NL—narrow-leaf lupine flour; CB—control bread; GPB10–GPB25—bread with 10, 15, 20, and 25% of grass pea flour; YLB10–YLB25—bread with 10, 15, 20, and 25% of yellow lupine flour; NLB10–NLB25—bread with 10, 15, 20, and 25% of narrow-leaf lupine flour. The values designated by the different letters [A–D] or [a–k] were significantly different ($p < 0.05$).

3.7. Sensory Evaluation Results

Currently, customers are increasingly seeking bakery products with enhanced nutritional value that retain sensory appeal. The nutritional value and sensory properties of bread depend on the type and quality of ingredients used as well as the applied technological process [71,72]. In our research, we used flour from seeds of selected legume species as an additional ingredient in the recipes. Additionally, the bread dough was prepared using a two-phase sourdough method, which is rarely used in industrial wheat bread production. When assessing the overall appearance of the loaf, the panelists paid attention to its shape, the degree of rising, and the appearance of the crust surface. The evaluators awarded the highest scores for these characteristics (8.5 points) to the control bread (CB) (Table 8), which had the most significant rise (Figure 1). The bread with a 10% addition of

GP, YL, or NL (GPB10, YLB10, and NLB10) as well as a 15% addition of YL or NL (YLB15 and NLB15) obtained comparable scores to the control sample. In general, the addition of legume seed flour primarily resulted in a reduction in the degree of rising of the loaf, which was particularly noticeable at the highest level of addition (25%). However, the evaluators had no major concerns regarding the loaves' shapes and the appearance of the crust surface. Therefore, all bread samples received ratings above 5 points on a 9-point hedonic scale for overall appearance, indicating consumer acceptability. The bread was also highly rated in terms of aroma and taste. The control bread received the highest ratings in these aspects (8.6 and 8.7 points, respectively), as it was exceptionally aromatic and had a delicate taste with a slightly perceptible sour note. According to the evaluators, the bread with a 10% addition of GP, YL, or NL (GPB10, YLB10, and NLB10) as well as a 15% addition of GP or NL (GPB15 and NLB15) had comparable aromas to the control sample. Similarly, bread with a 10% addition of GP, YL, or NL (GPB10, YLB10, and NLB10) as well as a 15% addition of GP or NL (GPB15 and NLB15) received scores comparable to the control sample in terms of taste. With a higher proportion of legume seed flour, a characteristic aroma and an aftertaste described as "bean-like" or "pea-like," were noticeable. According to some panelists, the bread with the highest proportion of legume seed flour (25%) had a slightly bitter aftertaste. Based on the scores given for the taste of the bread, the consumer acceptability threshold was set at a level of 15% inclusion of GP and NL and 20% YL. Klupsaite et al. [71] obtained higher scores for the taste and aroma of bread with the addition of lupine sourdough at levels of 3% and 6% compared to the control sample. According to the panelists, this bread was also characterized by a more pronounced acidic taste.

Table 8. Results of sensory evaluation of control and enriched bread samples (9-point hedonic scale).

Sample	Appearance	Smell	Taste	Texture	Color	OA
CB	8.5 ± 0.5 [a]	8.6 ± 1.0 [a]	8.7 ± 0.7 [a]	8.7 ± 0.7 [a]	8.1 ± 0.9 [a]	8.5 ± 0.6 [a]
GPB10	7.5 ± 0.5 [abc]	8.0 ± 0.8 [a]	8.3 ± 0.7 [ab]	8.0 ± 0.5 [ab]	7.7 ± 0.7 [a]	7.9 ± 0.5 [abc]
GPB15	7.0 ± 0.5 [bcd]	7.6 ± 0.7 [a]	7.6 ± 0.7 [ab]	7.7 ± 0.7 [ab]	7.4 ± 0.7 [a]	7.5 ± 0.4 [bc]
GPB20	6.5 ± 0.5 [cde]	5.2 ± 1.4 [h]	4.7 ± 2.0 [de]	4.3 ± 1.3 [cd]	3.8 ± 1.6 [bc]	4.8 ± 1.1 [de]
GPB25	5.1 ± 1.0 [f]	4.8 ± 1.8 [bc]	3.1 ± 1.5 [f]	1.9 ± 1.0 [e]	2.8 ± 1.1 [c]	3.2 ± 0.7 [f]
YLB10	8.3 ± 0.5 [a]	8.6 ± 1.0 [a]	8.2 ± 0.6 [ab]	8.6 ± 0.7 [a]	8.1 ± 0.9 [a]	8.4 ± 0.5 [ab]
YLB15	7.6 ± 0.5 [ab]	8.2 ± 0.9 [a]	7.0 ± 0.7 [bc]	8.4 ± 0.7 [ab]	8.0 ± 0.9 [a]	7.3 ± 0.5 [c]
YLB20	6.5 ± 0.5 [cde]	5.1 ± 1.1 [b]	5.6 ± 1.1 [cd]	5.3 ± 1.3 [c]	5.1 ± 1.3 [b]	5.5 ± 0.7 [d]
YLB25	6.2 ± 1.2 [e]	2.9 ± 1.7 [d]	3.4 ± 1.3 [ef]	2.3 ± 1.1 [e]	3.1 ± 0.7 [c]	3.4 ± 0.7 [f]
NLB10	8.3 ± 0.5 [a]	8.4 ± 0.8 [a]	7.5 ± 0.7 [ab]	8.3 ± 0.9 [ab]	7.5 ± 1.0 [a]	8.2 ± 0.4 [abc]
NLB15	7.5 ± 0.5 [abc]	7.6 ± 1.0 [a]	7.5 ± 0.5 [ab]	7.0 ± 0.9 [b]	6.8 ± 0.8 [a]	7.4 ± 0.5 [d]
NLB20	6.0 ± 0.5 [def]	4.6 ± 1.7 [bcd]	4.2 ± 0.8 [def]	3.9 ± 1.6 [cd]	4.9 ± 1.0 [b]	4.7 ± 0.6 [de]
NLB25	5.6 ± 1.2 [f]	3.6 ± 1.6 [bcd]	3.6 ± 1.2 [ef]	2.9 ± 0.9 [de]	4.2 ± 0.9 [bc]	4.0 ± 0.7 [ef]

CB—control bread; GPB10-GPB25—bread with 10, 15, 20, and 25% of grass pea flour; YLB10-YLB25—bread with 10, 15, 20, and 25% of yellow lupine flour; NLB10-NLB25—bread with 10, 15, 20, and 25% of narrow-leaf lupine flour; OA—overall acceptability. The values designated by the different letters [a–f,h] were significantly different ($p < 0.05$).

In terms of texture, the control bread received the highest rating (8.7 points) and was characterized by a uniform fine-pored structure of the crumb (Figure 2). The bread with a 10% addition of GP, YL, or NL (GPB10, YLB10, and NLB10) as well as a 15% addition of GP or YL (GPB15 and YLB15) obtained comparable scores for this characteristic. As the level of legume seed flour addition increased, the crumb became increasingly compact, and larger pores were also visible in the cross section. Therefore, the breads with a 20% proportion of GP or NL (GPB20 and NLB20) and a 25% proportion of YL (YLB25) were rated below the consumer acceptability threshold in terms of texture. The inclusion of legume seed flours in the recipe affected the color of both the crust and the crumb of the bread. The control bread had a light brown golden crust and a beige-colored crumb. As the proportion of legume seed flours increased, both the color of the crust and the crumb gradually darkened, with the crumb becoming more yellow in color. The consumer acceptability threshold for color was set at 15% for GP and YL and 20% for NL. A similar darkening of the crumb color was also observed by Klupsaite et al. [71] and Bartkiene et al. [58] when using lupine flour as an additive. In summary, the overall sensory evaluation scores indicated that the addition of GP and NL should not exceed 15%, while for YL, its maximum inclusion in the bread recipe could be 20%. On the other hand, Hall and Johnson [18] determined the maximum level of lupine flour addition to wheat bread accepted by consumers to be 10%.

Figure 1. Appearance of obtained bread loaves. CB—control bread; GPB10-GPB25—bread with 10, 15, 20, and 25% of grass pea flour; NLB10-NLB25—bread with 10, 15, 20, and 25% of narrow-leaf lupine flour; YLB10-YLB25—bread with 10, 15, 20, and 25% of yellow lupine flour.

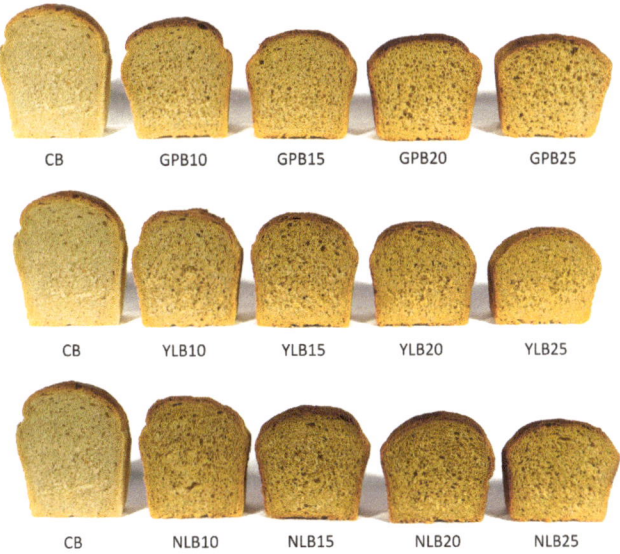

Figure 2. Crumb of obtained bread samples. CB—control bread; GPB10-GPB25—bread with 10, 15, 20, and 25% of grass pea flour; NLB10-NLB25—bread with 10, 15, 20, and 25% of narrow-leaf lupine flour; YLB10-YLB25—bread with 10, 15, 20, and 25% of yellow lupine flour.

4. Conclusions

The partial substitution of wheat flour with legume flour in the analyzed raw materials had several effects. It led to an increase in water absorption, the development time of the dough, and the bread yield. The highest flour water absorption and bread yield were found for bread with yellow lupine flour, whereas the lowest was for the grass pea flour bread. Legume flours positively influenced the bread composition, including higher contents of protein, fiber minerals, and phenolic compounds. These improvements were most pronounced when narrow-leaf lupine flour was added to the wheat flour. Moreover, the lightness of crumb decreased, while redness and yellowness increased as a result of bread enrichment with lupine and grass pea flour. Additionally, all the additives used increased the antioxidant activity of the bread against ABTS and DPPH radicals. However, there were some negative consequences of the bread enrichment as well. The volume of the bread decreased, and the bread crumb became harder. Furthermore, sensory properties like smell, taste, and texture were negatively affected, resulting in reduced consumer acceptance of the bread, especially when the legume raw materials were added in amounts exceeding 15% of the total flour weight.

Author Contributions: Conceptualization, G.C.-P., K.S., J.K., J.B. and D.D.; methodology, G.C.-P., K.S., J.K., J.B. and D.D.; software, G.C.-P., K.S. and D.D.; validation, G.C.-P., K.S. and D.D.; formal analysis, G.C.-P., K.S. and D.D.; investigation, G.C.-P., K.S. and D.D.; resources, G.C.-P., K.S., J.K., J.B. and D.D.; data curation, G.C.-P. and D.D.; writing—original draft preparation, G.C.-P., K.S. and D.D.; writing—review and editing, G.C.-P., K.S. and D.D.; visualization, G.C.-P.; supervision, K.S. and D.D.; project administration, J.K. and J.B.; funding acquisition, J.K. and J.B. All authors have read and agreed to the published version of the manuscript.

Funding: This research was funded by the Ministry of Agriculture and Rural Development under the topic "Research on the optimization of the selection of varieties in organic cultivation of agricultural plants, recommended for commercial field production, with particular emphasis on unfavorable climatic and soil conditions, especially related to water shortage, Determination of good practices of protection against pests in these crops, with particular emphasis on drought. Evaluation of the usefulness of seeds of selected leguminous plant species to improve the quality of bread" (Project No. DEJ.re.027.5202/1).

Institutional Review Board Statement: Not applicable.

Informed Consent Statement: Informed consent was obtained from all subjects involved in the study.

Data Availability Statement: The data presented in this study are available upon request from the corresponding author.

Acknowledgments: Research for this publication was conducted using research equipment purchased as part of the "Food and Nutrition Centre—modernisation of the WULS campus to create a Food and Nutrition Research and Development Centre (CZiZ)" co-financed by the European Union from the European Regional Development Fund under the Regional Operational Programme of the Mazowieckie Voivodeship for 2014–2020 (Project No. RPMA.01.01.00-14-8276/17).

Conflicts of Interest: The authors declare no conflict of interest.

References

1. López, E.P.; Goldner, M.C. Influence of storage time for the acceptability of bread formulated with lupine protein isolate and added brea gum. *LWT—Food Sci. Technol.* **2015**, *64*, 1171–1178. [CrossRef]
2. Cacak-Pietrzak, G.; Dziki, D.; Gawlik-Dziki, U.; Sułek, A.; Wójcik, M.; Krajewska, A. Dandelion Flowers as an Additive to Wheat Bread: Physical Properties of Dough and Bread Quality. *Appl. Sci.* **2023**, *13*, 477. [CrossRef]
3. Shewry, P.R.; Hey, S.J. The contribution of wheat to human diet and health. *Food Energy Secur.* **2015**, *4*, 178–202. [CrossRef]
4. Villarino, C.B.J.; Jayasena, V.; Coorey, R.; Chakrabarti-Bell, S.; Johnson, S. Nutritional, Health, and Technological Functionality of Lupin Flour Additionto Bread and Other Baked Products: Benefits and Challenges. *Crit. Rev. Food Sci. Nutr.* **2016**, *56*, 835–857. [CrossRef] [PubMed]
5. Rawat, M.; Varshney, A.; Rai, M.; Chikara, A.; Pohty, A.L.; Joshi, A.; Binjola, A.; Singh, C.P.; Rawat, K.; Rather, M.A.; et al. A comprehensive review on nutraceutical potential of underutilized cereals and cereal-based products. *J. Agric. Food Res.* **2023**, *12*, 100619. [CrossRef]

6. Sułek, A.; Cacak-Pietrzak, G.; Różewicz, M.; Nieróbca, A.; Grabiński, J.; Studnicki, M.; Sujka, K.; Dziki, D. Effect of Production Technology Intensity on the Grain Yield, Protein Content and Amino Acid Profile in Common and Durum Wheat Grain. *Plants* **2023**, *12*, 364. [CrossRef]
7. Cacak-Pietrzak, G.; Różyło, R.; Dziki, D.; Gawlik-Dziki, U.; Sułek, A.; Biernacka, B. *Cistus incanus* L. as an Innovative Functional Additive to Wheat Bread. *Foods* **2019**, *8*, 349. [CrossRef]
8. Cacak-Pietrzak, G.; Dziki, D.; Gawlik-Dziki, U.; Sułek, A.; Kalisz, S.; Sujka, K. Effect of the Addition of Dried Dandelion Roots (*Taraxacum officinale* F. H. Wigg.) on Wheat Dough and Bread Properties. *Molecules* **2021**, *26*, 7564. [CrossRef]
9. Dziki, D.; Cacak-Pietrzak, G.; Hassonn, W.H.; Gawlik-Dziki, U.; Sułek, A.; Różyło, R.; Suger, D. The fruit of sumac (*Rhus coriaria* L.) as a functional additive and salt replacement to wheat bread. *LWT—Food Sci. Technol.* **2021**, *136*, 110346. [CrossRef]
10. Wójcik, M.; Różyło, R.; Łysiak, G.; Kulig, R.; Cacak-Pietrzak, G. Textural and sensory properties of wheat bread fortified with nettle (*Urtica dioica* L.) produced by scalded flour method. *J. Food Process. Preserv.* **2021**, *45*, e15851. [CrossRef]
11. Tolve, R.; Simonato, B.; Rainero, G.; Bianchi, F.; Rizzi, C.; Cervini, M.; Giuberti, G. Wheat bread fortification by grape pomace powder: Nutritional, technological, antioxidant, and sensory properties. *Foods* **2021**, *10*, 75. [CrossRef]
12. Cantero, L.; Salmerón, J.; Miranda, J.; Larretxi, I.; Fernández-Gil, M.d.P.; Bustamante, M.Á.; Matias, S.; Navarro, V.; Simón, E.; Martínez, O. Performance of Apple Pomace for Gluten-Free Bread Manufacture: Effect on Physicochemical Characteristics and Nutritional Value. *Appl. Sci.* **2022**, *12*, 5934. [CrossRef]
13. Valková, V.; Ďúranová, H.; Havrlentová, M.; Ivanišová, E.; Mezey, J.; Tóthová, Z.; Gabríny, L.; Kačániová, M. Selected Physico-Chemical, Nutritional, Antioxidant and Sensory Properties of Wheat Bread Supplemented with Apple Pomace Powder as a By-Product from Juice Production. *Plants* **2022**, *11*, 1256. [CrossRef]
14. Cacak-Pietrzak, G.; Dziki, D.; Gawlik-Dziki, U.; Parol-Nadłonek, N.; Kalisz, S.; Krajewska, A.; Stępniewska, S. Wheat Bread Enriched with Black Chokeberry (*Aronia melanocarpa* L.) Pomace: Physicochemical Properties and Sensory Evaluation. *Appl. Sci.* **2023**, *13*, 6936. [CrossRef]
15. Stanciu, I.; Ungureanu, E.L.; Popa, E.E.; Geicu-Cristea, M.; Draghici, M.; Mitelut, A.C.; Mustatea, G.; Popa, M.E. The Experimental Development of Bread with Enriched Nutritional Properties Using Organic Sea Buckthorn Pomace. *Appl. Sci.* **2023**, *13*, 6513. [CrossRef]
16. Derkanosova, N.M.; Stakhurlova, A.A.; Pshenichnaya, I.A.; Ponomareva, I.N.; Peregonchaya, O.V.; Sokolova, S.A. Amaranth as a bread enriching ingredient. *Foods Raw Mater.* **2020**, *8*, 223–231. [CrossRef]
17. Cotovanu, I.; Ungureanu-Iuga, M.; Mironeasa, S. Investigation of Quinoa Seeds Fractions and Their Application in Wheat Bread Production. *Plants* **2021**, *10*, 2150. [CrossRef] [PubMed]
18. Hall, R.S.; Johnson, S.K. Sensory acceptability of foods containing Australian sweet lupin (*Lupinus angustifolius*) flour. *J. Food Sci.* **2004**, *69*, 92–97. [CrossRef]
19. Villarino, C.B.J.; Jayasena, V.; Coorey, R.; Chakrabarti-Bell, S.; Johnson, S. Optimization of formulation and process of Australian sweet lupin (ASL)—Wheat bread. *LWT—Food Sci. Technol.* **2015**, *61*, 359–367. [CrossRef]
20. Karamać, M.; Orak, H.H.; Amarowicz, R.; Orak, A.; Piekoszewski, W. Phenolic contents and antioxidant capacities of wild and cultivated white lupin (*Lupinus albus* L.) seeds. *Food Chem.* **2018**, *258*, 1–7. [CrossRef] [PubMed]
21. Carboni, D.A.; Salinas, V.M.; Puppo, C.M. Production of legume-wheat dough of optimum quality for breadmaking: Essential analyses required. *Curr. Opin. Food Sci.* **2023**, *49*, 100970. [CrossRef]
22. Bessada, S.M.F.; Barreira, J.C.M.; Oliveira, M.B.P.P. Pulses and food security: Dietary protein, digestibility, bioactive and functional properties. *Trends Food Sci. Technol.* **2019**, *93*, 53–68. [CrossRef]
23. FAOSTAT. Available online: https://www.fao.org/faostat/en/#data/QCL (accessed on 24 May 2023).
24. Roland, W.S.U.; Pouvreau, L.; Curran, J.; Van De Velde, F.; De Kok, P.M.T. Flavor aspects of pulse ingredients. *Cereal Chem.* **2017**, *94*, 58–65. [CrossRef]
25. Rajhi, I.; Baccouri, B.; Rajhi, F.; Mhadhbi, H.; Flamini, G. Monitoring the volatile compounds status of whole seeds and flours of legume cultivars. *Food Biosci.* **2021**, *41*, 101105. [CrossRef]
26. Tas, A.A.; Shah, A.U. The replacement of cereals by legumes in extruded snack foods: Science, technology and challenges. *Trends Food Sci. Technol.* **2021**, *116*, 701–711. [CrossRef]
27. Das, G.; Sharma, A.; Sarkar, P.K. Conventional and emerging processing techniques for the post-harvest reduction of antinutrients in edible legumes. *Appl. Food Res.* **2022**, *2*, 100112. [CrossRef]
28. Ulrike, M. Are legumes different? Origins and consequences of evolving nitrogen fixing symbioses. *J. Plant Physiol.* **2022**, *276*, 153765. [CrossRef]
29. Ogbole, O.O.; Akin-Ajani, O.D.; Ajala, T.O.; Ogunniyi, Q.A.; Fettke, J.; Odeku, O.A. Nutritional and pharmacological potentials of orphan legumes: Subfamily faboideae. *Heliyon* **2023**, *9*, e15493. [CrossRef]
30. Kalogeropoulos, N.; Chiou, A.; Ioannou, M.; Karathanos, V.T.; Hassapidou, M.; Andrikopoulos, N.K. Nutritional evaluation and bioactive microconstituents (phytosterols, tocopherols, polyphenols, triterpenic acids) in cooked dry legumes usually consumed in the Mediterranean countries. *Food Chem.* **2010**, *121*, 682–690. [CrossRef]
31. Rebello, C.J.; Greenway, F.L.; Finley, J.W. Whole grains and pulses: A comparison of the nutritional and health benefits. *J. Agric. Food Chem.* **2014**, *62*, 7029–7049. [CrossRef] [PubMed]
32. Temba, M.C.; Njobeh, P.B.; Adebo, O.A.; Olugbile, A.O.; Kayitesi, E. The role of compositing cereals with legumes to alleviate protein energy malnutrition in Africa. *Int. J. Food Sci. Technol.* **2016**, *51*, 543–554. [CrossRef]

33. Li, L.; Yuan, T.Z.; Setia, R.; Raja, R.B.; Zhang, B.; Ai, Y. Characteristics of pea, lentil and faba bean starches isolated from air-classified flours in comparison with commercial starches. *Food Chem.* **2019**, *276*, 599–607. [CrossRef] [PubMed]
34. Goldstein, N.; Reifen, R. The potential of legume-derived proteins in the food industry. *Grain Oil Sci. Technol.* **2022**, *5*, 167–178. [CrossRef]
35. de Almeida Costa, G.E.; da Silva Queiroz-Monici, K.; Reis, S.M.P.M.; de Oliveira, A.C. Chemical composition, dietary fibre and resistant starch contents of raw and cooked pea, common bean, chickpea and lentil legumes. *Food Chem.* **2006**, *94*, 327–330. [CrossRef]
36. Oyeyinka, A.S.; Singh, S.; Amonsou, E.O. A review on structural, digestibility and physicochemical properties of legume starch-lipid complexes. *Food Chem.* **2021**, *349*, 129165. [CrossRef]
37. Hutchins, A.M.; Winham, D.M.; Thompson, S.V. Phaseolus beans: Impact on glycaemic response and chronic disease risk in human subjects. *Br. J. Nutr.* **2012**, *108*, S52–S65. [CrossRef]
38. Samtiya, M.; Aluko, R.E.; Dhewa, T. Plant food anti-nutritional factors and their reduction strategies: An overview. *Food Prod. Process. Nutr.* **2020**, *2*, 6. [CrossRef]
39. Jenkins, D.J.; Kendall, C.W.; Augustin, L.S.; Mitchell, S.; Sahye-Pudaruth, S.; Mejia, S.B.; Chiavaroli, L.; Mirrahimi, A.; Ireland, C.; Bashyam, B.; et al. Effect of legumes as part of a low glycemic index diet on glycemic control and cardiovascular risk factors in type 2 diabetes mellitus: A randomized controlled trial. *Arch. Intern. Med.* **2012**, *172*, 1653–1660. [CrossRef]
40. Mudryj, A.N.; Yu, N.; Aukema, H.M. Nutritional and health benefits of pulses. *Appl. Physiol. Nutr. Metab.* **2014**, *39*, 1197–1204. [CrossRef]
41. Pastor-Cavada, E.; Juan, R.; Pastor, J.E.; Alaiz, M.; Vioque, J. Antioxidant activity of seed polyphenols in fifteen wild Lathyrus species from South Spain. *LWT—Food Sci. Technol.* **2009**, *42*, 705–709. [CrossRef]
42. Deshpande, S.S.; Campbell, C.G. Genotype variation in BOAA, condensed tannins, phenolics and enzyme-inhibitors of grass pea (*Lathyrus sativus*). *Can. J. Plant Sci.* **1992**, *72*, 1037–1047. [CrossRef]
43. Wang, X.F.; Warkentin, T.D.; Briggs, C.J.; Oomah, B.D.; Campbell, C.G.; Woods, S. Total phenolics and condensed tannins in field pea (*Pisum sativum* L.) and grass pea (*Lathyrus sativus* L.). *Euphytica* **1998**, *101*, 97–102. [CrossRef]
44. Chavan, U.D.; Amarowicz, R.; Shahidi, F. Antioxidant activity of phenolic fractions of beach pea (*Lathyrus maritimus* L.). *J. Food Lipids* **1999**, *6*, 1–11. [CrossRef]
45. Chavan, U.D.; McKenzie, D.B.; Amarowicz, R.; Shahidi, F. Phytochemical components of beach pea (*Lathyrus maritimus* L.). *Food Chem.* **2003**, *81*, 61–71. [CrossRef]
46. Shahidi, F.; Chavan, U.D.; Naczk, M.; Amarowicz, R. Nutrient distribution and phenolic antioxidants in air-classified fractions of beach pea (*Lathyrus maritimus* L.). *J. Agric. Food Chem.* **2001**, *49*, 926–933. [CrossRef]
47. Dixit, G.P.; Parihar, A.K.; Abhishek Bohra, A.; Singh, N.P. Achievements and prospects of grass pea (*Lathyrus sativus* L.) improvement for sustainable food production. *Crop J.* **2006**, *4*, 407–416. [CrossRef]
48. Łabuda, S.; Chwil, S. Rhythm of biomass and macroelements accumulation in grass pea (*Lathyrus sativus* L.). *Rocz. Glebozn.* **1996**, *47*, 79–87. (In Polish)
49. Rao, S.L. A look at the brighter facets of β-N-oxalyl-L-α,β-diaminopropionic acid, homoarginine and the grass pea. *Food Chem. Toxicol.* **2011**, *49*, 620–622. [CrossRef]
50. Singh, S.S.; Rao, S.L.N. Lessons from neurolathyrism: A disease of the past & the future of *Lathyrus sativus* (Khesari dal). *Indian J. Med. Res.* **2013**, *138*, 32–37.
51. Khandare, A.L.; Babu, J.J.; Ankulu, M.; Aparna, N.; Shirfule, A.; Rao, G.S. Grass pea consumption & present scenario of neurolathyrism in Maharashtra state of India. *Indian J. Med. Res.* **2014**, *140*, 96–101. [PubMed]
52. Cowling, W.A.; Buirchell, B.J.; Tapia, M.E. Lupin. *Promoting the Conservation and Use of Underutilized and Neglected Crops 23*; Institute of Plant Genetics and Crop Plant Research, Gatersleben/International Plant Genetic Resources Institute: Rome, Italy, 1998; pp. 1–100.
53. Gladstones, J.S. Distribution, origin, taxonomy, history and importance. In *Lupins as Crop Plants: Biology, Production and Utilisation*; Gladstones, J.S., Atkins, C.A., Hamblin, J., Eds.; CAB International: Wallingford, UK, 1998; pp. 1–37.
54. Lampart-Szczapa, E.; Korczak, J.; Nogala-Kalucka, M.; Zawirska-Wojtasiak, R. Antioxidant properties of lupin seed products. *Food Chem.* **2003**, *83*, 279–285. [CrossRef]
55. Khan, M.K.; Karnpanit, W.; Nasar-Abbas, S.M.; Zill-e-Huma; Jayasena, V. Phytochemical composition and bioactivities of lupin: A review. *Int. J. Food Sci. Technol.* **2015**, *50*, 2004–2012. [CrossRef]
56. Arnoldi, A.; Boschin, G.; Zanoni, C.; Lammi, C. The health benefits of sweet lupin seed flours and isolated proteins. *J. Funct. Foods* **2015**, *18*, 550–563. [CrossRef]
57. Starzyńska-Janiszewska, A.; Stodolak, B.; Jamróz, M. Antioxidant properties of extracts from fermented and cooked seeds of Polish cultivars of *Lathyrus sativus*. *Food Chem.* **2008**, *109*, 285–292. [CrossRef] [PubMed]
58. Bartkiene, E.; Juodeikiene, G.; Vidmantiene, D.; Viskelis, P.; Urbonaviciene, D. Nutritional and quality aspects of wheat sourdough bread using *L. luteus* and *L. angustifolius* flours fermented by *Pediococcus acidilactici*. *Int. J. Food Sci. Technol.* **2011**, *46*, 1724–1733. [CrossRef]
59. AACC. *American Association of Cereal Chemistry Approved Methods*, 10th ed.; AACC: St. Paul, MN, USA, 2000; Available online: http://methods.aaccnet.org/toc.aspx (accessed on 10 May 2023).

60. Romankiewicz, D.; Hassoon, W.H.; Cacak-Pietrzak, G.; Sobczyk, M.; Wirkowska-Wojdyła, M.; Ceglińska, A.; Dziki, D. The effect of chia seeds (*Salvia hispanica* L.) addition on quality and nutritional value of wheat bread. *J. Food Qual.* **2017**, *2017*, 7352631. [CrossRef]
61. Różyło, R.; Wójcik, M.; Dziki, D.; Biernacka, B.; Cacak-Pietrzak, G.; Gawłowski, S.; Zdybel, A. Freeze-dried elderberry and chokeberry as natural colorants for gluten-free wafer sheets. *Int. Agrophys.* **2018**, *33*, 217–225. [CrossRef]
62. Brand-Williams, W.; Cuvelier, E.; Berset, C. Use of a free radical method to evaluate antioxidant activity. *LWT—Food Sci. Technol.* **1995**, *28*, 25–30. [CrossRef]
63. Re, R.; Pellegrini, N.; Proteggente, A.; Pannala, A.; Yang, M.; Rice-Evans, C. Antioxidant activity applying an improved ABTS radical cation decolorization assay. *Free Radic. Biol. Med.* **1999**, *26*, 1231–1237. [CrossRef] [PubMed]
64. García-Gómez, B.; Fernández-Canto, N.; Vázquez-Odériz, M.L.; Quiroga-García, M.; Muñoz-Ferreiro, N.; Romero-Rodríguez, M.Á. Sensory descriptive analysis and hedonic consumer test for Galician type breads. *Food Control* **2022**, *134*, 108765. [CrossRef]
65. Dziki, D.; Cacak-Pietrzak, G.; Gawlik-Dziki, U.; Sułek, A.; Kocira, S.; Biernacka, B. Effect of Moldavian dragonhead (*Dracocephalum moldavica* L.) leaves on the baking properties of wheat flour and quality of bread. *CyTA—J. Food* **2019**, *17*, 536–543. [CrossRef]
66. Feledyn-Szewczyk, B.; Cacak-Pietrzak, G.; Lenc, L.; Gromadzka, K.; Dziki, D. Milling and Baking Quality of Spring Wheat (*Triticum aestivum* L.) from Organic Farming. *Agriculture* **2021**, *11*, 765. [CrossRef]
67. Rehman, S.; Alistair Paterson, A.; Hussain, S.; Murtaza, M.A.; Mehmood, S. Influence of partial substitution of wheat flour with vetch (*Lathyrus sativus* L.) flour on quality characteristics of doughnuts. *LWT—Food Sci. Technol.* **2007**, *40*, 73–82. [CrossRef]
68. Wandersleben, T.; Morales, E.; Burgos-Díaz, C.; Barahona, T.; Labra, E.; Rubilar, M.; Salvo-Garrido, H. Enhancement of functional and nutritional properties of bread using a mix of natural ingredients from novel varieties of flaxseed and lupine. *LWT—Food Sci. Technol.* **2018**, *91*, 48–54. [CrossRef]
69. Jaskulska, I.; Jaskulski, D.; Gałęzewski, L.; Knapowski, T.; Kozera, W.; Wacławowicz, R. Mineral Composition and Baking Value of the Winter Wheat Grain under Varied Environmental and Agronomic Conditions. *J. Chem.* **2018**, *2018*, 5013825. [CrossRef]
70. Steffolani, E.; Martinez, M.M.; León, A.E.; Gómez, M. Effect of pre-hydration of chia (*Salvia hispanica* L.) seed and flour on the quality of wheat flour breads. *LWT—Food Sci. Technol.* **2015**, *61*, 401–406. [CrossRef]
71. Klupsaite, D.; Juodeikiene, G.; Zadeike, D.; Bartkiene, E.; Maknickiene, Z.; Liutkute, G. The influence of lactic acid fermentation on functional properties of narrow-leaved lupine protein as functional additive for higher value wheat bread. *LWT—Food Sci. Technol.* **2017**, *75*, 180–186. [CrossRef]
72. Cappelli, A.; Lupori, L.; Cini, E. Baking technology: A systematic review of machines and plants and their effect on final products, including improvement strategies. *Trends Food Sci. Technol.* **2021**, *115*, 275–284. [CrossRef]

Disclaimer/Publisher's Note: The statements, opinions and data contained in all publications are solely those of the individual author(s) and contributor(s) and not of MDPI and/or the editor(s). MDPI and/or the editor(s) disclaim responsibility for any injury to people or property resulting from any ideas, methods, instructions or products referred to in the content.

Article

Effect of Type of Flour and Microalgae (*Chlorella vulgaris*) on the Rheological, Microstructural, Textural, and Sensory Properties of Vegan Muffins

Agata Marzec *, Patrycja Kramarczuk, Hanna Kowalska and Jolanta Kowalska

Department of Food Engineering and Process Management, Institute of Food Sciences, Warsaw University of Life Sciences—SGGW, 02-787 Warsaw, Poland; s173936@sggw.edu.pl (P.K.); hanna_kowalska@sggw.edu.pl (H.K.); jolanta_kowalska@sggw.edu.pl (J.K.)
* Correspondence: agata_marzec@sggw.edu.pl; Tel.: +48-22-593-75-65; Fax: +48-22-593-75-76

Abstract: The aim of this study was to develop a recipe for vegan muffins using wheat flour (100%) and a blend of whole-grain spelt flour (50%) and wheat flour (50%) enriched with microalgae (0, 0.5, 1.0, and 1.5% (g/100 g flour)). Replacing wheat flour with whole-grain spelt flour and adding microalgae while eliminating egg white from a recipe can affect the rheological properties of the dough and also the microstructure and texture of the muffins. The study analyzed the effects of the type of flour and the addition of microalgae on the rheological properties of the raw dough, measured through the oscillatory method, as well as the texture and microstructure, determined via X-ray microtomography. Additionally, the sensorial quality of the muffins was analyzed. The use of spelt flour in the formulation of muffins affected the rheological properties of the dough irrespective of the addition of microalgae. The dough made with spelt flour exhibited higher viscosity (consistency coefficient (K) was 74.7 Pa·s^n), but it was more cohesive and less springy compared to the dough made with wheat flour alone, which had a K = 58.3 Pa·s^n. Incorporating a mixture of spelt and wheat flour along with a 1.5% addition of microalgae made the dough more viscous (K = 118.6 Pa·s^n), leading to a fine, porous microstructure (porosity was 69.7%) and a crumbly texture (hardness was 52.2 N) in the muffins. On the other hand, the wheat flour dough with 1.5% microalgae had a consistency coefficient of 69.3 Pa·s^n, while the muffin porosity was 67.1% and the hardness 61.8 N. The microstructure had a strong effect on the texture of the muffin crumb. The new wheat flour products with microalgae exhibited a higher proportion of closed pores in their microstructure, whereas samples containing spelt flour and microalgae showed the opposite trend, with more open pores. The greatest difference in closed pores was observed with the addition of 1.5% of microalgae (33.4% in wheat muffins and 26.9% in spelled muffins). The presence of closed porosity contributed to the harder and less consistent texture observed in the muffins. However, despite the instrumental evaluation results, all the new products were accepted by consumers in terms of appearance, taste, and overall quality.

Keywords: microalgae; texture; color; microtomography; spelt flour; wheat flour

Citation: Marzec, A.; Kramarczuk, P.; Kowalska, H.; Kowalska, J. Effect of Type of Flour and Microalgae (*Chlorella vulgaris*) on the Rheological, Microstructural, Textural, and Sensory Properties of Vegan Muffins. *Appl. Sci.* **2023**, *13*, 7632. https://doi.org/10.3390/app13137632

Academic Editors: Urszula Pankiewicz, Piotr Zarzycki, Anna Wirkijowska and Agata Blicharz-Kania

Received: 9 June 2023
Revised: 23 June 2023
Accepted: 26 June 2023
Published: 28 June 2023

Copyright: © 2023 by the authors. Licensee MDPI, Basel, Switzerland. This article is an open access article distributed under the terms and conditions of the Creative Commons Attribution (CC BY) license (https://creativecommons.org/licenses/by/4.0/).

1. Introduction

By 2050, according to the UN, the world's population is projected to have risen from 7 to 9.7 billion. To sustain this growing population, food production must be increased by 60% while also shaping awareness about nutrition, promoting balanced and healthy diets. Scientists are actively seeking alternatives to full-fledged animal protein that can be produced efficiently, quickly, and cost-effectively while placing a low burden on the planet [1].

Microalgae have gained recognition as a "superfood" and hold the potential to become a valuable source of supermaterials in the future, enhancing both the nutritional and functional quality of food [2–5]. Gong et al. [5], based on Spirulina cells, developed a hybrid forming strategy for mass production of drugs and explored their therapeutic efficacy for cancer cells. The commonly used microalgae varieties are Spirulina and Chlorella. The annual production is about 7500 tons of dry biomass of Spirulina and Chlorella microalgae (5000 and 2500 tons, respectively) [5]. Both Spirulina (arthrospira) and Chlorella (vulgaris) exhibit high contents of complete protein (more than 50% dry weight), encompassing all essential amino acids, including endogenous and exogenous ones, pigments, long chain polyunsaturated fatty acids, sterols, and other compounds [6]. They also contain vitamins A, E, C, and B-group vitamins. This protein is characterized by a high biological value [3,6]. *Chlorella vulgaris* green is characterized by a relatively low fat content (5%) and a high total mineral content of 24% and is rich in calcium (4.7%) as well as in manganese and iron [2]. The literature describes the effects of adding microalgae biomass, such as Spirulina arthrospira, *Chlorella vulgaris*, *Tetraselmis suecica*, and *Phaeodactylum tricornutum*, at 2 and 6% (g/100 g) on the physicochemical and sensory properties and antioxidant activity of cakes and the in vitro digestibility of microalgae biomass and cakes [7,8]. Microalgae biomass has also been used as an alternative ingredient in snacks [9,10], pasta [11], and bread [12].

Since microalgae belong to the plant kingdom, they can be consumed by people following a vegan diet. Proteins are an important nutrient, and in a vegan diet, it is necessary to ensure the supply of complete proteins and B vitamins, especially B_{12} [13]. Scientific articles previously claimed that microalgae are the only plant-based source of vitamin B_{12}. However, about 64% of the vitamin B_{12} in Spirulina arthrospira algae biomass consists of inactive analogs that cannot be absorbed by humans. In contrast, research by Merchant et al. [13] suggests that *Chlorella* sp. algae contain a form of vitamin B_{12} that is assimilable by humans, making them potentially the only plant source. Furthermore, bioactive constituents found in algae exhibit antibacterial, antiviral, anticancer, anti-inflammatory, analgesic, and antioxidant properties [6].

Muffins are highly favored by consumers due to their versatility and the ease with which they can be modified to create a wide variety of muffin flavors, from sweet to savory. They can also be a very good carrier of nutritional or health-promoting ingredients. Unlike many other snack products, muffins possess a notable nutritional value, which contributes to their popularity. However, it is important to remember that muffin dough is a complex mixture comprising interacting ingredients such as sugar, fat, flour, eggs, and baking powder. Additional common ingredients include emulsifiers, preservatives, and milk powder [14–17]. Typically, muffins exhibit a porous structure and significant volume. This structure is achieved by incorporating foam stabilizers, such as eggs, egg whites, and—to a lesser extent—milk proteins, which slow down the coalescence of air bubbles. Fats and oils are used to create a moist texture and prevent a dry mouthfeel [14,15]. When preparing vegan muffins, ingredients like flour, sugar, oil, vegetable beverage, raising agents, and salt can be used as substitutes [17].

Wheat (*Triticum aestivum* L.) grains are rich in valuable nutrients of carbohydrates, protein, dietary fiber, and fat as well as minerals (including P, K, Ca, and Mg), B vitamins, vitamin E, and several antioxidant compounds (such as phenolic acids and carotenoids) [18].

Replacing wheat flour in baked goods poses a significant technological challenge due to the essential role of gluten, a structural protein that contributes to the appearance and crumb structure of many baked goods. The gluten matrix also plays a crucial role in determining the rheological characteristics of dough [19].

Spelt (*Triticum aestivum* var. *spelta*) is an ancient subspecies of common wheat that possesses slightly different technological properties compared to common wheat. Spelt is characterized by a higher nutrient content. It contains more protein with a more favorable amino acid composition than common wheat, including increased levels of essential amino acids, such as lysine, leucine, and isoleucine. Spelt also exhibits higher digestibility. Additionally, it contains a higher proportion of total fat, including unsaturated fatty acids such as oleic and linoleic acid. Spelt grain has a higher concentration of fat-soluble and B vitamins compared to common wheat. The abundant presence of total ash in spelt grain indicates a rich mineral content. Iron, zinc, copper, magnesium, potassium, selenium, and other minerals have been found to be more abundant in spelt grain compared to common wheat [20,21]. Wheat and cereals, including spelt, are the most important sources of dietary fiber in the human diet. The main components of dietary fiber in spelt is arabinoxylan [21]. Sinkovič et al. [21] showed that the total arabinoxylan content in spelt flour ranged from 11.4–16.0%, and that in whole-meal spelt flour ranged from 29.9–37.3%. The higher fiber content of spelt is expected to have an adverse effect on dough rheology. The compounds that make up dietary fiber have different binding capacities for water [22]. From a technological standpoint, processing spelt dough can be challenging due to its softness and stickiness after kneading [19].

Rheological, structural, and textural problems are commonly observed in bakery products that do not contain animal-derived raw materials, such as eggs and milk. Therefore, there is a continuous search for additives that can enhance the nutritional value of vegan products while providing them with the right structure, texture, and sensory characteristics. Enriching raw materials often have to be limited, as they significantly degrade the quality of the dough and the microstructure and texture of the final product. Our study may be important in expanding knowledge regarding dough rheological properties, color, microstructure, and texture of vegan muffins. To the best of our knowledge, the 3D microstructure of such products and its impact on texture is not yet described in the literature. The aim of this study was to evaluate the effect of the type of flour and the addition of microalgae on the rheologic properties of the dough, as well as on the microstructure, texture, and sensorial evaluation of muffins made without animal raw materials.

2. Materials and Methods

2.1. Materials

The study material included raw doughs of vegan muffins prepared using wheat flour type 450 (100%—referred to as sample CW) and a blend of whole-grain spelt flour type 2000 (50%) and wheat type 450 (50%) (referred to as sample SW). Microalgae C. vulgaris powder (MyVita, Proness, Legnica, Poland) was added to the dough at three different concentrations: 0.5, 1.0, and 1.5% (g/100 g flour). In samples marked CW, CWa0.5, CWa1.0, and CWa1.5, the base was wheat flour, while in SW, SWa0.5, SWa1.0, and SWa1.5, the base was a blend of whole-grain spelt flour (50%) and wheat flour (50%). The amounts of all ingredients in the dough recipe were expressed in % (g/100 g flour) and were the same in all samples: 93.3% of soy beverage (OraSi, Unigra S. r. I., Poland), 44.4% of sucrose (White Sugar, Sudzucker, Wrocław, Poland), 28.9% of rapeseed oil (Wielkopolski, EOL Poland), 1.8% of baking powder (sodium bicarbonate, Dr. Oetker, Bielefeld, Germany), 0.5% of soy lecithin (Młyn Oliwski, Gdańsk, Poland), and 0.4% iodized table salt (Cenos Sp. zo.o., Września, Poland). For the preparation of muffin dough, flours from domestic manufacturers were used: wheat flour type 450 (Lubella, Lublin, Poland) and whole-grain spelt flour type 2000 (Młyn Niedźwiady, Niedźwiady, Poland).

The wheat flour type 450 provided by the manufacturer contained 74 g/100 g of carbohydrates, 10 g/100 g of protein, 3.1 g/100 g of fiber, 1.1 g/100 g of fat, and 0.03 g/100 g of salt.

The whole-grain spelt flour type 2000 contained 59 g/100 g of carbohydrates, 13 g/100 g of protein, 13 g/100 g of fiber, 2.3 g/100 g of fat, and <0.01 g/100 g of salt.

Wheat flour type 450 contained water 14 g/100 g and was re-dried to have the same water content as whole-grain spelt flour. The water content was determined gravimetrically by drying the flour at 105 °C. Water contents of the wheat and whole-grain spelt flours were 10 ± 1.1 g/100 g and 11 ± 0.6 g/100 g, respectively, and were not statistically significantly different.

2.2. Dough Preparation and Baking

The dough was prepared using a Kitchen Aid Artisan 5 robot (USA) with the mixing speed set to "1" as indicated on the machine's scale. Precise measurements were taken using an analytical balance model PS 600/C/2 (Radwag, Poland).

The first step involved mixing the dry ingredients flour, sugar, baking powder, soy lecithin, salt, and microalgae for 1.5 min. Next, the liquid ingredients, namely soy beverage and rapeseed oil, were mixed for an additional 1.5 min. Then, the liquid ingredients were combined with the solid ingredients and mixed for another 1.5 min. Throughout the dough preparation process, the laboratory maintained a temperature of 21 °C. The dough was divided into 50 g portions and placed in paper molds (La Cucina, Wan Chai, Hong Kong), which were then arranged in a metal mold designed for baking muffins. Baking took place in an electric oven (Amica, Poland) at a temperature of 180 °C for 25 min. After baking, the muffins were cooled to room temperature, wrapped in polyethylene film, and stored at 21 °C for 24 h to allow the moisture content to equalize.

2.3. Rheological Properties of Dough

The rheological properties of the dough were tested using a Haake Mars 40 oscillating rheometer (Thermo Scientific, Karlsruhe, Germany). A plate-to-plate measuring system with a diameter of 35 mm (equipped with serrations to prevent spillage) and a measuring gap of 1 mm were employed. Dough samples were tested immediately after preparation to minimize changes in the dough's characteristics. Duplicate tests were conducted for each type of dough.

Constant shear tests were carried out in controlled rate mode, with a linearly increasing shear rate ranging from 1 to 100/s. The resulting experimental flow curves, depicting shear stress vs. shear rate, were compared using the Ostwald–de Waele equation: $\eta = K\gamma^{n-1}$ (where η represents the apparent viscosity, K is the consistency coefficient (Pa·s^n), γ denotes the shear rate (s^{-1}), and n signifies the flow rate. For shear-thinning fluids, n < 1, while for Newtonian fluids, n = 1 [14,15].

Two different dynamic rheological oscillation tests were conducted. The first was an amplitude sweep, in which the strain was varied from 0.1 to 100% to identify the linear viscoelastic region of the dough. The second test was a frequency sweep, which involved varying the frequency from 0.1 to 10 Hz while maintaining a constant strain of 1% at a temperature of 20 °C.

The mechanical spectra of the tested doughs were determined, and the changes in elastic moduli (G'), viscous moduli (G''), and loss angle tan(δ) were determined. These values were evaluated across an oscillation frequency range spanning from 0.1 to 100 Hz.

2.4. Water Content and Activity, Muffin Crumb Color

The muffins were cut in half, and from the center, pieces of crumb were taken to determine the water content and water activity.

The water content of the muffin samples was determined by measuring the weight loss during drying at 105 °C for 3 h until a constant weight was achieved.

The water activity of the muffins was tested using an Acqualab instrument (DECAGON DEVICES. Inc., Pullman, WA, USA).

To evaluate the crumb color of the muffins, they were cut transversely at a height of 2.5 cm. The color measurements were conducted using a CR-300 colorimeter (Konica Minolta, Japan) based on the CIELab color system. The color parameters were determined by averaging the results from 10 replicates. The obtained color parameters were then used to calculate the color chroma, $C^* = ((a^*)^2 + (b^*)^2)^{0.5}$, and hue angle, $h_{ab} = \arctan(b^*/a^*)$, where C^* is the chroma, a^* is the contribution of red color, b^* is the contribution of yellow color, and h_{ab} is the hue.

2.5. 2D and 3D Microstructure Examination of Muffin Crumb

The microstructure of the muffin was measured using a SkyScan 1272 microtomograph, specifically a micro-CT system (Brucker MicroCT, Kontich, Belgium). The scan was performed on specimens measuring 25 × 25 × 25 mm, and the scanning parameters and processing methods described in the literature [23] were followed. The resulting images had a pixel size of 20 μm.

2.6. Muffin Crumb Texture Examination

The textural properties of the muffins were tested using a TA-T2i Texture Analyser (Stable Micro System, Godalming, UK). The muffins were cut transversely at a height of 25 mm, and a profile texture analysis (TPA) test was conducted.

During the TPA test, the samples were compressed until they reached 50% deformation at a speed of 1 mm/s. There was a 5 s interval between the first and second compression. A piston with a diameter of 75 mm was used for the analysis. A total of ten samples for each type of muffin were tested to ensure reliable and representative results.

2.7. Sensorial Evaluation

For the evaluation, a group of 20 individuals who had undergone prior training participated. Among the respondents, 85% were women and 15% were men. The age distribution of the respondents was as follows: 95% were in the 18–25 age range, while 5% were in the 26–30 age range.

The participants were asked to rate various quality characteristics on a scale ranging from 1 (undesirable trait) to 5 (highly desirable trait). The quality characteristics assessed were as follows: external appearance, taste, smell, crumb structure and texture, and overall desirability.

2.8. Statistical Analysis

The obtained results were analyzed using Statistica 13.1 (StatSoft, Krakow, Poland). Analysis of variance was employed to evaluate the effect of both the type of flour and the addition of microalgae as well as to examine the differences between the samples. To determine significant differences between groups, the least significant differences were calculated using Duncan's test. The level of significance was set at $\alpha < 0.05$.

3. Results

3.1. Rheological Properties of Dough

The values of apparent viscosity as a function of shear rate, as well as the consistency coefficient and flow index, are shown in Figure 1. All of the tested raw doughs for vegan muffins exhibited shear thinning behavior, characterized by high viscosity. This finding aligns with previous studies by many authors [14–17].

High dough viscosity can favorably influence baking porosity and texture. Viscosity is a factor that controls the final porosity of the baked product due to its effect on the incorporation and movement of gas bubbles. Our research shows that the higher the viscosity of the dough (Figure 1a), the more pores and larger porosity the muffins had (Table 3). On the other hand, the pores had a smaller structure thickness, and the muffin texture was very soft and delicate (Table 4). The rate at which gas bubbles rise under buoyant force is inversely proportional to viscosity. Increased dough viscosity helps retain gas bubbles within the dough, contributing to greater stability throughout the baking process [14]. Our observations, however, show that too high a dough viscosity is not desirable; it creates a large number of pores but lower structure thickness, and this does not favor the texture.

Within the studied range of shear rates (1–100 s^{-1}), the Ostwald–de Waele power equation provided a good fit (r^2 ranging from 0.996 to 0.999) to describe the relationship. The consistency coefficient (K) of the dough made with wheat flour (CW) was 58.3 Pa·s^n, significantly lower than that of the dough made with a mixture of spelt and wheat flour (SW), which had a K value of 74.7 Pa·s^n (Figure 1). The addition of 1.5% microalgae (CWa1.5) resulted in an approximately 16% increase in the consistency coefficient compared to the CW sample. Similarly, the doughs based on the mixture of spelt and wheat flours with 1 and 1.5% microalgae additions (SWa1.0 and SWa1.5) exhibited significantly higher K values compared to the microalgae-free dough (SW), with increases of 25 and 37%, respectively. The flow index (n) was lower in the dough containing spelt flour, indicating higher viscosity compared to the dough made with wheat flour (Figure 1). Several studies have demonstrated that dough viscosity is influenced by the type and quantity of ingredients used [14,15]. The higher fiber content in spelt flour may have contributed to increased water binding and subsequently led to a higher consistency coefficient and a lower flow index. Additionally, the microalgae, known for their gelling properties [2,6], likely enhanced the dough structure when combined with spelt flour, resulting in higher K values and lower n values.

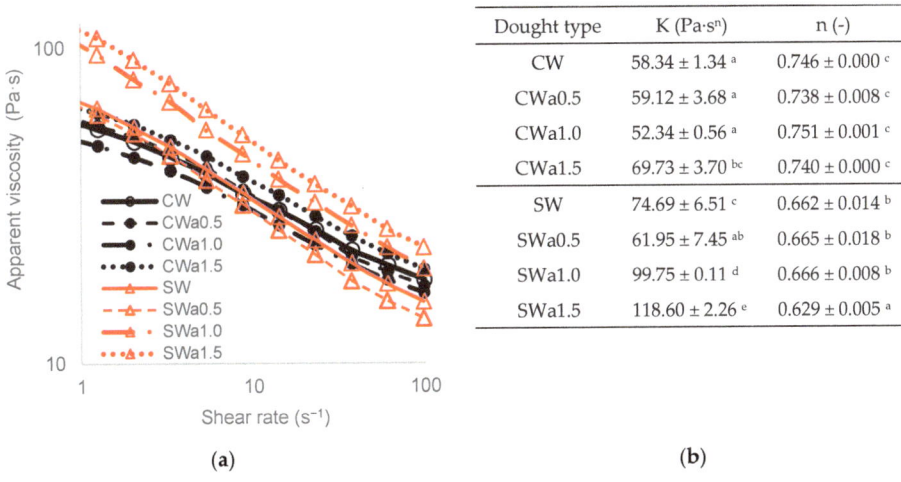

Dought type	K (Pa·s^n)	n (-)
CW	58.34 ± 1.34 [a]	0.746 ± 0.000 [c]
CWa0.5	59.12 ± 3.68 [a]	0.738 ± 0.008 [c]
CWa1.0	52.34 ± 0.56 [a]	0.751 ± 0.001 [c]
CWa1.5	69.73 ± 3.70 [bc]	0.740 ± 0.000 [c]
SW	74.69 ± 6.51 [c]	0.662 ± 0.014 [b]
SWa0.5	61.95 ± 7.45 [ab]	0.665 ± 0.018 [b]
SWa1.0	99.75 ± 0.11 [d]	0.666 ± 0.008 [b]
SWa1.5	118.60 ± 2.26 [e]	0.629 ± 0.005 [a]

(a)   (b)

Figure 1. (**a**) Flow curves of raw doughs. (**b**) The average value of consistency coefficient (K) and flow index (n) of raw dough. Explanations: CW—wheat flour (100%), SW—whole-grain spelt flour (50%) and wheat flour (50%), microalgae addition: a0.5, a1.0, and a1.5%. a, b, c, d, e—homogeneous groups, $p < 0.05$.

The rheological studies conducted on raw doughs provide valuable insights into the relationship between rheological parameters and dough composition and structure. Determining the ratio between elastic and viscous characteristics of the dough allows pastry and baking technologists to effectively model dough properties and achieve optimal results during reformulation and new product development [14,15,17].

Figure 2 presents the mechanical spectra of the raw doughs. All tested doughs exhibited elastic characteristics, with an increase in the values of the elastic modulus (G′) and viscous modulus (G″) as the sweep frequency increased. They displayed the typical behavior of soft gels, with G′ values higher than G″. The tgδ values, representing the loss angle, were lower than unity for all samples, indicating the weakly fluid nature of the doughs tested.

When formulating the dough, the inclusion of 50% whole-grain spelt flour (sample SW) resulted in a decrease in both G′ and G″ compared to the dough based on wheat flour (CW). This outcome aligns with expectations based on the available literature. Spelt flour contains significantly more fiber, which may lead to damage to the gluten network [17]. Although spelt flour has a higher protein content, it contains less gluten compared to wheat flour, resulting in a stronger and more elastic dough with better baking properties [20]. Pruska-Kędzior et al. [19] suggested that gluten proteins in spelt are less elastic and stretchier compared to those in common wheat proteins. The addition of microalgae influenced the viscoelastic behavior of the dough. Doughs made from a mixture of whole-grain spelt and wheat flour with microalgae exhibited higher G′ and G″ compared to doughs made solely from wheat flour (Figure 2). The most significant changes in rheological properties were observed with 1 and 1.5% microalgae additions. Sanz et al. [15] argued that increased elasticity reflects greater structural complexity in the doughs. However, the alteration of dough rheological properties is not solely attributable to the effect of microalgae on gluten. The muffin dough consists of ingredients mixed in a way that causes aeration (adding bubbles to the mix). The formation of fine bubbles provides nucleation sites for the CO_2 generated by the baking powder after starch gelatinization and protein denaturation during baking. This causes a porous crumb to form. The number and size of the bubbles depend on the time of mixing and the viscosity of the dough. Too high a viscosity may cause poor bubble retention [22]. The present study expands our knowledge of the rheological properties of doughs made from wheat flour and a mixture of whole-grain spelt and wheat flour with microalgae. It demonstrated that the modulus values increase nonlinearly with increasing amounts of microalgae in the dough. Furthermore, the combination of microalgae with whole-grain spelt flour creates a dough with enhanced stability, elasticity, and extensibility compared to a wheat flour dough with microalgae (Figure 2b). This finding is not easily explained, as the rheological properties of spelt gluten are predominantly influenced by gliadins, whereas those of common wheat gluten are primarily affected by glutenins [19]. The higher fiber content in whole-grain flour also affects the acidity of the dough matrix as well as the water-binding and rheological characteristics of the dough. Interactions between proteins, fiber, fat, and sucrose contribute to the overall rheological properties of the dough.

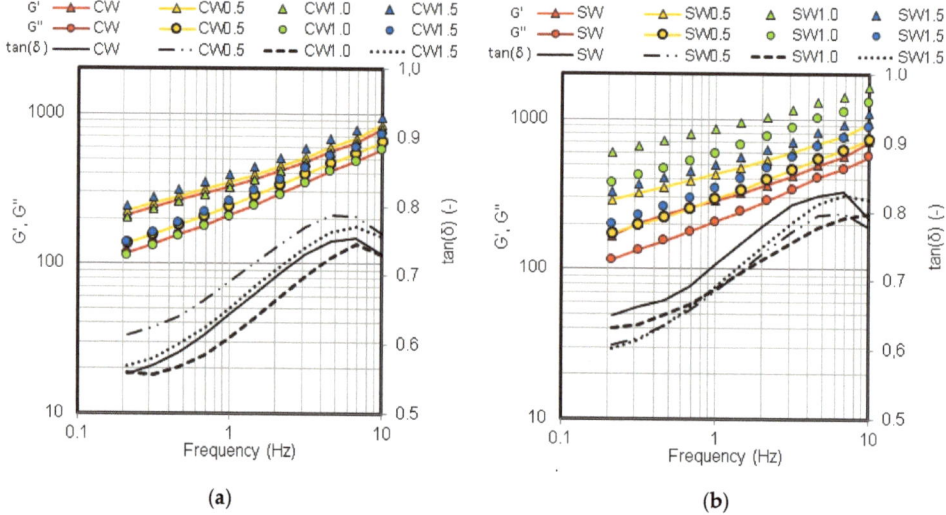

Figure 2. Mechanical spectra of raw doughs based on (**a**) wheat flour (CW) and (**b**) a mixture of whole-grain spelt flour (50%) and wheat flour (50%) (SW). Explanations: microalgae addition: a0.5, a1.0, and a1.5%, G′—preservation modulus, G″—loss modulus, and tgδ—tangent of phase lag angle.

3.2. Water Content, Water Activity (a_w), and Muffin Crumb Color

The replacement of 50% wheat flour with spelt flour did not significantly affect the moisture content of the muffins ($p = 0.059$) (Table 1). The addition of microalgae led to a significant reduction in moisture content across the samples ($p < 0.001$). Specifically, the addition of 0.5% microalgae resulted in a decrease in moisture content of about 1 p.p. (percentage point), and 1.5% microalgae reduced the moisture content by about 3 p.p. compared to samples without microalgae (Table 1). Similar results were observed in muffins enriched with brewer's spent grain flours, and grape pomace [17,24].

Table 1. Water content and activity (each value is presented as mean ± SD; a, b, c, d, e, f—homogenous group, α < 0.05).

Muffin Type	Water Content (%)	Water Activity (-)
CW	25.68 ± 0.93 [d]	0.889 ± 0.005 [cd]
CWa0.5	24.40 ± 0.09 [c]	0.875 ± 0.013 [abc]
CWa1.0	23.99 ± 0.21 [c]	0.860 ± 0.022 [ab]
CWa1.5	22.51 ± 0.23 [a]	0.845 ± 0.013 [a]
SW	25.48 ± 0.30 [d]	0.888 ± 0.003 [cd]
SWa0.5	24.25 ± 0.19 [c]	0.895 ± 0.003 [de]
SWa1.0	23.20 ± 0.26 [b]	0.908 ± 0.004 [e]
SWa1.5	22.53 ± 0.35 [a]	0.923 ± 0.003 [f]

ANOVA				
Factor	F	p	F	p
Flour type (X)	3.9	0.059	83.1	<0.001
Microalgae addition (Y)	81.8	<0.001	0.2	0.881
X × Y	1.5	0.231	19.0	<0.001

The water activity (a_w) of the muffins was influenced by the type of flour and the interaction between flour type and microalgae addition (Table 1). Muffins made with spelt flour and microalgae exhibited higher water activity compared to samples made with wheat flour and microalgae ($p < 0.001$). The inclusion of 1 and 1.5% microalgae had the effect of decreasing aw in wheat flour muffins, while it increased aw in samples containing both spelt and wheat flour (Table 1). The interactions between muffin ingredients can affect water binding and, consequently, contribute to variations in water activity. Despite similar water content, the differences in water activity observed may be attributed to the interactions between ingredients and the competition between biopolymers for water. Whole-grain flour, although containing more fiber, has fewer carbohydrates (starch) compared to wheat flour.

Color is an important parameter for muffins as it directly impacts the acceptability of the product and is influenced by the type of raw materials used. Table 2 presents various color parameters, including L* (brightness), a* (redness), b* (yellowing), C* (saturation), and hab (color tone). Both the use of whole spelt flour ($p < 0.001$) and the addition of microalgae ($p < 0.001$) significantly influence the L* value of the muffin (Table 2). Whole-grain spelt flour leads to a darker color of the muffin, as indicated by the lower L* value (Table 2). This dark color is attributed to the high concentration of relatively colorless polyphenolic compounds present in whole-grain spelt flour, such as flavan-3-ols, amino-phenolic compounds, benzoic and cinnamic acid derivatives, and proanthocyanidines [25]. In addition, the high fiber content of the spelt flour used may contribute to the darker color of the crumb, which aligns with findings from studies on muffins based on barnyard millet flour [26].

The addition of microalgae also leads to a darker color in the muffins. The green pigment present in microalgae significantly alters the a* and b* parameters, consequently affecting the C* (saturation) and hab (color tone) of the muffin. Color tone represents the dimension of color and describes the specific shade, ranging from red (0°) to yellow (90°), green (180°), blue (270°), and back to red (360°). A hab value above 90° indicates a yellower hue, while higher values suggest less yellow and more green [24]. Muffins made with wheat flour but without microalgae exhibited a yellow color, whereas the use of whole-grain spelt flour resulted in a change in color tone (259°), indicating a green–blue hue. Samples with added microalgae showed hab angles ranging from 95° to 109°, indicating a green color for the muffins (Table 2). Previous studies utilizing microalgae (A. platensis) in cakes have reported similar effects [7].

Table 2. Color parameters of vegan muffins with added microalgae (each value is presented as mean ± SD; a, b, c, d, e, f, g, h—homogenous group, α < 0.05).

Muffin Type	L*	a*	b*	C*	h_{ab} (°)
CW	70.20 ± 1.74 [g]	−0.66 ± 0.22 [g]	19.03 ± 0.62 [e]	19.04 ± 0.62 [de]	91.95 ± 0.68 [a]
CW0.5	59.91 ± 1.90 [e]	−5.04 ± 0.35 [c]	18.73 ± 0.95 [de]	19.40 ± 0.91 [e]	105.07 ± 1.34 [e]
CW1.0	55.36 ± 0.93 [c]	−5.91 ± 0.33 [b]	18.13 ± 0.60 [bc]	19.07 ± 0.65 [de]	108.02 ± 0.69 [f]
CW1.5	51.46 ± 1.14 [b]	−6.22 ± 0.41 [a]	17.82 ± 0.62 [c]	18.88 ± 0.70 [d]	109.18 ± 0.78 [g]
SW	63.01 ± 1.75 [f]	3.54 ± 0.40 [h]	18.56 ± 0.57 [d]	18.90 ± 0.59 [d]	259.24 ± 1.11 [h]
SW0.5	57.26 ± 1.71 [d]	−1.60 ± 0.36 [f]	18.16 ± 0.44 [c]	18.24 ± 0.45 [c]	94.99 ± 1.09 [b]
SW1.0	52.13 ± 1.08 [b]	−2.98 ± 0.30 [e]	17.50 ± 0.30 [b]	17.75 ± 0.31 [b]	99.61 ± 0.94 [c]
SW1.5	49.57 ± 1.05 [a]	−3.99 ± 0.22 [d]	16.81 ± 0.70 [a]	17.28 ± 0.69 [a]	103.34 ± 0.81 [d]

	ANOVA									
Factor	F	p	F	p	F	p	F	p	F	p
Flour type (X)	263.1	<0.001	3637.5	<0.001	45.5	<0.001	110.0	<0.001	55819	<0.001
Microalgae addition (Y)	919.5	<0.001	3131.0	<0.001	44.2	<0.001	16.2	<0.001	57274	<0.001
X × Y	26.2	<0.001	60.8	<0.001	1.5	0.227	10.0	<0.001	84054	<0.001

3.3. Two- and Three-Dimensional Microstructure of Muffin Crumb

High-quality muffins are characterized by a light, porous structure and high volume [26]. Figure 3 displays images obtained through X-ray microtomography, revealing the microstructure of the samples. All samples exhibited a highly porous microstructure. Wheat muffins exhibited a higher prevalence of closed pores, while open pores were more prominent in spelt muffins (Table 3). The average surface area of samples made with wheat flour was larger compared to those made with spelt flour. This variation in microstructure was likely influenced by the lower viscosity of the wheat dough.

The structure of muffins is not solely dependent on the number of pores but can also be influenced by the distribution of pore sizes [23]. The distribution of pore areas in the microstructure of wheat flour (CW) muffins exhibited the greatest variability (Figure 4). CW samples had 30% of pores with an area ranging from 0.1 to 0.2 mm², 54% in the range of 0.2 to 0.3 mm², and 15% >0.3 mm². In contrast, muffins made with spelt and wheat flour (SW) displayed finer pores in their microstructure: 16% with an area <0.1 mm², 54% in the range of 0.1–0.2 mm², and 27% in the range of 0.2–0.3 mm², with no pores >0.3 mm². The inclusion of 1% microalgae in wheat flour muffins (CWa1.0) resulted in the most uniform microstructure, with 70% of the pores falling within the 0.1–0.2 mm² range. Both wheat (CWa1.5) and spelt (SWa1.5) muffins with 1.5% microalgae exhibited approximately 50% of pores with an area of 0.1–0.2 mm², and 42 and 28% with an area of 0.2–0.3 mm², respectively. In our study, the addition of microalgae led to a more homogeneous microstructure, possibly due to the increased viscosity of the dough.

Table 3. The microstructure 2D and 3D vegan muffins (each value is presented as mean ± SD; a, b, c, d, e—homogenous group, α < 0.05.

Muffin Type	2D Microstructure (n = 541)				3D Microstructure (n = 2)				
	Closed Porosity (%)	Open Porosity (%)	Average Pores Area (Mm²)	Total Porosity (%)	Percent Object Volume (%)	Number of Pores	Structure Mode Index (-)	Structure Thickness (Mm)
CW	33.84 ± 6.59 [cd]	44.67 ± 10.24 [b]	0.24 ± 0.06 [g]	64.34 [b]	35.66 [b]	3036 [a]	−4.33	0.122 [c]
CWa0.5	37.17 ± 6.13 [e]	39.56 ± 8.46 [a]	0.16 ± 0.06 [d]	62.95 [a]	37.05 [b]	3955 [b]	−3.71	0.108 [a]
CWa1.0	37.48 ± 7.81 [e]	38.86 ± 10.04 [a]	0.13 ± 0.04 [b]	63.00 [a]	37.00 [b]	5234 [d]	−3.71	0.102 [a]
CWa1.5	33.41 ± 6.19 [c]	48.98 ± 11.42 [c]	0.20 ± 0.06 [f]	67.08 [c]	32.92 [a]	3376 [a]	−4.36	0.118 [c]
SW	28.14 ± 6.19 [b]	56.43 ± 11.04 [e]	0.17 ± 0.07 [e]	69.45 [d]	30.55 [a]	3407 [a]	−4.37	0.117 [c]
SWa0.5	34.34 ± 7.43 [d]	50.46 ± 9.80 [d]	0.11 ± 0.05 [a]	68.56 [d]	31.44 [a]	5896 [e]	−3.09	0.104 [a]
SWa1.0	36.80 ± 6.58 [e]	43.64 ± 9.22 [b]	0.14 ± 0.06 [c]	65.35 [b]	34.65 [b]	4309 [c]	−3.43	0.105 [a]
SWa1.5	26.88 ± 5.36 [a]	57.62 ± 5.43 [f]	0.16 ± 0.06 [d]	69.66 [d]	30.34 [a]	3691 [a]	−3.42	0.108 [a]

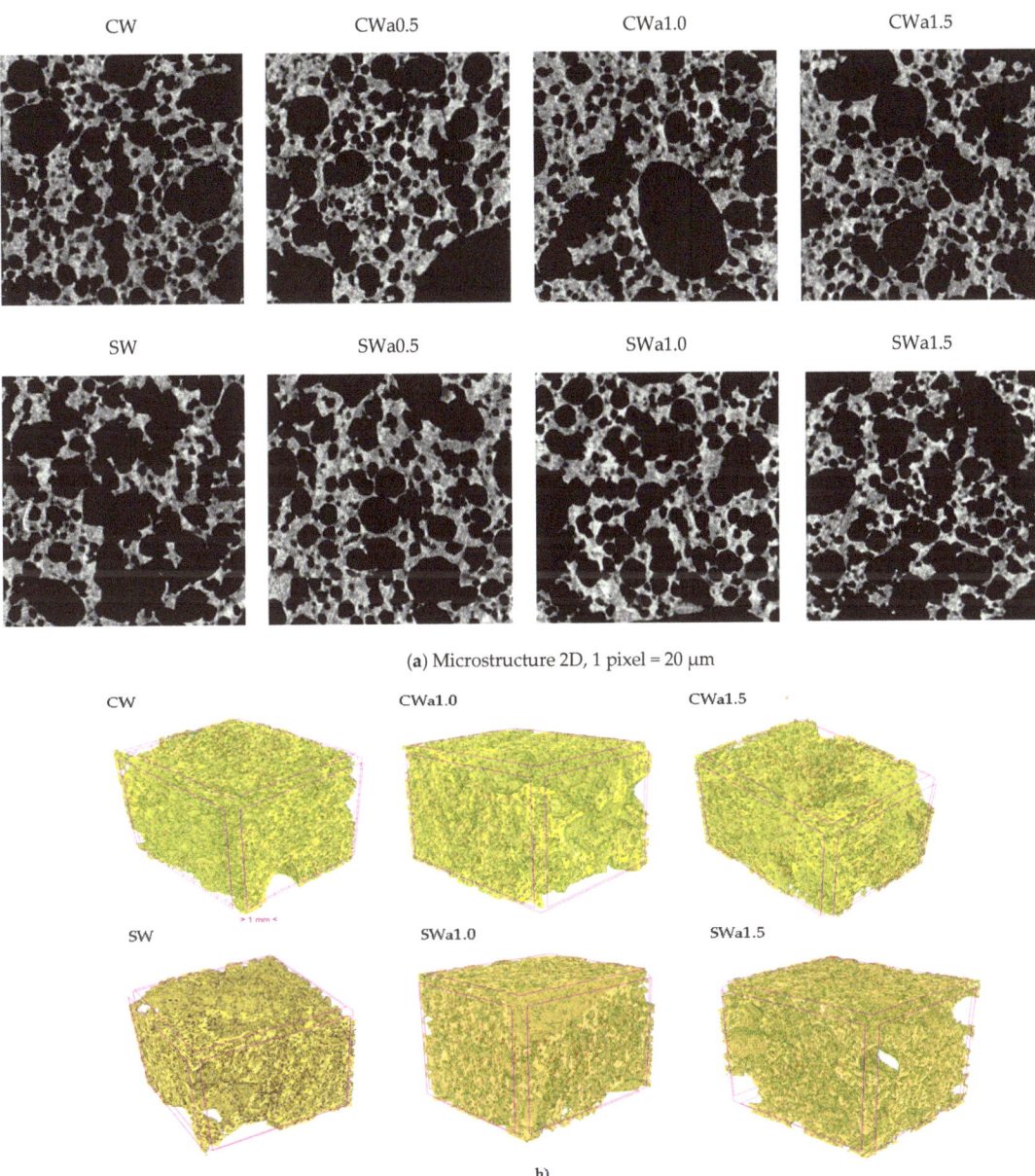

Figure 3. Microstructure X-ray CT images of vegan muffins: (**a**) 2D and (**b**) 3D. Explanations: CW—100% wheat flour, SW—whole-grain spelt flour (50%) and wheat flour (50%), microalgae addition: a0.5, a1.0, and a1.5%.

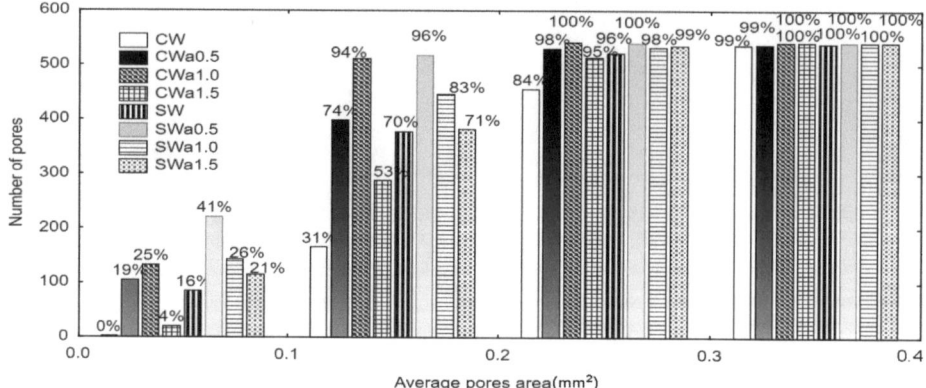

Figure 4. Cumulative distribution of the average pores area in vegan muffins. Explanations: CW—100% wheat flour, SW—whole spelt flour (50%), and wheat flour (50%), microalgae addition: a0.5, a1.0, a1.5%.

Spelt muffins exhibited a higher 3D total porosity (approximately 5 p.p.) compared to the corresponding wheat muffins in terms of microalgae content (Table 3). The addition of 0.5 and 1.0% microalgae resulted in a decrease in porosity, while the use of 1.5% microalgae resulted in porosity similar to that of samples without microalgae. Muffins made with wheat flour had a higher percentage of object volume, indicating a greater proportion of solids in the sample volume regardless of microalgae addition. Furthermore, they displayed a lower number of pores compared to samples made with spelt flour (Table 3). The examined muffin types exhibited similar pore shapes, as indicated by the structure model index values (Table 3). In our study, we proved that wheat flour alone affects the formation of closed pores to a greater extent than a blend of whole-grain spelt and wheat flour. The structure model index (SMI) indicates the relative prevalence of rods and plates in a 3D structure. The structure model index had a negative value. SMI involves the measurement of surface convexity. This parameter may be important in the sensory perception of porous food. An ideal plate, cylinder, and sphere have SMI values of 0, 3, and 4. Note that the concave surfaces of the closed pores represent negative convexity of the SMI, cause dilatation of the enclosed space decreased the surface area [27]. The thickness of the structure determines the thickness of the pore walls in the products. Regardless of the flour type, muffins without microalgae and wheat muffins with 1.5% microalgae had the thickest pore walls (0.122–0.117). In spelt muffins, a decrease in pore wall thickness was observed with increasing microalgae addition. Samples without microalgae (SW) had the highest structure thickness, and as the microalgae content increased, the structure thickness decreased, reaching its lowest point in muffins with 1.0 and 1.5% microalgae addition (SWa1.0 and SWa1.5) (Table 3). In the case of baked goods such as muffins, the structure of which is created by aerating the protein, it is extremely difficult to obtain the effect characteristic of traditional muffins containing structure-forming egg white [22]. The addition of dietary fiber may have a beneficial effect on the formation of the structure of the dough and the finished product [22,24], which is why the high content of fiber in spelt flour could have improved the structure.

3.4. Muffin Crumb Texture

The texture is a crucial characteristic that influences eating habits, serves as an indicator of food freshness and quality, and shapes consumer preferences. Muffins, being a sponge-fat dough product, should possess a soft, tender crumb, indicating minimal hardness and chewiness but high elasticity. These texture attributes are commonly associated with products containing sugars and fats [23]. Statistical analysis reveals that the hardness of muffins was influenced by the type of flour ($p < 0.001$) and the addition of microalgae ($p = 0.006$) (Table 4). Muffins made with wheat flour (CW) exhibited greater hardness compared to samples made with spelt flour (SW) (Table 4). The addition of 0.5% microalgae increased the hardness of the muffins, while higher microalgae concentrations did not significantly impact hardness in comparison to samples without microalgae. Elasticity, which demonstrates the product's ability to regain its shape after force application, and cohesion did not exhibit significant changes (Table 4). Chewiness, a parameter related to the ease or difficulty of chewing food and forming a bite before swallowing [26], was adversely affected by the type of flour ($p < 0.001$). Muffins made with a mixture of spelt and wheat flour displayed significantly lower chewiness (Table 4). Similarly, incorporating barnyard millet flour into muffin mixtures led to reduced hardness and cohesiveness of the products [26]. The authors explained these texture differences by the dilution of gluten. In our study, the variations in texture observed between muffins based on wheat flour and whole-grain spelt and wheat flour mixtures with the addition of microalgae may be attributed to the rheological properties of the different doughs, consequently leading to the formation of more pores (particularly open pores) and a more porous microstructure.

Table 4. Texture parameters of vegan muffins with added microalgae (each value is presented as mean ± SD; a, b, c, d—homogenous group, $\alpha < 0.05$).

Muffin Type	Hardness (N)		Elasticity (-)		Cohesiveness (-)		Chewiness (-)	
CW	62.55 ± 6.76 [c]		0.85 ± 0.03		0.49 ± 0.04		25.85 ± 3.63 [a]	
CWa0.5	64.65 ± 8.28 [d]		0.81 ± 0.04		0.46 ± 0.05		24.14 ± 2.71 [a]	
CWa1.0	62.17 ± 5.10 [c]		0.82 ± 0.02		0.46 ± 0.04		23.41 ± 1.83 [a]	
CWa1.5	61.75 ± 5.86 [c]		0.83 ± 0.02		0.46 ± 0.02		23.52 ± 2.08 [a]	
SW	52.75 ± 5.10 [a]		0.76 ± 0.06		0.42 ± 0.06		16.71 ± 2.77 [b]	
SWa0.5	57.41 ± 5.32 [b]		0.76 ± 0.03		0.42 ± 0.05		18.16 ± 1.52 [b]	
SWa1.0	52.80 ± 4.33 [a]		0.79 ± 0.03		0.45 ± 0.04		18.54 ± 1.33 [b]	
SWa1.5	52.25 ± 3.61 [a]		0.77 ± 0.05		0.43 ± 0.05		17.12 ± 2.66 [b]	
ANOVA								
Factor	F	p	F	p	F	p	F	p
Flour type (X)	100.97	<0.001	3.27	0.072	2.93	0.088	82.50	<0.001
Microalgae addition (Y)	4.28	0.006	1.48	0.221	0.61	0.609	1.02	0.387
X × Y	0.74	0.531	0.55	0.652	0.99	0.399	0.81	0.492

3.5. Sensorial Evaluation of Vegan Muffins

To assess the acceptability of the muffins, a sensory analysis was conducted. Figure 5 presents a summary of the results from the evaluation of sensory characteristics, providing the average values for all attributes assessed. It was observed that despite differences in microstructure and texture, there were no significant variations ($p > 0.05$) in the sensorial evaluation results for all attributes. However, it is worth noting that the muffins made with spelt flour and added microalgae exhibited a darker color and an intense "grassy" aroma. These findings demonstrate that microalgae can be successfully utilized in the production of vegan muffins. Similarly, Batista et al. [7] demonstrated that muffins containing 2 and 6% Chlorella, as well as Spirulina, were acceptable to the panelists. Furthermore, Lucas et al. [10] confirmed the satisfactory sensory quality of Spirulina bars, which were well-received by school-aged children despite variations in texture.

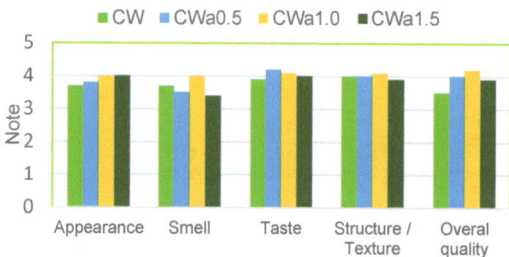

Figure 5. Sensorial evaluation of vegan muffins. Explanations: CW—100% wheat flour, SW—whole spelt flour (50%), and wheat flour (50%), microalgae addition: a0.5, a1.0, and a1.5%.

4. Conclusions

The primary objective of this study was to evaluate the impact of wheat flour and a combination of whole-grain spelt and wheat flours, along with the addition of microalgae as a functional ingredient at different levels (0.5, 1.0, and 1.5%), on the quality of vegan muffins. The study investigated the effects of flour type and microalgae addition on the rheological properties of the dough, as well as the color, microstructure, texture, and sensory properties of the muffins. Doughs containing spelt flour and microalgae exhibited a higher consistency coefficient index and lower flow index compared to doughs with wheat flour. The doughs with spelt flour and 1.0 and 1.5% microalgae additions demonstrated the highest consistency coefficients (99.7 Pa·s^n and 118.6 Pa·s^n, respectively), resulting in muffins with approximately 69% total porosity and a hardness of 52 N. In contrast, muffins made with wheat flour with 1.0 and 1.5% microalgae additions displayed low consistency coefficients (52.3 Pa·s^n and 69.7 Pa·s^n, respectively), resulting in greater total porosities (63% and 67%, respectively), more closed porosities, and larger average pores area in their microstructures. The taste and color of all samples were acceptable, but the addition of microalgae imparted a strong aroma. An important finding of this study is the successful development of vegan muffins enriched with microalgae using a blend of whole-grain spelt and wheat flour. With the addition of 1.5% microalgae, viscosity increased and structure and texture improved. The limitation above all is the grassy aroma. Our research shows that the addition of 1% microalgae is optimal for structure, texture, and sensory properties. However, more research is needed to confirm the nutritional value of the newly developed vegan muffins.

Author Contributions: Conceptualization, A.M. and P.K.; methodology, A.M.; software, A.M.; validation, A.M., H.K. and J.K.; formal analysis, A.M.; investigation, P.K.; resources, H.K. and J.K.; data curation, A.M., P.K., H.K. and J.K.; writing—original draft preparation, A.M.; writing—review and editing, A.M.; visualization, A.M.; supervision, A.M. and H.K. All authors have read and agreed to the published version of the manuscript.

Funding: This research received no external funding.

Institutional Review Board Statement: Not applicable.

Informed Consent Statement: Not applicable.

Data Availability Statement: Not applicable.

Acknowledgments: The research for this publication was performed using research equipment purchased as part of the "Food and Nutrition Centre—modernisation of the WULS campus to create a Food and Nutrition Research and Development Centre (CŻiŻ)" co-financed by the European Union from the European Regional Development Fund under the Regional Operational Programme of the Mazowieckie Voivodeship for 2014–2020 (Project No. RPMA.01.01.00-14-8276/17).

Conflicts of Interest: The authors declare no potential conflict of interest with respect to the research, authorship, and/or publication of this article.

Abbreviations

CW	Common wheat flour
SW	Whole spelt flour (50%), and wheat flour (50%), Microalgae addition: a0.5, a1.0, and a1.5%
G'	Elastic modulus
G''	Viscous modulus
tgδ	Loss angle
a_w	Water activity
τ	Shear stress (Pa)
γ	Shear rate (s^{-1})
K	Consistency coefficient (Pa·s^n)
n	Flow behavior index
r^2	Determination coefficient
L*	Lightness
a*	Redness
b*	Yellowness
C*	Chroma
h_{ab}	Hue

References

1. Available online: https://www.fao.org/fileadmin/templates/wsfs/docs/Issues_papers/HLEF2050_Global_Agriculture.pdf (accessed on 1 June 2023).
2. Batista, A.P.; Gouveia, L.; Bandarra, N.; Franco, J.M.; Raymundo, A. Comparison of microalgal biomass profiles as novel functional ingredient for food products. *Algal Res.* **2013**, *2*, 164–173. [CrossRef]
3. Barka, A.; Blecker, C. Microalgae as a potential source of single-cell proteins. *Biotechnol. Agron. Soc. Environ.* **2016**, *20*, 427–436. [CrossRef]
4. Ramírez-Rodrigues, M.M.; Estrada-Beristain, C.; Metri-Ojeda, J.; Pérez-Alva, A.; Baigts-Allende, D.K. *Spirulina platensis* protein as sustainable ingredient for nutritional food products development. *Sustainability* **2021**, *13*, 6849. [CrossRef]
5. Gong, D.; Sun, L.; Li, X.; Zhang, W.; Zhang, D.; Cai, J. Micro/Nanofabrication, Assembly, and Actuation Based on Microorganisms: Recent Advances and Perspectives. *Small Struct.* **2023**, 2200356. [CrossRef]
6. Andrade, L.M.; Andrade, C.J.; Dias, M.; Nascimento, C.A.O.; Mendes, M.A. *Chlorella* and *Spirulina* microalgae as sources offunctional foods, nutraceuticals, and food supplements; an overview. *MOJ Food Process. Technol.* **2018**, *6*, 45–58. [CrossRef]
7. Batista, A.P.; Niccolai, A.; Fradinho, P.; Fragoso, S.; Bursic, I.; Rodolfi, L. Microalgae biomass as an alternative ingredient in cookies: Sensory, physical and chemical properties, antioxidant activity and *in vitro* digestibility. *Algal Res.* **2017**, *26*, 161–171. [CrossRef]
8. Batista, A.P.; Niccolai, A.; Bursic, I.; Sousa, I.; Raymundo, A.; Rodolfi, L.; Biondi, N.; Tredici, M.R. Microalgae as functional ingredients in savory food products: Application to wheat crackers. *Foods* **2019**, *8*, 611. [CrossRef]
9. Lucas, B.F.; Morais, M.G.D.; Santos, T.D.; Costa, J.A.V. Spirulina for snack enrichment: Nutritional, physical and sensory evaluations. *LWT Food Sci.* **2018**, *90*, 270–276. [CrossRef]
10. Lucas, B.F.; da Rosa, A.P.C.; de Carvalho, L.F.; de Morais, M.G.; Santos, T.D.; Costa, J.A.V. Snack bars enriched with *Spirulina* for schoolchildren nutrition. *Food Sci. Technol.* **2020**, *40* (Suppl. S1), 146–152. [CrossRef]
11. De Marco Rodríguez, E.; Steffolani, M.E.; Martínez, C.S.; León, A.E. Effects of Spirulina biomass on the technological and nutritional quality of bread wheat pasta. *LWT Food Sci.* **2014**, *58*, 102–108. [CrossRef]
12. Różyło, R.; Hameed Hassoon, W.; Gawlik-Dziki, U.; Siastała, M.; Dziki, D. Study on the physical and antioxidant properties of gluten-free bread with Brown algae. *CyTA J. Food* **2017**, *15*, 196–203. [CrossRef]
13. Merchant, R.E.; Phillips, T.W.; Udani, J. Nutritional supplementation with *Chlorella pyrenoidosa* lowers serum methylmalonic acid in vegans and vegetarians with a suspected vitamin B$_{12}$ deficiency. *J. Med. Food* **2015**, *18*, 1357–1362. [CrossRef] [PubMed]
14. Baixauli, R.; Sanz, T.; Salvador, A.; Fiszman, S.M. Muffins with resistant starch: Baking performance in relation to the rheological properties of the batter. *J. Cereal Sci.* **2008**, *47*, 502–509. [CrossRef]
15. Sanz, T.; Salvador, Ć.A.; Fiszman, Ć.S.M. Evaluation of four types of resistant starch in muffin baking performance and relationship with batter rheology. *Eur. Food Res. Technol.* **2008**, *227*, 813–819. [CrossRef]
16. Rajiv, J.; Soumya, C.; Indrani, D.; Venkateswara Rao, G. Effect of replacement of wheat flour with finger millet flour (*Eleusine coracana*) on the batter microscopy, rheology and quality characteristics of muffins. *J. Texture Stud.* **2011**, *42*, 478–489. [CrossRef]
17. Bianchi, F.; Cervini, M.; Giuberti, G.; Rocchetti, G.; Lucini, L.; Simonato, B. Distilled grape pomace as a functional ingredient in vegan muffins: Effect on physicochemical, nutritional, rheological and sensory aspects. *Int. J. Food Sci. Technol.* **2022**, *57*, 4847–4858. [CrossRef]
18. Shewry, P.R.; Hey, S.J. The contribution of wheat to human diet and health. *Food Energy Secur.* **2015**, *4*, 178–202. [CrossRef]
19. Pruska-Kędzior, A.; Kędzior, Z.; Klockiewicz-Kaminska, E. Comparison of viscoelastic properties of gluten from spelt and common wheat. *Eur. Food Res. Technol.* **2008**, *227*, 199–207. [CrossRef]

20. Frakolaki, G.; Giannou, V.; Topakas, E.; Tzia, C. Chemical characterization and breadmaking potential of spelt versus wheat flour. *J. Cereal Sci.* **2018**, *79*, 50–56. [CrossRef]
21. Sinkovič, L.; Tóth, V.; Rakszegi, M.; Pipan, B. Elemental composition and nutritional characteristics of spelt flours and wholemeals. *J. Elementol.* **2023**, *28*, 27–39. [CrossRef]
22. Marcet, I.; Collado, S.; Paredes, B.; Díaz, M. Rheological and textural properties in a bakery product as a function of the proportions of the egg yolk fractions: Discussion and modelling. *Food Hydrocoll.* **2015**, *54*, 119–129. [CrossRef]
23. Marzec, A.; Kowalska, J.; Domian, E.; Galus, S.; Ciurzyńska, A.; Kowalska, H. Characteristics of dough rheology and the structural, mechanical, and sensory properties of sponge cakes with sweeteners. *Molecules* **2021**, *26*, 6638. [CrossRef] [PubMed]
24. Shih, Y.T.; Wang, W.; Hasenbeck, A.; Stone, D.; Zhao, Y. Investigation of physicochemical, nutritional, and sensory qualities of muffins incorporated with dried brewer's spent grain flours as a source of dietary fiber and protein. *J. Food Sci.* **2020**, *85*, 3943–3953. [CrossRef] [PubMed]
25. Čáslavková, P.; Bednářová, M.; Ošťádalová, M.; Štarha, P.; Bednář, J.; Pokorná, J.; Tremlová, B.; Řezačová Lukášková, Z. Colour change of bakery products influenced by used additions. *Acta Vet. Brno* **2014**, *83*, 111–120. [CrossRef]
26. Goswami, D.; Gupta, R.K.; Mridula, D.; Sharma, M.; Tyagi, S.K. Barnyard millet based muffins: Physical, textural and sensory properties. *LWT Food Sci.* **2015**, *64*, 374–380. [CrossRef]
27. Bruker. Morphometric Parameters Measured by Skyscan™ CT-analyser Sofware. In *Bruker-MicroCTCT-Analyser: Morphometric Parameters in 3D and 2D*; Bruker: Billerica, MA, USA, 2008; pp. 1–49.

Disclaimer/Publisher's Note: The statements, opinions and data contained in all publications are solely those of the individual author(s) and contributor(s) and not of MDPI and/or the editor(s). MDPI and/or the editor(s) disclaim responsibility for any injury to people or property resulting from any ideas, methods, instructions or products referred to in the content.

Review

Innovations in Wheat Bread: Using Food Industry By-Products for Better Quality and Nutrition

Piotr Zarzycki, Anna Wirkijowska *, Dorota Teterycz * and Paulina Łysakowska

Division of Engineering and Cereals Technology, Department of Plant Food Technology and Gastronomy, University of Life Sciences in Lublin, Skromna 8, 20-704 Lublin, Poland; piotr.zarzycki@up.lublin.pl (P.Z.); paulina.lysakowska@up.lublin.pl (P.Ł.)
* Correspondence: anna.wirkijowska@up.lublin.pl (A.W.); dorota.teterycz@up.lublin.pl (D.T.)

Abstract: The evolution of wheat bread as a dietary staple underscores its essential role in providing energy, protein, fiber, and vital nutrients. To address contemporary health challenges such as type 2 diabetes and cardiovascular diseases, fortifying wheat bread with health-promoting additives becomes imperative to mitigate deficiencies resulting from refined wheat flour consumption. Functional food innovations, aligned with sustainability goals and circular economy principles, offer promising approaches for addressing these concerns. Integrating by-products from fruits and oil crops into bread formulations enhances health benefits by boosting dietary fiber, bioactive compounds, and antioxidant potential. However, gaps persist in understanding anti-nutritional substances and contaminants in final products, necessitating further research for comprehensive safety assessments. The addition of by-product raw materials significantly influences dough rheology and sensory characteristics, potentially achieving quality comparable to traditional wheat bread. Challenges include inconsistencies in bread and by-product specifications across studies, hindering direct result comparison. Overcoming these obstacles is crucial for maximizing the potential of agri-food by-products in creating healthier, sustainable bread options while maintaining safety and quality standards.

Keywords: nutritional value; waste; by-products; apple pomace; olive pomace; grape pomace; flaxseed marc; bread

1. Introduction

Wheat bread, a staple of the human diet for centuries, serves not only as a source of energy but also provides protein, fiber, and essential nutrients. Its evolution, from the initial domestication processes in the Fertile Crescent around 10,000 years ago, through the development of agriculture to contemporary production techniques, illustrates the profound symbiosis between humans and their environment and the adaptability of plants to societal needs [1,2]. Health issues such as type 2 diabetes, coronary artery disease, chronic cardiovascular conditions, and colon cancer are increasingly associated with the heightened consumption of refined cereal products rich in easily digestible carbohydrates [2,3]. This highlights the necessity of revising human diets, focusing on addressing potential dietary deficiencies caused by the consumption of highly processed foodstuffs, such as refined wheat flour, through the fortification of wheat bread with health-promoting additives [3]. Foods rich in dietary fiber play crucial roles in the digestion and absorption of lipids in the small intestine, attenuation of blood glucose and cholesterol, weight control by increasing satiety and enhancing intestinal regularity, and protection against colon cancer [4].

Improving the nutritional quality of products consumed by a significant proportion of people is an essential strategy to meet the demands of consumers seeking better nutritional options and health benefits. Functional food can also be considered a promising alternative for the application of new ingredients, including from an economic, nutritional, technological, or environmental point of view. Current research on wheat bread focuses on its fortification, which involves enriching it with additional nutrients. This is aimed not

Citation: Zarzycki, P.; Wirkijowska, A.; Teterycz, D.; Łysakowska, P. Innovations in Wheat Bread: Using Food Industry By-Products for Better Quality and Nutrition. *Appl. Sci.* **2024**, *14*, 3976. https://doi.org/10.3390/app14103976

Academic Editor: Anna Lante

Received: 15 April 2024
Revised: 4 May 2024
Accepted: 6 May 2024
Published: 7 May 2024

Copyright: © 2024 by the authors. Licensee MDPI, Basel, Switzerland. This article is an open access article distributed under the terms and conditions of the Creative Commons Attribution (CC BY) license (https://creativecommons.org/licenses/by/4.0/).

only at enhancing its nutritional value but also at contributing to the reduction of dietary deficiencies in the population. Furthermore, in the face of the growing global challenge of food wastage, innovative approaches to bread production, such as utilizing by-products of the food industry, can significantly contribute to increasing resource utilization efficiency and promoting the principles of a circular economy (zero waste) [5–7].

The partial substitution of wheat flour in bread formulation with by-product ingredients leads to modifications not only in the chemical composition but also in the quality characteristics of the bread, significantly impacting its acceptance by consumers. Despite bread being one of the primary bakery products consumed worldwide, significant quantities of wheat bread are wasted at various stages of production and consumption. These losses are mainly due to unfavorable organoleptic properties resulting from microbiological activity and physical changes. Such wastage not only incurs economic losses but also has a detrimental impact on the environment [8]. Consumers play a pivotal role in determining the acceptability of bread, employing descriptive analysis and hedonic scale methods to assess its sensory properties, such as texture, taste, freshness, volume, and color. These attributes significantly influence the overall perception of wheat bread. Processes such as mixing, kneading, fermentation, and baking are crucial for the sensory quality of the final product, underscoring the importance of formulation and processing stages in bread production [9].

Every year, the agro-industrial sector produces substantial amounts of by-products, which are often discarded. The two primary categories of agro-industrial by-products are agricultural and industrial [10–14]. Agricultural residues are by-products resulting from the crop harvesting process, mainly left in the field. In contrast, damaged raw materials, pomaces, seeds, shells, brans, oilseed cakes, and molasses are examples of by-products obtained from food processing. Given global environmental concerns and resource scarcity, the food industry is increasingly acknowledging the importance of sustainable practices and waste reduction. There is a growing awareness that agri-food by-products, once considered waste materials, are valuable resources with untapped potential. These by-products contain rich bioactive compounds that can be utilized in various industrial applications, offering health and nutritional benefits [10,15–17]. A forward-looking approach to sustainability involves harnessing these cost-effective waste agri-food by-products to create value-added products. Research indicates that agri-food by-products can be integrated into wheat bread to enhance its bioactive profile, increase fiber content, and boost antioxidant capacity while maintaining satisfactory sensory acceptability [17–20]. In summary, the use of agri-food by-products in food formulation can contribute to the sustainability of the agri-food chain and positively impact consumer health.

Among food-processing by-products with interesting properties and significant potential are the residues from pressing fruits and vegetables and from pressing oilseeds. Processed fruits, such as juices, making of wine, jellies, chutney, and pulping, produce large amounts of solid residue known as pomace or marc, comprising husks, seeds, stalks, and remaining pulp, which ranges 20–50% of the fruit weight [21,22]. This by-product, produced in large quantities, offers potential as a high-nutritional-value component. It contains significant levels of dietary fiber and vital bioactive compounds such as polyphenols, carotenoids, and glucosinolates. Exploiting these nutritional qualities, the food sector can benefit from incorporating this by-product to create healthier and nutritionally rich foods [10,23]. During oil and olive oil production, from flaxseed and olive, a large amount, depending on the type of raw material and pressing system, of solid by-product known as cake or pomace is obtained. If not discarded, the cake is processed into meal for animal feed or fertilizer, providing energy for animals [14,24]. Olive pomace is also commonly repurposed as fuel and utilized as an ingredient for compost production, or as fertilizer for agricultural soils [25]. However, post-oil extraction, bioactive compounds remain in the cake, making it valuable. Both the widespread availability and high content of protein, dietary fiber, vitamins, minerals, unsaturated fatty acids, and other biologically active compounds make these raw materials exceptionally attractive. Thus, these by-products can be used in food product development, aligning with circular economy principles [17,26].

In the context of the information provided above, the aim of this review was to assess the potential of introducing new ingredients, such as residues from pressing fruits and oil, into the formulation of wheat bread to create a healthier version. The primary goal was to determine the impact of these ingredients on dough characteristics, physicochemical properties, and sensory acceptability of the bread, including changes in its nutritional profile especially dietary fiber content and overall health benefits.

Papers were selected from online databases such as Knovel, Science Direct, Springer, Google Scholar, and Wiley using descriptors like 'wheat bread', 'pomace', 'by-products', 'marc', 'oilseeds', 'apple', 'grape', 'flaxseed', 'olive', and their combinations. Articles containing these terms in the title, abstract, or keywords were selected, considering all articles available from 2014 until March 2024. The inclusion criteria involved compatibility with the main subject and accessibility for reading, while the exclusion criteria included lack of compatibility, literature reviews, theses, or books. Subsequently, chosen papers were read in their entirety to confirm if they covered the subject of the current study. The data evaluated included authors, year of publication, objectives, methods, and results. Selected papers offer comprehensive insights into the utilization of selected ingredients in wheat bread for potential health benefits and improved nutritional profiles.

2. Chemistry of Selected By-Products

The proper utilization of agricultural waste represents a crucial aspect in the context of sustainable development and efficient resource management. Among these raw materials, obtained as by-products of industrial food production processes, are apple, grape, olive, and flaxseed wastes. Despite their initial role as by-products, their potential as valuable resources for further utilization is increasingly being recognized. This chapter focuses on the chemical characterization of these wastes, emphasizing their value as sources of valuable nutrients and bioactive compounds.

Apples (*Malus domestica* L.) rank third among the most popular fruits worldwide, following bananas and watermelons [27]. They are extensively used for producing juices, ciders, alcoholic beverages, fruit preserves, dried products, and frozen goods. Globally, approximately 89 million tons of apples are produced annually, with 25% of them ending up as waste [11]. Apple pomace primarily consists of peels, seeds, and some pulp. After pressing, the moisture content is about 70–85%, rendering pomace highly susceptible to microbial growth. To maintain proper microbiological safety, pomace should be dried to a water content of no more than 10% [28]. The water content in dried pomace ranges from 4.4% to 10.8% according to literature data [29–31].

Apple pomace is rich in carbohydrates (45.1–84.7 g/100 g d.m.), primarily fructose, sucrose, and glucose, and total dietary fiber (35–82 g/100 g d.m.), with about 4.2–11.9 g being soluble fiber and 25.73–77.8 g insoluble fiber [15,32,33]. The main components of insoluble fiber in apple pomace are cellulose (6.7–40.4 g/100 g d.m.), lignin (14.1–18.9 g/100 g d.m.), and hemicelluloses (approximately 16.4 g/100 g) [32,34]. The main soluble fiber in apple pomace is pectin, comprising up to 15% of the d.m. in pomace [34]. Studies have shown that pectins in apples can reduce the absorption of cholesterol into the blood and decrease pancreatic lipase activity by up to 94.3%, indicating anti-obesity effects [35]. Additionally, pectin consumption has been associated with lowering blood glucose levels [36].

Ravn-Haren et al. [37] compared the effects of apple pomace, apples, and apple juice on plasma lipid profiles in a crossover study with healthy participants. They found that pectin consumption correlated with reduced plasma cholesterol, and apple pomace intake had no effect on serum cholesterol levels. Pomace is also a source of starch, comprising 14–17%, with immature fruits containing more starch [38]. It is also rich in mineral components such as potassium, calcium, and magnesium [34], and vitamins C (22.4 mg/100 g d.m.) and E, found in the seeds (5.5 mg/100 g d.m. in pomace) [39].

The polyphenolic components in apples include five main groups: flavanols, flavonols, hydroxycinnamates, dihydrochalcones, and anthocyanins. Apples have an antioxidant activity of about 100 mmol of vitamin C equivalents per gram of fruit, ranking second after cranberries in a study of fruit consumption in the USA. Apple pomace contains polyphenols such as catechin, p-coumaric acid, caffeic acid, and ferulic acid, which exhibit stronger antioxidant activity than vitamins E and C [34,40]. Apple pomace consumption showed a trend towards decreasing heart rate, blood pressure, and certain biomarkers associated with inflammation. Additionally, apple pomace improved gastrointestinal health, indicated by decreased lithocholic acid excretion [37]. Other studies suggest that apple pomace, rich in polyphenols, can benefit cholesterol levels, insulin sensitivity, and gut microbial functionality [40–43].

However, like any by-product, apple pomace also contains substances undesirable in food. The main anti-nutritional components in apple pomace are saponins, alkaloids, and tannins [44]. Therefore, further research is needed to determine the optimal dosage and safety of apple pomace for human consumption.

Grapes (*Vitis vinifera* L.) rank fifth in terms of fruit production volume, with approximately 74.94 million tons produced globally [27]. Of the total grape production in 2016, approximately 31.3% were table grapes, 6.3% were used for raisins, leaving around 62% to be crushed primarily for making wine, with about 30% potentially used for grape juice concentrate or distillation [22]. As reported by Antonić et al. [12], as much as 30% of grape mass used for wine production can become waste, posing a significant issue regarding disposal. Grape pomace, also known as wine pomace, is the leftover material after pressing and fermentation, primarily consisting of skins (up to 75%), grape seeds (up to 28%), seedless pulp, and stems [45,46]. Wine pomace also includes yeast cells resulting from the wine fermentation process [47]. Water can constitute up to 64% of pomace depending on the processing technique [48].

Large quantities of grape pomace, often discarded in landfills after harvests, can hinder biodegradation due to low pH and antibacterial polyphenols [12]. Although grape pomace contains some protein (up to about 14% d.m.), it is not efficiently digested by most animals for energy [12,49]. Using grape pomace as compost is not economically viable due to nutrient deficiencies, but it contains significant amounts of health-promoting compounds [50].

Grape pomace is mainly composed of dietary fiber (up to 89 g/100 g d.m., depending on grape variety), with about 13 g being soluble fiber and up to 63 g insoluble fiber [12]. Typically, seeds exhibit a higher fiber content than skins, with red wine pomace demonstrating greater fiber richness compared to its white wine counterpart [51]. The protein content of wine pomace, ranging from 6% to 15% d.m., is influenced by grape variety and harvesting conditions, with skins showing a slight superiority over separated seeds. Amino acid composition resembling cereals, it is abundant in glutamic acid and aspartic acid but deficient in tryptophan and sulfur-containing amino acids. Notably, skin protein is rich in alanine and lysine, in contrast to seed proteins [52].

Grape seed oil, extensively utilized in cosmetics and recognized for its antioxidant properties [53], contains an oil content ranging from 8% to 15%, primarily composed of oleic and linoleic acids, alongside palmitic acid [54,55]. It is rich in polyunsaturated and monounsaturated fatty acids, with β-sitosterol as the principal sterol and α-tocopherol as the predominant tocopherol, comprising about 70% [56].

The mineral content of wine pomace varies widely due to factors like edaphoclimatic conditions and winemaking processes. Potassium, phosphorus, sulfur, and magnesium accumulate mainly in grape skin, resulting in higher levels compared to seeds, which serve as reservoirs for calcium. The predominant potassium salts, such as potassium bitartrate, can constitute a significant portion of wine pomace [47,57].

The utilization of grape by-products in foods has limits due to the presence of antinutritional factors such as lectin and tannin [58]. Nevertheless, research highlights diverse phenolic compounds in wine pomace, influenced by grape properties and winemaking methods [59]. Skins are rich in hydroxycinnamic acids, while seeds contain gallic and protocatechuic acids. Flavonoids like anthocyanins and flavanols are abundant in both red and white pomace, with seeds having most flavanols. Certain grape varieties may contain significant compounds like quercetin 3-O-glucuronide, and wine pomace holds nonextractable polyphenols, including hydrolyzable polyphenols and nonextractable proanthocyanidins [60–62].

Grape seeds, as suggested by Bordiga et al. [54], are notable for containing a substantial quantity of oligosaccharides, mirroring those found in wine, thereby establishing grape seeds as a novel and promising reservoir of these bioactive compounds. Research suggests that grape pomace phenolic compounds may alleviate metabolic syndrome [63–65]. Understanding their metabolism in various health conditions is crucial [66,67]. Margalef et al. [68] found that flavanols have specific hypotensive effects on hypertension, with microbial metabolism influencing differences between healthy and hypertensive rats. These findings underscore the importance of tailored metabolic studies to fully grasp the health benefits of grape phenols.

The FAOSTAT data indicates that global olive (*Olea europaea* L.) production in 2022 exceeded 23 million tons, with approximately 5.3 million tons designated for table olives, while the remaining portion is allocated for olive oil production, yielding around 3.5 million tons annually [69]. During olive oil production, the quantity of olive pomace generated varies from 2.75 to 4 tons per ton of oil, influenced by fruit quality and extraction technology [13,70]. Olive pomace stands as a significant by-product in the olive oil industry, making up roughly 65% of the initial weight of pressed olives in a three-phased pressing system or 80% in a two-phased decanter [71,72]. Olive pomace encompasses pulp, skin, seeds, and stone fragments and has a high moisture content ranging from 65–75% [13]. Specifically, olive pomace is commonly repurposed as fuel and utilized as an ingredient for compost production or as fertilizer for agricultural soils [25]. Olive pomace contains between 4.5 to 9% residual oil, with cis-oleic acid being the predominant fatty acid [73–75]. The main component of olive pomace is dietary fiber (69.6–80.1 g/100 g d.m.). According to literature, the majority of the fiber consists of insoluble fiber (56.7–76.1 g/100 g d.m.), with soluble fiber accounting for only 3.5–12.9 g/100 g d.m.. The main fractions of fiber include lignin (25.5–42.6 g/100 g d.m.), hemicellulose (10–28.9 g/100 g d.m.), and cellulose (6.2–27 g/100 g d.m.) [16,76]. Sugars present in the pomace are mainly glucose (23.6–23.9 g/100 g d.m.), xylose (13 g/100 g d.m.), and arabinose (2 g/100 g d.m.) [16]. Olive pomace also contains 0.88–4.44 g/100 g d.m. of protein and 9.93–16.68 g of ash /100 g d.m., including minerals such as potassium (up to 2843 mg/100 g d.m.), calcium (up to 450 mg/100 g d.m.), iron (up to 61 mg/100 g d.m.), and copper (2.1 mg/100 g d.m.) [77–80]. They also contain certain amounts of vitamin E (0.87–2.25 mg/100 g) [13,75]. Olive oil by-products, rich in polyphenols (to 98% of the polyphenols found in olives; to 14.1 g/100 g d.m.), offer potential health benefits [81]. Main compounds include hydroxytyrosol, tyrosol, caffeic acid, p-coumaric acid, vanillic acid, syringic acid, gallic acid, luteolin, quercetin, cyanidin, and verbascoside [82,83], and fatty acids such as oleic, palmitic, and linoleic acids [84]. These by-products are cost-effective sources for extracting antioxidants used in various applications [25,85]. Phenolic compounds in olive pomace, particularly hydroxytyrosol derivatives, act as powerful antioxidants, offering various health benefits. These dietary antioxidants are essential for counteracting free radicals, which are implicated in oxidative stress and diseases such as cancer, cardiovascular issues, and diabetes. Olive-derived polyphenols also influence signaling pathways related to inflammation, oxidative stress, and insulin resistance. Moreover, they serve as natural food additives, prolonging shelf life and minimizing nutrient loss [86,87]. On the other hand, due to the presence of antinutrients like condensed tannins and insoluble fibers in dietary olive pomace, it was theorized that incorporating olive pomace into the diet would negatively impact serum biochemical parameters [88].

Flax, also known as linseed (*Linum usitatissimum* L.), is one of the most popular oil and fibrous crops worldwide. Data indicates that in 2022, global flaxseed production reached

3.64 million tons [89]. Historically, flaxseed has been primarily valued for its oil, which serves various purposes such as in paints, coatings, printing inks, soap making, core oils, brake linings, and herbicide adjuvants. When flaxseed is pressed, it yields oil and a solid residue called flaxseed cake. If not discarded, the cake is processed into meal for animal feed or fertilizer, providing energy for animals. Post-oil extraction, bioactive compounds remain in the cake, making it valuable. Thus, the cake can also be used in food product development, aligning with circular economy principles [14,24]. Flaxseed cake is often ground into flaxseed flour, facilitating its use in food production. The amount of waste generated during the pressing of flaxseed oil ranges from 70 to even 75%, depending on the oil extraction method [90]. Similarly to most cakes, the main component of flaxseed cake is dietary fiber, with content ranging from 32.78 g/100 g d.m. to 35.21 g/100 g d.m., of which 17.83–26.71 g/100 g d.m. is insoluble dietary fiber (IDF) and 8.5–14.95 g/100 g d.m. is soluble dietary fiber (SDF). The primary insoluble fiber fraction comprises cellulose and lignin, while the soluble fiber fractions include mucilage gums. Mucilages are hydrophilic compounds, and flaxseed mucilage (FM) comprises two distinct polysaccharides: a pectic-like material (acidic) and an arabinoxylan (neutral) [17,91,92]. The mucilage constitutes approximately 8% of the weight of flaxseed. Upon acid hydrolysis, these polysaccharides yield L-galactose, D-xylose, L-arabinose, L-rhamnose, D-galacturonic acid, and possibly traces of D-glucose. Mucilage gums become viscous when combined with water or other liquids, playing a crucial role in laxatives [93,94].

Protein content in flaxseed cake ranges from 29.20 to 35.07 g/100 g d.m. [17,95,96]. It primarily comprises globulins (linin) (58–66% of the protein) and albumins (conlinin), along with hirudin and oleosin [97]. Literature data indicates that the digestibility of flaxseed protein is 85% [95]. The residual fat content in the flaxseed cake after extraction ranges from 4.41% to 15.27 d.m. [17,92,95] and, similar to flaxseed oil, it consists mainly of polyunsaturated fatty acids (approximately 68%), with SFA and MUFA accounting for approximately 8–9% and 5–6% of the oil, respectively [98]. The main fatty acid in flaxseed oil is α-linolenic acid (C18:3), accounting for approximately 39–61% of the oil. The remaining fatty acids include linoleic acid (C18:2) 12.25–17.44%, oleic acid (C18:1) 13.44–19.39%, stearic acid (C18:0) 2.24–4.59%, and palmitic acid (C16:0) 4.9–8% [99,100]. The mineral content in the form of ash constitutes 6.08–9.45% of the dry matter of the flaxseed cake [17,92], primarily consisting of phosphorus, magnesium, calcium, iron, and zinc [98]. Flaxseed cake is also a rich source of phenolic compounds (7.40 mg GAE/g d.m.). The high presence of lignans (primarily secoisolariciresinol), predominantly found in the husk of flaxseed, is worth emphasizing. Lignans are non-nutrient, noncaloric, bioactive phenolic plant compounds. Lignans exhibit promising anticancer effects by modulating multiple targets of carcinogenesis. Additionally, they possess anti-inflammatory, antiviral, and antimicrobial properties, suggesting potential benefits in cancer prevention [101].

Cyanogenic glycosides, such as linustatin, neolinustatin, linamarin, lotaustralin, present in significant amounts in whole flaxseed, and phytic acid in flaxseed cake act as major antinutrients, hindering nutrient absorption. Despite the release of minimal hydrogen cyanide from flaxseed, well below toxic levels, roasting is commonly employed to mitigate cyanogenic glycosides' effects [98,102].

3. Dough Rheology

The utilization of by-products from plant food production, acting as natural raw materials rich in dietary fibers and antioxidants, provides an avenue for developing functional foods while concurrently promoting the valorization of generated by-products. However, the partial substitution of wheat flour in bread formulation with these fiber-rich ingredients leads to modifications in dough rheology, consequently affecting the properties of the final product [Table 1]. An in-depth comprehension of the rheological properties of wheat flour dough is crucial for bread producers striving to attain high-quality bakery products. Therefore, these properties must be meticulously considered to ensure the production of bakery items, such as bread, of superior quality.

Water absorption, in the context of dough preparation, denotes the quantity of water necessary to attain the desired consistency. This parameter is influenced by various factors such as the starch, damaged starch, protein, pentosan content, and the gluten network within the dough [72]. By-products like fruit pomaces and oil cakes, rich in dietary fiber and containing numerous hydroxyl groups in their structure, tend to form hydrogen bonds with water. Consequently, they enhance water absorption during dough preparation [18,20,103]. This increased water absorption can influence various dough properties, including texture, handling characteristics, and final product quality, often indicating good baking performance [18,104]. Tolve et al. [20] and Mironeasa and Mironeasa [105] observed such increases in water absorption after adding grape pomace (up to 10%) to wheat flour. Mironeasa and Mironeasa [105] also found that the type of grape pomace (red or white) could significantly impact changes in water absorption, while particle size showed no influence. Similarly, Kohajdová et al. [106], Usman et al. [103], and Lu et al. [107] reported similar increases in water absorption when adding apple pomace (up to 25%), attributing this effect to the rehydration properties of dried apple pomace. According to Lu et al. [107], a higher water content in wheat dough could enhance the organoleptic properties of bread, such as taste. Moreover, the studies conducted by these authors, similar to the results presented by Mironeasa and Mironeasa [105], did not demonstrate any impact of varying degrees of pulverization of apple pomace on the water absorption of wheat dough. In the case of by-products from oil extraction, Azadfar et al. [18] and Wirkijowska et al. [17] observed increases in water absorption for wheat dough supplemented with olive pomace and flaxseed cake up to 15%, respectively. Jiang et al. [19] found a similar increase in water absorption for flaxseed cake supplementation up to 50%. Conversely, Roozegar et al. [108] and Codina et al. [109] observed that the addition of ground whole flaxseed caused a decrease in water absorption (WA) of the dough. This decrease was mainly attributed to gluten dilution, requiring lower amounts of water to achieve the optimal consistency, and the higher content of oil, which can coat both starch and gluten, leading to a reduction in water absorption. In the study conducted by Dahdah et al. [72], a reduction in water absorption was noted as the supplementation levels of olive pomace increased, particularly with additions exceeding 2%. They utilized freeze-dried powder (<500 μm) obtained from olive pomace (from two olive cultivars) to supplement wheat flour. The authors attribute this behavior to the softer texture of the freeze-dried powder obtained from olive pomace compared to wheat, resulting in a higher water uptake rate and requiring less water to achieve the desired dough consistency. Additionally, the supplementation level used in their study (up to 5%) was low enough not to significantly affect the reduction in starch content, which could otherwise lead to an increase in the required water addition

Dough development time (DDT) and stability time are crucial parameters in evaluating flour strength. A longer dough development time indicates stronger gluten strength, resulting in a more robust and firmer dough. Conversely, wheat dough with a high stability time value is more likely to retain CO_2 during fermentation, enhancing the specific volume of bread compared to dough with low stability time values. Such characteristics are considered favorable for bread making [107,110,111]. The findings from Tolve et al. [20] revealed an increase in dough stability and the quality number with the rising proportion of grape pomace (0–10%). However, the development time remained unchanged, regardless of the grape pomace content. Similar results were reported by Šporin et al. [112], supporting the notion of increased stability time with elevated grape pomace levels. On the other hand, the study conducted by Mironeasa and Mironeasa [105] indicated an increase in development time but a decrease in stability time as the grape pomace level increased (0–9%). These alterations were attributed to the fibers in grape pomace, which slowed down the rate of hydration and gluten development. Notably, the type of grape pomace significantly influenced the range of changes observed for development time, with no discernible impact from particle size. However, concerning stability time, the participation, type, and particle size of grape pomace all exerted a significant effect on the observed alterations. Dough development time was also enhanced by the addition of both apple pomace and skimmed apple pomace [107]. A similar increase in dough development time was observed by Kohajdová et al. [106] and Usman et al. [103] after adding apple pomace powder to wheat dough. The authors attributed this effect to the elevated dietary fiber content in apple pomace, which slowed gluten development in the dough, resulting in increased development time. Additionally, Kohajdová et al. [106] suggested the possibility of fiber-gluten interaction, preventing protein hydration. Lu et al. [107] also noted a reduction in dough stability time with the addition of apple pomace. However, there was no significant difference in the stability time of wheat dough with varying particle sizes of apple pomace, and the defatting process applied to the apple pomace showed no discernible impact. Usman et al. [103] also reported a decrease in dough stability, while, in contrast, Kohajdová et al. [106] observed an increase in dough stability, possibly explained by higher interaction among dietary fiber, water, and flour proteins.

Also, when using by-products obtained from pressing oilseeds, a significant influence of supplementation on the studied rheological properties is evident, although it is not always possible to establish clear dependencies. In the study by Azadfar et al. [18], a fluctuating trend was observed for dough development time when wheat dough was supplemented with olive pomace. Initially, there was an increase in dough development time with up to 10% supplementation, followed by a subsequent decrease. This indicates that at high levels of supplementation with non-gluten components, gluten dilution can play a crucial role in influencing dough development time. Additionally, there was also an increase in dough stability and farinograph quality number, along with a decrease in the softening degree. These trends were similar to the effect of adding grape pomace to dough observed in a previous study by Tolve et al. [20]. The increase in dough stability and decrease in softening degree can be attributed to the hydroxyl groups present in phenolic compounds, which can directly bond with wheat flour proteins and affect the functional properties of the food. The study by Dahdah et al. [72], on the other hand, showed a decrease in dough development time and dough stability with increasing olive pomace content. However, at low supplementation levels (1–3%, depending on the olive variety), the changes in dough stability were insignificant compared to the control sample. Such a level of addition was also recommended by the above authors due to the rheological properties of the dough. Jiang et al. [19] point to similar tendencies, namely a decrease in dough development time and stability when supplementing dough with flaxseed cake. Wirkijowska et al. [17], also indicate a decrease in stability with increasing supplementation levels. Moreover, increased supplementation from 5 to 15% leads to a decrease in dough development time, although the dough development time for supplemented dough remains higher in each case compared to the control.

Increased water absorption, combined with a low degree of dough softening, is considered favorable, indicating good dough tolerance to mixing. Verheyen et al. [111] noted that bread made from softened wheat dough lacks a firm structure. The inclusion of high-fiber ingredients in the dough can weaken its structure, leading to an increase in the degree of dough softening [104]. However, as demonstrated in the study by Tolve et al. [20], supplementing wheat dough with 10% grape pomace led to a decrease in the degree of softening. On one hand, the addition of grape pomace, rich in insoluble fibers and other constituents that strongly interact with gluten proteins, can disrupt the development of desirable rheological properties. On the other hand, phenolic compounds in grape pomace, including tannins, which have a notable ability to form hydrogen bonds and hydrophobic interactions with glutenin fractions in wheat flour, may enhance the production of doughs resistant to mechanical stress [20,112]. Conversely, the study by Mironeasa and Mironeasa [105] did not demonstrate a significant impact of the level of grape pomace addition on the degree of softening. However, it was observed that the degree of softening increased as the particle size of grape pomace decreased. This effect, as suggested by the authors, may be related to the higher amount of soluble fibers compared to insoluble fibers present in smaller particles

In contrast, changes in the Mixing Tolerance Index (MTI) indicated an increase in dough softening with the addition of apple pomace and flaxseed cake [17,107]. The possible mechanism is that fibrous materials react with gluten, and the dilution of gluten protein in the dough with dietary fiber increases the MTI. Moreover, as shown by Lu et al. [107], apple pomace with smaller particle sizes, unlike the previously mentioned grape pomace, could potentially lead to limiting adverse changes in MTI. This underscores the complex influence of various factors on changes in the degree of dough softening, emphasizing the need for further research in this area. Lu et al. [107] also indicate that the degree of softening of wheat dough is closely associated with the farinograph quality number (FQN). As demonstrated in their study on the impact of apple pomace on the rheological properties of wheat dough, the increase in MTI was inversely correlated with FQN. Conversely, reverse relationships were noted for grape pomace by Tolve et al. [20], and for olive pomace by Azadfar et al. [18], confirming the ability of grape pomace and olive pomace to contribute to the production of doughs more resistant to mechanical stress.

The addition of grape pomace (GP) and apple pomace induces significant changes in the rheological properties of dough samples, as assessed by the alveograph parameters (extensibility value (L), dough tenacity (P), deformation energy (W), and P/L ratio). Tolve et al. [20] and Mironeasa and Mironeasa [105] indicated that the P value (a predictor of the dough's ability to retain gas) increases as the GP level increases, whereas L (an indicator of the dough's ability to expand without breakdown) decreases with the increase in GP level. The W value (an indicator of baking strength) decreased in GP fortified dough samples due to the higher P and lower L values. Additionally, Mironeasa and Mironeasa [105] showed a decrease in the P value with an increase in particle size of grape pomace powder. The increase in the P value can be related to the interactions that occur between the fiber structure and flour protein, while the increase in L value is associated with the high fiber content of the GP, which could compete with the gluten protein for available water in the dough system, forming a weaker gluten network, thus resulting in an inevitable decrease in extensibility [113]. The optimization of adding grape pomace from white grape varieties, conducted by Mironeasa and Mironeasa [105], revealed that to ensure optimal rheological characteristics, the supplementation of wheat flour should be at the level of 3.81%.

The third commonly used instrument for assessing the rheological behavior of wheat flour dough, in addition to the farinograph and alveograph, is the extensograph. The extensograph is a suitable tool for measuring the stretching properties of dough, enabling reliable assessments of the baking behavior of wheat flour dough in practical industrial applications and research. However, it is important to note that the extensograph method requires the use of a large amount of flour (300 g), which undoubtedly limits its applicability in certain areas of research Lu et al. [107] showed that the areas of wheat dough (parameters that provide information on the expected fermentation tolerance of dough) observed at 45, 90, and 135 min decreased with the addition of both apple pomace and de-fatted apple pomace. It indicated that wheat dough with low values of area and extensibility has weak gluten strength, confirming the results of MTI and FQN in farinograph properties of apple pomace dough. Extensibility of wheat dough, describing its elastic properties, was significantly lower with the addition of apple pomace compared to the control only after 45 min of fermentation. However, at 90 and 135 min, the presence of apple pomace did not show any significant effects on extensibility. The addition of apple pomace improved the resistance of the wheat dough compared to the control sample, regardless of the fermentation time. These dependencies resulted in an increase in the R/E ratio (the ratio of resistance and extensibility) compared to the control. Dough with a higher R/E ratio subsequently provides stiffening and elastic properties suitable for bread baking. The results obtained by Lu et al. [107] indicate the need for optimizing fermentation time and the addition of apple pomace to achieve bread with desirable characteristics.

Based on the findings from the aforementioned studies, the addition of plant by-products to wheat dough can lead to significant changes in its rheological properties, which in turn can impact the quality of the resulting bread. These alterations in specific rheological properties are influenced by factors such as the proportion, particle size, and type of by-products used. However, several challenges arise when interpreting the results across studies. Variations in the type of wheat flour used, lack of detailed specification of the by-products (such as their source and degree of pulverization), and the addition of other ingredients like salt for dough characteristics can hinder direct comparison of findings. Additionally, methodological differences in assessing rheological properties pose another challenge. While farinograph analysis using traditional farinographs or Mixolab is commonly used to evaluate dough rheology, other devices such as the alveograph or extensograph are employed to a lesser extent for dough characterization.

Table 1. Effect of selected by-products on wheat dough rheology.

Material and Level of Supplementation	Effects	Reference
Grape peels 3, 5, 7, and 9%	-Increase in water absorption, development time and dough tenacity -Decrease in stability time, deformation energy and the ability of the dough to expand -No changes in the degree of softening	Mironeasa and Mironeasa [105]
Wine grape pomace powder (without grape seeds) 5 and 10 g/100 g	-Increase in water absorption, dough stability, quality number (FQN), dough tenacity and in the gelatinization maximum of the dough -Decreased degree of dough softening, the ability of the dough to expand and deformation energy -No changes in development time	Tolve et al. [20]
Apple pomace and skimmed apple pomace 3, 6, and 9%	-Increase in water absorption, mixing tolerance index and development time -Decrease in stability time and farinograph quality number (FQN)	Lu et al. [107]
Apple pomace powders 5, 10, and 15%	-Increase in water absorption, dough stability, and development time	Kohajdová et al. [106]
Apple pomace powders 5, 10, 15, 20, and 25%	-Increase in water absorption and development time -Decrease in stability time	Usman et al. [103]
Olive pomace cellulose 2, 4, 6%	-Increase in water absorption and development time -Decrease in stability time and weakening value	Badawy and Smetanska [13]
Olive pomace 5, 10, and 15%	-Increase in water absorption, dough stability and quality number (FQN) -Decreased degree of dough softening	Azadfar et al. [18]
Olive pomace (freeze-dried powder) 1, 2, 3, and 5%	-Decrease in water absorption at high supplementation level, dough development time and stability	Dahdah et al. [72]
Flaxseed cake 5, 10, and 15%	-Increase in water absorption and in mixing time index at high supplementation level -Decrease dough development time and stability time	Wirkijowska et al. [17]
Flaxseed cake 5, 15, 25, 35, and 50%	-Increase in water absorption -Decrease dough development time and stability	Jiang et al. [19]

4. Bread Quality

The quality characterization of bread encompasses the evaluation of baking parameters such as dough and bread yield, baking loss, and a range of physical characteristics of bread including loaf volume, porosity, crumb moisture, and the color of the crumb and crust. Often, research works focus only on assessing selected parameters when defining bread quality. The most commonly evaluated aspects include the impact of components on loaf volume, crumb moisture, and color. Other parameters are described much less frequently and are often assessed using various methods [Table 2].

4.1. Baking Properties

The scientific reports confirm an increase in dough and bread yield with the increasing proportion of by-products, although this increase is not proportional to the quantity of the introduced component [17,114,115]. This phenomenon could be attributed to the increased water absorption capacity of fibers. Bread yield improved with the increasing amount of water added to the flour [116]. However, even with the same amount of water added to the flour, the bread yield may vary depending on the quantity and type of added flaxseed by-products and their processing (particle size, thermal treatment) [115]. The augmentation in dough absorption holds economic significance. Consequently, the incorporation of oil and fruit by-products into bread formulations could present an added value [117].

The high content of dietary fiber present in flaxseed by-products may promote water adsorption and water retention in bread, contributing to an increase in bread yield. Wirkijowska et al. [17] reported an increase in bread yield with the increasing supplementation level of flaxseed cake from 5% to 15%. At the maximum supplementation level, an 8% increase in bread yield was found compared to the control sample. However, a study by Jiang et al. [115] indicated that when the addition of flaxseed cake increased up to 25%, this trend can be interrupted. This suggests that an excessive addition of flaxseed cake could lead to deterioration of the gluten network, resulting in reduced water retention in the bread. Jiang et al. [115] also demonstrated that the particle size of the introduced component plays a crucial role in the structure and quality of bakery products. Comparing bread yield with a 25% addition of flaxseed cake with different particle sizes showed a higher value in the case of a by-product with a smaller particle size. A smaller particle size allows for better filling of the gluten network, reducing gluten structure damage and thereby retaining more water in the bread during baking. As reported by Lin et al. [118], a decrease in particle size could improve not only the gluten network but also lead to increased gas retention during fermentation.

Given the high fiber content and its potential influence on increased water absorption, it can be reasonably expected that in the case of other by-products such as olive, grape, and apple pomace, an increase in bread yield would also occur. Unfortunately, this characteristic was overlooked by the authors of the analyzed studies.

Another significant characteristic from an economic standpoint is oven loss and baking loss. These two parameters are associated with water loss during baking and cooling of the bread and, as shown in the analyzed study, depend on several factors such as the type of by-products, level of supplementation, and particle size of the raw material. As demonstrated by Azadfar et al. [18], substituting wheat flour with olive by-product flour resulted in a significant reduction in baking loss; decreasing from 14.33% observed for the control sample to 11.1% for bread with a 15% inclusion of olive by-products. This observed trend is attributed to the formation of hydrogen bonds between the hydroxyl groups of the dietary fiber structure. As a result, doughs containing a higher fiber content exhibited higher moisture content. This is confirmed by the high negative correlation observed between baking loss and crumb moisture after 24 h ($R = -0.942$) and after 72 h ($R = -0.950$). Kadirvelu and Fathima [119], indicated that some water molecules bind to the hydrophilic groups of fibers as bound water, which is more difficult to evaporate during the baking and cooling process, thus limiting the extent of baking losses. Such a reduction in baking loss was not observed when introducing flaxseed cake into bread. The total baking loss did not differ significantly for wheat bread with a 5–15% addition of flaxseed cake compared to the control [17]. However, as the authors note, the lack of a negative impact of supplementation on baking loss, combined with no noticeable changes in the weight of the bread, provides a good recommendation for bakery practice.

The influence of adding apple pomace on baking loss remains difficult to unequivocally determine. As reported by Bchir et al. [117], a 2% addition of apple pomace resulted in a significant increase in baking loss. The authors point out that as the amount of water needed for dough hydration increases with the amount of fiber added, greater water loss occurs during baking, leading to an increase in baking loss. Research conducted by Gumul et al. [120], also indicates the potential influence of the particle size of apple pomace on oven and total baking loss. The introduction of pomace in its whole form proved to be more favorable in terms of loss reduction, with a decrease in oven loss of 6.4–8.7% for 10 and 15% inclusion of apple by-products compared to control bread. On the other hand, an increase in both oven and total baking loss was noted for higher (15%) supplementation of milled apple pomace. Moreover, both oven loss and total baking loss were generally higher in the case of bread with milled pomace compared to loaves with whole pomace. The lower values of both parameters for bread with whole pomace may be due to the fact that larger fiber particles can absorb more water than small fragments, and the absorbed water is less likely to migrate during the baking process. This is confirmed by the water holding capacity values (whole pomace: 5.12 g/g water, milled pomace: 3.38 g/g water) [120]. However, it should be noted that this conclusion differs from the conclusions drawn by Bchir et al. [117]. It is possible that these reverse results are due to the thermal processing of the raw material, which occurred in the study conducted by Bchir et al. [117]. However, it should be noted that this conclusion differs from the conclusions drawn by Bchir et al. [117]. It is possible that these contrasting results are due to the thermal processing of the raw material in the study conducted by Bchir et al. [117].

Comparing physical characteristics such as volume, porosity, moisture, and color of bread fortified with various ingredients, which is well-known and widely accepted by most consumers, allows us to infer the degree of modification and potential acceptance of the product in the future. As shown in the analyzed study, the introduction of high-fiber raw materials, such as fruit pomace or oil industry by-products, into the bread recipe has a significant impact on changes in the physical properties of the bread [Table 2]. This is attributed, among other factors, to alterations in the rheological properties of the dough, resulting in the development of a less extensible and more tenacious dough in fortified samples, ultimately leading to a reduction in the volume and specific volume of the bread [12,121–123].

Walker et al. [123] reported a significant decrease in loaf volume for both red and white grape pomace. Bread with red grape pomace had a slightly smaller volume at the same level of addition as white grape pomace. In contrast, the study by Smith and Yu [121] indicates that the grape cultivar does not exhibit significant effects on both bread weight and loaf volume. Additionally, the results indicate that substituting 5% of wheat flour with grape pomace powder did not result in negative changes in these quality attributes. However, the bread with 10% GP exhibited a significantly lower loaf volume, accompanied by a slight decrease in weight, suggesting a denser crumb structure.

Hayta et al. [45] showed that the addition of grape pomace up to 10% caused a slight, though statistically insignificant, decrease in loaf volume. However, at the 10% level, it had a significantly lower specific volume compared to the control bread. The reduction in volume may be influenced by various factors, with the most commonly associated with a deterioration in crumb porosity. The amount of introduced component significantly influences the extent of bread volume and crumb porosity reduction. High-dietary-fiber ingredients, such as grape pomace, may extract water from starch granules and protein networks, potentially leading to a decrease in the volume of the bread. Research by Tolve et al. [20] additionally indicates that the decrease in the volume and specific volume of bread may be attributed to a reduction in pH. Acidic conditions could provide a more stressful environment, thus reducing yeast activity. Moreover, acidic conditions could promote the solubilization of gluten proteins, leading to the instability of the gluten network. It can be hypothesized that the decrease in yeast activity and instability of the gluten network may be the cause of poorer crumb porosity.

Regarding apple pomace, a 2% addition of this by-product from apples obtained during the cooking process does not result in a significant reduction in specific volume; however, a decrease in loaf volume is observed. Studies also show that thermal processing of apple pomace allows for a reduction in its negative impact on crumb porosity [117]. Significant reductions in specific volume were observed for bread supplemented with

5% apple pomace (AP) without and after enzymatic hydrolysis (variants hydrolyzed with Viscozyme® L, Pectinex® Ultra Tropical, and Celluclast® 1.5 L preparations) [124]. Researchers explain that the reduction in volume is caused by polysaccharides, which influence changes in the secondary structure of gluten proteins by altering the conformation of disulfide bridges and may partially dehydrate the gluten network through competitive water binding [125]. Natural apple pomace and those subjected to the mentioned enzymatic hydrolysis [124] resulted in a reduction in porosity from 80.06% to 70.71%. Only the variant of wheat bread prepared with apple pomace enzymatically hydrolyzed with Celluclast® 1.5 L did not differ significantly in terms of porosity from the control bread. Moreover, it exhibited better porosity than bread with pomace without hydrolysis.

Literature analysis does not provide a clear determination of the influence of oil industry by-products from flaxseed or olives on the specific volume and porosity of wheat bread. As reported by Wirkijowska et al. [17], an increase in the addition of flaxseed cake (from 5% to 15%) results in a decrease in the specific volume of bread; however, significant changes were noted with supplementation at levels of 10% and 15%. Supplementation of bread with flaxseed cake also led to a significant decrease in crumb porosity. The study indicated a porosity change from 77.7% for control bread to 70.3% for bread with a 15% addition of flaxseed cake.

However, there are reports that contradict the negative effect of flaxseed cake on bread volume and porosity. For instance, Guo et al. [126] observed a positive impact of flaxseed residue on specific volume with additions of 4% and 8%, especially at lower levels. The increase in specific volume compared to the control sample was 60% and 18%, respectively. Changes in dough strength and increased susceptibility to deformation due to the introduced flaxseed component explain this effect. A positive effect of incorporating flaxseed residue into bread was also observed by Jiang et al. [115], especially in the case of high-yield bread production with a high addition of flaxseed residue (at 25%). Lower levels of supplementation did not significantly affect the porosity of such bread.

Regarding olive pomace, data revealed by Azadfar et al. [18] showed that the introduction of olive pomace (from 5% to 15%) into flatbread results in a significant reduction in bread volume. Additionally, as shown, partial replacement of wheat flour with olive pomace leads to a reduction in gluten content, disruption of the gluten network, weakening of the dough structure, and consequently, a decrease not only in volume but also in crumb porosity was observed. Crumb porosity of flatbread changes from 24% for the control bread to 18% for bread with 15% olive pomace supplementation. In contrast, Cardinali et al. [26] did not demonstrate a negative impact of adding olive pomace on the volume of traditional bread, even with 20% supplementation. This difference may partially result from variations in the baking methods of flat and traditional bread. Moreover, the conducted research showed that the time (up to 6 months) and temperature of storing olive pomace (4 °C or −20 °C), as well as the type of wheat flour used (all-purpose white or whole wheat flour), do not cause significant changes in the volume of wheat bread.

One of the crucial physical characteristics of bread is its crumb moisture. An appropriately moist crumb is a guarantee of good-quality bread that retains freshness and does not crumble when sliced. Literature data also indicate that an increase in crumb moisture is negatively correlated with its energy density [17]. Literature reports on the influence of both grape and apple processing by-products on the moisture of fresh crumb are varied. While Tolve et al. [20] and Walker et al. [123] observed a slight reduction in crumb moisture for bread with a 10% addition of grape pomace, Smith and Yu [121] observed a significant increase in crumb moisture due to the introduction of 5% and 10% grape pomace. This increase in moisture was observed across four different grape varieties (Muscadine (Noble and Scuppernong) and Cabernet (Franc and Sauvignons)). Similarly, Gumul et al. [120] showed that the addition of apple pomace also leads to a significant increase in the moisture content of fresh crumb compared to wheat bread. Their research indicated that, in addition to the supplementation level, the degree of pomace fragmentation plays a significant role in crumb moisture. At a 15% supplementation level, there was a 12% and 19% increase in moisture compared to the control for bread supplemented with whole and milled pomace, respectively. Crumb taken from loaves containing milled pomace contained more hydrated parts of the pomace, while those from loaves with whole pomace contained less hydrated pomace. An increase in bread crumb moisture was also observed in studies on wheat bread with the addition of micronized dietary fiber obtained from apple pomace up to 20% [114].

Introducing olive pomace into bread at a 10% level results in a significant increase in bread moisture compared to wheat bread [18]. Both 24 and 72 h post-baking, bread supplemented with olive by-products exhibited significantly higher moisture content than the control sample. Hydroxyl groups within the dietary fiber structure form hydrogen bonds with water, leading to increased moisture levels in doughs with elevated fiber content. Some water molecules bind to the hydrophilic groups of fibers, forming bound water that resists evaporation during baking. Similarly, bread supplemented with flaxseed by-products behaves in the same way. The use of by-products from flaxseed, at a level up 15% in bread production resulted in a significant increase in the moisture of fresh crumb compared to wheat bread [17,126]. Authors suggest that the higher crumb moisture content of bread may result from the increased water retention ability of the soluble dietary fiber fraction, which, as a hydrocolloid, has high water-holding capacity [127]. Additionally, hydrocolloids could form a network that acts as a barrier to gas diffusion during baking, reducing vapor losses and leading to higher moisture content in bread crumb [128].

The increase in moisture content in breads with by-products is mostly attributed to the high water-binding capacity of dietary fiber. The hydration capacity of fiber depends mainly on its botanical origin and composition [129]. However, many studies lack information regarding both the origin of the raw materials and the fractional composition of dietary fiber. Moreover, it should be noted that direct comparisons of the moisture of so-called fresh crumb are challenging not only due to different types of bread production and the use of various base flours but also often because of imprecise determination of the time at which moisture was assessed, with this time often ranging from 1 to 24 h post-baking.

4.2. Color

Finally, one of the main sensory attributes that can considerably influence consumer acceptability is color. In the case of bread, from the consumer's perspective, the color of both the crumb and crust is important. The crumb color of bread is typically similar to the color of its ingredients because the crumb does not reach as high a temperature as the crust [130]. The crust color, to some extent, depends on the color of the introduced component, but primarily results from Maillard and sugar caramelization reactions due to contact with high temperatures in the baking chamber [131].

The crumb color of bread with grape components addition showed the lowest L* values (indicating whiteness (value 100) or blackness (value 0)) and b* values (indicating yellow (positive value) or blue (negative value)), but the highest a* values (indicating red (positive value) or green (negative value)) compared to the control [20,45,112,121]. The darkening of grape pomace (GP) breads is anticipated due to the substantial amount of polyphenols present in GP, especially anthocyanins and tannins, which exhibit a purple-red color at the baking pH. The color of grape skin is primarily influenced by the composition and content of anthocyanins, and their stability is significantly impacted by various processing conditions, including pH, temperature, light, oxygen, enzymes, ascorbic acid, flavonoids, proteins, and metallic ions [132,133]. In the case of bread crust, an increase in grape pomace proportion resulted in a decrease in a* value [20,45]. This may be attributed to a higher degradation of anthocyanins, responsible for the red GP pigmentation, resulting from the higher temperature and lower humidity on the crust compared to the conditions inside the loaf during baking.

Studies by Jannati et al. [134] have shown that, in the case of incorporating apple pomace in bread formula (from 1 to 7%), there was a decrease in L* and an increase in a* and b* values of crumb compared to the control. Similar trends were observed by Bchir et al. [117] for bread with a 2% addition of pomace subjected to previous thermal processing.

Conversely, reverse trends were observed for the crust of this bread, with a higher value of the L* parameter along with a significant reduction in both the a* and b* parameters compared to the control. In both crust and crumb, the total color difference (ΔE*) was 20.14 and 10.23, respectively, indicating very distinct differences in color.

Regarding olive pomace, Cardinali et al. [26] showed that both the crust and crumb color depend on the type of wheat flour used (soft type 0 or whole grain) and the amount of olive pomace used for baking. It was noted that the influence of olive pomace addition was less evident in bread samples containing whole wheat flour, likely due to the dark appearance of loaves with the presence of wheat bran. Concerning individual color parameters, a progressive decrease in brightness was detected in samples containing olive pomace, indicating an increase in the amount of pigments derived from olives. In this study, all samples with olive pomace addition had values in the red hue, which can be associated with a high content of anthocyanins noted in this component [135]. Meanwhile, the b* parameter values were in the yellow hue range, again reflecting a strong influence of the olive pomace addition, with the bread produced with 100% soft wheat flour showing the lowest average yellow levels. The results obtained in this study are consistent with those obtained by Cedola et al. [25], who found that bread samples containing olive pomace had a darker color compared to control loaves without this by-product.

Darkening of the crumb color was also noted as a result of introducing flaxseed residues into the bread recipe. Analyzing changes in the a* and b* parameters, a significant increase in the saturation of the red and blue colors was observed with increased supplementation of flaxseed cake [17,95,126]. The study by Wirkijowska et al. [17] indicates that even with a 5% addition, the color change is significant, as evidenced by the high ΔE* values of 9.7 and 17.2 for the 5% and 15% supplementation levels, respectively. Similar results were obtained by Taglieri et al. [14], who also showed that the color of bread with flaxseed cake addition depends on the leavening method used (sourdough or yeast). The researchers demonstrated that bread with flaxseed cake and sourdough had a lighter crumb and significantly lower a* values compared to bread with a similar addition of flaxseed cake and yeast. However, no differences in b* were observed between both methods (sourdough/yeast).

4.3. Texture

Textural parameters are crucial for assessing the sensory characteristics of food products. Among the fundamental texture parameters evaluated for bread, hardness or firmness, springiness, cohesiveness, and chewiness stand out [17,18,45,120]. Hardness of the crumb is particularly significant in bread assessment, serving as a primary indicator of its freshness [115,120]. It is typically defined as the maximum force experienced during the initial compression of the crumb. Springiness reflects the material's ability to recover after stress, indicating its delayed rebound following compressions. Cohesiveness measures the extent to which a material can deform before rupturing [45], and low values typically indicate susceptibility to fracture and crumble, which may negatively affect consumers' acceptance of bread [126,136]. Chewiness, meanwhile, signifies the time required to chew a food item until it reaches a suitable consistency for swallowing [137]. In Texture Profile Analysis (TPA), chewiness originally referred to the energy needed to masticate a solid food product, while gumminess described the energy required to disintegrate a semisolid food for swallowing [138]. It is essential to note that gumminess and chewiness are mutually exclusive, and therefore, when reporting TPA measurements, either chewiness or gumminess values should be provided, but not both for the same food.

The available literature examining the impact of non-conventional ingredients added to bread formulations, such as residues from pressing oilseeds and fruit residues, suggests significant alterations in textural properties for both fresh and stored wheat bread [17,18,45]. According to Hayta et al. [45], the inclusion of grape pomace at levels above 5% led to a notable increase in the hardness of fresh bread (measured 2 h after baking). This effect was attributed by the authors to the higher fiber content, which, by binding water, contributes to the observed increase in hardness. In the same study, there were generally no discernible differences in terms of springiness and cohesiveness between fresh bread with and without grape pomace. However, during consecutive days of storage (1 and 2 days), hardness gradually increased in all samples, with a greater range of changes observed as the proportion of grape pomace increased. For instance, after two days of storage, the hardness of the control sample increased by 60%, whereas for bread with a 10% addition of grape pomace, it increased by over threefold. While slight changes were noted for springiness and cohesiveness, with generally lower values observed as a result of storage, significant differences were not observed in most cases. Similarly, in the study by Walker et al. [123], an increase in grape pomace resulted in increased firmness and no changes in springiness. The increase in firmness with the addition of grape pomace is explained by the authors as a result of decreased volume. The reaction between gluten and fiber at high levels leads to a weakened gluten network, resulting in increased bread density and hardness. Additionally, an increase in chewiness was observed with the increase in grape pomace content. Tolve et al. [20] and Šporin et al. [112] reported a similar increase in the firmness of bread crumb, with grape pomace supplementation up to 10% and 15%, respectively. This, as suggested by the authors, may result from weak gluten network formation with poor gas retention ability, contributing to the hardening effect of bread crumb.

Gumul et al. [120] investigated the effects of incorporating whole and milled apple pomace (up to 15%) into wheat bread on its textural attributes. The study assessed the texture of the bread immediately after baking (fresh) and after 24 and 48 h of storage, a timeframe similar to that used by Hayta et al. [45] in their study on grape pomace addition, facilitating a direct comparison between these two additives. In the conducted studies, no significant influence of the level and type of addition was observed in terms of the cohesiveness of fresh bread and stored bread. Adding apple pomace above 5% levels, similar to grape pomace, significantly increased the bread hardness. Notably, when apple pomace levels were up to 10%, the type of pomace (whole or milled) did not significantly affect the texture parameters. However, at a 15% inclusion rate of milled apple pomace, the bread exhibited substantially higher hardness, with the bread's hardness more than quadrupling compared to the control bread. After two days of storage, a significant increase in hardness was observed for bread with apple pomace inclusion levels exceeding 5%. The most significant changes were noted with a 15% inclusion of milled apple pomace, indicating a negative influence of extensive particle size reduction on texture parameters. The lower hardness of bread supplemented with whole apple pomace is associated with its higher water-binding capacity and the subsequent release of absorbed water into the adjacent crumb throughout the storage period. However, this conclusion contradicts the findings of the study by Hayta et al. [45], where an increase in water-binding capacity was associated with increased hardness. It appears that changes in bread volume noted in the studies by Gumul et al. [120] have a greater impact on changes in hardness. A significant reduction in volume was observed for bread with the addition of milled apple pomace (especially at 15%) compared to whole apple pomace addition. This leads to a denser crumb texture and an increase in hardness, a phenomenon observed in the studies by other authors such as Walker et al. [123] and Tolve et al. [20]. Research conducted by Jagelaviciute et al. [124] also did not show a significant influence of 5% apple pomace addition on changes in hardness, and chewiness for fresh wheat bread. However, during a four-day storage period, hardness, and chewiness significantly increased, while cohesiveness and resilience significantly decreased. Apple pomace did not have a significant effect on wheat bread springiness or its changes during the four-day storage period. An interesting aspect of the conducted research was the assessment of the influence of enzymatic hydrolysis of apple pomace on changes in bread texture properties (hardness, springiness, chewiness, and resilience), which varied depending on the preparation used. It was noted that with the preparation causing a decrease in soluble fiber content, there was an increase in hardness, and chewiness of fresh bread, along with decreased cohesiveness and resilience.

Research by Jannati et al. [134] suggests the possibility of producing bread with reduced hardness when using a low level of apple pomace addition (up to 7%). The authors demonstrated that adding apple pomace up to 7% could slow down the bread aging process (specifically, Sangak, a flat type of Iranian bread), as evidenced by the lower hardness values of the supplemented bread throughout the storage period (from 24 to 96 h) compared to the control sample. According to the authors, this might be associated with the increased water absorption by the fiber compounds in apple pomace and the resulting higher moisture content of the bread, leading to reduced hardness. Regarding cohesiveness, only a slight decrease in values was observed with increased apple pomace addition, but this was only noticeable after 24 h of storage. In the subsequent storage period (48–96 h), no significant differences were noted between the supplemented bread and the control sample.

Based on the available literature regarding the effect of flaxseed cake on bread texture, the studies present contrasting results compared to the influence of fruit pomace (grape and apple). These studies generally showed lower or no changes in hardness [17,115,126]. This suggests that high amounts of flaxseed cake (even up to 25%) can be added to wheat flour to produce bread with an acceptable texture, comparable to wheat bread. Jiang et al. [115] investigated the effect of adding two types of flaxseed marc flours (roasted and unroasted) on fresh and 24-h stored bread. As shown in their study, both fresh and stored bread exhibited a significant decrease in hardness with the addition of flaxseed cake up to 15%, which the authors related to its high water-holding ability. Such trends confirm the previously demonstrated ambiguous influence of increased water-holding capacity on hardness changes, which are simultaneously influenced by other factors [45,120]. In this case, a 15% addition of flaxseed cake (both roasted and unroasted) resulted in an increase in lipid content, specific volume, and changes in crumb structure (lower cell diameter and thinner cell wall) compared to the control. This could also contribute to the decrease in hardness. It was shown that lipids present in flaxseed cake can promote a softer texture and prolonged freshness. The significant impact of specific volume on hardness changes is supported by the observed increase in hardness with a 25% flaxseed addition, which was accompanied by a reduced specific volume of the bread. However, it is important to emphasize that in each case, the hardness of the supplemented bread was either lower or did not significantly differ from the control sample. Changes in the proportion of flaxseed, regardless of the type, only slightly affected the crumb springiness and cohesiveness, with a noticeable decrease in springiness observed only in the case of fresh bread with a 25% addition. The minor impact of flaxseed cake addition (up to 15%) on springiness, cohesiveness, and chewiness is also confirmed by studies conducted by Wirkijowska et al. [17]. No significant changes in bread hardness were observed after 24 h. However, after 72 h, the bread with added flaxseed exhibited approximately 30% higher hardness compared to the control sample. The reduction in bread hardness noted by Jiang et al. [115] is consistent with the findings of Guo et al. [126] using flaxseed residue (at 4% and 8%). These results also confirm the minor impact of the addition on springiness and cohesiveness. However, contrary to the results presented by Wirkijowska et al. [17], a decrease in chewiness was noted.

Cardinali et al. [26] examined the impact of olive pomace on the hardness of bread made from white and whole wheat flour, fortified with fresh and stored olive pomace for 6 weeks at different temperatures (-4 °C and -20 °C). Fresh olive pomace up to 15% decreased bread hardness, but at 20%, hardness increased, although the values remained below the control sample. This trend was consistent with the observations made for flaxseed pomace by Jiang et al. [115]. Refrigerated olive pomace showed similar hardness trends, while frozen olive pomace at 15% and 20% increased bread hardness significantly compared to the non-fortified bread. As the results presented by Cardinali et al. [26] indicate no significant effect of the addition of olive pomace on the specific volume of the bread, it can be assumed that the changes in texture are mostly affected by changes in fat and dietary fiber content. As indicated earlier by Jiang et al. [115], an increased fat content in bread, associated with the type of additive used, can promote a softer bread texture. On the other hand, the increased dietary fiber content may compensate for the fat's impact on reducing hardness, especially at higher olive pomace inclusion levels. The potential influence of lipid content on bread hardness is also supported by the research of Azadfar et al. [18]. The authors demonstrated that when using defatted olive pomace, there is an increase in bread hardness (at 24 h) compared to the control sample, with a statistically significant increase observed only at a 15% inclusion rate. Additionally, the addition of defatted olive pomace had a minimal or no significant effect on adhesiveness, resilience, springiness, cohesiveness, and chewiness of the bread (at 24 h). During the 72-h storage period, an increase in hardness and crumbliness was observed, manifested by a decrease in cohesiveness and springiness, which are typical indicators of bread staling. However, it should be noted that the changes in individual characteristics were not uniform. While the increase in hardness for bread with a 15% addition of defatted olive pomace was 45%, the decrease in cohesiveness and springiness was approximately 15% and 7.5%, respectively. These changes result from processes occurring during bread storage, such as starch retrogradation, gluten dehydration, amylopectin recrystallization, and the transition from a rubbery to a glassy state of the protein network.

A general note on comparing the results of individual research studies should be highlighted. Difficulties arise when comparing results from different studies due to the lack of specification of all key Texture Profile Analysis (TPA) measurement parameters and the use of various measurement conditions. These conditions include different compression rates (e.g., 1 mm/s, 3 mm/s, 5 mm/s, or 10 mm/s) and varying compression levels (e.g., 25%, 40%, 50%). In some research studies, there is also an absence of a strictly defined time after which the bread texture analysis was conducted, as well as specified bread storage parameters like temperature. Due to significant texture changes occurring during bread storage, especially in the initial period, this makes it challenging to make more accurate comparisons between results concerning the use of different additional raw materials. Significant differences in the application of individual additives are also influenced by variations in the dough preparation and bread baking process. This includes the degree of comminution of individual ingredients, fermentation time, and the use of other additives in addition to the primary ingredient and supplement (discussed by-products), which also affect the bread's characteristics. Variations in the baking process itself, such as time and temperature, are also essential factors.

Table 2. Effect of selected by-products on wheat bread quality and sensory characteristics.

Material and Level of Supplementation	Effects	Reference
Grape pomace powder 2; 5 and 10%	-Decrease in loaf volume and specific volume -Darkening of crumb color; the color shifts towards red and blue hues -Increase in hardness with the level of supplementation and storage time -No significant changes in springiness and cohesiveness -Decrease in overall acceptability at 10% supplementation	Hayta et al. [45]
Wine grape pomace powder (without grape seeds) 5 and 10 g/100 g	-Decrease in loaf volume and specific volume -No significant changes in moisture content and baking loss -Increase in firmness -No significant impact on overall acceptability (despite significant changes in individual characteristics)	Tolve et al. [20]
Wine grape pomace powder 6; 10; and 15%	-Decrease in volume and specific volume -Darkening of crumb color; the color shifts towards red and blue hues -Increased in firmness -Significant differences were observed for all sensory attributes, except for yeast flavor, salty taste of the crumb, and crust thickness.	Šporin et al. [122]

Table 2. Cont.

Material and Level of Supplementation	Effects	Reference
Wine grape pomace powder 5; 10 and 15%	-Decrease in loaf volume and volume index -Darkening of crumb color -Increase in firmness and chewiness -No significant changes in springiness -No significant difference in all sensory attributes except for mouth feel and color	Walker et al. [123]
Wine grape pomace powder 5 and 10 g/100 g	-Decrease in loaf weight and volume -Darkening in crumb color; the color shifts towards red and blue hues -Increase in hardness -Decrease in consumer preferences for color, aroma, flavor, and texture	Smith and Yu [121]
Apple pomace (whole and milled) 5, 10, and 15%	-Increase in moisture content of crumb -Increase in oven loss (for milled apple pomace) -Decrease in specific volume -Decrease in oven loss, and total baking loss (for whole apple pomace) -Increase in firmness with the level of supplementation and storage time -No significant changes in cohesiveness -Wheat bread with 5% whole apple pomace received the best marks, thanks to good volume, low loss during baking, low crumb hardness compared to the control on the day of baking and during storage	Gumul et al. [120]
Apple pomace (non-treated and enzymatically hydrolyzed) 5%	-Decrease in specific volume and crumb porosity -No significant changes in hardness, gumminess, and chewiness for fresh bread (for non-treated apple pomace) -Changes in TPA properties depending on the type of enzyme used for enzymatically hydrolyzed apple pomace - Addition of 5% apple pomace enzymatically unprocessed and hydrolyzed with Celluclast® 1.5 L had no negative effect on sensory characteristics of wheat bread in most cases. While hydrolyzed with Viscozyme® L and Pectinex® Ultra Tropical had negative effect on textural characteristics of wheat bread.	Jagelaviciute et al. [124]
Apple pomace 1, 3, 5, and 7%	-Darkening of crumb color; the color shifts towards red and yellow hues -Decrease in hardness -A slight decrease in cohesiveness at 24 h of storage; no changes at 48–96 h of storage -Addition of 3% apple pomace powder to Sangak bread (i) consumers judged it to be perfectly acceptable, (ii) had a positive effect on aroma and texture compared to the control sample	Jannati et al. [134]
Olive pomace (defatted) 5, 10, and 15%	-Decrease in baking loss, specific volume and crumb porosity -Increase in crumb moisture after 24 and 72 h of storage -Increase in bread hardness at 24 and 72 h of storage -Minimal or no significant effect on adhesiveness, resilience, springiness, cohesiveness, and chewiness of the bread at 24 h -Replacing wheat flour with 10% olive pomace had no significant effect on the sensory parameters of Barbari bread	Azadfar et al. [18]
Olive pomace (fresh and stored at for 6 months at −20 °C or 4 °C) 10, 15, and 20%	-No significant effect on the specific volume -Darkening of crumb color; the color shifts towards red and yellow hues -Hardness was affected both by the addition and storage condition of olive pomace -no sensory testing	Cardinali et al. [26]
Flaxseed cake flour (unroasted and roasted) 5, 15, and 25%	-Minimal or no significant effect on specific volume and area of cells -Decrease in cell diameter -Decrease in hardness -Minimal or no significant effect on springiness and cohesiveness -Adding 25% roasted flax seed flour to wheat-rye bread improves its colour and flavour, making it as preferred by consumers as traditional wheat bread	Jiang et al. [115]

Table 2. Cont.

Material and Level of Supplementation	Effects	Reference
Flaxseed cake 5, 10, and 15%	-Increase in bread yield and crumb moisture -Decrease in baking loss and specific volume -Negative effect on the crumb porosity -Darkening of crumb color; the color shifts towards red and blue hues -No significant changes in hardness at 24 h of storage -A minor impact on springiness, cohesiveness, and chewiness -The 10% addition of flaxseed pomace produces a bread with acceptable sensory properties	Wirkijowska et al. [17]
Flaxseed residues (after oil extraction) 4 and 8%	-Increase in specific volume and crumb moisture -Darkening of crumb color; the color shifts towards red and blue hues -Decrease in hardness and chewiness -A minor impact on springiness and cohesiveness -darker color of the bread were less attractive to the assessors	Guo et al. [126]
Flaxseed cake 5, 7.5, and 10%	-Increase in the bitter taste (both in crumb and crust) -Significantly decreased the lightness -Significantly increase the greenness and yellowness -sensory analysis showed that the optimum level of flaxseed cake flour addition is 5% when using sourdough and 7.5% when using baker's yeast	Taglieri et al. [14]

5. Sensory Quality and Consumer Acceptance

Sensory properties are crucial in assessing the quality of food products and significantly influence consumer perception and acceptance in the food market [139]. Factors such as color, flavor, aroma, and texture are fundamental determinants of product perception and play a significant role in its market success. Sensory analysis, which involves evaluating perceptual signals received through human senses—including sight, hearing, taste, smell, and touch—plays a crucial function in studying the sensory properties of food products [140]. While traditional methods of sensory analysis, like trained sensory panels, colorimetry, and texture analysis, are effective, they often involve invasive procedures and are labor-intensive, limiting their application mainly to smaller studies. As research on the impact of additives, such as food industry by-products, on bread's sensory characteristics gains importance, the search for alternative ingredients to enhance its nutritional value continues.

Studies by Valková et al. [141], Lu et al. [107], Curutchet et al. [142], and Jagelaviciute et al. [124] analyze various aspects of the influence of apple pomace addition on the sensory evaluation of wheat bread. These studies employed different methods and evaluation techniques for sensory analysis. Valková et al. [141] used a semi-structured rating scale, Lu et al. [107] applied a fuzzy mathematical model, and both Curutchet et al. [142] and Jagelaviciute et al. [124] used CATA questionnaires.

In the study by Valková et al. [141], no significant differences in sensory parameters were observed between bread samples with varied concentrations of apple pomace and control samples. This suggests that this additive can be used in quantities up to 10% without significant deterioration in the sensory quality of bread. Similarly, Lu et al. [107] found that the optimal concentration of apple pomace was 3%, with higher concentrations potentially leading to deteriorations in bread sensory characteristics, primarily due to changes in texture and flavor. In contrast, Curutchet et al. [142] observed an improvement in consumer acceptance of bread with apple residues, although some still expressed concerns regarding taste changes. Jagelaviciute et al. [124] found that the addition of apple residues did not have a significant impact on the sensory properties of wheat bread. The review of these studies suggests that the addition of apple residues to wheat bread may be an effective strategy for enriching dietary fiber while maintaining sensory acceptability. During the development process of new bread recipes with added apple residues, it is important to consider consumer preferences and concerns regarding taste and healthiness. Additionally, information regarding the origin and sustainable development may influence consumer purchasing decisions, justifying their inclusion in marketing strategies for fiber-enriched products.

The integration of grape pomace (GP) and grape seed flour (GPP) into bread formulations has garnered considerable attention for its potential to enhance sensory properties while also improving nutritional profiles [20,45,121,123,141,143]. Over the past decade, research has provided a nuanced understanding of how these additions influence consumer perceptions of aroma, flavor, texture, and overall product acceptance.

Smith and Yu [121] illustrated that the cultivar of grape has a more pronounced effect on the sensory qualities of bread—such as aroma, flavor, and texture—than the quantity of grape pomace added. This suggests a nuanced interplay where both the specific type of GP and its proportion within the bread formulation are critical in maintaining the sensory appeal of the bread. Despite the potential benefits, their findings also highlight a general decline in qualitative sensory attributes with the inclusion of GP, emphasizing the need for careful consideration in the choice and amount of GP used. Supporting this, Hayta et al. [45] found that additions of 2% and 5% GP did not significantly affect the bread's sensory characteristics compared to a control, with no discernible difference in aspects such as shape symmetry, crumb color, and taste. However, a 10% inclusion rate led to a decrease in overall acceptability, primarily attributed to a reduction in taste quality.

Further investigation by Walker et al. [123] revealed that while 5% and 10% GP additions did not significantly alter most sensory attributes, there was a notable decline in Mouth Feel JAR ("Just About Right" scale) and Color JAR scores, suggesting that GP-enriched bread may be perceived as somewhat drier. Nevertheless, these changes did not affect the overall likability of the GP-fortified bread, indicating general consumer acceptance at these inclusion levels. Tolve et al. [20] expanded upon these insights by reporting that GP inclusion at 5% and 10% significantly enhanced global flavor and acidity, albeit at the cost of a sweeter taste and the bread's characteristic scent. This study also observed changes in bread appearance, such as porosity and hardness, underlining the significant but complex impact of GP on bread's sensory profiles. Parallel findings by Šporin et al. [122] echoed the significant sensory shifts induced by GP, particularly in increasing the bread's acidity and altering its texture to be more crumbly and less springy. These sensory changes, however, did not always align with instrumental texture analyses, suggesting a disparity between perceived and measured texture changes.

Research by Oprea et al. [143] and Valková et al. [144] introduced grape seed flour (GPP) as a variable, noting its beneficial impact on bread's sensory properties without compromising overall consumer acceptance. Oprea et al. [143] highlighted the potential of moderate GPP levels to introduce desirable changes in bread's texture and appearance, akin to those found in rye bread, without negative implications for consumer perception. Valková et al. [144] confirmed that even at levels up to 10%, GPP's effect on aroma, taste, and texture was positive, indicating a balance between nutritional enhancement and sensory appeal.

In conclusion, these collective findings suggest a promising avenue for incorporating GP and GPP into bread formulations. The critical determinant appears to be the careful selection of GP/GPP levels and types, which can enhance sensory characteristics—such as taste, aroma, texture, and appearance—without detracting from the overall product acceptance. Continued research in this domain is vital for optimizing recipes and fully leveraging the potential benefits of GP and GPP additions, thus opening new opportunities for the bakery industry to produce healthful, appealing, and innovative products.

Research conducted by Wirkijowska et al. [17], Guo et al. [126], Makowska et al. [145], Krupa-Kozak et al. [146], and Gao et al. [147] focused on assessing the impact of adding flaxseed cake, flour, and waste flaxseed extract on the sensory characteristics of bread. In the study by Wirkijowska et al. [17], it was observed that a 10% addition of flaxseed pomace results in bread with acceptable sensory properties. However, a higher addition of 15%

leads to a significant decrease in ratings related to both crust and crumb color. Nonetheless, for other analyzed attributes such as taste, aroma, elasticity, and crumb porosity, either no changes were observed, or they were minimal. Similarly, Guo et al. [126] reported a decrease in color assessment during sensory evaluation with additions of flaxseed cake, suggesting that the darker color of the bread was less attractive to the assessors. Makowska et al. [145] conducted a study on wheat bread using a sensory panel in accordance with ISO 8586-1:1993 [146]. The study involved evaluating the color, taste, aroma, texture, and overall acceptability of bread samples by ten judges. The results showed a significant influence of linseed cake fermentation on the sensory characteristics of bread, with high ratings obtained for samples fermented by lactic acid bacteria, especially L. plantarum. In contrast, Krupa-Kozak et al. [147] focused on evaluating the sensory properties of gluten-free bread with the addition of flaxseed extract. They employed a panel of trained experts following ISO guidelines and conducted descriptive sensory analysis. The addition of flaxseed extract improved the overall sensory quality of gluten-free bread, especially in the sample with the highest level of addition. Meanwhile, Gao et al.s' study [148] centered on Chinese steamed bread (CSB) enriched with flaxseed flour. They used an evaluation panel consisting of six assessors who assessed various sensory parameters of the bread. The addition of 10% flaxseed flour was found to be most acceptable to the panelists. A comparative analysis of the results from these studies suggests that flaxseed cake, similar to both flaxseed flour and waste flaxseed extract, can enhance the sensory characteristics of bread. Fermentation may also play a significant role in shaping these characteristics, particularly for wheat bread. It's worth noting that different types of bread (wheat, gluten-free, Chinese steamed bread) may respond differently to the addition of various types of flaxseed materials, possibly due to differences in production processes and raw material composition. The addition of 10% flaxseed cake and flour appears to be the optimal point for achieving the best sensory ratings in wheat and Chinese steamed bread. However, for gluten-free bread, a higher level of waste flaxseed extract may be more beneficial for overall sensory quality.

The incorporation of olive industry by-products may subtly but significantly influence the sensory attributes of bread, contingent upon the type of bread being supplemented. Depending on the specific bread type and the type as well as the quantity of olive by-products added, this could lead to alterations in taste, aroma, texture, and overall acceptability as perceived by consumers [18,53]. In a study focusing on Barbari bread enriched with olive pomace flour, sensory evaluation results indicated that the control sample received the highest sensory ratings, with the exception of odor. Bread enriched with olive pomace flour at varying concentrations (5%, 10%, 15%) garnered lower ratings, particularly in terms of texture and overall acceptability. It was observed that exceeding a 10% addition of olive pomace flour could have adverse effects on both texture and overall acceptability of the bread [18]. In contrast, a study by Cecchi et al. [53], which examined wheat bread supplemented with olive pulp (5%, 10%, 15%) revealed that bread enriched with olive pulp received higher ratings for taste, crust, crumb color, and overall acceptance compared to the control bread. The incorporation of olive pulp influenced the formation of the gluten network, impacting the final bubble structure in the bread, yet the olive pulp-enriched bread remained sensory acceptable.

The research reviewed in this section sheds light on the diverse impact of incorporating various additives into bread formulations on its sensory properties. Ranging from apple pomace and grape-derived products to flaxseed components and olive-based ingredients, these studies collectively emphasize the potential to enhance both the nutritional value and sensory appeal of bread. They also underscore the importance of carefully balancing additive concentrations to maintain or improve sensory characteristics such as taste, aroma, texture, and overall acceptability. With consumer preferences increasingly favoring healthier and more sustainable food options, the insights gleaned from these investigations are invaluable for the baking industry. They provide a roadmap for innovating product development that aligns with consumer demands without compromising the sensory qualities that make bread a staple food worldwide. Continued research in this area will be essential for further refining these formulations and ultimately thriving in the competitive food market.

6. Nutritional Value of Bread

Foods abundant in dietary fiber contribute significantly to various physiological processes, including the digestion and absorption of lipids, regulation of blood glucose and cholesterol levels, weight management through enhanced satiety, improved intestinal regularity, and protection against colon cancer [4]. The fortification of food items is a widespread strategy employed to augment both the nutritional content and functional characteristics of the products [Table 3].

Table 3. Effect of selected by-products on the nutritional value of wheat bread.

Material and Level of Supplementation	Effects	Reference
Grape pomace powder 5 and 10 g/100 g of flour	-Increase in phenolic compounds, particularly notable rise in anthocyanins; bioaccessibility of anthocyanins after in vitro digestion; antioxidant activity (ABTS, FRAP) -Decrease in the predicted glycemic index and starch hydrolysis	Rocchetti et al. [148]
Wine grape pomace powder 5 and 10 g/100 g of flour	-Increase in total dietary fiber and insoluble dietary fiber, ash, polyphenol and total flavonoid and antioxidant activity (Trolox) -Decrease in protein and carbohydrates content	Smith and Yu [121]
Wine grape pomace powder (without grape seeds) 5 and 10 g/100 g of flour	-Increase in the total dietary fiber, total starch, crude lipids, total phenolic content and flavonoid and antioxidant activity -Decrease in total starch -No significant changes in crude protein and free sugars content	Tolve et al. [20]
Wine grape pomace powder 5; 10 and 15%	-Increase in the total dietary fiber content, total phenolic content and radical scavenging activity	Walker et al. [123]
Grape pomace powder 2; 5 and 10%	-Increase in the total phenolic content and anti-radical activity (%)	Hayta et al. [45]
Apple pomace or skimmed apple pomace sieved by US-60 or US-100 3; 6 and 9%	-Increase in ash and dietary fiber content	Lu et al. [107]
Whole or milled apple pomace 5; 10 and 15%	-Increase in protein with 5% and 10% of whole apple pomace addition and in fat with whole apple pomace addition -Increase in total sugar, TDF and its fractions, anthocyanins content and antioxidant activity (Trolox) -Decrease in ash content with milled apple pomace addition	Gumul et al. [120]
Apple pomace powder 1; 2; 5 and 10%	-Increase in ash, carbohydrates and in antioxidant activity (Trolox) -Decrease in protein, fat and energy value	Valková et al. [141]
Olive mill wastewater instead of adding water and/or substituting 10% of flour with olive paste	-Increase in TPC and antioxidant activity (Trolox, FRAP)	Badawy and Smetanska [13]
Olive pomace cellulose 2; 4 and 6%	-Decrease in protein -Increase in dietary fiber and scavenging activity -No significant changes in ash, lipids and carbohydrate content	Cardinali et al. [26]
Fresh, frozen or refrigerated olive pomace 10; 15 and 20%	-Increase in TPC, antioxidant activity (DPPH, ABTS, FRAP) and dietary fiber	Cedola et al. [25]
Olive paste 10%	-Increase in total phenols and total flavonoids content, antioxidant activity (Trolox) and bioaccesibility of polyphenols -Decrease in glycemic index	Taglieri et al. [14]

Table 3. *Cont.*

Material and Level of Supplementation	Effects	Reference
Flaxseed cake 5, 7.5, 10% (substitution of dough)	-Increase in unsaturated fatty acids, total phenols, total flavonoids content, anti-radical activity (DPPH, Trolox), ratio of PUFA (Polyunsaturated Fatty Acids) to SFA (Saturated Fatty Acids) -Decrease in the ratio of n-6 to n-3 content	Wirkijowska et al. [17]
Flaxseed cake 0, 5, 10, 15%	-Increase in protein, dietary fibre, fat and ash content -Decrease in CHO content and energy value	Sanmartin et al. [95]
Flaxseed cake 0, 5, 7.5, 10% (substitution of dough)	- Increase in unsaturated fatty acids	Guo et al. [126]
Flaxseed residue 5 and 10%	-Increase in antioxidant activity (DPPH, ABTS, FRAP)	Rocchetti et al. [148]

Grape pomace, a by-product rich in dietary fiber and polyphenols, stands out as a valuable ingredient. Bread, being a staple and widely consumed food, serves as an effective carrier for delivering the health benefits associated with the inclusion of GP to consumers [20,45,121,123,149]. Smith and Yu [121] demonstrated that substituting 5–10% of white flour with GP in the bread formula resulted in a significant increase in the dietary fiber content of the bread. The total dietary fiber (TDF) in breads fortified with 10% GP is comparable to that in whole wheat bread. Regarding insoluble dietary fiber (IDF), even a 5% addition allowed for achieving values comparable to whole wheat bread. Moreover, a decrease in protein and an increase in ash content was observed. A significant increase in the fat content was observed only at the highest 10% supplementation level. Tolve et al. [20] demonstrated that at a 10% supplementation level, the obtained bread exhibited a TDF content of 6.3 g/100 g dry matter, surpassing the threshold of 6 g/100 g [150]. This categorizes the product as a food item high in dietary fiber. Additionally, GP supplementation increased the lipid content, while concurrently reducing total starch. However, no significant changes were observed in the content of crude protein and free sugars. Walker et al. [123] indicate that a 15% supplementation of GP allows for almost a twofold increase in the amount of dietary fiber, from 3.48 g to 6.33 g, in the served portion (serving sizes were 50 g), corresponding to bread without and with a 15% addition of GP, respectively.

According to Rocchetti et al. [149], fortification with GP resulted in a significant increase in TPC (total phenolic compounds), particularly anthocyanins, in the fortified wheat bread. With a 10% supplementation, the cumulative phenolic content reached 127.76 mg/100 g dry matter, approximately doubling that of the control bread, while the anthocyanin content reached 35.82 mg/100 g dry matter. These results are directly related to the chemical composition of the raw materials, as the grape pomace powder used in the study was characterized by a content of 24.36 mg/g of dry matter of total phenolic equivalents, with anthocyanins, the most abundant class, accounting for 11.60 mg/g of cyanidin equivalents. Hayta et al. [45] also indicated a significant increase, over 2.5-fold in the case of 10% supplementation, in TPC. The anti-radical activity (DPPH scavenging activity) of bread samples increased 5-fold with the increase in GP levels up to 10%. A higher increase, approximately 7-fold, in TPC was observed by Tolve et al. [20] for the same GP inclusion level, while the antioxidant activity, assessed by FRAP and ABTS, increased 7.9-fold and 6.4-fold, respectively. Smith and Yu [121], at a 10% supplementation level, reported an increase in TPC ranging from 3-fold to approximately 7.5-fold, depending on the grape variety. The antioxidant activity of bread (as TEAC) increased, depending on grape variety, from about 3-fold to 6-fold. In the same study, the authors demonstrated that 67–79% of the total polyphenols added during GP supplementation were retained in the bread formula, depending on the cultivar of GP added. The losses are caused by degradation/oxidation during baking. The differences in TPC and antioxidant activity can be explained by the grape variety and the presence/absence of seeds in the GP.

An equally important aspect related to the potential health benefits of phenolic compounds, in addition to their high content, is their bioavailability, bioaccessibility, and bioactivities. A factor that significantly influences the bioaccessibility of certain phenolic classes (phenolic acids, lignans, and flavones) may be dietary fiber, including soluble fractions [151]. Dietary fiber and phenolic compounds coexist in food along with other components. The bioavailability and bioaccessibility of phenolic compounds can be influenced by molecular interactions between dietary fiber and other compounds in the food matrix, such as lipids and proteins, as well as interactions between fiber and phenolic compounds [152]. In the study by Rocchetti et al. [149], a significant increase in the bioaccessibility of anthocyanins after in vitro digestion was noted in the bread with the addition of GP compared to the control sample. This increase was particularly noticeable during the transition from the gastric to the small intestine phase. An average bioaccessibility value of 24% for anthocyanins was recorded in the small intestine for both 5% and 10% GP fortification. Additionally, the authors note that the relatively high percentage bioaccessibility values observed at the end of the small intestine phase for other phenolic classes (flavones, and tyrosol equivalents) could promote an antioxidant environment in the digestive tract. The increase in bioaccessibility values observed at the end of the small intestine [149] confirms that the interactions between dietary fiber and phenolic compounds, and the resulting compounds, are key substrates for the colonic microbiota, enabling further processing of phenolics [150]. The increased inclusion of GP in bread led to reduced starch hydrolysis and a lower predicted glycemic index. At the 10% supplementation level, both of these characteristics exhibited approximately a 12–13% reduction [149]. Integrating these results with the previously discussed technological and sensory aspects implies that GP could be a beneficial ingredient for crafting enhanced wheat bread. Nevertheless, it's essential to note that fortifying with GP may influence the sensory attributes of the food, including factors like flavor, color, and texture.

Similar to the supplementation of bread with grape pomace (GP), incorporating apple pomace (AP) also enhances the dietary fiber content in the final product. In Lu et al. study [107], where apple pomace or skimmed apple pomace (SAP) was added at levels of 3, 6, or 9% relative to the flour mass, a notable increase in dietary fiber content was observed in the bread dough mixes. Initially, the dietary fiber content (DF) in wheat flour was 2.7% dry matter (d.m.). With 3% supplementation of AP and SAP, the DF content rose to 4.31% and 4.42% d.m., respectively, representing an increase of over 1.5 times. Incorporating 9% of AP or SAP led to respective increases of 2.78 and 2.82 times, categorizing these samples as high-fiber products (meeting the minimum requirement of 6 g/100 g) [152]. Although for the 3% supplementation, the apple raw materials were sieved through US-60 or US-100 mesh, the results showed no discernible differences in DF content resulting from this process. Dietary fiber content was also assessed in the study by Gumul et al. [120]. The authors applied 5, 10 or 15% additions of whole apple pomace (WAP) or milled apple pomace (MAP). The total dietary fiber (TDF) content for the control sample was 3.94% d.b., while for samples with only a 5% level of flour substitution, it rose to 8.18% d.b. (WAP) and 8.31% d.b. (MAP). Meanwhile, 15% supplementation resulted in further increases up to 12.95% d.b. and 13.35% d.b. The levels of individual fiber fractions were also determined, showing proportional increases with the supplementation level: IDF increased from 2.92% d.b. for CON to 10.15% d.b. for the 15% addition of WAP, and SDF increased from 1.02% d.b. to 3.16% d.b. for the same sample. It is noteworthy that the SDF content in the obtained bread increased over threefold, likely due to the high pectin content in the apple waste. This is a favorable development, as the positive impact of pectin consumption on health has been demonstrated, including its role in maintaining gut health and cancer therapy [153]. A similar trend was observed when supplementing apple pomace powder at levels from 5 to 25% into another bakery product, namely cookies. The increase in dietary fiber content ranged from 250 to 621% compared to the control sample [103].

Literature data suggest that by-products from apple processing are not significant sources of protein. Their addition resulted in either no differences [120] or a decrease in the protein content in bread [141]. Concerning fat content, a decrease was also observed: from 2.12% d.m. for control bread to 1.53% d.m. for 15% WAP [120] and from 6.72% d.m. for control to 5.82% d.m. for 10% APP [141]. As for the mineral component content in the form of ash, a significant increase was noted in studies on the addition of APP, from 0.54% d.m. to 0.95% for 10% APP. A similar trend was observed in Gumul et al. [120] research, but only for samples with 5% MAP addition and 10% WAP addition. In other trials, no statistically significant changes were noted, which the author attributes to randomness. The same author indicates a decrease in sugar content in bread with increasing proportions of apple components, from 2.03% d.m. for control to 1.32% d.m. for 15% MAP. However, Valková et al. [141] reported opposite results: their study showed a significant increase in carbohydrate content in bread after enrichment with APP, from 1.91% for 1% APP to 9.24% for 10% APP, which may result from the high carbohydrate content in the raw material [32].

The findings reveal a significant increase in both total polyphenol content (expressed as grams of gallic acid equivalents per kilogram dry weight) and AA (antioxidant activity expressed as grams of Trolox equivalents per kilogram dry weight) levels in wheat bread following the supplementation of APP, demonstrating a statistically significant ($p < 0.05$) surge compared to the control sample [141]. Furthermore, notable differences ($p < 0.05$) emerged among the experimental variants with incremental incorporations of APP. Particularly, bread loaves fortified with 10% APP exhibited a remarkable 4.27-fold increase in total polyphenols (from 0.6 g/kg for CON to 2.65 g/kg for APP 10%) and a significant 1.7-fold surge in AA levels (from 1.65 g/kg for CON to 2.79 g/kg), highlighting the robust impact of this supplementation strategy.

In the study conducted by Gumul et al. [120], the analysis of polyphenol content revealed a significant increase in breads enriched with apple pomace compared to the control. The total polyphenol content showed a notable increase, ranging from 0.29 mg catechin equivalent per gram dry matter (d.m.) for the control to 0.68 mg catechin equivalent per gram d.m. for 15% WAP (a 155–234% increase with all supplementations compared to the control). Additionally, polyphenol levels were, on average, 16% higher in loaves made with WAP than those made with MAP. While baking typically leads to polyphenol loss, the extent of degradation may vary depending on the form of introduction into the bread formulation. Thermal degradation was more pronounced when polyphenols were added in MAP, likely due to increased exposure to hot air [154]. Conversely, flavonoid fractions, specifically flavonols and anthocyanins, increased, especially in breads made with MAP. However, breads with WAP showed a higher flavonoid content compared to those with MAP and the control. This discrepancy may be attributed to the labeling of only flavonols and anthocyanins as markers of the entire range of flavonoids in this study. The remaining flavonoid fractions may have been more abundant in breads with WAP, resulting in higher total flavonoid and polyphenol levels compared to those with MAP. Additionally, WAP acts as a protective barrier for bioactive substances, preventing excessive losses during baking. This observation aligns with similar studies involving grape pomace and pomegranate peel powder, which also demonstrated increased phenolic content in enriched bread [121]. The antioxidant activity, measured in Trolox equivalent antioxidant capacity, varied between 7.80 μM Trolox equivalent per kilogram d.m. for the control sample and 25.37 μM Trolox equivalent per kilogram d.m. for 15% MAP (a 222–325% increase for all samples). However, differences in reported findings could also be ascribed to Maillard reaction products, impacting the antioxidant activity of bread [120]. These findings underscore the potential of apple pomace as a potent enhancer of the antioxidant profile of wheat bread, offering promising prospects for the development of functional food products with augmented health benefits.

Oilseed cakes, traditionally utilized as animal feed owing to their protein content, are garnering attention for human consumption due to their nutrient-rich composition. They serve as valuable sources of functional food ingredients such as proteins, dietary fiber, antioxidants, vitamins, and minerals, finding applications across various industries. Additionally, they can be refined into protein concentrates and isolates, offering high protein content ideal for fortifying food products [155–157]. Literature has already highlighted the potential utilization of oilseed cakes, such as olive pomace and flaxseed cake, in bread preparation. Like most by-products of plant processing, by-products from fruit and oilseed processing are also excellent sources of dietary fiber. As reported by Badawy and Smetanska [13], just a 2% addition of olive pomace cellulose increases the dietary fiber content in bread from 3.22% dry matter (d.m.) for the control sample to 3.90% d.m., representing a 21% increase, while a 6% addition increased the fiber content by almost 60% compared to the control sample. Similarly to fruit pomace, olive pomace is also not a good source of protein. The addition of olive pomace cellulose resulted in a decrease in bread protein content ranging from 3 to 12%; however, it was only a statistically significant decrease at a 6% addition [13]. In the study by Cardinali et al. [26], where fresh, refrigerated for 6 months, or frozen for 6 months olive pomace was added at levels of 10%, 15%, or 20% to white or whole wheat bread, a significant increase in dietary fiber content in the final product was also observed. The initial dietary fiber (DF) content in white bread was 3.27% d.m. for bread with the addition of fresh pomace, and 3.26% d.m. for bread with the addition of refrigerated and frozen pomace; 10% substitution increased these values to 4.43% d.m., 4.83% d.m., and 4.32% d.m., respectively, with a statistically significant increase observed only with the addition of fresh pomace. A 20% addition increased the DF content by 184% to 200% compared to the control, with the highest increase again observed for the addition of fresh pomace, although without statistically significant differences between different storage methods. Similar trends were observed for whole wheat bread; however, neither increasing the level of addition nor using a different storage method resulted in statistically significant differences [26]. Considering the ash, carbohydrates, and fat content, the addition of olive pomace cellulose did not result in any changes [13]. However, judging by the fat content in the olive pomace itself [75], unprocessed olive pomace should contribute to an increase in the fat content in the final product, as observed in the study by Caponio et al. [158] regarding the addition of olive pomace to cookies.

An important aspect of new food products is their health-promoting properties, often associated with the presence of bioactive compounds with antioxidant activity. Research by Cardinali et al. [26] demonstrated a significant increase in Total Phenolic Content (TPC), expressed in milligrams of Gallic Acid Equivalent per gram (mg GAE/g), with each bread supplementation, ranging from 2.5 to 9 times compared to the control, with higher values observed for white bread. A similar trend was observed for antioxidant activity against 2,2-diphenyl-1-picrylhydrazyl (DPPH), 2,2'-azino-bis(3-ethylbenzothiazoline-6-sulfonic acid) (ABTS), and Ferric Reducing Antioxidant Power (FRAP), increasing from 0.32–0.77 mg Trolox Equivalent Antioxidant Capacity (TEAC)/g in white bread to 1.24–2.64 mg GAE/g in bread supplemented with a 20% addition of olive raw materials. The highest values for both TPC and antioxidant activity were recorded for the supplementation of white bread with refrigerated pomace, although these differences were not statistically significant compared to other raw materials. Cedola et al. [25] observed a 7-fold increase in total phenol content with the supplementation of 10% dried olive paste flour, from 0.28 mg GAE/g dry matter (d.m.) for the control to 1.96 mg GAE/g d.m. for the supplemented sample. Flavonoid content for the control was 0.06 mg Quercetin Equivalent (QE)/g d.m., while for the fortified bread, it was 0.85 mg QE/g d.m. A significant increase, by 56-fold, was also noted for antioxidant activity (from 0.02 mg Trolox equivalent/g d.m. for the control to 1.12 mg Trolox equivalent/g d.m.). The research also aimed to determine the impact on the bioactive properties of bread with the addition of olive mill wastewater (OMWW), olive paste (OP), or both. The total polyphenol content of bread with OMWW instead of water was 6 mg GAE per g d.m., while with a 10% addition of OP, it was 4.3 mg GAE per g d.m. Combining both additives resulted in a total of 10.2 mg GAE per g d.m. The total phenol content increased from 0.14 mg GAE per g d.m. to 0.49 mg GAE per g d.m. for OMWW addition, 1.33 mg GAE per g d.m. for OP addition, and 1.8 mg GAE per g d.m. for both, representing a 950% increase compared to the control. Antioxidant activity (measured by Trolox and FRAP) also significantly increased with supplementation, particularly with OP addition, up to three times more for FRAP and over five times more for Trolox compared to OMWW. While the total polyphenol and phenol content showed a summation effect in bread with both additives, there was a synergy observed for antioxidant activity, which increased from 12% for FRAP to 34% for Trolox with both additives compared to the sum of this activity for supplementation with individual raw materials [25].

When evaluating the bioactivity of food products, it's crucial to consider not only the content of bioactive compounds but also their bioavailability. Cedola et al. [25] demonstrated that the stability of total polyphenols during in vitro digestion indicated their higher bio-accessibility in enriched bread compared to the control. This stability, attributed to milk proteins forming polyphenol-protein complexes, enhances antioxidant activity. Moreover, the food matrix influences compound release during digestion. Studies suggest that polyphenols from olive oil by-products are more bio-accessible when in the matrix, such as table olives.

The glycemic index (GI) ranks carbohydrate-containing foods from 0 to 100 based on their effect on blood glucose levels compared to a reference food, usually white wheat bread [159]. Bread enriched with olive paste exhibited a significantly lower GI compared to the control, likely due to its high fiber content. Dietary fibers, such as those found in olive paste, can reduce the glycemic response of carbohydrate-rich foods like bread. Additionally, the increased polyphenol content, particularly cyanidin-3-glucoside present in olive paste, may also modulate glucose absorption. Studies on other anthocyanin-rich foods like blueberries and pomegranates have reported similar effects on glucose metabolism, suggesting a potential role for anthocyanins in reducing blood sugar levels [25,160].

Similarly to other plant sources, waste from flaxseed oil pressing is a valuable source of dietary fiber. These by-products contain various components such as cellulose, hemicellulose, and lignin, contributing to the nutritional value of food products. Scientific research confirms that adding fiber to carbohydrate-rich products like bread and pasta can reduce the glycemic response [161]. According to Wirkijowska et al. [17], both the addition of flax flour (FF) and flax cake (FM) at levels of 5, 10, or 15% increase the TDF content in bread in a comparable manner, ranging from 40 to 74% for FF and from 28 to 81% for FM, while the TDF content in the control bread was 7.15% d.m. These studies also demonstrated an increase in the content of individual fiber fractions, especially SDF, with up to a 2.5-fold increase in trials with a 15% addition of flax materials compared to the control. This is a highly beneficial change, as SDF is often deficient in human diets [162]. In the studies by Wirkijowska et al. [17], the IDF:SDF ratio ranged from 1.79:1 for the control to as low as 0.95:1 for a 15% addition of flaxseed cake. This is mainly due to the high content of mucilage gum in flaxseed by-products, the presence of which is very beneficial due to its proven health-promoting effects [93]. Due to the increased dietary fiber content in the bread, the overall carbohydrate content decreased [17]. By-products from oilseed processing such as flaxseed, unlike that from fruit processing, not only serves as a good source of dietary fiber but also provides a very good source of protein. The increase in protein content in bread supplemented with flaxseed by-products is confirmed by studies conducted by Guo et al. [126] and Wirkijowska et al. [17]. The addition of flaxseed residue (FR) at levels of 5 or 10% increased the protein content from 11.23% d.m. for the control to 11.66% d.m. and 12.27% d.m. respectively [126]. In the studies by Wirkijowska et al. [17], this increase ranged from 13.36% d.m. for the control to 16.3% d.m. for a 15% addition of flax cake and 16.88% d.m. for a 15% addition of flax flour, representing an increase of 22% and 26% respectively compared to the control. Due to the high fat content remaining in the flaxseed residues, an expected increase in the fat content of supplemented bread was achieved. In the study by Wirkijowska et al. [17], the increase in lipid content was higher in bread supplemented with flax flour than flax cake, due to the initial fat content in the raw material. The lipid content in bread with a 15% addition of FM increased to 0.95% dry matter (d.m.), while the content of this macronutrient in the control bread was 0.18% d.m. On the other hand, a 15% addition of FF increased this level to 1.62% (a 9-fold increase). According to Sanmartin et al. [95] and Taglieri et al. [14], in sourdough or yeast bread supplemented with 5, 7.5, or 10% flaxseed cake flour relative to the dough mass, the content of unsaturated fatty acids such as linolenic acid increased (5.19–6.52-fold increase for sourdough bread and 2.93–5.94-fold increase for yeast bread) as well as oleic acid (1–41% increase for sourdough bread and 40–300% for yeast bread). A decrease in the content of fatty acids such as palmitic and linoleic acid was also noted. The same authors also indicate that in fortified bread, the overall content of PUFA n-3 and MUFA increased, while SFA and PUFA n-6 decreased. Notably, there was an improvement in the ratio of n-3 to n-6 fatty acids from 17.64 for control yeast bread and 16.81 for control sourdough bread to as low as 1.69 and 1.89, respectively, with 10% supplementation. This carries health benefits due to the proven role of n-3 acids in preventing cardiovascular and nervous system diseases [163]. The total phenol content in sourdough and yeast bread with 5–10% supplementation of flaxseed cake flour increased in direct proportion to the level of addition, with a predominance for yeast bread (from 0.301 mg GAE/g d.m. for CON to 1.212 mg GAE/g d.m. at 10% fortification). A similar trend was observed for the flavonoid content expressed as catechin equivalents (increase of 1.98–2.9 times in sourdough bread and 2.44–4.04 times in yeast bread) [14,95]. In the same study, the antioxidant activity against DPPH in sourdough and yeast bread with 10% supplementation was 2.826 mg Trolox equivalent/g d.m. and 2.71 mg Trolox equivalent/g d.m., respectively, while Guo et al. [126], with the same level of supplementation of flaxseed residue, achieved a value of 28.03 mg Trolox equivalent/g d.m. The same author also investigated the antioxidant activity against ABTS and FRAP, obtaining values higher than those for the control bread, by 113% and 23%, respectively.

7. Conclusions

The main conclusions drawn from the reviewed literature are as follows:

(a) Addition of by-products from the plant industry to bread significantly enhances its health benefits by increasing dietary fiber content, enriching it with bioactive substances, and boosting antioxidant potential. Specific ingredients found in these by-products, such as pectins in apple pomace, polyphenols in grape pomace, lignans in linseed oil residues, and fatty acids in olive pomace, exhibit health-promoting properties that could be leveraged in the development of new food products. Additionally, the high protein content in flaxseed marc suggests its potential to improve the nutritional profile of bread, which is typically low in this macronutrient.

(b) However, the literature lacks comprehensive information regarding the presence of anti-nutritional substances or contaminants in the final products derived from these by-products, highlighting the need for further supplementation. The occurrence of unwanted substances in food industry by-products is common, necessitating thorough analysis of products incorporating them. This is particularly crucial in today's food industry landscape, where there is heightened emphasis on food safety and health.

(c) The addition of by-product raw materials significantly affects the rheological properties of dough and, consequently, the characteristics of the final product. This influence is dependent not only on the type and origin of the by-product and the level of supplementation but also on the extent of prior processing (particle size, thermal and enzymatic treatment). The analysis of literature data reveals significant potential for modifying the sensory characteristics of bread, including taste, aroma, texture, and overall acceptability. Moreover, appropriate selection of by-products and their supplementation levels can result in bread with quality and sensory attributes comparable to wheat bread.

(d) Difficulties encountered across some studies include insufficient specification of the type of bread produced or the by-products utilized. Variations in the base wheat flour and the addition of other ingredients (e.g., powdered milk, hemicellulose), varying levels of salt and sugar, and the presence of additives like ascorbic acid or enzymatic improvers may complicate direct comparison of study results. Additionally, inadequate methodological details regarding measurements of specific bread properties (e.g., lack of precise information on when bread quality characteristics were measured, which is crucial for texture analysis) further contribute to challenges in data interpretation. Not always is the full specification of the used waste materials provided. This concerns, among other things, their origin, particle size and chemical composition.

Author Contributions: Conceptualization, P.Z. and A.W.; methodology, P.Z., A.W. and D.T.; resources, P.Z., A.W., D.T. and P.Ł.; data curation, D.T. and P.Ł.; writing—original draft preparation, P.Z., A.W., D.T. and P.Ł.; writing—review and editing, P.Z. and D.T.; visualization, P.Z.; supervision, P.Z. and A.W. All authors have read and agreed to the published version of the manuscript.

Funding: This research received no external funding.

Institutional Review Board Statement: Not applicable.

Informed Consent Statement: Not applicable.

Data Availability Statement: The data presented in this study are available on request from the corresponding author.

Conflicts of Interest: The authors declare no conflicts of interest.

References

1. Levy, A.A.; Feldman, M. Evolution and origin of bread wheat. *Plant Cell* **2022**, *34*, 2549–2567. [CrossRef] [PubMed]
2. Graça, C.; Raymundo, A.; Sousa, I. Wheat Bread with Dairy Products—Technology, Nutritional, and Sensory Properties. *Appl. Sci.* **2019**, *9*, 4101. [CrossRef]
3. Ma, S.; Wang, Z.; Liu, H.; Li, L.; Zheng, X.; Tian, X.; Sun, B.; Wang, X. Supplementation of wheat flour products with wheat bran dietary fiber: Purpose, mechanisms, and challenges. *Trends Food Sci. Technol.* **2022**, *123*, 281–289. [CrossRef]
4. Guan, Z.-W.; Yu, E.-Z.; Feng, Q. Soluble Dietary Fiber, One of the Most Important Nutrients for the Gut Microbiota. *Molecules* **2021**, *26*, 6802. [CrossRef] [PubMed]
5. Jung, J.-M.; Kim, J.Y.; Kim, J.-H.; Kim, S.M.; Jung, S.; Song, H.; Kwon, E.E.; Choi, Y.-E. Zero-waste strategy by means of valorization of bread waste. *J. Clean. Prod.* **2022**, *365*, 132795. [CrossRef]
6. Cox, R.; Narisetty, V.; Nagarajan, S.; Agrawal, D.; Ranade, V.V.; Salonitis, K.; Venus, J.; Kumar, V. High-Level fermentative production of Lactic acid from bread waste under Non-sterile conditions with a circular biorefining approach and zero waste discharge. *Fuel* **2022**, *313*, 122976. [CrossRef]
7. Dymchenko, A.; Geršl, M.; Gregor, T. Trends in bread waste utilisation. *Trends Food Sci. Technol.* **2023**, *132*, 93–102. [CrossRef]
8. Mollakhalili-Meybodi, N.; Sheidaei, Z.; Khorshidian, N.; Nematollahi, A.; Khanniri, E. Sensory attributes of wheat bread: A review of influential factors. *J. Food Meas. Charact.* **2023**, *17*, 2172–2181. [CrossRef]
9. Dong, Y.; Karboune, S. A review of bread qualities and current strategies for bread bioprotection: Flavor, sensory, rheological, and textural attributes. *Compr. Rev. Food Sci. Food Saf.* **2021**, *20*, 1937–1981. [CrossRef]
10. Rațu, R.N.; Veleșcu, I.D.; Stoica, F.; Usturoi, A.; Arsenoaia, V.N.; Crivei, I.C.; Postolache, A.N.; Lipșa, F.D.; Filipov, F.; Florea, A.M.; et al. Application of Agri-Food By-Products in the Food Industry. *Agriculture* **2023**, *13*, 1559. [CrossRef]
11. Magyar, M.; da Costa Sousa, L.; Jin, M.; Sarks, C.; Balan, V. Conversion of apple pomace waste to ethanol at industrial relevant conditions. *Appl. Microbiol. Biotechnol.* **2016**, *100*, 7349–7358. [CrossRef] [PubMed]
12. Antonić, B.; Jančíková, S.; Dordević, D.; Tremlová, B. Grape pomace valorization: A systematic review and meta-analysis. *Foods* **2020**, *9*, 1627. [CrossRef] [PubMed]
13. Badawy, W.; Smetanska, I. Utilization of olive pomace as a source of bioactive compounds in quality improving of toast bread. *Egypt. J. Food Sci.* **2020**, *48*, 27–40. [CrossRef]
14. Taglieri, I.; Sanmartin, C.; Venturi, F.; Macaluso, M.; Zinnai, A.; Tavarini, S.; Serra, A.; Conte, G.; Flamini, G.; Angelini, L.G. Effect of the leavening agent on the compositional and sensorial characteristics of bread fortified with flaxseed cake. *Appl. Sci.* **2020**, *10*, 5235. [CrossRef]
15. Asif, M.; Javaid, T.; Razzaq, Z.U.; Khan, M.K.I.; Maan, A.A.; Yousaf, S.; Usman, A.; Shahid, S. Sustainable utilization of apple pomace and its emerging potential for development of functional foods. *Environ. Sci. Pollut. Res.* **2024**, *31*, 17932–17950. [CrossRef] [PubMed]
16. Speroni, C.S.; Bender, A.B.B.; Stiebe, J.; Ballus, C.A.; Ávila, P.F.; Goldbeck, R.; Morisso, F.D.P.; da Silva, L.P.; Emanuelli, T. Granulometric fractionation and micronization: A process for increasing soluble dietary fiber content and improving technological and functional properties of olive pomace. *LWT* **2020**, *130*, 109526. [CrossRef]
17. Wirkijowska, A.; Zarzycki, P.; Sobota, A.; Nawrocka, A.; Blicharz-Kania, A.; Andrejko, D. The possibility of using by-products from the flaxseed industry for functional bread production. *LWT* **2020**, *118*, 108760. [CrossRef]
18. Azadfar, E.; Rad, A.H.; Sharifi, A.; Armin, M. Effect of olive pomace fiber on the baking properties of wheat flour and flat bread (Barbari Bread) quality. *J. Food Process. Preserv.* **2023**, *2023*, 1405758. [CrossRef]

19. Jiang, X.; Wang, X.; Zhou, S. Influence of roasted flaxseed marc flour on rheological, structural, fermentation, water distribution, and migration properties of wheat dough. *J. Food Sci.* **2023**, *88*, 4840–4852. [CrossRef]
20. Tolve, R.; Simonato, B.; Rainero, G.; Bianchi, F.; Rizzi, C.; Cervini, M.; Giuberti, G. Wheat Bread Fortification by Grape Pomace Powder: Nutritional, Technological, Antioxidant, and Sensory Properties. *Foods* **2021**, *10*, 75. [CrossRef]
21. Santos, L.F.D.; Lopes, S.T.; Nazari, M.T.; Biduski, B.; Pinto, V.Z.; Santos, J.S.D.; Bertolin, T.E.; dos Santos, L.R. Fruit pomace as a promising source to obtain biocompounds with antibacterial activity. *Crit. Rev. Food Sci. Nutr.* **2022**, *63*, 12597–12609. [CrossRef] [PubMed]
22. Alston, J.M.; Sambucci, O.S. Grapes in the World Economy. In *The Grape Genome*; Compendium of Plant Genomes; Springer: Cham, Switzerland, 2019; pp. 1–24.
23. Reguengo, L.M.; Salgaço, M.K.; Sivieri, K.; Júnior, M.R.M. Agro-industrial by-products: Valuable sources of bioactive compounds. *Food Res. Int.* **2022**, *152*, 110871. [CrossRef] [PubMed]
24. Bekhit, A.E.D.A.; Shavandi, A.; Jodjaja, T.; Birch, J.; Teh, S.; Ahmed, I.A.M.; Al-Juhaimi, F.Y.; Saeedi, P.; Bekhit, A.A. Flaxseed: Composition, detoxification, utilization, and opportunities. *Biocatal. Agric. Biotechnol.* **2018**, *13*, 129–152. [CrossRef]
25. Cedola, A.; Cardinali, A.; D'Antuono, I.; Conte, A.; Del Nobile, M.A. Cereal foods fortified with by-products from the olive oil industry. *Food Biosci.* **2020**, *33*, 100490. [CrossRef]
26. Cardinali, F.; Belleggia, L.; Reale, A.; Cirlini, M.; Boscaino, F.; Di Renzo, T.; Del Vecchio, L.; Cavalca, N.; Milanović, V.; Garofalo, C.; et al. Exploitation of Black Olive (*Olea europaea* L. cv. Piantone di Mogliano) Pomace for the Production of High-Value Bread. *Foods* **2024**, *13*, 460. [CrossRef]
27. Fruit: World Production by Type 2022 Statista. Available online: https://www.statista.com/statistics/264001/worldwideproduction-of-fruit-by-variety/ (accessed on 22 March 2024).
28. Waldbauer, K.; McKinnon, R.; Kopp, B. Apple pomace as potential source of natural active compounds. *Planta Med.* **2017**, *83*, 994–1010. [CrossRef] [PubMed]
29. Wang, X.; Kristo, E.; LaPointe, G. The effect of apple pomace on the texture, rheology and microstructure of set type yogurt. *Food Hydrocoll.* **2019**, *91*, 83–91. [CrossRef]
30. O'Shea, N.; Ktenioudaki, A.; Smyth, T.P.; McLoughlin, P.; Doran, L.; Auty, M.A.E.; Arendt, E.; Gallagher, E. Physicochemical assessment of two fruit by-products as functional ingredients: Apple and orange pomace. *J. Food Eng.* **2015**, *153*, 89–95. [CrossRef]
31. Kruczek, M.; Gumul, D.; IvaniÅ, E.; GambuÅ, H. Industrial apple pomace by-products as a potential source of pro-health compounds in functional food. *J. Microbiol. Biotechnol. Food Sci.* **2017**, *7*, 22–26. [CrossRef]
32. Bchir, B.; Karoui, R.; Danthine, S.; Blecker, C.; Besbes, S.; Attia, H. Date, apple, and pear by-products as functional ingredients in pasta: Cooking quality attributes and physicochemical, rheological, and sensorial properties. *Foods* **2022**, *11*, 1393. [CrossRef]
33. Sobczak, P.; Nadulski, R.; Kobus, Z.; Zawiślak, K. Technology for apple pomace utilization within a sustainable development policy framework. *Sustainability* **2022**, *14*, 5470. [CrossRef]
34. Skinner, R.C.; Gigliotti, J.C.; Ku, K.M.; Tou, J.C. A comprehensive analysis of the composition, health benefits, and safety of apple pomace. *Nutr. Rev.* **2018**, *76*, 893–909. [CrossRef] [PubMed]
35. Razak, N.Q.A.; Gan, C.Y.; Shafie, M.H. Unlocking the potential of Garcinia atroviridis fruit polysaccharides: A synergistic approach for obesity and hypertension management. *Food Biosci.* **2024**, *57*, 103553. [CrossRef]
36. Giuntini, E.B.; Sardá, F.A.H.; de Menezes, E.W. The effects of soluble dietary fibers on glycemic response: An overview and futures perspectives. *Foods* **2022**, *11*, 3934. [CrossRef]
37. Ravn-Haren, G.; Dragsted, L.O.; Buch-Andersen, T.; Jensen, E.N.; Jensen, R.I.; Nemeth-Balogh, M.; Paulovicsová, B.; Bergström, A.; Wilcks, A.; Licht, T.R.; et al. Intake of whole apples or clear apple juice has contrasting effects on plasma lipids in healthy volunteers. *Eur. J. Nutr.* **2013**, *52*, 1875–1889. [CrossRef]
38. Gustafsson, J.; Landberg, M.; Bátori, V.; Åkesson, D.; Taherzadeh, M.J.; Zamani, A. Development of bio-based films and 3D objects from apple pomace. *Polymers* **2019**, *11*, 289. [CrossRef] [PubMed]
39. Pieszka, M.; Gogol, P.; Pietras, M.; Pieszka, M. Valuable components of dried pomaces of chokeberry, black currant, strawberry, apple and carrot as a source of natural antioxidants and nutraceuticals in the animal diet. *Ann. Anim. Sci.* **2015**, *15*, 475–4912. [CrossRef]
40. Krawitzky, M.; Arias, E.; Peiro, J.M.; Negueruela, A.I.; Val, J.; Oria, R. Determination of color, antioxidant activity, and phenolic profile of different fruit tissue of Spanish 'Verde Doncella' apple cultivar. *Int. J. Food Prop.* **2014**, *17*, 2298–2311. [CrossRef]
41. Rago, D.; Gürdeniz, G.; Ravn-Haren, G.; Dragsted, L.O. An explorative study of the effect of apple and apple products on the human plasma metabolome investigated by LC–MS profiling. *Metabolomics* **2015**, *11*, 27–39. [CrossRef]
42. Ma, P.; Yao, L.; Lin, X.; Gu, T.; Rong, X.; Batey, R.; Yamahara, J.; Wang, J.; Li, Y. A mixture of apple pomace and rosemary extract improves fructose consumption-induced insulin resistance in rats: Modulation of sarcolemmal CD36 and glucose transporter-4. *Am. J. Transl. Res.* **2016**, *8*, 3791.
43. Cho, K.D.; Han, C.K.; Lee, B.H. Loss of body weight and fat and improved lipid profiles in obese rats fed apple pomace or apple juice concentrate. *J. Med. Food.* **2013**, *16*, 823–830. [CrossRef]
44. Yadav, S.; Gupta, R.K. Formulation of noodles using apple pomace and evaluation of its phytochemicals and antioxidant activity. *J. Pharmacogn. Phytochem.* **2015**, *4*, 99–106.
45. Hayta, M.; Özuğur, G.; Etgü, H.; Şeker, İ.T. Effect of Grape (*Vitis vinifera* L.) Pomace on the Quality, Total Phenolic Content and Anti-Radical Activity of Bread. *J. Food Process. Preserv.* **2014**, *38*, 980–986. [CrossRef]

46. Sirohi, R.; Tarafdar, A.; Singh, S.; Negi, T.; Gaur, V.K.; Gnansounou, E.; Bharathiraja, B. Green processing and biotechnological potential of grape pomace: Current trends and opportunities for sustainable biorefinery. *Bioresour. Technol.* **2020**, *314*, 123771. [CrossRef]
47. García-Lomillo, J.; González-SanJosé, M.L. Applications of wine pomace in the food industry: Approaches and functions. *Compr. Rev. Food Sci. Food Saf.* **2017**, *16*, 3–22. [CrossRef]
48. Tikhonova, A.; Ageeva, N.; Globa, E. Grape pomace as a promising source of biologically valuable components. *BIO Web Conf.* **2021**, *34*, 06002. [CrossRef]
49. Nistor, E.; Dobrei, A.; Bampidis, V.; Ciolac, V. Grape pomace in sheep and dairy cows feeding. *J. Hortic. Forestry Biotech.* **2014**, *18*, 146–150.
50. Dwyer, K.; Hosseinian, F.; Rod, M. The market potential of grape waste alternatives. *J. Food Res.* **2014**, *3*, 91–106. [CrossRef]
51. Gül, H.; Acun, S.; Şen, H.; Nayır, N.; Türk, S. Antioxidant activity, total phenolics and some chemical properties of öküzgözü and Narince grape pomace and grape seed flours. *J. Food Agric. Environ.* **2013**, *11*, 28–34.
52. Gazzola, D.; Vincenzi, S.; Gastaldon, L.; Tolin, S.; Pasini, G.; Curioni, A. The proteins of the grape (*Vitis vinifera* L.) seed endosperm: Fractionation and identification of the major components. *Food Chem.* **2014**, *155*, 132–139. [CrossRef]
53. Cecchi, L.; Innocenti, M.; Urciuoli, S.; Arlorio, M.; Paoli, P.; Mulinacci, N. In depth study of phenolic profile and PTP-1B inhibitory power of cold-pressed grape seed oils of different varieties. *Food Chem.* **2019**, *271*, 380–387. [CrossRef] [PubMed]
54. Bordiga, M.; Travaglia, F.; Locatelli, M.; Arlorio, M.; Coïsson, J.D. Spent grape pomace as a still potential by-product. *Int. J. Food Sci.* **2015**, *50*, 2022–2031. [CrossRef]
55. Mironeasa, S.; Codină, G.G.; Mironeasa, C. Optimization of wheat-grape seed composite flour to improve alpha-amylase activity and dough rheological behavior. *Int. J. Food Prop.* **2016**, *19*, 859–872. [CrossRef]
56. Fiori, L.; Lavelli, V.; Duba, K.S.; Harsha, P.S.C.S.; Mohamed, H.B.; Guella, G. Supercritical CO_2 extraction of oil from seeds of six grape cultivars: Modeling of mass transfer kinetics and evaluation of lipid profiles and tocol contents. *J. Supercrit. Fluids* **2014**, *94*, 71–80. [CrossRef]
57. García-Lomillo, J.; Gonzalez-SanJose, M.L.; Del Pino-García, R.; Rivero-Perez, M.D.; Muniz-Rodriguez, P. Antioxidant and antimicrobial properties of wine by products and their potential uses in the food industry. *J. Agric. Food Chem.* **2014**, *62*, 12595–12602. [CrossRef] [PubMed]
58. Bennato, F.; Ianni, A.; Florio, M.; Grotta, L.; Pomilio, F.; Saletti, M.A.; Martino, G. Nutritional properties of milk from dairy ewes fed with a diet containing grape pomace. *Foods* **2022**, *11*, 1878. [CrossRef] [PubMed]
59. Teixeira, A.; Baenas, N.; Dominguez-Perles, R.; Barros, A.; Rosa, E.; Moreno, D.A.; Garcia-Viguera, C. Natural bioactive compounds from winery by-products as health promoters: A review. *Int. J. Mol. Sci.* **2014**, *15*, 15638–15678. [CrossRef] [PubMed]
60. Deng, Q.; Penner, M.H.; Zhao, Y. Chemical composition of dietary fiber and polyphenols of five different varieties of wine grape pomace skins. *Food Res. Int.* **2011**, *44*, 2712–2720. [CrossRef]
61. Sheng, K.; Qu, H.; Liu, C.; Yan, L.; You, J.; Shui, S.; Zheng, L. A comparative assess of high hydrostatic pressure and superfine grinding on physicochemical and antioxidant properties of grape pomace. *Int. J. Food Sci. Technol.* **2017**, *52*, 2106–2114. [CrossRef]
62. Bordiga, M. *Post-Fermentation and Distillation Technology: Stabilization, Aging, and Spoilage*; CRC Press: Boca Raton, FL, USA, 2018.
63. Bocsan, I.C.; Măgureanu, D.C.; Pop, R.M.; Levai, A.M.; Macovei, Ș.O.; Pătrașca, I.M.; Buzoianu, A.D. Antioxidant and anti-inflammatory actions of polyphenols from red and white grape pomace in ischemic heart diseases. *Biomedicines* **2022**, *10*, 2337. [CrossRef]
64. Nassiri-Asl, M.; Hosseinzadeh, H. Review of the pharmacological effects of Vitis vinifera (Grape) and its bioactive constituents: An update. *Phytother. Res.* **2016**, *30*, 1392–1403. [CrossRef]
65. Averilla, J.N.; Oh, J.; Kim, H.J.; Kim, J.S.; Kim, J.S. Potential health benefits of phenolic compounds in grape processing by-products. *Food Sci. Biotechnol.* **2019**, *28*, 1607–1615. [CrossRef]
66. Chen, T.Y.; Ferruzzi, M.G.; Wu, Q.L.; Simon, J.E.; Talcott, S.T.; Wang, J.; Ho, L.; Todd, G.; Cooper, B.; Pasinetti, G.M.; et al. Influence of diabetes on plasma pharmacokinetics and brain bioavailability of grape polyphenols and their phase II metabolites in the Zucker diabetic fatty rat. *Mol. Nutr. Food Res.* **2017**, *61*, 1700111. [CrossRef]
67. Novotny, J.A.; Chen, T.Y.; Terekhov, A.I.; Gebauer, S.K.; Baer, D.J.; Ho, L.; Pasinetti, G.M.; Ferruzzi, M.G. The effect of obesity and repeated exposure on pharmacokinetic response to grape polyphenols in humans. *Mol. Nutr. Food Res.* **2017**, *61*, 1700043. [CrossRef]
68. Margalef, M.; Pons, Z.; Iglesias-Carres, L.; Quinones, M.; Bravo, F.I.; Arola-Arnal, A.; Muguerza, B. Rat health status affects bioavailability, target tissue levels, and bioactivity of grape seed flavanols. *Mol. Nutr. Food Res.* **2017**, *61*, 1600342. [CrossRef]
69. FAOSTAT. Food and Agriculture Organization of the United Nations. Food Balances. 2022. Available online: https://www.fao.org/faostat/en/#data/FBS (accessed on 22 March 2024).
70. Conterno, L.; Martinelli, F.; Tamburini, M.; Fava, F.; Mancini, A.; Sordo, M.; Pindo, M.; Martens, S.; Masuero, D.; Vrhovsek, U.; et al. Measuring the impact of olive pomace enriched biscuits on the gut microbiota and its metabolic activity in mildly hypercholesterolaemic subjects. *Eur. J. Nutr.* **2019**, *58*, 63–81. [CrossRef] [PubMed]
71. López-García, A.B.; Cotes-Palomino, T.; Uceda-Rodríguez, M.; Moreno-Maroto, J.M.; Cobo-Ceacero, C.J.; Andreola, N.F.; Martínez-García, C. Application of life cycle assessment in the environmental study of sustainable ceramic bricks made with 'alperujo' (Olive Pomace). *Appl. Sci.* **2021**, *11*, 2278. [CrossRef]

72. Dahdah, P.; Cabizza, R.; Farbo, M.G.; Fadda, C.; Mara, A.; Hassoun, G.; Piga, A. Improving the Rheological Properties of Dough Obtained by Partial Substitution of Wheat Flour with Freeze-Dried Olive Pomace. *Foods* **2024**, *13*, 478. [CrossRef]
73. Mennane, Z.; Tada, S.; Aki, I.; Faid, M.; Hassani, S.; Salmaoui, S. Physicochemical and microbiological characterization of the olive residue of 26 traditional oil mills in Beni Mellal (Morroco). *Les Technol. Lab.* **2010**, *5*, 4–9.
74. Bhanu, D.R.; Sabu, K.K. Fatty acid composition of the fruits of Syzygium Zeylanicum (L.) DC. VAR. Zeylanicum. *Int. J. Curr. Pharm. Res.* **2017**, *9*, 155–157. [CrossRef]
75. Nunes, M.A.; Palmeira, J.D.; Melo, D.; Machado, S.; Lobo, J.C.; Costa, A.S.G.; Oliveira, M.B.P.P. Chemical composition and antimicrobial activity of a new olive pomace functional ingredient. *Pharmaceuticals* **2021**, *14*, 913. [CrossRef] [PubMed]
76. Medouni-Haroune, L.; Zaidi, F.; Medouni-Adrar, S.; Kecha, M. Olive pomace: From an olive mill waste to a resource, an overview of the new treatments. *J. Crit. Rev.* **2018**, *5*, 1–6. [CrossRef]
77. International Olive Council. *Production Mondiale d'Huile d'Olive.* 2017. Available online: https://www.scoop.it/t/olivenews?r=0.00505805164182993#post_4012160171 (accessed on 20 March 2024).
78. Barbanera, M.; Lascaro, E.; Stanzione, V.; Esposito, A.; Altieri, R.; Bufacchi, M. Characterization of pellets from mixing olive pomace and olive tree pruning. *Renew. Energy* **2016**, *88*, 185–191. [CrossRef]
79. Innangi, M.; Niro, E.; D'Ascoli, R.; Danise, T.; Proietti, P.; Nasini, L.; Regni, L.; Castaldi, S.; Fioretto, A. Effects of olive pomace amendment on soil enzyme activities. *Appl. Soil Ecol.* **2017**, *119*, 242–249. [CrossRef]
80. Proietti, P.; Federici, E.; Fidati, L.; Scargetta, S.; Massaccesi, L.; Nasini, L.; Regni, L.; Ricci, A.; Cenci, G.; Gigliotti, G. Effects of amendment with oil mill waste and its derived-compost on soil chemical and microbiological characteristics and olive (*Olea europaea* L.) productivity. *Agric. Ecosys. Environ.* **2015**, *207*, 51–60. [CrossRef]
81. Chanioti, S.; Tzia, C. Optimization of ultrasound-assisted extraction of oil from olive pomace using response surface technology: Oil recovery, unsaponifiable matter, total phenol content and antioxidant activity. *LWT* **2017**, *79*, 178–189. [CrossRef]
82. D'Antuono, I.; Kontogianni, V.G.; Kotsiou, K.; Linsalata, V.; Logrieco, A.F.; Tasioula-Margari, M.; Cardinali, A. Polyphenolic characterization of olive mill wastewaters, coming from Italian and Greek olive cultivars, after membrane technology. *Food Res. Int.* **2014**, *65*, 301–310. [CrossRef]
83. Obied, H.K.; Prenzler, P.D.; Konczak, I.; Rehman, A.U.; Robards, K. Chemistry and bioactivity of olive biophenols in some antioxidant and antiproliferative in vitro bioassays. *Chem. Res. Toxicol.* **2009**, *22*, 227–234. [CrossRef] [PubMed]
84. Padalino, L.; D'Antuono, I.; Durante, M.; Conte, A.; Cardinali, A.; Linsalata, V.; Mita, G.; Logrieco, A.F.; Del Nobile, M.A. Use of olive oil industrial by-product for pasta enrichment. *Antioxidants* **2018**, *7*, 59. [CrossRef]
85. El-Abbassi, A.; Kiai, H.; Hafidi, A. Phenolic profile and antioxidant activities of olive mill wastewater. *Food Chem.* **2012**, *132*, 406–412. [CrossRef]
86. Echeverría, F.; Ortiz, M.; Valenzuela, R.; Videla, L.A. Hydroxytyrosol and cytoprotection: A projection for clinical interventions. *Int. J. Mol. Sci.* **2017**, *18*, 930. [CrossRef]
87. Vitali Čepo, D.; Radić, K.; Jurmanović, S.; Jug, M.; Grdić Rajković, M.; Pedisić, S.; Moslavac, T.; Albahari, P. Valorization of olive pomace-based nutraceuticals as antioxidants in chemical, food, and biological models. *Molecules* **2018**, *23*, 2070. [CrossRef]
88. Hlatshwayo, I.S.; Mnisi, C.M.; Egbu, C.F. Effect of dietary olive (*Olea europea*) pomace on productive performance, and physiological and meat quality parameters in Jumbo quail. *Sci. Rep.* **2023**, *13*, 6162. [CrossRef]
89. Mundus Agri, 2023. Flaxseed: Global Production Shrinks by 26%. Available online: https://www.mundus-agri.eu/news/flaxseed-global-production-shrinks-26.n31687.html (accessed on 22 March 2024).
90. Kulkarni, N.G.; Kar, J.R.; Singhal, R.S. Extraction of flaxseed oil: A comparative study of three-phase partitioning and supercritical carbon dioxide using response surface methodology. *Food Bioprocess Technol.* **2017**, *10*, 940–948. [CrossRef]
91. Cui, W.; Mazza, G.; Biliaderis, C.G. Chemical structure, molecular size distributions, and rheological properties of flaxseed gum. *J. Agric. Food Chem.* **1994**, *42*, 1891–1895. [CrossRef]
92. Zarzycki, P.; Sykut-Domańska, E.; Sobota, A.; Teterycz, D.; Krawęcka, A.; Blicharz-Kania, A.; Andrejko, D.; Zdybel, B. Flaxseed enriched pasta—Chemical composition and cooking quality. *Foods* **2020**, *9*, 404. [CrossRef]
93. Puligundla, P.; Lim, S. A review of extraction techniques and food applications of flaxseed mucilage. *Foods* **2022**, *11*, 1677. [CrossRef]
94. Singh, K.K.; Mridula, D.; Rehal, J.; Barnwal, P. Flaxseed: A potential source of food, feed and fiber. *Crit. Rev. Food Sci. Nutr.* **2011**, *51*, 210–222. [CrossRef]
95. Sanmartin, C.; Taglieri, I.; Venturi, F.; Macaluso, M.; Zinnai, A.; Tavarini, S.; Botto, A.; Serra, A.; Conte, G.; Flamini, G.; et al. Flaxseed Cake as a Tool for the Improvement of Nutraceutical and Sensorial Features of Sourdough Bread. *Foods* **2020**, *9*, 204. [CrossRef]
96. Rani, R.; Badwaik, L.S. Functional properties of oilseed cakes and defatted meals of mustard, soybean and flaxseed. *Waste Biomass Valori.* **2021**, *12*, 5639–5647. [CrossRef]
97. Waszkowiak, K.; Mikołajczak, B. The effect of roasting on the protein profile and antiradical capacity of flaxseed meal. *Foods* **2020**, *9*, 1383. [CrossRef]
98. Kaur, P.; Waghmare, R.; Kumar, V.; Rasane, P.; Kaur, S.; Gat, Y. Recent advances in utilization of flaxseed as potential source for value addition. *OCL* **2018**, *25*, A304. [CrossRef]
99. Goyal, A.; Sharma, V.; Upadhyay, N.; Gill, S.; Sihag, M. Flax and flaxseed oil: An ancient medicine & modern functional food. *J. Food Sci. Technol.* **2014**, *51*, 1633–1653. [CrossRef]

100. Ogunronbi, O.; Jooste, P.J.; Abu, J.O.; Van der Merwe, B. Chemical composition, storage stability and effect of cold-pressed flaxseed oil cake inclusion on bread quality. *J. Food Process. Preserv.* 2011, *35*, 64–79. [CrossRef]
101. De Silva, S.F.; Alcorn, J. Flaxseed lignans as important dietary polyphenols for cancer prevention and treatment: Chemistry, pharmacokinetics, and molecular targets. *Pharmaceuticals* 2019, *12*, 68. [CrossRef]
102. Łopusiewicz, Ł.; Drozłowska, E.; Siedlecka, P.; Mężyńska, M.; Bartkowiak, A.; Sienkiewicz, M.; Zielińska-Bliźniewska, H.; Kwiatkowski, P. Development, characterization, and bioactivity of non-dairy kefir-like fermented beverage based on flaxseed oil cake. *Foods* 2019, *8*, 544. [CrossRef]
103. Usman, M.; Ahmed, S.; Mehmood, A.; Bilal, M.; Patil, P.J.; Akram, K.; Farooq, U. Effect of apple pomace on nutrition, rheology of dough and cookies quality. *J. Food Sci. Technol.* 2020, *57*, 3244–3251. [CrossRef]
104. Zarzycki, P.; Wirkijowska, A.; Nawrocka, A.; Kozłowicz, K.; Krajewska, M.; Kłosok, K.; Krawęcka, A. Effect of Moldavian dragonhead seed residue on the baking properties of wheat flour and bread quality. *LWT* 2022, *155*, 112967. [CrossRef]
105. Mironeasa, S.; Mironeasa, C. Dough bread from refined wheat flour partially replaced by grape peels: Optimizing the rheological properties. *J. Food Process Eng.* 2019, *42*, e13207. [CrossRef]
106. Kohajdová, Z.; Karovičová, J.; Magala, M.; Kuchtová, V. Effect of apple pomace powder addition on farinographic properties of wheat dough and biscuits quality. *Chem. Pap.* 2014, *68*, 1059–1065. [CrossRef]
107. Lu, Q.; Liu, H.; Wang, Q.; Liu, J. Sensory and physical quality characteristics of bread fortified with apple pomace using fuzzy mathematical model. *Int. J. Food Sci. Technol.* 2017, *52*, 1092–1100. [CrossRef]
108. Roozegar, M.H.; Shahedi, M.; Keramet, J.; Hamdami, N.; Roshanak, S. Effect of coated and uncoated ground flaxseed addition on rheological, physical and sensory properties of Taftoon bread. *J. Food Sci. Technol.* 2015, *52*, 5102–5110. [CrossRef]
109. Codină, G.G.; Istrate, A.M.; Gontariu, I.; Mironeasa, S. Rheological properties of wheat–flaxseed composite flours assessed by mixolab and their relation to quality features. *Foods* 2019, *8*, 333. [CrossRef]
110. Wang, J.; Rosell, C.M.; de Barber, C.B. Effect of the addition of different fibres on wheat dough performance and bread quality. *Food Chem.* 2002, *79*, 221–226. [CrossRef]
111. Verheyen, C.; Albrecht, A.; Herrmann, J.; Strobl, M.; Jekle, M.; Becker, T. The contribution of glutathione to the destabilizing effect of yeast on wheat dough. *Food Chem.* 2015, *173*, 243–249. [CrossRef]
112. Šporin, M.; Avbelj, M.; Kovač, B.; Možina, S.S. Quality characteristics of wheat flour dough and bread containing grape pomace flour. *Food Sci. Technol. Int.* 2018, *24*, 251–263. [CrossRef]
113. Fendri, L.B.; Chaari, F.; Maaloul, M.; Kallel, F.; Abdelkafi, L.; Chaabouni, S.E.; Ghribi-Aydi, D. Wheat bread enrichment by pea and broad bean pods fibers: Effect on dough rheology and bread quality. *LWT* 2016, *73*, 584–591. [CrossRef]
114. Baca, E.; Kapka, A.; Karaś, M.; Zielińska, D. Influence of addition of apple fibre preparation to wheat flour on the functional properties of dough and bread quality. *Probl. Hig. Epidemiol.* 2011, *92*, 868–871. (In Polish)
115. Jiang, X.; Wang, X.; Zhou, S. Effect of flaxseed marc flour on high-yield wheat bread production: Comparison in baking, staling, antioxidant and digestion properties. *LWT* 2022, *169*, 113979. [CrossRef]
116. Miller, R.A.; Maningat, C.C.; Hoseney, R.C. Modified wheat starches increase bread yield. *Cereal Chem.* 2008, *85*, 713–715. [CrossRef]
117. Bchir, B.; Rabetafika, H.N.; Paquot, M.; Blecker, C. Effect of pear, apple and date fibres from cooked fruit by-products on dough performance and bread quality. *Food Bioproc. Technol.* 2014, *7*, 1114–1127. [CrossRef]
118. Lin, S.; Gao, J.; Jin, X.; Wang, Y.; Dong, Z.; Ying, J.; Zhou, W. Whole-wheat flour particle size influences dough properties, bread structure and in vitro starch digestibility. *Food Func.* 2020, *11*, 3610–3620. [CrossRef]
119. Kadirvelu, K.; Fathima, N.N. Deciphering mechanism of assembly of keratin within nanofibrous matrix: Expanding the horizon of electrospun polymer/protein composites. *ChemistrySelect* 2021, *6*, 10767–10775. [CrossRef]
120. Gumul, D.; Korus, J.; Ziobro, R.; Kruczek, M. Enrichment of wheat bread with apple pomace as a way to increase pro-health constituents. *Qual. Assur. Saf. Crops Foods* 2019, *11*, 231–240. [CrossRef]
121. Smith, I.N.; Yu, J. Nutritional and sensory quality of bread containing different quantities of grape pomace from different grape cultivars. *EC Nutr.* 2015, *2*, 291–301.
122. Šporin, M.; Avbelj, M.; Kovač, B.; Možina, S.S. Sensory properties of bread fortified with grape pomace. In Proceedings of the III International Congress, "Food Technology, Quality and Safety", Novi Sad, Serbia, 25–27 October 2016; pp. 169–174.
123. Walker, R.; Tseng, A.; Cavender, G.; Ross, A.; Zhao, Y. Physicochemical, nutritional, and sensory qualities of wine grape pomace fortified baked goods. *J. Food Sci.* 2014, *79*, S1811–S1822. [CrossRef]
124. Jagelaviciute, J.; Staniulyte, G.; Cizeikiene, D.; Basinskiene, L. Influence of enzymatic hydrolysis on composition and technological properties of apple pomace and its application for wheat bread making. *Plant Foods Hum. Nutr.* 2023, *78*, 307–313. [CrossRef]
125. Nawrocka, A.; Szymańska-Chargot, M.; Miś, A.; Wilczewska, A.Z.; Markiewicz, K.H. Effect of dietary fibre polysaccharides on structure and thermal properties of gluten proteins—A study on gluten dough with application of FT-Raman spectroscopy, TGA and DSC. *Food Hydrocoll.* 2017, *69*, 410–421. [CrossRef]
126. Guo, X.; Shi, L.; Yang, S.; Yang, R.; Dai, X.; Zhang, T.; Liu, R.; Chang, M.; Jin, Q.; Wang, X. Effect of sea-buckthorn pulp and flaxseed residues on quality and shelf life of bread. *Food Func.* 2019, *10*, 4220–4230. [CrossRef]
127. Liu, J.; Shim, Y.Y.; Tse, T.J.; Wang, Y.; Reaney, M.J.T. Flaxseed gum a versatile natural hydrocolloid for food and non-food applications. *Trends Food Sci. Technol.* 2018, *75*, 146–157. [CrossRef]

128. López, E.P.; Pérez, G.T.; Erramouspe, P.L.J.; Cuevas, C.M. Effect of Brea Gum on the characteristics of wheat bread at different storage times. *Food Sci. Technol.* **2013**, *33*, 745–752. [CrossRef]
129. Raghavendra, S.R.; Ramachandra, S.; Rastogi, N.K.; Raghavarao, K.S.M.S.; Sourav, K.; Tharanathan, R.N. Grinding characteristics and hydration properties of coconut residue: A source of dietary fiber. *J. Food Eng.* **2006**, *72*, 281–286. [CrossRef]
130. Gómez, M.; Ronda, F.; Blanco, C.A.; Pedro, A.; Apesteguia, A. Effect of dietary fibre on dough rheology and bread quality. *Eur. Food Res. Technol.* **2003**, *216*, 51–56. [CrossRef]
131. Shittu, T.A.; Dixon, A.; Awonorin, S.O.; Sanni, L.O.; Mazia-Dioxon, B. Bread from composite cassava-wheat flour: Effect of cassava genotype and nitrogen fertilizer on bread quality. *Food Res. Int.* **2008**, *41*, 569–578. [CrossRef]
132. Michalska, A.; Ceglinska, A.; Amarowicz, R.; Piskula, M.K.; Szawara-Nowak, D.; Zielinski, H. Antioxidant contents and antioxidative properties of traditional rye breads. *J. Agric. Food Chem.* **2007**, *55*, 734–740. [CrossRef]
133. Makris, D.P.; Boskou, G.; Andrikopoulos, N.K. Polyphenolic content and in vitro antioxidant characteristics of wine industry and other agri-food solid waste extracts. *J. Food Compos. Anal.* **2007**, *20*, 125–132. [CrossRef]
134. Jannati, N.; Hojjatoleslamy, M.; Hosseini, E.; Mozafari, H.R.; Siavoshi, M. Effect of apple pomace powder on rheological properties of dough and sangak bread texture. *Carpath. J. Food Sci. Technol.* **2018**, *10*, 77–84.
135. Vosloo, M.C. Some Factors Affecting the Digestion of Glycemic Carbohydrates and the Blood Glucose Response. *J. Fam. Ecol. Consum. Sci.* **2005**, *33*, 1–9. [CrossRef]
136. Xu, X.; Luo, Z.; Yang, Q.; Xiao, Z.; Lu, X. Effect of quinoa flour on baking performance, antioxidant properties and digestibility of wheat bread. *Food Chem.* **2019**, *294*, 87–95. [CrossRef]
137. Bourne, M.C. *Food Texture and Viscosity: Concept and Measurement*, 2nd ed.; Academic Press: San Diego, CA, USA, 2002. [CrossRef]
138. Szczesniak, A.S. Texture profile analysis-Methodology interpretation clarified (Reprinted from Journal of Food Science, vol 60 pg vii, 1995). *J. Texture Stud.* **1996**, *27*, R6–R7.
139. Gómez-Limia, L.; Carballo, J.; Rodríguez-González, M.; Martínez, S. Impact of the Filling Medium on the Colour and Sensory Characteristics of Canned European Eels (*Anguilla anguilla* L.). *Foods* **2022**, *11*, 1115. [CrossRef]
140. Özdoğan, G.; Lin, X.; Sun, D.W. Rapid and noninvasive sensory analyses of food products by hyperspectral imaging: Recent application developments. *Trends Food Sci. Technol.* **2021**, *111*, 151–165. [CrossRef]
141. Valková, V.; Ďúranová, H.; Havrlentová, M.; Ivanišová, E.; Mezey, J.; Tóthová, Z.; Gabríny, L.; Kačániová, M. Selected Physico-Chemical, Nutritional, Antioxidant and Sensory Properties of Wheat Bread Supplemented with Apple Pomace Powder as a By-Product from Juice Production. *Plants* **2022**, *11*, 1256. [CrossRef] [PubMed]
142. Curutchet, A.; Trias, J.; Tárrega, A.; Arcia, P. Consumer response to cake with apple pomace as a sustainable source of fibre. *Foods* **2021**, *10*, 499. [CrossRef] [PubMed]
143. Oprea, O.B.; Popa, M.E.; Apostol, L.; Gaceu, L. Research on the Potential Use of Grape Seed Flour in the Bakery Industry. *Foods* **2022**, *11*, 1589. [CrossRef]
144. Valková, V.; Ďúranová, H.; Štefániková, J.; Miškeje, M.; Tokár, M.; Gabríny, L.; Kowalczewski, P.Ł.; Kačániová, M. Wheat Bread with Grape Seeds Micropowder: Impact on Dough Rheology and Bread Properties. *Appl. Rheol.* **2020**, *30*, 138–150. [CrossRef]
145. Makowska, A.; Zielińska-Dawidziak, M.; Waszkowiak, K.; Myszka, K. Effect of Flax Cake and Lupine Flour Addition on the Physicochemical, Sensory Properties, and Composition of Wheat Bread. *Appl. Sci.* **2023**, *13*, 7840. [CrossRef]
146. *ISO 8586-1:1993*; Sensory Analysis. General Guidance for the Selection, Training and Monitoring of Assessors. ISO: Geneva, Switzerland, 1993.
147. Krupa-Kozak, U.; Bączek, N.; Capriles, V.D.; Łopusiewicz, Ł. Novel Gluten-Free Bread with an Extract from Flaxseed By-Product: The Relationship between Water Replacement Level and Nutritional Value, Antioxidant Properties, and Sensory Quality. *Molecules* **2022**, *27*, 2690. [CrossRef] [PubMed]
148. Gao, S.; Hong, J.; Liu, C.; Zheng, X.; Li, L.; Tian, X. Comparative study of different fermentation and cooking methods on dough rheology and the quality of Chinese steamed/baked bread. *J. Food Process. Preserv.* **2022**, *46*, e16221. [CrossRef]
149. Rocchetti, G.; Rizzi, C.; Cervini, M.; Rainero, G.; Bianchi, F.; Giuberti, G.; Lucini, L.; Simonato, B. Impact of grape pomace powder on the phenolic bioaccessibility and on in vitro starch digestibility of wheat based bread. *Foods* **2021**, *10*, 507. [CrossRef]
150. Regulation (EC) No 1924/2006 of the European Parliament and of the Council of 20 December 2006 on Nutrition and Health Claims Made on Foods. Available online: https://eur-lex.europa.eu/legal-content/en/TXT/?uri=CELEX:32006R1924 (accessed on 6 March 2023).
151. Tomas, M.; Rocchetti, G.; Ghisoni, S.; Giuberti, G.; Capanoglu, E.; Lucini, L. Effect of different soluble dietary fibres on the phenolic profile of blackberry puree subjected to in vitro gastrointestinal digestion and large intestine fermentation. *Food Res. Int.* **2020**, *130*, 108954. [CrossRef] [PubMed]
152. Jakobek, L.; Matić, P. Non-covalent dietary fiber-polyphenol interactions and their influence on polyphenol bioaccessibility. *Trends Food Sci. Technol.* **2019**, *83*, 235–247. [CrossRef]
153. Moslemi, M. Reviewing the recent advances in application of pectin for technical and health promotion purposes: From laboratory to market. *Carbohydr. Polym.* **2021**, *254*, 117324. [CrossRef]
154. Alvarez-Jubete, L.; Wijngaard, H.; Arendt, E.K.; Gallagher, E. Polyphenol composition and in vitro antioxidant activity of amaranth, quinoa, buckwheat, and wheat as affected by sprouting and baking. *Food Chem.* **2010**, *119*, 770–778. [CrossRef]

155. Bárta, J.; Bártová, V.; Jarošová, M.; Švajner, J.; Smetana, P.; Kadlec, J.; Filip, V.; Kyselka, J.; Berčíková, M.; Zdráhal, Z.; et al. Oilseed cake flour composition, functional properties and antioxidant potential as effects of sieving and species differences. *Foods* **2021**, *10*, 2766. [CrossRef]
156. Abedini, A.; Alizadeh, A.M.; Mahdavi, A.; Golzan, S.A.; Salimi, M.; Tajdar-Oranj, B.; Hosseini, H. Oilseed cakes in the food industry; a review on applications, challenges, and future perspectives. *Curr. Nutr. Food Sci.* **2022**, *18*, 345–362. [CrossRef]
157. Rakita, S.; Kokić, B.; Manoni, M.; Mazzoleni, S.; Lin, P.; Luciano, A.; Ottoboni, M.; Cheli, F.; Pinotti, L. Cold-pressed oilseed cakes as alternative and sustainable feed ingredients: A review. *Foods* **2023**, *12*, 432. [CrossRef] [PubMed]
158. Caponio, G.R.; Difonzo, G.; de Gennaro, G.; Calasso, M.; De Angelis, M.; Pasqualone, A. Nutritional improvement of gluten-free breadsticks by olive cake addition and sourdough fermentation: How texture, sensory, and aromatic profile were affected? *Front. Nutr.* **2022**, *9*, 830932. [CrossRef]
159. Jenkins, D.J.; Dehghan, M.; Mente, A.; Bangdiwala, S.I.; Rangarajan, S.; Srichaikul, K.; Mohan, V.; Avezum, A.; Díaz, R.; Rosengren, A.; et al. Glycemic index, glycemic load, and cardiovascular disease and mortality. *N. Engl. J. Med.* **2021**, *384*, 1312–1322. [CrossRef]
160. Barberis, A.; Garbetta, A.; Cardinali, A.; Bazzu, G.; D'Antuono, I.; Rocchitta, G.; Fadda, A.; Linsalata, V.; D'hallewin, G.; Serra, P.A.; et al. Real-time monitoring of glucose and phenols intestinal absorption through an integrated Caco-2TC7cells/biosensors telemetric device: Hypoglycemic effect of fruit phytochemicals. *Biosens. Bioelectron.* **2017**, *88*, 159–166. [CrossRef]
161. Hajiahmadi, S.; Hosseinzadeh, E.; Hosseinzadeh, M. Flaxseed and its products improve glycemic control: A systematic review and meta-analysis. *Obes. Med.* **2021**, *22*, 100311. [CrossRef]
162. Teterycz, D.; Sobota, A. Use of High-Protein and High-Dietary-Fibre Vegetable Processing Waste from Bell Pepper and Tomato for Pasta Fortification. *Foods* **2023**, *12*, 2567. [CrossRef]
163. Urlić, M.; Urlić, I.; Urlić, H.; Mašek, T.; Benzon, B.; Vitlov Uljević, M.; Vukojevic, K.; Filipovic, N. Effects of different n6/n3 PUFAs dietary ratio on cardiac diabetic neuropathy. *Nutrients* **2020**, *12*, 2761. [CrossRef]

Disclaimer/Publisher's Note: The statements, opinions and data contained in all publications are solely those of the individual author(s) and contributor(s) and not of MDPI and/or the editor(s). MDPI and/or the editor(s) disclaim responsibility for any injury to people or property resulting from any ideas, methods, instructions or products referred to in the content.

Review

The Potential of Aquafaba as a Structure-Shaping Additive in Plant-Derived Food Technology

Joanna Stasiak [1], Dariusz M. Stasiak [1] and Justyna Libera [2,*]

[1] Department of Animal Food Technology, University of Life Sciences in Lublin, 20-704 Lublin, Poland
[2] Department of Plant Food Technology and Gastronomy, University of Life Sciences in Lublin, 20-704 Lublin, Poland
* Correspondence: justyna.libera@up.lublin.pl; Tel.: +48-81-4623-316

Abstract: Aquafaba is the water solution left over from cooking legumes, mainly chickpeas. The liquid can also be obtained from canned beans. Aquafaba is currently very popular as an egg replacement in vegan diets. The chemical composition of aquafaba depends on the type of legume, variety, genotype and parameters during production, such as cooking time or proportions of water to seeds. Aquafaba can be used for its nutritional properties. Aquafaba is starting to be used more widely in food technology as well, due to its innovative texture-shaping properties. The foaming, emulsifying, gelling and thickening properties of aquafaba can be used in plant-based food recipes, but also in animal-based food recipes and 3D printing. So far, aquafaba has been used to make meringues, cakes, cookies, bread, crackers and vegan dairy substitutes. This raw material is used for the production of low-calorie food and for people on an egg-free diet. Perhaps the potential of this product is greater. The use of waste from legumes will be the answer from food producers to the needs of consumers, for whom environmental protection or the clean label trend are particularly important. In order to effectively use aquafaba in food technology, it is necessary to standardize its production process and conduct further research on the potential of using other legumes.

Keywords: legumes; aquafaba; reformulation; texture; confectionery

1. Introduction

As the world's population increases, so does the need for food [1]. In order to ensure food reserves and guarantee their appropriate quality and safety, new technological solutions are being sought [2,3]. High hopes are associated with the use of plants and waste. Estimates indicate that four and a half times less land is needed to produce plant products than to produce food of animal origin [3,4]. Six liters of water are needed to produce 1 kg of wheat, while 2500–6000 L are needed for 1 kg of meat [5]. Therefore, it is justified to develop food technology based on the use of plants. Production of legumes, rich in protein, is a partial alternative to animal sources food production. The greatest quantity of vegetable protein at the lowest production cost is obtained when growing soybeans, peas and beans [6,7]. According to FAOSTAT data, in 2021 the countries of the European Community produced about 483,000 tons of chickpeas, and 10 years earlier about 537,000 tons. This shows that a consistently high production of these legumes is maintained. Presumably, this will generate larger amounts of aquafaba, which until recently was treated only as post-production waste now, in line with the zero-waste trend, it can be used in many ways [8,9].

Currently, healthy eating is the right way of human development and is becoming more popular. People are more likely to reach for functional food, but they also carefully choose products from store shelves. Low-calorie or low-fat foods are very popular [10]. It should also be noted that more and more people, for various reasons, choose a meat-free diet [11–13]. These reasons include economic, health, religious, ethical or environmental considerations [14]. The growing demand for new and functional food products, especially of plant origin, contributes to the expansion of the assortment of food producers [15]. Both food technologists and scientists are constantly looking for new technologies and new possibilities to shape good quality food with the desired textural and physicochemical properties [16].

Aquafaba is a raw material that responds to the previously mentioned needs; it is reasonable to conduct research devoted to it. So far, researchers have conducted research in the field of understanding the chemical composition, physicochemical properties and use of aquafaba in products, mainly as a substitute for eggs [17].

The aim of this review is to present the current state of knowledge on aquafaba and to indicate potential directions for the development of food technology, with particular emphasis on the possibility of shaping the texture in the technology of food of plant origin, mainly in baking.

2. History and Etymology

Due to changing consumer needs, scientists and technologists have long been trying to develop a plant-based egg substitute [16]. The reasons for searching for an egg substitute are an increasing number of vegans, [11] the reduction of allergens—in this case for egg white—a growing interest in healthy nutrition, [10] facilitation of the technological process at the storage and pre-treatment stages in terms of safety, environmental sustainability and lower prices [18]. Eggs are characterized by many functional properties. These include binding, emulsifying, raising, thickening, gelling, antimicrobial and moisture retention properties. In addition, what should be noted is their high protein content, about 12.5% [18]. Currently, egg replacement products are soy lecithin, chia seeds, fruit or vegetable pulp, flaxseed, silk tofu, pulses flour, corn flour, agar, cane arrowroot and black Himalayan salt [16,18]. Unfortunately, none of these products has such versatile properties as eggs do, and it is often necessary to combine some substitutes with each other to achieve a satisfactory effect [16,18].

The first reports related to the use of aquafaba date back to 10 years ago (Figure 1). In March 2011, Miyoko Schinner published a post on the website artisanve-ganlife.com, in which she described how to make a meringue from linen gel. Unfortunately, the proposed recipe had a significant disadvantage: the foam fell during baking and the flax flavor was too strong. The preparation of the gel itself was also time-consuming, but this discovery turned out to be the basis for later experiments. In August 2012, another vegan meringue was created, in which saponin extract was used as an egg substitute [www.aquafaba.com]. Meringue prepared according to this recipe had a better texture and did not fall apart, but still had a significant disadvantage. Its big problem was the unpleasant taste, and saponin extract is difficult to access by the general public [www.aquafaba.com/history.html# (accessed on 3 January 2023)].

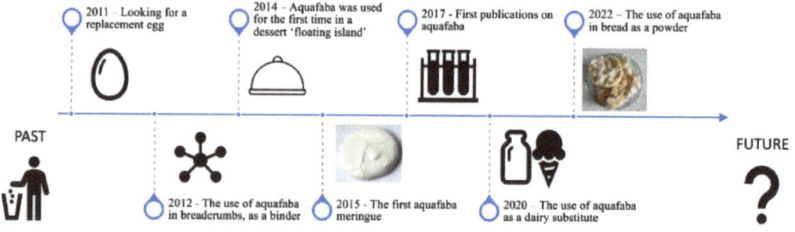

Figure 1. A simplified history of aquafaba.

A key discovery of aquafaba's properties was made in December 2014 by Joël Roessel, a French tenor who tested egg substitutes on the example of the 'floating island' dessert, which uses egg white foam [http://www.revolutionvegetale.com/en (accessed on 18 December 2022)]. He found that red bean and hearts of palm aquafaba could produce foam similar to that from egg whites, but it was not stable. It was necessary to add corn starch and guar gum. A little later, in February 2015, two Frenchmen prepared a ganache using aquafaba. At the same time, an American, Goose Wohlt, made the first vegan meringue from aquafaba. The foam from aquafaba after the addition of sugar was stable and did not require any other stabilizers [www.aquafaba.com/history.html# (accessed on 3 January 2023)].

The term 'aquafaba' was coined on 13 March 2015 by Goose Wohlt and was adopted by the local community in a Facebook group and then officially included in the Oxford English Dictionary, Merriam Webster and Scrabble Dictionary. 'Aquafaba' consists of two Latin words. 'Aqua' means water and 'faba' means beans. Aquafaba means water from boiling the seeds of edible legumes [16]. Currently, the most popular is chickpea aquafaba, due to the high consumption of chickpeas in the world [14]. Since 2015, aquafaba has been constantly gaining popularity thanks to its simplicity and accessibility. It is used by cooking enthusiasts, professional chefs and bartenders. Scientists and food technologists are trying to deepen their knowledge about it and find new applications for it to best meet the current needs of consumers [www.aquafaba.com/community.html (accessed on 3 January 2023)].

Aquafaba has become popular due to its diverse functional attributes such as gelling, foaming, emulsifying and thickening properties. It owes them to its unique chemical composition rich in oligosaccharides, soluble polysaccharides, low molecular and water-soluble protein, phenolic compounds and saponins. In addition, aquafaba is attractive to many consumers because of its ease of accessibility, plant origin, ecofriendliness and low calorie content [16].

3. Methods of Production and Storage of Aquafaba

Most aquafaba is produced during chickpea processing [17]. Ready-to-use aquafaba can be obtained from the finished product: canned chickpea seeds [16]. Self-preparation of aquafaba consists of soaking the seeds in water in order to hydrate them to extract anti-nutrients from the raw material and reduced the time of cooking the seeds. Wieczorek et al. [19] proved using the example of beans and peas that soaking in hot water for two hours causes greater losses of anti-nutrients than soaking in cold water for 10 h. In contrast, He et al. [20] showed that aquafaba from chickpeas soaked for 16 h at 4 °C has the best emulsifying properties. Not all scientists decide to soak seeds [21]. Example parameters of soaking and cooking seeds of legumes are shown in Table 1.

Table 1. Parameters of soaking and cooking seeds of legumes.

Legume Seeds	Soaking			Cooking			Reference
	Time, h	Temp., °C	S:W Ratio	Method	Time, min	S:W Ratio	
chickpea	10	ND	ND	traditional	40	1:4	[14]
whole peas, shelled peas, white beans	2	100 left at r. t.	1:4	traditional	40–42 (white beans), 20–21 (whole peas), 13–14 (shelled peas)	1:2.5	[19]
	10	4	1:4	pressure	6 (white beans), 5 (whole peas), 1 (shelled peas)	0.5:1.25	
chickpeas	1–16	4–85	1:4	pressure	20, 30, 60	1:1	[20]
chickpeas, black soybeans, black beans, yellow soybeans	-	-	-	pressure	160	2:3	[21]

Table 1. Cont.

Legume Seeds	Soaking			Cooking				Reference
	Time, h	Temp., °C	S:W Ratio	Method	Time, min	S:W Ratio		
chickpeas, lentils, peas, soybeans	12	ND	1:5	traditional	30	1:5		[22]
chickpeas	16	ND	1:3.3	traditional	90	1:1.75		[23]
haricot beans, chickpeas, whole green lentils, split yellow peas	16	ND	1:3.3	traditional	60, 90	1:1.75		[24]
yellow soybeans	16	r. t.	1:3.3	traditional	90	1:1.75		[25]
haricot beans, chickpeas, whole green lentils, split yellow peas	16	r. t.	1:1.75	traditional	60, 90	ND		[26]
chickpeas	24	bd	1:3	traditional	190	1:1.5; 1:3.25; 1:5		[27]
chickpeas	16	40	1:4	pressure	30	1:1		[28]
chickpeas	ND	ND	ND	traditional	30	1:5		[29]
chickpeas	2	40	ND	pressure	15, 30, 45	1:4, 1:2, 2:3		[30]
chickpeas	16	ND	1:3.3	pressure	20	1;3		[31]
lima beans	12	r. t.	1:4	pressure	bd	1:4		[32]
soybeans	-	-	-	pressure	90	1:1.5		[33]
chickpeas	8–10	ND	ND	traditional	45	1:3, 1:4, 1:5		[34]
chickpeas	16	5	1:3	pressure	30	1:2		[35]
chickpeas	ND	ND	ND	pressure	30	1:3		[36]

r.t.—room temperature; S:W—seed to water; ND—no data; "-"—not conducted.

The next step is to cook the legumes, usually in boiling water at normal atmospheric pressure. High pressure cooking is also possible [37]. Soaking and cooking seeds is not a standardized process, but standardization of the aquafaba production process should be a priority for future aquafaba research [21]. Baik and Han [22] proposed one method of preparing aquafaba, i.e., boiling chickpeas in water, in a ratio of 1:5, for 30 min at 98 °C.

Another challenge for researchers is to determine an effective storage method for aquafaba. Most often it is sterilized and stored in cans or jars. The liquid can be frozen, but there are still no extensive studies evaluating the effect of freezing on the quality of the raw material. Probably a good way to store aquafaba is to dry it at 70 °C [38].

4. Chemical Composition of Aquafaba

The composition of aquafaba is formed by the diffusion of chemical molecules from seeds into water during cooking. In the process of soaking and cooking the seeds of legumes, the shell is weakened, so that the components contained in the cotyledons transfer into the water [37]. Soaking and cooking cause hydration and denaturation of proteins, gelatinization of starch, as well as progressive solubilization, depolymerization and loss of pectin polysaccharides [39]. Temperature, water-to-seed ratio, seed size and seed variety determine the diffusion rate of the various components and thus affect the composition of the aquafaba [40].

The chemical composition of aquafaba varies (Table 2). It depends on the seed species, variety and genotype; environmental conditions during seed growth (e.g., climate, soil type, fertilization); the time and proportions of soaking the seeds; the time, proportions and method of cooking the seeds; and other factors [41]. The researchers demonstrated differences between chickpea genotypes in seed weight, cover thickness and chemical composition, justifying differences in aquafaba composition of samples prepared under the same conditions [42]. Chickpea aquafaba was also examined in terms of preparation steps to obtain aquafaba with the best possible parameters. The chemical composition of aquafaba formed because of cooking the remaining legumes is not yet precisely known. Already during the soaking of seeds, the diffusion of components from seeds into water begins. The dry matter of water for soaking chickpeas contains 0.25 g/100 g of insoluble carbohydrates, 0.19 g/100 g of water-soluble carbohydrates, 0.13 g/100 g of ash and 0.08 g/100 g of protein [22].

Table 2. Chemical composition of aquafaba.

Legume Seeds	Chickpea						Yellow Soybean	Bean; Green Lentil; Yellow Pea	Bean; Green Lentil; Yellow Pea
Energy; kJ/100 g	-	-	-	72	-	-	-	-	-
Dry matter; g/100 g	5.1	5.1	4.9–6.4	5.0	7.9	-	5.59	3.3; 4.7; 4.4	-
Ash; g/100 g	0.6	0.6	-	0.4	-	-	0.78	0.8; 0.5; 0.4	-
Protein; g/100 g	1.0	1.0	1.2–1.7	1.3	1.3	0.5–1.0	0.68	0.7; 1.5; 1.3	-
Fat; g/100 g	-	<DL	-	<DL	-	-	<DL	<DL	-
Available carbohydrates; g/100 g	-	3.6	-	2.6	-	-	4.12	1.8; 2.7; 2.7	-
LMW; g/100 g	1.2	1.2	-	0.6	-	-	1.66	0.7; 0.5; 1.0	-
HMW; g/100 g	-	0.04	-	0.7	-	-	-	0.2; 0.1; 0.1	-
Fiber; g/100 g	2.4	2.4	-	0.7	-	-	2.46	0.9; 2.1; 1.6	-
Saponins; mg/g	-	4.5	-	-	-	-	6.4	5.9; 12.0; 4.7	7.9; 14; 9.8
TPC; mg/g	-	-	-	0.3	-	-	-	-	0.3; 0.7; 0.6
Tocopherols; µg/mL	-	-	-	0.1	-	-	-	-	-
Tannins; mg/100 g	-	-	-	-	-	0.5–12.0	-	-	-
Reference	[23]	[24]	[42]	[43]	[44]	[45]	[25]	[24]	[26]

LMW—low molecular weight sugars; HMW—high molecular weight sugars; TPC—total phenolic content; "-"—not conducted; <DL—detection limit.

Shim et al. [42] performed tests on aquafaba from 10 different cans of chickpeas and showed that aquafaba is characterized by a high-water content and is a fat-free product. The total carbohydrate content in the dry matter of aquafaba is 55–74% (70% for chickpeas) [45]. Carbohydrates insoluble in chickpea aquafaba constitute approx. 47% [46]. Aquafaba does not contain starch, which is probably due to the fact that large granules are created with intertwined chains that are resistant to high temperature [46]. Proton-NMR analysis showed the presence of about 20 compounds in aquafaba, including sugar (glucose, sucrose), alcohol (isopropanol, ethanol, methanol), amino acid (alanine), organic acid (lactic acid, acetic acid, succinic acid, citrate, formate, malate) and nucleoside (inosine, adenosine) [42].

The ash content in aquafaba was for green beans 0.75 g/100 g, chickpeas 0.57 g/100 g, green lentils 0.48 g/100 g and yellow split peas 0.40 g/100 g [24]. Aquafaba has a high content of micronutrients, especially copper, potassium and manganese [26]. Heat treatment of chickpeas and aquafaba itself can cause losses of micronutrients [47].

It is assumed that the content of anti-nutrients in aquafaba is much lower than in raw seeds [47]. Other anti-nutrients (mainly carbohydrates) contained in chickpeas include phytates (5.9 mg/g), oxalates, phenolic compounds (0.72–6.10 mg/g), tannins (4.85 mg/g), saponins (0.75–0.91 mg/g) and oligosaccharides (3.87–6.98 g/100 g) [25]. Oligosaccharides include raffinose (0.62–1.45 g/100 g), stachyose (0.74–2.56 g/100 g) and verbascose (0–0.19 g/100 g) [48].

5. Functional Properties of Aquafaba in Food Technology

5.1. Foaming Properties

The foaming properties of aquafaba were discovered first. It turns out that the foaming of aquafaba is similar to egg white (1:1 ratio) [17]. The foaming properties of aquafaba result from the presence of albumin as well as polysaccharides and saponins. Thanks to its protein content, aquafaba can foam, and thanks to the carbohydrate content, it remains stable. Saponins are believed to be responsible for facilitating the formation of air bubbles because they have an amphiphilic structure. He et al. [33] showed in their research that the higher the protein content in aquafaba, the higher the foaming efficiency. It was observed that extending the foaming time of aquafaba did not adversely affect the foaming properties, as is the case with egg white foam [17]. The foaming ability of aquafaba can be used in mousses, meringues, biscuits and meat roasts. Foamed chickpea aquafaba is shown in Figure 2.

Figure 2. Meringue mass based on aquafaba (photo by Joanna Stasiak).

Other authors report that ultrasonic treatment can be used to enhance the foaming properties of aquafaba. Ultrasonication also improved foam stability, color and texture, as well as emulsifying capacity [31,45]. The foaming properties of aquafaba have been fairly well studied; however, the results of individual scientists vary depending on the other parameters of aquafaba (Table 3). Based on the examples of the collected publications, it can be concluded that one of the best yields and stability of aquafaba foaming can be obtained using chickpea seeds, which were previously soaked in water and then boiled in a ratio of 1:4 with water for 60 min.

Table 3. Foaming and emulsifying properties of aquafaba.

Legume Seeds	Foaming Capacity, %	Foaming Stability, %	Emulsifying Capacity, %	Emulsion Stability, %	Emulsifying Activity Index, m^2/g	Reference
chickpeas	521–685	86–99	-	-	-	[14]
	182–480	74–92	-	60–80	-	[17]
	-	-	-	72–76	-	[20]
	89	-	-	-	-	[24]
	-	-	-	-	39	[26]
	162–324	3.4–93	3.9–72	0–76	-	[27]
	127	95	-	-	-	[29]
	40–290	7–58	-	-	-	[30]
	259–548	42–77	-	-	-	[31]
	505–611	81–86	-	-	-	[34]

Table 3. Cont.

Legume Seeds	Foaming Capacity, %	Foaming Stability, %	Emulsifying Capacity, %	Emulsion Stability, %	Emulsifying Activity Index, m²/g	Reference
haricot beans; whole green lentils; split yellow peas	39; 97; 93	-	-	-	-	[24]
yellow soybeans	65	-	49	-	20	[25]
haricot beans; whole green lentils; split yellow peas	-	-	-	-	23; 47; 16	[26]
lima beans	348–660	23–82	-	-	-	[32]
green peas	575–725	75–90	-	-	-	[49]

"-"—not conducted.

5.2. Emulsifying Properties

The emulsion that is created using aquafaba is an 'oil-in-water' (O/W) emulsion. Using mechanical energy (e.g., a hand blender), oil molecules disperse in the aquafaba. The emulsifier is responsible for creating a layer separating oil from water [28]. It is thanks to the emulsifier that there is no stratification of the two fractions. Proteins that have amphiphilic properties are the emulsifier in aquafaba. They expose their hydrophilic part to the water contained in the aquafaba and their hydrophobic part to the oil. Saponins are considered surfactants that reduce the interfacial tension between water and oil. Polysaccharides contribute to increasing the stability of the emulsion by increasing the viscosity of the aqueous phase [16]. Aquafaba is characterized by a low content of dry matter (5–8%) and protein (0.85–1.5% in the wet state), which is another factor increasing the stability of the emulsion. Overall, more stable emulsions, protein–oil–water, contain low protein concentrations (0.2–1%) [16]. Aquafaba's emulsifying ability can be used in, e.g., vegan mayonnaise [45].

Foaming and emulsification depend on many different factors including diversity and seed species and aquafaba production conditions. One publication noted that the best emulsion was formed when the seeds were soaked at a refrigeration temperature for 16 h [20]. Buhl et al. [44] have shown that the best properties for forming and stabilizing emulsions occur at pH 7. In other studies, it was found that the best emulsion was obtained by using chickpeas and water in a 2:3 ratio and boiling for 60 min. [37]. Subjecting aquafaba to high pressure also positively affects its emulsifying ability [30].

5.3. Gelling and Thickening Properties

When cooking seeds, there is a complete or partial denaturation of proteins that interact with water-soluble carbohydrates and retain water molecules, forming a gel, coagulate or sediment. During cooking, there is also the Maillard reaction [16,21]. Chickpeas have been found to have the best gelling properties and that the ability to gel is inversely correlated with the content of insoluble fiber [24]. The gelling and thickening process takes place in products with a higher water content (e.g., mousse) [50]. In products with a high dry matter content that are heat-treated (e.g., meringue), it only occurs to a small extent [20]. Alsalman et al. [30] have proven that aquafaba subjected to high pressure treatment improves its structure and gelling ability.

A promising area of use for aquafaba is 3D printing of food. A major problem faced by researchers is the shaping of the rheological properties of materials (paints, pastes, filaments) used for printing [51]. The specific structural-forming properties of aquafaba may contribute to the development of this new food production technique [52].

6. The Use of Aquafaba in Baking and Confectionery

6.1. Meringue

The physicochemical properties of aquafaba have a huge and only partially discovered innovative potential in the design of food for vegans. The use of aquafaba began with vegan meringue, and now it is added to food as an egg substitute and a substance that imparts desirable sensory properties and texture. The first meringues prepared from aquafaba from beans, chickpeas, whole green lentils and yellow split peas were tested. Meringue with chickpea and yellow pea aquafaba most closely resembled egg meringue. Aquafaba meringues were generally characterized by higher water activity and lower hardness [24]. In another experiment, meringue was prepared from chickpea aquafaba. Aquafaba was characterized by low efficiency and foaming stability, which may be due to too long cooking time. In sensory evaluation, meringue from aquafaba has gained a general acceptance. No differences in taste and texture were observed [27]. In the next experiment, a French meringue from chickpea aquafaba was prepared. Ultrasound was used at 50% and 100% of the device's power, for 10, 20 and 30 min. The results showed that viscosity increased slightly, and foaming performance increased from 259% to 548% after 30 min of ultrasound use [31].

6.2. Crackers

Aquafaba has many unrecognized technological properties and nutritional values. When added to the dough for gluten-free crackers, it significantly changed the texture parameters of the product [25]. An increase in moisture content and a decrease in brittleness of crackers during 2-day storage at room temperature were found, probably because of increased water dynamics. The results obtained by Serventi et al. [25] show one of the limitations regarding the use of aquafaba, as a natural feature of crackers is their crunchiness.

6.3. Mousse

The foaming and emulsifying properties of aquafaba obtained from chickpeas and yellow peas make it possible to use it as an egg substitute in some dishes e.g., cream mousse [26]. The presence of specific chemical compounds (e.g., proteins, fiber, saponins) results in high emulsifying activity (46–54%). The aquafaba emulsions were extremely stable even after 1 day of storage (Figure 3).

Figure 3. Dessert with vegan chocolate mousse from aquafaba (photo by Joanna Stasiak).

Damian et al. [26] showed that surface-active saponins may modify emulsions' stability. Aquafaba showed a greater affinity for oil than for water. Aquafaba can replace eggs in raw confectionery products. This is a particularly valuable advantage in terms of food safety (microbial hazard, allergen). The panelists positively assessed the quality of the aquafaba product. They noticed a slightly lower sweetness, which may be due to the natural presence of calcium and sodium ions in the aquafaba.

6.4. Cake

A sponge cake was made with eggs replaced with aquafaba from canned chickpeas. The vegan sponge cake was similar to the traditional one. It had larger empty spaces and a darker skin [17]. A similar study also replaced eggs with chickpea aquafaba. The study prepared a control sample from eggs and four samples with varying degrees of egg replacement with aquafaba. It was concluded that replacing 50% of eggs with aquafaba does not adversely affect the physical properties of the dough, and the foaming efficiency is at a similar level [29]. Another product made of chickpea aquafaba was the muffin. Vegan muffins had similar characteristics to egg muffins. The best attempt turned out to be a muffin with the addition of citric acid [14]. In the production of dough, aquafaba can also replace palm oil. A lower level of color parameters in the crumb was observed. In addition, the dough with aquafaba retained moisture longer, which had a positive effect on sensory characteristics. It was found that aquafaba does not significantly alter the other parameters of the dough and can be used as a substitute for palm oil [53]. In another study, a gluten-free dough was made with eggs replaced with a mixture of aquafaba dry matter from chickpeas, lentil protein and citric acid. Physical characteristics were slightly lower than in the control sample with eggs, while sensory characteristics were at a similar level, and the final product contained more fiber [36]. Using aquafaba from chickpeas, Italian cookies were made—macaroons. The macaroons were subjected to sensory analysis, and quite a few testers did not distinguish between those made from aquafaba and the controls. Especially the texture of aquafaba macaroons was similar to the control sample [54].

6.5. Bread

The quality of various types of gluten-free bread was studied including the addition of aquafaba, xanthan gum, chickpea flour, cooked chickpea paste and water after soaking chickpeas. Bread with aquafaba was characterized by a softer consistency and a more homogeneous structure than the control sample. The remaining parameters were close to the control sample [23]. In another experiment, gluten-free bread was prepared with the addition of water after soaking the seeds (beans, garbanzo chickpeas, yellow split peas, whole green lentils and yellow soybeans). The seeds were soaked for 16 h in a ratio of 1: 3.3 (seeds/water). The structure of the bread with the addition of water after soaking the whole green lentils was the most porous and best represented the texture of the control sample [55].

6.6. Vegan Dairy Substitutes

Vegan whipped cream was prepared using aquafaba from chickpeas, sugar and xanthan gum. The product may correspond to Swiss meringue. Vegan whipped cream has been found to be a very good alternative to whipped cream in the production of vegan desserts [32]. A technology to produce vegan yogurt based on oat drink using aquafaba was also developed. Aquafaba had a beneficial effect on increasing water retention capacity and reducing syneresis. It has been found that aquafaba can serve as a gelling agent in vegan fermented products; however, the production process needs to be standardized [56]. Vegan ice cream was designed using chickpea aquafaba and yellow split peas. Aquafaba was used as an emulsifier. Ice cream using chickpea aquafaba was slightly darker, but in sensory assessment the difference was not noticeable; however, the overall acceptance was at a lower level [57,58].

7. Conclusions

Until recently, aquafaba was only seen as a waste product, but this view is changing. It was similar a long time ago with milk whey, which is now a valuable food raw material. Aquafaba possesses unique functional properties in food production and is an example of science's response to the specific needs of the food market, especially in terms of shaping the structure. The application potential of aquafaba prepared from legumes opens up new possibilities in food technology, especially in the field of modifying rheological properties.

In addition to the use of aquafaba as an egg replacement, new applications can be sought to improve the structural-shaping properties and nutritional value of food. It is necessary to optimize the production process in order to standardize the physical and chemical properties of aquafaba for industrial applications. The chemical composition and properties of many legume seeds remain unknown. The production and storage of aquafaba also needs to be addressed economically and logistically. Such efforts are highly empirical and require much experimentation. All the above-mentioned properties indicate the need for further research on aquafaba and its use in new products, not only in baking and confectionery, but also in the production of pasta or even in animal-based food recipes and 3D printing.

Author Contributions: Conceptualization, J.S., D.M.S. and J.L.; investigation and writing—original draft preparation, J.S.; writing—review and editing, J.L.; supervision, funding acquisition, D.M.S. All authors have read and agreed to the published version of the manuscript.

Funding: This research received no external funding.

Institutional Review Board Statement: Not applicable.

Informed Consent Statement: Not applicable.

Data Availability Statement: Not applicable.

Conflicts of Interest: The authors declare no conflict of interest.

References

1. De Queiroz, F.L.N.; Raposo, A.; Han, H.; Nader, M.; Ariza-Montes, A.; Zandonadi, R.P. Eating competence, food consumption and health outcomes: An overview. *Int. J. Env. Res. Public. Health* **2022**, *19*, 4484. [CrossRef] [PubMed]
2. Szczepaniak, I. Evaluation of food security and food self-sufficiency of Poland against the background of European Union countries. *Int. Bus. Glob. Econ.* **2008**, *37*, 168–182. (In Polish) [CrossRef]
3. Schepers, J.; Annemans, L. The potential health and economic effects of plant-based food patterns in Belgium and the United Kingdom. *Nutrition* **2018**, *48*, 24–32. [CrossRef] [PubMed]
4. Pérez-Escamilla, R. Food Security and the 2015–2030 sustainable development goals: From human to planetary health. *Curr. Dev. Nutr.* **2017**, *1*, 1007005. [CrossRef]
5. Tomczyk, E. Pro-ecological social attitudes as one of today's ways of understanding sustainable development: Contemporary nutritional trends: Vegetarianism and veganism. *Zrównoważony Rozw. Deb. Nauk.* **2018**, *3*, 111–118. (In Polish)
6. Boczar, P. Plant protein—Sources, production costs and quality. *Zesz. Nauk. SGGW Warszawie Probl. Rol. Swiat.* **2018**, *18*, 122–132. (In Polish) [CrossRef]
7. Sharif, H.; Williams, P.; Sharif, M.; Abbas, S.; Majeed, H.; Masamba, K.; Safdar, W.; Zhong, F. Current progress in the utilization of native and modified legume proteins as emulsifiers and encapsulants—A review. *Food Hydrocoll.* **2018**, *76*, 2–16. [CrossRef]
8. Szulc, K. Assessment of the possibility of using aquafaba in the production of vegetable emulsion. *Technol. Prog. Food Process.* **2021**, *2*, 56–61.
9. Erem, E.; Icyer, N.C.; Tatlisu, N.B.; Kilicli, M.; Kaderoglu, G.H.; Toker, Ö.S. A new trend among plant-based food ingredients in food processing technology: Aquafaba. *Crit. Rev. Food Sci. Nutr.* **2021**, *11*, 1–19. [CrossRef] [PubMed]
10. Seid, H.; Rosenbaum, M. Low carbohydrate and low-fat diets: What we don't know and why we should know it. *Nutrients* **2019**, *11*, 2749. [CrossRef]
11. Vainio, A.; Niva, M.; Jallinoja, P.; Latvala, T. From beef to beans: Eating motives and the replacement of animal proteins with plant proteins among Finnish consumers. *Appetite* **2016**, *106*, 92–100. [CrossRef] [PubMed]
12. Cader, P.; Lesiów, T. Veganism and vegetarianism as diets in the contemporary consumer society. *Eng. Sci. Technol.* **2021**, *1*, 9–33. (In Polish) [CrossRef]
13. Bakaloudi, D.R.; Halloran, A.; Rippin, H.L.; Oikonomidou, A.C.; Dardavesis, T.I.; Williams, J.; Wickramasinghe, K.; Breda, J.; Chourdakis, M. Intake and adequacy of the vegan diet. A systematic review of the evidence. *Clin. Nutr.* **2021**, *40*, 3503–3521. [CrossRef] [PubMed]
14. Nguyet, T.; Ngoc, N.; Quoc, L.; Tran, G. Application of chickpeas aquafaba with pre-treatment as egg replacer in cake production. *Chem. Eng. Trans.* **2021**, *89*, 7–12. [CrossRef]
15. McKeown, P.; Dunn, R.A. 'Life-style choice' or a philosophical belief?: The argument for veganism and vegetarianism to be a protected philosophical belief and the position in England and Wales. *Liverp. Law. Rev.* **2021**, *42*, 207–241. [CrossRef] [PubMed]
16. Mustafa, R.; Reaney, M. Aquafaba, from food waste to a value-added product. *Food Wastes By-Prod.* **2020**, *10*, 93–126. [CrossRef]
17. Mustafa, R.; He, Y.; Shim, Y.; Reaney, M. Aquafaba, wastewater from chickpea canning, functions as an egg replacer in sponge cake. *Int. J. Food Sci. Technol.* **2018**, *53*, 2247–2255. [CrossRef]

18. Grizio, M.; Specht, L.; The Good Food Institute. Plant-Based Egg Alternatives: Optimizing for Functional Properties and Applications. 2021. Available online: https://gfi.org/wp-content/uploads/2021/02/Plantbasedeggalternatives.pdf (accessed on 29 January 2023).
19. Wieczorek, C.; Sionek, B.; Przybylski, W.; Lahuta, L. The influence of culinary processing of legume seeds on the content of soluble carbohydrates. *Zesz. Probl. Postępów Nauk. Rol.* **2016**, *584*, 139–150. (In Polish)
20. He, Y.; Purdy, S.; Tse, T.; Tar'an, B.; Meda, V.; Reaney, M.; Mustafa, R. Standardization of aquafaba production and application in vegan mayonnaise analogs. *Foods* **2021**, *10*, 1978. [CrossRef]
21. Echeverria-Jaramillo, E.; Kim, Y.; Nam, Y.; Zheng, Y.; Cho, J.; Hong, W.; Kang, S.; Kim, J.; Shim, Y.; Shin, W. Revalorization of the cooking water (Aquafaba) from soybean varieties generated as a by-product of food manufacturing in Korea. *Foods* **2021**, *10*, 2287. [CrossRef]
22. Baik, B.; Han, I. Cooking, roasting, and fermentation of chickpeas, lentils, peas, and soybeans for fortification of leavened bread. *Cereal Chem.* **2012**, *89*, 269–275. [CrossRef]
23. Bird, L.; Pilkington, C.; Saputra, A.; Serventi, L. Products of chickpea processing as texture improvers in gluten-free bread. *Food Sci. Technol. Int.* **2017**, *23*, 690–698. [CrossRef]
24. Stantiall, S.; Dale, K.; Calizo, F.; Serventi, L. Application of pulses cooking water as functional ingredients: The foaming and gelling abilities. *Eur. Food Res. Technol.* **2018**, *244*, 97–104. [CrossRef]
25. Serventi, L.; Wang, S.; Zhu, J.; Liu, S.; Fei, F. Cooking water of yellow soybeans as emulsifier in gluten-free crackers. *Eur. Food Res. Technol.* **2018**, *244*, 2141–2148. [CrossRef]
26. Damian, J.; Huo, S.; Serventi, L. Phytochemical content and emulsifying ability of pulses cooking water. *Eur. Food Res. Technol.* **2018**, *244*, 1647–1655. [CrossRef]
27. Lafarga, T.; Villaró, S.; Bobo, G.; Aguiló-Aguayo, I. Optimization of the pH and boiling conditions needed to obtain improved foaming and emulsifying properties of chickpea aquafaba using a response surface methodology. *Int. J. Gastron. Food Sci.* **2019**, *18*, 100177. [CrossRef]
28. He, Y.; Shim, Y.; Mustafa, R.; Meda, V.; Reaney, M. Chickpea cultivar selection to produce aquafaba with superior emulsion properties. *Foods* **2019**, *8*, 685. [CrossRef]
29. Aslan, M.; Ertaş, N. Possibility of using 'chickpea aquafaba' as egg replacer in traditional cake formulation. *Harran Tarım Gıda Bilim. Derg.* **2020**, *24*, 1–8. [CrossRef]
30. Alsalman, F.; Tulbek, M.; Nickerson, M.; Ramaswamy, H. Evaluation and optimization of functional and antinutritional properties of aquafaba. *Legume Sci.* **2020**, *1*, 1–15. [CrossRef]
31. Meurer, M.; de Souza, D.; Ferreira Marczak, L. Effects of ultrasound on technological properties of chickpea cooking water (aquafaba). *J. Food Eng.* **2020**, *265*, 109688. [CrossRef]
32. Nguyet, T.; Nguyen, T.; Buu, T.; Quoc, L. Effect of processing methods on foam properties and application of lima bean (*Phaseolus lunatus* L.) aquafaba in eggless cupcakes. *J. Food Process. Preserv.* **2020**, *44*, e14886. [CrossRef]
33. He, Y.; Shim, Y.; Shen, J.; Kim, J.; Cho, J.; Hong, W.; Meda, V.; Reaney, M. Aquafaba from Korean Soybean II: Physicochemical properties and composition characterized by NMR analysis. *Foods* **2021**, *10*, 2589. [CrossRef] [PubMed]
34. Nguyet, T.; Quoc, L.; Buu, T. Evaluation of textural and microstructural properties of vegan aquafaba whipped cream from chickpeas. *Chem. Eng. Trans.* **2021**, *83*, 421–426. [CrossRef]
35. Karatay, G.; Galvão, A.; Hubinger, M. Storage stability of conventional and high internal phase emulsions stabilized solely by chickpea aquafaba. *Foods* **2022**, *11*, 1588. [CrossRef]
36. Silva, P.; Kalschne, D.; Salvati, D.; Bona, E.; Rodrigues, A. Aquafaba powder, lentil protein and citric acid as egg replacer in gluten-free cake: A model approach. *Appl. Food Res.* **2022**, *2*, 100188. [CrossRef]
37. Alsalman, F.; Tulbek, M.; Nickerson, M.; Ramaswamy, H. Evaluation of factors affecting aquafaba rheological and thermal properties. *LWT* **2020**, *1*, 1–33. [CrossRef]
38. Aslan, M.; Ertaş, N. Foam drying of aquafaba: Optimization with mixture design. *J. Food Process. Preserv.* **2021**, *4*, e15185. [CrossRef]
39. Chigwedere, C.M.; Olaoye, T.F.; Kyomugasho, C.; Jamsazzadeh Kermani, Z.; Pallares Pallares, A.; Van Loey, A.M.; Grauwet, T.; Hendrickx, M.E. Mechanistic insight into softening of Canadian wonder common beans (*Phaseolus vulgaris*) during cooking. *Food Res. Int.* **2018**, *106*, 522–531. [CrossRef]
40. Kinyanjui, P.; Njoroge, D.; Makokha, A.; Christiaens, S.; Ndaka, D.; Hendrickx, M. Hydration properties and texture fingerprints of easy-and hard-to-cook bean varieties. *Food Sci. Nutr.* **2015**, *3*, 39–47. [CrossRef]
41. Wood, J.A.; Tan, H.-T.; Collins, H.M.; Yap, K.; Khor, S.F.; Lim, W.L.; Xing, X.; Bulone, V.; Burton, R.A.; Fincher, G.B.; et al. Genetic and environmental factors contribute to variation in cell wall composition in mature desi chickpea (*Cicer arietinum* L.) cotyledons. *Plant. Cell. Env.* **2018**, *41*, 2195–2208. [CrossRef]
42. Shim, Y.; Mustafa, R.; Shen, J.; Ratanapariyanuch, K.; Reaney, M. Composition and properties of aquafaba: Water recovered from commercially canned chickpeas. *J. Vis. Exp.* **2018**, *132*, e56305. [CrossRef]
43. Raikos, V.; Hayes, H.; Ni, H. Aquafaba from commercially canned chickpeas as potential egg replacer for the development of vegan mayonnaise: Recipe optimization and storage stability. *Int. J. Food Sci. Technol.* **2020**, *55*, 1935–1942. [CrossRef]
44. Buhl, T.; Christensen, C.; Hammershøj, M. Aquafaba as an egg white substitute in food foams and emulsions: Protein composition and functional behavior. *Food Hydrocoll.* **2019**, *96*, 354–364. [CrossRef]

45. He, Y.; Meda, V.; Reaney, M.; Mustafa, R. Aquafaba, a new plant-based rheological additive for food applications. *Trends Food Sci. Technol.* **2021**, *111*, 27–42. [CrossRef]
46. Lamich, L. Aquafaba, an Egg Substitute for Food Applications. Available online: http://hdl.handle.net/2445/184718 (accessed on 6 December 2022).
47. El-Adawy, T. Nutritional composition and antinutritional factors of chickpeas (*Cicer arietinum* L.) undergoing different cooking methods and germination. *Plant. Food Hum. Nutr.* **2002**, *57*, 83–97. [CrossRef] [PubMed]
48. Rachwa-Rosiak, D.; Nebesny, E.; Budryn, G. Chickpeas—Composition, nutritional value, health benefits, application to bread and snacks: A review. *Crit. Rev. Food Sci. Nutr.* **2015**, *55*, 1137–1145. [CrossRef]
49. Kiliçli, M.; Bayram, M.; Said, O. *Usage of Green. Pea Aquafaba Modified with Ultrasound in Production of Whipped Cream*; Research Square: Durham, NC, USA, 2022.
50. Tsykhanovska, I.; Yevlash, V.; Trishch, R.; Lazarieva, T.; Alexandrov, A.; Nikulina, A. Functional and technological properties of food additive "Magnetofood" in production of shaped jelly marmalade on agar and pectin. *Food Sci. Technol.* **2021**, *15*, 143–154. [CrossRef]
51. Zhang, J.Y.; Pandya, J.K.; McClements, D.J.; Lu, J.; Kinchla, A.J. Advancements in 3D food printing: A comprehensive overview of properties and opportunities. *Crit. Rev. Food Sci. Nutr.* **2022**, *62*, 4752–4768. [CrossRef]
52. Baiano, A. 3D printed foods: A comprehensive review on technologies, nutritional value, safety, consumer attitude, regulatory framework, and economic and sustainability issues. *Food Rev. Int.* **2020**, *38*, 986–1016. [CrossRef]
53. Karatay, G.; Rebellato, A.; Joy Steel, C.; Dupas Hubinger, M. Chickpea aquafaba-based emulsions as a fat replacer in pound cake: Impact on cake properties and sensory analysis. *Foods* **2022**, *1*, 2484. [CrossRef]
54. Horner, D.; Huneycutt, E.; Ross, B. Nutrition and dietetic practice aquafaba and flax seed gel as a substitute for egg whites in french macaron cookies. *J. Nutr. Diet. Pr.* **2019**, *3*, 1–9.
55. Huang, S.; Liu, Y.; Zhang, W.; Dale, K.; Liu, S.; Zhu, J.; Serventi, L. Composition of legume soaking water and emulsifying properties in gluten-free bread. *Food Sci. Technol. Int.* **2018**, *24*, 232–241. [CrossRef] [PubMed]
56. Raikos, V.; Juskaite, L.; Vas, F.; Hayes, H. Physicochemical properties, texture, and probiotic survivability of oat-based yogurt using aquafaba as a gelling agent. *Food Sci. Nutr.* **2020**, *8*, 6426–6432. [CrossRef]
57. Serventi, L.; Yang, Y.; Bian, Y. Cooking water applications. In *Upcycling Legume Water: From Wastewater to Food Ingredients*, 1st ed.; Springer: Berlin/Heidelberg, Germany, 2020; pp. 105–120. [CrossRef]
58. Yazici, G.; Taspinar, T.; Ozer, M. Aquafaba: A multifunctional ingredient in food production. *Biol. Life Sci. Forum* **2022**, *18*, 24. [CrossRef]

Disclaimer/Publisher's Note: The statements, opinions and data contained in all publications are solely those of the individual author(s) and contributor(s) and not of MDPI and/or the editor(s). MDPI and/or the editor(s) disclaim responsibility for any injury to people or property resulting from any ideas, methods, instructions or products referred to in the content.

MDPI AG
Grosspeteranlage 5
4052 Basel
Switzerland
Tel.: +41 61 683 77 34

Applied Sciences Editorial Office
E-mail: applsci@mdpi.com
www.mdpi.com/journal/applsci

Disclaimer/Publisher's Note: The title and front matter of this reprint are at the discretion of the Guest Editors. The publisher is not responsible for their content or any associated concerns. The statements, opinions and data contained in all individual articles are solely those of the individual Editors and contributors and not of MDPI. MDPI disclaims responsibility for any injury to people or property resulting from any ideas, methods, instructions or products referred to in the content.

www.ingramcontent.com/pod-product-compliance
Lightning Source LLC
LaVergne TN
LVHW072251110526
838202LV00106B/2378